MW00720831

CompTIA Security+ SY0-201 Cert Guide

David L. Prowse

Pearson
800 East 96th Street
Indianapolis, Indiana 46240 USA

CompTIA® Security+ SY0-201 Cert Guide

CompTIA Official Academic Course Kit: Security+ SY0-201, With Voucher
ISBN-13: 978-0-7897-4747-1
ISBN-10: 0-7897-4747-2

CompTIA Official Academic Course Kit: Security+ SY0-201, Without Voucher
ISBN-13: 978-0-7897-4746-4
ISBN-10: 0-7897-4746-4

Library of Congress Cataloging-in-Publication data is on file.
Printed in the United States of America
First Printing: November 2010

Trademarks

All terms mentioned in this book that are known to be trademarks or service marks have been appropriately capitalized. Pearson IT Certification cannot attest to the accuracy of this information. Use of a term in this book should not be regarded as affecting the validity of any trademark or service mark.

Warning and Disclaimer

Every effort has been made to make this book as complete and as accurate as possible, but no warranty or fitness is implied. The information provided is on an "as is" basis. The author and the publisher shall have neither liability nor responsibility to any person or entity with respect to any loss or damages arising from the information contained in this book or from the use of the CD or programs accompanying it.

Bulk Sales

Pearson IT Certification offers excellent discounts on this book when ordered in quantity for bulk purchases or special sales. For more information, please contact

U.S. Corporate and Government Sales
1-800-382-3419
corpsales@pearsontechgroup.com

For sales outside of the U.S., please contact

International Sales
international@pearson.com

Associate Publisher
David Dusthimer

Acquisitions Editor
Betsy Brown

Development Editor
Andrew Cupp

Managing Editor
Sandra Schroeder

Senior Project Editor
Tonya Simpson

Copy Editor
Apostrophe Editing Services

Indexer
Cheryl Lenser

Proofreader
Sheri Cain

Technical Editor
Aubrey Adams

Publishing Coordinator
Vanessa Evans

Multimedia Developer
Dan Scherf

Book Designer
Gary Adair

Composition
Mark Shirar

Contents at a Glance

DVD

Table of Contents

About the Author

David L. Prowse is a computer network specialist, author, and technical trainer. As a consultant, he installs and secures the latest in computer and networking technology. Over the past several years, he has authored several titles for Pearson Education, including the well-received *CompTIA A+ Exam Cram*. In addition, over the past decade he has taught CompTIA A+, Network+, and Security+ certification courses, both in the classroom and via the Internet. He runs the website www.davidlprowse.com, where he gladly answers questions from students and readers.

About the Reviewer

Aubrey Adams (CCNA, Security+) is an electronic and computer system engineering lecturer and Cisco Networking Academy instructor at Central Institute of Technology in Perth, Western Australia. Coming from a background in telecommunications design, with qualifications in electronic engineering and management and graduate diplomas in computing and education, he teaches across a range of computer systems and networking vocational education and training areas. Aubrey also authors Networking Academy curriculum and assessments and is a Cisco Press author and Pearson Education technical editor.

Dedication

For my loyal website visitors, this one is for you!

Acknowledgments

This book and accompanying DVD wouldn't have been possible without my publisher, Pearson. I've been involved in many projects with Pearson for the past several years and give my thanks for the ongoing opportunities and support I have received.

One person in particular I'd like to acknowledge is Andrew Cupp. Drew, once again, your guidance during this project has been nothing short of greatness. You have definitely helped develop what I think is an exceptional product.

I'd also like to thank Aubrey Adams for his excellent feedback during the creation of this book. Good technical editors are difficult to find; I'm grateful to Aubrey for his dedication and hard work during this project. My thanks also go out to David Dusthimer, Betsy Brown, Sandra Schroeder, Tonya Simpson, Vanessa Evans, and Dan Scherf. It takes a lot of talented people to publish a book—I appreciate everything you did to make this book a reality.

And then there are the usually suspects—wife, family, friends; thank you for bearing with me on yet another crazy book-writing crusade!

Finally, I have dedicated this book to my website readers. Your input over the years has helped me tailor my book projects, making them more complete and helping them be successful. Many of you have requested I write a Security+ book; I am glad to oblige, and I hope that you benefit from it.

Foreword

This product is the third in a series of CompTIA Official Curriculum packages published by Pearson. These products were developed to provide best-in-class training for the CompTIA Security+ exam. CompTIA, the leading trade association for the information technology (IT) industry, endorses this Course Kit as its Official Curriculum for Security+. "We work closely with our partners around the world to help IT professionals advance their knowledge, skills and career credentials in order to raise on-the-job performance levels," said Terry Erdle, senior vice president, skills certification, CompTIA. "With the introduction of this program, CompTIA is expanding its commitment by adding substantial resources and working collaboratively with our partners to increase market impact and customer satisfaction."

This Course Kit includes a 650-page text for the study of security and Security+ preparation. The text is authored by David L. Prowse, a computer network specialist and trainer. The text provides complete coverage of the concepts, theory, and practice that a student will need to become a security technician, and a successful Security+ exam candidate.

In addition, the Course Kit includes five hours of instructional video by a team of accomplished trainers, designed to provide visual instruction on all topics for Security+. The author, Shon Harris, provides dozens of step-by-step procedures and reinforces the concepts you will read about in the book.

As you read and watch the video, you will have the opportunity to reinforce your learning with a product called MyITCertificationLab. This product enables you to test your skill level on each of the CompTIA Security+ subobjectives by taking a pretest. After you have completed the pretest you will be sent a personalized study plan based on the questions that you missed. You can then use the study plan to learn about what you missed on the pretest. When you are ready, you can take another test to confirm what you have learned. You can then take up to four practice tests to prepare you for the actual certification exam.

After you have completed all your work you will be ready to sit for the CompTIA Security+ exam. If you purchased the version of this package that comes with a test voucher, you can contact a Pearson VUE testing center and register to take the exam using the voucher numbers that came with your Course Kit. If you didn't purchase the Course Kit with the voucher, you can contact Pearson VUE and arrange to pay for the test and register with an exam location. You can contact Pearson VUE at www.pearsonvue.com.

Introduction

Welcome to the *CompTIA Security+ SY0-201 Cert Guide*. The CompTIA Security+ Certification is widely accepted as the first security certification you should attempt to attain in your information technology (IT) career. The CompTIA Security+ Certification is designed to be a vendor-neutral exam that measures your knowledge of industry-standard technologies and methodologies. It acts as a great stepping stone to other vendor-specific certifications and careers. I developed this book to be something you can study from for the exam and keep on your bookshelf for later use as a security resource.

I'd like to note that it's unfeasible to cover all security concepts in depth in a single book. However, the Security+ exam objectives are looking for a basic level of computer, networking, and organizational security knowledge. Keep this in mind while reading through this text, and remember that the main goal of this text is to help you pass the Security+ exam, not to be the master of all security. Not just yet at least!

Because this is a security book, it is a bit more serious than some of my other texts. This may come as a surprise to some, but levity should be used carefully when dealing with security concepts because too much humor can easily confuse the issue and be taken the wrong way. It is my belief that in this fast-paced world of ever-changing technology, an author needs to get right to the point. I understand that you don't have unlimited time for study, so you will notice me being blunt in the way I get to the core of concepts. Don't take offense! This is done by design to aid you in absorbing content quickly.

Good luck as you prepare to take the CompTIA Security+ exam. As you read through this book, you will be building an impenetrable castle of knowledge, culminating in hands-on familiarity and the know-how to pass the exam. If you have any questions while reading through this book, please feel free to ask them at my website: www.davidlprowse.com.

A NOTE TO INSTRUCTORS I developed this book not only for the individual reader, but also to work well in the classroom setting. To complement this book, I also designed an instructor guide that can be accessed for free from the following link:

www.pearsonhighered.com/educator

The supplemental instructor guide includes a breakdown of each chapter, a sample lesson plan, and plenty of teaching tips and tricks. You can also find PowerPoint presentations and a test bank of questions available for download. And of course, if you have questions about the guide, please let me know at my website. Good luck in your teaching endeavors!

Goals and Methods

The number one goal of this book is to help you pass the 2008 version of the CompTIA Security+ Certification Exam (number SY0-201). To that effect, I have added three 100-question practice exams with explanations. Two are in the text at the end of the book. A third is located on the accompanying DVD (print version of this book only). These tests are geared to check your knowledge and ready you for the real exam. If you would like to purchase more electronic practice questions, go to www.pearsonitcertification.com/0132303381.

The CompTIA Security+ Certification exam involves familiarity with computer security theory and hands-on know-how. To aid you in mastering and understanding the Security+ Certification objectives, this book uses the following methods:

- **Opening topics list**—This defines the topics to be covered in the chapter; it also lists the corresponding CompTIA Security+ objective numbers.
- **Topical coverage**—The heart of the chapter. Explains the topics from a theory-based standpoint, as well as from a hands-on perspective. This includes in-depth descriptions, tables, and figures that are geared to build your knowledge so that you can pass the exam. The chapters are broken down into two to three topics each.
- **Key Topics**—The Key Topics indicate important figures, tables, and lists of information that you should know for the exam. They are interspersed throughout the chapter and are listed in table format at the end of the chapter.
- **Memory Tables and Lists**—These can be found on the DVD as Appendix A, "Memory Tables," and Appendix B, "Memory Tables Answer Key." Use them to help memorize important information.
- **Key Terms**—Key terms without definitions are listed at the end of each chapter. See whether you can define them, and then check your work against the complete key term definitions in the glossary.
- **Hands-On Labs**—There are labs for each chapter (except Chapter 1, "Introduction to Security"). The step-by-step procedures appear at the end of the chapters and corresponding video solutions can be found on the DVD.
- **Review Questions**—At the end of each chapter is a quiz. The quizzes, and answers with explanations, are meant to gauge your knowledge of the subjects. If an answer to a question doesn't come readily to you, be sure to review that portion of the chapter.

Another goal of this book is to offer support for you—the reader. I have posted additional practice questions, videos, and errata on my website at the following link: www.davidlprowse.com/secplus. And if you have any questions to ask, you can post them in the "Ask Dave" section. Anyone can view the content on the website, but you must register to post questions. Registration is free; all that is needed is a valid e-mail address that is kept strictly confidential. I try my best to answer questions as soon as possible. On the site you can find some free extras as well. Visit often!

Who Should Read This Book?

This book is for anyone who wants to start or advance a career in IT security. Readers of this book can range from persons taking a Security+ course, to individuals already in the field who want to keep their skills sharp, or perhaps retain their job due to a company policy mandating they take the Security+ exam.

This book is also designed for people who plan on taking additional security-related certifications after the CompTIA Security+ exam. The book is designed in such a way to offer an easy transition to future certification studies.

Although not a prerequisite, it is recommended that CompTIA Security+ candidates have at least two years of technical networking experience with an emphasis on security. The CompTIA Network+ certification is also recommended as a prerequisite. It is expected that you understand computer topics such as how to install operating systems and applications, and networking topics such as how to configure IP, what a VLAN is, and so on. The focus of this book is to show how to secure these technologies and protect against possible exploits and attacks. Generally, for people looking to enter the IT field, the CompTIA Security+ certification is attained after the A+ and Network+ certifications.

Important! If you do not feel that you have the required experience, have never attempted to secure a computer or network, or are new to the IT field, I recommend considering an IT course that covers the CompTIA Security+ objectives. You can choose from plenty of technical training schools, community colleges, and online courses. Use this book with the course and any other course materials you obtain.

CompTIA Security+ Exam Topics

Table I-1 lists the exam topics for the CompTIA Security+ exam. This table lists the chapter in which each exam topic is covered. Chapter 1 is an introductory chapter and as such does not map to any specific exam objectives. Chapter 16 gives strategies for taking the exam and does not map to any specific objectives either.

Table I-1 CompTIA Security+ Exam Topics

Chapter	Exam Topic	CompTIA Security+ Exam Objectives Covered
1	Security 101 Think Like a Hacker	n/a
2	Computer Systems Security Threats Implementing Security Applications Securing Computer Hardware and Peripherals	Objectives 1.1, 1.2, and 1.5
3	Hardening Operating Systems Virtualization Technology	Objectives 1.3 and 1.6
4	Securing the Browser Securing Other Applications	Objective 1.4
5	Network Design Ports, Protocols, and Malicious Attacks	Objectives 2.1 and 2.2
6	Firewalls and Network Security NIDS Versus NIPS	Objectives 2.3 and 2.4
7	Securing Wired Networks and Devices Securing Wireless Networks	Objectives 2.5, 2.6, and 2.7
8	Physical Security Authentication Models and Components	Objectives 3.6, 3.7, 3.8, and 3.9
9	Access Control Models Defined Rights, Permissions, and Policies	Objectives 3.1, 3.2, 3.3, 3.4, and 3.5
10	Conducting Risk Assessments Assessing Vulnerability with Security Tools	Objectives 4.1, 4.2, and 4.3
11	Monitoring Methodologies Using Tools to Monitor Systems and Networks Conducting Audits	Objectives 4.4, 4.5, 4.6, and 4.7
12	Cryptography Concepts Encryption Algorithms Hashing Basics	Objectives 5.1, 5.2, and 5.3

Table I-1 CompTIA Security+ Exam Topics

Chapter	Exam Topic	CompTIA Security+ Exam Objectives Covered
13	Public Key Infrastructure Security Protocols	Objectives 5.4, 5.5, and 5.6
14	Redundancy Planning Disaster Recovery Planning and Procedures	Objective 6.1
15	Environmental Controls Social Engineering Legislative and Organizational Policies	Objectives 6.3, 6.4, 6.5, and 6.6
16	Getting Ready and the Exam Preparation Checklist Tips for Taking the Real Exam Beyond the CompTIA Security+ Certification	n/a

This chapter covers the following subjects:

- **Security 101**—School is in session. This section discusses some of the basic principles of security such as CIA and AAA, some basic threats, and various ways to mitigate those threats.
- **Think Like a Hacker**—To know your enemy, you must think like them. Sometimes the hacker is your enemy, sometimes not. This section describes the various hats worn in the hacker society.

CHAPTER 1

Introduction to Security

Welcome! Before we launch into heavy-duty security, I'd like to go over some foundation-level security concepts. I recommend that everyone read this chapter, but if you are a seasoned professional, you might opt to scan or skip it. For those of you new to the IT security field, this chapter (and the rest of the book) will act as the basis of your IT sleuthing career.

It is so important in today's organizations to protect information from unauthorized access and to prevent the modification, disruption, or destruction of data unless it is approved by the organization. That in a nutshell is information security. Companies consider it so important that many IT directors have become full-fledged executives—chief information officers (CIO) or chief technology officers (CTO). But let's not get ahead of ourselves! This book is for persons wanting to embark on, or continue along, the path as a network security administrator. Many other names are given to that particular position, but we'll stick with that one for the sake of continuity throughout this book.

This entire book is all about locating risks and vulnerabilities to your information and eliminating those risks, or at least reducing them to a point acceptable to your organization.

This first chapter talks about some basic fundamental security concepts and teaches you to think like a hacker but act like an administrator.

Let's begin!

Foundation Topics

Security 101

The first thing we need to get out of the way is that nothing is ever completely or truly secure. People might give clever definitions of something that *could* be completely secure, but it is a utopia—something that can be imagined but never achieved. There is always a way around or through any security precaution that we construct.

Now that it's understood that there is no perfect scenario, we can move on to some security basics that can help to build a solid foundation upon which proper mitigating of security risks can begin.

The CIA of Computer Security

No, we're not talking national security, but computers can be the victim of covert operations. To defend against the worst, IT people attempt to adhere to three core principles of information security: confidentiality, integrity, and availability.

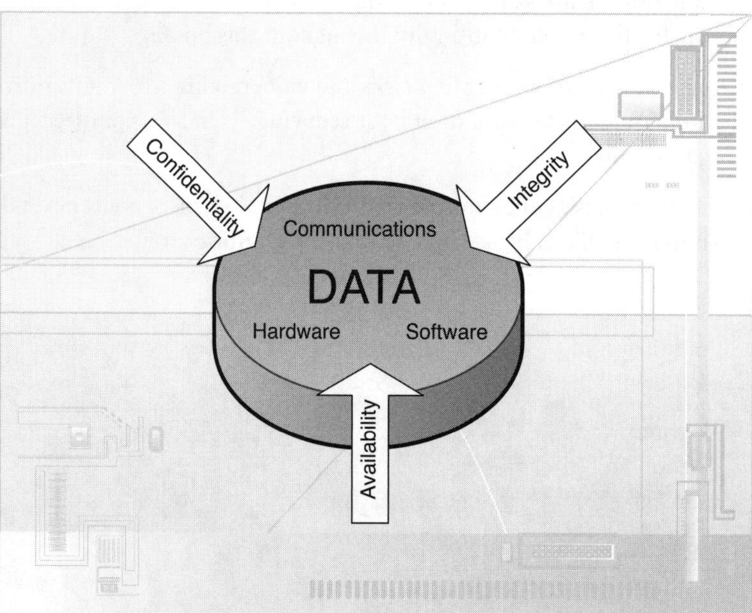

Figure 1-1 The CIA of Computer Security

By employing the concepts of confidentiality, integrity, and availability to your data, an organization's hardware, software, and communications can be secured properly. Let's discuss each of the three items of the CIA triad in a little more depth.

- **Confidentiality—**Preventing the disclosure of information to unauthorized persons. For the public it signifies Social Security numbers (or other country-specific identification), driver license information, bank accounts and passwords, and so on. For organizations this can include all the preceding information, but it actually denotes the confidentiality of data. To make data confidential, the organization must work hard to make sure that it can be accessed only by authorized individuals. This book spends a good amount of time discussing and showing how to accomplish this. For example, when you use a credit card number at a store or online, the number should be encrypted with a strong cipher so that the card number cannot be compromised. Next time you buy something online, take a look at how the credit card number is being kept confidential. As a security professional, confidentiality should be your number one goal. In keeping data confidential, you remove threats, absorb vulnerabilities, and reduce risk.
- **Integrity—**Authorization is necessary before data can be modified. If a person were to delete a file, either maliciously or inadvertently, the integrity of that file will have been violated. Here's a tip for you: Smart companies *do not* delete data!
- **Availability—**Securing computers and networks can be a strain on resources. Availability means that data is obtainable regardless of how information is stored, accessed, or protected. It also means that data should be available regardless of the malicious attack that might be perpetrated on it.

These three principles, known as the CIA triad, should be applied whenever dealing with the security of hardware, software, or communications.

Another acronym to live by is the AAA of computer security: authentication, authorization, and accounting.

- **Authentication—**When a person's identity is established with proof and confirmed by a system. Typically, this requires a digital identity of some sort, username/password, or other authentication scheme.
- **Authorization—**When a user is given access to certain data or areas of a building. Authorization happens after authentication and can be determined in several ways including permissions, access control lists, time-of-day, and other login restrictions and physical restrictions.
- **Accounting—**The tracking of data, computer usage, and network resources. Often it means logging, auditing, and monitoring of the data and resources. Accountability is quickly becoming more important in today's secure networks. Part of this concept is the burden of proof. You as the security person must provide proof if you believe that someone committed an unauthorized action.

When you have indisputable proof of something users have done and they cannot deny it, it is known as *nonrepudiation*.

The Basics of Data Security

Data security is the act of protecting data from threats and possible corruption. You need to be aware of several types of threats to be an effective network security administrator:

- **Malicious software**—Known as malware, this includes computer viruses, worms, Trojan horses, spyware, rootkits, adware, and other types of unwanted software. Everyone has heard of a scenario in which a user's computer was compromised to some extent due to malicious software.
- **Unauthorized access**—Access to computer resources and data without consent of the owner. It might include approaching the system, trespassing, communicating, storing and retrieving data, intercepting data, or any other methods that would interfere with a computer's normal work. Access to data must be controlled to ensure privacy. Improper administrative access would fall into this category as well.
- **System failure**—Computer crashes or individual application failure. This can happen due to three reasons: user error, malicious activity, or hardware failure.
- **Social engineering**—The act of manipulating users into revealing confidential information or performing other actions detrimental to the user. Almost everyone gets e-mails nowadays from unknown entities making false claims or asking for personal information (or money!); this is one example of social engineering.

Many data security technologies and concepts can protect against, or help recover from, the preceding threats. Several common ones are listed here:

- **User awareness**—The wiser the user, the less chance of security breaches. Employee training and education, easily accessible and understandable policies, security-awareness e-mails and online security resources all help to provide user awareness. These methods can help to protect from all the threats mentioned previously. Educating the user is an excellent method when attempting to protect against security attacks.
- **Authentication**—The verification of a person's identity that helps protect against unauthorized access. It is a preventative measure that can be broken down into three categories:
  - Something the user knows, for example a password or PIN
  - Something the user has, for example a smart card or other security token
  - Something the user is, for example the biometric reading of a fingerprint or retina scan
- **Antimalware software**—Protects a computer from the various forms of malware, and if necessary, detects and removes them. Types include antivirus and

antispyware software. Well-known examples include Norton AntiVirus, McAfee VirusScan, Windows Defender, and Spyware Doctor. Nowadays, a lot of the software named "antivirus" can protect against spyware as well.

- **Data backups—**Backups won't stop damage to data, but they can enable you to recover data after an attack or other compromise, or system failure. From programs such as NTbackup and Bacula to enterprise-level programs such as Tivoli and Veritas, data backup is an important part of security. Note that fault-tolerant methods such as RAID 1 and 5 are good preventative measures against hardware failure but might not offer protection from data corruption or erasure. For more information on RAID, see Chapter 14, "Redundancy and Disaster Recovery."
- **Encryption—**The act of changing information using an algorithm known as a cipher to make it unreadable to anyone except users who possess the proper "key" to the data. Examples of this include HTTPS, Kerberos, and PGP.
- **Data removal—**Proper data removal goes far beyond file deletion or the formatting of digital media. The problem with file deletion/formatting is data remanence, or the residue, that is left behind, from which re-creation of files can be accomplished by some less-than-reputable people with smart tools. Companies typically employ one of three options when met with the prospect of data removal: clearing, purging (also known as sanitizing) and destruction. We talk more about these in Chapter 15, "Policies, Procedures, and People."

Think Like a Hacker

I'm not condoning any malicious activity, but to think like a hacker, you have to understand the hacker. So ask yourself, why do people decide to become hackers? Why take advantage of users? In the minds of some malicious individuals, it may simply be because they are there to be taken advantage of! One common answer is greed—the act of hacking for illegal monetary gain. Other attackers have an agenda, or believe in a cause, or just want to get free access to movies and music. Still others just want to cause mayhem and anarchy. Consider this when you secure your organization's computers—they just might be a target!

Of course, people use different names to classify these types of individuals: hacker, cracker, cyber-criminal, and so on. It doesn't matter what you call them, but the accepted term in most network security circles is hacker.

Now consider this: Not all hackers are malicious. That's right! There are different types of hackers out there. Various names are used by different organizations, but some of the common labels include the following:

- **White hats—**These are nonmalicious; for example, an IT person who attempts to hack into a computer system before it goes live to test it. Generally, the person attempting the hack has a contractual agreement with the owner of the resource to be hacked. White hats will often be involved in something known as ethical hacking. An ethical hacker is an expert at breaking into systems and can attack systems on behalf of the system's owner and with the owner's consent. The ethical hacker will use penetration testing and intrusion testing to attempt to gain access to a target network or system.

- **Black hats**—These *are* malicious and attempt to break into computers and computer networks without authorization. Black hats are the ones who attempt identity theft, piracy, credit card fraud, and so on. Penalties for this type of activity are severe and black hats know it; keep this in mind if and when you come into contact with one of these seedy individuals—they can be brutal, especially when cornered. Of course, many vendors try to make the term "black hat" into something cuter and less dangerous. But for the purposes of this book and your job security, we need to call a spade a spade, or in this case, a black hat a malicious individual.
- **Gray hats**—These are possibly the most inexplicable people on the planet. They are individuals who do not have any affiliation with a company but risk breaking the law by attempting to hack a system and then notify the administrator of the system that they were successful in doing so—just to let them know! Not to do anything malicious (other than breaking in...). Some offer to fix security vulnerabilities at a price, but these types are also known as green hats or mercenaries.
- **Blue hats**—These are individuals who are asked to attempt to hack into a system by an organization, but the organization does not employ them. The organization relies on the fact that the person simply enjoys hacking into systems. Usually, this type of scenario occurs when testing systems.
- **Elite**—Elite hackers are the ones who first find out about vulnerabilities. Only 1 out of an estimated 10,000 hackers wears the Elite hat. The credit for their discoveries is usually appropriated by someone else more interested in fame. Many of these types of individuals don't usually care about "credit due" and are more interested in anonymity—perhaps a wise choice. You do not want to get on an Elites' bad side; they could crumple most networks within hours if they so desired.

We mentioned before that no system is truly secure. Hackers know this and count on it. It's a constant battle in which administrators and attackers are consistently building and breaking down better and better mouse traps. The scales are always tipping back and forth; a hacker develops a way to break into a system, then an administrator finds a way to block that attack, then the hacker looks for an alternative method, and so on. This seems to reek of the chicken and the egg—which came first? Answer: You have to take it on a case-by-case basis. The last few sentences of banter are there for one reason—to convince you that you need to be on your toes; that you need to review logs often; that you need to employ as many security precautions as possible; that you need to keep abreast of the latest attacks and ways to mitigate your risk; and to never underestimate the power and resilience of a hacker.

Exam Preparation Tasks

Review Key Topics

Review the most important topics in the chapter, noted with the Key Topics icon in the outer margin of the page. Table 1-1 lists a reference of these key topics and the page numbers on which each is found.

Table 1-1 Key Topics for Chapter 1

Key Topic Element	Description	Page Number
Figure 1-1	The CIA of computer security	4
Bulleted list	Definitions of confidentiality, integrity, and availability	5
Bulleted list	Definitions of authentication, authorization, and accounting	5

Define Key Terms

Define the following key terms from this chapter, and check your answers in the glossary.

confidentiality, integrity, availability, nonrepudiation, authentication, authorization, accounting

Answer Review Questions

Answer the following review questions. You can find the answers at the end of this chapter.

1. In information security, what are the three main goals? (Select the three best answers.)
   A. Auditing
   B. Integrity
   C. Nonrepudiation
   D. Confidentiality
   E. Risk Assessment
   F. Availability

2. To protect against malicious attacks, what should you think like?
   A. Hacker
   B. Network admin
   C. Spoofer
   D. Auditor

3. Tom sends out many e-mails containing secure information to other companies. What concept should be implemented to prove that Tom did indeed send the e-mails?
   A. Authenticity
   B. Nonrepudiation
   C. Confidentiality
   D. Integrity

4. Which of the following does the A in CIA stand for when it comes to IT security? Select the best answer.
   A. Accountability
   B. Assessment

C. Availability

D. Auditing

5. Which of the following is the greatest risk when it comes to removable storage?

A. Integrity of data

B. Availability of data

C. Confidentiality of data

D. Accountability of data

6. When it comes to information security, what is the I in CIA?

A. Insurrection

B. Information

C. Indigestion

D. Integrity

7. When is a system completely secure?

A. When it is updated

B. When it is assessed for vulnerabilities

C. When all anomalies have been removed

D. Never

Answers and Explanations

1. **B, D, and F.** Confidentiality, integrity, and availability (known as CIA or the CIA triad) are the three *main* goals when it comes to information security. Another goal within information security is accountability.
2. **A.** To protect against malicious attacks, think like a hacker. Then, protect and secure like a network security administrator.
3. **B.** You should use nonrepudiation to prevent Tom from denying that he sent the e-mails.
4. **C.** Availability is what the "A" in "CIA" stands for, as in "the availability of data." Together the acronym stands for confidentiality, integrity, and availability. Although accountability is important and is often included as a fourth component of the CIA triad, it is not the best answer. Assessment and auditing are both important concepts when checking for vulnerabilities and reviewing and logging, but they are not considered to be part of the CIA triad.

5. **C.** For removable storage, the confidentiality of data is the greatest risk because removable storage can easily be removed from the building and shared with others. Although the other factors of the CIA triad are important, any theft of removable storage can destroy the confidentiality of data, and that makes it the greatest risk.

6. **D.** The I in CIA stands for integrity. Together CIA stands for confidentiality, integrity, and availability. Accountability is also a core principle of information security.

7. **D.** A system can never truly be completely secure. The scales are always tipping back and forth; a hacker develops a way to break into a system, then an administrator finds a way to block that attack, and then the hacker looks for an alternative method. It goes on and on; be ready to wage the eternal battle!

This chapter covers the following subjects:

Computer Systems Security Threats—This portion of Chapter 2 can help you to differentiate between the various computer security threats you should be aware of for the exam including malware in all of its forms, spam, privilege escalation, and more. Then we discuss how to defend against those threats in a proactive way, and how to fix problems that do occur in the case that threats have already manifested themselves. By far, this is the most important section of this chapter; study it carefully!

Implementing Security Applications—In this section, you learn how to select, install, and configure security applications such as personal firewalls, antivirus programs, and host-based intrusion detection systems. You'll be able to distinguish between the various tools and decide which is best for the different situations you'll see in the field.

Securing Computer Hardware and Peripherals—Here we delve into the physical; how to protect a computer's hardware, BIOS, and peripherals. We also discuss how to protect cell phones and USB devices.

This chapter covers the CompTIA Security+ SY0-201 objectives 1.1, 1.2, and 1.5.

CHAPTER 2

Computer Systems Security

Simply stated, the most important part of a computer is the data. The data must be available, yet secured in such a way so that it can't be tampered with. Computer systems security is all about the security threats that can compromise an operating system and the data held within. Threats such as viruses, Trojans, and spyware are extremely prevalent in today's society. They are a big part of this chapter, and this chapter is an important part of the book. But it doesn't stop there, your computer can be accessed in other ways including via the BIOS and by external devices. And "computer" doesn't just mean that desktop computer at a user's desk. It also means laptops, PDAs, and cell phones—actually any other devices that have processing power and an operating system. These threats can be eliminated by implementing security applications on every one of your client computers on the network. Applications that can help to secure your computers against malware threats include antivirus programs, antispyware applications, personal firewalls, and host-based intrusion detection systems.

By implementing these security applications and ensuring that they are updated on a regular basis, you can stave off the majority of malicious attacks that can target a computer system.

Foundation Topics

Computer Systems Security Threats

To combat the various security threats that can occur on a computer system, we first need to classify them. Then we need to define how these threats can be delivered to the target computer. Afterward we can discuss how to prevent security threats from happening and troubleshoot them if they do occur. Let's start with the most common computer threat and probably the most deadly—malicious software.

Malicious Software

Malicious software, or *malware*, is software designed to infiltrate a computer system and possibly damage it without the user's knowledge or consent. Malware is a broad term used by computer professionals to include viruses, worms, Trojan horses, spyware, rootkits, adware, and other types of undesirable software.

Of course, we don't want malware to infect our computer system, but to defend against it we first need to define it and categorize it. Then we can put preventative measures into place. It's also important to locate and remove/quarantine malware from a computer system in the case that it does manifest itself.

For the exam, you need to know about several types of malware. For the past several years, an emphasis shift from viruses to spyware has occurred. Most people know about viruses and have some kind of antivirus software running. However, many people are still confused about exactly what spyware is, how it occurs, and how to protect against it. Because of this, computer professionals spend a lot of time fixing spyware issues and training users on how to protect against them in the future. However, viruses are still a valid foe; let's start by discussing them.

Viruses

A *virus* is code that runs on a computer without the user's knowledge; it infects the computer when the code is accessed and executed. For viruses to do their dirty work, they first need to be executed by the user in some way. A virus also has reproductive capability and can spread copies of itself throughout the computer if it is first executed by the user. By infecting files accessed by other computers, the virus can spread to those other systems as well. The problem is that computers can't call in sick on Monday; they need to be up and running as much as possible, more than your average human.

One well-known example of a virus is the Love Bug. Originating in 2000, this virus would arrive by an e-mail titled "I love you" with an attachment named *love-letter-for-you.txt.vbs*, or one of several other permutations of this fictitious love. Some users would be tricked into thinking this was a text file, but the extension was actually

.vbs, short for Visual Basic script. This virus deleted files, sent usernames and passwords to its creator, infected 15 million computers, and supposedly caused $5 billion in damage. Educate your users on how to screen their e-mail!

You might encounter several different types of viruses:

- **Boot sector—**Initially loads into the first sector of the hard drive; when the computer boots, the virus then loads into memory.
- **Macro—**Usually placed in documents and e-mailed to users in the hopes that the user will open the document, thus executing the virus.
- **Program—**Infects executable files.
- **Polymorphic—**Can change every time is it executed in an attempt to avoid antivirus detection.
- **Stealth—**Uses various techniques to go unnoticed by antivirus programs.
- **Armored—**These protect themselves from antivirus programs by tricking the program into thinking that it is located in a different place from where it actually resides. Essentially, it has a layer of protection that it can use against the person who tries to analyze it; it will thwart attempts by analysts to examine its code.
- **Multipartite—**A hybrid of boot and program viruses that attacks the boot sector or system files first and then attacks the other.

Worms

Worms are much like viruses except they self-replicate whereas a virus does not. Worms take advantage of backdoors and security holes in operating systems and applications. They look for other systems on the network or through the Internet that are running the same applications and replicate to those other systems. With worms, the user doesn't need to access and execute the malware. A virus needs some sort of carrier to get it where it wants to go and needs explicit instructions to be executed, or it must be executed by the user. The worm does not need this carrier or explicit instructions to be executed.

A well-known example of a worm is Nimda (admin backward), which propagated automatically through the Internet in 22 minutes in 2001, causing widespread damage. It propagated through network shares, mass e-mailing, and operating system vulnerabilities.

Trojan Horses

Trojan horses, or simply Trojans, appear to perform wanted functions but are actually performing malicious functions behind the scenes. These are not technically viruses and can easily be downloaded without noticing them. Remote access Trojans (RATs) are the most common type of Trojan, for example Back Orifice or NetBus; their capability to allow an attacker higher administration privileges than the owner of the system makes them dangerous as well. Another example of a remote access Trojan (also known as a backdoor Trojan) is SubSeven, as shown in Figure 2-1. As you can see in the figure, this program has the capability to scan for unprotected hosts and make all kinds of changes to a host when connected. A program like this was not designed to be used maliciously, but programs like these are easy for an average person to download and use. When a target computer is controlled by an attacker, it could easily become a robot (or simply a *bot*), carrying out the plans of the attackers at their command.

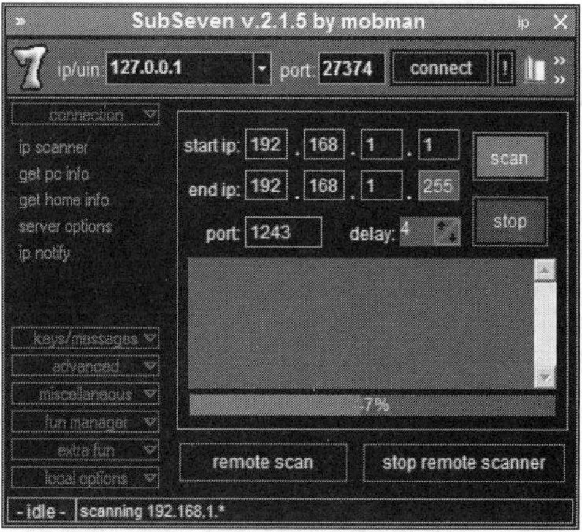

Figure 2-1 Example of a Remote Access Trojan Program

NOTE: It should go without mentioning, but I'll mention it anyway. Take extreme care when dealing with applications such as SubSeven; they are dangerous! During the writing of this book, I set up a test computer on a segregated network as my guinea pig, so to speak. This computer is where I run tests on viruses, spyware, Trojans, and malicious applications. I call it a "clean computer." This computer never sees any of my other live networks, does not connect to the Internet, and is wiped when tests are complete. Please be careful and use test systems and test networks when assessing malware and antimalware applications.

Spyware

Spyware is a type of malicious software either downloaded unwittingly from a website or installed along with some other third-party software. Usually, this malware collects information about the user without the user's consent. It could be as simple as a piece of code that logs what websites you access, or go as far as a program that records your keystrokes. Spyware is also associated with advertising (those pop-ups that just won't go away!) and could possibly change the computer configuration without any user interaction; for example, redirecting a browser to access websites other than those wanted. *Adware* usually falls into the realm of spyware because it pops up advertisements based on what it has learned from spying on the user. *Grayware* is another general term that describes applications that are behaving improperly but without serious consequences. It is associated with spyware, adware, and joke programs. Very funny...not. One example (of many) of spyware is the Internet Optimizer, which redirects IE error pages out to other website's advertising pages.

Rootkits

A *rootkit* is a type of software designed to gain administrator-level control over a computer system without being detected. The term is a combination of the words "root" (meaning the root user in a UNIX/Linux system or administrator in a Windows system) and "kit" (meaning software kit). Usually, the purpose is to perform malicious operations on a target computer at a later date without the knowledge of the administrators or users of that computer. Rootkits can target the BIOS, boot loader, kernel, and more. An example of a boot loader rootkit is the Evil Maid Attack; this attack can extract the encryption keys of a full disk encryption system, which we discuss more later. Rootkits are difficult to detect because they are activated before the operating system has fully booted. A rootkit might install hidden files, processes, and hidden user accounts. Because rootkits can be installed in hardware or software, they can intercept data from network connections, keyboards, and so on.

Spam

Spam is the abuse of electronic messaging systems such as e-mail, broadcast media, instant messaging, and so on. Spammers send unsolicited bulk messages indiscriminately, usually without benefit to the actual spammer, because the majority of spam is either deflected or ignored. Companies with questionable ethics condone this type of marketing (usually set up as a pyramid scheme) so that the people at the top of the marketing chain can benefit; however, it's usually not worthwhile for the actual person that sends out spam.

The most common form of spam is e-mail spam, which is one of the worst banes of network administrators. Spam can clog up resources and possibly cause a type of denial of service to an e-mail server if there is enough of it. It can also mislead users, in an attempt at social engineering. And the bulk of network-based viruses are transferred through spam e-mails. Yikes! The worst type of spamming is when a person uses another organization's e-mail server to send the spam. Obviously illegal, it could also create legal issues for the organization that owns the e-mail server. Just about everyone has seen a spam e-mail, and in the rare case that you haven't, check out this link for some pretty horrific examples:

www.antespam.co.uk/spam-resource/

Summary of Malware Threats

Table 2-1 summarizes the malware threats discussed up to this point.

Table 2-1 Summary of Malware Threats

Malware Threat	Definition	Example
Virus	Code that runs on a computer without the user's knowledge; it infects the computer when the code is accessed and executed.	Love Bug virus Ex: *love-letter-for-you.txt.vbs*
Worm	Similar to viruses except that it self-replicates whereas a virus does not.	Nimda Propagated through network shares and mass e-mailing
Trojan horse	Appears to perform desired functions but are actually performing malicious functions behind the scenes.	Remote access Trojan Ex: SubSeven malware application
Spyware	Malicious software either downloaded unwittingly from a website or installed along with some other third-party software.	Internet Optimizer (aka DyFuCA)
Rootkit	Software designed to gain administrator-level control over a computer system without being detected.	Boot loader rootkits Ex: Evil Maid Attack
Spam	The abuse of electronic messaging systems such as e-mail, broadcast media, and instant messaging.	Phishing identity theft e-mails Lottery scam e-mails

Ways to Deliver Malicious Software

Malware is not sentient (...not yet) and can't just appear out of thin air; it needs to be transported and delivered to a computer or installed on a computer system in some manner. This can be done in several ways. The simplest way would be for attackers to gain physical access to an unprotected computer and perform their malicious work locally. But because it can be difficult to obtain physical access, this can be done in several other ways, as shown in the upcoming sections. Some of the methods listed next can also be used by an attacker to simply gain access to a computer, make modifications, and so on, in addition to delivering the malware.

Via Software, Messaging, and Media

Malware can be delivered via software in a lot of different ways. A person who e-mails a zipped file might not even know that malware also exists in that file. The recipients of the e-mail will have no idea that the extra malware exists unless they have software to scan their e-mail attachments for it. Malware could also be delivered via FTP. Because FTP servers are inherently insecure, it's easier than you might think to upload insidious files and other software. Malware is often found among P2P networks and bit torrents. Great care should be taken by users who use these technologies. Malware can also be embedded within, and distributed by, websites through the use of corrupting code or bad downloads. Malware can even be distributed by advertisements. And of course, removable media can victimize a computer as well. CD-ROMs, DVDs, and USB flash drives can easily be manipulated to automatically run malware when they are inserted into the computer. This is when AutoRun is not your friend! The removable media could also have hidden viruses or worms and possibly logic bombs configured to set that malware off at specific times.

Active Interception

Active interception (also known as *active inception*) normally includes a computer placed between the sender and the receiver in an effort to capture and possibly modify information. If a person can eavesdrop on your computer's data session, then that data can be stolen, modified, or exploited in other ways. Examples of this include session theft and man-in-the-middle attacks. For more information on these attacks, see the section titled "Ports, Protocols, and Malicious Attacks" in Chapter 5, "Network Design Elements and Threats."

Privilege Escalation

Privilege escalation is the act of exploiting a bug or design flaw in a software or firmware application to gain access to resources that normally would've been protected from an application or user. This results in a user gaining additional privileges, more than were originally intended by the developer of the application; for example, if a regular user gains administrative control, or if a particular user can read another user's e-mail without authorization.

Backdoors

Backdoors are used in computer programs to bypass normal authentication and other security mechanisms in place. Originally, backdoors were used by developers as a legitimate way of accessing an application, but soon after they were implemented by attackers who would use backdoors to make changes to operating systems, websites, and network devices. Or the attacker would create a completely new application that would act as a backdoor, for example Back Orifice, which enables a user to control a Windows computer from a remote location. Quite often, it is installed via a Trojan horse; this particular one is known as a remote access Trojan or RAT. Some worms install backdoors on computers so that remote spammers can send junk e-mail from the infected computers, or so an attacker can attempt privilege escalation. Unfortunately, there isn't much that can be done about backdoors aside from updating or patching the system infected and keeping on top of updates. However, if network administrators were to find out about a new backdoor, they should inform the manufacturer of the device or the application as soon as possible. Backdoors are less common nowadays, because their practice is usually discouraged by software manufacturers and by makers of network devices.

Logic Bombs

Logic bombs are code that has, in some way, been inserted into software; it is meant to initiate one of many types of malicious functions when specific criteria are met. Logic bombs blur the line between malware and a malware delivery system. They are indeed unwanted software but are intended to activate viruses, worms, or Trojans at a specific time. Trojans set off on a certain date are also referred to as *time bombs*. The logic bomb ticks away until the correct time, date, and other parameters have been met. So, some of the worst bombs do not incorporate an explosion whatsoever. The logic bomb could be contained within a virus or loaded separately. Logic bombs are more common in the movies than they are in real life, but they do happen, and with grave consequences; but more often than not, they are detected before they are set off. If you, as a systems administrator, suspect that you have found a logic bomb, or a portion of the code of a logic bomb, you should notify your superior immediately and check your organization's policies to see if you should take any other actions. Action could include placing network disaster recovery processes on stand-by; notifying the software vendor; and closely managing usage of the software including, perhaps, withdrawing it from service until the threat is mitigated. Logic bombs are the evil cousin of the Easter egg.

Easter eggs historically have been a platonic extra that was added to an OS or application as a sort of joke; quite often, it was missed by quality control and subsequently released by the manufacturer of the software. An example of an Easter egg is the capability to force a win in Windows XP's Solitaire by pressing the ALT+Shift+2 keys simultaneously. Easter eggs are not normally documented (being tossed in last minute by humorous programmers) and are meant to be harmless, but nowadays they are not allowed by responsible software companies and are thoroughly scanned for. Because an Easter egg (and who knows what else) can possibly slip past quality control, and the growing concerns about malware in general, many companies have adopted the idea of Trustworthy Computing, which is a newer concept that sets standards for how software is designed, coded, and checked for quality control. Sadly, as far as software goes, the Easter egg's day has passed.

Botnets and Zombies

I know what you are thinking—the names of these attacks and delivery methods are getting a bit ridiculous. But bear with me; they make sense and are deadly serious. Allow me to explain—malware can be distributed throughout the Internet by a group of compromised computers, known as a *botnet*, and controlled by a master computer (where the attacker resides). The individual compromised computers in the botnet are called *zombies*. This is because they are unaware of the malware that has been installed on them. This can occur in several ways, including automated distribution of the malware from one zombie computer to another. Now imagine if all the zombie computers had a specific virus or other attack loaded, and a logic bomb was also installed, ready to set off the malware at a specific time. If this were done to hundreds or thousands of computers, a synchronized attack of great proportions could be enacted on just about any target. Often, this is known as a distributed denial of service, or DDoS, attack, and is usually perpetuated on a particularly popular server, one that serves many requests.

Preventing and Troubleshooting Malware

Now that we know the types of malware, and the ways that they can be delivered to a computer, let's talk about how to stop them before they happen, and how to troubleshoot them if they do happen. Unfortunately, given the amount of computers you will work on, they *will* happen.

If a system is affected by malware, it might be sluggish in its response time or display unwanted pop-ups and incorrect home pages; or applications (and maybe even the whole system) could lock up or shut down unexpectedly. Quite often, malware uses CPU and memory resources directly or behind the scenes, causing the system to run slower than usual. In general, a technician should look for erratic behavior from the computer, as if it had a mind of its own! Let's go over viruses and spyware, and show how to prevent them, and finally how to troubleshoot them if they do occur.

Preventing and Troubleshooting Viruses

We can do several things to protect a computer system from viruses. First, every computer should have antivirus software running on it. McAfee, Norton, and Vipre are examples of manufacturers of AV software, but there are many others. Second, the AV software should be updated, which means that the software will require a current license; this is renewed yearly with most providers. When updating, be sure to update the AV engine *and* the definitions if you are doing it manually. Otherwise, set the AV software to automatically update at periodic intervals, for example, every day or every week. It's a good idea to schedule regular full scans of the system within the AV software. Figure 2-2 shows an example of a scan that has detected a virus. It recommends that the virus be quarantined; this is the cleaning action that will be taken if you click the **Clean** button. This is actually one of many test viruses that can be created on a system; it doesn't do any particular damage, but it verifies that your AV software can live up to its name.

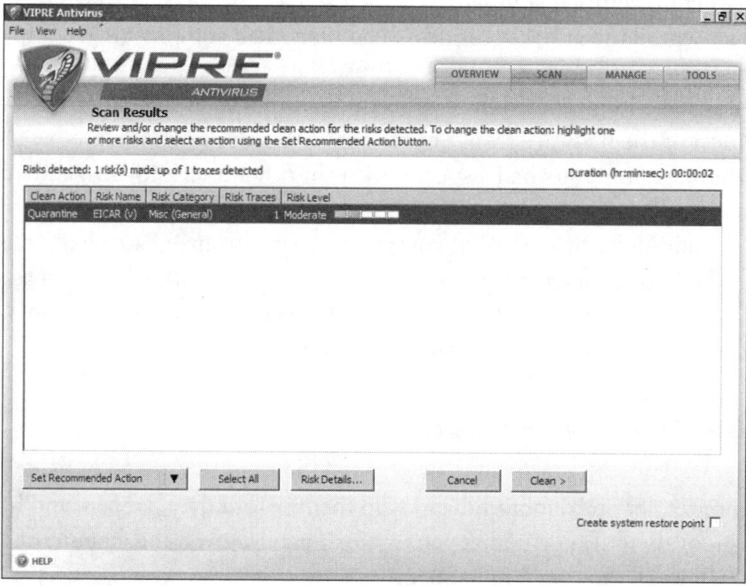

Figure 2-2 Example of Detected Virus

NOTE: For a quick video of the Vipre AV software quarantining some malware, see the following link:

www.davidlprowse.com/forums/showthread.php?t=1630

Next, we want to make sure that the computer has the latest service packs and updates available. This goes for the operating system and applications such as Microsoft Office. Backdoors into operating systems and other applications are not uncommon, and the OS manufacturers often release fixes for these breaches of security. In Windows XP, Automatic Updates can be configured by going to **Start > Control Panel > Automatic Updates**. In Windows Vista go to **Start > Control Panel > System Maintenance > Windows Update**. Then click the **Change settings** link.

Configure Automatic Updates according to your company's policy. You can also check if your computer is up to date by going to **Start > All Programs > Windows Update**. In Windows XP, it directs you to a website that prompts you to install a Windows Update component and then checks if the computer has the latest security (and other) patches. In Windows Vista you can check for updates directly within the Automatic Updates program.

It's also important to make sure that a firewall is available, enabled, and updated. A firewall closes all the inbound ports to your computer (or network) in an attempt to block intruders. The Windows Firewall is a built-in feature of Windows XP/Vista, and you might also have a SOHO router with a built-in firewall. By using both, you have two layers of protection from viruses and other attacks. You can access the Windows Firewall by navigating to **Start > Control Panel > Windows Firewall**. Keep in mind that you might need to set exceptions for programs that need to access the Internet. This can be done by the program, or the port used by the protocol, and can be configured in the Exceptions tab, enabling specific applications to communicate through the firewall while keeping the rest of the ports closed.

Another way to help prevent viruses is to use what I call "separation of OS and data" (similar to the term "separation of church and state" in concept but not in content!). This method calls for two hard drives. The operating system is installed to the C: drive, and the data is stored on the D: drive (or whatever letter you use for the second drive). This compartmentalizes the system and data, making it more difficult for viruses to spread and easier to isolate them when scanning. It also enables for easy reinstallation without having to back up data! You can accomplish a similar scenario by using two partitions on the same drive.

NOTE: There are other viruses that can affect other types of computers. PDAs, micro computers, Mac, and Linux are all susceptible, although not as commonly targeted as Windows operating systems. For example, the Phage virus can infect Palm PDA applications. Although this virus occurs rarely, Palm released an update to its operating system for the virus. It might seem to be a hassle to update a PC, Mac, or PDA, but quite often it is necessary, especially if your computer or mobile device is promiscuous; meaning that it has contact with foreign removable media, questionable websites, and unknown networks.

Finally, educate users as to how viruses can infect a system. Instruct them on how to screen their e-mails and tell them not to open unknown attachments. Show them how to scan removable media before copying files to their computer, or set up the computer to scan removable media automatically. Sometimes user education works; sometimes it doesn't. One way to make user education more effective is to have a technical trainer educate your users, instead of doing it yourself. This can provide for a more engaging learning environment.

By using these methods, virus infection can be severely reduced. However, if a computer is infected by a virus, you want to know what to look for so that you can "cure" the computer.

Here are some typical symptoms of viruses:

- Computer runs slower than usual.
- Computer locks up frequently or stops responding altogether.
- Computer restarts on its own or crashes frequently.
- Disk drives and applications are not accessible or don't work properly.
- Strange sounds occur.
- You receive unusual error messages.
- Display or print distortion occurs.
- New icons appear or old icons (and applications) disappear.
- There is a double extension on a file attached to an e-mail that was opened, for example: .txt.vbs or .txt.exe.
- Antivirus programs will not run or can't be installed.
- Files have been corrupted or folders are created automatically.

Before making any changes to the computer, make sure that you back up critical data and verify that the latest updates have been installed to the OS and the AV software. Then, perform a thorough scan of the system using the AV software's scan utility; if allowed by the software, run the scan in Safe Mode. Another option is to move the affected drive to a "clean machine," a computer that is used solely for the purpose of scanning for malware, that does not connect to the Internet. This can be done by slaving the affected drive to an IDE, SATA, or eSATA port of the other computer and running the AV software on the clean machine to scan that drive. PC repair shops have this kind of isolated clean machine.

Hopefully, the AV software will find and quarantine the virus on the system. In the case that the AV software's scan does not find the issue, or if the AV software has been infected and won't run, you can try using an online scanner such as Trend Micro's HouseCall: http://housecall.trendmicro.com/ or download Microsoft's Malicious Software Removal Tool: www.microsoft.com/security/malwareremove/default.mspx.

In rare cases, you might need to delete individual files and remove Registry entries. This might be the only solution when a new virus has infected a system and there is no antivirus definition released. Instructions on how to remove viruses in this manner can be found on AV software manufacturers' websites.

When it comes to boot sector viruses, your AV software is still the best bet. The AV software might use a boot disk to accomplish scanning of the boot sector, or it might have boot shielding built in. Some BIOS programs have the capability to scan the boot sector of the hard drive at startup; this might need to be enabled in the BIOS setup first. It is also possible to use the DOS **SYS** command to restore the first sector or the **FDISK/MBR** command to repair the master boot record within the boot sector, but a DOS-based boot disk is necessary to do this; it needs to be created on a DOS-based computer or downloaded from the Internet. Windows 2000 and XP offer the **FIXMBR** command available from the Recovery Console. Windows Vista offers the bootrec /fixmbr command from within the System Recovery Options Command Prompt. Keep in mind that the DOS, Recovery Console, and System Recovery Options Command Prompt methods might not fix the problem; they might render the hard drive inoperable depending on the type of virus. It is best to use the AV software's various utilities that you have purchased for the system.

Preventing and Troubleshooting Worms and Trojans

Worms and Trojans can be prevented and troubleshot in the same manner as viruses. There are scanners for Trojans as well, for example: www.windowsecurity.com/trojanscan/. In some cases, AV software scans for worms and Trojans in addition to viruses. The application at this link and most AV software can easily detect RATs such as SubSeven, which was mentioned previously in the chapter, regardless of whether it is the actual attacker's application or any .exe files that are part of the application and are used at the victim computer.

Preventing and Troubleshooting Spyware

Preventing spyware works in much the same manner as preventing viruses when it comes to updating the operating system and using a firewall. Also, because spyware has become much more common, antivirus companies have begun adding antispyware components to their software. Here are a few more things you can do to protect your computer in the hopes of preventing spyware:

- Download and install antispyware protection software. For example, Windows Defender, available at the following link: www.microsoft.com/windows/products/winfamily/defender/default.mspx. Other options include Spyware Doctor with Antivirus, SpyBot S&D (free), or one of the antivirus programs previously mentioned if it includes spyware protection. Be sure to keep the antispyware software updated.

- Adjust Internet Explorer security settings. This can be done by clicking **Tools** on the menu bar, selecting **Internet Options**, and accessing the **Security** tab.

From there, the security level can be increased, and trusted and restricted sites can be established. (It's a good thing.) Internet Explorer 7 and higher also have a phishing filter that you can turn on by going to **Tools > Phishing Filter** and clicking **Turn on Automatic Website Checking**. This attempts to filter out fraudulent online requests for usernames, passwords, and credit card information, which is also known as web-page spoofing. Higher security settings can also help to fend off session hijacking that is the act of taking control of a user session after obtaining or generating an authentication ID. Similar security settings are available on most of today's web browsers.

- Uninstall unnecessary applications and turn off superfluous services (for example, Telnet and FTP if they are not used).
- Educate users on how to surf the web safely. User education is actually the number one method of preventing malware! Access only sites believed to be safe, and download only programs from reputable websites. Don't click OK or Agree to close a window; instead press **Alt+F4** on the keyboard to close that window. Be wary of file-sharing websites and the content stored on those sites. Be careful of e-mails with links to downloadable software that could be malicious.
- Consider technologies that discourage spyware. For example, use a browser that is less susceptible to spyware. Consider running a browser within a virtual machine, or take it to the next level and use a thin-client computer!

Here are some common symptoms of spyware:

- The web browser's default home page has been modified.
- A particular website comes up every time you perform a search.
- Excessive pop-up windows appear.
- The network adapter's activity LED blinks frequently when the computer shouldn't be transmitting data.
- The firewall and antivirus programs turn off automatically.
- New programs, icons, and favorites appear.
- Odd problems occur within windows (slow system, applications behaving strangely, and such).
- The Java console appears randomly.

To troubleshoot and repair systems infected with spyware, first disconnect the system from the Internet. Then, try uninstalling the program from Add/Remove Programs in Windows XP, or Programs and Features in Windows Vista. Some of the less malicious spyware programs can be fully uninstalled without any residual damage. Be sure to reboot the computer afterward and verify that the spyware was actually uninstalled! Next, scan your system with the AV software to remove any viruses that might have infested the system, which might get in the way of a successful spyware removal. Again, do this in Safe Mode if the AV software offers that option.

NOTE: In some cases, Safe Mode is not enough, and you need to boot off of a CD (Knoppix or BartPE, for example) and then rerun the scans.

Next, scan the computer with the antispyware software of your choice in an attempt to quarantine and remove the spyware. You can use other programs, such as HijackThis, in an attempt to remove malware, but be careful with these programs because you will probably need to modify the Registry. Remove only that which is part of the infection.

Finally, you need to make sure that the malware will not reemerge on your system. To do this, check your home page setting in your browser, verify that your host's file hasn't been hijacked (located in C:\WINDOWS\system32\drivers\etc), and make sure that unwanted websites haven't been added to the Trusted Sites within the browser.

Preventing and Troubleshooting Rootkits

A successfully installed rootkit enables unauthorized users to gain access to a system acting as the root or administrator user. Rootkits are copied to a computer as a binary file; this binary file can be detected by signature-based and heuristic-based antivirus programs, which we speak more to later in this chapter in the "Host-Based Intrusion Detection Systems" section. However, after the rootkit is executed, it can be difficult to detect. This is because most rootkits are collections of programs working together that can make many modifications to the system. When subversion of the operating system takes place, that OS can't be trusted, and it is difficult to tell if your antivirus programs run properly, or if any of your other efforts have any effect. Although security software manufacturers are attempting to detect running rootkits, it is doubtful that they will be successful. The best way to identify a rootkit is to use removable media (USB flash drive, or a special rescue CD-ROM) to boot the computer. This way, the operating system is not running, and therefore, the rootkit is not running, making it much easier to detect by the external media. Programs that can be used to detect rootkits include the following:

- Microsoft Sysinternals Rootkit Revealer: http://technet.microsoft.com/en-us/sysinternals/bb897445.aspx (for Windows systems)
- chkrootkit: www.chkrootkit.org/ (for UNIX-based systems)

Unfortunately, because of the difficulty involved in removing a rootkit, the best way to combat rootkits is to reinstall all software. Generally, a PC technician, upon detecting a rootkit, will do just this, because it usually takes less time than attempting to fix all the rootkit issues, plus it can verify that the rootkit has been removed completely.

Preventing and Troubleshooting Spam

The Internet needs to be conserved, just like our environment. Might sound crazy, but it's true. There is only so much space to store information, and only so much bandwidth that can be used to transfer data. It is estimated that spam causes billions of dollars in fraud, damage, lost productivity and so on every year; it's the single biggest gobbler of Internet resources. The worst part is that most spammers do not bear the burden of the costs involved; someone else usually does. So the key is to block as much spam as possible, report those who do it, and train your users. Here are several ways that spam can be reduced:

- **Use a spam filter**—This can be purchased for the server-side as software or as an appliance. One example of an appliance is the Barracuda Networks Spam Firewall (www.barracudanetworks.com). Barracuda monitors spam activity and creates and updates whitelists and blacklists, all of which can be downloaded to the appliance automatically. Network administrators should also block any e-mails that include attachments that do not comply with company rules. For example, some companies enable only .zip, .txt, and .doc to go through their e-mail attachment filter. If your company uses a web-hosting company for its website and for e-mail, that company often has many spam filtering options. And on the client-side, you can configure Outlook and other mail programs to a higher level of security against spam; this is usually in the Junk E-mail Options area, as shown in Figure 2-3. Spam filters can also be installed on individual clients. Many popular antivirus suites have built-in spam filtering. Make sure it is enabled! Just as an example, my personal e-mail account (which I try to keep private) has a filter at the web hosting company, plus my antivirus software package filters the e-mails, and Outlook is set to High in the Junk E-mail Options page, and of course, I still get at least 30 or 40 spams to my inbox every single day.
- **Close open mail relays**—SMTP servers can be configured as *open mail relays*, this enables anyone on the Internet to send e-mail through the SMTP server. Although this is desirable to customers of the company who runs the SMTP server, it is not desirable to the company to have a completely open mail relay. So, open mail relays should either be closed or configured in such a way that only customers and properly authenticated users can use them. Open mail relays are also known as *SMTP open relays*.
- **Remove e-mail address links from the company website**—Replace these with online forms (secure PHP or CGI forms) that enable a person to contact the company but not enable them to see any company e-mail addresses. Use a

separate advertising e-mail address for any literature or ads. Consider changing this often; marketing people might already do this as a form of tracking leads.

- **Use whitelists and blacklists—**Whitelists are lists of e-mail addresses or entire e-mail domains that are trusted, whereas blacklists are not trusted. These can be set up on e-mail servers, e-mail appliances, and within mail client programs such as Outlook.
- **Train your users—**Have them create and use a free e-mail address whenever they post to forums and newsgroups, and not to use their company e-mail for anything except company-related purposes. Make sure that they screen their e-mail carefully; this is also known as e-mail vetting. E-mail with attachments should be considered volatile unless the user knows exactly where it comes from. Train your employees never to make a purchase from an unsolicited e-mail. Also, explain the reasoning behind using BCC when sending an e-mail to multiple users. Let's not beat around the bush; we all know that this is the most difficult thing to ask of a company and its employees who have more important things to do. However, some companies enforce this as policy and monitor users' e-mail habits. Some companies have a policy in place in which users must create a "safe" list. This means that only the addresses on that list can send e-mail to the user and have it show up in the inbox.

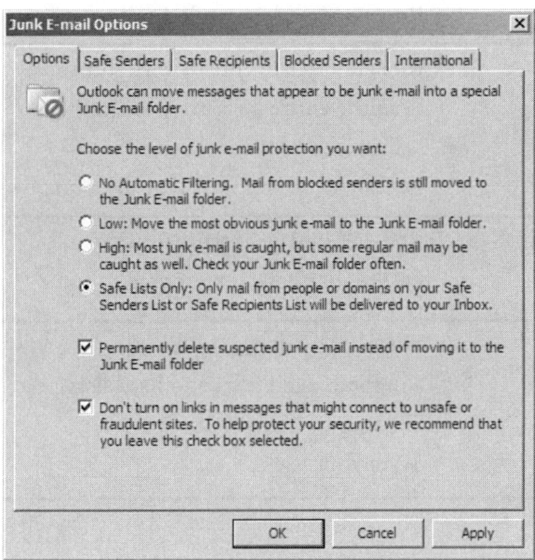

Figure 2-3 Outlook 2003 Junk E-mail Options Set at Highest Level of Security

You Can't Save Every Computer from Malware!

On a final and sad note, sometimes computers become so infected with malware that they cannot be saved. In this case, the data should be backed up (if necessary by removing the hard drive and slaving it to another system), and the operating system and applications reinstalled. The BIOS of the computer should also be flashed. After the reinstall, the system should be thoroughly checked to make sure that there were no residual effects and that the system's hard drive performs properly.

Summary of Malware Prevention Techniques

Table 2-2 summarizes the malware prevention techniques we have discussed up to this point.

Table 2-2 Summary of Malware Prevention Techniques

Malware Threat	Prevention Techniques
Virus	Run and update antivirus software. Scan the entire system periodically. Update the operating system. Use a firewall.
Worm	Run and update antivirus software. Scan the entire system periodically.
Trojan horse	Run and update antivirus software. Scan the entire system periodically. Run a Trojan scan periodically.
Spyware	Run and update antispyware software. Scan the entire system periodically. Adjust web browser settings. Consider technologies that discourage spyware.
Rootkit	Run and update antivirus software. Use rootkit detector programs.
Spam	Use a spam filter. Configure whitelists and blacklists. Close open mail relays. Train your users.

Implementing Security Applications

In the preceding section, we discussed antivirus suites such as McAfee, Norton, and so on. These application suites usually have antivirus, antispyware, and antispam components. Quite often, they also have a built-in firewall as well, known as a personal firewall. And perhaps the application suite also has a built-in *intrusion detection system (IDS)*; a piece of software that monitors and analyzes the system in an attempt to detect malicious activities. The type of IDS that a client computer would have is a *host-based intrusion detection systems (HIDS)*. But there are other types of standalone software firewalls and HIDS; we cover these in just a bit. Another type of built-in security is the pop-up blocker. Integrated into web browsers and web browser add-ons, pop-up blockers help users to avoid websites that could be malicious. Let's discuss these security applications in a little more depth, starting with personal firewalls.

Personal Software Firewalls

Personal firewalls are applications that protect an individual computer from unwanted Internet traffic. They do so by way of a set of rules and policies. Some personal firewalls prompt the user for permission to enable particular applications to access the Internet. In addition, some personal firewalls now also have the capability to detect intrusions to a computer and block that intrusion; this is a basic form of a HIDS that we talk more about in the next section.

Examples of software-based personal firewalls include the following:

- **Windows Firewall**—Built in to Windows, the basic version is accessible from the Control Panel in Windows Vista and later and from the network adapter's Properties window in older versions of Windows (XP and 2000). The advanced version, the Windows Firewall with Advanced Security, can be accessed (for example in Windows Vista) by navigating to **Start > Administrative Tools > Windows Firewall with Advanced Security**. This advanced version enables a user to complete more in-depth configurations such as custom rules.

NOTE: For a quick tutorial on using the Windows Firewall with Advanced Security, see the following link:
www.davidlprowse.com/forums/showthread.php?t=1628

- **ZoneAlarm**—Originally a free product that is still available (see the following link), this was purchased by Check Point and is now also offered as part of a suite of security applications. Go to www.zonealarm.com/security/en-us/zonealarm-pc-security-free-firewall.htm.
- **ipfirewall**—Built in to Mac OS and some versions of FreeBSD.

Antivirus application suites, such as Norton 360, McAfee Total Protection, Kaspersky Internet Security, and so on, include personal firewalls as well. This has become a common trend over the past few years, and you can expect to see personal firewall applications built in to most antivirus application suites in the future.

Because they are software, and because of the ever-increasing level of Internet attacks, personal firewalls should be updated often, and in many cases it is preferable to have them auto-update, although this depends on your organization's policies.

A personal firewall is software, and as such, it can utilize some of the computer's resources. In the late '90s and early 2000s, there were some complaints that particular antivirus suites used too much CPU power and RAM, sometimes to the point of crashing the computer; in some cases this was because of the resources used by the firewall. So a smart systems administrator will select an application suite that has a small footprint. Some organizations opt not to use personal firewalls on client computers and instead focus more on the network-based firewalls and other security precautions. This can vary but should be carefully analyzed before a decision is made.

Personal firewalls (like any software application) can also be the victim of attack. If worms or other malware compromise a system, the firewall could be affected. This just reinforces the concept that antivirus suites should be updated often; daily updates would be the optimal solution.

A common scenario for security in small offices and home offices is to have a 4-port SOHO router/firewall protecting the network and updated personal firewalls on every client computer. This combination provides two levels of protection for the average user, which is usually adequate. But larger networks usually concentrate more on the network firewall (or firewalls) and network-based IDSs than on personal firewalls; although, it is common to see both levels of firewall security in larger network as well.

Host-Based Intrusion Detection Systems

Let's start by talking about intrusion detection systems (IDS) in general. An IDS is used to monitor an individual computer system or a network, or portion of a network and analyze data that passes through to identify incidents, attacks, and so forth. You should be aware of two types of IDSs for the exam:

- **Host-based intrusion detection system (HIDS)—**Loaded on an individual computer; it analyzes and monitors what happens inside that computer, for example, if any changes have been made to file integrity. A HIDS is installed directly within an operating system, so it is not considered to be an "inline" device, unlike other network-based IDS solutions. One of the advantages of using a HIDS is that it can interpret encrypted traffic. Disadvantages include price and resource-intensive, and by default the HIDS object database is stored locally; if something happens to the computer the database will be unavailable.

- **Network intrusion detection system (NIDS)—**Can be loaded on the computer, or can be a standalone appliance, but it checks all the packets that pass through the network interfaces, enabling it to "see" more than just one computer; because of this, a NIDS is considered to be an "inline" device. Advantages include the fact that it is less expensive and less resource intensive, and an entire network can be scanned for malicious activity as opposed to just one computer. Of course, the disadvantage is that a NIDS cannot monitor for things that happen within an operating system. For more information about NIDS, see the section "NIDS Versus NIPS" in Chapter 6, "Network Perimeter Security."

Following are two main types of monitoring that an IDS can carry out:

- **Statistical anomaly—**Establishes a performance baseline based on normal network traffic evaluations. It then compares current network traffic activity with the baseline to detect whether it is within baseline parameters. If the sampled traffic is outside baseline parameters, an alarm is triggered and sent to the administrator.
- **Signature-based—**Network traffic is analyzed for predetermined attack patterns, which are known as signatures. These signatures are stored in a database that must be updated regularly to have effect. Many attacks today have their own distinct signatures. However, only the specific attack that matches the signature will be detected. Malicious activity with a slightly different signature might be missed.

For more information about the various types of on a monitoring methodologies, see the section "Monitoring Methodologies" in Chapter 11, "Monitoring and Auditing."

IDS solutions need to be accurate and updated often to avoid the misidentification of legitimate traffic or, worse, the misidentification of attacks. Following are two main types of misidentification you need to know for the exam:

- **False positive—**If the IPS identifies legitimate activity as something malicious, it would be known as a *false positive.*
- **False negative—**If the IPS does not have a particular attack's signature in its database, and lets that attack run its course thinking it is legitimate, it is known as a *false negative*. More information about false positives, false negatives, and other IDS terminology can be found in Chapter 8, "Physical Security and Authentication Models."

Some antivirus application suites have basic HIDS functionality, but true HIDS solutions are individual and separate applications that monitor log files, check for file integrity, monitor policies, detect rootkits, and alert the administrator in real-time of any changes to the host. This is all done in the hopes to detect malicious activity such as spamming, zombie/botnet activity, identify theft, keystroke logging, and so on. A few examples of HIDS applications include the following:

- **Trend Micro OSSEC** (www.ossec.net)—A free solution with versions for Windows, Mac, Linux and UNIX
- **Osiris** (http://osiris.shmoo.com)—Another free download for Windows or Linux
- **Verisys** (www.ionx.co.uk/products/verisys)—A commercial HIDS solution for Windows

It is important to protect the HIDS database because this can be a target for attackers. It should either be encrypted, stored on some sort of read-only memory, or stored outside the system.

If an IDS observes an incident, it notifies the systems or network administrator so that she might quarantine and fix the problem. However, over time, the need for prevention has become more desirable, and so *intrusion prevention systems (IPS)* and intrusion detection and prevention systems (IDPS) were developed. These not only detect incidents and attacks, but also attempt to prevent them from doing any real damage to the computer or to the network.

Pop-Up Blockers

For a website to generate revenue, a webmaster quite often advertises other products and services, charging fees to the organization that creates these products and services. The only way that an organization can continually advertise on the website is if it is positive it will get a certain amount of click-through response for its ads. However, web users quickly learn to define which windows are advertisements and which aren't. So advertisers need to constantly create new and exciting ways to advertise their products. The traditional JavaScript-based pop-up window doesn't do as good of a job as it used to because many web browsers have built-in pop-up blockers, but you still see tons of them on the Internet, and they can take their toll on user productivity—and can be detrimental to the user's computer. For example, some pop-up ads, if clicked, force the user to go to one or more separate websites that could have harmful code. Or worse yet, the pop-up itself could have malicious code built in; perhaps the Close button within the ad launches some other process altogether. Some attackers create entire websites with malicious pop-ups just to infect as many computers as they can. As mentioned in Chapter 1, "Introduction to Security,": "Why take advantage of users? Because they are there to be taken advantage of!" Not that I condone this behavior, but this mentality is infectious, making pop-ups and all their cousins common; so systems administrators should try their best to block pop-ups. One way to do this is with a *pop-up blocker*. Following are some examples of web browsers that have built-in pop-up blocking functionality, and web browser add-on pop-up blocking tools:

- Internet Explorer
- Mozilla Firefox

- Google Chrome
- Google Toolbar (add-on) http://toolbar.google.com
- Adblock Plus (add-on) http://adblockplus.org/en/
- IE7Pro (add-on) www.ie7pro.com/

One of the problems with pop-up blocking is that it might block content that is not an advertisement but instead is integral to the actual website. For example, on my website www.davidlprowse.com, I run a bulletin board system that has the capability to enable users to know that they have new private messages from other users; one of the options is for this alert to show up as a pop-up window. Because so many users do not see this alert, and instead get a message from the browser that says "Pop-up blocked" or something similar, which can look sort of suspicious to the user, I decided to turn that functionality off and instead let the main login page of the website (and e-mails) notify the user of new messages. This type of philosophy should be taken into account by webmasters when they define what the purpose of their website will be. Proper website functionality should be integrated directly into the actual web page, because most users ignore pop-ups or consider them malicious and attempt to close them, or block them, if they weren't otherwise blocked automatically by their browser.

When dealing with the previously listed applications and add-ons, pop-up blocking is known as *ad filtering*; but this can be taken to another level, known as *content filtering*. Content filters block external files that use JavaScript or images from loading into the browser. Content filtering continues to become more and more important as advertisers become more and more clever. Internet Explorer version 8 has built-in content filtering, and Adblock Plus can provide the same functionality for Mozilla Firefox, plus there are proxy-based programs such as Squid that can filter content (among other things) for multiple computers. For more about proxy servers, see the section "Firewalls and Network Security" in Chapter 6.

Of course, advertisers have some new tricks in an attempt to get past the pop-up blockers and content filters: flash-based pop-ups, pop-*under* ads, DHTML hover ads, and so on. Advertisers continue to battle for ad space with smart new ad types, so systems administrators should be prepared to update their clients' web browsers and browser add-ons on a regular basis.

Securing Computer Hardware and Peripherals

Now that the operating system is better secured, let's talk about securing other types of computer hardware, external peripheral devices, and the BIOS.

Although it's important to secure PCs, Macs, the servers, and other hosts on the network, we can't forget about wireless devices such as laptops, PDAs, and cell phones. And also a plethora of devices can be connected to a computer system, for example, USB flash drives, external SATA hard drives, and removable media such as CD-ROMs and DVDs.

Then of course, there's the underlying firmware without which our computer could not run; I'm speaking of the BIOS.

Securing the BIOS

The BIOS can be the victim of malicious attacks; for mischievous persons it can also act as the gateway to the rest of the system. Protect it! Or your computer just might not boot. Following are a few ways to do so:

- **Use a BIOS password—**The password that blocks unwanted persons from gaining access to the BIOS is the supervisor password. Don't confuse it with the user password (or power-on password) employed so that the BIOS can verify a user's identity before accessing the operating system. Both of these are shown in Figure 2-4. Because BIOS passwords are relatively weak compared to other types of passwords, organizations often use one password for the BIOS on every computer in the network; in this scenario, there is all the more reason to change the password at regular intervals. Because most computers' BIOS password can be cleared by opening the computer (and either removing the battery or changing the BIOS jumper), some organizations opt to use locking cables or a similar locking device that deters a person from opening the computer.

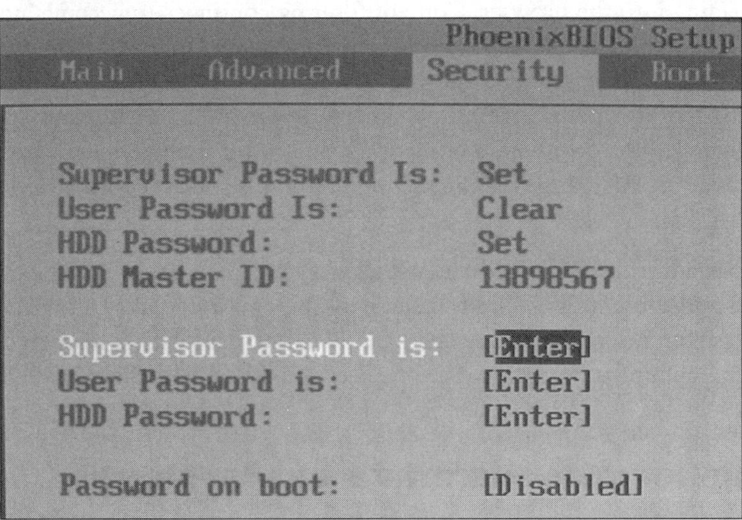

Figure 2-4 BIOS and Drive Lock Passwords

On a semi-related note, many laptops come equipped with *drive lock* technology; this might simply be referred to as an HDD password. If enabled, it prompts the user to enter a password for the hard drive when the computer is first booted. If the user of the computer doesn't know the password for the hard drive, the drive locks and the OS does not boot. An 8-digit, or like, hard drive ID usually associates the laptop with the hard drive installed (refer to Figure 2-4). On most systems this password is clear by default, but if the password is set and forgotten, it can usually be reset within the BIOS. Some laptops come with documentation clearly stating the BIOS and drive lock passwords.

- **Flash the BIOS**—Flashing describes the updating of the BIOS. By updating the BIOS to the latest version, you can avoid possible exploits and BIOS errors that might occur. All new motherboards issue at least one new BIOS version within the first 6 months of the motherboard's release.
- **Configure the BIOS**—Set up the BIOS to reduce the risk of infiltration. For example, change the BIOS boot order (boot device priority) so that it looks for a hard disk first and not any type of removable media. Also, if a company policy requires it, disable removable media including the floppy drives and eSATA and USB ports.

Securing Storage Devices

Removable Storage

Removable storage, or removable media, includes CD-ROMs, DVDs, USB devices, eSATA devices, and even floppy disks in some cases. A network administrator can prevent access to removable media from within the BIOS and within the operating system policies. In many companies, all removable media is blocked except for specifically necessary devices, which are approved on a case-by-case basis. Users should be trained on the proper usage of removable media and should *not* be allowed to take any data home with them. Users who sometimes work from home should do so via a VPN connection to keep the data confidential, yet accessible.

USB devices must be carefully considered. They are small but can transport a lot of data. These devices can be the victim of attacks and the delivery mechanism for attacks to a computer. For example, a USB flash drive might have data files or entire virtual operating systems that can be exploited by viruses and worms. Also, an attacker can attempt to install a special type of virus or worm onto the flash drive executed when the flash drive connects to the computer; in this scenario the computer is the target for the malware. Organizations must decide whether to allow USB devices to be used. Operating system group policies can be implemented to enforce what users are allowed to use USB devices. As mentioned earlier, the BIOS can also disable the use of USB devices on a local computer. Finally, the data on a USB device can be encrypted with various programs, for example, TrueCrypt (www.truecrypt.org/), or you might opt to purchase a secure USB flash drive, for example, a flash drive by Ironkey (https://www.ironkey.com/).

Network Attached Storage

Network attached storage (NAS) is a storage device that connects directly to your Ethernet network. Examples of NAS include simple devices such as the D-Link DNS 323. This device contains two hard drives enabling you to set up RAID 1 mirroring, which protects your data if one drive fails. A more advanced example of NAS would be a device that looks more like a computer and might house up to 32 drives and contain terabytes of data. Possibly hot-swappable, these drives can be physically replaced, and the data can be rebuilt in a short amount of time. A NAS device might be part of a larger storage area network (SAN); therefore, network security should also be considered when implementing any type of NAS. For more information on network security, see Chapters 5 through 7. To protect a single NAS device consider data encryption, authentication, and constant secure logging of the device.

Whole Disk Encryption

Encryption is a huge component of today's computer security. By encrypting information, the data is rearranged in such a way in which only the persons with proper authentication can read it. To encrypt an entire hard disk, you need some kind of full disk encryption software. Several are currently available on the market; one developed by Microsoft is called BitLocker—available only on Vista Ultimate and Vista Enterprise. This software can encrypt the entire disk which, after complete, is transparent to the user. Following are some requirements for this:

- Trusted Platform Module (TPM)—A chip residing on the motherboard that actually stores the encrypted keys.
  or
- An external USB key to store the encrypted keys.
  and
- A hard drive with two volumes, preferably created during the installation of Windows. One volume is for the operating system (most likely C:) that will be encrypted; the other is the active volume that remains unencrypted so that the computer can boot. If a second volume needs to be created, the BitLocker Drive Preparation Tool can be of assistance and can be downloaded from Windows Update.

BitLocker software is based on the Advanced Encryption Standard (AES) and uses a 128-bit key. Keep in mind that a drive encrypted with BitLocker usually suffers in performance compared to a nonencrypted drive and could have a shorter shelf life as well.

BitLocker can be accessed via the following steps:

Step 1. Navigate to Start > Accessories > Run.

Step 2. Type **gpedit.msc** and press **Enter**.

Step 3. In the Group Policy window, navigate to **Computer Configuration** > **Administrative Templates** > **Windows Components** > **BitLocker Drive Encryption**.

Figure 2-5 shows a screen capture of the BitLocker configuration screen.

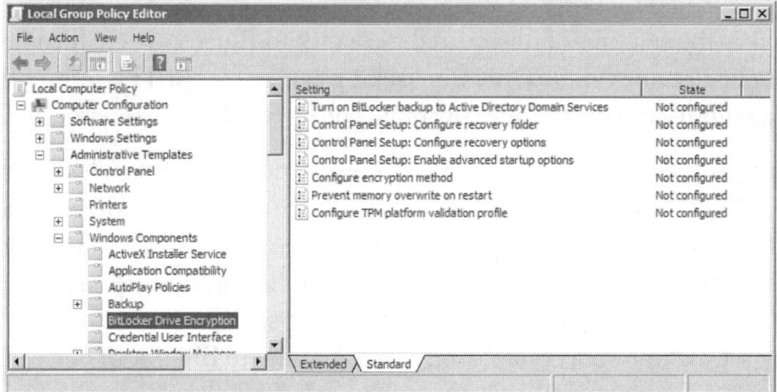

Figure 2-5 BitLocker Configuration Screen

NOTE: For more information about BitLocker and how to use it, see the following link: http://technet.microsoft.com/en-us/library/cc766295(WS.10).aspx.

Securing Cell Phones and PDAs

Unfortunately, cell phones and PDAs can be the victims of attack as well. Attackers might choose to abuse your service or use your cell phone as part of a larger scale attack, and possibly to gain access to your account information.

Users of cell phones and PDAs should be careful who they give their cell phone number to, and to try not to list their cell phone on any websites, especially when purchasing products. Train your users not to follow any links sent by e-mail or by text messages if these are unsolicited. Explain the issues with much of the downloadable software, such as games and ringtones, to your users. Use a locking code/password that's hard to guess; this will lock the phone after a specific amount of time has lapsed, and use complex passwords when necessary.

Cell phones and PDA software must be updated just like computer software; keep these devices up to date, and there will be less of a chance that they will be affected by viruses and other malware. You can encrypt data in several ways, and some organizations have policies that specify how data will be encrypted. More good tips are available at the following National Cyber Alert System website links:

- www.us-cert.gov/cas/tips/ST05-017.html
- www.us-cert.gov/cas/tips/ST04-020.html

Any time a cell phone or PDA connects, it uses some type of wireless service. Whether it's GSM, Wi-Fi, infrared, RFID or Bluetooth, security implications exist. The best solution is to turn off the particular service when not in use, or simply turn the phone/PDA off altogether. Bluetooth is especially vulnerable to virus attacks including bluejacking and bluesnarfing.

Bluejacking is the sending of unsolicited messages to Bluetooth-enabled devices such as mobile phones and PDAs. Bluejacking can be stopped by setting the affected Bluetooth device to "undiscoverable" or by turning off Bluetooth altogether.

Bluesnarfing is the unauthorized access of information from a wireless device through a Bluetooth connection. Generally, Bluesnarfing is the theft of data (calendar information, phonebook contacts, and so on). Ways of discouraging Bluesnarfing include using a pairing key that is not easy to guess; for example, stay away from 0000 or similar default Bluetooth pairing keys! Otherwise, Bluetooth devices should be set to "undiscoverable" (only after legitimate Bluetooth devices have been set up, of course), or Bluetooth can be turned off altogether.

For more information about Bluetooth vulnerabilities see the section "Securing Wireless Networks" in Chapter 7, "Securing Network Media and Devices."

Exam Preparation Tasks

Review Key Topics

Review the most important topics in the chapter, noted with the Key Topics icon in the outer margin of the page. Table 2-3 lists a reference of these key topics and the page numbers on which each is found.

Table 2-3 Key Topics for Chapter 2

Key Topic Element	Description	Page Number
Bullet list	Types of viruses	17
Table 2-1	Summary of Malware Threats	20
Table 2-2	Summary of Malware Prevention Techniques	32
Figure 2-4	BIOS and Drive Lock Passwords	38

Complete Tables and Lists from Memory

Print a copy of Appendix A, "Memory Tables," (found on the DVD), or at least the section for this chapter, and complete the tables and lists from memory. Appendix B, "Memory Tables Answer Key," also on the DVD, includes completed tables and lists to check your work.

Define Key Terms

Define the following key terms from this chapter, and check your answers in the glossary:

malware, virus, worm, Trojan horse, spyware, adware, grayware, rootkit, logic bomb, Easter egg, time bomb, botnet, zombie, spam, active interception, open mail relay, host-based intrusion detection system (HIDS), pop-up blocker, ad filtering, content filters, personal firewall, privilege escalation, backdoors, bluejacking, bluesnarfing

Hands-On Labs

Complete the following written step-by-step scenarios. After you finish (or if you do not have adequate equipment to complete the scenario), watch the corresponding video solutions on the DVD.

If you have additional questions, feel free to post them at my website: www.davidlprowse.com in the Ask Dave forum. (Free registration is required to post on the website.)

Equipment Needed

- A computer with Internet access. A test computer or virtual machine is strongly recommended for these labs and not your every-day computer.
- Web browser: Internet Explorer version 6 and higher or Firefox are recommended.
- Microsoft Virtual PC 2007. Freely downloaded from the following link: www.microsoft.com/downloads/details.aspx?FamilyId=04D26402-3199-48A3-AFA2-2DC0B40A73B6&displaylang=en, or simply do a search for **Microsoft Virtual PC**.

Lab 2-1: Using Free Malware Scanning Programs

In this lab, you download and install free Trend Micro programs and use them to scan your computer for malware. You should use a test computer or virtual machine for this lab. The steps are as follows:

Step 1. Download Trend Micro's HouseCall software from http://housecall.trendmicro.com/.

Step 2. When it finishes downloading, install the program.

Step 3. The program should run automatically; use it to scan your computer for malware. You can click settings to select different partitions or folders. If you find any malware, quarantine it!

Step 4. Consider downloading and utilizing other tools in the Free Tools list such as HijackThis, Rootkit Buster, and so on.

Step 5. When you finish working with the free malware scanning programs, uninstall each of them from the computer.

Watch the solution video in the Hands-On Scenarios section of the DVD.

Lab 2-2: How to Secure the BIOS

In this lab, you use the virtual BIOS in Microsoft Virtual PC to make some configuration changes, thus securing the BIOS. The steps are as follows:

Step 1. Download and install Microsoft Virtual PC 2007.

Step 2. Run the Virtual PC program; this should display the Virtual PC console.

Step 3. Create a new virtual machine:

A. In the Virtual PC Console, click the **New** button.

B. In the New Virtual Machine window, click **Next**.

C. Click the **Create a virtual machine** radio button and click **Next.**

D. Name the virtual machine **Bios Test**. If you want to save the virtual machine (VM) somewhere else, do so now. Then click **Next**.

E. Leave the Operating system drop-down menu selection as Other and click Next.

F. Leave the default settings for RAM and click **Next**.

G. Select the **A new virtual hard disk** radio button and click **Next**.

H. Leave the settings as the default, or select a new location for the virtual hard disk if you want; then click **Next**.

I. Click **Finish**; your VM is now created. For a more detailed lab about how to create a virtual machine in Virtual PC, see Lab 3-2 in Chapter 3, "OS Hardening and Virtualization."

Step 4. Access the VM BIOS:

A. Make sure the VM is highlighted in the Virtual PC Console window.

B. Either double-click the new VM, or click the **Start** button.

C. Immediately press the **Del** key to access the virtual BIOS. You get only a second or two to do so. If you miss the timeout, simply restart the VM by clicking **Action** on the menu bar and select **Reset**.

D. This should display the BIOS Setup Utility window. At this point, you need to use the keyboard (especially the arrow keys) to navigate through the VM's BIOS; the mouse will not function.

Step 5. Change the Boot device priority order:

A. Arrow over to the **Boot** menu.

B. Verify that **Boot Device Priority** is highlighted and press **Enter**.

C. Press the **+** sign until the Hard Drive option is listed first. Adjust the rest of the boot devices as you see fit.

Step 6. Disable the floppy drive:

A. Press the **Esc** key to return to the main menu.

B. Arrow over to the **Advanced** menu.

C. Arrow down to **Floppy Configuration** and press **Enter**.

D. Highlight **Floppy A** and press **Enter**.

E. Arrow up to **Disabled** and press **Enter**.

F. Press **Esc**; this should display the Floppy Configuration screen, and **Floppy A** should be set to **Disabled**.

Step 7. Configure a complex supervisor password:

A. Press the **Esc** key to return to the main menu.

B. Arrow over to the **Security** menu.

C. Highlight **Change Supervisor Password** and press **Enter**.

D. Type a complex password, for example **ABc123** and press **Enter**.

E. Confirm the password by typing it again.

F. In the **Supervisor Password** field, it should now say **Installed**.

Step 8. Return the virtual BIOS settings to normal. To return the BIOS password, you need to type the old password, and then simply press **Enter** to configure a blank password. If you choose to secure the virtual BIOS in the future, you need to save the virtual machine settings by selecting **Action > Close > Save State** (in the drop-down menu).

Watch the solution video in the "Hands-On Scenarios" section of the DVD.

View Recommended Resources

For readers who want to brush up on their CompTIA A+ topics:

- Prowse, David L. *CompTIA A+ Exam Cram*, Fourth Edition. Que. 2010.

Links to antimalware companies:

- McAfee Total Protection: www.mcafee.com
- Norton Internet Security 2010: http://antivirus.norton.com
- Vipre Antivirus: www.vipreantivirus.com/

Windows Defender:

www.microsoft.com/windows/products/winfamily/defender/default.mspx.

Barracuda Networks:
www.barracudanetworks.com

Microsoft Sysinternals Rootkit Revealer:
http://technet.microsoft.com/en-us/sysinternals/bb897445.aspx (for Windows systems)

chkrootkit:
www.chkrootkit.org/ (for UNIX-based systems)

Windows BitLocker Drive Encryption Step-by-Step Guide:
http://technet.microsoft.com/en-us/library/cc766295(WS.10).aspx

National Cyber Alert System links:
www.us-cert.gov/cas/tips/ST05-017.html
www.us-cert.gov/cas/tips/ST04-020.html

Answer Review Questions

Answer the following review questions. You can find the answers at the end of this chapter.

1. A group of compromised computers that have software installed by a worm is known as which of the following?

A. Botnet

B. Virus

C. Honeypot

D. Zombie

2. What are some of the drawbacks to using HIDS instead of NIDS on a server?

A. A HIDS may use a lot of resources that can slow server performance.

B. A HIDS cannot detect operating system attacks.

C. A HIDS has a low level of detection of operating system attacks.

D. A HIDS cannot detect network attacks.

3. Which of the following computer security threats can be updated automatically and remotely? (Select the best answer.)

A. Virus

B. Worm

C. Zombie

D. Malware

4. Which of the following is the best mode to use when scanning for viruses?

A. Safe Mode

B. Last Known Good Configuration

C. Command Prompt only

D. Boot into Windows normally

5. Which of the following is a common symptom of spyware?

A. Infected files

B. Computer shuts down

C. Applications freeze

D. Pop-up windows

6. What are two ways to secure the computer within the BIOS? (Select the two best answers.)

A. Configure a supervisor password.

B. Turn on BIOS shadowing.

C. Flash the BIOS.

D. Set the hard drive first in the boot order.

7. Dan is a network administrator. One day he notices that his DHCP server is flooded with information. He analyzes it and finds that the information is coming from more than 50 computers on the network. Which of the following is the most likely reason?

A. Virus

B. Worm

C. Zombie

D. PHP script

8. Which of the following is not an example of malicious software?

A. Rootkits

B. Spyware

C. Viruses

D. Browser

9. Which type of attack uses more than one computer?

A. Virus

B. DoS

C. Worm

D. DDoS

10. What are the two ways that you can stop employees from using USB flash drives? (Select the two best answers.)

A. Utilize RBAC.

B. Disable USB devices in the BIOS.

C. Disable the USB root hub.

D. Enable MAC filtering.

11. Which of the following does not need updating?

A. HIDS

B. Antivirus software

C. Pop-up blockers
D. Antispyware

12. Which of the following are Bluetooth threats? (Select the two best answers.)

A. Bluesnarfing
B. Blue bearding
C. Bluejacking
D. Distributed denial of service

13. What is a malicious attack that executes at the same time every week?

A. Virus
B. Worm
C. Bluejacking
D. Logic bomb

14. Which of these is true for active inception?

A. When a computer is put between a sender and receiver
B. When a person overhears a conversation
C. When a person looks through files
D. When a person hardens an operating system

15. Tim believes that his computer has a worm. What is the best tool to use to remove that worm?

A. Antivirus software
B. Antispyware software
C. HIDS
D. NIDS

16. Which of the following types of scanners can locate a rootkit on a computer?

A. Image scanner
B. Barcode scanner
C. Malware scanner
D. Adware scanner

17. Which type of malware does *not* require a user to execute a program to distribute the software?

A. Worm
B. Virus

C. Trojan Horse

D. Stealth

18. Which of these is not considered to be an inline device?

A. Firewall

B. Router

C. CSU/DSU

D. HIDS

19. Whitelisting, blacklisting, and closing open relays are all mitigation techniques addressing what kind of threat?

A. Spyware

B. Spam

C. Viruses

D. Botnets

20. How do most network-based viruses spread?

A. By CD and DVD

B. Through e-mail

C. By USB flash drive

D. By floppy disk

21. Which of the following defines the difference between a Trojan horse and a worm? (Select the best answer.)

A. Worms self-replicate but Trojan horses do not.

B. The two are the same.

C. Worms are sent via e-mail; Trojan horses or not.

D. Trojan horses are malicious attacks; worms are not.

22. Which of the following types of viruses hides its code to mask itself?

A. Stealth virus

B. Polymorphic virus

C. Worm

D. Armored virus

23. Which of the following types of malware appears to the user as legitimate but actually enables unauthorized access to the user's computer?

A. Worm

B. Virus

C. Trojan

D. Spam

24. Which of the following would be considered detrimental effects of a virus hoax? (Select the two best answers.)

A. Technical support resources are consumed by increased user calls.

B. Users are at risk for identity theft.

C. Users are tricked into changing the system configuration.

D. The e-mail server capacity is consumed by message traffic.

25. To mitigate risks when users accesses company e-mail with their cell phone, what security policy should be implemented on the cell phone?

A. Data connection capabilities should be disabled.

B. A password should be set on the phone.

C. Cell phone data should be encrypted.

D. Cell phone should be only for company use.

26. Your manager wants you to implement a type of intrusion detection system (IDS) that can be matched to certain types of traffic patterns. What kind of IDS is this?

A. Anomaly based IDS

B. Signature-based IDS

C. Behavior-based IDS

D. Heuristic-based IDS

Answers and Explanations

1. **A.** A botnet is a group of compromised computers, usually working together, with malware that was installed by a worm or a Trojan horse.
2. **A and D.** Host-based intrusion detection systems (HIDS) run within the operating system of a computer. Because of this, they can slow a computer's performance. Most HIDS do not detect network attacks well (if at all). However, a HIDS can detect operating system attack, and will usually have a high-level of detection for those attacks.
3. **C.** Zombies (also known as zombie computers) are systems that have been compromised without the knowledge of the owner. A prerequisite is the computer must be connected to the Internet so that the hacker or malicious attack can make its way to the computer and be controlled remotely. Multiple zombies working in concert often form a botnet. See the section "Computer Systems Security Threats" in Chapter 2, "Computer Systems Security," for more information.

4. **A.** Safe Mode should be used (if your AV software supports it) when scanning for viruses.
5. **D.** Pop-up windows are common to spyware. The rest of the answers are more common symptoms of viruses.
6. **A and D.** Configuring a supervisor password in the BIOS disallows any other user to enter the BIOS and make changes. Setting the hard drive first in the BIOS boot order disables any other devices from being booted off, including floppy drives, optical drives, and USB flash drives. BIOS shadowing doesn't have anything to do with computer security, and although flashing the BIOS may include some security updates, it's not the best answer.
7. **B.** A worm is most likely the reason that the server is being bombarded with information by the clients; perhaps it is perpetuated by a botnet. Because worms self-replicate, the damage can quickly become critical.
8. **D.** A web browser (for example, Internet Explorer) is the only one listed that is not an example of malicious software. Although a browser can be compromised in a variety of ways by malicious software, the application itself is not the malware.
9. **D.** A DDoS, or distributed denial of service, attack uses multiple computers to make its attack, usually perpetuated on a server. None of the other answers use multiple computers.
10. **B and C.** By disabling all USB devices in the BIOS, a user cannot use their flash drive. Also, the user cannot use the device if you disable the USB root hub within the operating system.
11. **C.** Pop-up blockers do not require updating to be accurate. However, host-based intrusion detection systems, antivirus software, and antispyware all need to be updated to be accurate.
12. **A and C.** Bluesnarfing and bluejacking are the names of a couple Bluetooth threats. Another attack could be aimed at a Bluetooth device's discovery mode. To date there is no such thing as blue bearding, and a distributed denial of service attack uses multiple computers attacking one host.
13. **D.** A logic bomb is a malicious attack that executes at a specific time. Viruses normally execute when a user inadvertently runs them. Worms can self-replicate at will. And bluejacking deals with Bluetooth devices.
14. **A.** Active inception (aka active interception) normally includes a computer placed between the sender and the receiver to capture information.
15. **A.** Antivirus software is the best option when removing a worm. It may be necessary to boot into safe mode to remove this worm when using antivirus software.

16. **C.** Malware scanners can locate rootkits and other types of malware. These types of scanners are often found in antimalware software from manufacturers such as McAfee, Norton, Viper, and so on. Adware scanners (quite often free) can scan for only adware. Always have some kind of antimalware software running on live client computers!

17. **A.** Worms self-replicate and do not require a user to execute a program to distribute the software across networks. All the other answers do require user intervention. Stealth refers to a type of virus.

18. **D.** HIDS or host-based intrusion detection systems are not considered to be an inline device. This is because they run on an individual computer. Firewalls, routers, and CSU/DSUs are inline devices.

19. **B.** Closing open relays, whitelisting, and blacklisting bar all mitigation techniques that address spam. Spam e-mail is a serious problem for all companies and must be filtered as much is possible.

20. **B.** E-mail is the number one reason why network-based viruses spread. All a person needs to do is double-click the attachment within the e-mail, and the virus will do its thing, which is most likely to spread through the user's address book. Removable media such as CDs, DVDs, USB flash drives, and floppy disks can spread viruses but are not nearly as common as e-mail.

21. **A.** The primary difference between a Trojan horse and a worm is that worms will self-replicate without any user intervention; Trojan horses do not self-replicate.

22. **D.** An armored virus attempts to make disassembly difficult for an antivirus software program. It thwarts attempts at code examination. Stealth viruses attempt to avoid detection by antivirus software altogether. Polymorphic viruses change every time they run. Worms are not viruses.

23. **C.** A Trojan, or a Trojan horse, will appear to be legitimate and will look like it'll perform desirable functions, but in reality it is designed to enable unauthorized access to the user's computer.

24. **A and C.** Because a virus can affect many users, technical support resources can be consumed by an increase in user phone calls and e-mails. This can be detrimental to the company because all companies have a limited amount of technical support personnel. Another detrimental effect is that unwitting users may be tricked into changing some of their computer system configurations. The key term in the question is "virus hoax." If the e-mail server is consumed by message traffic, that would be a detrimental effect caused by the person who sent the virus and by the virus itself but not necessarily by the hoax. Although users may be at risk for identity theft, it is not one of the most detrimental effects of the virus hoax.

25. **B.** A password should be set on the phone, and the phone should lock after a set period of time. When the user wants to use the phone again, the user should be prompted for a password. Disabling the data connection altogether would make access to e-mail impossible on the cell phone. Cell phone encryption of data is possible, but it could use a lot of processing power that may make it unfeasible. Whether the cell phone is used only for company use is up to the policies of the company.

26. **B.** When using an IDS, particular types of traffic patterns refers to signature-based IDS.

This chapter covers the following subjects:

Hardening Operating Systems—Service packs, patches, hotfixes—This section details what you need to know to make your operating system strong as steel. Group policies, security templates, and baselining put on the finishing touches to attain that bullet-proof system.

Virtualization Technology—This section delves into virtual machines and other virtual implementations with an eye on applying real-world virtualization scenarios.

This chapter covers the CompTIA Security+ SY0-201 objectives 1.3 and 1.6.

CHAPTER 3

OS Hardening and Virtualization

Imagine a computer with a freshly installed server operating system (OS) placed on the Internet or on a DMZ that went live without any updating, service packs, or hotfixes. How long do you think it would take for this computer to be compromised? Probably within a week—maybe sooner, depending on the size and popularity of the organization. And its not just servers! Workstations, routers, switches: You name it; they all need to be updated on a regular basis, or they *will* fall victim to attack. By updating systems frequently and by employing other methods such as group policies and baselining, we are *hardening* the system, making it tough to withstand the pounding that it will probably take from today's technology...and society.

Another way to create a secure environment is to run OSs *virtually*. Virtual systems allow for a high degree of security, portability, and ease of use. However, they are resource-intensive, so a balance needs to be found, and virtualization needs to be used according to the resources of the organization. Of course, these systems need to maintained and updated (hardened) as well.

By utilizing virtualization properly and by implementing an intelligent update plan, OSs, and the relationships between OSs, can be more secure and last a long time.

Foundation Topics

Hardening Operating Systems

An OS that has been installed out-of-the-box is inherently insecure. This can be attributed to several things, including initial code issues and backdoors, the age of the product, and the fact that most systems start off with a basic and insecure set of rules and policies. How many times have you heard of an OS where the controlling user account had no password? Although these types of oversights are constantly being improved upon, making an out-of-the-box experience more pleasant, new applications and new technologies offer new security implications as well. So regardless of the product, we must try to protect it after the installation is complete.

Hardening of the OS is the act of configuring an OS securely, updating it, creating rules and policies to help govern the system in a secure manner, and removing unnecessary applications and services. This is done to minimize a computer OS's exposure to threats and to mitigate possible risk. Although it is impossible to reduce risk to zero, I'll show some tips and tricks that can enable you to diminish current and future risk to an acceptable level.

This section demonstrates how to harden the OS through the use of service packs, patches and patch management, hotfixes, group policies, security templates, and configuration baselines. We then discuss a little bit about how to secure the file system and hard drives. But first, let's discuss how to go about analyzing the system and deciding which applications and services are unnecessary, and then remove them.

Removing Unnecessary Applications and Services

Unnecessary applications and services use valuable hard drive space and processing power. Plus, they can be vulnerabilities to an operating system.

For example, instant messaging programs might be fun for a user but usually are not productive in the workplace (to put it nicely); plus, they often have backdoors that are easily accessible to attackers. They should be discouraged or disallowed by rules and policies. Be proactive when it comes to these types of programs. If users can't install an IM program on their computer, you will never have to go about removing it from the system. But if you do have to remove an application like this, be sure to remove all traces that it ever existed. Make sure that related services are turned off and disabled. Then verify that their inbound ports are no longer functional, and that they are closed and secured. For example, AOL Instant Messenger uses inbound port 5190, which is well known to attackers, as are other inbound ports of other IM programs, such as ICQ or Trillian. Confirm that any shares created by an app are disabled as well. Basically, remove all instances of the application or, if necessary, re-image the computer! That is just one example of many, but it can be applied to most superfluous programs. Another type of program you should watch out for are remote control programs. Applications that enable remote control of a computer should be avoided if possible.

Personally, I use a *lot* of programs. But over time, some of them fall by the wayside and are replaced by better programs. The best procedure is to check a system periodically for any unnecessary programs. For example, in Windows Vista we can look at the list of installed programs by going to the **Control Panel** and accessing **Programs and Features**, as shown in Figure 3-1.

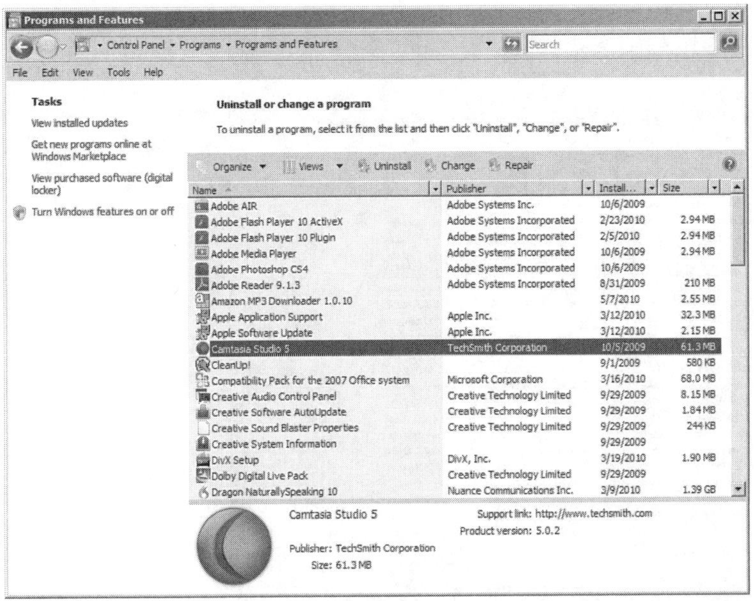

Figure 3-1 Windows Vista Programs and Features Window

Notice in the figure that Camtasia Studio 5 is installed. If in the future I decide to use another program, such as Adobe Captivate or something similar, and Camtasia is no longer necessary, it should be removed. This can be done by right-clicking the application and selecting **Uninstall**. Or an application might have an uninstall feature built in to the Start menu that you can use. Camtasia takes up 61 MB, so it makes sense to remove apps like this to conserve hard drive space. This becomes more important when you deal with audio/video departments that would use an application (and many others like it) such as Camtasia. They are always battling for hard drive space, and it can get ugly! Not only that, but a lot of applications out there place a piece of themselves in the system tray. So a part of the program actually is running behind the scenes using processor and especially RAM resources. If the application is necessary, there are quite often ways to eliminate it from the system tray, either by right-clicking the system tray icon and accessing its properties, or by turning it off with a configuration program such as MSconfig.

Consider also that apps like this might also attempt to communicate with the Internet in an attempt to download updates, or for other reasons. It makes this issue not only a resource problem, but also a security concern, so it should be removed if it is unused. Only software that is deemed necessary should be installed in the future.

Services are used by applications and the OS. They too can be a burden on system resources and pose security concerns. Examine Figure 3-2 and note the highlighted service.

Key Topic

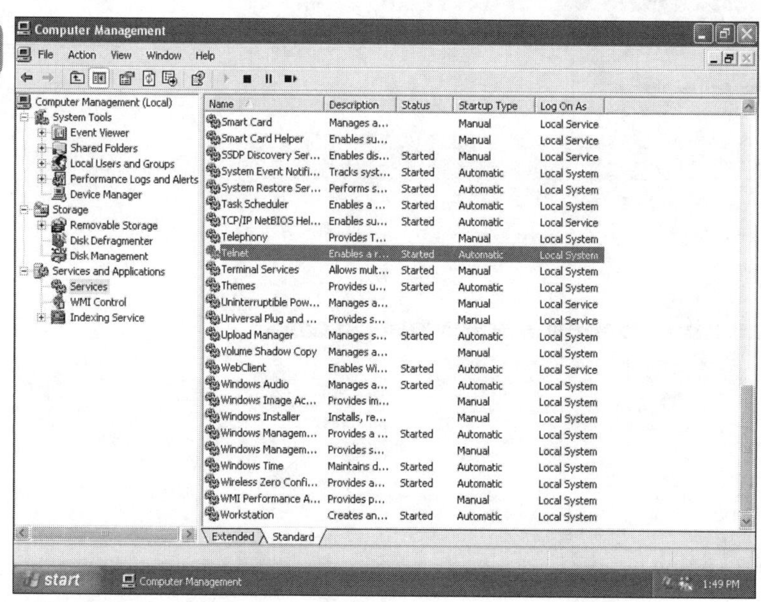

Figure 3-2 Services Window in Windows XP

The OS shown in the figure is Windows XP. Windows XP was the last Microsoft OS to have Telnet installed by default, even though it was already well-known that Telnet was a security risk. This is an example of an out-of-box security risk. But to make matter worse, the Telnet service in the figure is started! Instead of using Telnet, a more secure application/protocol should be utilized such as SSH. Then Telnet should be stopped and disabled. To do so, just right-click the service, select **Properties**, then click the **Stop** button, and change the Startup type drop-down menu to the **Disabled** option, as shown in Figure 3-3. This should be done for all unnecessary services, for example, the Trivial File Transfer Protocol (TFTP). By disabling services such as this one we can reduce the risk of attacker access to the computer and we trim the amount of resources used. This is especially important on Windows servers, because they run a lot more services and are a more common target. By disabling unnecessary services, we *reduce the size of the attack surface.* Services can be disabled in the Windows Command Prompt by using the **sc config** command, and can be started and stopped with the **net start** and **net stop** commands, respectively.

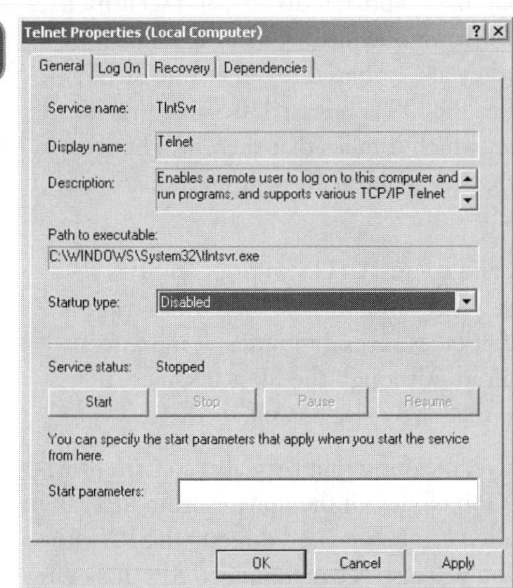

Figure 3-3 Telnet Properties Dialog Box

Services can be stopped in the Linux command-line in a few ways:

- By typing the following syntax:

  ```
  /etc/init.d/<service> stop
  ```
  where <service> is the service name.

- By typing the following syntax in select versions:

  ```
  service <service> stop
  ```

Some services require a different set of syntax. For example, Telnet can be deactivated in Red Hat by typing **chkconfig telnet off**. Check the MAN pages within the command-line or online for your particular version of Linux to obtain exact syntax and any previous commands that need to be issued. Or use a generic Linux online MAN page, for example: http://linux.die.net/man/1/telnet.

In Mac OS X, services can be stopped in the command-line by using the following syntax:

```
% sudo /sbin/service <service> stop
```

Don't confuse services with *service packs*. Although a service controls a specific function of an OS or application, a service pack is used to update a system. The service pack probably will update services as well, but the similarity in names is purely coincidental.

Service Packs

A *service pack (SP)* is a group of updates, bug fixes, updated drivers, and security fixes installed from one downloadable package or from one disc. When the number of patches for an OS reaches a certain limit, they are gathered together into an SP. This might take one-to-several months after the OS is released. Because organizations know an SP will follow an OS release, which implies that there will be security issues with a brand new out-of-the-box OS, they will usually wait until the first SP is released before embracing a new OS.

SPs are numbered; for example SP1, SP2, and so on. An OS without an SP is referred to as SP0. Installing an SP is relatively easy and only asks a few basic questions. When those questions are answered, it takes several minutes or more to complete the update; then a restart is required. Although the SP is installed, it rewrites many files and copies new ones to the hard drive as well.

Historically, many SPs have been cumulative, meaning that they also contain previous SPs. For example, SP2 for Windows XP includes all the updates from SP1; a Windows XP installation with no SP installed can be updated directly to SP2 without having to install SP1 first. However, you will also see incremental SPs, for example, Windows XP SP3. A Windows XP installation with no SP *cannot* be updated directly to SP3; it needs to have SP1 or SP2 installed first before the SP3 update. Another example of an incremental SP is Windows Vista SP2; SP 1 must be installed before updating to SP2 in Windows Vista. This is becoming more common with Microsoft software. Before installing an SP, read the instructions that accompany it, or the instructions on the download page on the company's website.

To find out an OS's current SP level, click **Start**, right-click **Computer**, and select **Properties**, and the SP should be listed. If there is no SP installed, it will be blank. An example of Windows Vista's System window is shown in Figure 3-4; it shows that SP2 is installed. An example of Windows XP's System Properties dialog box is shown in Figure 3-5; it has no SP installed (SP0). If an SP were installed, the SP number would be displayed under Version 2002; otherwise the area is left blank. Windows Server OSs work in the same fashion.

NOTE: You can also find out which service pack your operating system uses by opening the System Information tool (open the Run prompt and type **msinfo32.exe**). It will be listed directly in the system summary. In addition, you can use the **systeminfo** command in the Command Prompt (a GREAT information gatherer!).

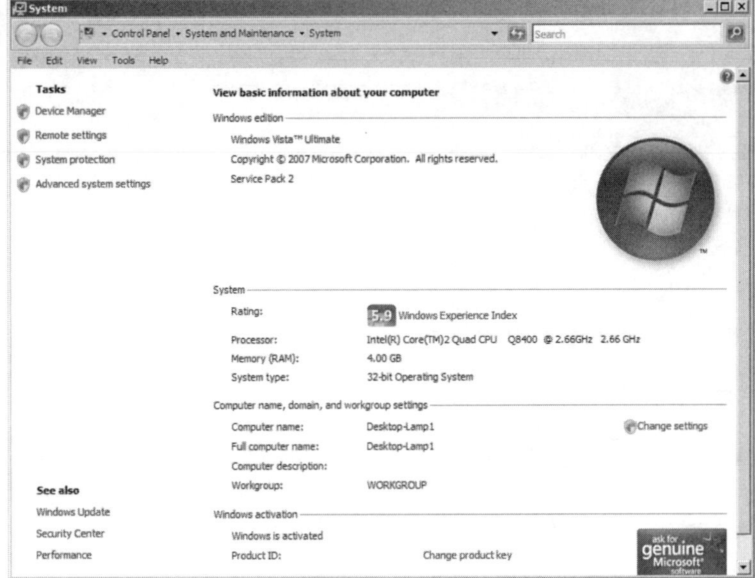

Figure 3-4 Windows Vista System Window

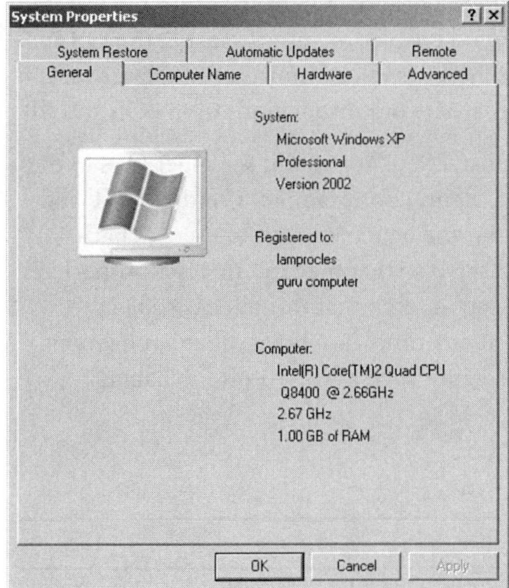

Figure 3-5 Windows XP System Properties Dialog Box

To find out what SP a particular version of Office is running, click **Help** on the menu bar and select **About Microsoft Office <Application Name>** where the application name could be Outlook, Word, and so on, depending on what app you use. An example of this in Outlook is shown in Figure 3-6. Office SPs affect all the applications within the Office suite.

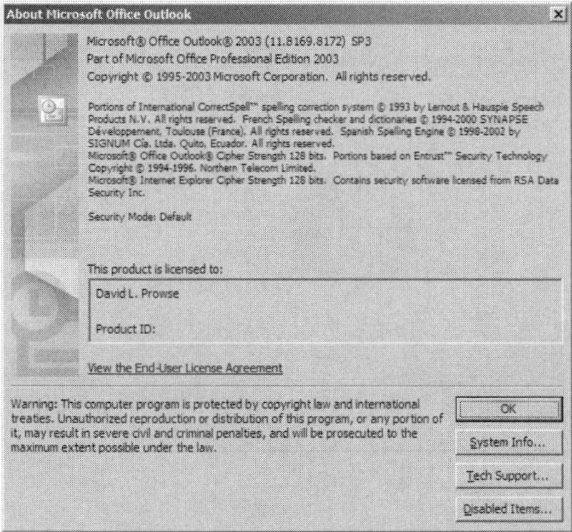

Figure 3-6 Office 2003 Outlook About Window

SPs can be acquired through Windows Update, at www.microsoft.com on CD/DVD and through a Microsoft Developer Network (MSDN) subscription. An SP might also have been incorporated into the original OS distribution DVD/CD. This is known as slipstreaming. This method enables the user to install the OS and the SP at the same time in a seamless manner. System administrators can create slipstreamed images for simplified over-the-network installations of the OS and SP.

Table 3-1 defines the latest SPs as of August, 2010. You might see older OSs in the field. (If something works, why replace it, right?) For example, Windows NT and 2000 servers might be happily churning out the data necessary to users. That's okay; just make sure that they use the latest SP so that they can interact properly with other computers on the network. Keep in mind that this table is subject to change because new SPs can be released at any time. Note that other applications such as Microsoft Office, and server-based apps such as Microsoft Exchange Server, use SPs as well.

Table 3-1 Latest Windows SPs as of August 2010

Operating System	Service Pack
Windows 7	None as of the publishing of this book. (SP1 to be released the first half of 2011, according to Microsoft.)
Windows Vista	SP2
Windows XP	SP3
Windows Server 2008	None as of the publishing of this book. (SP1 to be released the first half of 2011, according to Microsoft.)

Table 3-1 Latest Windows SPs as of August 2010

Operating System	Service Pack
Windows Server 2003	SP2
Windows 2000 (Server and Professional)	SP4
Windows NT 4.0 (Server and Workstation)	SP6
Office 2007	SP2
Office 2003	SP3
Office 2000	SP3

NOTE: Some companies choose to stay with an older SP so that the OS in question can interoperate properly with specific applications. Though this is not recommended, you should check your organization's policies governing this subject.

If possible, service pack installations should be done offline. Disconnect the computer from the network by disabling the network adapter before initiating the SP upgrade. Again, because brand new OSs are inherently insecure to some extent (no matter what a manufacturer might say), organizations usually wait for the release of the first SP before implementing the OS on a live network. However, SPs are not the only type of updating you need to do to your computers. Microsoft OSs require further patching with the Windows Update program, and other applications require their own patches and hotfixes.

Windows Update, Patches, and Hotfixes

OSs should be updated regularly. For example, Microsoft recognizes the deficiencies in an OS, and possible exploits that could occur, and releases patches to increase OS performance and protect the system. After the latest SP has been installed, the next step is to see if any additional updates are available for download.

For example, if you want to install additional updates for Windows through Windows Update, you can do the following:

Step 1. Click **Start > All Programs > Windows Update**.

Step 2. Different OSs have different results at this point. For example, Windows Vista opens the Window Update window in which you can click the **Install Updates** button. Windows XP opens a web page in which you can select **Express** or **Custom** installation of updates. Follow the prompts to install the latest version of the Windows Update software if necessary.

NOTE: Do not select Express or let Microsoft automatically install all updates if you do not want to use newer applications, for example Internet Explorer 8 or XP SP3.

Step 3. The system (or web page) automatically scans for updates. Updates are divided into the following categories:

- **Critical updates and SPs—**These include the latest SP and other security and stability updates. Some updates must be installed individually; others can be installed as a group.
- **Windows updates—**Recommended updates to fix noncritical problems certain users might encounter; also adds features and updates to features bundled into Windows.
- **Driver updates—**Updated device drivers for installed hardware.

If your system is in need of updates, a shield (for the Windows Security Center) appears in the system tray. Double-clicking this brings up the Security Center window in which you can turn on automatic updates. To modify how you are alerted to updates, and how they are downloaded and installed, do the following in Windows Vista:

- Click **Start** > **All Programs** > **Windows Update**; then click the **Change Settings** link.

  It might require slightly different navigation in other OSs to access this.

From here, there will be four options (In other OSs, the options might be slightly different):

- **Install Updates Automatically—**This is the recommended option by Microsoft. You can schedule when and how often the updates should be downloaded and installed.
- **Download Updates but Let Me Choose Whether to Install Them—**This automatically download updates when they become available, but Windows prompts you to install them instead of installing them automatically. Each update has a checkbox, so you can select individual updates to install.
- **Check for Updates but Let Me Choose Whether to Download and Install Them—**This enables you know when updates are available, but you are in control as to when they are downloaded and installed.
- **Never Check for Updates—**This is not recommended by Microsoft because it can be a security risk but might be necessary in some environments in which updates could cause conflicts over the network. In some networks, the administrator takes care of updates from a server and sets the local computers to this option.

Another tool that can be used online is Microsoft Update, which is similar to Windows Update, but it can update for other Microsoft applications as well. It can be found at the following link: http://windowsupdate.microsoft.com/. For newer versions of Windows, this will simply open the Windows Update program on you local computer automatically.

Patches and Hotfixes

The best place to obtain patches and hotfixes is from the manufacturer's website. The terms "patches" and "hotfixes" are often used interchangeably. Windows Updates are made up of *hotfixes*. Originally, a hotfix was defined as a single problem-fixing patch to an individual OS or application installed live while the system was up and running and without a reboot necessary. However, this term has changed over time and varies from vendor to vendor. (Vendors may even use both terms to describe the same thing.) For example, if you run the **systeminfo** command in the Command Prompt of a Windows Vista computer, you see a list of Hotfix(s), similar to Figure 3-7. The figure doesn't show all of them because there are 88 in total. However, they can be identified with the letters KB followed by six numbers. Some of these are single patches to individual applications, but others affect the entire system, such as #88, which is called KB948465. This hotfix is actually Windows Vista Service Pack 2!—which includes program compatibility changes, additional hardware support, and general OS updates. And a Service Pack 2 installation definitely requires a restart.

Key Topic

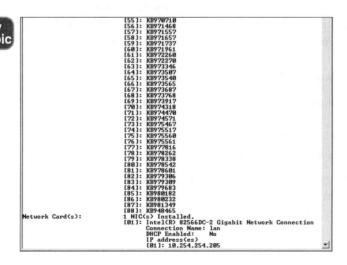

Figure 3-7 Systeminfo Command in Windows Vista

On the other side of the spectrum, World of Warcraft defines hotfixes as a "hot" change to the server with no downtime (or a quick world restart), and no client download is necessary. The organization releases these if they are critical, instead of waiting for a full patch version. The gaming world commonly uses the terms *patch version*, *point release*, or *maintenance release* to describe a group of file updates to a particular gaming version. For example, a game might start at version 1 and later release an update known as 1.17. The .17 is the point release. (This could be any number depending on the amount of code rewrites.) Later, the game might release 1.32, in which .32 is the point release, again otherwise referred to as the patch version. This is common with other programs as well. For example, the aforementioned Camtasia program that is running on the computer we showed is version 5.0.2. The second dot (.2) represents very small changes to the program, whereas a patch version called 5.1 would be a larger change, and 6.0 would be a completely new version of the software. If you look at my website (www.davidlprowse.com), note I am running a bulletin board system, also referred to as a forum or portal. If you scroll to the bottom, you will see that the bulletin board software is at least patch version 3.7.6. As new threats are discovered (and they are extremely common in the blogging world) new patch versions are released. They should be downloaded by the administrator, tested, and installed without delay. Admins should keep in touch with their software manufacturers, either through phone or e-mail, or by frequenting their web pages. This keeps the admin "in the know" when it comes to the latest updates. And this applies to server and client operating systems, server add-ons such as Microsoft Exchange or SQL Server, Office programs, web browsers, and the plethora of third-party programs that an organization might use. Your job just got a bit busier!

Of course, we are usually not concerned with updating games in the working world; they should be removed from a computer if they are found (unless perhaps if you work for a gaming company). But multimedia software such as Camtasia is prevalent in most companies, and web-based software such as bulletin-board systems are also common and susceptible to attack.

Patches generally carry the connotation of a small fix in the mind of the user or system administrator, so larger patches are often referred to as software updates, service packs, or something similar. However, if you were asked to fix a single security issue on a computer, a patch would be the solution you would want.

Sometimes, patches are designed poorly, and although they might fix one problem, they could possibly create another, which is a form of software regression. Because you never know exactly what a patch to a system might do, or how it might react or interact with other systems, it is wise to incorporate patch management.

Patch Management

It is not wise to go running around the network randomly updating computers, not to say that you would do so! Patching, like any other process, should be managed properly. *Patch management* is the planning, testing, implementing, and auditing of patches. Now, these four steps are ones that I use; other companies might have a slightly different patch management strategy, but each of the four concepts should be included:

- **Planning—**Before actually doing anything, a plan should be set into motion. The first thing that needs to be decided is whether the patch is necessary and if it will be compatible with other systems. Microsoft Baseline Security Analyzer (MBSA) is one example of a program that can identify security misconfigurations on the computers in your network, letting you know if patching is needed. If the patch is deemed necessary, the plan should consist of a way to test the patch in a "clean" network on clean systems, how and when the patch will be implemented, and how the patch will be checked after it is installed.
- **Testing—**Before automating the deployment of a patch among a thousand computers, it makes sense to test it on a single system or small group of systems first. These systems should be reserved for testing purposes only and should not be used by "civilians" or regular users on the network. I know, this is asking a lot, especially given the amount of resources some companies have. But the more you can push for at least a single testing system that is not a part of the main network, the less you will have to cover your tracks if a failure occurs!
- **Implementing—**If the test is successful, the patch should be deployed to all the necessary systems. In many cases this will be done in the evening or over the weekend for larger updates. Patches can be deployed automatically using software such as Microsoft's Systems Management Server (SMS).
- **Auditing—**When the implementation is complete, the systems (or at least a sample of systems) should be audited; first, to make sure the patch has taken hold properly, and second, to check for any changes or failures due to the patch. SMS, and other third-party tools can be used in this endeavor.

There are also Linux-based and Mac-based programs and services developed to help manage patching and the auditing of patches. Red Hat has services to help sys admins with all the RPMs they need to download and install, which can become a mountain of work quickly! And for those people who run GPL Linux, there are third-party services as well. Sometimes, patch management is just too much for one person, or for an entire IT department, and an organization might opt to contract that work out.

Group Policies, Security Templates, and Configuration Baselines

Although they are important; removing applications, disabling services, patching, hotfixing, and installing service packs are not the only ways to harden an operating system. Administrative privileges should be used sparingly, and policies should be in place to enforce your organization's rules. *Group policies* are used in Microsoft environments to govern user and computer accounts through a set of rules. Built-in or administrator-designed security templates can be applied to these to configure many rules at one time. And configuration baselines should be created and used to measure server and network activity.

To access the group policy in Windows, go to the Run prompt and type **gpedit.msc**. This should display the Local Group Policy Editor console window. Figure 3-8 shows an example of this in Windows Vista.

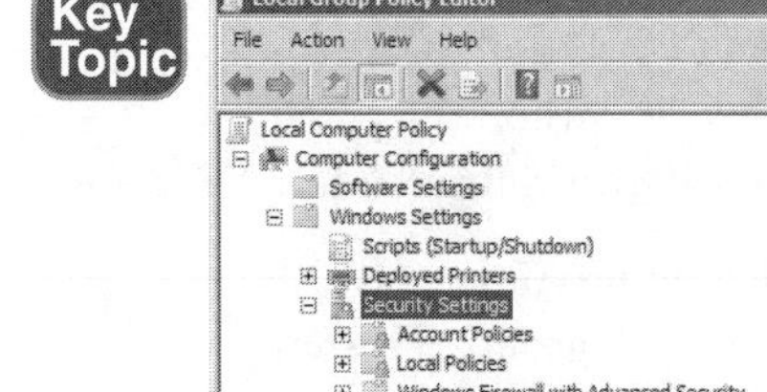

Figure 3-8 Local Group Policy Editor in Windows Vista

Although there are lots of configuration changes you can make, this figure focuses on the computer's security settings that can be accessed by navigating to **Local Computer Policy > Computer Configuration > Windows Settings > Security Settings**. From here you can make changes to the password policies, for example how long a password lasts before having to be changed, account lockout policies, public key policies, and so on. We talk about these different types of policies and the best way to apply them in future chapters. The group policy editor in the figure is known as the Local Group Policy and only governs that particular machine and the local users of that machine. It is a basic version of the group policy used by Windows Server 2003 domain controllers that have Active Directory loaded.

It is also from here where you can add security templates as well. *Security templates* are groups of policies that can be loaded in one procedure; they are commonly used in corporate environments. Different security templates have different security levels. These can be installed by right-clicking **Security Settings** and selecting **Import Policy**. This brings up the **Import Policy From** window. Figure 3-9 shows an example of this in Windows Server 2003. For example, securedc.inf file is an information file filled with policy configurations more secure than the default you would find in a Windows Server 2003 domain controller that runs Active Directory. And hisecdc.inf is even more secure, perhaps too secure and limiting for some organizations. Generally, these policy templates are applied to organizational units on a domain controller. But they can be used for other types of systems and policies as well. Templates are generally stored in c:\Windows\Security\templates.

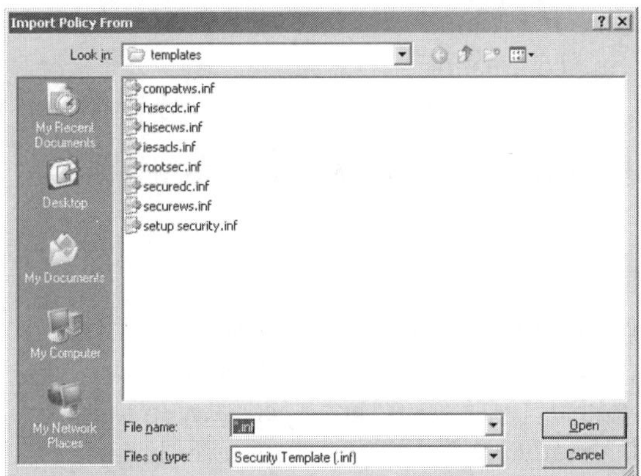

Figure 3-9 Import Policy From Window in Windows Server 2003

Baselining is the process of measuring changes in networking, hardware, software, and so on. Creating a baseline consists of selecting something to measure and measuring it consistently for a period of time. For example, I might want to know what the average hourly data transfer is to and from a server. There are a lot of ways to measure this, but I could possibly use a protocol analyzer to find out how many packets cross through the server's network adapter. This could be run for 1 hour (during business hours of course) every day for 2 weeks. Selecting different hours for each day would add more randomness to the final results. By averaging the results together, we get a baseline. Then we can compare future measurements of the server to the baseline. This can help us to define what the standard load of our server is and the requirements our server needs on a consistent basis. It can also help when installing additional, like computers on the network. The term baselining is most often used to refer to monitoring network performance, but it actually can be used to describe just about any type of performance monitoring. Baselining and benchmarking are extremely important when testing equipment and when monitoring already installed devices. We discuss this further in Chapter 11, "Monitoring and Auditing."

Hardening File Systems and Hard Drives

Last topic about hardening your system, I promise! Not! The rest of the book constantly refers to more advanced and in-depth ways to harden a computer system.

But for this chapter, let's conclude this section by giving a few tips on hardening a hard drive and the file system it houses.

First, the file system used dictates a certain level of security. On Microsoft computers, the best option is to use NTFS, which is more secure, enables for logging (oh so important), supports encryption, and has support for a much larger maximum partition size and larger file sizes. Just about the only place where FAT32 and NTFS are on a level playing field is that they support the same amount of file formats. So, by far, NTFS is the best option. If a volume uses FAT or FAT32, it can be *converted* to NTFS using the following command:

```
Convert volume /FS:NTFS
```

For example, if I want to convert a USB flash drive named M: to NTFS the syntax would be

```
Convert M: /FS:NTFS
```

There are additional options for the **convert** command. To see these, simply type **convert /?** in the Command Prompt. NTFS enables for file-level security and tracks permissions within access control lists (ACLs) that are a necessity in today's environment. Most systems today will already use NTFS, but you never know about flash-based and other removable media. A quick **chkdsk** command in the Command Prompt or right-clicking the drive in the GUI and selecting **Properties** can tell you what type of file system it runs.

System files and folders by default are hidden from view to protect a Windows system, but you never know. To permanently configure the system to not show hidden files and folders, navigate to Windows Explorer, click the **Tools** menu, and click **Folder Options**. Then select the **View** tab, and under Hidden Files and Folders select the **Do not show hidden files and folders** radio button. Note that in Windows Vista, the menu bar can also be hidden; to view it press **Alt+T** on the keyboard. To configure the system to hide protected system files, select the **Hide protected operating system files** checkbox, located three lines below the radio button previously mentioned. This disables the ability to view files such as ntldr, boot.ini, or bootmgr. You might also need to secure a system by turning off file sharing. For example, this can be done in Windows Vista within the Network and Sharing Center, and within Windows XP in the Local Area Connection Properties dialog box.

In the past, I have made a bold statement: "Hard disks *will* fail." But it's all too true; it's not a matter of *if*; it's a matter of *when*. By maintaining and hardening the hard disk with various hard disk utilities, we attempt to stave off that dark day as long as possible. You can implement several things when maintaining and hardening a hard disk:

- **Remove temporary files—**Temporary files and older files can clog up a hard disk and cause a decrease in performance and pose a security threat. It is recommended that Disk Cleanup or a similar program be used. Policies can be configured (or written) to run Disk Cleanup every day or at logoff for all the computers on the network.

- **Defragment drives**—Drives also become defragmented over time. For a server, this could be disaster, because the server cannot serve requests in a timely fashion if the drive is too thoroughly fragmented. Defragmenting the drive can be done with Microsoft's Disk Defragmenter, with the command-line **defrag** command, or with other third-party programs.
- **Back up data**—Backing up data is critical for a company. It is not enough to rely on a fault tolerant array. Individual files or the entire system can be backed up to another set of hard disks, to optical discs, or to tape. Microsoft domain controllers' Active Directory databases are particularly susceptible to attack; the System State for these OSs should be backed up, in the case that the server fails and the Active Directory needs to be recovered in the future.
- **Create restore points**—Restore points should also be created on a regular basis for servers and workstations. System Restore can fix issues caused by defective hardware or software by reverting back to an earlier time. Registry changes made by hardware or software are reversed in an attempt to force the computer to work the way it did previously. Restore points can be created manually and are also created automatically by the OS before new applications or hardware is installed.
- **Consider whole disk encryption**—Finally, whole disk encryption can be used to secure the contents of the drive, making it harder for attackers to obtain and interpret its contents.

A recommendation I give to all my students and readers is to separate the OS from the data physically. If you can have each on a separate hard drive, it can make things a bit easier just in case the OS is infected with malware. The hard drive that the OS inhabits can be completely wiped and re-installed without worrying about data loss, and applications can always be reloaded. Of course, settings should be backed up (or stored on the second drive). If a second drive isn't available, consider configuring the one hard drive as two partitions, one for the OS (or system) and one for the data. By doing this, and keeping a well-maintained computer, you are effectively hardening the OS.

Keeping a Well-Maintained Computer

This is an excerpt of an article I wrote that I give to all my customers and students. By maintaining the workstation or server, you are hardening it as well. I break it down into six steps:

Step 1. Use a surge protector or UPS—Make sure the computer and other equipment connect to a surge protector, or better yet a UPS if you are concerned about power loss.

Step 2. **Update the BIOS**—Flashing the BIOS isn't always necessary; check the manufacturer's website for your motherboard to see if an update is needed.

Step 3. **Update Windows**—This includes the latest SPs and any Windows updates beyond that and setting Windows to alert if there are any new updates.

Step 4. **Update antimalware**—This includes making sure that there is a current license for the antimalware (antivirus and antispyware) and verifying that updates are turned on and the software is regularly scanning the system.

Step 5. **Update the firewall**—Be sure to have some kind of firewall installed and enabled; then update it. If it is the Windows Firewall, updates should happen automatically through Windows Update. However, if you have a SOHO router with a built-in firewall, or other firewall device, you need to update the device's ROM by downloading the latest image from the manufacturer's website.

Step 6. **Maintain the disks**—This means running a disk cleanup program regularly and checking to see if the hard disk needs to be defragmented from once a week to once a month depending on the amount of usage. It also means creating restore points, doing Complete PC Backups, or using third-party backup or drive imaging software.

Virtualization Technology

Let's define virtualization. *Virtualization* is the creation of a virtual entity, as opposed to a true or actual entity. The most common type of entity created through virtualization is the virtual machine—usually as an OS. In this section we discuss types of virtualizations, their purposes, and define some of the various virtual applications.

Types of Virtualization and Their Purposes

Virtualization in the computing world is also referred to as v12n and may be referred to as other things depending on the virtual software vendor.

Many types of virtualization exist, from network and storage to hardware and software. The CompTIA Security+ exam focuses mostly on virtual machine software. The *virtual machines (VMs)* that are created by this software run operating systems or individual applications. These virtual OSs are designed to run *inside* of a real OS. So the beauty behind this is that you can run multiple various OSs simultaneously from just one PC. This has great advantages for programmers, developers, and systems administrators, and can facilitate a great testing environment. Security researchers in particular utilize virtual machines so they can execute and test malware without risk to an actual OS and the hardware it resides on. Nowadays, many

VMs are also used in live production environments. Plus, an entire OS can be dropped onto a DVD or even a flash drive and transported where you want to go. Of course, there are drawbacks. Processor and RAM resources and hard drive space are eaten up by virtual machines. And hardware compatibility can pose some problems as well. Also, if the physical computer that houses the virtual OS fails, the virtual OS will go offline immediately. All other virtual computers that run on that physical system will also go offline. There is added administration as well. Some technicians forget that virtual machines need to be updated with the latest service packs and patches just like regular OSs.

Virtual machines can be broken down into two categories:

- **System virtual machine—**A complete platform meant to take the place of an entire computer that enables you to run an entire OS virtually.
- **Process virtual machine—**Designed to run a single application, for example, if you ran a virtual web browser.

Whichever VM you select, the VM cannot cross the software boundaries set in place. For example, a virus might infect a computer when executed and spread to other files in the OS. However, a virus executed in a VM will spread through the VM but not affect the underlying *actual* OS. So this provides a secure platform to run tests, analyze malware, and so on...and creates an *isolated* system. If there are adverse effects to the VM, those effects (and the VM) can be compartmentalized to stop the spread of those effects. This is all because the virtual machine inhabits a separate area of the hard drive from the actual OS. This enables us to isolate network services and roles that a virtual server might play on the network.

Virtual machines are, for all intents and purposes, emulators. The terms emulation, simulation, and virtualization are often used interchangeably.

Emulators can also be web-based. An example of a web-based emulator is D-Link's DIR-655 router emulator (we use this in Chapters 5–7), which you can find at the following link: http://support.dlink.com/emulators/dir655/133NA/login.html.

You might remember older emulators such as Basilisk, or the DOSBox, but nowadays, anything that runs an OS virtually is generally referred to as a virtual machine or virtual appliance.

A *virtual appliance* is a virtual machine image designed to run on virtualization platforms; it can refer to an entire OS image or an individual application image. Generally, companies such as VMware refer to the images as virtual appliances, and companies such as Microsoft refer to images as virtual machines. One example of a virtual appliance that runs a single app is a virtual browser. VMware developed a virtual browser appliance that protects the underlying OS from malware installations from malicious websites. If the website succeeds in its attempt to install the malware to the virtual browser, the browser can be deleted and either a new one can be created or an older saved version of the virtual browser can be brought online!

Other examples of virtualization include the virtual private network (VPN), which is covered in Chapter 8, "Physical Security and Authentication Models," and the virtual local area network (VLAN), which is covered in Chapter 5, "Network Design Elements and Threats."

Working with Virtual Machines

Several companies offer virtual software including Microsoft and VMware. Let's take a look at some of those programs now.

Microsoft Virtual PC

Microsoft's Virtual PC is commonly used to host workstation OSs, server OSs, and sometimes other OSs such as DOS or even Linux. There are 32-bit and 64-bit versions that can be downloaded for free and run on most Windows systems. The latest version is Virtual PC 2007 that can be downloaded from the following link: www.microsoft.com/downlOAds/details.aspx?familyid=04D26402-3199-48A3-AFA2-2DC0B40A73B6&displaylang=en.

After a quick installation, running the program displays the Virtual PC Console window, as shown in Figure 3-10.

Key Topic

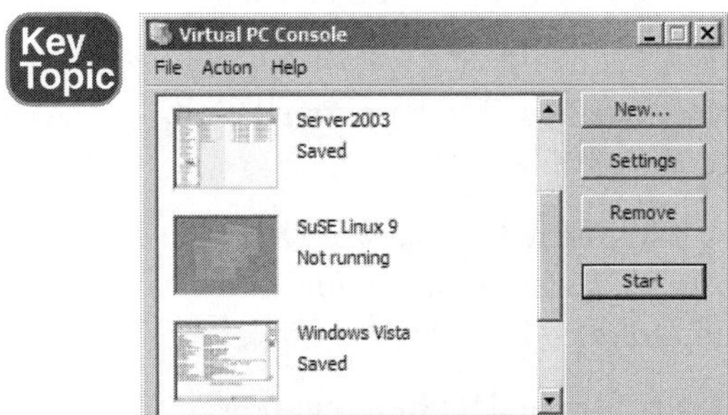

Figure 3-10 Virtual PC Console

After a fresh install of Virtual PC, there won't be any virtual machines listed. However, in Figure 3-10, you can note a Windows Server 2003 VM, a SuSE Linux 9 VM, and a Windows Vista VM. Personally, I run all kinds of platforms with Virtual PC, but it is not the only virtual software I use.

A virtual machine can be created by clicking the **New** button and following the directions. The virtual machine consists of two parts when you are done:

- Virtual machine configuration file or .vmc
- Virtual hard drive file or .vhd

In addition to this, you can save the state of the virtual machine. Let's say you needed to restart your main computer but don't want to restart the virtual machine. You could simply "save the state" of the VM that will save it, remember all the files that were open, and where you were last working, and close the VM. Even after rebooting the actual PC, you can immediately reload the last place you were working in a VM. When a VM's state is saved, an additional file called a .vsv file is stored adjacent to the .vhd. Figure 3-11 shows an example of a Windows Server 2003 virtual machine.

See Lab 2 in the Work Through Hands-On Scenarios at the end of this chapter for a quick tutorial/lab on using Virtual PC to create a virtual machine.

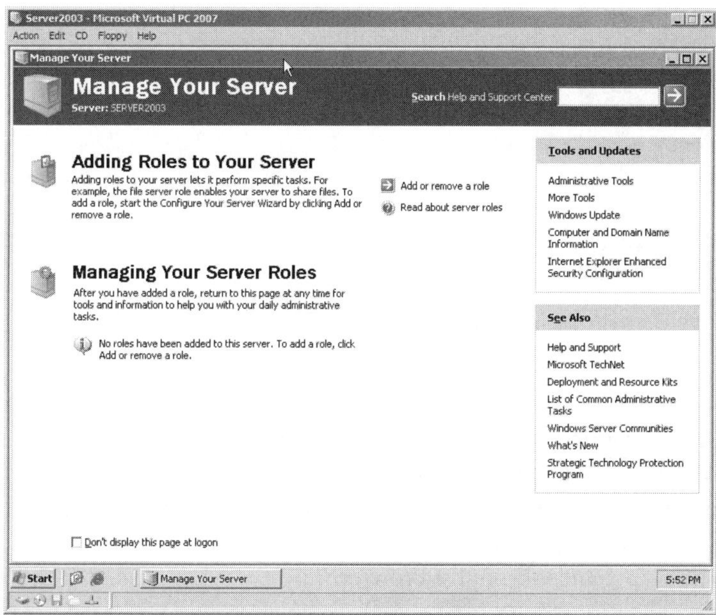

Figure 3-11 Windows Server 2003 Virtual Machine

NOTE: Also, if you are interested, I have demonstrations of several virtual machine OS installations on my website including the following:

Vista: www.davidlprowse.com/forums/showthread.php?t=1520

XP: www.davidlprowse.com/forums/showthread.php?t=1519

Server 2003: www.davidlprowse.com/forums/showthread.php?t=1515

Microsoft Windows XP Mode

Windows 7 can emulate the entire Windows XP OS if you so want. To do so, you must install Windows XP Mode, then Virtual PC, and then the Windows XP Mode update. This is done to help with program compatibility. These components can be downloaded for free (as long as you have a valid copy of Windows 7) from the following link: www.microsoft.com/windows/virtual-pc/download.aspx.

Microsoft Virtual Server

Virtual Server is similar to Virtual PC but is far more powerful and is meant for running server OSs in particular. It is not free like Virtual PC, and an install of Internet Information Services (IIS) is required prior to the install of Virtual Server to take full advantage of the program. When servers are created, they can be connected to by using the Virtual Machine Remote Control (VMRC) client, as shown in Figure 3-12.

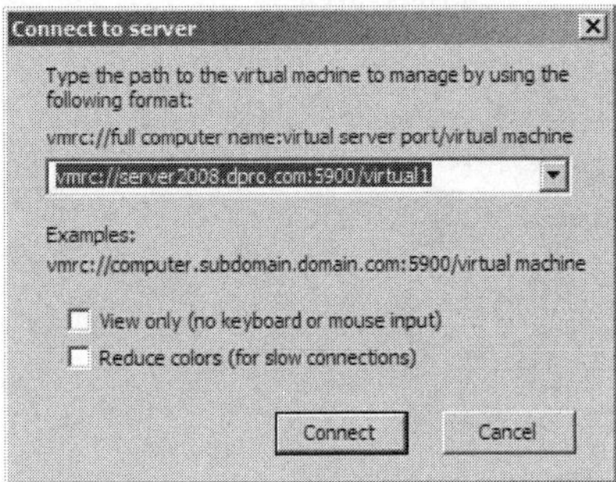

Figure 3-12 Virtual Machine Remote Client in Virtual Server 2005

VMware

VMware (part of EMC Corporation) runs on Windows, Linux, and Mac OSs. Some versions of VMware (for example VMware ESX Server) can run on server hardware without any underlying OS. These programs are extremely powerful, may require a lot of resources, and are generally web-based, meaning that you would control the virtual appliance through a browser.

Exam Preparation Tasks

Review Key Topics

Review the most important topics in the chapter, noted with the Key Topics icon in the outer margin of the page. Table 3-2 lists a reference of these key topics and the page numbers on which each is found.

Table 3-2 Key Topics for Chapter 3

Key Topic Element	Description	Page Number
Figure 3-2	Services Window in Windows XP	60
Figure 3-3	Telnet Properties Dialog Box	61
Bullet list	Stopping services in Linux	61
Figures 3-4 and 3-5 and Note	Identifying the SP level	62–63
Table 3-1	Latest Windows Service Packs	64
Numbered list	Windows update	65
Figure 3-7	**systeminfo** Command in Windows Vista	67
Bulleted list	Patch management four steps	69
Figure 3-8	Local Group Policy Editor in Windows Vista	70
Figure 3-9	Import Policy from Window Windows Server 2003	71
Numbered list	Keeping a well-maintained computer	73
Figure 3-10	Virtual PC Console	76

Complete Tables and Lists from Memory

Print a copy of Appendix A, "Memory Tables," (found on the DVD), or at least the section for this chapter, and complete the tables and lists from memory. Appendix B, "Memory Tables Answer Key," also on the DVD, includes completed tables and lists to check your work.

Define Key Terms

Define the following key terms from this chapter, and check your answers in the glossary:

hardening, service pack (SP), hotfix, patch, patch management, group policy, security template, baselining, virtualization, virtual machine

Hands-On Labs

Complete the following written step-by-step scenarios. After you finish (or if you do not have adequate equipment to complete the scenario), watch the corresponding video solutions on the DVD.

If you have additional questions, feel free to post them at my website: www.davidlprowse.com in the Ask Dave forum. (Free registration is required to post on the website.)

Equipment Needed

- Computer with Internet access.
- Web browser: Internet Explorer version 6 and higher or Firefox are recommended.
- Virtual PC 2007: This can be downloaded at the following link: www.microsoft.com/downloads/details.aspx?FamilyID=04d26402-3199-48a3-afa2-2dc0b40a73b6&displaylang=en.

Lab 3-1: Discerning and Updating the Service Pack Level

In this lab, you observe the service pack currently used on a Windows Vista computer and show where to go to update the SP to the latest version. The steps are as follows:

Step 1. Access Windows Vista (other Windows OSs will be similar in appearance and in navigation).

Step 2. View the SP level:

A. Click **Start**.

B. Right-click **Computer** and select **Properties**. This brings up the System window. From here, you can see the SP level in the Windows edition section.

Step 3. Access Windows Update:

A. Click **Start**.

B. Click **All Programs**.

C. Click **Windows Update**.

Step 4. Modify Windows Update:

A. Click the **View Advanced Options** link.

B. Select the **Check for Updates but Let Me Choose Whether to Download Them or Install Them** radio button.

C. Click **OK**.

Step 5. Locate Windows Vista Service Pack 2 at support.microsoft.com.

You can find information about Windows Vista SP2 at the following link: http://support.microsoft.com/kb/948465.

Watch the solution video in the "Hands-On Scenarios" section of the DVD.

Lab 3-2: Creating a Virtual Machine in Virtual PC 2007

In this lab, you learn how to create a basic virtual machine (VM) in Virtual PC 2007. The steps are as follows:

Step 1. Download the Virtual PC 2007 application. It is a free download available at the following link:
www.microsoft.com/downloads/details.aspx?FamilyID=04d26402-3199-48a3-afa2-2dc0b40a73b6&displaylang=en.

You can also search the phrase **virtual PC 2007 download**.

Step 2. Install Virtual PC 2007. Install the program with the default settings unless you want to modify them.

Step 3. Run Virtual PC 2007 by navigating to **Start > All Programs > Microsoft Virtual PC**. This displays the Virtual PC Console.

Step 4. Create a new virtual machine:

A. Click the **New** button.

B. Click **Next** for the wizard.

C. Select **Create a virtual machine** radio button and click **Next**.

D. Type a name for the virtual machine. Try to keep the name close to the name of the OS you plan to install. For example, if you install Windows Vista, type **Windows Vista**. Virtual PC can recognize these names. Keep in mind that you do not have to install an OS; this lab is simply to show how to create the virtual machine. This virtual machine will be available to you to use later on if you want, and you can load any OS into the VM that want.

E. Select where you want to save the virtual machine by clicking the **Browse** button, or simply leave the default. Then click **Next**.

F. Select the OS you want to install from the drop-down menu. If you are not planning on installing an OS, select **Other**. Then click **Next**.

G. Select the amount of RAM you would like the VM to use. You can increase the default by clicking the **Adjusting the RAM** radio button. As a rule of thumb it is recommended that you use no more than half of the physical RAM on your system for a single VM. Then click **Next**.

H. Select the **A New Virtual Hard Disk** radio button, and select where you want to save the virtual hard disk (.vhd file). Then click **Next**.

I. Review the summary and click **Finish**.
The new VM should now be listed in the Virtual PC Console.

Step 5. Run the VM:

A. Highlight the new VM.

B. Click **Start**.

Step 6. (Optional) Install an OS. Be sure to select **CD** from the menu bar and click **Use Physical Drive**. This way, the VM can use the physical CD-ROM drive.

Step 7. Save the VM:

A. Click **Action** on the menu bar.

B. Select **Close**.

C. From the drop-down menu in the Close dialog box, select **Save State** and click **OK**.

Step 8. Modify the VM settings:

A. Highlight the new VM.

B. Click the **Settings** button.

C. Click **OK** for the pop-up note.

D. Examine the various settings for each device within the VM. Note that you cannot make changes to some of the settings when the VM is in a saved state. To modify these, you need to turn off the VM either within Virtual PC or by shutting down the OS normally. Watch the solution video in the "Hands-On Scenarios" section of the DVD.

View Recommended Resources

For readers who want to brush up on their CompTIA A+ topics:

- Prowse, David L. *CompTIA A+ Exam Cram*, Fourth Edition. Que. 2010.

Virtualization software links:

- Microsoft Virtual PC: www.microsoft.com/downlOAds/details.aspx?familyid=04D26402-3199-48A3-AFA2-2DC0B40A73B6&displaylang=en
- Windows XP Mode: www.microsoft.com/windows/virtual-pc/download.aspx
- Virtual Server 2005: www.microsoft.com/windowsserversystem/virtualserver/
- VMware: www.vmware.com/

Answer Review Questions

Answer the following review questions. You can find the answers at the end of this chapter.

1. Virtualization technology is often implemented as operating systems and applications that run in software. Quite often, it is implemented as a virtual machine. Of the following, which can be a security benefit when using virtualization?
   A. Patching a computer will patch all virtual machines running on the computer.
   B. If one virtual machine is compromised, none of the other virtual machines can be compromised.
   C. If a virtual machine is compromised, the adverse effects can be compartmentalized.
   D. Virtual machines cannot be affected by hacking techniques.

2. Eric wants to install an isolated operating system. What is the best tool to use?
   A. Virtualization
   B. UAC
   C. HIDS
   D. NIDS

3. Where would you turn off file sharing in Windows Vista?
   A. Control Panel
   B. Local Area Connection
   C. Network and Sharing Center
   D. Firewall properties

4. Which option enables you to hide ntldr?
   A. Enable Hide Protected Operating System Files
   B. Disable Show Hidden Files and Folders

C. Disable Hide Protected operating system Files

D. Remove the –R Attribute

5. Which of the following should be implemented to harden an operating system? (Select the two best answers.)

A. Install the latest service pack.

B. Install Windows Defender.

C. Install a virtual operating system.

D. Execute PHP scripts.

6. In Windows XP and Windows Vista, what is the best file system to use?

A. FAT

B. NTFS

C. DFS

D. FAT32

7. A customer's computer uses FAT16 as its file system. What file system can you upgrade it to when using the **`convert`** **command?**

A. NTFS

B. HPFS

C. FAT32

D. NFS

8. Which of the following is not an advantage of NTFS over FAT32?

A. NTFS supports file encryption.

B. NTFS supports larger file sizes.

C. NTFS supports larger volumes.

D. NTFS supports more file formats.

9. What is the deadliest risk of a virtual computer?

A. If a virtual computer fails, all other virtual computers immediately go offline.

B. If a virtual computer fails, the physical server goes offline.

C. If the physical server fails, all other physical servers immediately go offline.

D. If the physical server fails, all the virtual computers immediately go offline.

10. Virtualized browsers can protect the OS that they are installed within from which of the following?

A. DDoS attacks against the underlying OS

B. Phishing and spam attacks

C. Man-in-the-middle attacks

D. Malware installation from Internet websites

11. Which of the following needs to be backed up on a domain controller to recover Active Directory?

A. User data

B. System files

C. Operating system

D. System state

12. Which of the following should you implement to fix a single security issue on the computer?

A. Service pack

B. Support website

C. Patch

D. Baseline

13. An administrator wants to reduce the size of the attack surface of Windows server 2003. Which of the following is the best answer to accomplish this?

A. Update antivirus software.

B. Install service packs

C. Disable unnecessary services.

D. Install network intrusion detection systems.

14. You finished installing the operating system for a home user. What are three good methods to implement in order to secure that operating system? (Select the three best answers.)

A. Install the latest service pack.

B. Install a hardware- or software-based firewall.

C. Install the latest patches.

D. Install pcAnywhere.

15. Which of the following is a security reason to implement virtualization in your network?

A. To isolate network services and roles

B. To analyze network traffic

C. To add network services at lower costs

D. To centralize patch management

Answers and Explanations

1. **C.** By using a virtual machine (which is one example of a virtual instance) any ill effects can be compartmentalized to that particular virtual machine, usually without any ill effects to the main operating system on the computer. Patching a computer does not automatically patch virtual machines existing on the computer. Other virtual machines can be compromised, especially if nothing is done about the problem. Finally, virtual machines can definitely be affected by hacking techniques. Be sure to secure them!
2. **A.** Virtualization enables a person to install operating systems (or applications) in an isolated area of the computer's hard drive, separate from the computer's main operating system.
3. **C.** The Network and Sharing Center is where you can disable file sharing in Windows Vista.
4. **A.** To hide ntldr you need to enable the **Hide Protected Operating System Files** checkbox. Keep in mind that you should have already enabled the **Show Hidden Files and Folders** radio button.
5. **A and B.** Two ways to harden an operating system include installing the latest service pack and installing Windows defender. However, virtualization is a separate concept altogether, and PHP scripts will generally not be used to harden an operating system.
6. **B.** NTFS is the most secure file system for use with Windows XP and Windows Vista. FAT and FAT32 are older file systems, and DFS is the distributed file system used in more advanced networking.
7. **A.** The `Convert` command is used to upgrade FAT and FAT32 volumes to the more secure NTFS without loss of data. HPFS is the High Performance File System developed by IBM and not used by Windows. NFS is the Network File System, something you would see in a storage area network.
8. **D.** NTFS and FAT32 support the same number of file formats.
9. **D.** The biggest risk of running a virtual computer is that it will go offline immediately if the server that it is housed on fails. All other virtual computers on that particular server will also go offline immediately.
10. **D.** The beauty of a virtualized browser is that regardless of whether a virus or other malware damages it, the underlying operating system will remain unharmed. The virtual browser can be deleted and a new one can be created; or if the old virtual browser was backed up previous to the malware attack, it can be restored.
11. **D.** The system state needs to be backed up on a domain controller to recover the active directory database in the future. The system state includes user data and system files but does not include the entire operating system. If a server

fails, the operating system would have to be reinstalled, and then the system state would need to be restored.

12. **C.** A patch can fix a single security issue on a computer. A service pack addresses many issues and rewrites many files on a computer; it may be overkill to use a service pack when only a patch is necessary. You might obtain the patch from a support website. A baseline can measure a server or a network and to obtain averages of usage.
13. **C.** Quite often, operating system manufacturers such as Microsoft refer to the attack surface as all the services that run on the operating system. By conducting an analysis of which services are necessary and which are unnecessary, an administrator can find out which ones need to be disabled, thereby reducing the attack surface. Service packs, antivirus software, and network intrusion detection systems (NIDS) are good tools to use to secure an individual computer and the network but do not help to reduce the size of the attack surface of the operating system.
14. **A, B, and C.** After installing an operating system, it's important to install the latest service pack, patches, and a firewall. These three methods can help to secure the operating system. However, pcAnywhere can actually make a computer less secure and should be installed only if the user requests it. PcAnywhere is just one of many examples of remote control software.
15. **A.** Virtualization of computer servers enables a network administrator to isolate the various network services and roles that a server may play. Analyzing network traffic would have to do more with assessing risk and vulnerability and monitoring and auditing. Adding network services at lower costs deals more with budgeting than with virtualization; although, virtualization can be less expensive. Centralizing patch management has to do with hardening the operating systems on the network scale.

This chapter covers the following subjects:

- **Securing the Browser—**What is a client computer without a web browser? Some might answer "worthless." Well, a compromised browser is worse than no browser at all. The web browser must be secured to have a productive and enjoyable web experience. In this section, we concentrate on Internet Explorer and Firefox, and show various ways to secure them.
- **Securing Other Applications—**Organizations use many applications, and they each have their own group of security vulnerabilities. In this section, we spend a little time on common applications such as Microsoft Office and demonstrate how to make those applications safe.

This chapter covers the CompTIA Security+ SY0-201 objective 1.4.

CHAPTER 4

Application Security

This is a shorter chapter, but another important one. Browser security should be at the top of any network security administrator's list. It's another example of inherently insecure software "out of the box". Browsers are becoming more secure as time goes on, but malware and especially adware are presenting more of a challenge—as we mentioned in Chapter 1, "Introduction to Security," the scales are always tipping back and forth.

Most browsers have plenty of built-in options that you can enable to make them more secure, and third-party programs can help in this endeavor as well. This chapter concentrates on Internet Explorer and Firefox, but the concepts we cover can be applied to most other browsers. However, users don't just work with web browsers. They use office applications frequently as well, so these should be secured, too. Also, other applications, such as the command-line, though a great tool, can also be a target. Be sure to secure any application used on your network. It takes only one vulnerable application to compromise the security of your network.

Let's start with discussing how to secure web browsers.

Foundation Topics

Securing the Browser

There is a great debate as to which web browser to use. The two front runners are Internet Explorer and Firefox. Personally, it doesn't matter too much to me, because as a security guy, I am going to spend a decent amount of time securing either one. However, each does have advantages, and one might work better than the other depending on the environment. So if you are also in charge of implementing a browser solution, be sure to plan for performance *and* security right from the start. As to planning for, and configuring security, I do make some standard recommendations to customers, students, and readers. Let's discuss a few of those now.

The first recommendation is to *not* use the latest browser. (Same advice I always give for any application it seems). Let the people at the top of the marketing pyramid, the innovators, mess around with the "latest and greatest;" let those people find out about the issues, back doors, and whatever other problems a new application might have; at worst, let their computer crash! For the average user, and especially for a fast-paced organization, the browser needs to be rock-solid; these organizations will not tolerate any downtime. As an example, as of the writing of this book, Internet Explorer 8 has been released (Windows 7 comes with it standard), but I still don't recommend it to customers running other Windows operating systems. Of course, that will change over time, but I always allow for some time to pass before fully embracing and recommending software. (My lead time for new software is between 6 and 12 months depending on what it is.) The reason I bring this up is because most companies share the same view.

The next recommendation is to consider what type of computer, or computers, will be running the browser. Generally, Linux computers run Firefox or another browser besides IE; however, you can run a type of IE on Linux, but WINE must be installed first. IE dominates the Windows market, but Firefox works well on Windows PCs, too. And many other applications such as Microsoft Office are linked to IE, so it is wise to consider other applications that are in use when deciding on a browser. Another important point is whether you will be centrally managing multiple client computers' browsers. IE can be centrally managed through the use of Group Policy Objects (GPOs) on a domain; I'll show a quick demonstration of this later in the chapter.

You might also want to consider how the two browser companies fix vulnerabilities. If vulnerability is found in Firefox, it generally becomes common knowledge quickly, which could lead to rapid exploits of the vulnerability before the folks at Mozilla have a chance to fix it. However, an advantage of Firefox is that vulnerabilities appear to be fixed faster than IE vulnerabilities the majority of the time. On the flipside, Microsoft will find out about vulnerabilities but will keep them secret, which pretty much eliminates any possible exploits born from company-presented information. But...Microsoft might take longer to fix the vulnerability. When it comes to functionality, they both work very well. Personally, I use Internet Explorer for sites that I frequent often such as banking websites and my personal website. But I use Firefox for researching of data. It should be noted that some sites do not allow connections by any browser except IE. This is a "security feature" of those websites and should be investigated before implementing other browsers in your organization. If your company makes connections to those types of sites, no other browser will be appropriate. As far as security in general, IE received a poor reputation during older versions. However, Microsoft has worked on this in recent years, resulting in a much more secure version 7 and higher. Firefox has been known all along for its security, but it would seem that the two are quite evenly matched at this point. If you were to research the total number of discovered vulnerabilities for each browser, it would probably be close to the same number. Anyway, I think that's enough yappin' about the two for now—we'll cover some security techniques for each in just a little bit.

General Browser Security Procedures

First, some general procedures should be implemented regardless of the browser your organization uses:

- Implement policies.
- Train your users.
- Use a proxy and content filter.
- Secure against malicious code.

Each of these is discussed in more detail in the following sections.

Implement Policies

The policy could be written, configured at the browser, implemented within the computer operating system, or better yet, configured on a server centrally. Policies can be configured to manage add-ons, and disallow access to websites known to be malicious, have Flash content, or use a lot of bandwidth. As an example, Figure 4-1 displays Internet Explorer Security Features within the Local Group Policy of a Windows Vista computer. You can access it by opening the computer's Local Computer Policy (in the figure it was added as a snap-in to an MMC) and navigating to **User Configuration > Administrative Templates > Windows Components > Internet Explorer > Security Features**. Of course, there are literally hundreds of settings that can be changed for Internet Explorer. You can also modify Internet Explorer Maintenance Security by navigating to **User Configuration > Windows**

Settings > Internet Explorer Maintenance > Security, as shown in Figure 4-2. The Security Zones and Content Ratings object was double-clicked to show the dialog box of the same name. Some versions of Windows will not enable you to access to the Local Computer Policy; however, most security features can be configured directly within the browser.

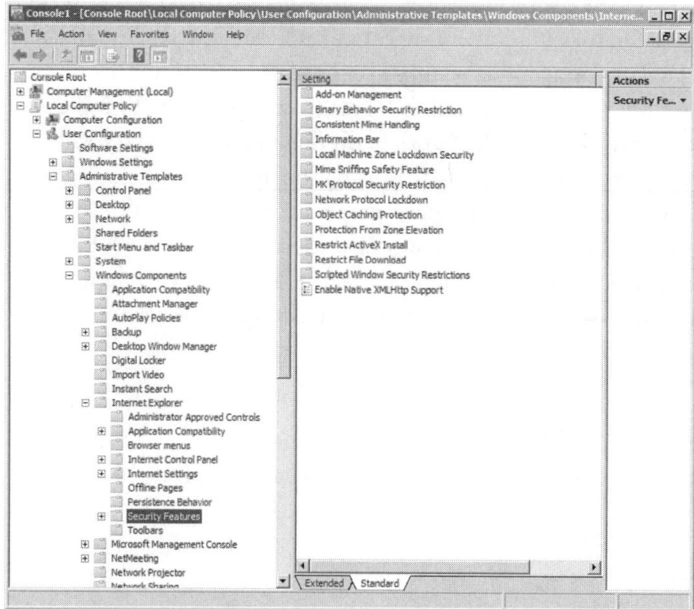

Figure 4-1 Internet Explorer Security Features in the Local Computer Policy

Now, you wouldn't want to configure these policy settings on many more than a few computers individually. If you have multiple computers that need their IE security policies updated, consider using a template (described in Chapter 3, "OS Hardening and Virtualization"), or if you have a domain controller, consider making the changes from that central location. From there, much more in-depth security can be configured and deployed to the IE browsers within multiple computers. An example of the IE policies, as managed from a domain controller, is shown in Figure 4-3. For this, I set up a Windows Server 2003 as a domain controller (controlling the domain dpro2.com), created an organizational unit named Marketing, and then created a Group Policy Object named Marketing-Policy that I added to the MMC. From that policy the Internet Explorer settings, which can affect all computers within the Marketing organizational unit (OU), can be accessed by navigating to **Computer Configuration > Administrative Templates > Windows Components > Internet Explorer**. From here we can configure trusted and nontrusted sites, zones, and advanced security features in one shot for all the computers in the OU. A real time-saver!

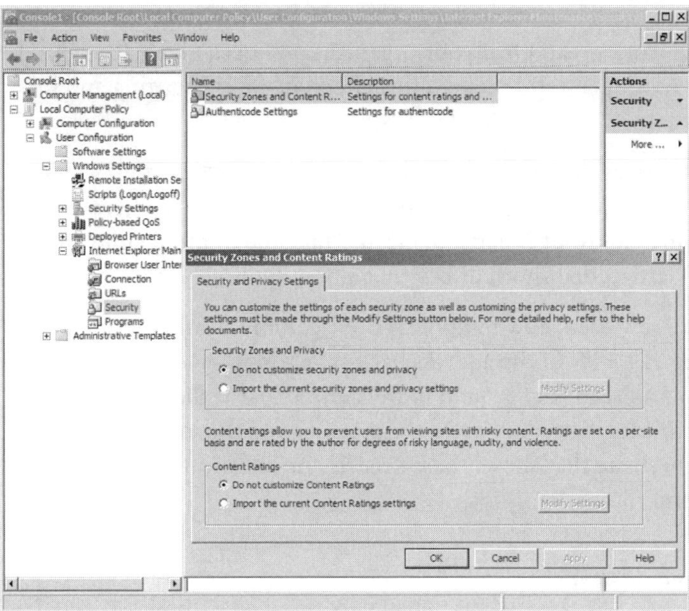

Figure 4-2 Internet Explorer Maintenance Security in the Local Computer Policy

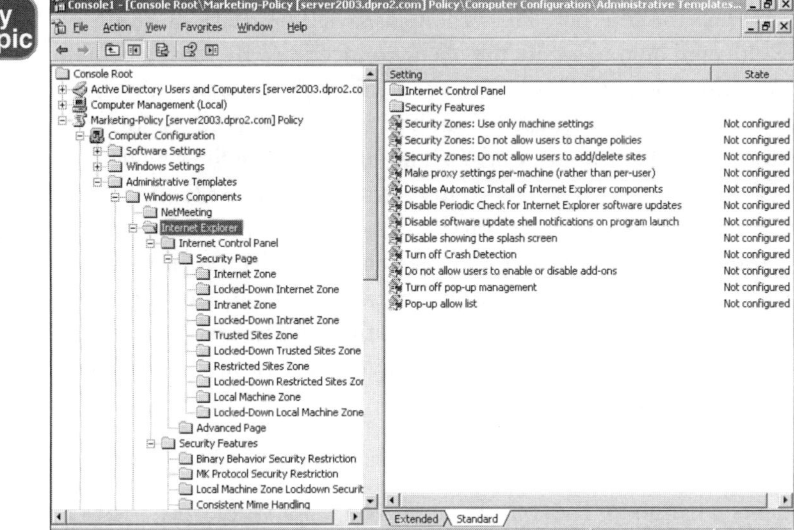

Figure 4-3 Internet Explorer Policies in the Marketing-Policy GPO

Train Your Users

User training is important to determine what websites to access, how to use search engines, and what to do if pop-ups appear on the screen. The more users you can reach with your wisdom, the better! On-site training classes, webinars, and downloadable screencasts all work great. Or if your organization doesn't have those kinds of resources, consider writing a web article to this effect, make it engaging and interesting, yet educational.

For example, explain to users the value of pressing **Alt+F4** to close pop-up windows instead of clicking No or an X. Pop-ups could be coded in such a way where No actually means Yes, and the close-out X actually means "take me to more annoying websites!" Alt+F4 is a hard-coded shortcut key that closes applications.

Another example is to show users how to know if their communications are secure on the web. Just typing HTTPS in the address bar isn't enough. Today, Internet Explorer and Firefox show a green background in the address bar if the website uses a proper encryption certificate. Some browsers use a padlock in the locked position to show it is secure. One website that shows these security notifications in action is https://www.paypal.com.

Use a Proxy and Content Filter

HTTP proxies (known as proxy servers) act as a go-between for the clients on the network and the Internet. Simply stated, they cache website information for the clients, reducing the amount of requests that need to be forwarded to the actual corresponding web server on the Internet. This is done to save time, make more efficient use of bandwidth, and help to secure the client connections. By using a content filter in combination with this, specific websites can be filtered out, especially ones that can potentially be malicious, or ones that can be a waste of man hours, for example P2P websites/servers. I know—I'm such a buzzkill. But these filtering devices are common in today's networks; we talk more about them in Chapter 6, "Network Perimeter Security." For now, it is important to know how to connect to them with a browser. We use Internet Explorer as an example. Remember that the proxy server is a mediator between the client and the Internet. So the client's web browser must be configured to connect to them. You can either have the browser automatically detect a proxy server or (and this is more common) configure it statically. Here's how:

Step 1. Open **Internet Explorer.** (For this exercise I used IE 7, but other versions will be similar.)

Step 2. On the menu bar go to **Tools**. If the menu bar is not visible, press **Alt+T** on the keyboard to bring up the menu.

Step 3. Select **Internet Options**. This should display the Internet Options dialog box.

Step 4. Click the **Connections** tab.

Step 5. Click the **LAN Settings** button. This displays the Local Area Network (LAN) Settings window, as shown in Figure 4-4.

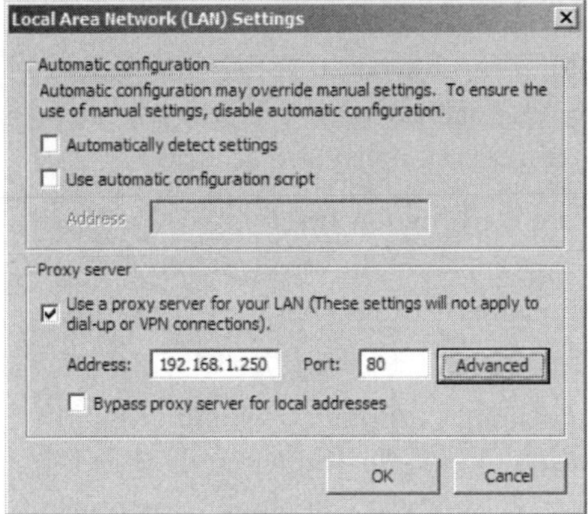

Figure 4-4 Configuring the Proxy Server Connection in Internet Explorer

Step 6. Check the **Use a proxy server for your LAN** checkbox. This enables the Proxy server field.

Step 7. In the **Address** field, type in the IP address or name of the proxy server, for example 192.168.1.250.

Step 8. Select a port; by default 80 is selected because it corresponds with HTTP and most web requests. However, your proxy might use a different port. Consult your network documentation for details.

Step 9. If your proxy server also acts as a go-between for other services such as FTP or secure web transactions, configure these by clicking the **Advanced** button.

Step 10. Click **OK** for the Local Area Network (LAN) Settings dialog box.

Step 11. Click **OK** for the Internet Options dialog box. The client should now be configured to use a proxy server for all its HTTP transactions. To remove the proxy server at any time, simply deselect the **Use a proxy server for your LAN** checkbox.

NOTE: This setting can also be configured within an organizational unit's Group Policy Object on the domain controller. This way, it can be configured one time but will affect all the computers within the particular OU.

Secure Against Malicious Code

Depending on your company's policies and procedures, you might need to configure a higher level of security concerning ActiveX controls, Java, JavaScript, Flash media, Phishing, and much more. We show a few of these configurations in the subsequent sections.

Securing Internet Explorer

There are lots of ways to make Internet Explorer more secure. Be warned, though, that the more a browser is secured, the less functional it becomes. Generally, the best solution is to find a happy medium between functionality and security.

The first thing that should be done is to update the browser. Internet Explorer can be updated directly through the Windows Update feature; however, watch for completely new versions as well. Whenever updating, always check the list of updates before installing them.

Next, install pop-up blocking and other ad-blocking solutions. Many antivirus suites have pop-up blocking tools. There is also the Google Toolbar and other tools like it. And of course, newer versions of web browsers will block some pop-ups on their own.

Now we move on to configuring security within the browser itself. By adjusting Internet Explorer settings, you can add a layer of defense that helps to prevent spyware and other malicious attacks.

First we configure security zones. This and many other security configurations can be completed in the Internet Options dialog box, which can be accessed by going to **Tools** on the menu bar and selecting **Internet Options**. (If the menu bar is not visible, press **Alt+T** on the keyboard to bring up the Tools menu.) Then click the **Security** tab to show the Internet Explorer security zones. Remember, just because they are called security zones doesn't necessarily make them secure. Adjust the security level for the zone named Internet. Many organizations set this to High, as shown in Figure 4-5.

Key Topic

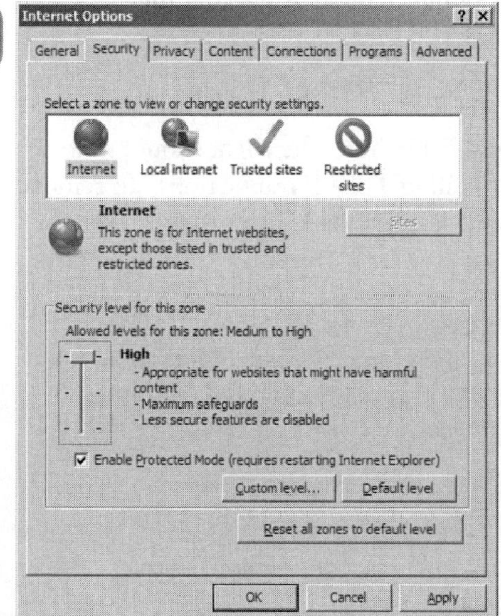

Figure 4-5 Internet Options Dialog Box—Security Zones

You can set the security level in the same manner for the Local intranet zone, Trusted sites zone, and Restricted sites zone. In addition, you can set custom levels by clicking the **Custom Level** button. Here you can disable ActiveX controls and plug-ins, turn the scripting of Java applets on and off, and much more. The Security tab is also where you can add trusted sites to the computer. For example, if you have a high security level, and IE always asks if a particular website is okay to visit, and it's a site you visit everyday that you know to be legitimate, you can add it to the trusted sites by clicking the **Trusted sites** zone, clicking the **Sites** button, and adding the URL of the site in question. Conversely, you can restrict sites by clicking the **Restricted sites** zone and again clicking the **Sites** button.

Cookies can also pose a security threat. The next tab in the Internet Options window is the Privacy tab. This is where you can select how cookies will be handled. *Cookies* are text files placed on the client computer that store information about it, which could include your computer's browsing habits and possibly user credentials. By adjusting the slider, you can either accept all cookies, deny all cookies, or select one of several options in between. Figure 4-6 displays this slider set to High, which blocks cookies that save information that can be used to contact the user or do not have a compact privacy policy.

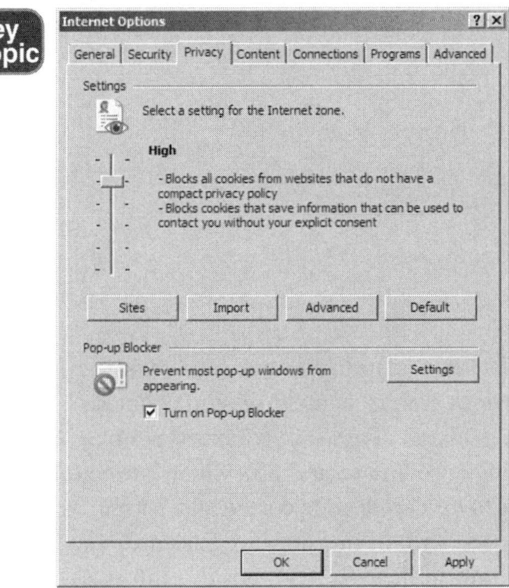

Figure 4-6 Internet Options Dialog Box—Privacy Tab

You can also override any automatic cookie handling that might occur by clicking the **Advanced** button (this displays the Advanced Privacy Settings dialog box), check marking the box and selecting **Prompt** for example. This way, a user will be prompted when a website attempts to create a cookie. With this setting in place, IE will display a window similar to Figure 4-7. In this example, my website www.davidlprowse.com was accessed. My site automatically tries to create a cookie due to the bulletin board system code. IE sees this, stops it before it occurs, and verifies with the user whether to accept it. This particular cookie is harmless, so in this case I would accept it. There is a learning curve for users when it comes to knowing which cookies to accept. I guarantee that once or twice they will block a cookie that subsequently blocks functionality of the website. In some cases, an organization deals with too many websites that have too many cookies, so this particular security configuration is not an option.

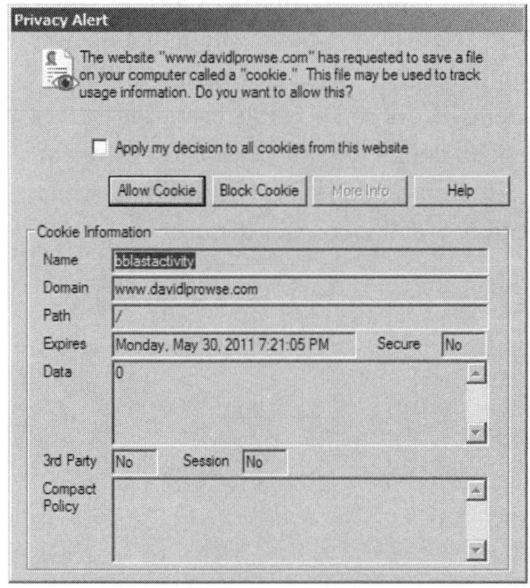

Figure 4-7 IE Cookie Privacy Alert

Tracking cookies are used by spyware to collect information about a web user's activities. Cookies can also be the target for various attacks; namely, session cookies are used when an attacker attempts to hijack a session. There are various types of session hijacking including Cross-site scripting (also known as XSS), which is when the attacker manipulates a client computer into executing code considered trusted as if it came from the server the client was connected to. In this way, the hacker can acquire the client computer's session cookie (allowing them to steal sensitive information) or exploit the computer in other ways. We cover more about session hijacking in Chapter 5, "Network Design Elements and Network Threats."

Pop-ups are the bane of any web surfer. There is a pop-up blocker in the Privacy tab of Internet Explorer, this is on by default, but is worth checking if a user is getting a lot of pop-ups.

The Content tab allows for parental controls and a content advisor, both of which can help secure the browser. This tab is also where you can find encryption certificates. You can find more information on certificates in Chapter 13, "PKI and Encryption Protocols."

The Connections tab enables a user to make secure connections through a VPN and also connect to the Internet via a proxy server as mentioned earlier. You can find more information on VPNs in Chapter 8, "Physical Security and Authentication Models."

The Advanced tab has more than a dozen security settings that you can find by scrolling toward the bottom of the Settings box. For example, a hotel that offers Internet access as a service for guests might check mark the Empty Temporary Internet Files folder option. This way, the history of users are erased when they close the browser. On a related note, salespeople, field technicians, and other remote users should be trained to delete temporary files and cookies when they are using computers on the road. From here, you can also configure whether to check if SSL certificates have been revoked. You can also check if the proper version of SSL is used. At the time of this book's publishing, it is wise to have SSL 3.0 selected and SSL 2.0 deselected. Some organizations also disable third-party browser extensions from this tab in the Browsing section.

You can enable and disable add-on programs in the Programs tab by clicking the **Manage add-ons** button. (This can also be accessed directly within the Tools menu.) IE will always ask before installing add-ons, but over time a company might decide that certain add-ons (that were already installed) could be vulnerabilities. For example, in Figure 4-8, an audio ActiveX Control is selected. Perhaps this control is causing IE to close or the system to crash; it could be turned off by clicking the **Disable** radio button in the Settings box. Most add-ons are ActiveX controls, and ActiveX could also be turned off altogether as mentioned previously.

ActiveX controls are small program building blocks used to allow a web browser to execute a program. They are similar to Java applets; however, Java applets can run on any platform, whereas ActiveX can run only on Internet Explorer (and Windows operating systems). You can see how a downloadable, executable ActiveX control or Java applet from a suspect website could possibly contain viruses, spyware, or worse. Flash scripts can also be a security threat. Generally, you can disable undesirable scripts on either the Advanced tab or the Custom level of a security site. If a particular script technology cannot be disabled within the browser, consider using a content filtering solution.

Of course, this only scrapes the surface as you can see, but it gives you an idea of some of the ways to secure Internet Explorer.

In Chapter 3 we mentioned that removing applications that aren't used is important. But removing web browsers can be difficult, if not downright impossible, and should be voided. Web browsers become one with the operating system, especially so in the case of IE and Windows.

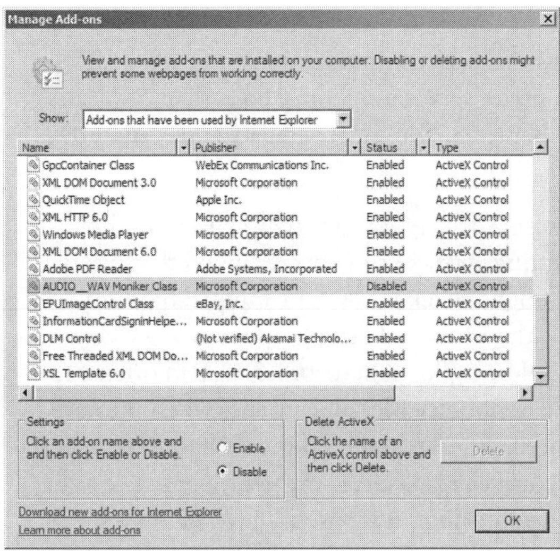

Figure 4-8 Managing Add-Ons

If a computer has multiple browsers, and your organization decides to use Internet Explorer as the *default* browser, you can make this so by going to the **Programs** tab and selecting the **Make default** button. But even if a computer uses Firefox in lieu of IE, it isn't practical to attempt the removal of IE. The same goes for the converse.

Securing Firefox

If an organization decides to use Mozilla Firefox instead of IE, Firefox can be set as the default by opening the browser, navigating to the **Tools** menu, clicking **Options**, clicking **Advanced**, and on the **General** tab clicking the **Check Now** button. This can tell you whether it is default and offer if you want to set it as default. A FYI; we used version 3.6.3 on a Windows Vista platform in the figures. You can also check mark the **Always check to see if Firefox is the default browser on startup** option, as shown in Figure 4-9, just in case another browser has become the default for some strange reason.

The Options dialog box is where most security configurations appear. Many of the security features we mentioned in the Internet Explorer section can be enabled in Firefox as well, but the navigation to them will be slightly different. Firefox does not offer security zones in the way that IE does and does not offer features that enable the management of ActiveX controls.

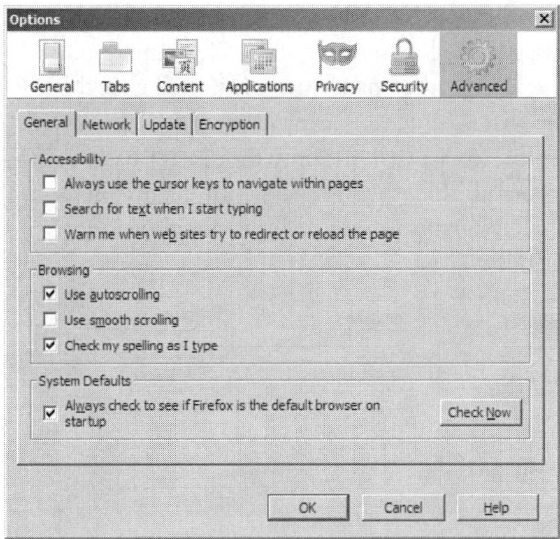

Figure 4-9 Firefox General Tab of the Advanced Options

Cookies can be configured by clicking the **Privacy** options at the top of the Options dialog box, as shown in Figure 4-10. Exceptions can be configured as to which sites cookies will be allowed. You can also view the list of cookies currently stored on the computer. Allowed cookies are also known as whitelists.

Key Topic

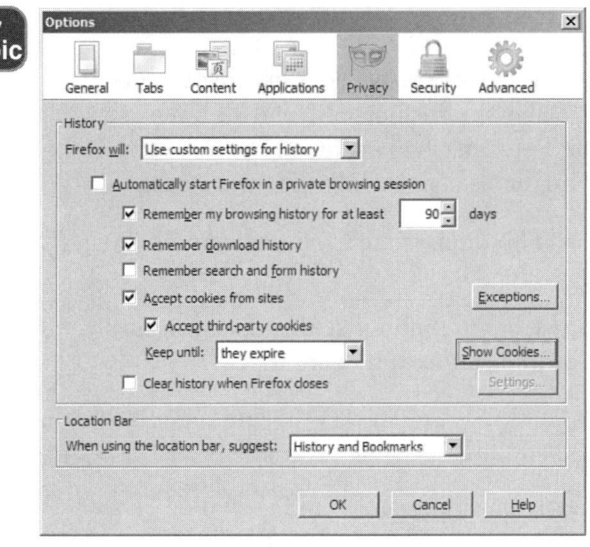

Figure 4-10 Firefox Privacy Options

The **Security** option houses configurations such as add-on warnings, password remembrance, and other warning messages, as shown in Figure 4-11. Some organizations make it a policy to disable the **Remember passwords for sites** checkbox. If you do save passwords, it would be wise to enter a master password. This way, when saved passwords are necessary, Firefox will ask for only the master password; and you don't have to type or remember all the others. A password quality meter tells you how strong the password is. Personally, I don't recommend allowing any web browser to store passwords. Period.

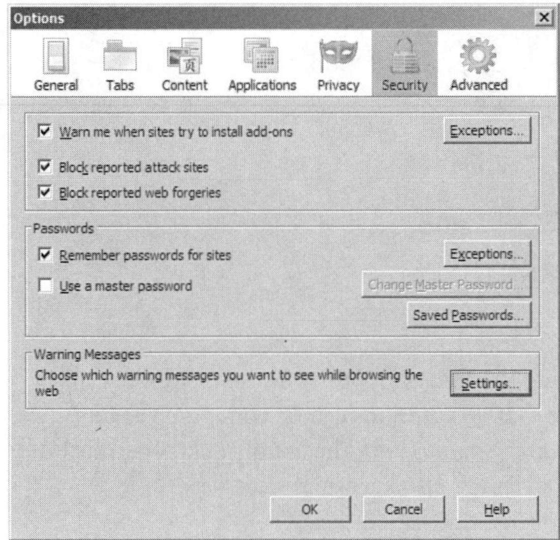

Figure 4-11 Firefox Security Options

The Advanced option has several tabs where various portions of Firefox can be configured and include the Encryption tab that includes SSL and TLS versions and certificate information. Also, the Network tab offers the capability to connect to the Internet via a proxy server. This can be done by following these steps:

Step 1. Click the **Settings** button. This displays the Connection Settings dialog box.

Step 2. Proxies can be auto-detected, but to continue setting up one manually, click the **Manual proxy configuration radio** button

Step 3. Type in the IP address or name of the proxy server followed by the inbound port it uses

The resulting configuration would look something similar to Figure 4-12. This figure shows a configured HTTP proxy. You can also enable automatic proxy configurations if your proxy server allows for that. A specific URL would be needed that points to the appropriate server and configuration script.

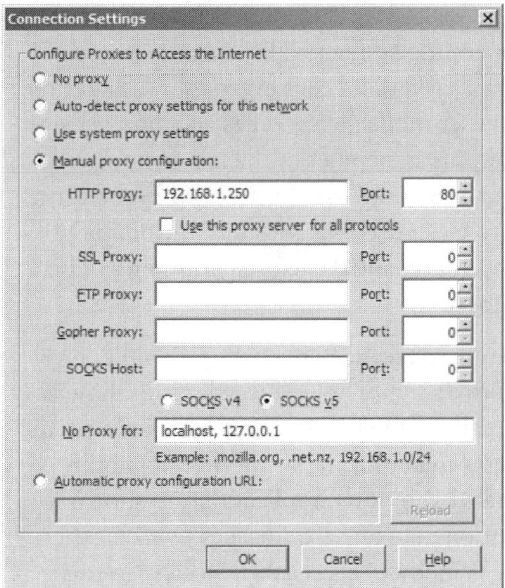

Figure 4-12 Firefox Proxy Connection

Another way to secure Firefox is to use third-party pop-up blocking software such as Adblock Plus. This is an extension to Firefox, or add-on, so the use of add-ons needs to be enabled. However, programs like this one will automatically update as new types of advertisement pop-ups are released.

Firefox has an entire site dedicated to browser add-ons at https://addons.mozilla.org/en-US/firefox/. One example of a smart add-on is NoScript. You can install this to protect against possible malicious JavaScript, Flash, and XSS code. This helps to ward off hijacking and click-jacking attempts. Check out the site to find more smart add-ons that help to make Firefox more secure and efficient. There are add-ons to get a handhold on the amount of Google ads you encounter, antiphishing tools, and lots more.

Keep in mind that the technology world is changing quickly, especially when it comes to the Internet, browsing, web browsers, and attacks. Be sure to periodically review your security policies for web browsing and keep up to date with the latest browser functionality, security settings, and malicious attacks.

Securing Other Applications

Typical users shouldn't have access to any applications other than the ones they specifically need. For instance, would you want a typical user to have full control over the Command Prompt in Windows? Doubtful—and protective measures should be put into place to make sure the typical user does not have access.

One way to do this is to use User Account Control or UAC. User Account Control should be used on qualifying Windows operating systems. *User Account Control (UAC)* is a security component of Windows Vista that keeps every user (besides the actual Administrator account) in standard user mode instead of as an administrator with full administrative rights—even if they are a member of the administrators group. It is meant to prevent unauthorized access and avoid user error in the form of accidental changes. A user attempting to execute commands in the Command Prompt will be blocked, and will be asked for credentials before continuing. This applies to other applications within Windows.

Another way to deny access to applications is to create a policy. For example, on a Windows Server 2003, you can do this in two ways. The first way is to disallow access to specific applications; this policy is called Don't Run Specified Windows Applications. However, the list could be longer than Florida, so another possibility would be to configure the Run Only Allowed Windows Applications, as shown in Figure 4-13. This and the previously mentioned policy are adjacent to each other and can be found at the following path in Windows Server 2003: **Policy** (in this case we use the Marketing-Policy again) **> User Configuration > Administrative Templates > System**.

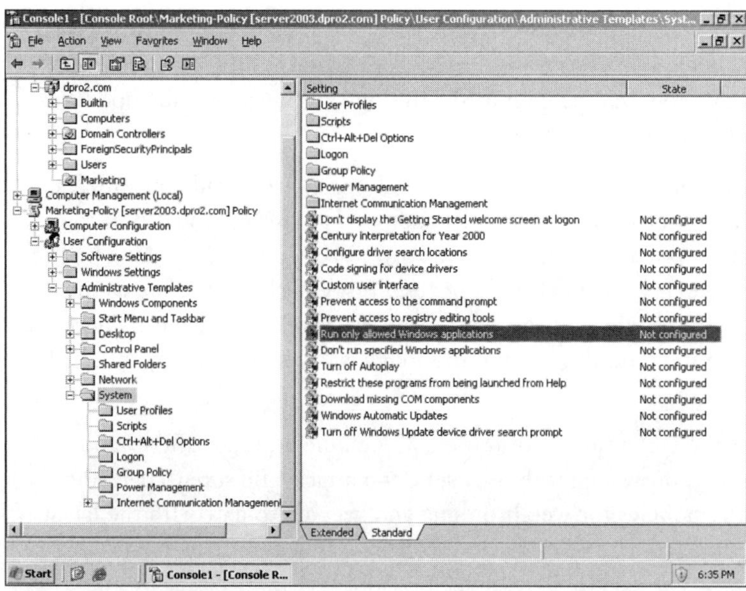

Figure 4-13 Run Only Allowed Windows Applications Policy

When double-clicked, the policy opens and you can enable it and specify one or more applications that are allowed. All other applications will be denied to the user (if the user is logged onto the domain and is a member of the Marketing organizational unit to which the policy is applied). Maybe you as the systems administrator decide that the marketing people should be using only Microsoft PowerPoint. A rather narrow view, but let's use that just for the sake of argument. All you need to do is click the **Enabled** radio button, click the **Show** button, and in the Show Contents window, add the application—in this case, PowerPoint, which is Powerpnt.exe. An example of this is shown in Figure 4-14.

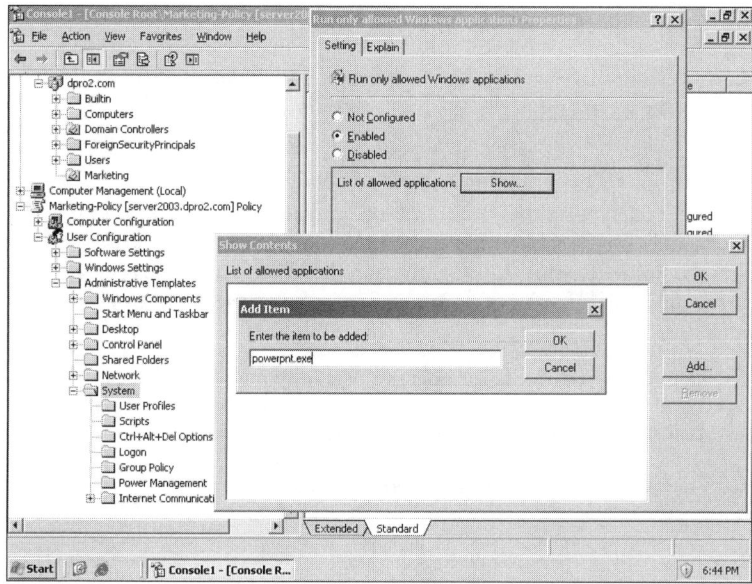

Figure 4-14 Adding a Single Allowed Application

This is in-depth stuff, and the CompTIA Security+ won't test you on exact procedures for this, but you should be aware that there are various ways to disallow access to just about anything you can think of. Of course, the more practice you can get on various servers including Windows Server 2003 and 2008, the better.

For those applications that users are allowed to work with, they should be secured accordingly. Table 4-1 shows some common applications and some simple safeguards that can be implemented for them.

Table 4-1 Common Applications and Safeguards

Application Name	Safeguards
Outlook	Install the latest Office service pack. (This applies to all Office suite applications.)
	Keep Office up to date with Windows Update. (This also applies to all Office suite applications.)
	Increase the junk e-mail security level or use a whitelist.
	Read messages in plain text instead of HTML.
	Enable attachment blocking.
	Use a version that enables Object model guard functionality, or download it for older versions.
	Password protect any .PST files.
	Consider encrypting the authentication scheme, and possibly other traffic, including message traffic between Outlook clients and Exchange servers. Secure Password Authentication (SPA) can be used to secure the login and S/MIME, and PGP can be used to secure actual e-mail transmissions.
Word	Consider using passwords for opening or modifying documents.
	Use read-only or comments only (tracking changes) settings.
	Consider using a digital certificate to seal the document.
Excel	Use password protection on worksheets.
	Set macro security levels.
	Consider Excel encryption.

Whatever the application you use, attempt to secure it by updating and configuring it. Access the manufacturer's website for more information on how to secure the application. Just remember that users still need to work with the program. Don't make it so secure that a user gets locked out!

Applications should be analyzed for backdoors, possible buffer overflows, and proper data input validation. Let's discuss these three briefly.

As mentioned in 2, "Computer Systems Security," backdoors are used in computer programs to bypass normal authentication and other security mechanisms in place. These can be avoided by updating the operating system and applications and firmware on devices.

Applications in general should be protected from buffer overflows. A *buffer overflow* is when a process stores data outside of the memory that the developer intended. This could cause erratic behavior in the application, especially if the memory already had other data in it. Stacks and heaps are data structures that can be affected by buffer overflows. Value types are stored in a stack, whereas reference types are stored in a heap. An ethical coder will try to keep these running efficiently. An unethical coder will attempt to use a buffer overflow to affect heaps and stacks that in turn could affect the application in question or the operating system. The buffer overflow might be initiated by certain inputs and can be prevented by bounds checking. It can also be prevented by using correct code and the right programming language for the job in question. Without getting too much into the programming side of things, special values called "canaries" are used to protect against buffer overflows.

Input validation is important for website design and applications development. *Input validation* or data validation is a process that ensures the correct usage of data. If data is not validated correctly, it can lead to security vulnerabilities and data corruption. You can check data in many ways, from data checks to consistency checks to spelling and grammar checks, and so on. Whatever data is being dealt with, it should be checked to make sure it is being entered correctly and won't create or take advantage of a security flaw. For example, if an organization has a web page with a contact form, the data entered by the visitor should be checked for errors or vulnerabilities. Sometimes, web developers will run web scripts in a sandbox. A *sandbox* is when a Web script runs in its own environment for the express purpose of not interfering with other processes, possibly for testing. Table 4-2 summarizes the programming vulnerabilities we have covered in this section.

Table 4-2 Summary of Programming Vulnerabilities

Vulnerability	Description
Backdoor	Placed by programmers, knowingly or inadvertently, to bypass normal authentication, and other security mechanisms in place
Buffer overflow	When a process stores data outside of the memory that the developer intended
Input validation	The process that ensures the correct usage of data
Sandbox	When a Web script runs in its own environment for the express purpose of not interfering with other processes

Organizations use lots of applications specific to their type of business. Stay on top of the various vendors that supply your organization with updates and new versions of software. Always test what effects one new piece of software will have on the rest of your installed software before implementation.

Exam Preparation Tasks

Review Key Topics

Review the most important topics in the chapter, noted with the Key Topics icon in the outer margin of the page. Table 4-3 lists a reference of these key topics and the page numbers on which each is found.

Table 4-3 Key Topics for Chapter 4

Key Topic Element	Description	Page Number
Figure 4-1	Internet Explorer Security Features in the Local Computer Policy	92
Figure 4-3	Internet Explorer Policies in the Marketing-Policy GPO	93
Figure 4-4	Configuring the Proxy Server Connection in Internet Explorer	95
Figure 4-5	Internet Options Dialog Box—Security Zones	96
Figure 4-6	Internet Options Dialog Box—Privacy Tab	97
Figure 4-10	Firefox Privacy Options	101
Figure 4-11	Firefox Security Options	102
Table 4-2	Summary of Programming Vulnerabilities	107

Complete Tables and Lists from Memory

Print a copy of Appendix A, "Memory Tables," (found on the DVD), or at least the section for this chapter, and complete the tables and lists from memory. Appendix B, "Memory Tables Answer Key," also on the DVD, includes completed tables and lists to check your work.

Define Key Terms

Define the following key terms from this chapter, and check your answers in the glossary:

cookies, buffer overflow, cross-site scripting, User Account Control, input validation, sandbox

Hands-On Labs

Complete the following written step-by-step scenarios. After you finish (or if you do not have adequate equipment to complete the scenario), watch the corresponding video solutions on the DVD.

If you have additional questions, feel free to post them at my website at www.davidlprowse.com in the Ask Dave forum. (Free registration is required to post on the website.)

Equipment Needed

- A computer with Internet access and Internet Explorer 7 or higher
- Windows Server 2003 (or Server 2008) that has been promoted to a domain controller

Lab 4-1: Securing the Browser

In this lab, you secure Internet Explorer by turning on the pop-up blocker, enabling the phishing filter, increasing zone and cookies security, and enabling advanced features. The steps are as follows:

Step 1. Open Internet Explorer.

Step 2. Access the Tools menu by pressing **ALT+T**:

A. Select **Pop-up Blocker > Turn on Pop-up Blocker**.

B. Next, select **Phishing Filter > Turn On Automatic Website Checking**.

Step 3. Go back to the Tools menu, and select **Internet Options**. This displays the Internet Options dialog box.

Step 4. Increase security of the browser's zones:

A. Click the **Security** tab.

B. Select the **Internet** zone.

C. Set the slider to **High** for maximum security.

Step 5. Increase security for cookies:

A. Click the **Privacy** tab.

B. Set the slider to **High**.

Step 6. View other security configurations:

A. Click the **Advanced** tab.

B. Scroll down to the **Security** section.

C. Check mark the **Empty Temporary Internet Files folder when the browser is closed** checkbox.

D. Scroll down further, and verify that **SSL 3.0** is enabled and that **SSL 2.0** is disabled.

E. Scroll back up to the **Browsing** section. Deselect the **Enable third-party browser extensions*** checkbox.

Step 7. Set up websites to be trusted and restricted:

A. Click the **Security** tab.

B. Click the **Restricted sites** zone, and then click the **Sites** button.

C. Add a website to the list. Be sure to remove it when you finish with this lab.

D. Click **Close**.

E. Click the **Trusted sites** zone, and click the **Sites** button.

F. Add a website to the list such as https://www.paypal.com. Be sure to remove it when you finish with this lab.

Watch the solution video in the "Hands-On Scenarios" section of the DVD.

Lab 4-2: Disabling Applications with a Windows Server 2003 Policy

In this lab, you restrict users from applications by configuring a group policy. We use Windows Server 2003 as our example, but Windows Server 2008 will be quite similar. Remember that the server must have been previously promoted to a domain controller so that you can create organization units and the corresponding policies.

NOTE: For more information about promoting a server to a domain controller, see my video on my website at the following link: www.davidlprowse.com/forums/showthread.php?t=1548.

The steps are as follows:

Step 1. Access the Windows Server.

Step 2. Open your MMC if you have one. If not, create a new one so that you can keep all of your snap-ins organized in one window. Add the **Active Directory Users and Computers** snap-in.

Step 3. Create a new OU:

A. Navigate to **Active Directory** Users and Computers > [domain name]. In this example I use the domain name Dpro2.com.

B. Right-click the domain name.

C. Select **New > Organization Unit**.

D. Name the OU. For example: **accounting**. Then click **OK**. This should add the new OU to the domain.

Step 4. Create a new policy based off the OU:

A. Right-click the new OU and select **Properties**. This displays the accounting Properties dialog box.

B. Click the **Group Policy** tab.

C. Click the **New** button. Name the policy, for example **acct-policy** and press **Enter**. Then click **Close**.

Step 5. Add the new policy to the MMC:

A. Go to **File > Add/Remove Snap-in**.

B. In the Add/Remove Snap-in dialog box, click **Add**.

C. Select the **Group Policy Object Editor** and click **Add**.

D. In the Select Group Policy Object dialog box, click **Browse**.

E. Double-click the **accounting.dpro2.com** folder.

F. Highlight the policy (for example **acct-policy**) and click **OK**.

G. Click **Finish**, **Close**, and **OK** for the other open dialog boxes. This should add the acct-policy to the MMC.

Step 6. Configure the policy:

A. Expand the **acct-policy**.

B. Navigate to **User Configuration > Administrative Templates > System**.

C. Double-click **Don't run specified Windows applications**.

D. Click the **Enabled** radio button.

E. Click **Show**.

F. Click **Add** and add an application, for example winword.exe (the executable for Microsoft Word). Then click **OK**. Be sure to reset this at the end of the lab if it will affect any computers or users.

G. Click **OK** for the policy's Properties window. This brings you back to the MMC. The policy will now be enabled.

H. Double-click the **Run only allowed Windows applications** policy.

I. Enable the policy; then click **Show**.

J. Add an application by clicking the **Add** button and typing the name of an application, for example **excel.exe** (the executable for Microsoft Excel), and clicking **OK**.

K. Click **OK** for the policy's Properties window. This brings you back to the MMC. The policy will now be enabled.

Step 7. Save your MMC.

Watch the solution video in the "Hands-On Scenarios" section of the DVD.

View Recommended Resources

For readers who want to brush up on their CompTIA A+ topics:

- Prowse, David L. *CompTIA A+ Exam Cram*, Fourth Edition. Que. 2010.

Firefox add-on links:

- Adblock Plus Firefox add-on: https://addons.mozilla.org/en-US/firefox/addon/1865/
- NoScript Firefox add-on: https://addons.mozilla.org/en-US/firefox/addon/722/

Answer Review Questions

Answer the following review questions. You can find the answers at the end of this chapter.

1. Which of the following is one way of preventing spyware from being downloaded?

A. Use firewall exceptions.

B. Adjust Internet Explorer security settings.

C. Adjust the Internet Explorer home page.

D. Remove the spyware from Add/Remove Programs.

2. What key combination should be used to close a popup window?

A. Windows+R

B. Ctrl+Shift+Esc

C. Ctrl+Alt+Del

D. Alt+F4

3. Which protocol can be used to secure the e-mail login from an Outlook client using POP3 and SMTP?

A. SMTP

B. SPA

C. SAP

D. Exchange

4. What are two ways to secure Internet Explorer? (Select the two best answers.)

A. Set the Internet zone's security level to **High**.

B. Disable the pop-up blocker.

C. Disable ActiveX controls.

D. Add malicious sites to the **Trusted Sites** zone.

5. Heaps and stacks can be affected by which of the following attacks?

   A. Buffer overflows

   B. Root kits

   C. SQL injection

   D. Cross-site scripting

6. As part of your user awareness training, you recommend that users remove which of the following when they finish accessing the Internet?

   A. Instant messaging

   B. Cookies

   C. Group policies

   D. Temporary files

7. Which statement best applies to the term Java Applet?

   A. It decreases the usability of web-enabled systems.

   B. It is a programming language.

   C. A Web browser must have the capability to run Java applets.

   D. It uses digital signatures for authentication.

8. Which of the following concepts can ease administration but can be the victim of malicious attack?

   A. Zombies

   B. Backdoors

   C. Buffer overflow

   D. Group policy

9. In an attempt to collect information about a user's activities, which of the following will be used by spyware?

   A. Tracking cookie

   B. Session cookie

   C. Shopping cart

   D. Persistent cookie

10. What is it known as when a Web script runs in its own environment and does not interfere with other processes?

    A. Quarantine

    B. Honeynet

    C. Sandbox

    D. VPN

11. How can you train a user to easily determine whether a web page has a valid security certificate? (Select the best answer.)

A. Have the user contact the webmaster.

B. Have the user check for HTTPS://.

C. Have the user click the padlock in the browser and verify the certificate.

D. Have the user called the ISP.

12. To code applications in a secure manner, what is the best practice to use?

A. Cross-site scripting

B. Flash version 3

C. Input validation

D. HTML version 5

Answers and Explanations

1. **B.** Adjust the Internet Explorer security settings so that security is at a higher level, and add trusted and restricted websites.
2. **D.** Alt+F4 is the key combination that is used to close an active window. Sometimes it is okay to click the X, but malware creators are getting smarter all the time; the X could be a ruse.
3. **B.** SPA (Secure Password Authentication) is a Microsoft protocol used to authenticate e-mail clients. S/MIME and PGP can be used to secure the actual e-mail transmissions.
4. **A and C.** By increasing the Internet zone security level to high, you employ the maximum safeguards for that zone. ActiveX controls can be used for malicious purposes; disabling them makes it so that they do not show up in the browser. Disabling a pop-up blocker and adding malicious sites to the Trusted Sites zone would make Internet Explorer less secure.
5. **A.** Stacks and heaps are data structures that can be affected by buffer overflows. Value types are stored in a stack, whereas reference types are stored in a heap. An ethical coder will try to keep these running efficiently. An unethical coder will attempt to use a buffer overflow to affect heaps and stacks that in turn could affect the application in question or the operating system. The buffer overflow might be initiated by certain inputs and can be prevented by bounds checking.
6. **B.** The best answer is cookies, which can be used for authentication and session tracking and can be read as plain text. They can be used by spyware and can track people without their permission. It is also wise to delete temporary Internet files as opposed to temporary files.

7. **C.** To run Java applets, a Web browser must have that option enabled. Java increases the usability of web-enabled systems, and Java is a programming language. It does not use digital signatures for authentication.
8. **B.** Backdoors were originally created to ease administration. However, hackers quickly found that they could use these backdoors for a malicious attack.
9. **A.** A tracking cookie will be used, or misused, by spyware in an attempt to access a user's activities. Tracking cookies are also known as browser cookies or HTTP cookies, or simply a cookie. Shopping carts take advantage of cookies to keep the shopping cart reliable.
10. **C.** When a Web script runs in its own environment for the express purpose of not interfering with other processes, it is known as running in a sandbox. Quite often, the sandbox will be used to create sample scripts before they are actually implemented. Quarantining is a method used to isolate viruses. A honeynet is a collection of servers used to attract hackers and isolate them in an area where they can do no damage. VPN is short for virtual private network, which enables the connection of two hosts from remote networks.
11. **C.** In Internet Explorer, the user should click the padlock in the browser; this will show the certificate information. Quite often, the address bar will have different colors as the background; for example, blue or green means that the certificate is valid, whereas red or pink indicates a problem. In Firefox, click the name of the website listed in the address bar just before where it says HTTPS to find out the validity of the certificate. Contacting the webmaster and calling the ISP are time-consuming, not easily done, and not something that an end user should do. Although HTTPS:// can tell a person that the browser is now using the hypertext transfer protocol secure, it does not necessarily determine whether the certificate is valid.
12. **C.** Input validation is the best practice to use when coding applications. This is important when creating web applications or web pages that require information to be inputted by the user.

This chapter covers the following subjects:

- **Network Design**—This section discusses network design elements such as hubs, switches, and routers, and how to protect those devices from attack. It also talks about network address translation, private versus public IP addresses, and the private IP ranges. Afterward you learn about network zones and interconnections, for example, intranets and extranets, demilitarized zones, LANs, and WANs. Finally, you learn how to defend against attacks on your virtual local area networks, IP subnets, and telephony devices.
- **Ports, Protocols, and Malicious Attacks**—In this section, you learn the ports and their associated protocols you need to know for the exam and how to secure those ports. The end of the chapter covers the basics about network attacks and how to defend against them.

This chapter covers the CompTIA Security+ SY0-201 objectives 2.1 and 2.2.

CHAPTER 5

Network Design Elements and Network Threats

Up until now we have focused on the individual computer system. Let's expand our security perimeter to now include networks. Network design is extremely important in a secure network. The elements that you include in your design can help to defend against many different types of network attacks. Being able to identify these network threats is the next step in securing your network. If you apply the strategies and defense mechanisms included in this chapter, you should be able to stave off most network attacks. This chapter and the following two chapters assume that you have a working knowledge of networks and that you have the CompTIA Network+ certification or commensurate experience. Let's begin with network design.

Foundation Topics

Network Design

Proper network design is critical for the security of your network, servers, and client computers. You need to protect your network devices so that they and the clients that they connect together will be less subject to attack. Implementing network address translation and having a good understanding of the standard private IP ranges can further protect all the computers in a standard network. A thorough knowledge of network zones, for example local area networks and demilitarized zones, is also important when designing a secure network. Finally, by utilizing subnetting, virtual local area networks, network access control, and secure telephony devices, you can put the final touches on your network design. We start with a relatively easy topic: network devices.

Network Devices

Let's begin with the network devices that are common on today's networks. Central connecting devices such as hubs and switches need to be secured and monitored; it makes sense because these devices will connect all the computers on your local area network. Attacks aimed at these devices could bring down the entire LAN. And of course, routers are extremely important when interconnecting local area networks and subnets. Because many routers have visible IP addresses on the Internet, you should expand your line of thinking to include securing these devices from attackers that might come from inside and outside your network. It is more common that attackers will be situated outside your network, but you never know!

Hub

A hub is a central connecting device used in a physical star topology. It is used in Ethernet networks only. A hub is actually a simple device, connecting multiple computers together and amplifying and passing on the electrical signal. Internally, the hub just has one trunk circuit to which all the ports connect. The hub *broadcasts* information out to all ports. Because of this, it can be easily compromised. A mischievous person could connect a laptop to any port on the hub, or any Ethernet jack that connects to the hub, and access all network traffic with the aid of a protocol analyzer.

NOTE: Protocol analyzers are also known as network sniffers, or packet sniffers. For more information on protocol analyzers, see Chapter 10, "Vulnerability and Risk Assessment."

A hub resides on the Physical Layer of the OSI model; therefore, when attempting to secure a hub, you have to think in physical, tangible terms. For example, the hub should be located in a secure area—server room, locked wiring closet, and so on. Further security precautions should be made to monitor traffic, which is covered in Chapter 11, "Monitoring and Auditing." However, the best way to secure a hub is to remove it! Basic hubs are deprecated devices and should be replaced with a switch or other more current device. Most companies today rely on the switch instead of the hub.

Switch

Ethernet switching was developed in 1996 and quickly took hold as the preferred method of networking, taking the place of deprecated devices such as hubs and bridges. This is due to the switch's improvement in the areas of data transfer and security. Like a hub, a switch is a central connecting device to which all computers on the network connect. Again, like a hub, a switch will regenerate the signal. That's where the similarity ends, however. Unlike a hub, a switch sends the signal in a *unicast* fashion to the correct computer, instead of broadcasting it out to every port. It does this by mapping computers' MAC addresses to their corresponding physical port. This can effectively make every port an individual entity, thus securing the network, and exponentially increasing data throughput. Switches employ a matrix of copper wiring instead of the standard trunk circuit, and intelligence to pass information to the correct port. Although there are Layer 1 through Layer 4 switches, the type generally covered on the Security+ exam is the Layer 2 switch. This switch sends information to each computer via MAC addresses.

Although the switch is by far the superior solution compared to a hub, there are still some security implications involved with it. These include but are not limited to the following:

Key Topic

- **MAC flooding—**Switches have memory that is set aside to store the MAC address to the port translation table, known as the Content Addressable Memory table, or *CAM table*. A MAC flood can send numerous packets to the switch, each of which has a different source MAC address, in an attempt to use up the memory on the switch. If this is successful, the switch changes state to what is known as *failopen mode*. At this point, the switch broadcasts data on all ports the way a hub does. This means two things: First, that network bandwidth will be dramatically reduced, and second, that a mischievous person could now use a protocol analyzer, running in promiscuous mode, to capture data from any other computer on the network. Yikes!

  Some switches are equipped with the capability to shut down a particular port if it receives a certain amount of packets with different source MAC addresses. For example, Cisco switches use port-security. This restricts a port by limiting and identifying MAC addresses of the computers that are permitted to access that port. A Cisco switch defines three categories of secure MAC addresses as part of a policy on the switch. Other providers have like policies that can be implemented. Other ways to secure against MAC flooding and constrain connectivity include using 802.1X-compliant devices, Dynamic VLANs, and network intrusion detection systems (NIDS), and to consistently monitor the network. We speak more to these concepts later in this chapter and in future chapters.

- **Physical tampering—**Some switches have a dedicated monitoring port. If this is accessible, a person could perpetuate a variety of attacks on the network. Even if a single port of the switch is accessible, a person could attempt the aforementioned MAC flooding attack and move on from there. So remember that the switch needs to be physically secured, most likely in a server room with some type of access control system. It sounds so simple, but it is commonly overlooked by many companies.

Router

A router connects two or more networks to form an internetwork. They are used in LANs, in WANs, and on the Internet. This device routes data from one location to another, usually by way of the IP address and IP network numbers. Routers function on the Network Layer of the OSI model.

NOTE: For a primer about the OSI Model and its layers, see the following link: www.davidlprowse.com/forums/showthread.php?t=1556.

Routers come in several forms including SOHO routers, those four port devices used in homes and small offices to connect to the Internet; servers, which can be configured for routing if they have multiple network adapters and the proper software; and most commonly, black box devices such as Cisco routers. Routers are intelligent and even have their own operating system, for example Cisco routers use an IOS (Internetwork Operating System). Quite often, a DMZ will be set up within a router, especially SOHO router devices; we speak more about the DMZ later in this chapter.

Routers can be the victim of denial-of-service attacks, malware intrusions, and other attacks that we cover in more depth later in this chapter and can spread these attacks and malware to other sections of the network. Routers can be protected from these attacks in the following ways:

- **Firewalls—**Firewalls protect against and filter out unwanted traffic. A firewall can be an individual device or can be added to a router. For example, most SOHO routers have a firewall built in, and Cisco Integrated Services Routers include the Cisco IOS Firewall. You can find more information on firewalls in Chapter 6, "Network Perimeter Security."

- **Intrusion prevention systems (IPS)**—An IPS will not only detect, but will also prevent directed attacks, botnet attacks, malware, and other forms of attacks. An IPS can be installed as a network-based solution or on a particular computer and some routers. More information on network-based IPS (and IDS) solutions can be found in Chapter 6.
- **Secure VPN connectivity**—Instead of connecting directly to a router, virtual private networks enable for secure connections utilizing IPSec and SSL. Secure VPN connectivity can be used on SOHO routers, advanced routers like ones offered by Cisco, or implemented with Windows server. You can find more information about VPNs in Chapter 8, "Physical Security and Authentication Models."
- **Content filtering**—Content filtering blocks or restricts access to certain websites. This provides protection from malicious websites. Content filtering can be installed as a server, as an appliance or on some routers. You can find more information about content filters in Chapter 6.
- **Access control lists (ACLs)**—Access control lists enable or deny traffic. These can be implemented on a router and within firewalls; in some cases the two will be the same physical device. For example, an ACL can be configured to deny any connections by computers that have IP addresses outside of the network number. You can find more information about access control lists in Chapter 9, "Access Control Methods and Models."

Network Address Translation, and Private Versus Public IP

Network address translation (NAT) is the process of changing an IP address while it is in transit across a router. This is usually so one larger address space (private) can be remapped to another address space, or single IP address (public). In this case it is known as network masquerading, or IP masquerading, and was originally implemented to alleviate the problem of IPv4 address exhaustion. Today, NAT provides protection by hiding a person's private internal IP address. Basic routers only allow for basic NAT, which is IP address-translation-only. But more advanced routers allow for PAT, or *port address translation*, which translates both IP addresses and port numbers. A NAT implementation on a firewall hides an entire private network of IP addresses (for example, the 192.168.1.0 network), behind a single publicly displayed IP address. Many SOHO routers, servers, and more advanced routers offer this technology to protect a company's computers on the LAN. Generally, when an individual computer attempts to communicate through the router, *static NAT* is employed, meaning that the single private IP address will translate to a single public IP address. This is also called *one-to-one mapping*.

It is also important to know the difference between private and public addresses. A private address is one not displayed directly to the Internet and is normally behind a firewall (or NAT-enabled device). Typically these are addresses that a SOHO router or DHCP server would assign automatically to clients. A list of reserved private IP ranges is shown in Table 5-1. Public addresses are addresses displayed directly to the Internet; they are addresses that anyone can possibly connect to around the world. Most addresses besides the private ones listed in Table 5-1 are considered public addresses. Figure 5-1 shows an example of a router/firewall implementing NAT. The router's public address is 207.172.15.50, and its private address is 10.0.0.1. Computers to the left of the router are on the LAN, and all their IP addresses are private, protected by NAT, which occurs at the router. Servers outside the Internet cloud have public IP addresses (for example, 208.96.234.193) so that they can be accessed by anyone on the Internet.

Key Topic

Table 5-1 Private IP Ranges (as Assigned by the IANA)

IP Class	Assigned Range
Class A	10.0.0.0–10.255.255.255
Class B	172.16.0.0–172.31.255.255
Class C	192.168.0.0–192.168.255.255

Key Topic

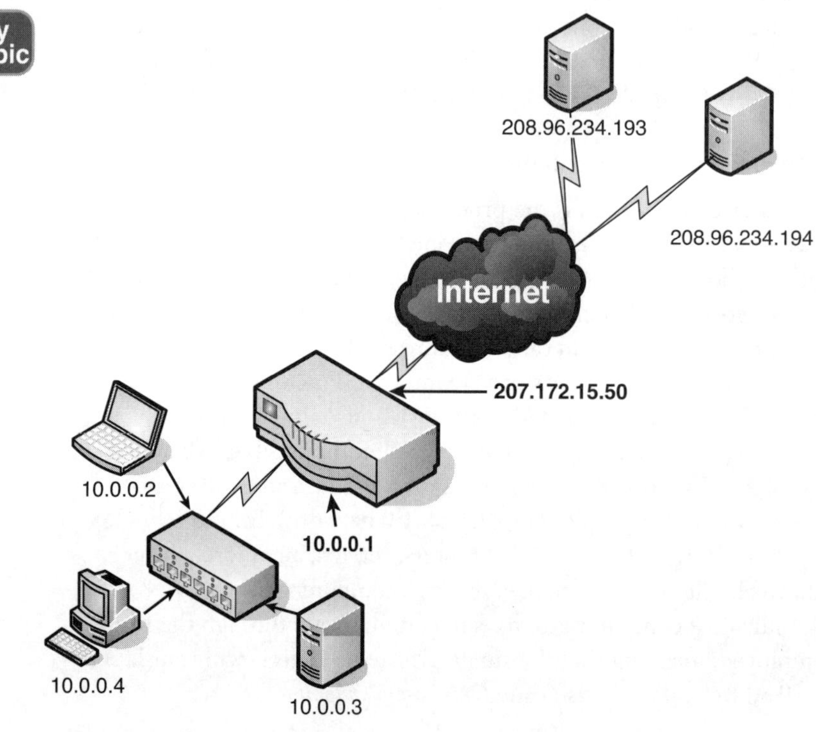

Figure 5-1 Example of Public and Private IP Addresses

Network Zones and Interconnections

When designing your network, think about all the pieces of the network and all the connections your network might make to other networks. Are you in charge of a local area network, or more than one local area network that perhaps form a wide area network? What kind of, and how many Internet connections do you have? Will you have servers that need to be accessed by users on the Internet? And will you need to share information with company employees that work from home or with other organizations, while securing that information from the average user on the Internet? The more interconnections and network zones that you have, the more security risk you are taking on. Keep this in mind as you read through the section.

LAN Versus WAN

A local area network, or LAN, is a group of networked computers contained in a small space like a small office, a school, or one or two close-knit buildings. Generally, the computers in the LAN are all assigned private IP addresses and are behind a firewall. Although computers on a LAN do not have to connect to the Internet, they usually will, but will do so via a router that acts as an IP proxy and employs NAT. It is important to secure computers on the LAN by placing them behind the router, assigning private IPs, and verifying that antimalware programs are installed.

A wide area network, or WAN, is one or more LANs connected together. The big difference between a LAN and a WAN is that a WAN covers a larger geographic area. This implies that the services of a telecommunications or data communications provider is necessary. The security implications of a WAN are great; the more connections your network has, the more likely attacks will become. All connections should be monitored and firewalled if possible. Consider that there might be connections to other states or countries...and, to the biggest WAN of them all—the Internet.

Internet

The Internet is the worldwide interconnection of individual computers and computer networks. Because it is a public arena, anyone on the Internet can possibly be a target, or an attacker. All types of sessions on the Internet should be protected at all times. For example, voice calls should be done within a protected VoIP system; data sessions should be protected by being run within a virtual private network; and so on. Individual computers should be protected by firewalls and antimalware programs. Networks should be protected by firewalls as well. But what about systems that need to access the LAN and also need to be accessed by clients on the Internet? Well, one option is to create an area that is not quite the LAN, and not quite the Internet; this is a demilitarized zone, or DMZ.

Demilitarized Zone (DMZ)

When talking about computer security, a *Demilitarized Zone (DMZ)* is a special area of the network (sometimes referred to as a subnetwork) that houses servers which host information accessed by clients or other networks on the Internet. Some of these servers might include web, FTP, mail, and database computers. These servers might also be accessible to clients on the LAN. There are several ways to set up a DMZ; a common way is the *3-leg perimeter* DMZ, as shown in Figure 5-2. Notice the third "leg" that branches off the firewall to the right. This leads to a special switch that has WWW and FTP servers connected to it. Also note that the DMZ is on a different IP network than the LAN, although both the LAN and DMZ are private IP network numbers. The firewall can (and usually will) be configured in a secure fashion on the DMZ connection (172.29.250.200) and an even more secure fashion on the LAN connection (192.168.100.200). The DMZ connection in Figure 5-2 needs to have only inbound ports 80 (WWW) and 21 (FTP) open; all other ports can be closed, thus filtering inbound traffic. The LAN connection can be completely shielded on the inbound side. Although DMZs can be created logically, they are most often found as physical implementations. There are several other implementations of a DMZ. For example, a DMZ can be set up with two firewalls that surround it, also known as a *back-to-back perimeter* network configuration; in this case the DMZ would be located between the LAN and the Internet. A DMZ might also be set up within a router, especially in small organizations that use basic SOHO router devices. It all depends on the network architecture and security concerns of the organization.

Intranets and Extranets

Intranets and extranets are implemented so that a company (or companies) can share its data using all the features and benefits of the Internet, while keeping that data secure within the organization, select organizations, and specific users. In the case of an intranet, only one company is involved; it could be as simple as an internal company website, or a more advanced architecture of servers, operational systems, and networks that deploy tools, applications, and of course data. In the case of an extranet, multiple companies can be involved, or an organization can opt to share its data and resources with users that are not part of the organization(s). This sharing is done via the Internet, but again, is secured so that only particular people and organizations can connect. Whether you have an intranet or an extranet, security is a major concern. Proper authentication schemes should be implemented to ensure that only the appropriate users can access data and resources. Only certain types of information should be stored on an intranet or extranet. Confidential, secret, and top secret information should not be hosted within an intranet or extranet. Finally, the deployment of a firewall(s) should be thoroughly planned out in advance. An example of a company that hosts an intranet and an extranet is shown in Figure 5-3. Note that data commuters from Company A can access the intranet because they work for the company. Also note that Company B can access the extranet, but not the intranet. In this example, the company (Company A) has created two DMZs, one for its intranet and one for its extranet. Of course, it is possible to set this up using only one DMZ, but the access control lists on the firewall and other devices would have to be planned and monitored more carefully. If possible, separating the data into two distinct physical locations will have several benefits, namely being more secure; although, it will cost more money to do so. This will all depend on the acceptable risk level of the organization and its budget!

Key Topic

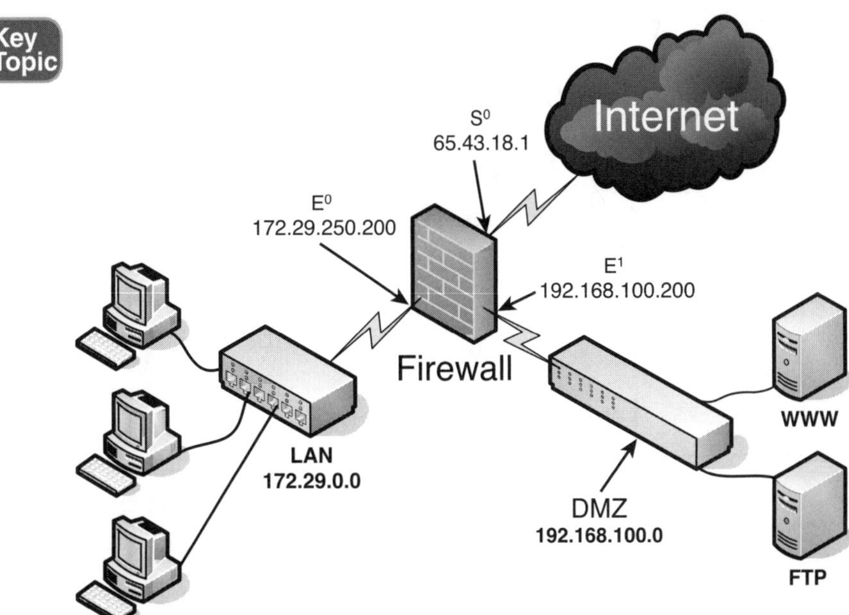

Figure 5-2 3-Leg Perimeter DMZ

Network Access Control (NAC)

In this chapter, we have mentioned several types of networking technologies and design elements. But whichever you choose to use, they need to be controlled in a secure fashion. *Network Access Control* (NAC) does this by setting the rules by which connections to a network are governed. Computers attempting to connect to a network are denied access unless they comply with rules including levels of antivirus protection, system updates, and so on...effectively weeding out those who would perpetuate malicious attacks. The client computer will continue to be denied until it has been properly updated, which in some cases can be taken care of by the NAC solution automatically. This would often require some kind of pre-installed software (an agent) on the client computer, or the computer would be scanned by the NAC solution remotely.

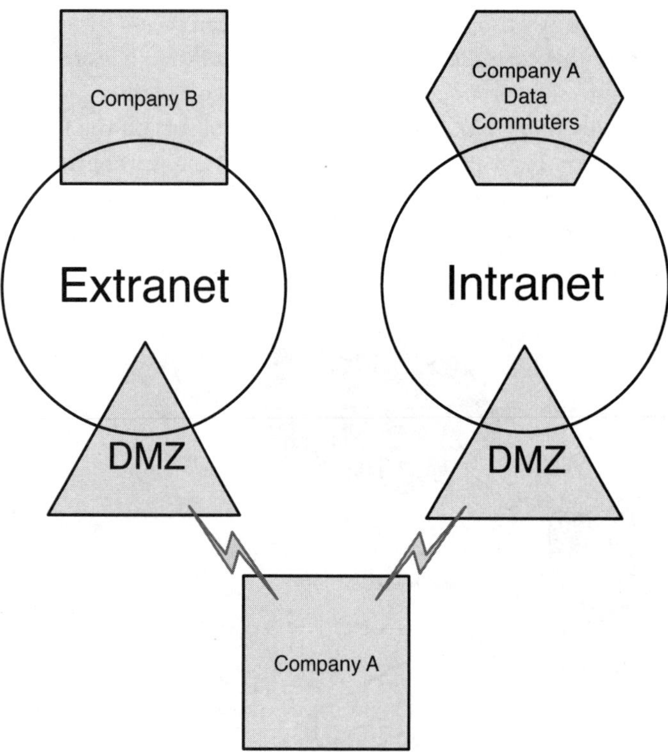

Figure 5-3 Example of an Intranet and Extranet

Some companies offer hardware-based NAC solutions, for example the Nortel Secure Network Access Switch, whereas other organizations offer software-based NAC solutions such as FreeNAC (http://freenac.net/) or PacketFence (www.packetfence.org), which are both open source.

The IEEE 802.1X standard, known as port-based Network Access Control, or PNAC, is a basic form of NAC that enables the establishment of authenticated point-to-point connections, but NAC has grown to include software; 802.1X is now considered a subset of NAC. See the section "Authentication Models and Components" in Chapter 8 for more information about IEEE 802.1X.

Subnetting

Subnetting is the act of creating subnetworks logically through the manipulation of IP addresses. These subnetworks are distinct portions of a single IP network.

Subnetting is implemented for a few reasons:

- It increases security by compartmentalizing the network.
- It is a more efficient use of IP address space.
- It reduces broadcast traffic and collisions.

To illustrate the first bullet point, examine Figure 5-4. This shows a simple diagram of two subnets within the 192.168.50.0 network using the subnet mask 255.255.255.240; this would also be known as 192.168.50.0/28 in CIDR notation. You can see that the subnets are divided; this implies that traffic is isolated—it can not travel from one subnet to another without a route set up specifically for that purpose. So, computers within Subnet ID 2 can communicate with each other by default, and computers within Subnet ID 8 can communicate with each other, but computers on Subnet 2 *cannot* communicate with computer on Subnet 8, and vice versa.

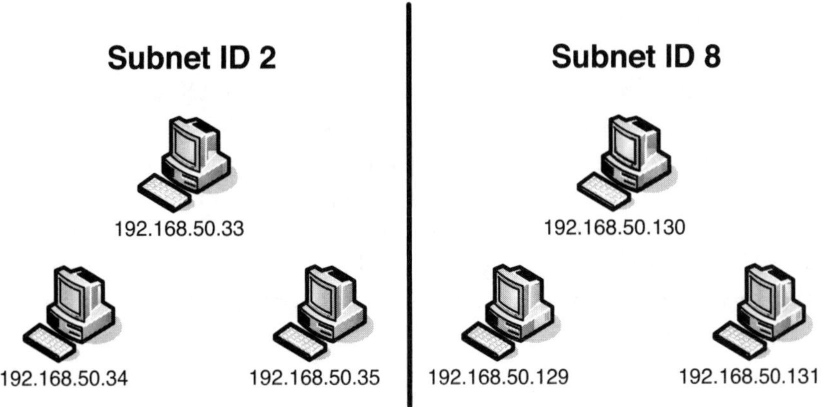

Figure 5-4 Example of a Subnetted Network

As a security precaution, using subnet zero is discouraged, and instead a network administrator should start with subnet 1, which in the preceding example would be 192.168.50.16. This avoids any possible confusion regarding the actual network number (192.168.50.0) and its subnets. If a network administrator were to use the first subnet and then inadvertently use a default subnet mask (such as 255.255.255.0) the hosts on that subnet would have access to more of the network than they should. This kind of mistake is common when using the first subnet and is the main reason it is discouraged.

When compartmentalizing the network through subnetting, an organization's departments can be assigned to individual subnets, and varying degrees of security policies can be associated with each subnet. Incidents and attacks are normally isolated to the subnet that they occur on. Any router that makes the logical connections for subnets should have its firmware updated regularly, and traffic should be occasionally monitored to verify that it is isolated.

NOTE: The CompTIA Security+ objectives speak to *securing* subnetted IP networks and expect the examinee to be well versed with *how* to set up subnetworks; the "how" portion is covered in the Network+ exam. For more information about how to subnet as it applies to the CompTIA Network+ exam, purchase the *CompTIA Network+ Video Mentor* (by yours truly) and access my website: www.davidlprowse.com

Virtual Local Area Network (VLAN)

A VLAN is implemented to segment the network, reduce collisions, organize the network, boost performance, and hopefully, increase security. A device such as a switch can control the VLAN. Like subnetting, a VLAN compartmentalizes the network and can isolate traffic. But unlike subnetting, a VLAN can be set up in a physical manner; an example of this would be the port-based VLAN, as shown in Figure 5-5. In this example, each group of computers such as Classroom 1 have its own VLAN; however, computers in the VLAN can be located anywhere on the *physical* network. For example, Staff computers could be located in several physical areas in the building, but regardless of where they are located, they are associated with the Staff VLAN because of the physical port they connect to. Due to this, it is important to place physical network jacks in secure locations for VLANs that have access to confidential data.

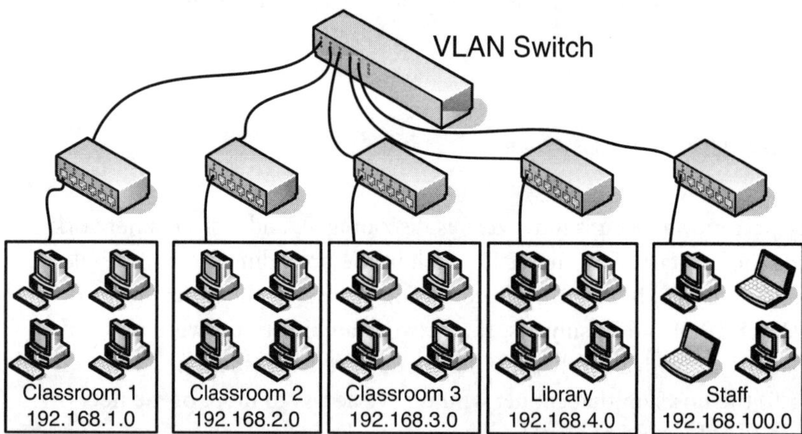

Figure 5-5 Example of a VLAN

There are also logical types of VLANs, such as the protocol-based VLAN and the MAC address-based VLAN, that have a whole separate set of security precautions, but those precautions go beyond the scope of the CompTIA Security+ exam.

The most common standard associated with VLANs is IEEE 802.1Q; which modifies Ethernet frames by "tagging" them with the appropriate VLAN information, based on which VLAN the Ethernet frame should be directed to.

VLANs restrict access to network resources, but this can be bypassed through the use of *VLAN hopping*. VLAN hopping can be divided into two categories, as shown in Table 5-2.

Table 5-2 Types of VLAN Hopping

VLAN Hopping Method	How It Works	How to Defend
Switch spoofing	The attacking computer must be capable of speaking the tagging and trunking protocols used by the VLAN trunking switch to imitate the switch. If successful, traffic for one or more VLANs is then accessible to the attacking computer.	■ Put unplugged ports on the switch into an unused VLAN. ■ Configure the switch ports in charge of passing tagged frames to be trunks and to explicitly forward specific tags. ■ Avoid using default VLAN names such as VLAN or VLAN1.
Double tagging	In a double-tagging attack, an attacking host attaches two VLAN tags to the frames it transmits. The first, proper header is stripped off by the first switch the frame encounters, and the frame is then forwarded. The second, false header is then visible to the second switch that the frame encounters.	■ Upgrade firmware or software. ■ Pick an unused VLAN as the default VLAN (also known as a native VLAN) for all trunks, and do not use it for any other intent. ■ Consider redesigning the VLAN if multiple 802.1Q switches are used.

MAC flooding attacks can also be perpetuated on a VLAN, but because the flood of packets will be constrained to an individual VLAN, VLAN hopping will not be possible as a result of a MAC flood.

VLANs can also be the victims of ARP attacks, brute force attacks, spanning-tree attacks, and more of which we discuss in later chapters.

Telephony Devices

Telephony aims at providing voice communication for your users and requires various equipment to accomplish this goal. Older devices such as modems can be the victim of an attack, but nowadays computers are also heavily involved in telephony; this is known as computer telephony integration or CTI. What does this mean for you, the network security administrator? Well, for one thing, special telephones and servers require particular security, for a whole new level of attacks and ways of targeting this equipment. The telephone, regardless of what type, is still one of the primary communication methods and therefore needs to be up and running all the time.

Modems

In networking environments such as a network operations center (NOC) or server room, modems are still used by network administrators to connect to servers and networking equipment via dial-up lines. Often, this is a redundant, worst-case scenario implementation—sometimes, it is the default way for an admins to access and configure their networking equipment. In some cases, this is done without any authentication, and to make matters worse, sometimes admins use Telnet to configure their equipment. Of course, this is insecure, to say the least. A modem can be the victim of *wardialing*, which is the act of scanning telephone numbers by dialing them one at a time. Computers will usually pick up on the first ring, and the wardialing system will make a note of that and add that number to the list. Besides the obvious social annoyance this could create, a hacker would then use the list to attempt to access computer networks. Now think back to the system that has *no authentication scheme in place*!

So to protect modem connections, a network admin should 1) use the callback feature in the modem software and set it to call the person back at a preset phone number; 2) use some type of username/password authentication scheme and select only strong passwords because wardialers will most likely try at password guessing; and 3) use dial-up modems sparingly, only in secure locations, and try to keep the modem's phone number secret. And by the way, a quick word on Telnet; it is not secure and should be substituted with SSH or another more secure way of configuring a remote device.

For the typical user who still uses a modem on a client computer, set the modem to not answer incoming calls, and be sure not to use any remote control software on the system that houses the modem. Finally, consider upgrading to a faster and more secure Internet access solution!

PBX Equipment

A private branch exchange (PBX) makes all of an organization's internal phone connections and also provides connectivity to the PSTN. Originally, they were simple devices, but as time progressed they incorporated many new features and along the way became more of a security concern. For example, a hacker might attempt to exploit a PBX to obtain free long distance service or to employ social engineering to obtain information from people at the organization that owns the PBX. To secure a standard PBX, make sure it is in a secure room (server room, locked wiring closet, and so on); usually they should be mounted to the wall but could be fixed to the floor as well. Also, change passwords regularly, and only allow authorized maintenance; log any authorized maintenance done as well. PBX computers will often have a remote port (basically a built-in modem or other device) for monitoring and maintenance; ensure that this port is not exploited and that only authorized personnel know how to access it. Today's PBX devices might act as servers on the network and might incorporate VoIP, which is also known as an IP-PBX.

VoIP

Voice over Internet Protocol (VoIP) is a broad term that deals with the transmission of voice data over IP networks such as the Internet. It is used by organizations and in homes. In an organization, IP phones can be the victim of attacks much like individual computers can. In addition, VoIP servers can be exploited the same way that other servers can; for example, by way of denial-of-service attacks. When securing a VoIP server, a network security administrator should implement many of the same precautions that they would make for more traditional servers, such as file servers and FTP servers. Some VoIP solutions, especially for home use, use the Session Initiation Protocol (SIP), which can be exploited by man-in-the-middle attacks. To help reduce risk, VoIP systems should be updated regularly and use encryption and an authentication scheme. We could talk about VoIP for days, but luckily for you, the exam requires that you have only a basic understanding of what VoIP is and how to protect it in a general sense. Most of the ways that you will mitigate risk on a VoIP system are the same as you would for other server systems, and these are covered in the following section.

Ports, Protocols, and Malicious Attacks

I can't stress enough how important it is to secure a host's ports and protocols. They are the doorways into an operating system. Think about it, an open doorway is a plain and simple invitation for disaster. And that disaster could be caused by one of many different types of malicious network attacks. The network security administrator must be ever vigilant in monitoring, auditing, and implementing updated defense mechanisms to combat malicious attacks. Understanding ports and protocols is the first step in this endeavor.

Ports and Protocols

Although many readers of this book are familiar with ports used by the network adapter and operating system, a review of them is necessary because they play a big role in securing hosts and will most definitely appear on the exam in some way, shape, or form.

Ports act as logical communications endpoints for computers and are used on the Transport Layer of the OSI model by protocols such as the Transmission Control Protocol (TCP) and User Datagram Protocol (UDP). There are 65,536 ports altogether, numbering between 0 and 65,535. The ports are divided into categories, as shown in Table 5-3.

Table 5-3 Port Ranges

Port Range	Category Type	Description
0–1023	Well-Known Ports	This range defines commonly used protocols, for example HTTP uses port 80. They are designated by the IANA (Internet Assigned Numbers Authority), which is operated by the ICANN (Internet Corporation for Assigned Names and Numbers).
1024–49,151	Registered Ports	Ports used by vendors for proprietary applications. These must be registered with the IANA For example, Microsoft registered 3,389 for use with the Remote Desktop Protocol (RDP), aka Microsoft Terminal Server.
49,152–65,535	Dynamic and Private Ports	These ports can be used by applications but cannot be registered by vendors.

You need to understand the difference between inbound and outbound ports as described in the following two bullets and as illustrated in Figure 5-6.

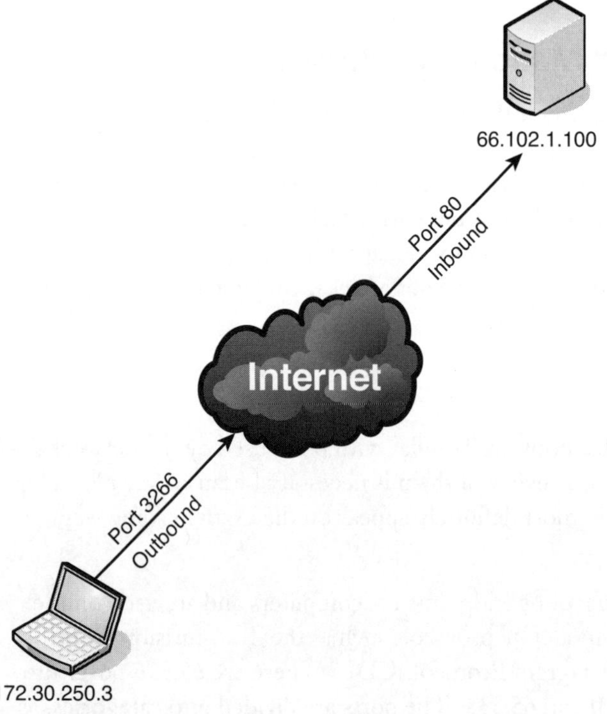

Figure 5-6 Inbound Versus Outbound Ports

- **Inbound ports—**Used when another computer wants to connect to a service or application running on your computer. Servers primarily use inbound ports so that they can accept incoming connections and serve data. For example, in Figure 5-6, the server with the IP address 66.102.1.100 has inbound port 80 open to accept incoming web page requests.
- **Outbound ports—**Used when your computer wants to connect to a service or application running on another computer. Client computers primarily use outbound ports that are assigned dynamically by the operating system. For example, in Figure 5-6, the client computer with the IP address 172.30.250.3 has outbound port 3266 open to make a web page request to the server.

NOTE: For a refresher about TCP, UDP, and ports, see the short 5-minute video at the following link:

www.davidlprowse.com/forums/showthread.php?t=1614

It's the inbound ports that a network security administrator should be most concerned with. Web servers, FTP servers, database servers, and so on have specific inbound ports opened to the public. Any other unnecessary ports should be closed, and any open ports should be protected and monitored carefully. Although there are 1,024 well-known ports, for the exam you need to know only a handful of them, as shown in Table 5-4. Remember that these inbound port numbers relate to the applications, services, and protocols that run on a server.

Table 5-4 23 Ports and Their Associated Protocols

Port Number	Associated Protocol	Full Name
7	Echo	Echo
19	CHARGEN	Character Generator
21	FTP	File Transfer Protocol
22	SSH	Secure Shell
23	Telnet	TErminaL NETwork
25	SMTP	Simple Mail Transfer Protocol
49	TACACS	Terminal Access Controller Access-Control System

continues

Table 5-4 23 Ports and Their Associated Protocols (continued)

Port Number	Associated Protocol	Full Name
53	DNS	Domain Name System
69	TFTP	Trivial File Transfer Protocol
80	HTTP	Hypertext Transfer Protocol
88	Kerberos	Kerberos
110	POP3	Post Office Protocol Version 3
119	NNTP	Network News Transfer Protocol
137-139	NetBIOS	NetBIOS Name, Datagram, and Session Services, respectively
143	IMAP	Internet Access Message Protocol
161	SNMP	Simple Network Management Protocol
389	LDAP	Lightweight Directory Access Protocol
443	HTTPS	Hypertext Transfer Protocol Secure (Uses TLS or SSL)
445	SMB	Server Message Block
636	LDAP over TLS/SSL	Lightweight Directory Access Protocol (over TLS/SSL)
1701	L2TP	Layer 2 Tunneling Protocol
1723	PPTP	Point-to-Point Tunneling Protocol
3389	RDP	Remote Desktop Protocol (Microsoft Terminal Server)

NOTE: You can find a complete list of ports and their corresponding protocols at the following link: www.iana.org/assignments/port-numbers.

The IP address of a computer and the port number it is sending or receiving on are combined together to form a network socket address. An example of this would be 66.102.1.100:80. That illustrates the IP address of the server in Figure 5-6 and the inbound port number accepting a connection from the client computer. Notice that the two are separated by a colon.

Figure 5-7 illustrates a few more examples of this within a Windows Vista client computer. It shows some of the results of a **netstat –an** command after FTP, WWW, and mail connections were made by the client to two separate servers. Examine the following figure and then read on.

The first callout in the figure is FTP Control Connection. This happens when a user first connects to an FTP server with FTP client software. Notice that the local computer has the IP address 10.254.254.205 and uses the dynamically assigned outbound port 55768 to connect to the FTP server. The remote computer on the other hand has the IP address 216.97.236.245 and uses inbound port 21 to accept the connection. Keep in mind that this is only the initial connection and login to the FTP server. Subsequent data connections are normally done on the server side via dynamically assigned ports. For example, the second callout, FTP Data Connection, occurred when the client downloaded a file. It is a separate session in which the client used the dynamically assigned port number 55769. In reality, this isn't quite dynamic anymore; the client operating system is simply selecting the next port number available; afterward, a subsequent and concurrent download would probably use port 55770. The server, on the other hand used the dynamically assigned port number 31290. Many FTP servers randomly select a different inbound port to use for each data connection to increase security. However, some FTP connections still use the original port 20 for data connections, which is not as secure, not only because it is well known, but also because it is static. To secure FTP communications, consider using software that enables dynamically assigned ports during data transfers; for example, Pure-FTPd (www.pureftpd.org) on the server-side and FileZilla (http://filezilla-project.org/) on the client-side. If your FTP server enables it, you can also consider IPv6 connections, and as always, be sure to use strong, complex passwords. (I don't mean to sound like a broken record!) The third callout shows an HTTP connection. Note that this is being made to a different server (208.80.152.118) and uses port 80. And finally, a POP3 connection that was previously made to the same server IP enabled the FTP connection, but note that the port number reflects POP3—it shows port number 110. These are just a few examples of many that occur between clients and servers all the time. Try making some connections to various servers from your client computer and view those sessions in the command-line.

Key Topic

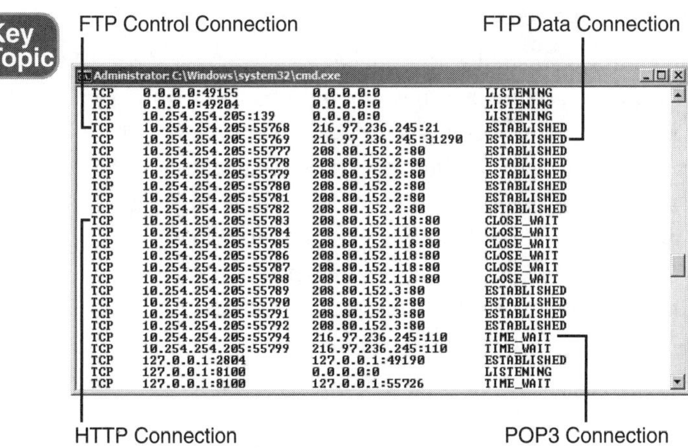

Figure 5-7 IP Addresses and Ports

Aside from servers, ports also become particularly important on router/firewall devices. These devices operate on the *implicit deny* concept, which means they will deny all traffic unless a rule is made to open the port associated with the type of traffic desired to be let through. We talk more about firewalls in Chapter 6.

You need to scan your servers, routers, and firewall devices to discern which ports are open. This can be done with the aforementioned **netstat** command or with an application such as Nmap (http://nmap.org/) or with an online scanner from a website such as GRC's ShieldsUP! (www.grc.com). The most effective way is with an actual scanning application which we show in depth in Chapter 10. However, there is a basic lab on port scanning referenced at the end of this chapter in the "Work Through Hands-On Scenarios" section.

Afterward, unnecessary ports should be closed. This can be done in a few ways:

- **Within the operating system GUI**—For example, in Windows, open the **Computer Management** console. Then go to **Services and Applications** > **Services**. Right-click the appropriate service and select **Properties**. From here the service can be stopped and disabled.
- **Within the CLI**—For example, a service can be stopped in Windows by using the **net stop** *service* command. A service can be disabled with the **SC** command. In Red Hat Linux a service can be stopped with the command **# service httpd stop** for example, and the same service can be disabled with the command **# chkconfig httpd off**. (Different versions of Linux have varying commands.)
- **Within a firewall**—Simply setting up a firewall normally closes and shields all ports by default. But you might have a service that was used previously on a server, and therefore a rule might have been created on the firewall to enable traffic through on that port. Within the firewall software, the rule can be deleted, disabled, or modified as needed.

Unnecessary ports also include ports associated with nonessential protocols. For example, TFTP (port 69) is usually considered a nonessential protocol, as is Finger (port 79). Telnet (port 23) is insecure and as such is also considered nonessential. However, the list of nonessential protocols will differ from one organization to the next. Always rescan the host to make sure that the ports are indeed closed. Then, make the necessary changes in documentation. Depending on company policy, you might need to follow change management procedures before making modifications to ports and services. For more information on this type of documentation and procedures, see Chapter 15, "Policies, Procedures, and People."

Port Zero Security

Let's talk about port zero for a moment. Although there are a total of 65,536 ports, only 65,535 of them can normally be exploited. The reason is that port zero usually redirects to another dynamically assigned port. Although the IANA listings say it is reserved, it does not officially exist and is defined as an invalid port number. But programmers use port zero as a wildcard port, designing their applications to ask the operating system to assign a nonzero port. So, normally malware that exploits port zero will simply be redirected to another valid port. Again, this means that only 65,535 of the 65,536 ports can be exploited. In the future, port zero may become more of a security concern with the growth of legitimate raw socket programming. This is programming directly to network ports, bypassing the Transport Layer; an example would be the Internet Control Message Protocol (ICMP) such as ping operations. However, historically raw sockets have been used by hackers to perform *TCP reset attacks*, which set the reset flag in a TCP header to 1, telling the respective computer to kill the TCP session immediately. Until recently, raw socket programming has been generally frowned upon.

Malicious Network Attacks

There are many types of network attacks. Some are similar to others, making it difficult to differentiate between them. Because of this, I've listed simple definitions and examples of each, plus mitigating techniques, and summarized them at the end of this section.

DoS

Denial of Service *(DoS)* is a broad term given to many different types of network attacks that attempt to make computer resources unavailable. Generally this will be done to servers but could also be perpetuated against routers and other hosts. DoS attacks can be implemented in several ways as listed here.

- **Flood attacks**—Deals with sending many packets to a single server or other host in an attempt to disable it. There are a few ways to accomplish this including:
  - **Ping flood**—Also known as an ICMP flood attack, is when an attacker attempts to send many ICMP echo request packets (pings) to a host in an attempt to use up all available bandwidth. This will work only if the attacker has more bandwidth available than the target. To deter this attack, configure the system not to respond to ICMP echoes. You might have noticed that several years ago, you could ping large companies' websites and get replies. But after Ping floods became prevalent, a lot of these companies disabled ICMP echo replies. For example, try opening the command prompt and typing **ping microsoft.com** (Internet connection required). It should result in Request Timed Out, which tells you that Microsoft has disabled this.
  - **Smurf attack**—Also sends large amounts of ICMP echoes, but this particular attack goes a bit further. The attacking computer broadcasts the ICMP echo requests to every computer on its network or subnetwork. In addi-

tion, in the header of the ICMP echo requests will have a spoofed IP address. That IP address is the target of the Smurf attack. Every computer that replies to the ICMP echo requests will do so to the spoofed IP. Don't forget that the original attack was broadcast, so, the more systems on the network (or subnetwork), the more echo replies that are sent to the target computer. There are several defenses for this attack, including configuring hosts not to respond to pings or ICMP echoes, configuring routers not to forward packets directed to broadcast addresses, implement subnetting with smaller subnetworks, and employing network ingress filtering in an attempt to drop packets that contain forged or spoofed IP addresses (especially addresses on other networks). These defenses have enabled most network administrators to make their networks immune to Smurf and other ICMP-based attacks. The attack can be automated and modified using the exploit code known as Smurf.c.

- **Fraggle—**Similar to the Smurf attack, but the traffic sent is *UDP* echoes. The traffic is directed to port 7 (Echo) and port 19 (CHARGEN). To protect against this attack, again, configure routers not to forward packets directed to broadcast addresses, employ network filtering, and disable ports 7 and 19. These ports are not normally used in most networks. The attack can be automated and modified using the exploit code known as Fraggle.c.

NOTE: A similar attack is known as a *UDP flood attack*, which also uses the connectionless User Datagram Protocol. It is enticing to attackers because it does not require a synchronization process.

- **SYN flood—**Occurs when an attacker sends a large amount of SYN request packets to a server in an attempt to deny service. Remember that in the TCP three-way handshake, a synchronization (SYN) packet is sent from the client to the server, then a SYN/ACK packet is sent from the server to the client, and finally, an acknowledgment (ACK) packet is sent from the client to the server. Attackers attempting a SYN flood will either simply skip sending the ACK or will spoof the source IP address in the original SYN. Either way, the server will never receive the final ACK packet. This ends up being a half-open connection. By doing this multiple times, an attacker seeks to use up all connection-oriented resources so that no real connections can be made. A couple ways to defend against this are to recycle half-open connections after a predetermined amount of time and use Intrusion Detection Systems (IDS) to detect the attack. You can find more information about IDS in Chapter 6 and more information about SYN flood attacks and mitigation techniques at the following link:

  http://tools.ietf.org/html/rfc4987

- **Ping of Death—**POD is an attack that sends an oversized and malformed packet to another computer. It is an older attack; most computer operating systems today will not be affected by it, and most firewalls will block it before it enters a network. It entails sending a packet that is larger than 65,535 bytes in length, which according to RFC 791 is the largest size packet that can be used on a TCP/IP network without fragmentation. If a packet is sent that is larger than 65,535 bytes, it might overflow the target system's memory buffers, which can cause several types of problems including system crashes. Windows computers do not allow ping sizes beyond 65,500 bytes. For example, **ping** *destination* **–l 65500** will work, but **ping** *destination* **–l 66000** will not work. However, on some systems, this maximum limitation can be hacked in the Registry, and there are also third-party applications that can send these "larger than life" packets. To protect against this type of attack, configure hosts not to respond to pings or ICMP echoes, make sure that operating systems run the latest service packs and updates, update the firmware on any hardware-based firewalls, and update any software-based firewalls as well. POD can be combined with a ping flood, but because most firewalls will block one or more PODs, it doesn't make much sense to attempt the attack, so most hackers will opt for some other sort of packet flooding nowadays. This was one of the first DoS attacks. It and other attacks such as Nuke and WinNuke are considered to be deprecated.
- **Teardrop attack—**Sends mangled IP fragments with overlapping and oversized payloads to the target machine. This can crash and reboot various operating systems due to a bug in their TCP/IP fragmentation re-assembly code. For example, Windows 7 and Vista are particularly susceptible to Teardrop attacks. Linux and Windows systems should be upgraded to protect from this attack. There are also software downloads available on the Internet for Teardrop detection.
- **Permanent DoS attack—**Generally consists of an attacker exploiting security flaws in routers and other networking hardware by flashing the firmware of the device and replacing it with a modified image. This is also known as Phlashing, or PDoS.
- **Fork bomb—**Works by quickly creating a large number of processes to saturate the available processing space in the computer's operating system. Running processes can be "forked" to create other running processes, and so on. They are not considered viruses or worms but are known as "wabbits" or "bacteria" because they might self-replicate but do not infect programs or use the network to spread.

There are other types of DoS attacks, but that should suffice for now. Keep in mind that new DoS attacks are always being dreamed up (and implemented), so as a network security administrator, you need to be ready for new attacks and prepared to exercise new mitigation techniques.

DDoS

A *distributed denial-of-service (DDoS)* attack is when a group of compromised systems attack a single target, causing a DoS to occur at that host. A DDoS attack often utilizes a botnet. The unsuspecting computers in the botnet that act as attackers are known as zombies. A hacker starts the DDoS attack by exploiting a single vulnerability in a computer system and making that computer the zombie master, or DDoS master. The master system communicates with the other systems in the botnet. The attacker often loads malicious software on many computers (zombies). The attacker can launch a flood of attacks by all zombies in the botnet with a single command.

DoS and DDoS attacks are difficult to defend against. Other than the methods mentioned previously in the DoS section, these attacks can be prevented to some extent by updated stateful firewalls, switches, and routers with access control lists, intrusion-prevention systems (IPS), and proactive testing. Several companies offer products that simulate DoS and DDoS attacks. By creating a test server and assessing its vulnerabilities with simulated DoS tests, you can find holes in the security of your server before you take it live. A quick search for **DoS testing** shows a few of these simulation test companies. An organization could also opt for a "clean pipe," which attempts to weed out DDoS attacks, among other attacks. This solution is offered as a service by Verisign and other companies. Finally, if you do realize that a DDoS attack is being carried out on your network, call your ISP and request that this traffic be redirected.

Spoofing

A spoofing attack is when an attacker masquerades as another person by falsifying information. There are several types of spoofing attacks. The man-in-the-middle attack is not only a form of session hijacking, but it is also considered spoofing. Internet protocols and their associated applications can also be spoofed, especially if the protocol were poorly programmed in the first place. Web pages can also be spoofed in an attempt to fool users into thinking they are logging into a trusted website; this is known as URL spoofing and is used when attackers are fraudulently *phishing* for information such as usernames, passwords, credit card information, and identities. Phishing can also be done through a false e-mail that looks like it comes from a valid source. Quite often, this will be combined with e-mail address spoofing, which hides or disguises the sender information. Defending against these types of spoofing attacks is difficult, but by carefully selecting and updating applications that your organization uses, and through user awareness, spoofing can be held down to a minimum and when necessary ignored.

Just about anything can be spoofed if enough work is put into it, and IP addresses are no exception. IP address spoofing is when IP packets are created with a forged source IP address in the header. This conceals where the packets originated from. Packet filtering and sessions that repeat authentication can defend against this type of spoofing. Also, updating OSs and firmware and using newer OSs and network devices helps to mitigate risks involved with IP spoofing. IP spoofing is commonly used in DoS attacks as mentioned earlier and is also common in TCP/IP hijacking, which we discuss more in the next section.

Session Hijacking

Session hijacking is the exploitation of a computer session in an attempt to gain unauthorized access to data, services, or other resources on a computer. A few types of session hijacks can occur:

- **Session theft—**Can be accomplished by stealing a cookie from the client computer, which authenticates the client computer to a server. This is done at the Application Layer, and the cookies involved are often based off of their corresponding web applications (such as WWW sessions). This can be combated by using encryption and long random numbers for the session key, and regeneration of the session after a successful login. The Challenge Handshake Authentication Protocol (CHAP) can also be employed to require clients to periodically re-authenticate. However, session hijacking can also occur at the Network Layer, for example TCP/IP hijacking.
- **TCP/IP hijacking—**A common type of session hijacking, due to its popularity among hackers. It is when a hacker takes over a TCP session between two computers without the need of a cookie or any other type of host access. Because most communications' authentication occurs only at the beginning of a standard TCP session, a hacker can attempt to gain access to a client computer anytime after the session begins. One way would be to spoof the client computer's IP address, then find out what was the last packet sequence number sent to the server, and then inject data into the session before the client sends another packet of information to the server. Remember the three-way handshake that occurs at the beginning of a session; this is the only authentication that occurs during the session. A synchronization (SYN) packet is sent by the client to the server, then a SYN/ACK packet is sent by the server to the client, and finally, an acknowledgment (ACK) packet is sent by the client to the server. An attacker can jump in any time after this process and attempt to steal the session by injecting data into the data stream. This is the more difficult part; the attacker might need to perform a DoS attack on the client to stop it from sending anymore packets so that the packet sequence number doesn't increase. In contrast, UDP sessions are easier to hijack because no packet sequence numbers exist. Targets for this type of attack include online games such as Quake and Halo, and also DNS queries.

To mitigate the risk of TCP/IP hijacking, employ encrypted transport protocols such as SSL, IPSec, and SSH. For more information about these encryption protocols, see Chapter 13, "PKI and Encryption Protocols."

- **Blind hijacking—**When an attacker blindly injects data into a data stream without being able to see whether the injection was successful. The attacker could be attempting to create a new administrator account or gain access to one.
- **Man-in-the-middle (MITM)—**Attacks intercept all data between a client and a server. It is a type of active interception. If successful, all communications now go through the MITM attacking computer. The attacking computer can at this point modify the data and send it to the receiving computer. This type of eavesdropping is only successful when the attacker can properly impersonate each endpoint. Cryptographic protocols such as Secure Socket Layer (SSL) and Transport Layer Security (TLS) address MITM attacks by using a mutually trusted third-party certification authority. These public key infrastructures (PKI) should use strong mutual authentication such as secret keys and strong passwords. For more information about PKI, see Chapter 13.

On a semirelated note, *cross-site scripting* is a type of vulnerability found in web applications that is used with session hijacking. The attacker manipulates a client computer into executing code that is considered trusted as if it came from the server the client was connected to. In this way, the hacker can acquire the client computer's session cookie (enabling them to steal sensitive information) or exploit the computer in other ways.

Replay

A *replay attack* is a network attack in which a valid data transmission is maliciously or fraudulently repeated or delayed. An attacker might use a packet sniffer to intercept data and retransmit it later. This differs from session hijacking in that the original session is simply intercepted and analyzed for later use. In this way a hacker can impersonate the entity that originally sent the data. For example, if customers were to log in to a banking website with their credentials while an attacker was watching, the attacker could possibly sniff out the packets that include the usernames and passwords and then possibly connect with those credentials later on. Of course, if the bank uses SSL or TLS to secure login sessions, then the hacker would have to decrypt the data as well, which could prove more difficult. An organization can defend against this attack in several ways. The first is to use session tokens that are transmitted to people the first time they attempt to connect, and identify them subsequently. They are handed out randomly so that attackers cannot guess at token numbers. The second way is to implement timestamping and synchronization as in a Kerberos environment. A third way would be to use a timestamped *nonce* that is a random number issued by an authentication protocol that can only be used one time. We talk more about SSL, TLS, Kerberos, and other cryptographic solutions in Chapter 13.

NOTE: A replay attack should not be confused with SMTP relay, which is when one server forwards e-mail to other e-mail servers.

Null Sessions

A null session is a connection to the Windows interprocess communications share (IPC$). The null session attack is a type of exploit that makes unauthenticated NetBIOS connections to a target computer. The attack uses ports 139 and 445, which are the NetBIOS session port and the Server Message Block port respectively. If successful, an attacker could find user IDs, share names, and various settings and could possibly gain access to files, folders, and other resources. An example of the initial code an attacker might use is

```
net use \\IP address\ipc$ "" /U: ""
```

Afterward, the attacker might use a program such as enum.exe or something similar to extract information from the remote computer, such as usernames. Finally, an attacker might use a brute force attack in an attempt at cracking passwords and gaining more access.

To protect against this computers should be updated as soon as possible, for example Windows XP should be upgraded to service pack 3. However, the best way to defend against this attack is to filter out traffic on ports 139 and 445, with a firewall or a host-based intrusion prevention system. When a firewall is enabled, ports 139 and 445 will not appear to exist.

DNS Poisoning and Other DNS Attacks

DNS poisoning or DNS cache poisoning is the modification of name resolution information that should be in a DNS server's cache. It is done to redirect client computers to incorrect websites. This can happen through improper software design, misconfiguration of name servers, and maliciously designed scenarios exploiting the traditionally open architecture of the DNS system. Let's say a client wants to go to www.comptia.org. That client's DNS server will have a cache of information about domain names and their corresponding IP addresses. If CompTIA's site were visited in the recent past by any client accessing the DNS server, its domain name and IP should be in the DNS server's cache. If the cache is poisoned, it could be modified in such a way to redirect requests for www.comptia.org to a different IP address and website. This other site could be a phishing site or could be malicious in some other way. This attack can be countered by using Transport Layer Security (TLS) and digital signatures or by using Secure DNS (DNSSEC) that uses encrypted electronic signatures when passing DNS information, and finally, by patching the DNS server.

Unauthorized zone transfers are another bane to DNS servers. Zone transfers replicate the database that contains DNS data. If a zone transfer is initiated, say through a reconnaissance attack, server name and IP address information can be stolen, resulting in the attacker accessing various hosts by IP address. To defend against this, zone transfers should be restricted and audited in an attempt to eliminate unauthorized zone transfers and to identify anyone who tries to exploit the DNS server in this manner. Vigilant logging of the DNS server and the regular checking of DNS records can help detect unauthorized zone transfers.

A Windows computer's hosts file can also be the victim of attack. The hosts file is used on a local computer to translate or resolve hostnames to IP addresses. This is the predecessor to DNS but can still be used on local computers if DNS or another name service is not available. Attackers may attempt to hijack the hosts file in an attempt to alter or poison it or to try to have the client bypass DNS altogether. The best defense for this is to modify the computer's hosts file permissions to read-only. It is located at the following path: \%systemroot%\System32\drivers\etc.

Although it is less of an actual attack, *domain name kiting* or simply domain kiting is the process of deleting a domain name during the 5-day grace period (known as the add grace period or AGP) and immediately reregistering it for another 5-day period. This process is repeated any number of times with the end result of having the domain registered without ever actually paying for it. It is a malicious attack on the entire domain name system by misusing the domain tasting grace period. The result is that a legitimate company or organization quite often cannot secure the domain name of its choice.

As you can see, the DNS server can be the victim of many attacks due to its visibility on the Internet. It should be closely monitored at all times. Other highly visible servers such as web servers and mail servers should be likewise monitored, audited, and patched as soon as updates are available.

ARP Poisoning

The Address Resolution Protocol (ARP) resolves MAC addresses to IP addresses. Any resolutions that occur over a set amount of time are stored in the ARP table. The ARP table can be poisoned or spoofed. ARP poisoning is an attack that exploits Ethernet networks, and it may enable an attacker to sniff frames of information, modify that information, or stop it from getting to its intended destination. The spoofed frames of data will contain a false source MAC address, which will deceive other devices on the network. The idea behind this is to associate the attackers MAC address with an IP address of another device, such as a default gateway or router so that any traffic that would normally go to the gateway would end up at the attacker's computer. The attacker could then perpetuate a man-in-the-middle attack, or a denial-of-service attack, in addition to MAC flooding. Some of the defenses for ARP poisoning include DHCP snooping and an open source program called ArpON (http://arpon.sourceforge.net/).

Summary of Network Attacks

Table 5-5 lists important network attacks and mitigation techniques.

Table 5-5 Summary of Important Network Attacks and Mitigation Techniques to Know for the Exam

Network Attack	Description	Mitigation Techniques
MAC flooding	A MAC Flood will send numerous packets to the switch, each of which has a different source MAC address, in an attempt to use up the memory on the switch.	■ Implement 802.1X. ■ Use port-security. ■ Implement dynamic VLANs and NIDS. ■ Consistently monitor the network.
VLAN hopping	The act of gaining access to traffic on other VLANs that would not normally be accessible by jumping from one VLAN to another.	■ Put unplugged ports on the switch into an unused VLAN. ■ Configure the switch ports in charge of passing tagged frames to be trunks and to explicitly forward specific tags. ■ Pick an unused VLAN as the default VLAN for all trunks, and do not use it for any other intent. ■ Avoid using default VLAN names such as VLAN or VLAN1. ■ Upgrade firmware or software. ■ Consider redesigning the VLAN if multiple 802.1Q switches are being used.
Ping flood	Type of DoS. When an attacker attempts to send many ICMP echo request packets (pings) to a host in an attempt to use up all available bandwidth.	Configure the system not to respond to ICMP echoes.

continues

Table 5-5 Summary of Important Network Attacks and Mitigation Techniques to Know for the Exam

Network Attack	Description	Mitigation Techniques
Smurf attack	Type of DoS. Sends large amounts of ICMP echoes, broadcasting the ICMP echo requests to every computer on its network or subnetwork. The header of the ICMP echo requests will have a spoofed IP address. That IP address is the target of the Smurf attack. Every computer that replies to the ICMP echo requests will do so to the spoofed IP.	■ Configure hosts not to respond to pings or ICMP echoes. ■ Configure routers not to forward packets directed to broadcast addresses. ■ Implement subnetting with smaller subnetworks. ■ Employ network ingress filtering.
Fraggle	Type of DoS. Similar to the Smurf attack, but the traffic sent is *UDP* echo traffic as opposed to ICMP echo traffic.	■ Configure routers not to forward packets directed to broadcast addresses. ■ Employ network filtering, disabling ports 7 and 19.
SYN flood	Type of DoS. When an attacker sends a large amount of SYN request packets to a server in an attempt to deny service.	■ Recycle half-open connections after a predetermined amount of time. ■ Use Intrusion Detection Systems (IDS) to detect the attack.
Ping of Death	Type of DoS. Sends an oversized and malformed packet to another computer.	■ Configure hosts not to respond to pings or ICMP echoes. ■ Verify operating systems are running the latest service packs and updates. ■ Update the firmware on any hardware-based firewalls, and update any software-based firewalls as well.
Teardrop attack	Type of DoS. Sends mangled IP fragments with overlapping and oversized payloads to the target machine.	■ Upgrade operating systems. ■ Consider third-party downloads.
DDoS	When a group of compromised systems attack a single target, causing a DoS to occur at that host, usually using a botnet.	■ Update firewalls. ■ Use IPS. ■ Utilize a "clean pipe."

Table 5-5 Summary of Important Network Attacks and Mitigation Techniques to Know for the Exam

Network Attack	Description	Mitigation Techniques
Spoofing	When an attacker masquerades as another person by falsifying information.	■ Carefully select applications.. ■ User awareness ■ In the case of IP spoofing, incorporate packet filtering, and repeat authentication schemes.
Session theft	When an attacker attempts to steal a user's session using the owner's cookie and authentication information.	■ Use encryption. ■ Use CHAP.
TCP/IP hijacking	When a hacker takes over a TCP session between two computers without the need of a cookie or any other type of host access.	■ Employ encrypted transport protocols such as SSL, IPSec, and SSH.
Man-in-the-middle (MITM)	Form of eavesdropping that intercepts all data between a client and a server, relaying that information back and forth.	■ Implement SSL/TLS using a mutually trusted third-party certification authority.
Replay attack	Valid data transmission is maliciously or fraudulently repeated or delayed.	■ Use session tokens. ■ Implement timestamping and synchronization. ■ Use a nonce.
Null session	A connection to the Windows interprocess communications share (IPC$).	■ Update computers. ■ Filter ports 139 and 445.
DNS poisoning	The modification of name resolution information that should be in a DNS server's cache.	■ Use TLS. ■ Utilize Secure DNS.
Unauthorized zone transfers	Unauthorized transfer of DNS information from a DNS server.	■ Log the DNS server. ■ Restrict and audit the DNS server.

continues

Table 5-5 Summary of Important Network Attacks and Mitigation Techniques to Know for the Exam

Network Attack	Description	Mitigation Techniques
Altered hosts file	When an attacker attempts to hijack the hosts file and have the client bypass the DNS server or access incorrect websites.	■ Change permission on the hosts file to read-only.
Domain name kiting	The process of deleting a domain name during the 5-day grace period (known as the add grace period, or AGP) and immediately reregistering it for another 5-day period.	■ Not many ways to defend against this other than created rules that charge fees for people who kite domain names.
ARP poisoning	An attack that exploits Ethernet networks, and it may enable an attacker to sniff frames of information, modify that information, or stop it from getting to its intended destination.	■ DHCP snooping ■ Third-party tools like ArpON.

Exam Preparation Tasks

Review Key Topics

Review the most important topics in the chapter, noted with the Key Topics icon in the outer margin of the page. Table 5-6 lists a reference of these key topics and the page numbers on which each is found.

Table 5-6 Key Topics for Chapter 5

Key Topic Element	Description	Page Number
Bullet list	Description of MAC flooding and defense techniques	119
Table 5-1	Private IP Ranges (as Assigned by the IANA)	122
Figure 5-1	Example of Public and Private IP Addresses	122
Figure 5-2	3-Leg Perimeter DMZ	125
Table 5-2	Types of VLAN Hopping	129
Table 5-4	23 Ports and Their Associated Protocols	133
Figure 5-7	IP Addresses and Ports	135
Table 5-5	Summary of Network Attacks and Mitigation Techniques	145

Complete Tables and Lists from Memory

Print a copy of Appendix A, "Memory Tables," (found on the DVD), or at least the section for this chapter, and complete the tables and lists from memory. Appendix B, "Memory Tables Answer Key," also on the DVD, includes completed tables and lists to check your work.

Define Key Terms

Define the following key terms from this chapter, and check your answers in the glossary:

MAC flooding, failopen mode, CAM table, network address translation, static NAT, port address translation, demilitarized zone, 3-leg perimeter, back-to-back perimeter, Network Access Control, VLAN hopping, wardialing, TCP reset attack, implicit deny, TCP/IP hijacking, man-in-the-middle attack, cross-site scripting, Denial of Service, ping flood, Smurf attack, fraggle, permanent DoS attack, Ping of Death, fork bomb, SYN flood, teardrop attack, Distributed Denial of Service, spoofing, phishing, replay attack, nonce, null session, domain name kiting, DNS poisoning, ARP poisoning, UDP flood attack

Hands-On Labs

Complete the following written step-by-step scenarios. After you finish (or if you do not have adequate equipment to complete the scenario), watch the corresponding video solutions on the DVD.

If you have additional questions, feel free to post them at my website: www.davidlprowse.com in the Ask Dave forum. (Free registration is required to post on the website.)

Equipment Needed

- Two Windows computers, at least one with Internet access.
- Web browser: Internet Explorer version 6 and higher or Firefox are recommended. This will be used to access the ShieldsUP! Program at www.grc.com and to download Nmap.
- Nmap software: This can be downloaded from www.nmap.com.

Lab 5-1: Port Scanning Basics

This lab demonstrates how to scan the ports of a computer with the Nmap program and with the Internet utility ShieldsUP! The steps are as follows:

Step 1. Download and install the command-line version of the Nmap program from http://nmap.org/download.html.

Step 2. Extract the contents to a folder of your choice. In the video, we use the nmap folder.

Step 3. Write down the IP address of a Windows host on your network.

Step 4. Scan the ports of that host with the **–sS** parameter; for example,

```
nmap -sS 172.29.250.200
```

Step 5. If there are nonessential ports open, turn off their corresponding unnecessary services, such as FTP, HTTP, or Telnet. This can be done in a variety of places including Computer Management. If there are no services that you want to turn off, enable one (such as Telnet), then rescan the ports with Nmap (to show that the service is running), turn off the service, and move on to the next step.

Step 6. Scan the ports of that host a second time, again with the **–sS** parameter. This time you are verifying that the services are turned off by identifying that the corresponding ports are closed.

Step 7. Scan the ports of a 4-port SOHO router/firewall or a computer with a firewall running. Use the **–P0** parameter. For example:

```
nmap -P0 65.43.18.1
```

This may take up to five minutes. It will verify whether the firewall is running properly by displaying that all the ports are filtered.

Step 8. With a web browser, connect to **www.grc.com**.

Step 9. Click the **ShieldsUP!! Picture**.

Step 10. Scroll down and click the **ShieldsUP! Link**. (This is a necessary second step.)

Step 11. Click the **Proceed** button.

Step 12. Select the **Common Ports** scan. This initiates a scan of the computer or device that is displayed to the Internet. If you access the Internet through a router/firewall, this will be the device scanned. If your computer connects directly to the Internet, the computer will be scanned.

Step 13. Make note of the results. It should show the public IP that was scanned. Then it lists the ports that were scanned and their status. The desired result for all ports listed is Stealth, all the way down the line for each of the listed ports. If there are Open or Closed ports, you should check to make sure that the firewall is enabled and operating properly.

Step 14. Try a few other scans, such as All Service Ports, or File Sharing.

Watch the solution video in the "Hands-On Scenarios" section of the DVD.

View Recommended Resources

For readers who wish to brush up on their networking topics:

- Prowse, David L. *CompTIA Network+ Video Mentor*, First Edition. Que. 2009.
- Harwood, Mike. *CompTIA Network+ Cert Guide*. 2010.
- Comer, Douglas. *Computer Networks and Internets* (Fifth Edition). Prentice Hall. 2008.
- Video: OSI Model Primer: www.davidlprowse.com/forums/showthread.php?t=1556
- Internetworking Basics: www.cisco.com/en/US/docs/internetworking/technology/handbook/Intro-to-Internet.html

- Video: TCP, UDP, and Ports Refresher: www.davidlprowse.com/forums/showthread.php?t=1614

Port Numbers: www.iana.org/assignments/port-numbers

FreeNAC: http://freenac.net/

Pure-FTPd: www.pureftpd.org

FileZilla: http://filezilla-project.org/

Nmap: http://nmap.org/

GRC's ShieldsUP!: www.grc.com

More information on SYN Flood attacks, see tools.ietf.org/html/rfc4987.

Answer Review Questions

Answer the following review questions. You can find the answers at the end of this chapter.

1. Which of the following would you set up in a router?

A. DMZ

B. DOS

C. OSI

D. ARP

2. Which of the following is an example of a nonessential protocol?

A. DNS

B. ARP

C. DMZ

D. TFTP

3. A person attempts to access a server during a zone transfer to get access to a zone file. What type of server are they trying to manipulate?

A. Proxy server

B. DNS server

C. File server

D. Web server

4. Which of the following is a private IP address?

A. 11.16.0.1

B. 127.0.0.1

C. 172.16.0.1

D. 208.0.0.1

5. Which of these hides an entire network of IP addresses?

A. SPI

B. NAT

C. SSH

D. FTP

6. Which one of the following can monitor and protect a DNS server?

A. Ping the DNS server.

B. Block port 53 on the firewall.

C. Purge PTR records daily.

D. Check DNS records regularly.

7. Which TCP port does LDAP use?

A. 389

B. 80

C. 443

D. 143

8. From the list of ports select two that are used for e-mail. (Select the two best answers.)

A. 110

B. 3389

C. 143

D. 389

9. Which port number does the domain name system use?

A. 53

B. 80

C. 110

D. 88

10. Which of the following statements best describes a static NAT?

A. Static NAT uses a one-to-one mapping.

B. Static NAT uses a many-to-many mapping.

C. Static NAT uses a one-to-many mapping.

D. Static NAT uses a many-to-one mapping.

11. John needs to install a web server that can offer SSL-based encryption. Which of the following ports is required for SSL transactions?

A. Port 80 inbound

B. Port 80 outbound

C. Port 443 inbound

D. Port 443 outbound

12. If a person takes control of a session between a server and a client, it is known as what type of attack?

A. DDoS

B. Smurf

C. Session hijacking

D. Malicious software

13. Making data appear as if it is coming from somewhere other than its original source is known as what?

A. Hacking

B. Phishing

C. Cracking

D. Spoofing

14. Which of the following enables a hacker to float a domain registration for a maximum of 5 days?

A. Kiting

B. DNS poisoning

C. Domain hijacking

D. Spoofing

15. What is the best definition for ARP?

A. Resolves IP addresses to DNS names

B. Resolves IP addresses to host names

C. Resolves IP addresses to MAC addresses

D. Resolves IP addresses to DNS addresses

16. Which of the following should be placed between the LAN and the Internet?

A. DMZ

B. HIDS

C. Domain controller

D. Extranet

17. You have three e-mail servers. What is it called when one server forwards e-mail to another?

A. SMTP relay

B. Buffer overflows

C. POP3

D. Cookies

18. You want to reduce network traffic on a particular network segment to limit the amount of user visibility. Which of the following is the best device to use in this scenario?

A. Switch

B. Hub

C. Router

D. Firewall

19. A coworker goes to a website but notices that the browser brings her to a different website and that the URL has changed. What type of attack is this?

A. DNS poisoning

B. Denial of service

C. Buffer overflow

D. ARP poisoning

20. Which of the following misuses the transmission control protocol handshake process?

A. Man-in-the-middle attack

B. SYN attack

C. WPA attack

D. Replay attack

21. For a remote tech to log in to a user's computer in another state, what inbound port must be open on the user's computer?

A. 21

B. 389

C. 3389

D. 8080

22. A DDoS attack can be best defined as what?

A. Privilege escalation

B. Multiple computers attacking a single server

C. A computer placed between a sender and receiver to capture data

D. Overhearing parts of a conversation

23. When users in your company attempt to access a particular website, the attempts are redirected to a spoofed website. What are two possible reasons for this?

A. DoS

B. DNS poisoning

C. Modified hosts file

D. Domain name kiting

24. What kind of attack is it when the packets sent do not require a synchronization process and are not connection-oriented?

A. Man-in-the-middle

B. TCP/IP hijacking

C. UDP attack

D. ICMP flood

25. How many of the TCP/IP ports can be attacked?

A. 1,024 ports

B. 65,535

C. 256

D. 16,777,216

26. Which of the following attacks is a type of DoS attack that sends large amounts of UDP echoes to port 7 and 19?

A. Teardrop

B. IP spoofing

C. Fraggle

D. Replay

27. Don must configure his firewall to support TACACS. Which port(s) should he open on the firewall?

A. Port 53

B. Port 49

C. Port 161

D. Port 22

28. Which of the following ports is used by Kerberos by default?

A. 21

B. 80

C. 88

D. 443

Answers and Explanations

1. **A.** A DMZ, or demilitarized zone, can be set up on a router to create a sort of safe haven for servers. It is neither the LAN nor the Internet, but instead, a location in between the two.
2. **D.** The Trivial File Transfer Protocol (TFTP) is a simpler version of FTP that uses a small amount of memory. It is generally considered to be a nonessential protocol. The Domain Name System service (or DNS service) is required for Internet access and on Microsoft domains. The Address Resolution Protocol (ARP) is necessary in Ethernets that use TCP/IP. And a demilitarized zone (DMZ) is not a protocol but more of a network design element.
3. **B.** DNS servers are the only types of servers listed that do zone transfers. The purpose of accessing the zone file is to find out what hosts are on the network.
4. **C.** 172.16.0.1 is the only address listed that is private. The private assigned ranges can be seen in Table 5-1 earlier in the chapter. 11.16.0.1 is a public IP address, as is 208.0.0.1. 127.0.0.1 is the loopback address.
5. **B.** Network Address Translation hides an entire network of IP Addresses. SPI, or Stateful Packet Inspection, is the other type of firewall that today's SOHO routers incorporate.
6. **D.** By checking a DNS server's records regularly, a security admin can monitor *and* protect it. Blocking port 53 on a firewall might protect it (it also might make it inaccessible depending on the network configuration) but won't enable you to monitor it. Pinging the server can simply tell you whether the server is alive. Purging pointer records (PTR) cannot help to secure or monitor the server.

7. **A.** The Lightweight Directory Access Protocol (LDAP) uses port TCP 389. Port 80 is used by HTTP. Port 443 is used by HTTPS. Port 143 is used by IMAP.
8. **A and C.** POP3 uses port 110; IMAP uses port 143; 3389 is used by the remote desktop protocol; and 389 is used by LDAP.
9. **A.** The domain name system or DNS uses port 53. Port 80 is used by HTTP; port 110 is used by POP3; and port 88 is used by Kerberos.
10. **A.** Static network address translation will normally use a one-to-one mapping when dealing with IP addresses.
11. **C.** For clients to connect to the server via SSL, the server must have inbound port 443 open. The outbound ports on the server are of little consequence for this concept, and inbound port 80 is used by HTTP.
12. **C.** Session hijacking (or TCP/IP hijacking) is when an unwanted mediator takes control of the session between a client and a server (for example, an FTP or HTTP session).
13. **D.** Spoofing is when a malicious user makes data or e-mail appears to be coming from somewhere else.
14. **A.** Kiting is the practice of monopolizing domain names without paying for them. Newly registered domain names can be canceled with a full refund during an initial 5-day window known as an AGP, or add grace period.
15. **C.** The address resolution protocol, or ARP, resolves IP addresses to MAC addresses. DNS resolves from IP addresses to hostnames, word domain names, and vice versa. RARP resolves MAC addresses to IP addresses.
16. **A.** A demilitarized zone, or DMZ, can be placed between the LAN and the Internet; this is known as a back-to-back perimeter configuration. In some cases, it will be part of a 3-leg firewall scheme. Host-based intrusion detection systems are placed on an individual computer, usually within the LAN. Domain controllers should be protected and are normally on the LAN as well. An extranet can include parts of the Internet and parts of one or more LANs; normally it connects two companies utilizing the power of the Internet.
17. **A.** The SMTP relay is when one server forwards e-mail to other e-mail servers. Buffer overflows are attacks that can be perpetuated on web pages. POP3 is another type of e-mail protocol, and cookies are small text files stored on the client computer that remember information about that computer's session with a website.
18. **A.** A switch can reduce network traffic on a particular network segment. It does this by keeping a table of information about computers on that segment. Instead of broadcasting information to all ports of the switch, the switch selectively chooses where the information goes.

19. **A.** DNS poisoning can occur at a DNS server and can affect all clients on the network. It can also occur at an individual computer. Another possibility is that spyware has compromised the browser. A denial of service is a single attack that attempts to stop a server from functioning. A buffer overflow is an attack that, for example, could be perpetuated on a web page. ARP poisoning is the poisoning of an ARP table, creating confusion when it comes to IP address-to-MAC address resolutions.
20. **B.** A synchronize (SYN) attack misuses the TCP three-way handshake process. The idea behind this is to overload servers and deny access to users.
21. **C.** Port 3389 must be open on the inbound side of the user's computer to enable a remote tech to log in remotely and take control of that computer. Port 21 is the port used by FTP, and 389 is used by LDAP. 8080 is another port used by web browsers that takes the place of port 80.
22. **B.** When multiple computers attack a single server, it is known as a Distributed Denial of Service attack, or DDoS. Privilege escalation is when a person that is not normally authorized to a server manages to get administrative permissions to resources. If a computer is placed between a sender and receiver, it is known as a man-in-the-middle attack. Overhearing parts of a conversation is known as eavesdropping.
23. **B and C.** DNS poisoning and a DNS server's modified hosts files are possible causes for why a person would be redirected to a spoofed website. DoS, or a Denial of Service, is when a computer attempts to attack a server to stop it from functioning. Domain name kiting is when a person renews and cancels domains within 5-day periods.
24. **C.** User Datagram Protocol (UDP) attacks, or UDP flood attacks, are DoS attacks that use a computer to send a large number of UDP packets to a remote host. The remote host will reply to each of these with an ICMP Destination Unreachable packet, which ultimately, makes it inaccessible to clients.
25. **B.** The best answer to this question is 65,535. The Internet Assigned Numbers Authority (IANA) list of ports starts at 0 and ends at 65,535. Although this equals 65,536 ports, it should be known that normally port 0 (zero) will forward packets to another port number that is dynamically assigned. So port 0 should not be affected by attacks, because it actually doesn't act as a normal port.
26. **C.** A Fraggle attack is a type of DoS attack that sends large amounts of UDP echoes to port 7 and 19. This is similar to the Smurf attack. Teardrop DoS attacks send many IP fragments with over-sized payloads to a target.
27. **B.** Port 49 is used by TACACS. Port 53 is used by DNS, Port 161 is used by SNMP, and Port 22 is used by SSH.
28. **C.** Port 88 is used by Kerberos by default. Port 21 is used by FTP. Port 80 is used by HTTP. Port 443 is used by HTTPS (TLS/SSL).

This chapter covers the following subjects:

- **Firewalls and Network Security—**In this section, you will find out about one of the most important strategic pieces in your network security design—the firewall. Then we discuss other network security concepts such as packet filtering, access control lists, proxy servers, and honeypots.
- **NIDS Versus NIPS—**This section delves into the characteristics, advantages, disadvantages, and differences of network intrusion detection systems and network intrusion prevention systems.

This chapter covers the CompTIA Security+ SY0-201 objectives 2.3 and 2.4.

CHAPTER 6

Network Perimeter Security

This chapter is all about the network border, also known as the *network perimeter*. This should be a network administrator's primary focus when it comes to securing the network because it contains the entrances that attackers attempt to use.

Allow me to analogize for a few moments. I've said it before; as you read this book, you are building yourself an impenetrable castle of knowledge, culminating in hands-on familiarity and the know-how to pass the exam. But we can use the castle analogy for your network as well. Imagine a big stone castle with tall walls, an expanse of clear land around the castle, or perhaps a moat surrounding it (with alligators, of course), and one or more drawbridges. The tall walls are meant to keep the average person out, sort of like a firewall in a computer network, not perfect, but necessary. The open area around the castle makes it difficult for people to sneak up on your castle; they would quickly be *detected*, just like malicious packets detected by a network intrusion detection system. Or better yet, if you had a moat, people trying to cross it would have a difficult time, would be easy targets for your bowmen, and would probably be gobbled up by your pet alligators. This would represent a network intrusion *prevention* system, which not only detects threats, but also eliminates those threats to the network. The drawbridge, or drawbridges, could be seen as network ports open to the network. As drawbridges are part of the castle wall, so network ports are part of the firewall. You, as the network administrator, have the ability and the right to close these ports at any time. At the risk of taking this analogy even further, you might decide to set traps for people; like a pool of quicksand that has a bag of pyrite suspended above it, or maybe a false entry to the castle that, after a long corridor, is walled off on the inside, ultimately trapping the unwary. In a network environment, these would be known as honeypots. Of course, every once in a while, legitimate traffic needs to enter and exit your network, too! To do this in a more secure fashion, you can set up proxy servers to act as go-betweens for the computers inside your network, and the servers they talk to on the Internet. Kind of like a sentry in the tower of the castle that would relay an outsider's messages to someone inside the castle.

The network perimeter is less tangible in an actual network environment. Most networking devices will commonly be located in one single server room! To better envision your network, one of the best tips I can give you is to map out your network on paper, or create network documentation using programs such as

Microsoft Visio and by utilizing network mapping tools (more on these tools in Chapter 10, "Vulnerability and Risk Assessment").

So before we end up playing Dungeons & Dragons, let's talk about one of the most important parts of your strategic defense—the firewall.

Foundation Topics

Firewalls and Network Security

Nowadays, firewalls are everywhere. Businesses large and small use them, and many households have simpler versions of these protective devices as well. You need to be aware of several types of firewalls, and you definitely want to spend some time configuring a firewall, which we do in the "Work-Through Hands-On Scenarios" section. The firewall is there to protect the entire network, but other tools are often implemented as well; for example proxy servers that help protect users and computers by keeping them anonymous, and honeypots meant to attract hackers, crackers, and other types of attackers into a false computer or network. But by far, the most important element in your network will be the firewall, so let's begin with that.

Firewalls

In Chapter 2, "Computer Systems Security," we discussed personal firewalls—you remember, the kind installed to an individual computer. Now let's broaden the scope of your knowledge with network-based firewalls. Network-based firewalls are primarily used to section off and protect one network from another. They are a primary line of defense and are *extremely* important in network security. There are several types of firewalls; some run as software on server computers, some as a standalone dedicated appliances, and some that work as just one function of many on a single device. They are commonly represented as a sort of "brick wall" between a LAN and the Internet, as shown in Figure 6-1.

Just as a firewall in a physical building is there to slow the spread of a fire and contain it until the fire department arrives, a firewall in a computer network is there to keep fire at bay in the form of malicious attacks. Quite often, a firewall (or the device the firewall resides on) will have NAT in operation as well. In Figure 6-1, note that the firewall has a local address of 172.29.250.200; this connects it to the LAN. It also has an Internet address of 65.43.18.1, enabling connectivity for the entire LAN to the Internet, while hiding the LAN IP addresses. By default, the IP address 65.43.18.1 is completely shielded. This means that all inbound ports are effectively closed and will not enable incoming traffic, unless a LAN computer initiates a session with another system on the Internet. However, a good network security administrator always checks this to make sure; first, by accessing the firewall's firmware (or software application as the case may be) and verifying that the firewall is on, and next by scanning the firewall with a third-party application such as Nmap (www.nmap.org) or with a web-based port scanning utility such as ShieldsUP! (www.grc.com), as was shown in the Chapter 5 lab, "Port Scanning Basics." If any ports are open, or unshielded, they should be dealt with immediately. Then the firewall should be rescanned for vulnerabilities. You can find more information on port scanning and vulnerability assessments in Chapter 10. Firewalls should be used only as they were intended. The company firewall should not be handling any other extraneous services, for example acting as a web server or SMTP server. By using a firewall as it was intended, its vulnerability is reduced.

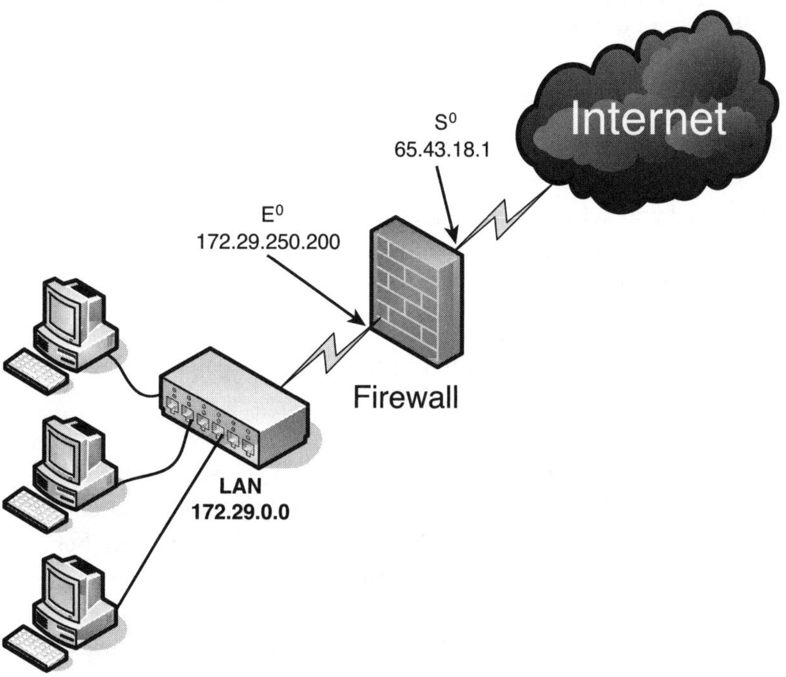

Figure 6-1 Diagram of a Basic Firewall Implementation

Generally, a firewall inspects traffic that passes through it and permits or denies that traffic based on rules set by an administrator. For example, this can be done through the use of port forwarding and virtual servers, or it can be based on the IP address of the external computer.

NOTE: For a quick tutorial on setting up virtual servers and port forwarding on a typical SOHO router/firewall, see the following link:

www.davidlprowse.com/forums/showthread.php?t=1620

A lot of today's firewalls have two types of firewall technologies built-in to them: SPI and NAT. However, there are a couple other types of firewall methodologies that you should be aware of; all these are covered in the following list.

- **Packet filtering—**Inspects each packet passing through the firewall and accepts or rejects it based on rules. However, there are two types: stateless packet inspection, and *stateful packet inspection* (also known as SPI or a stateful firewall). A stateless packet filter, also known as pure packet filtering, does not retain memory of packets that have passed through the firewall; due to this, a stateless packet filter can be vulnerable to IP spoofing attacks. But a firewall running stateful packet inspection is normally not vulnerable to this because it keeps track of the state of network connections by examining the header in each packet. It can distinguish between legitimate and illegitimate packets. This function operates at the Network Layer of the OSI model.
- **NAT filtering—**Also known as NAT endpoint filtering, filters traffic according to ports (TCP or UDP). This can be done in three ways: by way of basic endpoint connections, by matching incoming traffic to the corresponding outbound IP address connection, or by matching incoming traffic to the corresponding IP address *and* port.

NOTE: See the step-by-step lab on packet filtering and NAT firewalls in the "Hands-On Labs" section.

- **Application-level gateway (ALG)—**Applies security mechanisms to specific applications, such as FTP and or BitTorrent. It supports address and port translation and checks whether the type of application traffic is allowed. For example, your company might allow FTP traffic through the firewall, but might decide to disable Telnet traffic (probably a wise choice). The ALG will check each type of packet coming in and discard those that are Telnet packets. Although this adds a powerful layer of security, the price is that it is resource-intensive, which could lead to performance degradation.
- **Circuit-level gateway—**Works at the Session Layer of the OSI model, and applies security mechanisms when a TCP or UDP connection is established; they act as a go between for the Transport and Application Layers in TCP/IP. After the connection has been made, packets can flow between the hosts without further checking. Circuit-level gateways hide information about the private network, but they do not filter individual packets.

A firewall can be set up in several different physical configurations. For example, in Chapter 5, "Network Design Elements and Network Threats," we discussed implementing a DMZ. This could be done in a back-to-back configuration (two firewalls surrounding the DMZ), as shown in Figure 6-2, or as a 3-leg perimeter configuration.

Key Topic

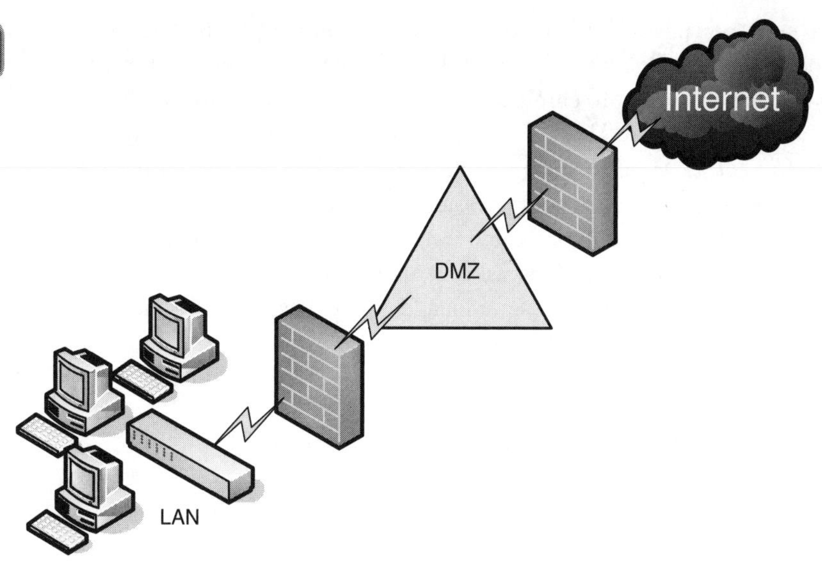

Figure 6-2 Back-to-Back Firewall/DMZ Configuration

NOTE: For a quick tutorial on setting up a 3-leg perimeter firewall/DMZ configuration with ISA, see the following link:
www.davidlprowse.com/forums/showthread.php?t=1621

Generally, there will be one firewall with the network and all devices and computers residing "behind" it. By the way, if a device is "behind" the firewall, it is also considered to be "after" the firewall, and if the device is "in front of" the firewall, it is also known as being "before" the firewall. Think of the firewall as the drawbridge of a castle. When you are trying to gain admittance to the castle, the drawbridge will probably be closed. You would be in front of the drawbridge, and the people inside the castle would be behind the drawbridge. This is a basic analogy, but should help to understand the whole "in front of" and "behind" business as it relates to data attempting to enter the network and devices that reside on your network.

Logging is also important when it comes to a firewall. Firewall logs should be the first thing you check when an intrusion has been detected. You should know how to access the logs, and how to read them. For example, Figure 6-3 shows two screen captures: The first displays the Internet sessions on a basic D-Link router/firewall, and the second shows log events such as blocked packets. Look at the blocked Gnutella packet that is pointed out. I know it is a Gnutella packet because the inbound port on my firewall that the external computer is trying to connect to shows as port 6346; this associates with Gnutella. Gnutella is a P2P file-sharing network. None of the computers on this particular network use or are in any way connected to the Gnutella service. These external computers are just random clients of the Gnutella P2P network trying to connect to every one possible. It's good that these packets have been blocked, but maybe you don't want the IP address shown (24.253.3.20) to have any capability to connect to your network at all. To eliminate that IP, you could add it to an inbound filter (which you will do in the "Work-Through Hands-On Scenarios" section) or to an *access control list (ACL)*. When dealing with firewalls, an ACL is a set of rules that apply to a list of network names, IP addresses, and port numbers. These rules can be configured to control inbound and outbound traffic. This is a bit different than ACLs with respect to operating systems, which we cover in Chapter 9, "Access Control Methods and Models," but the same basic principles apply: Basically, one entity is granted or denied permission to another entity.

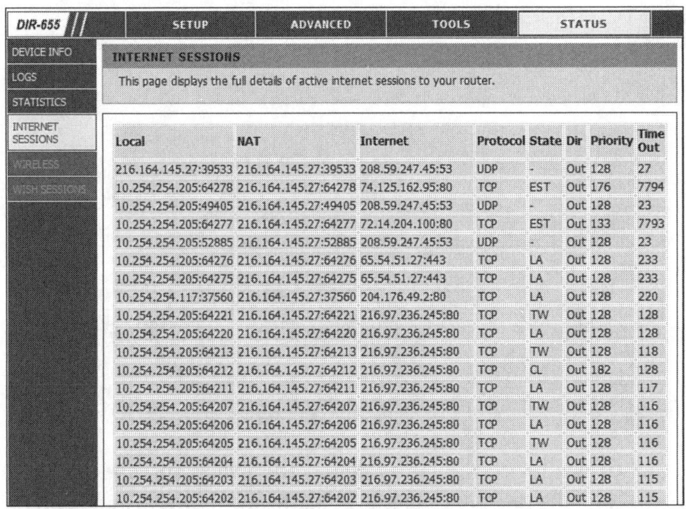

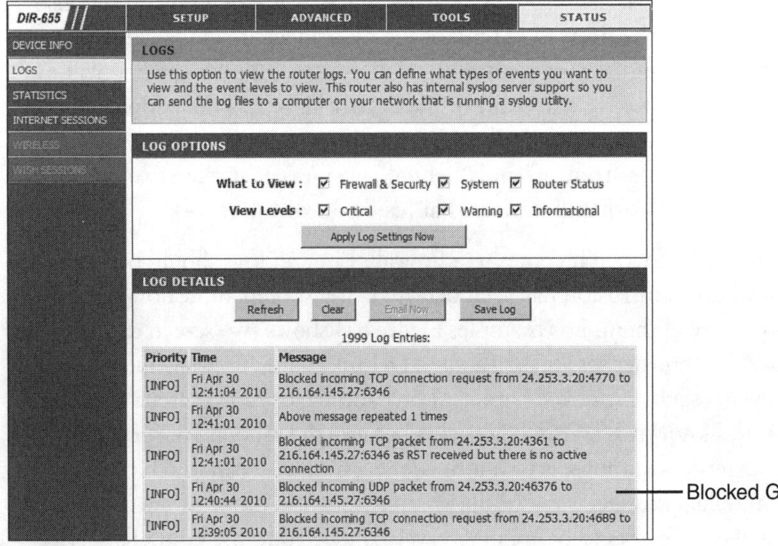

Figure 6-3 D-Link Router/Firewall Internet Sessions

Examples of network firewalls include basic devices such as the D-Link DIR-655 SOHO router/firewall, as shown in Figure 6-3, and more advanced appliances such as Cisco PIX/ASA Security Appliances and Juniper NetScreens. A firewall could also be incorporated into a server, for instance Microsoft's Internet Security & Acceleration Server (ISA). A firewall will usually have more than one network adapter so that it can connect to more than one network; this is known as a multi-homed connection. An ISA server needs to be dual-homed at minimum (two adapters), and it is recommended that the server has three network adapters, in the case that you want to implement a DMZ or another perimeter security technique.

Firewalls are often considered to be all-in-one devices, but actually they provide specific functionality as we have discussed in this section. Still, it is common to hear people refer to a firewall when they are really talking about another technology, or even another device. For example, many home users and small office users will have an all-in-one multifunction network device. This device will have four ports for wired connections, plus a wireless antenna; it will connect all the computers to the Internet, and finally will have a firewall built-in. Because some users consider this to be simply a firewall, you should teach them about the benefits of disabling SSID broadcasting, and enabling MAC filtering. By disabling Service Set Identifier (SSID) broadcasting, the average user cannot connect wirelessly to the device. An attacker will know how to bypass this, but it is an important element of security that you should implement, after all trusted computers have been connected wirelessly. MAC filtering denies access to any computer that does not have one of the MAC addresses you list, another powerful tool. See Lab 3, "Enabling MAC Filtering" in the "Work Through Hands-On Scenarios" on the DVD for more information.

To make matters a bit more confusing, a firewall can also act as, or in combination with, a proxy server, which we discuss in the following section.

Proxy Servers

A *proxy server* acts as an intermediary for clients usually located on a LAN, and the servers that they want to access that are usually located on the Internet. By definition, proxy means go-between, or mediator, acting as such a mediator in between a private and a public network. The proxy server will evaluate requests from clients, and if they meet certain criteria, forward them to the appropriate server. There are several types of proxies, including a couple you should know for the exam:

- **IP proxy—**Secures a network by keeping machines behind it anonymous; it does this through the use of NAT. For example, a basic four-port router can act as an IP proxy for the clients on the LAN it protects. An IP proxy can be the victim of many of the network attacks mentioned in Chapter 5, especially

DoS attacks. Regardless of whether the IP proxy is an appliance, or a computer, it should be updated regularly, and its log files should be monitored periodically and audited according to organization policies.

- **Caching proxy—**Attempts to serve client requests without actually contacting the remote server. Although there are FTP and SMTP proxies among others, the most common caching proxy is the *HTTP proxy*, also known as a *web proxy*, which caches web pages from servers on the Internet for a set amount of time. Examples of caching proxies include Microsoft ISA Server and Privoxy. An example of a caching proxy is illustrated in Figure 6-4. For example, let's say a coworker of yours (Client A) accessed www.google.com, and that she was the first person to do so on the network. This client request will go through the HTTP proxy and be redirected to Google's web server. As the data for Google's home page comes in, the HTTP proxy will store or cache that information. When another person on your network (Client B) makes a subsequent request for www.google.com, the bulk of that information will come from the HTTP proxy instead of from Google's web server. This is done to save bandwidth on the company's Internet connection and to increase the speed at which client requests are carried out. Most HTTP proxies check websites to verify that nothing has changed since the last request. Because information changes quickly on the Internet, a time limit of 24 hours is common for storing cached information before it is deleted.

Key Topic

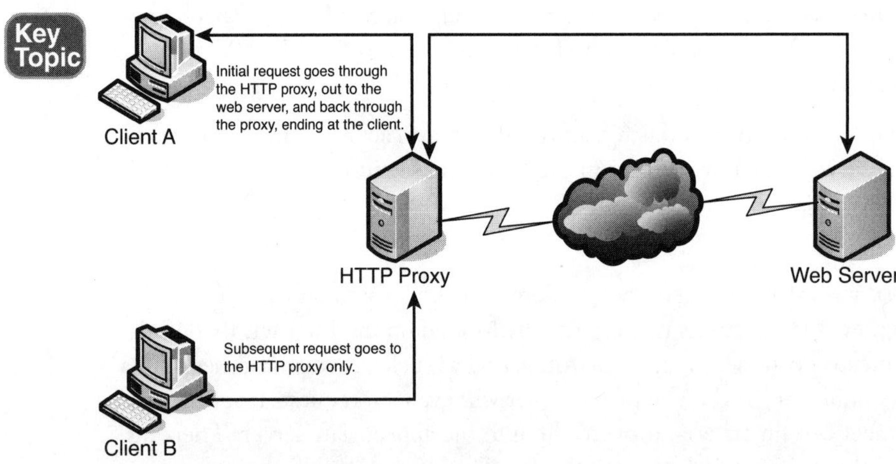

Figure 6-4 Illustration of an HTTP Proxy in Action

Other types of proxies are available to apply policies, block undesirable websites, audit employee usage, and scan for malware. One device or computer might do all these things or just one or two. It depends on the software used or appliance installed. Reverse proxies can also be implemented to protect a DMZ server's identity or to provide authentication and other secure tasks. This is done when users on the Internet are accessing server resources on your network. Generally, a proxy server will have more than one network adapter so that it can connect to the various networks it is acting as a mediator for. Each of the network adapters in a proxy should be periodically monitored for improper traffic and for possible network attacks and other vulnerabilities. A proxy server might be the same device as a firewall, or it could be separate. Because of this, there are a multitude of network configurations possible. Proxy servers, especially HTTP proxies, can be used maliciously to record traffic sent through them; because most of the traffic is sent in unencrypted form, this could be a security risk. A possible mitigation for this is to chain multiple proxies together in an attempt to confuse any onlookers and potential attackers.

Another example of a proxy in action is Internet content filtering. An *Internet content filter*, or simply a content filter, is usually applied as software at the Application Layer and can filter out various types of Internet activities such as websites accessed, e-mail, instant messaging, and more. It is used most often to disallow access to inappropriate web material (estimated to be a big percentage of the Internet!) or websites that take up far too much of an organization's Internet bandwidth. Internet content filters can be installed on individual clients, but by far the more efficient implementation is as an individual proxy that acts as a mediator between all the clients and the Internet. These proxy versions of content filters secure the network in two ways: one, by forbidding access to potentially malicious websites, and two, by blocking access to objectionable material that employees might feel is offensive. Even if employees inadvertently type an incorrect URL, they can rest assured that any objectionable material will not show up on their display. Internet filtering appliances will analyze just about all the data that comes through it including Internet content, URLs, and security certificates such as the kind you would automatically receive when going to a secure site that starts with https.

Honeypots and Honeynets

Honeypots and honeynets attract and trap potential attackers to counteract any attempts at unauthorized access of the network. This isolates the potential attacker in a monitored area and contains dummy resources that look to be of value to the perpetrator. While an attacker is trapped in one of these, their methods can be studied and analyzed, and the results of those analyses can be applied to the general security of the functional network.

A *honeypot* is generally a single computer but could also be a file, group of files, or an area of unused IP address space, whereas a *honeynet* is one or more computers, servers, or an area of a network; these are used when a single honeypot is not sufficient. Either way, the individual computer, or group of servers, will *usually* not house any important company information. Various analysis tools are implemented to study the attacker; these tools, along with a centralized group of honeypots (or a honeynet), are known collectively as a honeyfarm.

One example of a honeypot in action is the spam honeypot. Spam e-mail is one of the worst banes known to a network administrator; a spam honeypot can lure spammers in enabling the network administrators to study the spammer's techniques and habits, thus allowing the network admins to better protect their actual e-mail servers, SMTP relays, SMTP proxies, and so on, over the long term. It might ultimately keep the spammers away from the real e-mail addresses, because the spammers are occupied elsewhere. Some of the information gained by studying spammers is often shared with other network admins or organizations' websites dedicated to reducing spam. A spam honeypot could be as simple as a single e-mail address or as complex as an entire e-mail domain with multiple SMTP servers.

Of course, as with any technology that will study attackers, honeypots also bear risks to the legitimate network. The honeypot or honeynet should be carefully firewalled off from the legitimate network to ensure that the attacker can't break through.

Quite often, honeypots and honeynets are used as part of a more complex solution known as a network intrusion detection system.

NIDS Versus NIPS

It's not a battle royale, but you should be able to differentiate between a network intrusion *detection* system (NIDS) and a network intrusion *prevention* system (NIPS) for the exam. Previously, in Chapter 3, "OS Hardening and Virtualization," we discussed host-based intrusion detection systems (or HIDS). Although a great many attacks can hamper an individual computer, there are just as many network attacks that could possibly take down a server, switch, router, or even an entire network. Network-based IDSs were developed to detect these malicious network attacks, and network-based IPSs were developed in an attempt to prevent them.

NIDS

A *network intrusion detection system (NIDS)* by definition is a type of IDS that attempts to detect malicious network activities, for example port scans and DoS attacks, by constantly monitoring network traffic. Examples of NIDS include open source instances such as Snort (www.snort.org/), Bro (www.bro-ids.org/), and products from Enterasys (www.enterasys.com). A NIDS should be situated at the entrance or gateway to your network. It is not a firewall but should be used with a firewall. Because the NIDS will be inspecting every packet that traverses through your network, it needs to be fast; basically the slower the NIDS, the slower the network. So the solution itself, the computer/device it is installed on and the network connections of that computer/device all need to be planned out accordingly, to ensure that the NIDS does not cause network performance degradation.

Figure 6-5 illustrates how a NIDS might be implemented on a network. Quite often it will be placed in front of a firewall. The NIDS will detect attacks and anomalies and alert the administrator if they occur, whereas the firewall will do its best to prevent those attacks from entering the network. However, a NIDS could be placed behind the firewall, or you might have multiple NIDS points strategically placed around the network. If the NIDS is placed in front of the firewall, it will generate a lot more administrator alerts, but these can usually be whittled down within the firmware or software of the device running the NIDS. Regardless of where the NIDS is located, a network administrator should monitor traffic from time to time; to do so, the computer, server, or appliance that has the NIDS installed should have a network adapter configured to work in *promiscuous mode*. This passes all traffic to the CPU, not just the frames addressed to it.

Key Topic

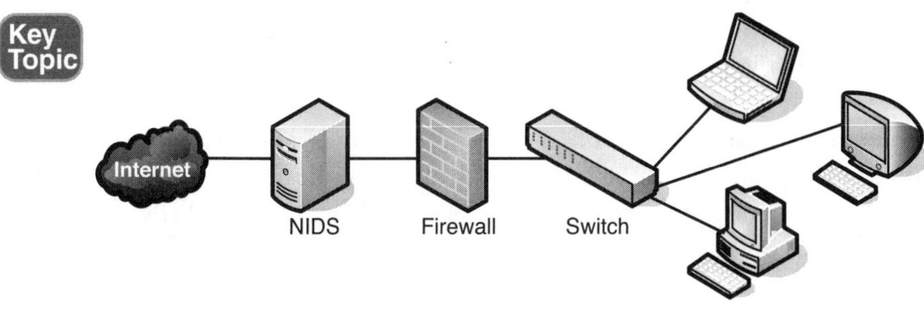

Figure 6-5 Illustration of NIDS Placement in a Network

The beauty of a NIDS is that you might get away with one or two NIDS points on the network, and do away with some or all the HIDS installed on individual computers, effectively lowering the bottom line while still doing a decent job of mitigating risk. A couple of the disadvantage of a NIDS, aside from possible network performance issues, is that it might not be able to read encrypted packets of information and will not detect problems that occur on an individual computer. Therefore, to secure a network and its hosts, many organizations will implement a mixture of NIDS and HIDS. If a NIDS is placed in front of the firewall, it is subject to attack; therefore it should be monitored and updated regularly. Some NIDS solutions will auto-update. Finally, the biggest disadvantage of a NIDS is that it *detects* only attacks; to protect against, or *prevent*, these attacks, you would need a NIPS.

NIPS

A *network intrusion prevention system (NIPS)* is designed to inspect traffic, and based on its configuration or security policy, it can remove, detain, or redirect malicious traffic. More and more companies are offering NIPS solutions in addition to, or instead of, NIDS solutions. Examples of NIPS include Enterasys Intrusion Prevention System (also known as Dragon IPS), Check Point Security Appliances (www.checkpoint.com), McAfee IntruShield (www.mcafee.com), and the aforementioned Snort, which is actually an NIDS/NIPS software package that should be installed on a dual or multihomed server. Not only can a NIPS go above and beyond a NIDS by removing or redirecting malicious traffic, it can also redirect a recognized attacker to a single computer known as a padded cell, which contains no information of value, and has no way out.

Like a NIDS, a NIPS should sit inline on the network, often in front of the firewall, although it could be placed elsewhere, depending on the network segment it protects and the network architecture. Whereas many NIPS solutions have two connections only and are known as perimeter solutions, other NIPS appliances will have up to 16 ports enabling many points of detection on the network—these would be known as network "core" devices. Regardless of the solution you select, as packets pass through the device, they are inspected for possible attacks. These devices need to be accurate and updated often (hopefully automatically) to avoid the misidentification of legitimate traffic, or worse, the misidentification of attacks. If the NIPS blocks legitimate traffic, it would be known as a *false positive*, and effectively could deny service to legitimate customers, creating a self-inflicted denial of service of sorts. If the IPS does not have a particular attack's signature in its database, and lets that attack through thinking it is legitimate traffic, it is known as a *false negative*, also bad for obvious reasons! Many IPS systems can monitor for attack signatures and anomalies. More information about false positives and false negatives can be found in Chapter 8, "Physical Security and Authentication Models." More information on signatures can be found in Chapter 3 and Chapter 11, "Monitoring and Auditing." Another type of error that can occur with NIDS and NIPS is a subversion error; this is when the NIDS/NIPS has been altered by an attacker to allow for false negatives, ultimately leading to attacks creeping into the network. This can be deadly because the NIDS/NIPS will often be the first point of resistance in the network. To protect against this, some devices will have the capability to hide or mask their IP address. They might also come with an internal firewall. It is also important to select an IPS solution that has a secure channel for the management console interface.

The beauty of a NIPS compared to a host-based IPS is that it can protect noncomputer-based network devices such as switches, routers, and firewalls. However, the NIPS is considered a single point of failure because it sits inline on the network. Due to this, some organizations will opt to install a bypass switch, which also enables the NIPS to be taken offline when maintenance needs to be done.

Another advantage of newer NIPS solutions is that some of them can act as protocol analyzers by reading encrypted traffic and stopping encrypted attacks.

Summary of NIDS Versus NIPS

Table 6-1 summarizes NIDS versus NIPS.

Table 6-1 Summary of NIDS Versus NIPS

Type of System	Summary	Disadvantage/Advantage	Example
NIDS	Detects malicious network activities	Pro: Only a limited amount of NIDS are necessary on a network. Con: Only *detects* malicious activities.	Snort Bro-IDS
NIPS	Detects, removes, detains, and redirects traffic	Pro: Detects and mitigates malicious activity. Pro: Can act as a protocol analyzer. Con: Uses more resources. Con: Possibility of false positives and false negatives.	Dragon IPS McAfee IntruShield

The Protocol Analyzer's Role in NIDS and NIPS

You might be familiar already with protocol analyzers such as Wireshark (Ethereal) or Network Monitor. These are loaded on a computer and are controlled by the user in a GUI environment; they capture packets enabling the user to analyze them and view their contents. However, some NIDS/NIPS are considered to be full protocol analyzers with no user intervention required. The protocol analyzer is built into the NIDS/NIPS appliance. It decodes Application Layer protocols, such as HTTP, FTP, or SMTP, and forwards the results to the IDS or IPS analysis engine. Then the analysis engine will study the information for anomalous or behavioral exploits. This type of analysis can block many exploits based on a single signature. This is superior to basic signature pattern recognition (without protocol analysis), because with signature-based IDS/IPS solutions, many signatures have to be constantly downloaded and stored in the device's database, and they don't enable dynamic understanding of new attacks. However, as with any powerful analysis, like protocol analysis, there is a premium placed on processing power, and the price of these types of IDS/IPS solutions will undoubtedly be higher.

Exam Preparation Tasks

Review Key Topics

Review the most important topics in the chapter, noted with the Key Topics icon in the outer margin of the page. Table 6-2 lists a reference of these key topics and the page numbers on which each is found.

Table 6-2 Key Topics for Chapter 6

Key Topic Element	Description	Page Number
Bullet list	Types of firewalls	164
Figure 6-2	Back-to-Back Firewall/DMZ Configuration	165
Bullet list	Types of proxies	167
Figure 6-4	Illustration of an HTTP Proxy in Action	168
Figure 6-5	Illustration of NIDS Placement in a Network	171
Table 6-1	Summary of NIDS Versus NIPS	173

Complete Tables and Lists from Memory

Print a copy of Appendix A, "Memory Tables," (found on the DVD), or at least the section for this chapter, and complete the tables and lists from memory. Appendix B, "Memory Tables Answer Key," also on the DVD, includes completed tables and lists to check your work.

Define Key Terms

Define the following key terms from this chapter, and check your answers in the glossary:

stateful packet inspection, firewall, packet filtering, application-level gateway, circuit-level gateway, proxy server, IP proxy, HTTP proxy (web proxy), Internet content filter, honeypot, honeynet, network intrusion detection system, network intrusion prevention system, false positive, false negative, access control list, network perimeter, promiscuous mode

Hands-On Labs

Complete the following written step-by-step scenarios. After you finish (or if you do not have adequate equipment to complete the scenario), watch the correspon-ding video solutions on the DVD.

If you have additional questions, feel free to post them at my website: www.davidlprowse.com in the Ask Dave forum. (Free registration is required to post on the website.)

Equipment Needed

- Computer with Internet access.
- Web browser: Internet Explorer version 6 and higher or Firefox are recommended.
- D-Link DIR-655 router:
  - If you have access to an actual DIR-655, make sure that it is updated to the latest firmware. Then connect to it by opening a web browser and typing the IP address of the router in the URL field, for example, 192.168.0.1. Next, at the login screen, type the password for the router, and click the **Log In** button. This should display the Device Information page. Start at this page for each of the three labs.
  - If you do not have access to an actual DIR-655, use the D-Link simulator located at http://support.dlink.com/Emulators/dir655/index.html. Then select the 1st option: **DIR-655 Device UI**. Next, at the login screen, click the **Log In** button. (No password is necessary.) This should display the Device Information page. Start at this page for each of the three labs.

Lab 6-1: Packet Filtering and NAT Firewalls

In this lab, you view where to turn on stateful packet inspection (SPI) and configure the NAT firewall. The steps are as follows:

Step 1. On the main **Device Information** page, click the **Advanced** link near the top of the window. This should bring up the Advanced page.

Step 2. On the left side, click the **Firewall Settings** link. This should display the Firewall Settings window.

Step 3. Take note of the first setting: **Enable SPI**. This is stateful packet inspection. It should be selected by default, but if not, select it, and move on to the next step.

Step 4. View the NAT Endpoint Filtering section directly under the Firewall Settings. Increase the security of UDP Endpoint Filtering by clicking the radio button **Port and Address Restricted**. This is the highest level of security you can select.

Step 5. Next, enable antispoofing by clicking the **Enable anti-spoofing checking** checkbox.

Step 6. Finally, scroll down and view the Application Level Gateway (ALG) Configuration. **PPTP**, **IPSec (VPN)**, **RTSP**, and **SIP** should all be selected.

Watch the solution video in the “Hands-On Scenarios” section of the DVD.

Lab 6-2: Configuring an Inbound Filter on a SOHO Router/Firewall

In this lab, you view the firewall logs and set up an inbound filter to deny access to a remote computer’s IP address. The steps are as follows:

Step 1. On the main **Device Information** page, click the **Logs** link on the left side. This should display the Logs window.

Step 2. View the Log Details. If you are using an actual D-Link DIR-655, you will most likely see blocked packets. If you are using the simulator, you will see only basic entries, for example the wireless link is up, and so on.

Step 3. If there is an IP address that you want to block, write down the number now. Otherwise, write down the IP address: **12.46.14.66** (at one time a known Spam IP address).

Step 4. Click the **Advanced** link near the top of the window. This should bring up the Advanced page.

Step 5. On the left side, click the **Inbound Filter** link. This should display the Inbound Filter window.

Step 6. Give a name to your new rule in the **Name** field; for example, **Block IP 12.46.14.66**.

Step 7. Leave the Action drop-down box set to **Deny**. This denies access to the IP address or addresses you select.

Step 8. Click the first checkbox under where it says Remote IP Range.

Step 9. Enter the IP address you want to deny in the Remote IP Start and Remote IP End fields. If you want to block a range of addresses, you could do this as well, for example type: **12.46.14.66** in the Remote IP Start field and **12.46.14.70** in the Remote IP End field.

Step 10. Click the **Add** button. This should add the filter rule to the list. If you are using the D-Link simulator, you might not see the addition; reference the video solution for this.

Step 11. View the Inbound Filter Rules List. When finished, return the computer to normal. Remove the rule by clicking the garbage can and clicking **OK**.

Watch the solution video in the “Hands-On Scenarios” section of the DVD.

Lab 6-3: Enabling MAC Filtering

In this lab, you turn on Media Access Control (MAC) filtering at the firewall by allowing only one computer on your network access to the firewall. The steps are as follows:

Step 1. Discover and write down your local computer's MAC address.

On a Windows computer, open the Command Prompt and type ipconfig/all. The MAC address is a hexadecimal number listed in the Physical Address field. Write this number down. If you have more than one network adapter, write down the MAC address associated with the network adapter you are currently using to access the D-Link DIR-655.

On a Linux computer, open the CLI and type ifconfig. The MAC address is a hexadecimal number listed in the HWaddr field. Write this number down. If you have more than one network adapter, write down the MAC address associated with the network adapter you are currently using to access the D-Link DIR-655.

Step 2. On the main **Device Information** page of the D-Link DIR-655, click the **Advanced** link near the top of the window. This should bring up the Advanced page.

Step 3. On the left side, click the **Network Filter** link. This should display the MAC Address Filter window.

Step 4. Click the drop-down menu for the Configure MAC Filtering below field. Select **Turn MAC Filtering ON and ALLOW computers listed to access the network**.

Step 5. Type the MAC address you wrote down previously into the first blank field. You can use hyphens or colons to separate the numbers, for example: **00-1C-C0-A1-55-16** or **00:1C:C0:A1:55:16**.

Step 6. Click the **Save Settings** button. The simulator version of the D-Link DIR-655 will usually clear these automatically, but if you want to clear a MAC address that is listed, click the **Clear** button.

Step 7. Finally, when you finish, click the drop-down menu to turn MAC Filtering off.

Watch the solution video in the "Hands-On Scenarios" section of the DVD.

View Recommended Resources

If you want to brush up on your networking topics:

- Prowse, David L. *CompTIA Network+ Video Mentor*, First edition. Que. 2009.
- Harwood, Mike. *CompTIA Network+ N10-004 Cert Guide*, Third edition. Que. 2009.
- Comer, Douglas. *Computer Networks and Internets* (5th Edition). Prentice Hall. 2008.

Article: Intrusion Detection Overview:
www.informit.com/articles/article.aspx?p=174342

Video: Setting up virtual servers and port forwarding on a typical SOHO router/firewall: www.davidlprowse.com/forums/showthread.php?t=1620

Video: Setting up a 3-leg perimeter firewall/DMZ configuration with ISA:
www.davidlprowse.com/forums/showthread.php?t=1621

Nmap: http://nmap.org/

GRC's ShieldsUP!: www.grc.com

Answer Review Questions

Answer the following review questions. You can find the answers at the end of this chapter.

1. Which tool would you use if you want to view the contents of a packet?
   A. TDR
   B. Port scanner
   C. Protocol analyzer
   D. Loopback adapter

2. The honeypot concept is enticing to administrators because
   A. It enables them to observe attacks.
   B. It traps an attacker in a network.
   C. It bounces attacks back at the attacker.
   D. It traps a person physically between two locked doors.

3. James has detected an intrusion in his company. What should he check first?
   A. DNS Logs
   B. Firewall logs

C. The Event Viewer

D. Performance logs

4. Which of the following devices should you employ to protect your network? (Select the best answer.)

A. Protocol analyzer

B. Firewall

C. DMZ

D. Proxy server

5. Which device's log file will show access control lists and who was allowed access and who wasn't?

A. Firewall

B. PDA

C. Performance monitor

D. IP proxy

6. Where are software firewalls usually located?

A. On routers

B. On servers

C. On clients

D. On every computer

7. Where is the optimal place to have a proxy server?

A. In between two private networks

B. In between a private and a public network

C. In between two public networks

D. On all of the servers

8. A coworker has installed an SMTP server on the company firewall. What security principle does this violate?

A. Chain of custody

B. Use of a device as it was intended

C. Man trap

D. Use of multifunction network devices

9. You are working on a server and are busy implementing a network intrusion detection system on the network. You need to monitor the network traffic from the server. What mode should you configure the network adapter to work in?

   A. Half-duplex mode

   B. Full-duplex mode

   C. Auto configuration mode

   D. Promiscuous mode

10. Which of the following displays a single public IP address to the Internet while hiding a group of internal private IP addresses?

    A. HTTP proxy

    B. Protocol analyzer

    C. IP proxy

    D. SMTP proxy

11. If your ISP blocks objectionable material, what device would you guess has been implemented?

    A. Proxy server

    B. Firewall

    C. Internet content filter

    D. NIDS

12. Of the following, which is a collection of servers that was set up to attract hackers?

    A. DMZ

    B. Honeypot

    C. Honeynet

    D. VLAN

13. Which of the following will detect malicious packets and discard them?

    A. Proxy server

    B. NIDS

    C. NIPS

    D. PAT

14. Which of the following will an Internet filtering appliance analyze? (Select the three best answers.)
    A. Content
    B. Certificates
    C. Certificate revocation lists
    D. URLs certificates were goals

Answers and Explanations

1. **C.** A protocol analyzer has the capability to "drill" down through a packet and show the contents of that packet as they correspond to the OSI model.
2. **A.** By creating a honeypot, the administrator can monitor attacks without sustaining damage to a server or other computer. Don't confuse this with a honeynet (answer B), which is meant to attract and trap malicious attackers in an entire false network. Answer C is not something that an administrator would normally do, and answer D is defining a man trap.
3. **B.** If there were an intrusion, the first thing you should check are the firewall logs. DNS logs in the event viewer and the performance logs will most likely not show intrusions to the company. The best place to look first is the firewall logs.
4. **B.** Install a firewall to protect the network. Protocol analyzers will not help to protect a network but are valuable as vulnerability assessment and monitoring tools. Although a DMZ and a proxy server could possibly help to protect a portion of the network to a certain extent, the best answer is firewall.
5. **A.** A firewall contains one or more access control lists (ACLs) defining who is enabled to access to the network. The firewall can also show attempts at access and whether they succeeded or failed. A personal digital assistant (PDA) might list who called or e-mailed but as of the writing of this book does not use ACLs. Performance Monitor analyzes the performance of a computer, and an IP proxy deals with network address translation, hiding many private IP addresses behind one public address. Although the function of an IP proxy is often built into a firewall, the best answer would be firewall.
6. **C.** Software-based firewalls, such as the Windows Firewall, are normally running on the client computers. Although a software-based firewall could also be run on a server, it is not as common. Also, a SOHO router might have a built-in firewall, but not all routers will have firewalls.
7. **B.** Proxy servers should normally be between the private and the public network. This way they can act as a go between for all the computers located on the private network. This applies especially to IP proxy servers but might also include HTTP proxy servers.

8. **B.** And SMTP servers should not be installed on a company firewall. This is not the intention of a firewall device. The SMTP server should most likely be installed within a DMZ.
9. **D.** To monitor the implementation of NIDS on the network, you should configure the network adapter to work in promiscuous mode; this forces the network adapter to pass all the traffic it receives to the processor, not just the frames that were addressed to that particular network adapter. The other three answers have to do with duplexing—whether the network adapter can send *and* receive simultaneously.
10. **C.** An IP proxy displays a single public IP address to the Internet while hiding a group of internal private IP addresses. It sends data back and forth between the IP addresses by using Network Address Translation (NAT). This functionality is usually built into SOHO routers and is one of the main functions of those routers. HTTP proxies store commonly accessed Internet information. Protocol analyzers enable the capture and viewing of network data. SMTP proxies act as a go between for e-mail.
11. **C.** An Internet content filter, usually implemented as content-control software can block objectionable material before it ever gets to the user. This is common in schools, government, and many companies.
12. **C.** A honeynet is a collection of servers set up to attract hackers. A honeypot is usually one computer or one server that has the same purpose. A DMZ is the demilitarized zone that is in between the LAN and the Internet. A VLAN is a virtual LAN.
13. **C.** NIPS, or a network intrusion prevention system, will detect *and* discard malicious packets. A NIDS only detects them and alerts the administrator. A proxy server acts as a go-between for clients sending data to systems on the Internet. PAT is port-based address translation.
14. **A, B, and D.** However, certificate revocation lists will most likely not be analyzed. Remember that CRLs are published only periodically.

This chapter covers the following subjects:

- **Securing Wired Networks and Devices—**In this section, you learn about how to reduce the risk of attack to your wired networks and the central connecting devices that control access to those networks. Concepts covered include security for common network devices such as SOHO routers and firewalls, and how to secure twisted-pair, fiber-optic, and coaxial cables.
- **Securing Wireless Networks—**Here, we delve into wireless networks, how you can secure your wireless access points and protect your wireless network from intruders, inside or outside the building. Wireless concepts covered include Wi-Fi security and Bluetooth security.

This chapter covers the CompTIA Security+ SY0-201 objectives 2.5, 2.6, and 2.7.

CHAPTER 7

Securing Network Media and Devices

Imagine if you will that you are in charge of securing your organization's wired and wireless networks, and all of the devices associated with them. There are several questions you should ask yourself: What kind of cables does your network use, what are the vulnerabilities of those cables, and how can they be secured? What are your future cabling plans? Do you have wireless networks, and if so, how can you protect data that is flinging through the air? How many devices can be accessed either from users on the network or remotely? And are there any older devices that need to be updated, or simply removed?

Verifying that all network devices, cables, and other mediums are secure might sound like a daunting task at first, but let's take it step by step and discuss how this can be done. We'll begin with wired networks, cables, and the devices you might find on a wired network; then we'll move onto wireless transmissions. At the end of the chapter, we will show a final piece of network documentation that sums up a lot of the security precautions that we've implemented in Chapters 5 through 7.

Foundation Topics

Securing Wired Networks and Devices

Implementing a security plan for your wired network is critical. In Chapter 5, "Network Design Elements and Network Threats," we talked about the design elements of your network and the possible threats to those design elements and to the computers and servers on the network. In Chapter 6, "Network Perimeter Security," we talked about some of the security tools such as firewalls that could be used to protect the network. But what connects it altogether?—Usually the wired network. Now let's get into the nitty-gritty of the wired network. Not only are the devices wired to the network targets for attack, but the wires could be targets as well. Some attacks could come from inside the network, whereas other attacks could be external. Let's start with some of the common vulnerabilities to network devices.

Network Device Vulnerabilities

Devices that reside on your network might include hubs, switches, routers, firewalls, NIDS/NIPS appliances, and more. Each of these devices can be vulnerable in their default state. Most devices are sold with simple default accounts and blank or weak passwords. In some cases, it's easy for users to escalate their privileges to gain access to resources that they normally would not have access to. Some devices and computers can be the victim of backdoors that programmers did not remove, or forgot to remove, which enable access for attackers. And of course, a good network administrator will protect against network attacks such as denial of service. Let's go through each of these one by one and show how to protect against these vulnerabilities to help mitigate risk.

Default Accounts

A lot of the networking devices available to organizations are initially installed with a default set of user credentials; this is the *default account*. The default account might be called administrator, or admin, or something else similar. If possible, this default account should be changed to a new name, because attackers are aware of default account names. This also applies to computers and servers, as we mentioned in Chapter 3, "OS Hardening and Virtualization." By renaming the default account, or by removing it altogether, you add a layer of security that makes it more difficult for an attacker to figure out which account has administrative access to the device. One example of this is the D-Link DIR-655 SOHO router we have mentioned in previous chapters. It is common knowledge that these devices (and many other SOHO routers) are set up by default with the username admin and a blank password. This is one of the first things you should change before you connect it to the Internet. Although the DIR-655 does not enable you to change the username, it certainly enables you to change the password. And a lot of these devices allow a separate user account as well, which might have varying levels of access depending on the device. This should either be set with a complex password or disabled altogether.

If any guest accounts exist, it is recommended that you disable these accounts. And again, this applies to network devices and computers. The guest account will usually not be enabled, but you should always check this just in case. Of course, more important than the account name or the username is the password. If you have to use a guest account, set a complex password! More on passwords in just a little bit.

Weak Passwords

Passwords should be as complex as possible. A weak password can be cracked by an attacker in a short time. Many network devices come stock with no password at all; so, your first order of business should be to create a complex password. It is common knowledge that a strong password is important for protecting a user account, whether the account is with a bank, at work, or elsewhere. The same goes for network devices. But what is a strong password? Many organizations define a *strong* password as a password with at least 8 characters, including at least one uppercase letter, one number, and one special character. The *best* passwords have the same requirements but are 14 characters or more. Many password checker programs are available on the Internet, for example Microsoft's password checker at www.microsoft.com/protect/yourself/password/checker.mspx.

Let's look at Table 7-1. This table gives some examples of weak passwords and strong passwords.

Table 7-1 Weak, Strong, and Stronger Passwords

Password	Strength of Password
Prowse	Weak
DavidProwse	Medium
|ocrian7	Strong
This1sV#ryS3cure	Very strong or "best"

The first password in Table 7-1 is weak; even though it has an uppercase P, it is only 6 characters in length. The second password is only medium strength; it has 11 characters but only two uppercase characters, and nothing else is special about it. However, notice the third password is using the | pipe symbol instead of the letter L. This is a special character that shares the \ backslash key on the keyboard. Because it has a special character, and a number, and that it has 8 characters in total, it is considered to be a strong password. In the last password, we have 16 characters, including 3 uppercase letters, 2 numbers, and 1 special character. These methods make for an extremely strong password that would take a super-computer many years to crack.

Privilege Escalation

Privilege escalation is the act of exploiting a bug or design flaw in a software or firmware application to gain access to resources that normally would be protected from an application or user. This results in a user gaining additional privileges, more than were originally intended by the developer of the application. For example, if a particular user can read another user's e-mail without authorization. Other programs, such as Cisco Call Manager, have also been the victim of privilege escalations, although patches are regularly released if issues like these are discovered. Buffer overflows are used on Windows computers to elevate privileges as well. To bypass digital rights management (DRM), attackers use a method known as a jail break, another type of privilege escalation. Malware will also attempt to exploit privilege escalation vulnerabilities, if any exist on the system. Privilege escalation can also be attempted on network devices. Generally, the fix for this is simply to update the device and to check on a regular basis if any updates are available. For example, our D-Link DIR-655 mentioned previously has a user account and an admin account. If a device like this isn't properly updated, an attacker can take advantage of a bug in the firmware to elevate the privileges of the user account. Couple this with the fact that a person forgot to put a password on the user account (or disable it) and your network could be in for some "fun." It is also possible on some devices to encrypt the firmware component. Following are a couple different types of privilege escalation:

- **Vertical privilege escalation—**When a lower privileged user accesses functions reserved for higher privilege users, for example, if a standard user can access functions of an administrator. This is also known as privilege elevation and is the most common description.
- **Horizontal privilege escalation—**When a normal user accesses functions or content reserved for other normal users, for example, if one user reads another's e-mail. This can be done through hacking or by a person walking over to other people's computers and simply reading their e-mail! Always have your users lock their computer (or log off) when they are not physically at their desk!

There is also privilege de-escalation, when high privileged but segregated users can downgrade their access level to access normal users' functions. Sneaky admins can attempt this to glean confidential information from an organization. It's a two-way street when it comes to security; you should think three-dimensionally when securing your network!

Back Doors

Backdoors are used in computer programs to bypass normal authentication and other security mechanisms in place. Originally backdoors were used by developers as a legitimate way of accessing an application, but soon after they were implemented, attackers would use backdoors to either make changes on network devices, or the attacker would create a completely new application that would act as a backdoor, for example Back Orifice, which enables a user to control a Windows computer from a remote location. Often, it is installed via a Trojan horse; this particular one is known as a remote access Trojan or RAT. Some worms install backdoors on computers so that remote spammers can send junk e-mail from the infected computers, or so an attacker can attempt privilege escalation. Unfortunately, there isn't much that can be done about backdoors aside from updating or patching the infected system and keeping on top of updates. However, if network administrators were to find out about a new backdoor, they should inform the manufacturer of the device or the application as soon as possible. Backdoors are less common nowadays, because their practice is usually discouraged by software manufacturers and by makers of network devices.

Network Attacks

Denial of service and many other network attacks can cause havoc on your network devices. It is important to keep abreast of these latest attacks and to verify that all systems and network devices are updated accordingly. Use smart network intrusion prevention systems (NIPS) to identify new attacks and prevent them from causing trouble on your networks. For more information on denial of service attacks and other types of network attacks, see the section titled "Ports, Protocols, and Malicious Attacks" in Chapter 5.

Other Network Device Considerations

Some network administrators use remote ports on their network devices to remotely administer that device. These ports can be used maliciously as well. If the remote port is not to be used, it should be disabled. If it is to be used, a strong authentication system should be employed, and data encryption should be considered. This applies to routers, switches, servers, and PBX equipment. For more specific ways to protect your network devices, see the section "Network Design" in Chapter 5.

In some cases a network administrator uses the Telnet program to access network equipment remotely from another site or from within the local area network. This practice should be shunned because Telnet by default is not secure; it does not encrypt data, including passwords, and default implementations of Telnet have no authentication scheme that ensures that communications will not be intercepted. In addition most Telnet programs have other vulnerabilities and risk associated with them. Instead of using Telnet, administrators should opt for another protocol such as Secure Shell (SSH).

Cable Media Vulnerabilities

The most commonly overlooked item in a network is the cabling. The entire cabling infrastructure (or cabling plant) includes the cables themselves, network jacks, patch panels, punch blocks, and so on. You need to think about what types of cabling you are using, what vulnerabilities they have, and how to combat those vulnerabilities in an attempt to reduce risk. Following are three types of cabling that you might have implemented in your network:

- **Twisted-pair**—A copper-based cable with four pairs of wires (for a total of eight wires), each of which is twisted together along the length of the cable. It is the most common type of network cable; it sends electrical signals to transfer data and uses RJ45 plugs to connect to ports on hosts. The most common security problem with twisted-pair cable is crosstalk, which we discuss later.
- **Fiber-optic**—A glass/plastic-based cable that sends light (photons) instead of electricity. It is composed of one or more thin strands known as fibers that transfer the data. Generally, this is the most secure type of cable that can be used in a network. It is not susceptible to EMI, RFI, or data emanations and is the least susceptible cable to wiretapping.
- **Coaxial**—A less used copper-based cable that has a single copper core. Although not used for connections to hosts anymore, you might see it used with special connections, perhaps for the Internet or for video. In smaller companies' networks, it is common to see an RG-6 cable used for the Internet connection. The most common security risk with coaxial cable is data emanation, which we discuss later.

Each of these cables has its own inherent vulnerabilities; let's talk about a few of these now.

Interference

Interference is anything that disrupts or modifies a signal traveling along a wire. There are many types of interference but you should know about only a few for the exam, including the following:

- **Electromagnetic interference (EMI)**—A disturbance that can affect electrical circuits, devices, and cables due to electromagnetic conduction or radiation. Just about any type of electrical device can cause EMI: TVs, microwaves, air conditioning units, motors, unshielded electrical lines, and so on. Copper-based cables and network devices should be kept away from these electrical devices if at all possible. If not possible, shielded cables can be used, for example shielded twisted pair (STP). Or the device that is emanating EMI can be shielded. For example, an air conditioning unit could be boxed in with aluminum shielding in an attempt to keep the EMI generated by the AC unit's motor to a minimum. In addition, electrical cables should be BX (encased in metal), and not Romex (not encased in metal); most municipalities require this to meet industrial and office space building code. EMI can also be used in a mischievous manner, known as radio jamming. But the methods listed here can help defend against this as well.

- **Radio frequency interference (RFI)—**Interference that can come from AM/FM transmissions and cell towers. It is often considered to be part of the EMI family and will sometimes be referred to as EMI. The closer a business is to one of these towers, the greater the chance of interference. The methods mentioned for EMI can be employed to help defend against RFI. In addition, filters can be installed on the network to eliminate the signal frequency broadcast by a radio tower, though this usually does not affect standard-wired Ethernet networks. Wireless signals from wireless networks and cell phones can interfere with speakers and other devices; try to keep speakers and monitors away from cell phones and wireless network adapters. Try to keep wireless access points away from computers, printers, monitors, and speakers, ands switches, routers, and other network equipment.

Another common type of interference is crosstalk that we discuss in next.

Crosstalk

Crosstalk is when a signal transmitted on one copper wire creates an undesired effect on another wire; the signal "bleeds" over, so to speak. This first occurred when telephone lines were placed in close proximity to each other. Because the phone lines were so close, the signal could jump from one line to the next intermittently. If you have ever heard another conversation while talking on your home phone (not cell phones mind you) you have been the victim of crosstalk. This can happen with connections made by a modem as well, causing considerable havoc on the data transfer.

NOTE: With cell phones, crosstalk is also known as co-channel interference or CCI, a different type not covered on the 2008 Security+ objectives.

To combat crosstalk, you can use twisted-pair cable. This helps when regular analog signals are sent across the wires and applies only to standard POTS connections and computer modems that use POTS connections. The beauty of the twists in twisted-pair cabling is that the signal has less chance of leaking to other wires, in comparison to straight wires next to each other and bundled together. If the signals are digital, for example, Ethernet data transfers or voice over IP, you already have an environment less susceptible to crosstalk, in comparison to an analog environment. Data can still bleed over to other wires, but it is less common, because the twists of the wires have been precisely calculated by the manufacturer. Sometimes this occurs due to bunches of cables bundled too tightly, which could also cause crimping or other damage to the cable. If this is the case, a trusty continuity tester will let you know which cable has failed; normally this would have to be replaced. When it comes to twisted-pair cabling, crosstalk is broken down into two categories: near end crosstalk (NEXT) and far end crosstalk (FEXT). NEXT is when measured interference occurs between two pairs in a single cable, measured on the cable end nearest the transmitter. FEXT is when like interference occurs but is measured at the cable end farthest from the transmitter.

If crosstalk is still a problem, even though twisted-pair cable has been employed, and digital data transmissions have been implemented, shielded twisted pair (STP) could be used. Although twisting individual pairs can minimize crosstalk between wire pairs within a cable, shielding an entire cable will minimize crosstalk between cables. Normally, companies opt for regular twisted-pair cabling, which is unshielded (also known as UTP), but sometimes, too much interference exists in the environment to send data effectively, and STP must be utilized.

Data Emanation

Data emanation (or signal emanation) is the electromagnetic (EM) field generated by a network cable or network device, which can be manipulated to eavesdrop on conversations or to steal data. Data emanation is sometimes also referred to as eavesdropping, although this is not accurate.

Data emanation is the most commonly seen security risk when using coaxial cable, depending on the type of coaxial cable but can also be a security risk for other copper-based cables. There are various ways to tap into these (EM) fields to get unauthorized access to confidential data. To alleviate the situation, there are several solutions. For example, you could use shielded cabling or run the cabling through metal conduits. Secondly, you could use electromagnetic shielding on devices that might be emanating an electromagnetic field. This could be done on a small scale by shielding the single device or on a larger scale shielding an entire room, perhaps a server room; this would be an example of a *Faraday cage*. If an entire room is shielded, electromagnetic energy cannot pass through the walls in either direction. So, if a person attempts to use a cell phone inside the cage, it will not function properly, because the signal cannot go beyond the cage walls. More important, devices such as cell phones, motors, and wireless access points that create electromagnetic fields and are outside the cage cannot disrupt electromagnetic-sensitive devices that reside inside the cage. Server rooms and cabling should be protected in some way, especially if the data that travels through them is confidential. Studies are constantly done about signal emanations and how to contain them. A group of standards known as *TEMPEST* refers to the investigations of conducted emissions from electrical and mechanical devices, which could be compromising to an organization.

Tapping into Data and Conversations

This is a huge subject, and we could talk about it for days without scratching the surface. One item of note: ANY system can be tapped or hacked. It's just the lengths you must go to that can vary; it depends on the network, cabling, and security precautions already in place.

One of the items on the Security+ exam is "vampire taps"; this is number 2.6 in the 2008 Security+ objectives. This type of tap deals with coaxial cable, namely 10BASE5 or "thicknet," which uses a bus topology. Although this is a deprecated network type, the vampire tap is nevertheless still on the objectives, so you should know it for the exam. The *vampire tap* works by piercing into the 10BASE5 cable. The device surrounds the cable and actually taps into the copper core. It has an Attachment User Interface (AUI) that enables a new connection to be made to a PC, as shown in Figure 7-1; some have RG-58 coaxial connections as well. The point of the device is to enable an administrator to tap into the network and add a PC to it, without having to bring the entire network down. Without the device, a network admin would have to cut the cable and attach a T-connector, which would indeed require stopping the network until the job is done. Now, it stands to reason that the vampire tap could be used for more insidious purposes by attackers, but only if they have physical access to the coaxial cable. When attackers have access by using a vampire tap, they can monitor the network in a transparent fashion; meaning, the network admin won't even know that the monitoring is taking place. Again, this is an older type of technology, and an older way of hacking in to a system, but it should make you realize that any network can be tapped.

Key Topic

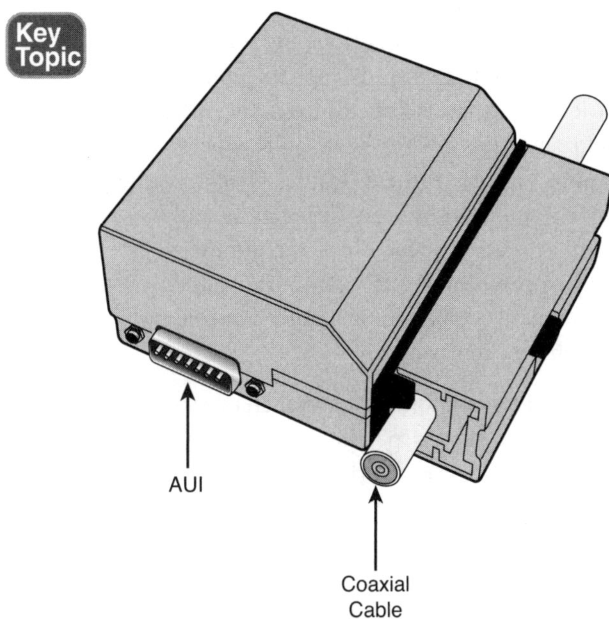

Figure 7-1 Illustration of a Vampire Tap

"Tapping" today takes on a whole new meaning. Instead of tapping directly onto a coaxial cable, tapping can mean any one of the following and more:

- **Connecting to a punch block, or RJ11 jack with a butt set**—A *butt set* (or lineman's handset) is a device that looks similar to a phone but has alligator clips that can connect to the various terminals used by phone equipment enabling a person to test a new line or listen in to a conversation. The device is used primarily by telecommunications technicians but can obviously be used for malicious purposes as well. There are analog versions of this device (for POTS systems) and digital versions (for digital systems such as VoIP and so on) that act as packet capturing devices (sniffers). To protect against this, keep all punch blocks and other phone equipment in a locked server room or wiring closet. Although expensive, there are also lockable RJ11 jacks, but it would probably be less costly to install a network of cameras in the building, especially if your organization wants them for other purposes as well.
- **Plugging into an open port of a twisted-pair network**—This could be either at a RJ45 wall plate or in the server room (not as easy) at an open port of a hub or switch. Unused ports, whether on a hub or switch, or at a computer station's RJ45 jack, should be disabled. Also, central connecting devices such as hubs and switches should be locked in the server room, and only properly authenticated individuals should have access.
- **Splitting the wires of a twisted-pair connection**—This can be done anywhere along a cable but would disrupt communications for that individual computer or segment while it is being done. By cutting the twisted-pair cable and soldering a second twisted-pair cable to the appropriate wires (for example, Ethernet 568B networks use the orange and green pairs of wires by default), a person could eavesdrop on all communications on that segment. Cables should not be exposed if at all possible. Cable runs should be above the drop ceiling and inside the walls, perhaps run in conduit. It is understandable that computers need to connect to RJ45 jacks by way of patch cables; if a computer suddenly loses its connection to the network, an alert can be sent to junior administrators, prompting them to investigate why it occurred.
- **Using a spectral analyzer to access data emanations**—Spectral analyzers can measure the composition of electrical waveforms at specific frequencies (for example 100 MHz on a 100BASE-T twisted-pair network). These can also decode encrypted transmissions. These types of devices should not be allowed in the building (unless used by authorized personnel). A metal detector could be used at the entrance of the building, and again, video cameras can help detect this, and perhaps even prevent mischievous people from attempting to do so, just because they think they might be under surveillance.
- **Using a passive optical splitter for fiber-optic networks**—This is a more expensive device and would need access to a cable. Plus the process of getting it to work is difficult. (And again, this would disrupt communications for a time.) The preceding listed methods apply to defending against this as well. Because

it is difficult to implement an optical splitter properly, this could cause chromatic dispersion on the particular fiber segment. Chromatic dispersion (and subsequent loss of data) could also occur if the fiber optic cable is too long. Administrators could monitor the network for dispersion and have alerts sent to them in the case that it occurs. The most common example of chromatic dispersion is the rainbow. For example, if light is sent through a prism, the light will be refracted (dispersed) into the rainbow of colors. Although not exactly how it would occur on a fiber optic cable, if this were to happen, data transmissions would fail.

Keep in mind that the Security+ exam does not go too far in depth for this subject, but realize that you might get a question on wire tapping, and remember that any network can be hacked! It is more common to attempt hacking into wireless networks. So let's delve into the basics of that immense subject next.

Securing Wireless Networks

Wireless networks pose a whole new set of problems for a network administrator. Wireless access points and wireless network adapters need to be secure from attackers that could be just about anywhere as long as they're within range of the wireless network. There are several points we cover that can help you secure your wireless access point, wireless network adapters, and any other wireless devices. In this section, you learn how to watch out for wireless transmission vulnerabilities and some of the Bluetooth vulnerabilities that you should be aware of.

Wireless Access Point Vulnerabilities

The wireless access point is the central connecting device for wireless network adapters that might exist in PCs, laptops, handheld computers, PDAs, and other similar devices. You need to secure any broadcasts that the wireless access point might make and verify that transmissions are encrypted with a strong encryption technique. It's also important to watch out for rogue access points and round up any nomads on your network.

Secure the Administration Interface

The first thing you should look at when it comes to wireless access points is the administration interface, or console. The act of accessing the administration interface is sometimes referred to as "romming" into the access point. By default, most access points have a blank password or a simple and weak password, for example "password." The first step you want to take is to access the administration interface and modify the password; change it to a complex password. Next, consider disabling remote administration if it is not necessary. Your organization might require it, but it depends on several factors. If you are dead set on leaving it enabled, be completely sure that the remote administration password is complex.

SSID Broadcast

The *service set identifier (SSID)* is one of several broadcasts that a wireless access point makes. It identifies the network and is the name of the access point used by clients to connect to the wireless network. It is on by default. After all your clients have been connected to the wireless network, consider disabling the SSID broadcast. Though there will still be ways for hackers to get into your access point, this at least provides a preliminary level of security. The average user cannot see the SSID and cannot connect to the wireless network. In the future if you need to add clients, simply enable the SSID temporarily, connect the client, and then disable the SSID. This might not be a factor if you are in a large building. But if you are in a smaller structure, the wireless access point's broadcast range may leak out beyond your organization's property. You can also try reducing the transmitter power of the wireless access point. Although not all access points have this function, some do and it can help to fine-tune the area that the access point serves.

Rogue Access Points

Sometimes companies lose track of the wireless access points on their network. Keep track of all your devices with network documentation. Use network mapping programs and Microsoft Visio to detect and document any rogue access points. Older access points, especially ones with weak encryption, should be updated, disabled, or simply disconnected from the network. Some companies may have a dozen wireless access points and additional wireless devices such as repeaters, and it may be difficult to keep track of these. In this case, a network mapping program can be one of your best friends. In addition, you can search for rogue access points with a laptop or handheld computer with Microsoft's Wireless Zero Configuration tool, the wireless network adapter's built-in software, or third-party applications such as AirMagnet or NetStumbler.

Weak Encryption

Weak encryption or no encryption can be a couple of the worst things that can happen to a wireless network. This can occur for several reasons, for example if someone wanted to connect an older device or a device that hasn't been updated, and that device can run only a weaker, older type of encryption. It's important to have strong encryption in your network; as of the writing of this book, WPA2 is the strongest encryption you can use. It can be used with TKIP or AES. Remember that the encryption level of the wireless access point and the network adapters that connect to it need to be the same. Table 7-2 defines some of the available wireless encryption types.

Table 7-2 Wireless Encryption Methods

Wireless Encryption Protocol	Description	Encryption Level (Key Size)
WEP	Wired Equivalent Privacy	64-bit
WPA2	Wi-Fi Protected Access	256-bit
TKIP	Temporal Key Integrity Protocol	128-bit
AES	Advanced Encryption Standard	128-bit, 192-bit, and 256-bit

WEP is the weakest type of encryption; WPA is stronger, and WPA2 is the strongest of the three. However, it is better to have WEP as opposed to nothing. If this is the case, use encryption keys that are difficult to guess, and consider changing those keys often. Some devices can be updated to support WPA, whether it is through a firmware upgrade or through the use of a software add-on. Figure 7-2 shows a typical wireless access point with WPA2 and AES configured; AES is the cipher type. The preshared key used to enable connectivity between wireless clients and the access point is a complex pass-phrase.

WIRELESS SECURITY MODE
To protect your privacy you can configure wireless security features. This device supports three wireless security modes, including WEP, WPA-Personal, and WPA-Enterprise. WEP is the original wireless encryption standard. WPA provides a higher level of security. WPA-Personal does not require an authentication server. The WPA-Enterprise option requires an external RADIUS server.
Security Mode : WPA-Personal
WPA
Use WPA or WPA2 mode to achieve a balance of strong security and best compatibility. This mode uses WPA for legacy clients while maintaining higher security with stations that are WPA2 capable. Also the strongest cipher that the client supports will be used. For best security, use WPA2 Only mode. This mode uses AES(CCMP) cipher and legacy stations are not allowed access with WPA security. For maximum compatibility, use WPA Only. This mode uses TKIP cipher. Some gaming and legacy devices work only in this mode.
To achieve better wireless performance use WPA2 Only security mode (or in other words AES cipher).
WPA Mode : WPA2 Only
Cipher Type : AES
Group Key Update Interval : 3600 (seconds)
PRE-SHARED KEY
Enter an 8- to 63-character alphanumeric pass-phrase. For good security it should be of ample length and should not be a commonly known phrase.
Pre-Shared Key : ••••••••••••

Figure 7-2 Wireless Security Configuration on a Typical Access Point

Other Wireless Access Point Security Strategies

Strategic placement of a WAP is vital. Usually, the best place for a WAP is in the center of the building. This way, equal access can be given to everyone on the perimeter of the organization's property, and there is the least chance of the signal bleeding over to other organizations. If needed, attempt to reduce the transmission power of the antenna; which can reduce the broadcast range of the WAP. Also, to avoid interference in the form of EMI or RFI, keep wireless access points away from any electrical panels, cables, devices, motors, or other pieces of equipment that might give off an electromagnetic field. If necessary, shield the device creating the EM field, or shield the access point itself. Sheesh, I am starting to sound bossy!

Many wireless access points come with a built-in firewall. If the firewall is utilized, the stateful packet inspection (SPI) option and NAT filtering should be enabled. The wireless access point might also have the capability to be configured for MAC filtering, which can filter out which computers can access the wireless network. The WAP does this by consulting a list of MAC addresses that have been previously entered. Only the network adapters with those corresponding MAC addresses can connect; everyone else cannot join the wireless network. In some cases, a device might broadcast this MAC table. If this is the case, look for an update for the firmware of the access point, and again, attempt to fine-tune the broadcast range of the device so that it does not leak out to other organizations.

It is also possible to include the IEEE 802.1x standard for port-based network access control that can provide for strong authentication. For a wireless access point to incorporate this kind of technology, it must also act as a router, which adds the duty of wireless gateway to the access point.

Another option is to consider encryption technologies on the Application Layer, such as SSL, SSH, or PGP; these and others can help to secure data transmissions from attackers that have already gained access to the wireless network. For more information on encryption types see the section "Security Protocols" in Chapter 13, "Encryption Protocols, Keys, and Certificates," When it comes down to it, authentication and a strong encryption protocol such as WPA (or WPA2) are the two security precautions that will best help to protect against network attacks.

NOTE: See the step-by-step lab on securing a wireless access point in the "Hands-On Labs" section.

Finally, another option is to not run wireless at all. It's quite tough to hack into a wireless network that doesn't exist! Some companies opt for this as strange as it may seem, because they have deduced that the costs of implementation, administration, maintenance, and security outweigh the benefits of having a wireless network. Personally, I don't run any wireless networks at my home (aside from any testing purposes), my home is cabled up 100%; bedrooms, bathrooms, attic, you name it! J However, if you decide to go down this road, make sure that any devices that enable wireless access have those wireless functions disabled. This includes wireless access points, laptops, and other mobile devices that have wireless adapters, and any Bluetooth, infrared, or other wireless transmitters.

Wireless Transmission Vulnerabilities

Because wireless networks can transmit information through air or space, data emanations are everywhere and can easily be identified by people using the right tools. One deed that can be considered an attack on wireless networks is known as *wardriving*; this is the act of searching for wireless networks by a person in a vehicle, through the use of a device with a wireless antenna, often times a particularly strong antenna. A basic example of this would be a person in a car with a laptop, utilizing the freely downloadable NetStumbler software. When wardrivers find a network, they can attempt to crack the password or pass-phrase to gain access to the wireless network. This might be done by guessing; you'd be surprised how much this works; it is estimated that more than 40% of wireless networks are unprotected. It could also be done with dictionary or brute force attacks. You can find more information on password cracking in the section "Assessing Vulnerability with Security Tools" in Chapter 10, "Vulnerability and Risk Assessment."

NOTE: See the step-by-step lab showing a basic wardriving example and how to protect against this in the "Hands-On Labs" section.

Ways to protect against wardriving include hiding the SSID of the wireless access point, proper positioning of the WAP, using strong encryption, and changing the pass-phrase (encryption key) at regular intervals.

Bluetooth Vulnerabilities

Bluetooth, like any wireless technology, is vulnerable to attack as well. Bluejacking and Bluesnarfing are two types of vulnerabilities to Bluetooth-enabled devices. Bluetooth is also vulnerable to conflicts with other wireless technologies. For example, some WLAN (or Wi-Fi) standards use the 2.4-GHz frequency range, as does Bluetooth, and even though Bluetooth uses frequency hopping, conflicts can occur between 802.11g or 802.11b networks, and Bluetooth personal area networks. To avoid this, use Bluetooth version 1.2 devices or greater, which employ adaptive frequency-hopping, improving resistance to radio interference. Also, consider placing Bluetooth access points (if they are used) and WLAN access points in different areas of the building. Some companies have policies governing Bluetooth usage; in some cases, it is not allowed if 802.11 standards are in place, and in some cases a company will enforce rules that say Bluetooth can be used only outside the building. In other cases, a company will put its 802.11 devices on specific channels or use WLAN standards that use the 5-GHz range.

Bluejacking

Bluejacking is the sending of unsolicited messages to Bluetooth-enabled devices such as mobile phones and PDAs. Bluejacking is usually harmless but may appear that the Bluetooth device is malfunctioning. Originally, bluejackers would send only text messages, but with newer Bluetooth-enabled cell phones and PDAs, it is possible to send images and sounds as well. Bluejacking is used in less-than-reputable marketing campaigns. Bluejacking can be stopped by setting the affected Bluetooth device to "undiscoverable" or by turning off Bluetooth altogether.

Bluesnarfing

I known what you are thinking: The names of these attacks are starting to get a bit ridiculous! I guarantee it will improve as we progress through the rest of this book! Anyways, *bluesnarfing* is the unauthorized access of information from a wireless device through a Bluetooth connection. Generally, bluesnarfing is the theft of data (calendar information, phonebook contacts, and so on). It is possible to steal other information as well, but to pilfer any of this data, a pairing must be made between the attacking Bluetooth device and the Bluetooth victim. Sony, Nokia, and Ericsson phones are among the most common victims of bluesnarfing. Ways of discouraging bluesnarfing include using a pairing key that is not easy to guess; for example, stay away from 0000 or similar default Bluetooth pairing keys! Otherwise, Bluetooth devices should be set to "undiscoverable" (only after legitimate Bluetooth devices have been set up, of course), or Bluetooth can be turned off altogether, especially in areas that might be bluesnarfing playgrounds, for example, Times Square, NY. Bluesnarfing is considered by some to be a component of bluejacking, but for the exam, try to differentiate between the two.

Final Network Documentation

As promised in the beginning of this chapter, Figure 7-3 sums up a lot of the devices and security implementations that we have discussed in Chapters 5–7. Note the different network elements, devices, cabling, and wireless connectivity included in the illustration. You will also note that the firewall has four connections, one each to the LAN, DMZ, extranet, and Internet. Also worth noting is that the 802.11g WAP and the Bluetooth access point are located in different areas of the network. Try to define each network element that you see, and remember the various ways to secure them. Then create your own set of documentation for your own dream network (with security implementations, of course) that includes all the elements (or as many as you can) discussed in Chapters 5–7.

Key Topic

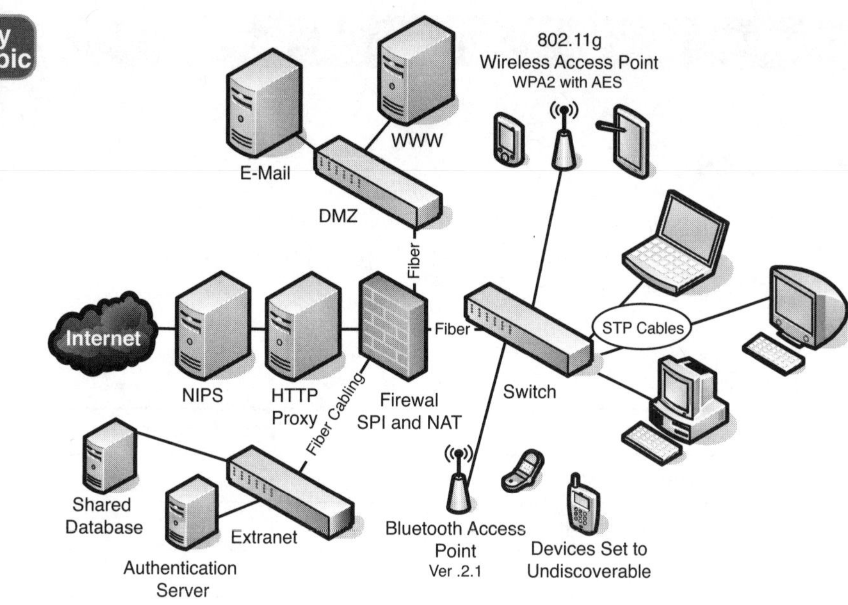

Figure 7-3 Final Network Documentation

Exam Preparation Tasks

Review Key Topics

Review the most important topics in the chapter, noted with the Key Topics icon in the outer margin of the page. Table 7-3 lists a reference of these key topics and the page numbers on which each is found.

Table 7-3 Key Topics for Chapter 7

Key Topic Element	Description	Page Number
Table 7-1	Strong and Stronger Passwords	187
Bullet list	Privilege escalation types	188
Bullet list	Cable types	190
Bullet list	Interference types	190
Figure 7-1	Illustration of a Vampire Tap	193
Table 7-2	Wireless Encryption Methods	197
Figure 7-3	Final Network Documentation	201

Complete Tables and Lists from Memory

Print a copy of Appendix A, "Memory Tables," (found on the DVD), or at least the section for this chapter, and complete the tables and lists from memory. Appendix B, "Memory Tables Answer Key," also on the DVD, includes completed tables and lists to check your work.

Define Key Terms

Define the following key terms from this chapter, and check your answers in the glossary:

default account, privilege escalation, backdoors, crosstalk, data emanation, vampire tap, wiretapping, chromatic dispersion, electromagnetic interference (EMI), radio frequency interference, TEMPEST, Faraday cage, butt set, service set identifier (SSID), Wired Equivalent Privacy (WEP), Wi-Fi Protected Access (WPA), Advanced Encryption Standard (AES), Temporal Key Integrity Protocol (TKIP), MAC filtering, wardriving, bluejacking, bluesnarfing

Hands-On Labs

Complete the following written step-by-step scenarios. After you finish (or if you do not have adequate equipment to complete the scenario), watch the corresponding video solution on the DVD.

If you have additional questions, feel free to post them at my website: www.davidlprowse.com in the Ask Dave forum. (Free registration is required to post on the website.)

Equipment Needed

- A computer with Internet access and a wireless network adapter.
- Web browser: Internet Explorer version 6 and higher or Firefox are recommended.
- D-Link DIR-655 or similar router:
  - If you have access to an actual DIR-655, make sure that it is updated to the latest firmware. Then connect to it by opening a web browser and typing the IP address of the router in the URL field, for example, 192.168.0.1. Next, at the login screen, type the password for the router, and click the **Log In** button. This should display the Device Information page. Start at this page for each of the three labs.
  - If you do not have access to an actual DIR-655, use the D-Link simulator located at http://support.dlink.com/Emulators/dir655/index.html. Then select the 1st option: **DIR-655 Device UI**. Next, at the login screen, click the **Log In** button. (A password is necessary.) This should display the Device Information page. Start at this page for each of the three labs.
  - NetStumbler software: www.netstumbler.com/downloads/

Lab 7-1: Securing a Wireless Device: 8 Steps to a Secure Network

In this lab, you secure a wireless access point and make it virtually unhackable. The steps are as follows:

Step 1. Update firmware.

A. On the main **Device Information** page, click the **Tools** link near the top of the window. This should bring up the Tools page.

B. On the left side, click the **Firmware** link. This should display the Firewall Settings window.

C. If you have an actual DIR-655, click the **Check Now** button. This looks for the latest firmware version. The DIR-655 simulator will be updated to the latest version. If you must download the firmware, note where it is downloaded.

D. Back at the Firmware page of the device, click the **Browse** button to search for the downloaded firmware. Then click the **Upload** button to install the new firmware. A restart is required.

Consider checking the **Automatically Check Online** and **Email Notification** checkboxes so that the device will look for upgrades and let you know as they become available.

Step 2. Set passwords!

A. Still on the Tools page, click the **Admin** link to the left.

B. In the Admin Password section, enter a complex password and verify it.

C. In the User Password section, enter a different complex password and verify it.

Step 3. Disable remote administration.

A. On the same Tools > Admin page deselect the **Enable Remote Management** checkbox. Then, click the **Remote Admin Inbound Filter** drop-down menu and select **Deny All**. This eliminates remote management even if the Enable Remote Management checkbox is somehow selected in the future.

Step 4. Disable SSID broadcasting.

A. Click the **Setup** link in the top banner.

B. Click the **Wireless Setting** link on the left side.

C. Click the **Manual Wireless Network Setup** button.

D. Change the Visibility Status by clicking the **Invisible** radio button. It is also wise to change the default SSID to a different name; **dlink** is commonly known and should be modified even if you disable the SSID.

Step 5. Enable WPA2 and AES.

A. Still on the Wireless page, click the **Security Mode** drop-down menu.

B. Select **WPA-Personal**.

C. Scroll down and in the **WPA Mode** drop-down menu select **WPA2 only**.

D. In the **Cipher Type** drop-down menu select **AES**.

E. Type a complex preshared key!!! Change this key as often as you change your toothbrush!

F. Click the **Save Settings** button at the top of the window. A router restart is usually required.

Consider also using Wi-Fi Protected Setup under the **Advanced** section.

Step 6. Reduce the output transmitting power of the WAP. This is not possible on the DIR-655, but if you have a WAP that incorporates this functionality, you should use it to "shape" your wireless network and prevent leakage to other organizations.

Step 7. Enable MAC filtering.

A. Click the **Advanced** link in the top banner.

B. Click the **Network Filter** link on the left side.

C. Add MAC addresses that are either allowed or denied access.

If you haven't already, check out the Chapter 6, Lab 3: MAC filtering video.

Step 8. Configure other rules and ACLs. This might include inbound filters, access control policies, application rules, and so on, each of which are located in the **Advanced** page.

Watch the solution video in the "Hands-On Scenarios" section of the DVD.

Lab 7-2: Wardriving...and The Cure

In this lab, you see a basic example of wardriving and how to defend against this. The steps are as follows:

Step 1. Make sure your computer's wireless adapter is enabled and functioning properly.

Step 2. Attempt to access wireless networks with the Wireless Zero Configuration tool (built in to Microsoft).

Step 3. Attempt to access wireless networks with proprietary software from the network adapter's manufacturer.

Step 4. Use NetStumbler to view available wireless networks.

A. Download and install the NetStumbler program from www.netstumbler.com/downloads/.

B. Open and run the program to view possible networks.

Step 5. Defend against people attempting to wardrive by

A. Configuring a strong password

B. Configuring strong encryption

C. Disabling SSID

D. Enabling MAC filtering

Watch the solution video in the "Hands-On Scenarios" section of the DVD.

View Recommended Resources

For readers who want to brush up on their networking topics:

- Prowse, David L. *CompTIA Network+ Video Mentor*, First Edition. Que. 2009.
- Harwood, Mike. *CompTIA Exam Prep Network+ N10-004*, Third Edition. Que. 2009.
- Comer, Douglas. *Computer Networks and Internets* (Fifth Edition). Prentice Hall. 2008.

AirMagnet: www.airmagnet.com/

NetStumbler: www.netstumbler.com/

Some decent security websites (there are many more!):

- Security Focus: www.securityfocus.com/
- Cert: www.cert.org/

Answer Review Questions

Answer the following review questions. You can find the answers at the end of this chapter.

1. Which of the following is the most secure protocol to use when accessing a wireless network?

A. WEP

B. WPA

C. WPA2

D. WEP2

2. What type of cabling is the most secure for networks?

A. STP

B. UTP

C. Fiber optic

D. Coaxial

3. What should you configure to improve wireless security?

A. Enable the SSID

B. IP spoofing

C. Remove repeaters

D. MAC filtering

4. In a wireless network, why is an SSID used?
   A. To secure the wireless access point
   B. To identify the network
   C. To encrypt data
   D. To enforce MAC filtering

5. What is the most commonly seen security risk of using coaxial cable?
   A. Data that emanates from the core of the cable
   B. Crosstalk between the different wires
   C. Chromatic dispersion
   D. Time domain reflection

6. Of the following, what is the most common problem associated with UTP cable?
   A. Crosstalk
   B. Data emanation
   C. Chromatic dispersion
   D. Vampire tapping

7. What two security precautions can best help to protect against wireless network attacks?
   A. Authentication and the WEP
   B. Access control lists and WEP
   C. Identification and WPA2
   D. Authentication and WPA

8. Which of the following cables suffers from chromatic dispersion if the cable is too long?
   A. Twisted-pair cable
   B. Fiber optic cable
   C. Coaxial cable
   D. USB cables

9. Which of the following cable media is the least susceptible to a tap?
   A. Coaxial cable
   B. Twisted-pair cable
   C. Fiber optic cable
   D. CATV cable

10. Which of the following, when removed, can increase the security of a wireless access point?

A. MAC filtering

B. SSID

C. WPA

D. Firewall

11. A wireless network switch has connectivity issues but only when the air-conditioning system is running. What can be added to fix the problem?

A. Shielding

B. A wireless network

C. A key deflector

D. Redundant air-conditioning systems

12. Which of the following is the most secure type of cabling?

A. Unshielded twisted pair

B. Shielded twisted pair

C. Coaxial

D. Category five

13. Which of the following is the least secure type of wireless encryption?

A. WEP 64-bit

B. WEP 128-bit

C. WPA with TKIP

D. WPA2 with AES

14. Which of the following is the unauthorized access of information from a Bluetooth device?

A. Bluejacking

B. Bluesnarfing

C. Blue privileges

D. The Blues Brothers

15. Which of the following can be described as the act of exploiting a bug or flaw in software to gain access to resources which normally would be protected?

A. Privilege escalation

B. Chain of custody

C. Default account

D. Backdoor

Answers and Explanations

1. **C.** Wi-Fi Protected Access 2 (WPA2) is the most secure protocol listed for connecting to wireless networks. It is more secure than WPA and WEP. Wired Equivalent Privacy (WEP) is actually a deprecated protocol that should be avoided, as is WEP2. The WEP and WEP2 algorithms are considered deficient for encrypted wireless networks.
2. **C.** Fiber optic is the most secure because it cannot be tapped like the other three copper-based cables; it does not emit EMI. Although shielded twisted pair (STP) offers a level of security due to it's shielding, it does not offer a level of security like to that of fiber optic and is not the best answer.
3. **D.** MAC filtering disallows connections from any wireless clients unless the wireless client's MAC address is on the MAC filtering list.
4. **B.** The SSID is used to identify the wireless network. It does not secure the wireless access point; one of the ways to secure a wireless access point is by masking the word disabling the SSID. The SSID does not encrypt data or enforce MAC filtering.
5. **A.** Some types of coaxial cables suffer from the emanation of data from the core of the cable, which can be accessed. Crosstalk occurs on twisted-pair cable. Chromatic dispersion occurs on fiber-optic cable. Time domain reflection is a concept that is used by a TDR.
6. **A.** Of the listed answers, crosstalk is the most common problem associated with UTP cable. Older versions of UTP cable (for example Category 3 or 5) are more susceptible to crosstalk than newer versions such as Cat 5e or Cat6. Although data emanation can be a problem with UTP cable, it is more common with coaxial cable, as is vampire tapping. Chromatic dispersion is a problem with fiber-optic cable.
7. **D.** The best two security precautions are authentication and WPA. Although WPA2 is more secure than WPA, the term identification is not correct. WEP is a deprecated wireless encryption protocol and should be avoided.
8. **B.** Fiber-optic cable is the only one listed that might suffer from chromatic dispersion, because it is the only cable based on light. All the other answers are based on electricity.
9. **C.** Fiber-optic cable is the least susceptible to a tap because it operates on the principle of light as opposed to electricity. All the other answers suffer from data emanation because they are all copper-based.
10. **B.** By removing the security set identifier or SSID, the wireless access point will be more secure and will be tougher for wardrivers to access that network. Of course, no new clients can connect to the wireless access point. MAC filtering, WPA, and firewalls are all components that increase the security of a wireless access point.

11. **A.** By shielding the network switch, we hope to deflect any interference from the air conditioning system. Another option would be to move the network switch to another location.
12. **B.** Shielded twisted pair is the most secure type of cabling listed. It adds an aluminum sheath around the wires that can help mitigate data emanation. By far, fiber optic would be the most secure type of cabling because it does not suffer from data emanation because the medium is glass instead of copper.
13. **A.** WEP 64-bit is the least secure type of wireless encryption listed in the possible answers. The answers are listed in order from least secure to most secure.
14. **B.** Bluesnarfing is the unauthorized access of information from a Bluetooth device, for example, calendar information, phonebook contacts, and so on. Bluejacking is the sending of unsolicited messages to Bluetooth-enabled devices. Blue privileges is not a valid answer, and if you answered the Blues Brothers, you should reread this entire chapter.
15. **A.** Privilege escalation is as the act of exploiting a bug or flaw in software to gain access to resources that normally would be protected. Chain of custody is the chronological paper trail used as evidence. A default account is an account such as admin set up by the manufacturer on a device; it usually has a blank or simple password. A backdoor is used in computer programs to bypass normal authentication and other security mechanisms that might be in place.

This chapter covers the following subjects:

- **Physical Security**—An organization's building is one of its greatest assets and as such it should be properly protected. This section details door access, biometric readers, access logs, and video surveillance to teach you some of the ways to protect the building, its contents, and its inhabitants and to ensure proper authentication when a person enters a building.
- **Authentication Models and Components**—You can use various methods and models to authenticate a person who wants to access computer networks and resources. This section delves into local authentication technologies such as Kerberos, LDAP, and 802.1X and remote authentication types, for instance RAS and VPN.

This chapter covers the CompTIA Security+ SY0-201 objectives 3.6, 3.7, 3.8, and 3.9.

CHAPTER 8

Physical Security and Authentication Models

I suppose that at times life on this planet is all about proving oneself. The world of security is no different. To gain access to an organization's building and ultimately to its resources, you must first prove yourself in a physical manner, providing indisputable evidence of your identity. Then, perhaps you can gain access by being authenticated, as long as the system authenticating you accepts your identification. Finally, if all this goes through properly, you should be authorized to specific resources such as data files, printers, and so on.

Some people use the terms identification, authentication, and authorization synonymously. Although this might be somewhat acceptable in everyday conversation, we need to delve a bit deeper and attempt to make some distinctions between the three.

- **Identification—**When a person is in a state of being identified. It can also be described as something that identifies a person such as an ID card.
- **Authentication—**When a person's identity is confirmed or verified through the use of a specific system. Authorization to specific resources cannot be accomplished without previous authentication of the user. This might also be referred to as access control, but generally authentication is considered to be a component of access control.
- **Authorization—**When a user is given permission to access certain resources. This can be accomplished only when authentication is complete.

The CompTIA Security+ exam concentrates most on the terms authentication and access control. This chapter focuses mostly on the authentication portion of access control. The rest of access control is covered in Chapter 9, "Access Control Methods and Models."

First, we cover the physical ways that a person can be authenticated. Then, we move on to ways that a person can be authenticated to a computer network, whether they are attempting to connect locally (for example, on the LAN), or if they are connecting remotely (for example, via a VPN).

Authentication is required to gain access to a secure area of the building or to gain access to secure data. A person might authenticate themselves in one of several ways depending on the authentication scheme used, by presenting one of the following:

- **Something the user knows—**Such as a password or pin
- **Something the user has—**Such as a smartcard or ID card
- **Something the user is—**Such as a thumbprint or retina scan or other biometric
- **Something the user does—**Such as a signature or voice recognition

Where a person is will also affect the authentication process. In this chapter, we cover local and remote types of authentication methods.

Another term you might hear in your travels is *identity proofing*, which is an initial validation of an identity. For example, if employees working for the government tried to enter a restricted building, the first thing they would do is show their ID. A guard or similar person would then do an initial check of that ID. Additional authentication systems would undoubtedly ensue. Identity proofing is also when an entity validates the identity of a person applying for a certain credential with that entity. It could be used for anonymous access as well.

As you go through this chapter and read about the following physical and logical authentication technologies, try to remember this introduction and apply these concepts to each of those authentication types.

Foundation Topics

Physical Security

To control access, physical security can be considered the first line of defense, sort of like a firewall is the first line of defense for a network. Implementing physical access security methods should be a top priority for an organization. Unfortunately, securing physical access to the organization's building sometimes slumps to the bottom of the list. Or a system is employed, but it fails to mitigate risk properly. In some cases, the system is not maintained well. Proper building entrance access and secure access to physical equipment is vital. And anyone coming and going should be logged and surveyed. Let's discuss a few of the ways that we can secure physical access to an organization's building.

General Building and Server Room Security

Protecting an organization's building is an important step in general security. The more security a building has, the less you will have to depend on your authentication system. A building's perimeter should be surveyed for possible breaches; this includes all doors, windows, loading docks, and even the roof. The area around the building should be scanned for hiding places; if there are any they should be removed. The area surrounding the building should be well lit at night. Some companies may opt to use security guards and guard dogs. It is important that these are trained properly; usually an organization will enlist the services of a third party. Video surveillance can also be employed to track an individual's movements. Video cameras should be placed on the exterior perimeter of the building in an area hard to access, for example 12 feet or higher with no lateral or climbing access. The more hidden the cameras are the better. Video cameras can also be placed inside the building especially in secure areas such as executive offices, wiring closets, and server rooms, and research and development areas. Many organizations use closed circuit television (CCTV) but some will opt for a wired/wireless IP-based solution. Either way, the video stream may be watched and recorded, but it should not be broadcast. Video cameras are an excellent way of tracking user identities. Motion detectors are also common as part of a total alarm system. They are often infrared-based (set off by heat) or ultrasonic-based (set off by certain higher frequencies). We could go on and on about general building security, but this chapter focuses on authentication. Besides, I think you get the idea. If your organization is extremely concerned about building security, and doubts that it has the knowledge to protect the building and its contents properly, consider hiring a professional.

The server room is the lifeblood in today's organizations. If anything happens to the server room, the company could be in for a disaster. We talk more about how an organization can recover from disasters in Chapter 14, "Redundancy and Disaster Recovery," but the best policy is to try to avoid disasters before they happen. So there are some things you should think about when it comes to server room security. First, where is the server room to be placed? It's wise to avoid basements or any other areas that might be prone to water damage. Secondly, the room should be accessible only to authorized IT persons. This can be accomplished by using one of many door access systems. The room should also have video surveillance saved to a hard drive located in a different room of the building or stored off site. All devices and servers in the server room should have complex passwords that only the authorized IT personnel have knowledge of. Devices and servers should be physically locked down to prevent theft. We talk more about server room security and building security in Chapter 14 and Chapter 15, "Policies, Procedures, and People." However for now, door access is the number one way to stop intruders from getting into the building or server room. If the system is set up properly, the intruder cannot be authenticated. Let's talk about door access in a little more depth.

Door Access

Lock the door! Sounds so simple, yet it is often overlooked. As a person in charge of security for a small business or even a mid-sized business, you have to think about all type of security, including entrances to the building. Door locks are essential. When deciding on a locking system to use, you should take into account the type of area your building is in and the crime rate, and who will have authorized access to the building. If you purchase regular door locks that work with a key, it is recommended that you get two or three of them. The first one should be tested. Can you break in to it with a credit card, jeweler's screwdriver, or other tools? And a backup should always be on hand in case the current door lock gets jimmied in an attempt to force a break-in. Cipher locks are a decent solution when regular key locks are not enough, but you don't want to implement an electronic system. The cipher lock uses a punch code to lock the door and unlock it. Though it will have a relatively low amount of combinations, that they have to be attempted manually makes it difficult to get past them.

Of course, many companies get more technical with their door access systems. Electronic access control systems such as cardkey are common. These use scanning devices on each door used for access to the building. They read the cardkeys that you give out to employees and visitors. These cardkeys should be logged; it should be known exactly who has which key at all times. The whole system is guided by a cardkey controller. This controller should be placed in a wiring closet or in a server room, and that room should be locked as well (and protected by the cardkey system). Some companies implement separate cardkey systems for the server room and for the main entrances. Some systems use ID badges for identification and authentication to a building's entrance. They might have a magnetic stripe similar to a credit card, or they might have a barcode, or use an RFID chip. A key card door access system is another good practice for tracking user identities.

> **NOTE:** Hardware-based *security tokens* are physical devices given to authorized users to help with authentication. These devices might be attached to a keychain or are part of a card system. Hardware-based tokens might be used as part of the door access system or as something that gives access to an individual computer.

Another possibility is the smart card. The smart card falls into the category of "something a person has," and is known as a token. It's the size of a credit card and has an embedded chip that stores and transacts data for use in secure applications such as hotel guest room access, prepaid phone services, and more. Smart cards have multiple applications, one of which is to authenticate users by swiping the device against a scanner, thus securing a computer or a computer room. It might also be used as part of a multifactor authentication scheme in which there is a combination of username/password (or PIN) and a smart card. Advanced smart cards have specialized cryptographic hardware that uses algorithms such as RSA and 3DES but will generally use private keys to encrypt data. (More on encryption and these encryption types later in Chapter 12, "Encryption and Hashing Concepts.") A smart card might incorporate a processor or an RFID chip as well. A smart card security system will usually be composed of the smart card itself, smart card readers, and a back-office database that stores all the smart card access control lists and history.

Older technologies use proximity sensors, but this is not considered very secure today. However, the more complex the technology, the more it will cost. Quite often, in these situations, budgeting becomes more important to organizations than mitigating risk; and generally the amount of acceptable risk increases as the budget decreases. So, you will probably see proximity-based door access systems. HID (also known as HID Global) is an example of a company that offers various levels of door access control systems. Figure 8-1 shows an example of a proximity-based door access card.

To increase security of the entrances of the building, some organizations implement *mantraps*, which is an area between two doorways, meant to hold people until they are identified and authenticated. This might be coupled with security guards, video surveillance, multifactor authentication, and sign-in logs. The main purpose of a physical access log or sign-in log is to show who entered the facility and when.

Door access systems are considered by many to be the weakest link in an enterprise. This can be taken to the next level by also incorporating biometrics, thus creating a different type of multifactor authentication scheme.

Biometric Readers

Biometrics is the science of recognizing humans based on one or more physical characteristics. Biometrics is used as a form of authentication and access control. It is also used to identify persons that might be under surveillance.

Figure 8-1 Example of a Proximity-Based Door Access Card

Biometrics falls into the category of "something a person is." Examples of bodily characteristics that are measured include fingerprints, retinal patterns, iris patterns, and even bone structure. Biometric readers, for example fingerprint scanners, are becoming more common in door access systems and on laptops or as USB devices. Biometric information can also be incorporated into smart card technology. An example of a biometric door access system is Suprema, which has various levels of access systems including some that incorporate smart cards and biometrics, together forming a multifactor authentication system. One example of biometric hardware for a local computer is the Microsoft Fingerprint Scanner, which is USB-based.

Biometrics can be seen in many movies and TV shows. However, many biometric systems over the past decade have been easily compromised. It has only been of late that readily available biometric systems have started to live up to the hype. Thorough investigation and testing of a biometric system is necessary before purchase and installation. In addition, it should be used in a multifactor authentication scheme. The more factors the better, as long as your users can handle it. (You would be surprised what a little bit of training can do.) Voice recognition software has made great leaps and bounds since the turn of the millennium. A combination of biometrics, voice recognition, and pin access would make for an excellent three-factor authentication system. But as always, only if you can get it through budgeting!

Authentication Models and Components

Now that we've covered some physical authentication methods, let's move into authentication models, components and technologies used to grant or deny access to operating systems and computer networks.

The first thing a security administrator should do is plan what type of authentication model they will use. Then, consider what type of authentication technology and how many factors of authentication will be implemented. Also for consideration is how the authentication system will be monitored and logged. Getting more into the specifics, will only local authentication be necessary? Or will remote authentication also be needed? And which type of technology should be utilized? Will it be Windows-based or a third-party solution? Let's discuss these concepts now and give some different examples of the possible solutions you can implement.

Authentication Models

A lot of small businesses and even some midsize businesses often have one type of authentication to gain access to a computer network—the username and password. In today's security conscious world, this is not enough for the average organization. Some companies share passwords or fail to enforce password complexity. In addition password cracking, programs are becoming more and more powerful and work much more quickly than they did just five years ago, making the username and password authentication scheme limiting. Not to say that it shouldn't be used but perhaps it should be enforced, enhanced, and integrated with other technologies.

Because of the limitations of a single type of authentication such as username and password, organizations will sometimes use multiple factors of authentication. *Multifactor authentication* is when two or more types of authentication are used when dealing with user access control. An example of multifactor authentication would be when a user needs to sign in with a username and password and swipe some type of smart card or use some other type of physical token at the same time. Adding factors of authentication makes it more difficult for a malicious person to gain access to a computer network or an individual computer system. Sometimes an organization uses three factors of authentication; perhaps a smartcard, biometrics, and a username/password. The disadvantages of a multifactor authentication scheme are that users need to remember more information and remember to bring more identification with them, and more IT costs and more administration will be involved.

Some organizations have several or more computer systems that an individual user might need access to. By default, each of these systems will have a separate login. It can be difficult for users to remember the various logins. *Single sign-on (SSO)* is when a user can log in once but gain access to multiple systems without being asked to log in again. This is complemented by single sign-off, which is basically the reverse; logging off signs a person off of multiple systems. Single sign-on is meant to reduce password fatigue, or password chaos, which is when a person can become confused and possibly even disoriented when having to login with several different usernames and passwords. It is also meant to reduce IT help desk calls and password resets. By implementing a more centralized authentication scheme such as single sign-on, many companies have reduced IT costs significantly. If implemented properly, single sign-on can also reduce phishing. In large networks and enterprise scenarios, it might not be possible for users to have a single sign-on, and in these cases it might be referred to as *reduced* sign-on. Single sign-on can be Kerberos-based, integrated with Windows authentication, or token- or smart card-based.

Whatever the type of authentication scheme used, it needs to be monitored periodically to make sure that it's working properly. The system should block people who cannot furnish proper identification and should allow access to people who do have proper identification. Sometimes there are failures in which an authentication system will improperly authenticate people. A few examples of these include the following:

- **False positive—**This is when a system authenticates a user who should not be allowed access to the system. This is also known as a Type I error.
- **False negative—**This is when a system denies a user who actually should be allowed access to the system. This is known as a Type II error.

The previous two examples are the ones you should know for the exam. Other terminology used when dealing with authentication systems includes true positive, which is when legitimate persons are authenticated properly and given access to the system, and true negative, which is when illegitimate persons are denied access as they should be. Both of these are proper functions so they usually don't come up as a conversation piece.

The type of authentication technology used will factor into the amount of false positives and false negatives that occur in any authentication scheme. Let's talk about some of those authentication technologies now.

Localized Authentication Technologies

There are several types of technologies for authenticating a user to a local area network. Examples that are software-based including LDAP and Kerberos, whereas an example that includes physical characteristics would be 802.1X. Keep in mind that there is a gray area between localized and remote authentication technologies. I've placed each technology in the category that it is used the most commonly.

During this section and the next one, we mention several encryption concepts that work with the various authentication technologies. These encryption concepts and protocols will be covered in detail in Chapter 12 and Chapter 13, "PKI and Encryption Protocols."

802.1X and EAP

802.1X is an IEEE standard that defines port-based Network Access Control (PNAC). Not to be confused with 802.*11*x WLAN standards, *802.1X* is a Data Link Layer authentication technology used to connect hosts to a LAN or WLAN. It all starts with the central connecting device such as a switch or wireless access point. These devices must first enable 802.1X connections; they must have the 802.1X protocol (and supporting protocols) installed. Vendors that offer 802.1X-compliant devices (for example switches and wireless access points) include Cisco, Symbol, and Intel. Next, the client computer needs to have an operating system, or additional software, that supports 802.1X. The client computer is known as the supplicant. Examples of operating systems that support 802.1X include Windows XP, Windows Vista, and Windows 7, though each comes with its own set of advantages and disadvantages. Mac OS X offers support as well, and Linux computers can use Open1X to enable client access to networks that require 802.1X authentication.

802.1X encapsulates the *Extensible Authentication Protocol (EAP)* over wired or wireless connections. EAP is not an authentication mechanism in itself, but instead defines message formats. 802.1X is the authentication mechanism and defines how EAP is encapsulated within messages. An example of an 802.1X-enabled network adapter is shown in Figure 8-2. In the figure, you can see that 802.1X has been checked, and that the type of network authentication method for 802.1X is EAP.

Key Topic

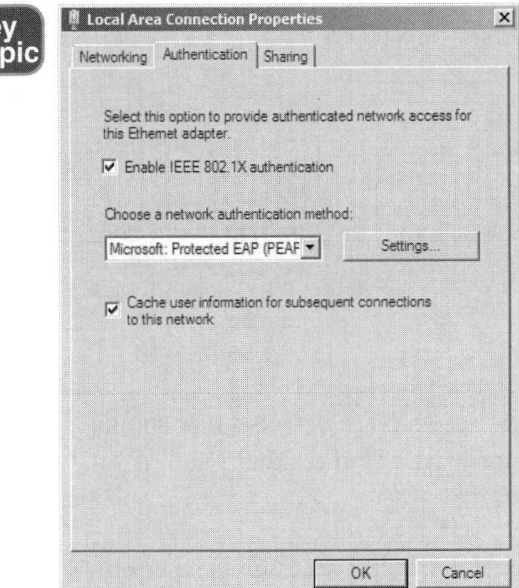

Figure 8-2 Example of an 802.1X-Enabled Network Adapter in Windows Vista

NOTE: 802.1X can be enabled in Windows by accessing the Local Area Connection Properties page.

Lab 1 in the "Hands-On Labs" section shows how to enable 802.1X on a network adapter.

Following are three components to an 802.1X connection:

- **Supplicant**—A software client running on a workstation
- **Authenticator**—A wireless access point or switch
- **Authentication server**—An authentication database, most likely a RADIUS server

The typical 802.1X authentication procedure has four steps. The components used in these steps are illustrated in Figure 8-3.

Key Topic

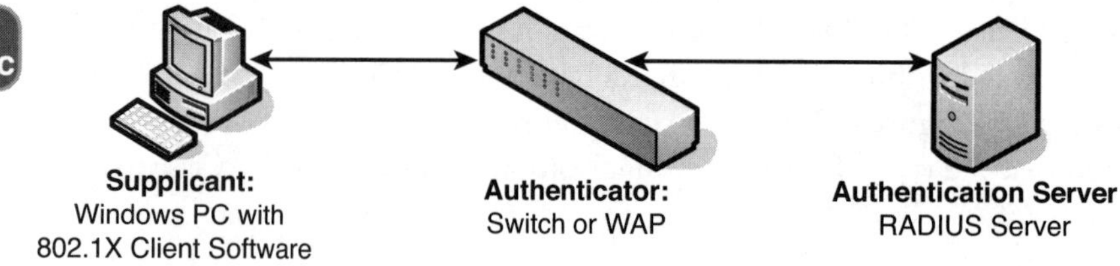

Figure 8-3 Components of a Typical 802.1X Authentication Procedure

NOTE: 802.1X authentication components include a supplicant, authenticator, and authentication server.

Step 1. **Initialization**—If a switch or wireless access point detects a new supplicant, the port connection enables port 802.1X traffic; other types of traffic are dropped.

Step 2. **Initiation**—The authenticator (switch or wireless access point) periodically sends EAP requests to a MAC address on the network. The supplicant listens for this address and sends an EAP response that might include a user ID or other similar information. The authenticator encapsulates this response and sends it to the authentication server.

Step 3. **Negotiation**—The authentication server then sends a reply to the authenticator. The authentication server specifies which EAP method to use. (these are listed next.) Then the authenticator transmits that request to the supplicant.

Step 4. **Authentication**—If the supplicant and the authentication server agree on an EAP method, the two transmit until there is either success or failure to authenticate the supplicant computer.

Following are several types of EAP authentication:

- **EAP-MD5**—This is a challenge-based authentication providing basic EAP support. It enables only one-way authentication and not mutual authentication.
- **EAP-TLS**—This version uses Transport Layer Security, which is a certificate-based system that does enable mutual authentication. This does not work well in enterprise scenarios because certificates must be configured or managed on the client- and server side.
- **EAP-TTLS**—This version is Tunneled Transport Layer Security and is basically the same as TLS except that it is done through an encrypted channel, and it requires only server-side certificates.
- **EAP-FAST**—This uses a protected access credential instead of a certificate to achieve mutual authentication. FAST stands for flexible authentication via secure tunneling.
- **PEAP**—This is the protected extensible authentication protocol. It competes with TTLS and includes legacy password-based protocols.

Cisco also created a proprietary protocol called LEAP (Lightweight EAP), and it is just that—proprietary. To use LEAP, you must have a Cisco device such as an Aironet WAP or Catalyst switch, or another vendor's device that complies with the Cisco Compatible Extensions program. Then you must download a third-party client on Windows computers to connect to the Cisco device. Most WLAN vendors offer an 802.1X LEAP download for their wireless network adapters.

Although 802.1X is often used for port-based network access control on the LAN, especially VLANs, it can also be used with VPNs as a way of remote authentication. Central connecting devices such as switches and wireless access points remain the same, but on the client side 802.1X would need to be configured on a VPN adapter, instead of a network adapter.

Many vendors, such as Intel and Cisco, refer to 802.1X with a lowercase x; however, the IEEE displays this on its website with an uppercase X. The protocol was originally defined in 2001 (802.1X-2001) and has been redefined in 2004 and 2010 (802.1X-2004 and 802.1X-2010, respectively). There are several links to more information about 802.1X at the end of the chapter.

LDAP

The *Lightweight Directory Access Protocol (LDAP)* is an Application Layer protocol used for accessing and modifying directory services data. It is part of the TCP/IP suite. Originally used in WAN connections, it has developed over time into a protocol commonly used by services such as Microsoft Active Directory on Windows Server domain controllers. LDAP acts as the protocol that controls the directory service. This is the service that organizes the users, computers, and other objects within the Active Directory. An example of the Active Directory is shown in Figure 8-4. Note the list of users (known as objects of the Active Directory) from the **Users** folder that is highlighted and other folders such as **Computers** that house other objects.

Key Topic

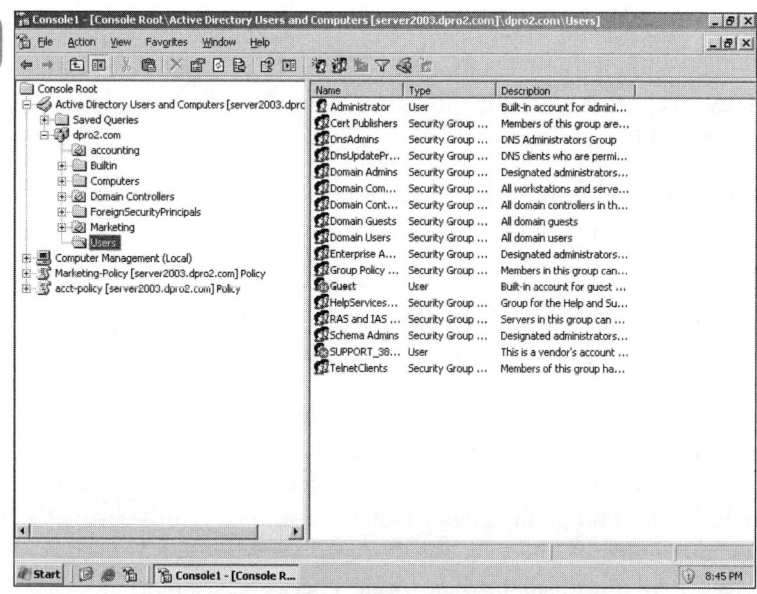

Figure 8-4 Example of Active Directory Showing User Objects

A Microsoft server that has Active Directory and LDAP running will have inbound port 389 open by default. To protect Active Directory from being tampered with, Secure LDAP can be used, which brings into play SSL (Secure Sockets Layer) on top of LDAP and uses inbound port 636 by default. Other implementations of LDAP use TLS (Transport Layer Security) over LDAP.

NOTE: LDAP uses port 389 and is most commonly found in Windows domain controllers.

Kerberos and Mutual Authentication

Kerberos is an authentication protocol designed at MIT that enables computers to prove their identity to each other in a secure manner. It is used most often in a client-server environment; the client and the server both verify each other's identity. This is known as two-way authentication or *mutual authentication*. Often, Kerberos protects a network server from illegitimate login attempts, just as the mythological three-headed guard dog of the same name (also known as Cerberus) guards Hades.

A common implementation of Kerberos occurs when a user logs on to a Microsoft domain. (Of course, I am not saying that Microsoft domains are analogous to Hades!) The domain controller in the Microsoft domain is known as the KDC or key distribution center. This server works with *tickets* that prove the identity of users. The KDC is composed of two logical parts: the authentication server and the ticket granting server. Basically, a client computer attempts to authenticate itself to the authentication server portion of the KDC. When done, the client receives a ticket. This is actually a ticket to get other tickets. The client uses this preliminary ticket to demonstrate its identity to a ticket granting server in the hopes of ultimately getting access to a service, for example, making a connection to the Active Directory of a domain controller.

The domain controller running Kerberos will have inbound port 88 open to the service log on requests from clients. Figure 8-5 shows a **netstat –an** command run on a Windows Server 2003 that has been promoted to a domain controller. It points out port 88 (used by Kerberos) and port 389 (used by LDAP) on the same domain controller.

NOTE: Kerberos uses Port 88. Microsoft domain controllers use this protocol.

Kerberos is designed to protect against replay attacks and eavesdropping. One of the drawbacks of Kerberos is that it relies on a centralized server such as a domain controller. This can be a single point of failure. To alleviate this problem, secondary and tertiary domain controllers can be installed that keep a copy of the Active Directory and are available with no downtime in the case the first domain controller fails. Another possible issue is one of synchronicity. Time between the clients and the domain controller must be synchronized for Kerberos to work properly. If for some reason a client attempting to connect to a domain controller becomes desynchronized, it cannot complete the Kerberos authentication, and as an end result the user cannot log on to the domain. This can be fixed by logging on to the affected client locally and synchronizing the client's time to the domain controller by using the **net time** command. For example, to synchronize to the domain controller in Figure 8-5, the command would be

```
net time \\10.254.254.252 /set.
```

Key Topic

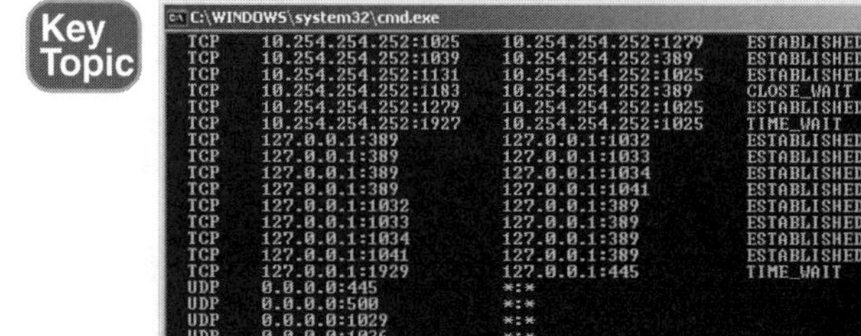

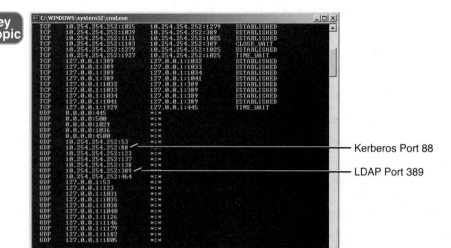

Figure 8-5 Results of the **netstat—an** Command on a Windows Server 2003

Afterward, the client should be able to connect to the domain. We revisit Kerberos and how it makes use of encryption keys in Chapter 12.

Terminal Services

Terminal Services enable the remote control of Windows servers from a client computer. This client computer could be on the LAN or out on the Internet; so the term "remote" is used loosely. It can also be used to enable clients access to specific applications.

The Terminal Services application is in charge of authenticating terminal users and will do so if the user has been configured properly. For example, in Windows Server 2003, users in question must have Remote Access permissions enabled within the properties of their account. Terminal Services authentication integrates directly with standard Windows Server authentication.

The terminal server will have inbound port 3389 open to accept connections from remote clients. Their sessions are stored at the terminal server, enabling for disconnections and later reuse. Terminal Services is now referred to as Remote Desktop Services in newer versions of Windows.

Remote Authentication Technologies

Even more important than authenticating local users is authenticating remote users. The chances of illegitimate connections increase when you allow remote users to connect to your network. Examples of remote authentication technologies include RAS, VPN, RADIUS, TACACS, and CHAP. Let's discuss these now.

Remote Access Service

Remote Access Service (RAS) began as a service that enabled dial-up connections from remote clients. Nowadays, more and more remote connections are made with high-speed Internet technologies such as cable Internet, DSL, and FIOS. But we can't discount the dial-up connection. It is used in certain areas where other Internet connections are not available and is still used as a fail-safe in many network operation centers and server rooms to take control of networking equipment.

One of the best things you can do to secure a RAS server is to deny access to individuals who don't require it. Even if the user or user group is set to "not configured," it is wise to specifically deny them access. Allow access to only those users who need it. And monitor the logs that list who connect on a daily basis. If there are any unknowns, investigate immediately. Be sure to update the permissions list often in the case that a remote user is terminated or otherwise leaves the organization.

The next most important security precaution is to set up RAS authentication. One secure way is to use the *challenge-handshake authentication protocol (CHAP)*., which is an authentication scheme used by the Point-to-Point Protocol (PPP), which is the standard for dial-up connections. It uses a challenge-response mechanism with one-way encryption. Due to this, it is not capable of mutual authentication in the way that Kerberos is, for example. CHAP uses DES and MD5 encryption types which we cover in Chapter 12. Microsoft developed its own version of CHAP known as MS-CHAP, an example of this is shown in Figure 8-6. The figure shows the Advanced Security Settings dialog box of a dial-up connection. Notice that this particular configuration shows that encryption is required, and that the only protocol allowed is MS-CHAP V2. Of course, the RAS server will have to be configured to accept MS-CHAP connections as well. You also have the option to enable EAP for the dial-up connection. Other RAS authentication protocols include SPAP, which is of lesser security, and PAP, which sends usernames and passwords in clear text—obviously insecure and to be avoided.

NOTE: Use CHAP, MS-CHAP, or EAP for dial-up connections. Verify that it is configured properly on the RAS server and dial-up client to ensure a proper handshake.

The CHAP authentication scheme consists of several steps. It authenticates a user or a network host to entities such as Internet access providers. CHAP periodically verifies the identity of the client by using a three-way handshake. The verification is based on a shared secret. After the link has been established, the authenticator sends a challenge message to the peer. The encrypted results are compared, and finally the client is either authorized or denied access.

Key Topic

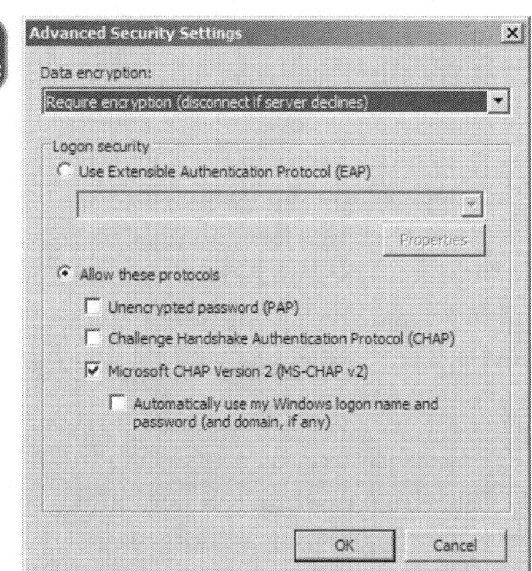

Figure 8-6 MS-CHAP Enabled on a Dial-Up Connection

The actual data transmitted in these RAS connections is encrypted as well. By default Microsoft RAS connections are encrypted by the RSA RC4 algorithm. More information on this can also be found in Chapter 12.

Now you might say, "But Dave, who cares about dial-up connections?" Well, there are two reasons that this is important. First, these protocols, authentication types, and encryption types are used in other technologies; this is the basis for those systems. Second, as I mentioned before, some organizations still use the dial-up connection—for remote users or for administrative purposes. And hey, don't downplay the dial-up connection. Old-school dial-up guys used to tweak the connection to the point where it was as fast as some DSL versions and as reliable. So there are going to be die-hards out there as well.

However, RAS now has morphed into something that goes beyond just dial-up. VPN connections that use dial-up, cable Internet, DSL, and so on are all considered remote access.

Virtual Private Networks

A *virtual private network (VPN)* is a connection between two or more computers or devices not on the same private network. Generally, VPNs use the Internet to connect one host to another. It is desirable that only proper users and data sessions make their way to a VPN device; because of this, data encapsulation and encryption are used. A "tunnel' is created through any LANs and WANs that might intervene; this tunnel connects the two VPN devices together. Every time a new session is initiated, a new tunnel is created, which makes the connection secure.

VPNs normally use one of two tunneling protocols, as shown in Table 8-1.

Table 8-1 VPN Tunneling Protocols

Tunneling Protocol	Description	Port Used
Point-to-Point Tunneling Protocol (PPTP)	This is the more commonly used tunneling protocol (although that is quickly changing) but the less secure solution of the two listed here. PPTP generally includes security mechanisms and no additional software or protocols need to be loaded. A VPN device or server must have inbound port 1723 open to enable incoming PPTP connections. PPTP works within the Point-to-Point Protocol (PPP) that is also used for dial-up connections, as we mentioned earlier.	Port 1723
Layer 2 Tunneling Protocol (L2TP)	This is quickly gaining popularity due to the inclusion of IPSec as its security protocol. Although this is a separate protocol and L2TP doesn't have any inherent security, L2TP will be considered the more secure solution because IPSec is required in most L2TP implementations. A VPN device or server must have inbound port 1701 open to enable incoming L2TP connections.	Port 1701

PPTP and L2TP can cause a lot of havoc if the security settings are not configured properly on the client and the server side. This can cause errors; you can find a link to the list of these error codes at the end of the chapter in the "View Recommended Resources" section. We cover PPTP and L2TP encryption in Chapter 13.

Figure 8-7 shows an illustration of a VPN. Note that the VPN server is on one side of the cloud and the VPN client is on the other. It should be known that the VPN client will have a standard IP address to connect to its own LAN. However, it will receive a second IP address from the VPN server or a DHCP device. This second IP address works "inside" of the original IP address. So, the client computer will have two IP addresses; in essence, the VPN address is encapsulated within the logical IP address. As we mentioned before, dial-up authentication protocols such as CHAP are also used in other technologies; this is one of those examples. VPN adapters, regardless of the Internet connection used, can use MS-CHAP, as shown in the figure. To further increase authentication security, a separate RADIUS server can be used with the VPN server—we will talk more about RADIUS in the next section.

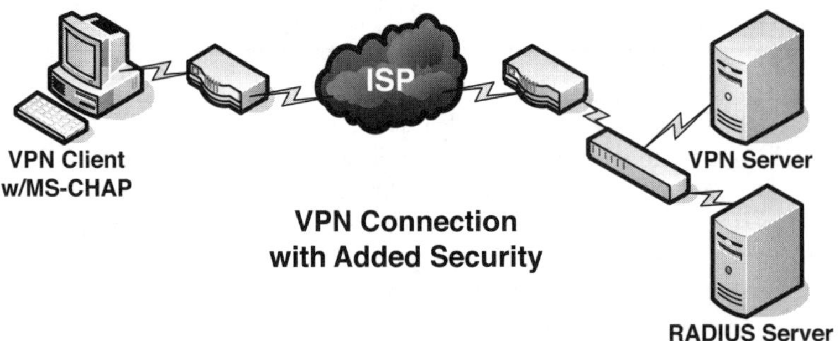

Figure 8-7 Illustration of a VPN

NOTE: VPNs use either PPTP (Port 1723) or L2TP (Port 1701) and can also incorporate CHAP on the client side and RADIUS servers for authentication.

A Microsoft VPN can be set up on a standard Windows Server by configuring Routing and Remote Access Service (RRAS). Remote access policies can be created from here that permit or deny access to groups of users for dial-in or VPN connections. An example of this is illustrated in Figure 8-8. Note the Remote Access Policies section within Server2003 in the MMC. By right-clicking this, you can create a new policy. The New Remote Access Policy Wizard window is open and is in the process of creating a policy for VPN connections.

NOTE: Remote access policies can be configured in the RRAS snap-in of Windows Server to permit or deny access to remote users and groups.

Of course, you can run a VPN locally as well, and some companies do. We do just that in Lab 2 in the "Hands-On Labs" section at the end of the chapter to demonstrate the setup of a working VPN.

RADIUS Versus TACACS

The *Remote Authentication Dial-In User Service (RADIUS)* provides centralized administration of dial-up, VPN, and wireless authentication and can be used with EAP and 802.1X. To set this up on a Windows Server, the Internet Authentication Service must be loaded; it is usually set up on a separate physical server. RADIUS is a client-server protocol that runs on the Application Layer of the OSI model.

RADIUS works with the AAA concept: It is used to **a**uthenticate users, **a**uthorize them to services, and **a**ccount for the usage of those services. RADIUS checks if the correct authentication scheme such as CHAP or EAP is used by connecting clients. RADIUS commonly uses port 1812 for authentication messages and port 1813 for accounting messages. These are the ports you should memorize for the exam. In rarer cases, it will use ports 1645 and 1646 for these messages, respectively.

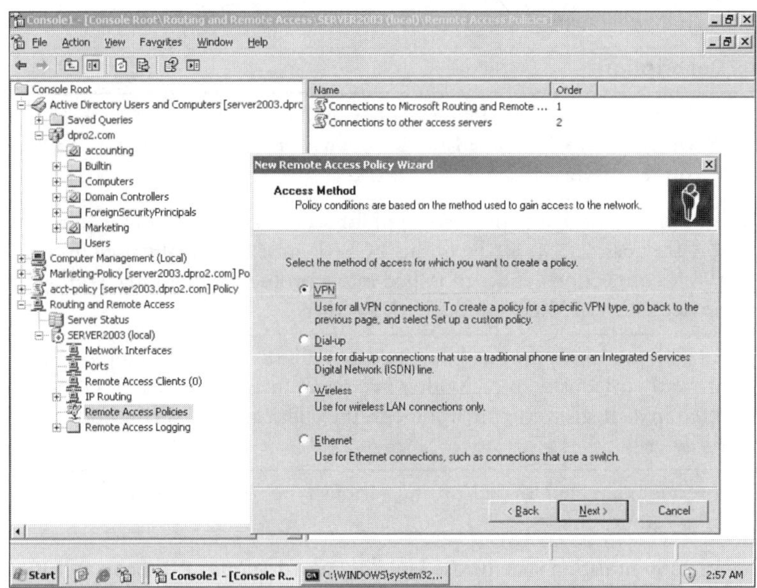

Figure 8-8 A RRAS VPN Policy on a Windows Server 2003

NOTE: In the section "Hands-On Labs," which appears at the end of this chapter, Lab 8-3 shows you how to set up a RADIUS server.

The *Terminal Access Controller Access-Control System (TACACS)* is one of the most confusing sounding acronyms ever. Now that we have reached the pinnacle of computer acronyms, let's really discuss what it is. TACACS is another remote authentication protocol used more often in UNIX networks. In UNIX, the TACACS service is known as the TACACS daemon. The newer and more commonly used implementation of TACACS is called TACACS+. It is not backward compatible with TACACS. TACACS+ was developed by Cisco and uses inbound port 49.

There are a few differences between RADIUS and TACACS+. RADIUS uses UDP as its Transport Layer protocol. TACACS+ uses TCP as its Transport Layer protocol, which is usually seen as a more reliable transport protocol. Also, RADIUS combines the authentication and authorization functions together when dealing with users; however, TACACS+ separates these two functions into two separate operations that introduce another layer of security. TACACS encrypts client-server dialogues whereas RADIUS does not. Finally, TACACS+ provides for more types of authentication requests than RADIUS.

Table 8-2 summarizes the local and remote authentication technologies we have covered thus far.

Table 8-2 Summary of Authentication Technologies

Authentication Type	Description
802.1X	An IEEE standard that defines port-based Network Access Control (PNAC). 802.1X is a Data Link Layer authentication technology used to connect devices to a LAN or WLAN.
LDAP	An Application Layer protocol used for accessing and modifying directory services data. It is part of the TCP/IP suite. Originally used in WAN connections, it has morphed into a protocol commonly used by services such as Microsoft Active Directory.
Kerberos	An authentication protocol designed at MIT that enables computers to prove their identity to each other in a secure manner. It is used most often in a client-server environment; the client and the server both verify each other's identity.
RAS	A service that enables dial-up and various types of VPN connections from remote clients.
CHAP	An authentication scheme used by the Point-to-Point Protocol (PPP) that is the standard for dial-up connections. It utilizes a challenge-response mechanism with one-way encryption.
RADIUS	Used to provide centralized administration of dial-up, VPN, and wireless authentication. It can be used with EAP and 802.1X.
TACACS	Another remote authentication protocol, similar to RADIUS, and used more often in UNIX networks.

Exam Preparation Tasks

Review Key Topics

Review the most important topics in the chapter, noted with the Key Topics icon in the outer margin of the page. Table 8-3 lists a reference of these key topics and the page numbers on which each is found.

Table 8-3 Key Topics for Chapter 8

Key Topic Element	Description	Page Number
Bulleted list	Authentication Types	214
Figure 8-2	Example of an 802.1X-Enabled Network Adapter in Windows Vista	221
Figure 8-3	Components of a Typical 802.1X Authentication Procedure	222
Figure 8-4	Example of Active Directory	224
Figure 8-5	Results of the **netstat –an** Command on a Windows Server 2003	226
Figure 8-6	MS-CHAP Enabled on a Dial-Up Connection	228
Table 8-1	VPN Tunneling Protocols	229
Table 8-2	Summary of Authentication Technologies	232

Complete Tables and Lists from Memory

Print a copy of Appendix A, "Memory Tables," (found on the DVD), or at least the section for this chapter, and complete the tables and lists from memory. Appendix B, "Memory Tables Answer Key," also on the DVD, includes completed tables and lists to check your work.

Define Key Terms

Define the following key terms from this chapter, and check your answers in the glossary:

identification, authentication, authorization, identity proofing, security tokens, multifactor authentication, biometrics, Mantrap, 802.1X, Extensible Authentication Protocol (EAP), single sign-on (SSO), false positive, false negative, Lightweight Directory Access Protocol (LDAP), Kerberos, mutual authentication, Tickets, Challenge-Handshake Authentication Protocol (CHAP), Remote Access

Service (RAS), virtual private network (VPN), Point-to-Point Tunneling Protocol (PPTP), Layer 2 Tunneling Protocol (L2TP), Remote Authentication Dial-In User Service (RADIUS), Terminal Access Controller Access-Control System (TACACS)

Hands-On Labs

Complete the following written step-by-step scenarios. After you finish (or if you do not have adequate equipment to complete the scenario), watch the corresponding video solution on the DVD.

If you have additional questions, feel free to post them at my website: www.davidlprowse.com in the Ask Dave forum. (Free registration is required to post on the website.)

Equipment Needed

A computer network including the following:

- Windows client computer (Windows Vista or Windows 7 preferred)
- Windows Server 2003 or 2008
- D-Link DIR-655 or similar router:
  - If you have access to an actual DIR-655, make sure that it is updated to the latest firmware. Then connect to it by opening a web browser and typing the IP address of the router in the URL field, for example, **192.168.0.1**. Next, at the login screen, type the password for the router, and click the **Log In** button. This should display the Device Information page. Start at this page for each of the three labs.
  - If you do not have access to an actual DIR-655, use the D-Link simulator located at http://support.dlink.com/Emulators/dir655/index.html. Then select the first option: **DIR-655 Device UI**. Next, at the login screen, click the **Log In** button. (No password is necessary.) This should display the Device Information page. Start at this page for each of the three labs.

Lab 8-1: Enabling 802.1X on a Network Adapter

In this lab, you turn on the 802.1X feature in Windows Vista. The steps are as follows:

Step 1. Open the Network and Sharing Center.

Step 2. Click the **Manage network connections** link. This displays the Network Connections window.

Step 3. Right-click the **Local Area Connection** and select **Properties**. This displays the Local Area Connection Properties window.

Step 4. Click the **Authentication** tab.

Step 5. Check the **Enable IEEE 802.1X authentication** checkbox.

Step 6. Select **Microsoft: Protected EAP (PEAP)** from the drop-down menu.

Step 7. Explore the additional settings by clicking the **Settings** button.

Watch the solution video in the "Hands-On Scenarios" section of the DVD.

Lab 8-2: Setting Up a VPN

In this lab, we demonstrate how to set up a VPN using a Windows Server 2008 as the VPN server and a Windows Vista computer as the client. Windows Server 2003 works in a similar fashion. The steps are as follows:

Step 1. Access the server.

Step 2. Open your MMC. If you don't have one, create one now and add the Server Manager and Computer Management snap-ins.

Step 3. If you use Windows Server 2008, you need to have the Network Policy and Access Services role installed within the Roles section of Server Manager. Windows Server 2003 does not need this.

Step 4. Add the RRAS snap-in.

A. Click **File**; then click **Add/Remove Snap-In**.

B. Scroll down to Routing and Remote Access and click **Add**.

C. Click **OK**.

Step 5. Add the local server into the RRAS snap-in.

A. Expand the newly added Routing and Remote Access snap-in, right-click **Server Status**, and click **Add Server**.

B. Select the **This computer** radio button and click **OK**.

Step 6. Configure RRAS.

A. Right-click the server name.

B. Select **Configure and Enable Routing and Remote Access**.

C. Click **Next** for the wizard intro.

D. Select the **Custom configuration** radio button, and click **Next**.

E. Check **VPN access**, and click **Next**.

F. Click **Finish**.

Step 7. Expand the server. Verify that there is a green arrow pointing up. This indicates that the service is indeed started. If it is not, check the service status within Computer Management.

Step 8. Check the ports used on the server by accessing the Command Prompt and typing **netstat –an**.

Step 9. Verify that the proper accounts are allowed dial-in and VPN access.

A. Navigate to **Computer Management > System Tools > Local Users and Groups > Users**.

B. Right-click the **Administrator** account, and select **Properties**. You can use another account (or accounts) if you want. Just remember to connect as that account from the VPN client later.

C. Click the **Dial-in** tab.

D. Select the **Allow Access** radio button and click **OK**. Do this for any other accounts that you want to have access to the VPN server.

Step 10. Configure the VPN adapter on Windows Vista. (Other operating systems such as Windows 7 will be similar in navigation and configuration.)

A. Access the Network and Sharing Center.

B. Click the **Set up a connection or network** link.

C. Select **Connect to a workplace** and click **Next**.

D. Select **Use my Internet connection (VPN)**.

E. Type the IP address of the VPN server in the **Internet address:** field. For example, 10.254.254.252.

F. Give a name to the VPN connection in the **Destination name:** field and click **Next**.

G. Type the username and password of the account on the VPN server that has VPN access enabled. Then click **Connect**.

Step 11. Check the VPN adapter's IP configuration by accessing the Command Prompt and typing **ipconfig/all**. Note the VPN adapter IP address and the Local Area Connection IP address.

Keep the VPN adapter so that you can use it in Lab 3.

Watch the solution video in the "Hands-On Scenarios" section of the DVD.

Lab 8-3: Setting Up a RADIUS Server

In this lab, we demonstrate how to set up a RADIUS server using a Windows Server 2003. We also show how to point to a RADIUS server from a

SOHO 4-port router. Finally, we show some different authentication techniques on the server and the client side. The steps are as follows:

Step 1. Access the server and install the Internet Authentication Service.

A. Click **Start > Control Panel > Add or Remove Programs**.

B. Click **Add/Remove Windows Components**.

C. Scroll down to Networking Services and click **Details**.

D. Check **Internet Authentication Service** and click **OK**.

E. Click **Next**. This installs the service. Click **Finish** when complete.

Step 2. Open the MMC and add the Internet Authentication Service snap-in.

Step 3. Add a RADIUS client.

A. Expand the Internet Authentication Service snap-in, right-click **RADIUS Clients** and click **New RADIUS client**.

B. Type a friendly name for the client and the IP address of the computer that will be connecting to the RADIUS server. Then click **Next**.

C. Select **RADIUS Standard** for the client-vendor attribute.

D. Create a pass-phrase and confirm it. Click **Finish**.

Step 4. Create a Remote Access Policy.

A. Right-click **Remote Access Policies** and select **New Remote Access Policy**.

B. Click **Next** for the wizard.

C. Use the wizard to set up the policy and name the policy. Then click **Next**.

D. Select the **VPN** radio button. Then click **Next**.

E. Select the **User** radio button. Then click **Next**.

F. Checkmark the **Extensible Authentication Protocol (EAP)** and select **Protected EAP (PEAP)** as the type. Then click **Next**.

G. Leave the default encryption options. Then click **Next**.

H. Click **Finish** to complete the configuration.

Step 5. Configure the Windows Vista client.

A. Right-click the client computer's VPN adapter and select **Properties**.

B. Click the **Security** tab.

C. Select the **Advanced (custom settings)** radio button. Then click the **Settings** button.

D. Click the **Use Extensible Authentication Protocol (EAP)**.

E. Click the drop-down menu, and select **Protected EAP (PEAP)**.

F. Click **OK** for all dialog boxes.

Step 6. Configure a SOHO 4-port router to point to a VPN server and a RADIUS server.

A. Log in to the DIR-655 router. If you do not have an actual device, use the emulator online at the link given in the beginning of this lab document.

B. Click the **SETUP** link.

C. Click the **Manual Internet Connection Setup** button.

D. In the My Internet Connection Is drop down menu, select **PPTP**.

E. Add the IP address of the VPN server in the **PPTP Server IP Address** field.

F. Click the **SETUP** link.

G. Click the **Wireless Settings** link on the left side.

H. Click the **Manual Wireless Network Setup** button.

I. Enable wireless.

J. Scroll down, and in the Security Mode drop-down menu, select **WPA-Enterprise**.

K. Scroll down further, and type the IP address of the RADIUS server into the **RADIUS Server IP Address** field.

L. Check the port used. By default, this is **1812**. but if the server is using a different port, you have to change it.

Watch the solution video in the "Hands-On Scenarios" section of the DVD.

View Recommended Resources

Recommended reading:

- Harper, Jim. "Identity Crisis: How Identification is Overused and Misunderstood." Cato Institute 2006.

Internet links:

- HID Door Access Control Systems: www.hidglobal.com/products/readers.php

802.1X links:

- Official IEEE 802.1X PDF download: http://standards.ieee.org/getieee802/download/802.1X-2004.pdf
- Intel: Wireless Networking 802.1X Overview: www.intel.com/support/wireless/wlan/sb/cs-008413.htm
- Cisco: Deploying 802.1X Technology with Cisco Integrated Service Routers: www.cisco.com/en/US/prod/collateral/routers/ps5853/prod_white_paper0900aecd806c6d65.html
- Open1X: http://open1x.sourceforge.net/

LDAP links:

- IETF Technical Specifications: http://tools.ietf.org/html/rfc4510
- Open LDAP: www.openldap.org/
- Microsoft: How to enable LDAP over SSL: http://support.microsoft.com/kb/321051

Kerberos links:

- Kerberos Explained: http://technet.microsoft.com/en-us/library/bb742516.aspx
- Kerberos: The Network Authentication Protocol: http://web.mit.edu/Kerberos/
- Kerberos Consortium: www.kerberos.org/

RAS links:

- RAS Security: http://technet.microsoft.com/en-us/library/cc751466.aspx
- How to Enforce a Remote Access Policy in Windows Server: http://support.microsoft.com/kb/313082
- List of Microsoft dial-up and VPN error codes: http://support.microsoft.com/kb/824864

RADIUS and TACACS links:

- Microsoft RADIUS Protocol Security and Best Practices: http://technet.microsoft.com/en-us/library/bb742489.aspx
- Free GNU RADIUS: www.gnu.org/software/radius/
- http://freeradius.org/
- TACACS+ and RADIUS Comparison: www.cisco.com/en/US/tech/tk59/technologies_tech_note09186a0080094e99.shtml

Answer Review Questions

Answer the following review questions. You can find the answers at the end of this chapter.

1. Which of the following is the verification of a person's identity?
   - A. Authorization
   - B. Accountability
   - C. Authentication
   - D. Password

2. Which of the following would fall into the category of "something a person is"?
   - A. Passwords
   - B. Passphrases
   - C. Fingerprints
   - D. Smart Cards

3. Which of the following are good practices for tracking user identities? (Select the two best answers.)
   - A. Video cameras
   - B. Key card door access systems
   - C. Sign-in sheets
   - D. Security guards

4. What are two examples of common single sign-on authentication configurations? (Select the two best answers.)
   - A. Biometrics-based
   - B. Multifactor authentication
   - C. Kerberos-based
   - D. Smart card-based

5. Which of the following is an example of two factor authentication?
   - A. L2TP and IPSec
   - B. Username and password
   - C. Thumb print and key card
   - D. Client and server

6. What is the main purpose of a physical access log?

A. To enable authorized employee access

B. To show who exited the facility

C. To show who entered the facility

D. To prevent unauthorized employee access

7. Which of the following is not a common criteria when authenticating users?

A. Something you do

B. Something you are

C. Something you know

D. Something you like

8. Of the following, what two authentication mechanisms require something you physically possess? (Select the two best answers.)

A. Smartcard

B. Certificate

C. USB flash drive

D. Username and password

9. Which of the following is the final step a user needs to take before that user can access domain resources?

A. Verification

B. Validation

C. Authorization

D. Authentication

10. To gain access to your network, users must provide a thumbprint and a username and password. What type of authentication model is this?

A. Biometrics

B. Domain logon

C. Multifactor

D. Single sign-on

11. The IT director has asked you to set up an authentication model in which users can enter their credentials one time, yet still access multiple server resources. What type of authentication model should you implement?

A. Smartcard and biometrics

B. Three factor authentication

C. SSO

D. VPN

12. Which of the following about authentication is false?

A. RADIUS is a client/server system that provides authentication, authorization, and accounting services.

B. PAP is insecure because usernames and passwords are sent as clear text.

C. MS-CHAPv1 is capable of mutual authentication of the client and server.

D. CHAP is more secure than PAP because it encrypts usernames and passwords.

13. What types of technologies are used by external motion detectors? (Select the two best answers.)

A. Infrared

B. RFID

C. Gamma rays

D. Ultrasonic

14. In a secure environment, which authentication mechanism performs better?

A. RADIUS because it is a remote access authentication service.

B. RADIUS because it encrypts client/server passwords.

C. TACACS because it is a remote access authentication service.

D. TACACS because it encrypts client/server negotiation dialogues.

15. Which port number does the protocol LDAP use when it is secured?

A. 389

B. 443

C. 636

D. 3389

16. Which of the following results occurs when a biometric system identifies a legitimate user as unauthorized?

A. False rejection

B. False positive

C. False negative

D. False exception

17. Of the following, which is not a logical method of access control?

A. Username/password

B. Access control lists

C. Biometrics

D. Software-based policy

18. Which of the following permits or denies access to resources through the use of ports?

A. Hub

B. 802.11n

C. 802.11x

D. 802.1X

19. Your data center has highly critical information. Because of this you want to improve upon physical security. The data center already has a video surveillance system. What else can you add to increase physical security? (Select the two best answers.)

A. A software-based token system

B. Access control lists

C. A man trap

D. Biometrics

20. Which authentication method completes the following in order: Logon request, encrypts value response, server, challenge, compare encrypts results, and authorize or fail referred to?

A. Security tokens

B. Certificates

C. Kerberos

D. CHAP

21. What does a virtual private network use to connect one remote host to another? (Select the best answer.)

A. Modem

B. Network adapter

C. Internet

D. Cell phone

22. Two items are needed before a user can be given access to the network. What are these two items? (Select the two best answers.)

A. Authentication and authorization

B. Authorization and identification

C. Identification and authentication

D. Password and authentication

23. Kerberos uses which of the following? (Select the two best answers.)

A. Ticket distribution service

B. The Faraday cage

C. Port 389

D. Authentication service

24. Which of the following authentication systems make use of a Key Distribution Center?

A. Security tokens

B. CHAP

C. Kerberos

D. Certificates

25. Of the following, which best describes the difference between RADIUS and TACACS?

A. RADIUS is a remote access authentication service.

B. RADIUS separates authentication, authorization, and auditing capabilities.

C. TACACS is a remote access authentication service.

D. TACACS separates authentication, authorization, and auditing capabilities.

Answers and Explanations

1. C. Authentication is the verification of a person's identity. Authorization to specific resources cannot be accomplished without previous authentication of the user.

2. C. Fingerprints are an example of something a person is. The process of measuring that characteristic is known as biometrics.

3. A and B. Video cameras enable a person to view and visually identify users as they enter and traverse through a building. Key card access systems can be configured to identify a person as well, as long as the right person is carrying the key card!

4. **C and D.** Kerberos and smart card setups are common single sign-on configurations.
5. **C.** Two-factor authentication (or dual-factor) means that two pieces of identity are needed prior to authentication. A thumb print and key card would fall into this category. L2TP and IPSec are protocols used to connect through a VPN, which by default require only a username and password. Username and password is considered one-factor authentication. There is no client and server authentication model.
6. **C.** A physical access log's main purpose is to show who entered the facility and when. Different access control and authentication models will be used to permit or prevent employee access.
7. **D.** Common criteria when authenticating users includes something you do, something you are, something you know, and something you have. A person's likes and dislikes are not common criteria; although, they may be asked as secondary questions when logging into a system.
8. **A and C.** Two of the authentication mechanisms that require something you physically possess include smart cards and USB flash drives. Key fobs and card keys would also be part of this category. Certificates are granted from a server and are stored on a computer as software. The username/password mechanism is a common authentication scheme but they are something that you type and not something that you physically possess.
9. **C.** Before a user can gain access to domain resources, the final step is to be authorized to those resources. Previously the user should have provided identification to be authenticated.
10. **C.** Multifactor authentication means that the user must provide two different types of identification. The thumbprint is an example of biometrics. Username and password are example of a domain logon. Single sign-on would only be one type of authentication that enables the user access to multiple resources.
11. **C.** Single sign-on or SSO enables users to access multiple servers and multiple resources while entering their credentials only once. The type of authentication can vary but will generally be a username and password. Smart cards and biometrics as an example of two-factor authentication. VPN is short for virtual private network.
12. **C.** MS-CHAPv1 is not capable of mutual authentication of the client and server. Mutual authentication is accomplished with Kerberos. All the other statements are true.
13. **A and D.** Motion detectors often use infrared technology; heat would set them off. They also use ultrasonic technology; sounds in higher spectrums that humans cannot hear would set these detectors off.

14. **D.** Unlike RADIUS, TACACS (Terminal Access Control or Access Control System) encrypts client/server negotiation dialogues. Both protocols are remote authentication protocols.
15. **C.** Port 636 is the port used to secure LDAP. Port 389 is the standard LDAP port number. Port 443 is used by HTTPS (SSL/TLS), and Port 3389 is used by RDP.
16. **C.** False rejection happens when a biometric system fails to identify a legitimate user. A false positive is a Type I error, which rejects a null hypothesis when it is actually true. A false negative is a Type II error, which rejects a null hypothesis when it is not true. False exceptions have to do with software that has failed and needs to be debugged.
17. **C.** The only answer that is not a logical method of access control is biometrics. Biometrics deals with the physical attributes of a person and is the most tangible of the answers. All the rest deal with software, so they are logical methods.
18. **D.** 802.1X permits or denies access to resources through the use of ports. It implements port-based Network Access Control or PNAC. This is part of the 802.1 group of IEEE protocols. 802.1X should not be confused with 802.11x, which is an informal term used to denote any of the 802.11 standards including 802.11b, 802.11g, and 802.11n. A hub connects computers by way of physical ports but does not permit or deny access to any particular resources; it is a simple physical connector of computers.
19. **C and D.** A man trap is a device made to capture a person. It is usually an area with two doorways, the first of which leads to the outside and locks when the person enters, the second of which leads to the secure area and is locked until the person is granted access. Biometrics can help in the granting of this access by authenticating the user in a secure way, such as thumb print, retina scan, and so on. Software-based token systems and access control lists are both logical and do not play into physical security.
20. **D.** CHAP, the Challenge Handshake Authentication Protocol, authenticates a user or a network host to entities like Internet access providers. CHAP periodically verifies the identity of the client by using a three-way handshake; the verification is based on a shared secret. After a link has been established, the authenticator sends a challenge message to the peer; this does not happen in the other three authentication methods listed.
21. **C.** The Internet is used to connect hosts to each other in virtual private networks. A particular computer will probably also use a VPN adapter and/or a network adapter. Modems are generally used in dial-up connections and not used in VPNs.

22. **C.** Before users can be given access to the network, the network needs to identify them and authenticate them. Later users may be authorized to use particular resources on the network. Part of the authentication scheme may include a username and password. This would be known as an access control method.
23. **A and D.** Kerberos uses a ticket distribution service and an authentication service. This is provided by the Key Distribution Center. A Faraday cage is used to block data emanations. Port 389 is used by LDAP. One of the more common ports that Kerberos uses is port 88.
24. **C.** Kerberos uses a KDC or Key Distribution Center to centralize the distribution of certificate keys and keep a list of revoked keys.
25. **D.** Unlike RADIUS, TACACS separates authentication, authorization, and auditing capabilities. The other three answers are incorrect and are not differences between RADIUS and TACACS.

This chapter covers the following subjects:

- **Access Control Models Defined**—This section gets into access control models, such as MAC, DAC, and RBAC, plus methodologies such as implicit deny and job rotation. Before creating and enforcing policies, a plan of action has to be developed, and the access control model to be used should be at the core of that plan.
- **Rights, Permissions, and Policies**—Here, we delve into users, groups, permissions, rights, and policies that can be created on a computer network. By configuring users, templates, and groups in a smart fashion, you can ease administration and increase security at the same time. Policies can control just about anything a user does on the network or on an individual computer. And security templates make it easier than ever to implement a secure set of policies.

This chapter covers the CompTIA Security+ SY0-201 objectives 3.6, 3.7, 3.8, and 3.9.

CHAPTER 9

Access Control Methods and Models

Controlling user access is of paramount importance. You don't want just any Tom, Dick, or Harry to gain admittance to your computer network! The first step in controlling user access is to define who needs to have access and what they need to have access to. After this is done, an access control plan must be developed. This primarily consists of choosing an access control model. The model you choose will depend on your organization's procedures and written policies, and on the level of security you need, and the amount of IT resources at your disposal. After a model has been selected, you should implement as many safe practices as possible to bolster the model's effectiveness. Then, you can actually implement security on the computers and network. This includes creating and organizing secure users, groups, and other network objects such as organizational units. More important, it incorporates the use of policies and group policy objects. By configuring computer-based policies for your users, groups, and computers, you are forcing them to abide by your organization's rules.

Foundation Topics

Access Control Models Defined

Access control models are methodologies in which admission to physical areas, and more important, computer systems, is managed and organized. Access control, also known as an access policy, is extremely important when it comes to users accessing secure or confidential data. Some organizations also practice concepts such as separation of duties, job rotation, and least privilege. By combining these best practices along with an access control model, a robust plan can be developed concerning how users will access confidential data and secure areas of a building.

There are several models for access control, each with its own special characteristics that you should know for the exam. The three most commonly recognized models are discretionary access control (DAC), mandatory access control (MAC), and role-based access control (RBAC). Let's discuss these now.

Discretionary Access Control

Discretionary access control (DAC) is an access control policy generally determined by the owner. Objects such as files and printers can be created and accessed by the owner. Also, the owner decides what users are allowed to have access to the objects, and what level of access they may have. The levels of access, or permissions, are stored in access control lists (ACLs).

Originally, DAC was described in *The Orange Book* as the Discretionary Security Policy and was meant to enforce a consistent set of rules governing limited access to identified individuals. The Orange Book's proper name is the Trusted Computer System Evaluation Criteria, or TCSEC, and was developed by the DoD; however, *The Orange Book* is old (they refer to it in the movie *Hackers* in the '90s!), the standard was superseded by new policies in 2002. But the DAC methodology lives on in most of today's personal computers and client-server networks.

NOTE: An entire set of security standards was published by the DoD in the '80s and '90s known as the "Rainbow Series." Although *The Orange Book* is the centerpiece of the series (maybe not in the color spectrum, but as far as security content), there are other ones you might come into contact with such as *The Red Book*, which is the Trusted Network Interpretation standard. Some of the standards have been superseded, but they contain the basis for many of today's security procedures.

An example of DAC would be a typical Windows computer with two users. User A can log on to the computer, create a folder, stock it with data, and then finally configure permissions so that only she can access the folder. User B can log on to the computer, but cannot access User A's folder by default, unless User A says so, and configures it as so! However, User B can create his own folder and lock down permissions in the same way. Let's say that there was a third user, User C, who wanted both User A and User B to have limited access to a folder of their creation. That is also possible by setting specific permission levels, as shown in Figure 9-1. The first Properties window shows that User C (the owner) has full control permissions. This is normal because User C created the folder. But in the second Properties window, you see that User A has limited permissions, which were set by User C.

Key Topic

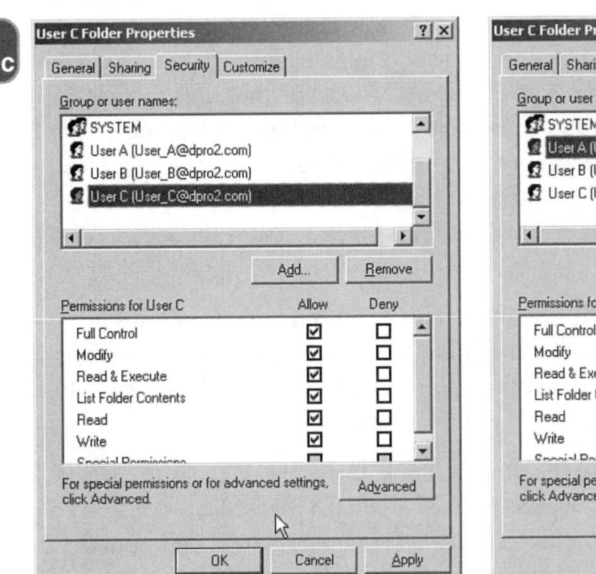

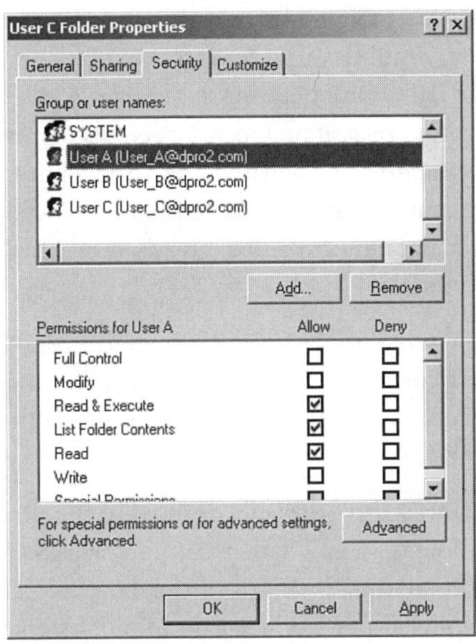

Figure 9-1 Example of Discretionary Access in Windows

NOTE: The owner of a resource controls the permissions to that resource! This is the core of the DAC model.

Windows networks/domains work in the same fashion. Access to objects is based on what user created them and what permissions they assign to those objects. However, in Windows networks we can group users together and assign permissions by way of roles as well. More on that in the role-based access control (RBAC) section.

In a way, DAC, when implemented in client-server networks is sort of a decentralized administration model. Even though an administrator will still have control over most, or all, resources, (depending on company policy) the owners will retain a certain amount of power over their own resources. But, many companies will take away the ability for users to configure permissions. They may create folders, and save data to them, but the permissions list is often generated on a parent folder by someone else and is inherited by the subfolder.

There are two important points to remember when talking about the DAC model: First, that every object in the system has an owner and that the owner has control over its access policy; and second, access rights, or permissions, can be assigned by the owner to users to specifically control object access.

Mandatory Access Control

Mandatory access control (MAC) is an access control policy determined by a computer system, not by a user or owner, as it is in DAC. Permissions are predefined in the MAC model. Historically, it has been used in highly classified government and military multilevel systems, but you will find lesser implementations of it in today's more common operating systems as well. The MAC model defines sensitivity labels that are assigned to subjects (users) and objects (files and folders). A subject's label dictates its security level, or level of trust. An object's label dictates what level of clearance is needed to access it, also known as a trust level. Also, in the MAC model data import and export is controlled. MAC is the strictest of the access control models.

An example of MAC can be seen in FreeBSD version 5.0 and higher. In this OS, access control modules can be installed that allow for security policies which label subjects and objects. The enforcement of the policies is done by administrators or by the OS; this is what makes it mandatory and sets it apart from DAC.

MAC was also originally defined in the Orange Book, but as the Mandatory Security Policy—a policy that enforces access control based on a user's clearance, and by the confidentiality levels of the data. Even though *The Orange Book* is deprecated, the concept of MAC lives on in today's systems and is implemented in two ways:

- **Rule-based access control—**Also known as label-based access control, this defines whether access should be granted or denied to objects by comparing the object label and the subject label.
- **Lattice-based access control—**Used for more complex determinations of object access by subjects. Somewhat advanced mathematics are used to create sets of objects and subjects and define how the two interact.

NOTE: Rule-based access control uses labels, is part of mandatory access control, and should not be confused with *role*-based access control.

NOTE: Other related access control models include Bell-La Padula, Biba, and Clark-Wilson. Bell-La Padula is a state machine model used for enforcing access control in government applications. It is a less common multilevel security derivative of mandatory access control. This model focuses on data confidentiality and controlled access to classified information. The Biba Integrity Model describes rules for the protection of data integrity. Clark-Wilson is another integrity model that provides a foundation for specifying and analyzing an integrity policy for computing system.

Role-Based Access Control (RBAC)

Role-based access control (RBAC) is an access model that, like MAC, is controlled by the system, and unlike DAC, not by the owner of a resource. However, RBAC is different than MAC in the way that permissions are configured. RBAC works with sets of permissions, instead of individual permissions that are label-based. A set of permissions will constitute a role. When users are assigned to roles, they can then gain access to resources. A role might be the ability to complete a specific operation in an organization as opposed to accessing a single data file. For example, a person in a bank who wants to check a prospective client's credit score would be attempting to perform a transaction that is allowed only if that person holds the proper role. So roles are created for various job functions in an organization. Roles might have overlapping privileges and responsibilities. Also, some general operations can be completed by all the employees of an organization. Because there is overlap, an administrator can develop role hierarchies; these define roles that can contain other roles, or have exclusive attributes.

Think about it. Did you ever notice that an administrator or root user is extremely powerful? Perhaps too powerful? And standard users are quite often not powerful enough to respond to their own needs or fix their own problems. Some operating systems counter this problem by creating mid-level accounts such as Power Users (Microsoft) or Operators (Solaris), but for large organizations, this is not flexible enough. Currently, more levels of roles and special groups of users are implemented in newer operating systems. RBAC is used in database access as well and is becoming more common in the healthcare industry and government.

Table 9-1 summarizes the access control models we discussed in the last three sections: DAC, MAC, and RBAC.

Table 9-1 Summary of Access Control Models

Tunneling Protocol	Key Points
DAC	Every object in the system has an owner. Permissions are determined by the owner.
MAC	Permissions are determined by the system. Can be rule-based or lattice-based. Labels are used to identify security levels of subjects and objects.

continues

Table 9-1 Summary of Access Control Models (continued)

Tunneling Protocol	Key Points
RBAC	Based on roles, or sets of permissions involved in an operation. Controlled by the system.

NOTE: Another type of access control method is known as anonymous access control, for example access to a FTP server. This method uses attributes before access is granted to an object. Authentication is usually not required.

Access Control Wise Practices

After you decide on an access control model that fits your needs, you should consider employing some other concepts. Some of these are used in operating systems automatically to some extent:

- **Implicit deny—**This concept denies all traffic to a resource unless the users generating that traffic are specifically granted access to the resource. Even if permissions haven't been configured for the user in question, that person will still be denied access. This is a default setting for access control lists on a Cisco router. It is also used by default on Microsoft computers to a certain extent. Figure 9-2 shows an example of this. In the folder's permissions, you can see that the Users group has the Read & Execute, List Folder Contents, and Read permissions set to Allow. But other permissions such as Modify are not configured at all—not set to Allow *or* Deny. Therefore, the users in the Users group cannot modify data inside the folder because that permission is implicitly denied. Likewise, they can't take full control of the folder.

NOTE: Implicit deny will deny users access to a resource unless they are specifically allowed access.

- **Least privilege—**This is when users are given only the amount of privileges needed to do their job and not one iota more. A basic example of this would be the Guest account in a Windows computer. This account (when enabled) can surf the web, and use other basic applications, but cannot make any modifications to the computer system. However, least privilege as a principle goes much further. One of the ideas behind the principle is to run the user session with only the processes necessary, thus reducing the amount of CPU power needed. This hopefully leads to better system stability and system security. Have you ever noticed that many crashed systems are due to users trying to do more than they really should be allowed? Or more than the computer can handle? The concept of *least* privilege tends to be absolute, where an absolute solution isn't quite possible in the real world. It is difficult to gauge exactly what the "least" amount of privileges and processes would be. Instead, a security administrator should practice the implementation of minimal privilege, reducing what a user has access to as much as possible. Programmers will also practice this when developing applications and operating systems, making sure that the app has only the least privilege necessary to accomplish what it needs to do. This concept is also known as "the principle of least privilege."

Key Topic

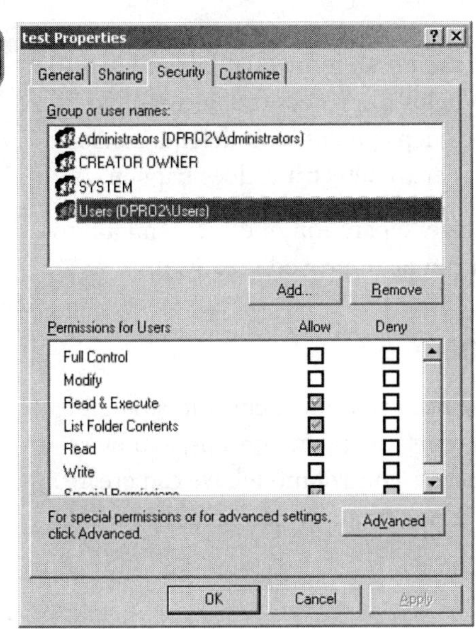

Figure 9-2 Example of Implicit Deny on a Windows Folder

- **Separation of Duties (SoD)—**This is when more than one person is required to complete a particular task or operation. If one person has too much control, and completes too many portions of a task, it can become a security risk. The more people involved, the less the chance that a job can be compromised. Checks and balances are employed to make sure that the proper equilibrium of users is maintained. One example of this would be the securing of a new network. There might be one or more security administrators in charge of doing the actual planning, and a couple more doing the actual implementation, and finally another group for testing; or perhaps, a third-party company will do the testing, keeping everything on the up and up. It all depends on the size of the organization and the internal trust level (and the IT budget!).

  SoD can also be applied to a single user. For example, if a typical user on a Windows 7 computer has a specific set of privileges. But if they want to do something on the system that requires administrative access, User Account Control (UAC) will kick in and ask for the proper credentials to perform the actions of that role. If the credentials cannot be supplied, UAC will block the action, keeping the various duties separate.

- **Job rotation**—This is one of the checks and balances that might be employed to enforce the proper separation of duties. Job rotation is when users are cycled through various assignments to
  - Increase user insight as to overall operations
  - Reduce employee boredom
  - Enhance employee skill level
  - Increase operation security

  Job rotation creates a pool of people that can do an individual job and discourages hoarding of information. It also helps to protect the purity of an operation. By cross-training people in each department, you defend against fraud and increase awareness making it easier to detect if it does happen.

By incorporating the implicit deny, least privilege, separation of duties, and job rotation concepts, your total access control plan can be improved greatly.

Rights, Permissions, and Policies

Now that we have a plan for access control, we need to implement it in a tangible way. By strategically setting up organizational units, users, and groups, and by assigning permissions according to our chosen access control model, we can create a safe, guarded working area for all employees. In so doing, we can protect the data on the network.

Users, Groups, and Permissions

User accounts can be added to individual computers or to networks. For example, a Windows client, Linux computer, or Mac can have multiple users. And larger networks that have a controlling server, for example a Windows domain controller, enable user accounts that can access one or more computers on the domain. In a Microsoft domain, users are added in Active Directory Users and Computers (ADUC), as shown in Figure 9-3.

ADUC can be accessed from Administrative Tools or added as a snap-in to an MMC. Users can be added in one of two places:

- **In the Users folder**—This is located inside the domain name within ADUC.
- **In an OU**—Organizational units can be created within the domain. These are often made to mimic the departments of a company. In the figure, there are accounting and marketing OUs; users can be created within these OUs.

User rights can be modified within the particular user's Properties window. There are many more rights associated with a user account that is stored on a Windows Server domain controller than there are on an individual Windows client computer.

For example, the Account tab can be configured so that the user account has an expiration date. You can see this in Figure 9-4 where at the bottom of the Properties window, we have configured Megan's account to expire on April 1, 2012—and that's no April Fools! Immediately after expiration, the user cannot log on to the domain unless her account is reconfigured or she logs on as someone else.

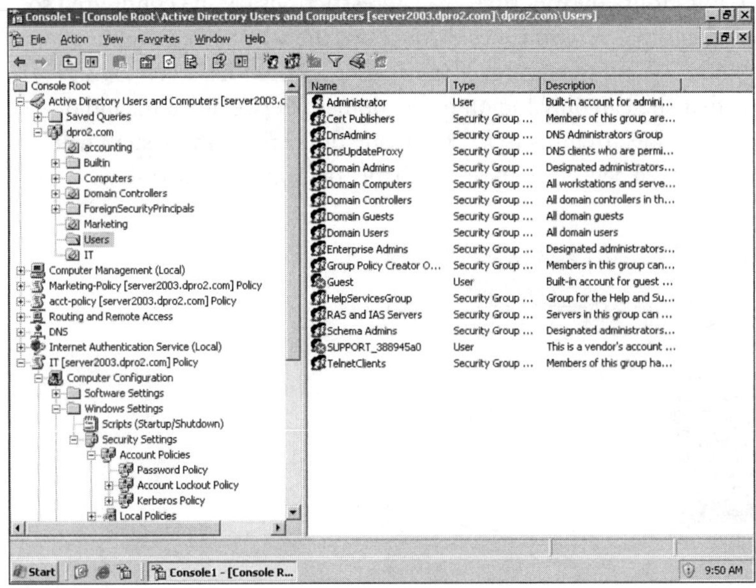

Figure 9-3 The Users Folder Within ADUC on a Windows Server 2003

Key Topic

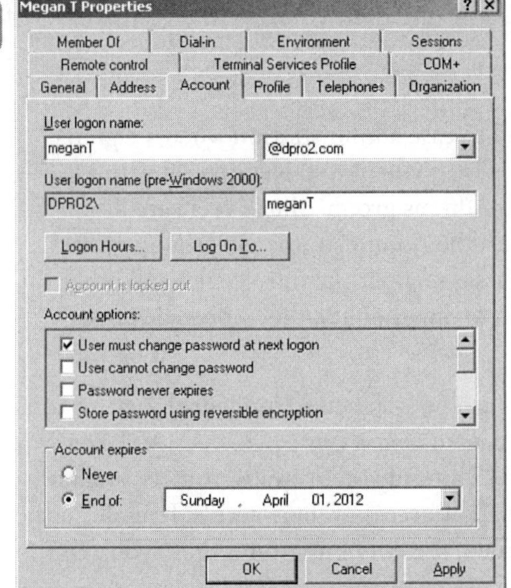

Figure 9-4 User Account Expiration Date

NOTE: Users cannot log on to a network after their account has expired. The Account Expiration date in Windows controls this.

By clicking the Logon Hours button, time-of-day restrictions can be configured so that a user can only log on at certain times throughout the week. An example of this is shown in Figure 9-5. In the figure, Megan's user account has been configured in such a way that she can only log on to the domain between 8 a.m. and 6 p.m. Monday–Friday. If she attempts to log on at any other time, the system will deny access. These kinds of access rights are available on domain controllers.

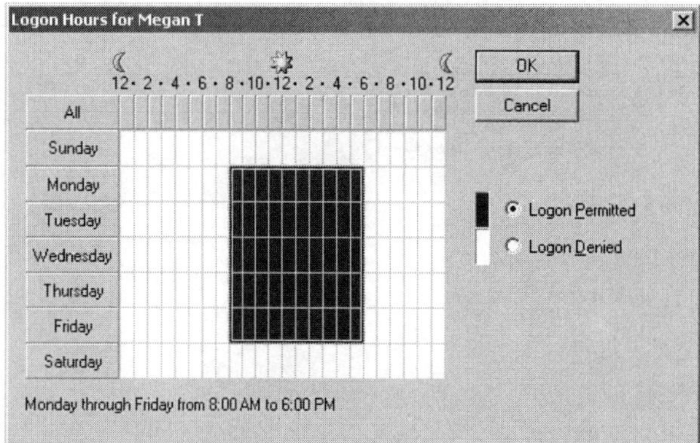

Figure 9-5 Time-of-Day Restrictions for a Standard User

NOTE: Users can only log on to the network during their configured logon hours.

Groups can be created to classify users and to ease administration when assigning permissions. If you refer to Figure 9-3, you see that a group is displayed with a two-headed icon, for example the Domain Admins group. Single users are displayed with a single head, as is the case with the Administrator. By grouping users together, you can save a lot of time when assigning permissions to files and other resources; instead of assigning permissions to one user at a time, it can be done to the entire group in one shot.

Permissions such as file and printer access can be assigned to individual users or to groups. These permissions are examples of *access control lists (ACLs)*. An ACL is a list of permissions attached to an object. ACLs reside on firewalls, routers, and on computers. Permissions in an ACL might allow access or deny access. It all depends on who is required to have access; then, the configuration is up to you.

In Windows there are two types of permissions. Sharing permissions are basic permissions including Full Control, Change, and Read, which are applied to folders only. These are often ignored in favor of the more powerful (and superseding) NTFS permissions, also called security permissions, which can secure folders and individual files. In a standard Windows folder on a domain, the types of NTFS permissions include the following:

- Full Control
- Modify
- Read & Execute
- List Folder Contents
- Read
- Write

These are shown in Figure 9-6 on a Window Server 2003 in the Properties dialog box of a folder named "test folder." Note that the Administrators group has full control of the folder. Also note that you can allow particular permissions, or specifically deny those permissions. If a permission is not set to Allow, it will be implicitly denied.

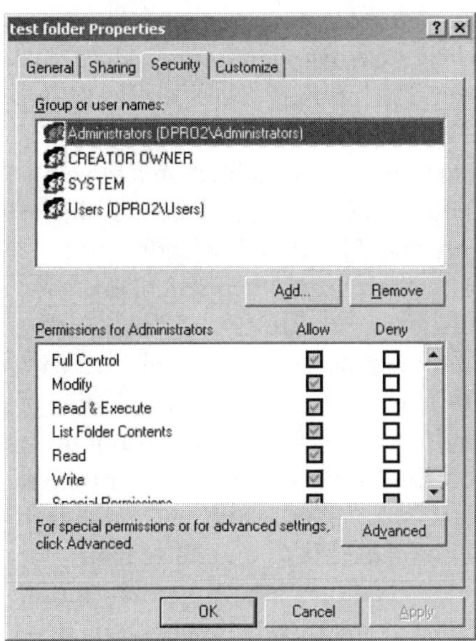

Figure 9-6 NTFS Permissions

Permissions similar to these are used for individual files and printers, and work in a related fashion on other operating systems such as Linux, Novell, and Mac. Navigation to, and configuration of, permissions in GUI-based OSs is similar to Windows. However, modifying permissions in the command-line, for example in Linux or UNIX is done differently. If a particular file, say test.txt needed to be modified, the command to be used would be **chmod**. Chmod is short for change mode. The type of mode dictates the "permissions" of the file among other things. For example, in **chmod 755 test.txt**, the first digit (7) represents the permission associated with the owner of the file. The second digit (5) represents permissions for the group. The third digit (5) represents the permissions for everyone else, also known as the everyone group.

When working with permissions, the "least privilege" or "minimal privilege" concept should be implemented. Give the users only the amount of access that they absolutely need. Also, if a company has a particularly high attrition rate (hiring and terminating of employees), the administrator should periodically review user permissions and access control lists. This will verify that users no longer with the company cannot log on to the network and cannot gain access to resources. It also ensures that new users can gain access to necessary resources.

Permission Inheritance and Propagation

If you create a folder, the default action it takes is to inherit permissions from the parent folder, which ultimately come from the root folder. So any permissions set in the parent will be inherited by the subfolder. To view an example of this, locate any folder within an NTFS volume (besides the root folder), right-click it, and select **Properties**, access the **Security** tab, and click the **Advanced** button. Here, you see an enabled check box named Inherit from Parent the Permission Entries... toward the bottom of the window, as shown in Figure 9-7. This means that any permissions added or removed in the parent folder will also be added or removed in the current folder. In addition, those permissions inherited cannot be modified in the current folder. To make modifications you would have to deselect the **Inherit from Parent the Permission Entries...** check box. When you do so, you have the option to copy the permissions from the parent to the current folder or remove them entirely. To summarize, by default the parent is automatically propagating permissions to the subfolder, and the subfolder is inheriting its permissions from the parent. You can also propagate permission changes to subfolders not inheriting from the current folder. To do so, select the **Replace Permission Entries on All Child Objects...** check box. This might all seem a bit confusing, and you will probably not be asked many questions on the subject. Just remember that folders automatically inherit from the parent unless you turn inheriting off—and you can propagate permission entries to subfolders at any time by selecting the Replace option.

Moving and Copying Folders and Files

This subject and the previous one are actually more advanced Microsoft concepts, the type you would be asked on a Microsoft exam, and less likely to be asked on a CompTIA exam, so we'll try to keep this simple. Moving and copying folders have different results when it comes to permissions. Basically, it breaks down like this:

- If you *copy* a folder on the same volume or to a different volume, the folder inherits the permissions of the parent folder it was copied to (target directory).
- If you *move* a folder to a different location on the same volume, the folder retains its original permissions. (You cannot move a folder to a separate volume; if you attempt to do so it will automatically be copied to the other volume.)

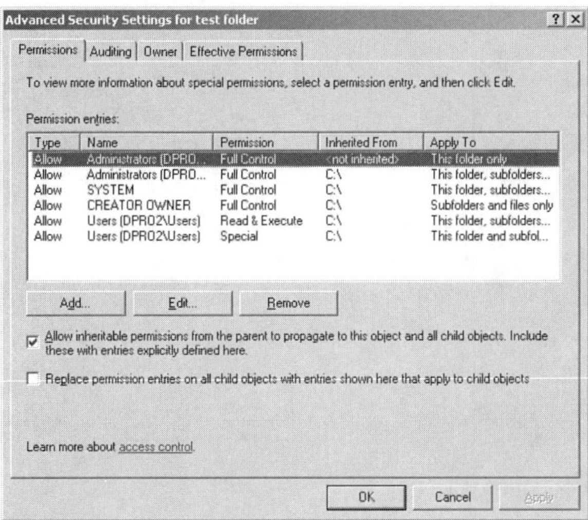

Figure 9-7 Inheritable Permissions

> **NOTE:** Keep in mind that when you move data within a volume, the data isn't actually relocated; instead the pointer to the file or folder is modified. Accordingly, permissions are not really moved either, so they remain the same.

Usernames and Passwords

The most common type of authentication is the username/password combination. Usernames are usually based on a person's real name. Large organizations will use the *firstname.lastname* convention (for example, david.prowse@company.com) or first initial and last name (dprowse@company.com). Smaller organizations might use the first name and last initial. The naming convention decided upon should be easy for you to implement without name confusion and have the capability to be utilized for all systems on the network including login, e-mail, database, and file access, and so on.

The password is either set by the user or created automatically for the user by an administrator. Figure 9-8 shows an example of a password that was created by the administrator. However, in this case, the user is not blocked from changing the password (unless a policy was created for that purpose). Note that the second checkbox **User Cannot Change Password** is not selected. As an administrator, you also have the option to select **User Must Change Password at Next Logon**. A user would have to pick a password when he first logs on to the domain, one that meets whatever complexity requirements your network calls for. This with the self-service password resetting (when users reset their own passwords at regular intervals) is necessary in larger networks to ease administration and increase security. The only caveat to this is account lockouts. Unlocking accounts that were locked by the system should only be done by an administrator or system operator.

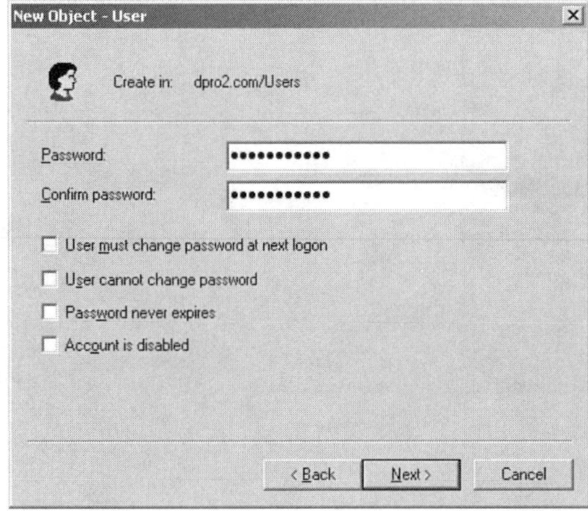

Figure 9-8 Password Phase of User Account Creation

At this point, it is common knowledge that a strong password is important for protecting a user account. Nowadays, a lot of user accounts are compromised because of laziness; laziness on the part of the user for not configuring a strong password, or lethargic complacency on the part of the administrator for not enforcing the use of strong passwords.

But what is a strong password? That will depend on the organization you deal with, but generally it is broken down into a few easy to remember points. Passwords should comply with the following:

- Contain uppercase letters
- Contain lowercase letters
- Contain numbers
- Contain special characters (symbols)
- Should be 8 characters or more. Some organizations that have extremely sensitive data will require 12 or 14 characters as a minimum.

Many password checker programs are available on the web including:

- Microsoft's password checker: www.microsoft.com/protect/yourself/password/checker.mspx
- The Password Meter: www.passwordmeter.com/

Try some of your favorite passwords—test them with the checkers. You might be surprised what you find! Your goal is to have a very strong or 100% strong password. Keep in mind that different checkers might have slightly different criteria.

Table 9-2 shows several passwords, each stronger than the last, all of which were checked by The Password Meter.

Table 9-2 Password Strength as Checked by www.passwordmeter.com

Password	Strength of Password
|ocrian#	Weak–38%
Thisisverysecure	Good–50%
Marqu1sD3S0d	Very Strong–98%
This1sV#ryS3cure	Very strong–100%

Notice the first password is using the | pipe symbol instead of the letter L. Although the password is 8 characters, and has special characters, it is considered weak; however, this is a stronger password than the majority of passwords used in the United States! To make this password more complex, increasing the size of the password and adding uppercase letters would be the best course of action. The last password has 16 characters, 3 uppercase letters, 2 numbers, and a partridge in a pear tree, um, I mean one special character. Just checking if you are still with me! Of course, a partridge wouldn't help your password security, but the other methods make for an extremely strong password that would take a super-computer many years to crack. I have placed this password on security testing websites and several persons have attempted to crack it without a positive result. (Actually, it was positive for me because it wasn't cracked!)

A password that has 12 characters including uppercase, numbers, and special characters is currently considered to be effectively uncrackable. And 72-bit or higher passwords are the standard for networks that contain confidential data. We talk more about password strength and password cracking in Chapter 10, "Vulnerability and Risk Assessment."

Changing your password at regular intervals is important as well. The general rule of thumb is to change your password as often as you change your toothbrush. However, because this is a subjective concept (to put it nicely!), many organizations have policies concerning your password that we will speak to in the next section. It might need to meet certain requirements, or be changed at regular intervals, and so forth.

Here are a couple more tips when it comes to user accounts, passwords, and logons:

- **Rename and password protect the Administrator account**—It's nice that Windows has incorporated a separate administrator account: The problem is that by default the account has no password. To configure this account, navigate to **Computer Management > System Tools > Local Users and Groups > Users** and locate the **Administrator** account. In a domain, this would be in **ADUC > Domain name > Users**. By right-clicking the account, you see a drop-down menu in which you can rename it and/or give it a password. (Just remember the new username and password!) Now it's great to have this additional administrator account on the shelf just in case the primary account fails; however, some OSs such as Vista disable the account by default. To enable it, right-click the account and select **Properties**. In the General tab, deselect the **Account Is Disabled** check box. Alternatively, open the command line and type **`net user administrator /active:yes`**. The way that the administrator account behaves by default will depend on the version of Windows. The Linux/UNIX counterpart is the root account. The same types of measures should be employed when dealing with this account.
- **Verify that the Guest account (and other unnecessary accounts) are disabled**—This can be done by right-clicking the account in question, selecting **Properties** and then selecting the checkbox named **Account Is Disabled**. It is also possible to delete accounts (aside from built-in accounts such as the Guest account); however, companies usually opt to have them disabled instead so that the company can retain information linking to the account.
- **Use Ctrl+Alt+Del**—Pressing Ctrl+Alt+Del before the logon adds a layer of security to the logon process. This can be added as a policy on individual Windows computers. It is implemented by default with computers that are members of a domain.
- **Use policies**—Policies governing user accounts, passwords, and so on can help you to enforce your rules, as discussed in the next section. Large organizations with a lot of users will usually implement a self-service password management system. This means that users reset their own passwords after a given amount of time (set in a group policy); the administrator does not create passwords for users.

Policies

Policies are rules or guidelines used to guide decisions and achieve outcomes. They can be written or configured on a computer. The former are more difficult to enforce, whereas the latter would have to be hacked to be bypassed. Local computer policies and network policies are what really make an access control model effective.

Password policies can be implemented to enforce the usage of complex passwords and regulate how long passwords last. They can be configured on local computers, such as Windows XP and Vista, by navigating to **Start > All Programs > Administrative Tools > Local Security Policy**. When in the Local Security Settings window, continue to **Security Settings > Account Policies > Password Policy**.

More important, they can be configured for an entire network, for example on a Microsoft domain. The policy can affect the entire domain or individual organizational units. This would be known as a group policy and would be configured on a domain controller. For example, a Windows Server 2003 domain controller can be configured by completing the following steps:

Step 1. Access the domain controller.

Step 2. Create an MMC.

Step 3. Add the Default Domain Policy to the MMC. (Done by adding a Group Policy Object Editor snap-in.)

Step 4. In the Default Domain Policy, navigate to **Computer Configuration > Windows Settings > Security Settings > Account Policies > Password Policy**.

> **NOTE:** The Default Domain Policy will affect all users. This is okay for small networks, but for larger networks, separate organizational units should be created, each with its own security policy. More information about how to go about this can be found in Lab 9-1 in the "Hands-On Labs" section.

When in the Password Policy, you see the following policies:

- **Enforce password history—**When this is defined, users cannot use any of the passwords remembered in the history. If you set the history to 3, the last three passwords cannot be used again when it is time to change the password.
- **Maximum and minimum password age—**This defines exactly how long a password can be used. The maximum is initially set to 42 days but does not affect the default Administrator account. To enforce effective password history, the minimum must be higher than zero.
- **Minimum password length—**This requires that the password must be at least the specified amount of characters. For a strong password policy, set this to 8 or more.
- **Passwords must meet complexity requirements—**This means that passwords must meet three of these four criteria: uppercase characters, lowercase characters, digits between 0 and 9, and nonalphabetic characters (special characters).

Remember that these policies, when enabled, affect all users that the policy applies to. If it is the Default Domain Policy (usually not recommended for configuration), it affects all users; if it is an OU policy, it affects all users in the OU.

NOTE: For more information on password best practices, see the following link: http://technet.microsoft.com/en-us/library/cc784090.aspx.

There are plenty of other policies that you can configure. You can pretty much configure any policy on a domain. You can't configure how a person should shave in the morning, but anything computer-related can be modified and policed. One example is how many attempts a person will be allowed when typing in a password. This is known as the Account lockout threshold, as shown in Figure 9-9. By default, this is set to 5 attempts on a Windows Server 2003, but many companies will adjust this to 3; this is known as the 3 strikes and you're out rule.

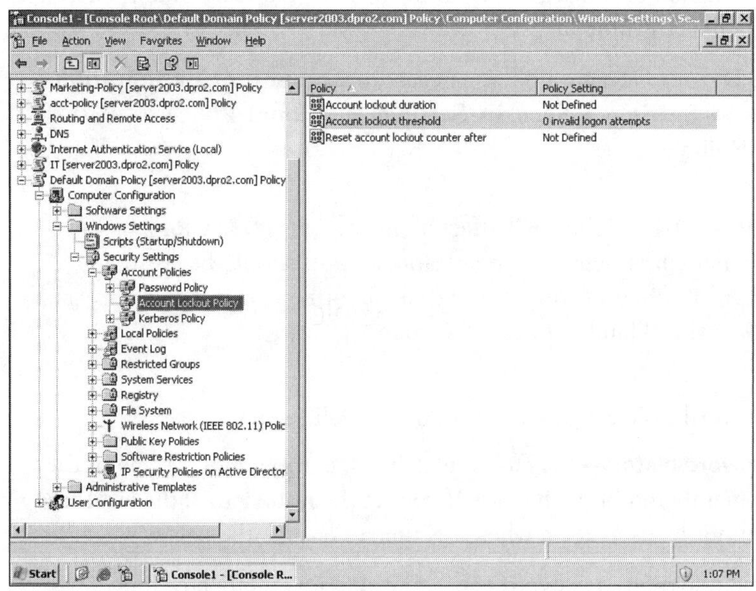

Figure 9-9 Account Lockout Threshold Policy

Another great tool is previous logon notification. This can be configured in a policy and will show the user the last time the account logged in successfully— generally during the logon process. If users suspects that their account was compromised, they could check the previous logon notification and compare that with when they remember logging in.

It's important to note that when logging on to a Microsoft network, the logon process is secured by the Kerberos protocol, which is run by the Domain Controller. This adds a layer of protection for the username and password as they are authenticated across the network. When users take a break or go to lunch, they should lock the computer. This can be done by pressing **Windows+L**. When doing so, the operating system goes into a locked state, and the only way to unlock the computer is to enter the username and password of the person who locked the computer. The difference between this and logging out is that a locked computer keeps all the session's applications and files open, whereas logging out closes all applications and open files. A policy can also be configured to force locking after a certain amount of time has elapsed. There are literally hundreds of policies that are configurable. You could spend weeks doing it! Microsoft understands this and offers various levels of security templates that can be imported into your OU policy, making your job as an administrator a bit easier. A particular template might be just what you are looking for, or it might need a bit of tweaking. But in most cases it beats starting from scratch!

Policies can be developed on all kinds of software and systems, not just operating systems. For example, many organizations have websites, and a good portion of those organizations now set up bulletin board systems where authorized users can post messages. Bulletin boards are also known as forums or portals. Bulletin boards are often the playground for malicious activity, for example, users or bots who post spam messages. Various policies can be implemented on an interactive bulletin board system to prevent these types of problems. For example, when people first register, they would need to answer a question that requires something they knows such as 2+4 = *blank*. The user would enter the answer (6) and continue on their merry way. Another viable option is to use CAPTCHA, which can display an image that has letters and numbers in it. The user must type the letters and numbers *that they see* before they can register, or perhaps to post any messages at all. This is a good deterrent for bots!

User Account Control (UAC)

User Account Control (UAC) is a security component of Windows Server 2008, Windows Vista, and Windows 7 that keeps users (besides the actual Administrator account) in standard user mode instead of as an administrator with full administrative rights—even if they are a member of the administrators group. It is a built-in security policy meant to prevent unauthorized access and avoid user error in the form of accidental changes. With UAC enabled users perform common tasks as nonadministrators, and when necessary, as administrators, without having to switch users, log off, or use Run As.

Basically, UAC was created with two goals in mind: First, to eliminate unnecessary requests for excessive administrative-level access to Windows resources; and second, to reduce the risk of malicious software using the administrator's access control to infect operating system files. When a standard end user requires administrator privileges to perform certain tasks such as installing an application, a small pop-up UAC window appears notifying the user that an administrator credential is necessary. If users have administrative rights and click **Continue**, the task will be carried out, but if they do not have sufficient rights, the attempt fails. Note that these pop-up UAC windows do not appear if the person is logged on with the actual Administrator account.

Turning UAC on and off can be done by going to **Start > Control Panel > User Accounts and Family Safety**. Then select **User Accounts** and **Turn User Account Control On or Off**. From there UAC can be turned on and off by checking or unchecking the box. If a change is made to UAC, the system needs to be restarted. Note that if you use the Classic View in the Control Panel, User Accounts and Family Safety is bypassed.

Exam Preparation Tasks

Review Key Topics

Review the most important topics in the chapter, noted with the Key Topics icon in the outer margin of the page. Table 9-3 lists a reference of these key topics and the page numbers on which each is found.

Table 9-3 Key Topics for Chapter 9

Key Topic Element	Description	Page Number
Figure 9-1	Example of Discretionary Access in Windows	251
Table 9-1	Summary of Access Control Models	253
Figure 9-2	Example of Implicit Deny on a Windows Folder	255
Figure 9-4	User Account Expiration Date	257
Figure 9-5	Time-of-Day Restrictions for a Standard User	258
Bulleted list	Password compliance	262
Table 9-2	Password Strength as Checked by www.passwordmeter.com	263

Complete Tables and Lists from Memory

Print a copy of Appendix A, "Memory Tables," (found on the DVD), or at least the section for this chapter, and complete the tables and lists from memory. Appendix B, "Memory Tables Answer Key," also on the DVD, includes completed tables and lists to check your work.

Define Key Terms

Define the following key terms from this chapter, and check your answers in the glossary:

access control model, discretionary access control (DAC), Trusted Computer System Evaluation Criteria (TCSEC), mandatory access control (MAC), role-based access control (RBAC), implicit deny, job rotation, Separation of Duties (SoD), least privilege, account expiration, permissions, time-of-day restriction, access control list (ACL), policy

Hands-On Labs

Complete the following written step-by-step scenarios. After you have finished (or if you do not have adequate equipment to complete the scenario), watch the corresponding video solutions on the DVD.

If you have additional questions, feel free to post them at my website: www.davidlprowse.com in the Ask Dave forum. (Free registration is required to post on the website.)

Equipment Needed

- A Windows Server (2003 or 2008 preferred). This server must be promoted to a domain controller.

Lab 9-1: Configuring Password Policies and User Account Restrictions

In this lab, you create an organizational unit and policy within a Windows Server 2003 domain controller. Then, you configure group policy objects and user restrictions. The steps are as follows:

Step 1. Access the Windows Server 2003 MMC. If you don't have one, create one now, and add the Active Directory Users and Computers (ADUC) snap-in.

Step 2. Create a new organizational unit (OU):

A. Expand the ADUC snap-in.

B. Right-click the domain name and select **New > Organizational Unit**.

C. Name the OU and click **OK**. Generally, OUs will be named after departments in a company such as accounting, marketing, and so on.

D. Add a user to the OU by right-clicking the work area and selecting **New > User**. Call the user **Template**.

Step 3. Create a policy associated with the OU:

A. Right-click the new OU and select **Properties**.

B. Click the **Group Policy** tab.

C. Click the **New** button.

D. Name the policy. Choose a name that will associate the policy with the OU.

E. Click **Close**.

Step 4. Add the new policy as a snap-in to the MMC:

A. Click **File > Add/Remove Snap-In**.

B. Click **Add**.

C. Select **Group Policy Editor** and click **Add**.

D. Click **Browse**; then double-click the folder with the name of your new OU.

E. Highlight the new policy and click **OK**.

F. Click **Finish**. Close all other dialog boxes. The new policy should now be added to the MMC as a snap-in.

Step 5. Make changes to the policy:

A. Navigate to **Computer Configuration** > **Windows Settings** > **Security Settings** > **Account Policies** > **Password Policy**.

B. Modify the password age and length as you want. For example, to change the Maximum password age to 30 days, double-click that policy object, select **Define this policy setting**, and change the amount to **30**.

C. Enable password complexity requirements.

Step 6. Make changes to the Account Lockout Policy within Account Policies:

A. Click Account Lockout Policy.

B. Define the account lockout duration as 30 minutes.

C. Define the account lockout threshold to after 3 invalid logon attempts.

Step 7. Examine the importable policies:

A. Right-click **Security Settings** and select **Import Policy**.

B. View the policy options. Cancel out when finished.

Step 8. Modify the template user account:

A. Right-click the account and select **Properties**.

B. Click the **Account** tab.

C. Click **Logon Hours**.

D. Modify this setting by clicking and dragging within the days so that the template user can only logon between 9 a.m. and 5 p.m. Monday–Friday.

E. Click **OK** for the logon hours. Then click **OK** for the Template account Properties dialog box.

Step 9. Create users by making copies of the template account:

A. Right-click the Template account and select **Copy**.

B. Name the new user and give is a logon name. For example, someone's first initial and last name. Then click **Next**.

C. Give a password for the user that meets your complexity requirements.

D. Deselect **User Must Change Password at Logon** and click **Next**.

E. Click **Finish**. The new account should be listed in the OU.

F. Right-click the new user and select **Properties**.

G. Review the Logon hours in the Account tab and verify that they are the same as the Template account.

Watch the solution video in the "Hands-On Scenarios" section of the DVD.

Lab 9-2: Configuring User and Group Permissions

In this lab, you configure user and group permissions for a shared resource on a Windows Server 2003 domain controller. This lab is written to be a little more intuitive. The step-by-step is slightly less informative. Use your imagination to fill in the gaps! The steps are as follows:

Step 1. Create two more user accounts in the new OU that you created in the previous lab.

Step 2. Create a group:

A. Right-click the new OU and select **New > Group**.

B. Name the group, for example: IT1 and click **OK**.

Step 3. Add members to the group:

A. Right-click the group and select **Properties**.

B. Click the **Members** tab.

C. Click **Add**. Then click **Advanced** and **Find Now**. Add the new users you created to the IT group. Select each one at a time or use **Ctrl+Click** to select all of them at one time. Click **OK** for all dialog boxes to add them to the group.

Step 4. Apply permissions for a shared folder to the entire group:

A. Create a folder specifically for the new group of users.

B. Share the folder.

C. Click the **Security** tab.

D. Click the **Advanced** button. Remove inheritable permissions by deselecting the checkbox and selecting **Copy**.

E. Click the **Add** button and add the new group of users to the share.

F. Remove other groups and users besides the Administrators group.

G. Click **OK** when finished.

Watch the solution video in the "Hands-On Scenarios" section of the DVD.

View Recommended Resources

- TCSEC *The Orange Book*. http://csrc.ncsl.nist.gov/publications/secpubs/rainbow/std001.txt
- DOD Directive 8500.01E (replacement for *The Orange Book*) www.dtic.mil/whs/directives/corres/pdf/850001p.pdf
- Role-based access control Introduction http://csrc.nist.gov/groups/SNS/rbac/documents/design_implementation/Intro_role_based_access.htm

Password checking tools:

- Microsoft's password checker: www.microsoft.com/protect/yourself/password/checker.mspx
- The Password Meter: www.passwordmeter.com/
- Password Best Practices: http://technet.microsoft.com/en-us/library/cc784090.aspx
- User Account Control Step-by-Step Guide: http://technet.microsoft.com/en-us/library/cc709691%28WS.10%29.aspx

Answer Review Questions

Answer the following review questions. You can find the answers at the end of this chapter.

1. Which of the following is the strongest password?
   A. |ocrian#
   B. Marqu1sD3S0d
   C. This1sV#ryS3cure
   D. Thisisverysecure
2. Which of these is a security component of Windows Vista?
   A. UAC
   B. UPS
   C. Gadgets
   D. Control Panel
3. What key combination helps to secure the logon process?
   A. Windows+R
   B. Ctrl+Shift+Esc

C. Ctrl+Alt+Del

D. Alt+F4

4. Which of the following is the most common authentication model?

A. Username and password

B. Biometrics

C. Key cards

D. Tokens

5. Which of the following access control methods uses rules to govern whether object access will be allowed? (Select the best answer.)

A. Rule-based access control

B. Role-based access control

C. Discretionary access control

D. Mandatory access control

6. When using the mandatory access control model, what component is needed?

A. Labels

B. Certificates

C. Tokens

D. RBAC

7. Which of the following statements regarding the MAC access control model is true?

A. Mandatory access control is a dynamic model.

B. Mandatory access control enables an owner to establish access privileges to a resource.

C. Mandatory access control is not restrictive.

D. Mandatory access control users cannot share resources dynamically.

8. In the DAC model, how are permissions identified?

A. Role membership.

B. Access control lists.

C. They are predefined.

D. It is automatic.

9. Robert needs to access a resource. In the DAC model, what is used to identify him or other users?

A. Roles

B. ACLs

C. MAC

D. Rules

10. A company has a high attrition rate. What should you ask the network administrator do first? (Select the best answer.)

A. Review user permissions and access control lists.

B. Review group policies.

C. Review Performance logs.

D. Review the Application log.

11. Your company has 1,000 users. Which of the following password management systems will work best for your company?

A. Multiple access methods

B. Synchronize passwords

C. Historical passwords

D. Self-service password resetting

12. In a discretionary access control model, who is in charge of setting permissions to a resource?

A. The owner of the resource

B. The administrator

C. Any user of the computer

D. The administrator and the owner

13. Jason needs to add several users to a group. Which of the following will help him to get the job done faster?

A. Propagation

B. Inheritance

C. Template

D. Access control lists

14. How are permissions defined in the mandatory access control model?

A. Access control lists

B. User roles

C. Defined by the user

D. Predefined access privileges

15. Which of the following would lower the level of password security?

A. After a set number of failed attempts, the server will lock the user out, forcing them to call the administrator to reenable their account.

B. Passwords must be greater than eight characters and contain at least one special character.

C. All passwords are set to expire after 30 days.

D. Complex passwords that users cannot change are randomly generated by the administrator.

16. Of the following access control models, which use object labels? (Select the best answer.)

A. Discretionary access control

B. Role-based access control

C. Rule-based access control

D. Mandatory access control

17. Which of the following methods could identify when an unauthorized access has occurred?

A. Two -factor authentication

B. Session termination

C. Previous logon notification

D. Session lock

18. What would you use to control the traffic that is allowed in or out of a network? (Select the best answer.)

A. Access control lists

B. Firewall

C. Address resolution protocol

D. Discretionary access control

19. In an attempt to detect fraud and defend against it, your company cross-trains people in each department. What is this an example of?

A. Separation of duties

B. Chain of custody

C. Job rotation

D. Least privilege

20. What is a definition of implicit deny?

A. Everything is denied by default.

B. All traffic from one network to another is denied.

C. ACLs are used to secure the firewall.

D. Resources that are not given access are denied by default.

21. In an environment where administrators, the accounting department, and the marketing department all have different levels of access, which of the following access control models is being used?

A. Role-based access control (RBAC)

B. Mandatory access control (MAC)

C. Discretionary access control (DAC)

D. Rule-based access control (RBAC)

22. Which security measure should be included when implementing access control?

A. Disabling SSID broadcast

B. Time-of-day restrictions

C. Changing default passwords

D. Password complexity requirements

23. Which password management system best provides for a system with a large number of users?

A. Locally saved passwords management systems

B. Synchronized passwords management systems

C. Multiple access methods management systems

D. Self-service password reset management systems

24. You administer a bulletin board system for a rock and roll band. While reviewing logs for the board, you see one particular IP address posting spam multiple times per day. What is the best way to prevent type of problem?

    A. Block the IP address of the user.

    B. Ban the user.

    C. Disable ActiveX.

    D. Implement CAPTCHA.

Answers and Explanations

1. **C.** Answer C incorporates case-sensitive letters, numbers, and special characters and is 16 characters long. The other answers do not have the complexity of answer C.
2. **A.** User Account Control (UAC) adds a layer of security to Windows Server 2008, Windows Vista, and Windows 7 to protect against malware and user error and conserve resources. It enforces a type of separation of duties.
3. **C.** Ctrl+Alt+Del is the key combination used to help secure the logon process. It can be added by configuring the Local Security policy.
4. **A.** By far the username and password combination is the most common authentication model. Although biometrics, key cards, and tokens are also used, the password is still the most common.
5. **A.** Rule-based access control uses rules to govern if an object can be accessed. It is a type of mandatory access control.
6. **A.** Labels are required in the mandatory access control model (MAC).
7. **D.** In MAC (mandatory access control) users cannot share resources dynamically. MAC is not a dynamic model; it is a static model. Owners cannot establish access privileges to a resource; this would be done by the administrator. MAC is indeed very restrictive, as restrictive as the administrator wants it to be.
8. **B.** In the discretionary access control model, permissions to files are identified by access control lists or ACLs. Role membership is used in RBAC. The mandatory access control model predefines permissions. Either way, it is not identified automatically.
9. **B.** Access control lists (ACLs) are used in the Discretionary Access Control model. This is different from role-based, rule-based, and MAC (Mandatory Access Control) models.
10. **A.** The first thing administrators should do when they notice that the company has a high attrition rate (high turnover of employees) is to conduct a thorough review of user permissions, rights, and access control lists. A review of

group policies might also be necessary but is not as imperative. Performance logs and the Application log will probably not pertain to the fact that the company has a lot of employees being hired and leaving the company.

11. **D.** It would be difficult for administrators to deal with thousands of users passwords; therefore, the best management system for a company with 1,000 users would be self-service password resetting.
12. **A.** In the discretionary access control model (DAC), the owner of the resource is in charge of setting permissions. In a mandatory access control model, the administrator is in charge.
13. **C.** By using a template, you can add many users to a group at once simply by applying the template to the users. Propagation and inheritance deal with how permissions are exchanged between parent folders and subfolders. Access control lists show who was allowed access to a particular resource.
14. **D.** The mandatory access control model uses predefined access privileges to define which users have permission to resources.
15. **D.** To have a secure password scheme, passwords should be changed by the user. They should not be generated by the administrator. If an administrator were to generate the password for the user, it would have to be submitted in written (and unencrypted) form in some way to the user. This creates a security issue, especially if the user does not memorize the password and leaves a written version of it lying around. All the other answers would increase the level of password security.
16. **D.** The mandatory access control (MAC) model uses object and subject labels. DAC and RBAC (role-based access control) do not. Rule-based access control is a portion of MAC, and although it might use labels, MAC is the best answer.
17. **C.** Previous logon notification can identify if unauthorized access has occurred. Two-factor authentication means that person will supply two forms of identity before being authenticated to a network or system. Session termination is a mechanism that can be implemented to end an unauthorized access. Session lock mechanisms can be employed to lock a particular user or IP address out of the system.
18. **A.** Access control lists can be used to control the traffic that is allowed in or out of a network. They are usually included as part of a firewall, and they are the better answer because they specifically will control the traffic. Address resolution protocol or ARP resolves IP addresses to MAC addresses. In the discretionary access control model, the owner controls permissions of resources.

19. **C.** When a company cross-trains people, it is known as job rotation. Separation of duties is in a way the opposite; this is when multiple people are needed to complete a single task. Chain of custody has to do with the legal paper trail of a particular occurrence. Least privilege is a mitigation technique to defend against privilege escalation attacks.

20. **D.** If a resource is not given specific access, it will be implicitly denied by default. Access control lists are used to permit or deny access from one network to another and are often implemented on a firewall.

21. **A.** Role-based access control is when different groups or roles are assigned different levels of permissions; rights and permissions are based on an ob function. In the mandatory access control model, an administrator centrally controls permissions. In the discretionary access control model, the owner of the user sets permissions. In the rule-based access control model, rules are defined by the administrator and are stored in an ACL.

22. **D.** By implementing password complexity requirements, users will be forced to select and enter complex passwords, for example, eight characters or more, uppercase characters, special characters, and more. Disabling the SSID deals with wireless networks, time-of-day restrictions is applied only after persons logs in with their username and password, and changing default passwords should be part of a password policy.

23. **D.** If a network has a large number of users, the administrator should set up a system and policies to enforce the system that will allow for users to reset their own passwords. The passwords should be stored centrally, not locally. Also, it would be best if single sign-on were implemented and not a multiple access method.

24. **D.** By implementing CAPTCHA, another level of security is added that users have to complete before they can register to and/or post to a bulletin board. Although banning a user or the user's IP address can help to eliminate that particular person from spamming the site, the best way is to add another level of security, such as CAPTCHA. This applies to all persons who attempt to attack the bulletin board.

This chapter covers the following subjects:

- **Conducting Risk Assessments—**This section covers risk management and assessment. It discusses the differences between qualitative and quantitative risk and describes the methodologies of an important part of risk management—vulnerability management. Also covered are various ways to assess vulnerabilities and how to perform penetration tests.
- **Assessing Vulnerability with Security Tools—**In this section, you learn how to use common network security tools to measure the vulnerability of your computer systems and network devices. These tools include network mappers, vulnerability scanners, protocol analyzers, packet sniffers, and password crackers.

This chapter covers the CompTIA Security+ SY0-201 objectives 4.1, 4.2, and 4.3.

CHAPTER 10

Vulnerability and Risk Assessment

Let's take it to the next level and talk some serious security. As people, we're all vulnerable to something. They say that you need to "manage your own healthcare"—our computers are no different. The potential health of your computers and network is based on vulnerabilities. One of the most important tasks of a network security administrator is to find vulnerabilities and either remove them or secure them as much as possible—within acceptable parameters. *Vulnerabilities* are weaknesses in your computer network design and individual host configuration. Vulnerabilities, such as open ports, unnecessary services, weak passwords, systems that aren't updated, lack of policy, and so on, are invitations to threats such as malicious attacks. Of course, your computer network can be vulnerable to other types of threats as well, such as environmental or natural threats, but these are covered in more depth in Chapter 14, "Redundancy and Disaster Recovery," and Chapter 15, "Policies, Procedures, and People."

Vulnerability assessment is just part of overall risk management. Risk includes computer vulnerabilities, potential dangers, possible hardware and software failure, man hours wasted, and of course, monetary loss. Having a computer network is inherently a risky business, so we need to conduct risk assessments to define what an organization's risks are and how to reduce those risks.

Foundation Topics

Conducting Risk Assessments

When dealing with computer security, a *risk* is the possibility of a malicious attack or other threat causing damage or downtime to a computer system. Generally, this is done by exploiting vulnerabilities in a computer system or network. The more vulnerability—the more risk. Smart organizations are extremely interested in managing vulnerabilities, and thereby managing risk. *Risk management* can be defined as the identification, assessment, and prioritization of risks, and the mitigating and monitoring of those risks. Organizations usually employ one of the four following general strategies when managing a particular risk:

- Transfer the risk to another organization or third party.
- Avoid the risk.
- Reduce the risk.
- Accept some or all of the consequences of a risk.

The ultimate goal of risk management is to reduce all risk to a level acceptable to the organization. It is impossible to remove all risk, but it should be mitigated as much as possible within reason. Usually, budgeting and IT resources will dictate how much risk can be reduced. For example, installing antivirus/firewall software on every client computer is common; most companies will do this. However, installing a high-end, hardware-based firewall at every computer is not common. Although it would probably make for a secure network, the amount of money and administration needed to implement that solution would make it unacceptable. Most organizations are willing to accept the risk of threats exploiting vulnerabilities that would otherwise be mitigated by the use of that type of equipment. IT budgeting is always on the mind of a network security administrator. This concept would be an example of *residual risk*, which is the risk left over after a security and disaster recovery plan have been implemented. There is always risk, as a company cannot possibly foresee every future event, nor can it secure against every single threat. Senior management as a collective whole is ultimately responsible for deciding how much residual risk there will be in a company's network. Quite often, no one person will be in charge of this, but it will be decided on as a group.

There are many different types of risks to computers and computer networks. Of course, before you can decide what to do about a particular risk, you need to assess what those risks are.

Risk assessment is the attempt to determine the amount of threats or hazards that could possibly occur in a given amount of time to your computers and networks. When you assess risks, they are often recognized threats—but risk assessment can also take into account new types of threats that might occur. When risk has been assessed, it can be mitigated up until the point in which the organization will accept any additional risk. Generally, risk assessments follow a particular order, for example:

Step 1. Identify the organization's assets.

Step 2. Identify vulnerabilities.

Step 3. Identify threats and threat likelihood.

Step 4. Identify potential monetary impact.

The fourth step is also known as impact assessment. This is when you determine the potential monetary costs related to a threat. See the section "Vulnerability Management" later in this chapter for more on information on Steps 2 and 3, including how to mitigate potential threats.

The two most common risk assessment methods are qualitative and quantitative. Let's discuss these now.

Qualitative Risk Assessment

Qualitative risk assessment is an assessment that assigns numeric values to the probability of a risk, and the impact it can have on the system or network. Unlike its counterpart, it does not assign monetary values to assets or possible losses. It is the easier, quicker, and cheaper way to assess risk but cannot assign asset value or give a total for possible monetary loss.

With this method, ranges can be assigned, for example 1 to 10 or 1 to 100. The higher the number, the higher the probability of risk, or the greater the impact on the system. As a basic example, a computer without antivirus software that is connected to the Internet will most likely have a high probability of risk; it will also most likely have a great impact on the system. We could assign the number 99 as the probability of risk. We are not sure exactly when it will happen but are 99% sure that it will happen at some point. Next, we could assign the number 90 as the impact of the risk. 90 out of 100 implies a heavy impact; probably either the system has crashed or has been rendered unusable at some point. There is a 10% chance that the system will remain usable, but it is unlikely. Finally, we multiply the two numbers together to find out the qualitative risk: $99 \times 90 = 8{,}910$. That's 8,910 out of a possible 10,000, which is a high level of risk. *Risk mitigation* is when a risk is reduced or eliminated altogether. The way to mitigate risk in this example would be to install antivirus software and verify that it is configured to auto-update. By assigning these types of qualitative values to various risks, we can make comparisons from one risk to another and get a better idea of what needs to be mitigated and what doesn't.

The main issue with this type of risk assessment is that it is difficult to place an exact value on many types of risks. The type of qualitative system will vary from organization to organization, even from person to person; it is a common source of debate as well. This makes qualitative risk assessments more descriptive than truly measurable. However, by relying on group surveys, company history, and personal experience, you can get a basic idea of the risk involved.

Quantitative Risk Assessment

Quantitative risk assessment measures risk by using exact monetary values. It attempts to give an expected yearly loss in dollars for any given risk. It also defines asset values to servers, routers, and other network equipment.

Three values are used when making quantitative risk calculations:

- **Single loss expectancy (SLE)**—The loss of value in dollars based on a single incident.
- **Annualized rate of occurrence (ARO)**—The amount of times per year that the specific incident occurs.
- **Annualized loss expectancy (ALE)**—The total loss in dollars per year due to a specific incident. The incident might happen once, or more than once; either way, this number is the total loss in dollars for that particular type of incident. It is computed with the following calculation:

  SLE × ARO = ALE

So, for example, suppose you wanted to find out how much an e-commerce web server's downtime would cost the company per year. We would need some additional information such as the average web server downtime in minutes and the amount of times this occurs per year. We also would need to know the average sale amount in dollars and how many sales are made per minute on this e-commerce web server. This information can be deduced by using accounting reports and by further security analysis of the web server, which we discuss later. For now, let's just say that over the past year our web server failed 7 times. The average downtime for each failure was 45 minutes. That equals a total of 315 minutes of downtime per year, close to 99.9% uptime. (The more years we can measure, the better our estimate will be.) Now let's say that this web server processes an average of 10 orders per minute with an average revenue of $35. That means that $350 of revenue comes in per minute. As we mentioned, a single downtime averages 45 minutes, corresponding to a $15,750 loss per occurrence. So, the SLE is $15,750. Ouch! Some salespeople are going to be quite unhappy with your 99.9% uptime! But we're not done. We want to know the annualized loss expectancy (ALE). This can be calculated by multiplying the SLE ($15,750) by the annualized rate of occurrence (ARO). We said that the web server failed 7 times last year, so the SLE × ARO would be $15,750 × 7, which equals $110,250 (the ALE). This is shown in Table 10-1.

Table 10-1 Example of Quantitative Risk Assessment

SLE	ARO	ALE
$15,750	7	$110,250
Revenue lost due to each web server failure	Total web server failures over the past year	Total loss due to web server failure per year

Whoa! Apparently, we need to increase the uptime of our e-commerce web server! Many organizations will demand 99.99% or even 99.999% uptime; 99.999% uptime means that the server will only have 5 minutes of downtime over the entire course of the year. Of course, to accomplish this we first need to scrutinize our server to see precisely why it fails so often. What exactly are the vulnerabilities of the web server? Which ones were exploited? Which threats exploited those vulnerabilities? By exploring the server's logs, configurations, and policies, and by using security tools, we can discern exactly why this happens so often. However, this analysis should be done carefully because the server does so much business for the company. We continue this example and show the specific tools you can use in the section "Assessing Vulnerability with Security Tools."

It isn't possible to assign a specific ALE to incidents that will happen in the future, so new technologies should be monitored carefully. Any failures should be documented thoroughly. For example, a spreadsheet could be maintained that contains the various technologies your organization uses, their failure history, their SLE, ARO, and SLE, and mitigation techniques that you have employed, and when they were implemented.

Table 10-2 Summary of Risk Assessment Types

Risk Assessment Type	Description	Key Points
Qualitative risk assessment	Assigns numeric values to the probability of a risk, and the impact it can have on the system or network.	Numbers are arbitrary. Examples: 1–10 or 1–100.
Quantitative risk assessment	Measures risk by using exact monetary values. It attempts to give an expected yearly loss in dollars for any given risk.	Values are specific monetary amounts. SLE × ARO = ALE

Security Analysis Methodologies

To assess risk properly, we must analyze the security of our computers, servers, and network devices. But before making an analysis, the computer, server, or other device should be backed up accordingly. This might require a backup of files, a complete image backup, or a backup of firmware. It all depends on the device in question. When this is done, an analysis can be made. Hosts should be analyzed to discern whether a firewall is in place, what type of configuration is used (or worse if the device is using a default configuration), what antimalware software is installed if any, and what updates have been made. A list of vulnerabilities should be developed, and a security person should watch for threats that could exploit these vulnerabilities; they might occur naturally, or be perpetuated by malicious persons, or could be due to user error.

Security analysis can be done in one of two ways: actively or passively.

Active security analysis is when actual hands-on tests are run on the system in question. These tests might require a device to be taken off the network for a short time, or it might cause a loss in productivity. Active scanning is used to find out if ports are open on a specific device, or to find out what IP addresses are in use on the network. A backup of the systems to be analyzed should be accomplished before the scan takes place. Active scanning can be detrimental to systems or the entire network, especially if you are dealing with a mission-critical network that requires close to 100% uptime. In some cases, you can pull systems off the network or run your test on off hours. But in other cases you must rely on passive security analysis.

Passive security analysis is when servers, devices, and networks are not affected by your analyses, scans, and other tests. It could be as simple as using documentation only to test the security of a system. For example, if an organization's network documentation shows computers, switches, servers, and routers, but no firewall, you have found a vulnerability to the network (a rather large one). Passive security analysis might be required in real-time, mission-critical networks or if you are conducting computer forensics analysis; but even if you are performing a passive security analysis, a backup of the system is normal procedure.

One example of the difference between active and passive is fingerprinting, which is when a security person (or hacker) scans hosts to find out what ports are open, ultimately helping the person to distinguish the operating system used by the computer. It is also known as OS fingerprinting or TCP/IP fingerprinting. Active fingerprinting is when a direct connection is made to the computer starting with ICMP requests. This type of test could cause the system to respond slowly to other requests from legitimate computers. Passive fingerprinting is when the scanning host sniffs the network by chance, classifying hosts as the scanning host observes its traffic on the occasion that it occurs. This method is less common in port scanners but can help to reduce stress on the system being scanned.

Vulnerability Management

Vulnerability management is the practice of finding and mitigating software vulnerabilities in computers and networks. It consists of analyzing network documentation, testing computers and networks with a variety of security tools, mitigating vulnerabilities, and periodically monitoring for effects and changes. Vulnerability management can be broken down into five steps:

Step 1. **Define the desired state of security—**An organization might have written policies defining the desired state of security, or you as the network security administrator might have to create those policies. These policies include access control rules, device configurations, network configurations, network documentation, and so on.

Step 2. **Create baselines—**After the desired state of security is defined, baselines should be taken to assess the current security state of computers, servers, network devices, and the network in general. These baselines are known as *vulnerability assessments*. The baselines should find as many vulnerabilities as possible. These baselines will be known as premitigation baselines and should be saved for later comparison.

Step 3. **Prioritize vulnerabilities—**Which vulnerabilities should take precedence? For example, the e-commerce web server we talked about earlier should definitely have a higher priority than a single client computer that does not have antivirus software installed. Prioritize all the vulnerabilities; this creates a list of items that need to be mitigated in order.

Step 4. **Mitigate vulnerabilities—**Go through the prioritized list and mitigate as many of the vulnerabilities as possible. This depends on the level of acceptable risk your organization will allow.

Step 5. **Monitor the environment—**When you finish mitigation, monitor the environment and compare the results to the original baseline. Use the new results as the post-mitigation baseline to be compared against future analyses. Because new vulnerabilities are always being discovered, and because company policies may change over time, you should periodically monitor the environment and compare your results to the post-mitigation baseline. Do this any time policies change or the environment changes.

This five-step process has helped me when managing vulnerabilities for customers. It should be noted again that some organizations already have a defined policy for their desired security level. You might come into a company as an employee or consultant who needs to work within their pre-existing mindset. In other cases, an organization won't have a policy defined; it might not even know what type of security it needs. Just don't jump the gun assuming that you need to complete Step 1 from scratch.

The most important parts of vulnerability management are the finding and mitigating of vulnerabilities. Actual tools used to conduct vulnerability assessments include network mappers, port scanners, and other vulnerability scanners, ping scanners, protocol analyzers (also called network sniffers), and password crackers. Vulnerability assessments might discover confidential data or sensitive data that is not properly protected, open ports, weak passwords, default configurations, prior attacks, system failures, and so on. Vulnerability assessments or vulnerability scanning can be taken to the next level by administering a penetration test.

Penetration Testing

Penetration testing is a method of evaluating the security of a system by simulating one or more attacks on that system. One of the differences between regular vulnerability scanning and penetration testing is that vulnerability scanning *may* be passive or active, whereas penetration testing *will* be active. Penetration tests can be done blind, as in black box testing, where testers have no knowledge of the computer, infrastructure, or environment that they are testing. This simulates an attack from a person who is unfamiliar with the system. White box testing is the converse, where the tester is provided with complete knowledge of the computer, infrastructure, or environment to be tested. Generally, penetration testing is performed on servers or network devices that will face the Internet publicly. This would be an example of external security testing—when a test is conducted from outside the organization's security perimeter. Following are a couple methodologies for accomplishing penetration testing:

- **The *Open Source Security Testing Methodology Manual* (OSSTMM)—**This manual and corresponding methodology define the proper way to conduct security testing. It adheres to the scientific method. The manual is freely obtained from ISECOM (link at the end of the chapter).
- **NIST penetration testing—**This is discussed in the document SP800-115 (link at the end of the chapter). This document and methodology is less thorough than the OSSTMM; however, many organizations find it satisfactory because it comes from a department of the U.S. government. At times, it refers to the OSSTMM instead of going into more detail.

OVAL

The *Open Vulnerability and Assessment Language (OVAL)* is a standard designed to regulate the transfer of secure public information across networks and the Internet utilizing any security tools and services available at the time. It is an international standard but is funded by the U.S. Department of Homeland Security. There is a worldwide OVAL community that contributes to the standard, storing OVAL content in several locations, such as the MITRE Corporation (http://oval.mitre.org/). OVAL can be defined in two parts: the OVAL Language and the OVAL Interpreter.

- **OVAL Language—**Three different XML schemas have been developed that act as the framework of OVAL:
  1. System testing information
  2. System state analysis
  3. Assessment results reporting

  OVAL is not a language like C++ but is an XML schema that defines and describes the XML documents to be created for use with OVAL.
- **OVAL Interpreter—**A reference developed to ensure that the correct syntax is used by comparing it to OVAL schemas and definitions. There are several downloads associated with the OVAL Interpreter and help files and forums that enable security people to check their work for accuracy.

  OVAL has several uses, for example as a tool to standardize security advisory distributions. Software vendors need to publish vulnerabilities in a standard, machine-readable format. By including an authoring tool, definitions repository, and definition evaluator, OVAL enables users to regulate their security advisories. Other uses for OVAL include vulnerability assessment, patch management, auditing, threat indicators, and so on.

Some of the entities that use OVAL include Hewlett-Packard, Red Hat Inc., CA Inc., and the U.S. Army CERDEC (Communications-Electronics Research, Development and Engineering Center).

Assessing Vulnerability with Security Tools

Up until now, we have talked about processes, methodologies, and concepts. But without actual security tools, testing, analyzing, and assessing cannot be accomplished. This section delves into the tools you might use in the field today.

Computer and networks are naturally vulnerable. Whether it is an operating system or appliance installed out-of-the-box, they are inherently insecure. Vulnerabilities could come in the form of backdoors or open ports. They could also be caused after installation due to poor design.

To understand what can be affected, network security administrators should possess thorough computer and network documentation, and if they don't already, they should develop it themselves. Tools such as LAN Surveyor, Network Magic, and Microsoft Visio can help to create proper network documentation. Then, tools such as vulnerability scanners, protocol analyzers, and password crackers should be used to assess the level of vulnerability on a computer network. When vulnerabilities are found, they should be eliminated or reduced as much as possible. Finally, scanning tools should be used again to prove that the vulnerabilities to the computer network have been removed.

You will find that most of the tools described in this section will be used by network security administrators and hackers alike. One uses the tools to find vulnerabilities and mitigate risk. The other uses the tools to exploit those vulnerabilities. However, remember that not all hackers are malevolent. Some are just curious, but they can cause just as much damage and down time as any other hacker.

Network Mapping

Network documentation is an important part of defining the desired state of security. To develop adequate detailed network documentation, network mapping software should be used with network diagramming software. *Network mapping* is the study of physical and logical connectivity of networks. One example of network mapping software is LAN Surveyor by Solarwinds. This product can map elements on Layers 1–3 of the OSI model giving you a thorough representation of what is on the network. This type of network scan is not for the "weak of bandwidth." It should be attempted only during off hours (if there is such a thing nowadays). Otherwise, when the network is at its lowest point of usage. Figure 10-1 shows an example of a test network mapped with LAN Surveyor. It was configured to map the 10.254.254.0 network but can be arranged to analyze a larger network space. You will notice that a computer named Server2003 is listed twice. This could be a possible security issue, or it could mean that the computer is multihomed or has two IP addresses bound to the same network adapter. Either way, it should be verified and possibly fixed during the mitigation phase of vulnerability assessment. This program shows routers, Layer 3 switches, client computers, servers, and virtual machines. It can also export the mapped contents directly to Microsoft Visio, a handy time-saver.

Another example of a network mapping tool is Network Magic, available as a free trial from the Cisco Pure Networks Solutions website. This tool also comes as a full or lite version with various models of routers. You just might have the software in your possession if you have a Linksys or D-Link router. This tool is easy to use and works well in small networks. An example of another test network mapped with Network Magic is shown in Figure 10-2. There are plenty of other free and pay versions of network mapping software. A quick Google search will display a list. Try out different programs, get to know them, and decide what works best for your infrastructure.

Wireless networks can be surveyed in a similar fashion. Applications such as AirMagnet can map out the wireless clients on your network and output the information as you want to aid in your network documentation efforts.

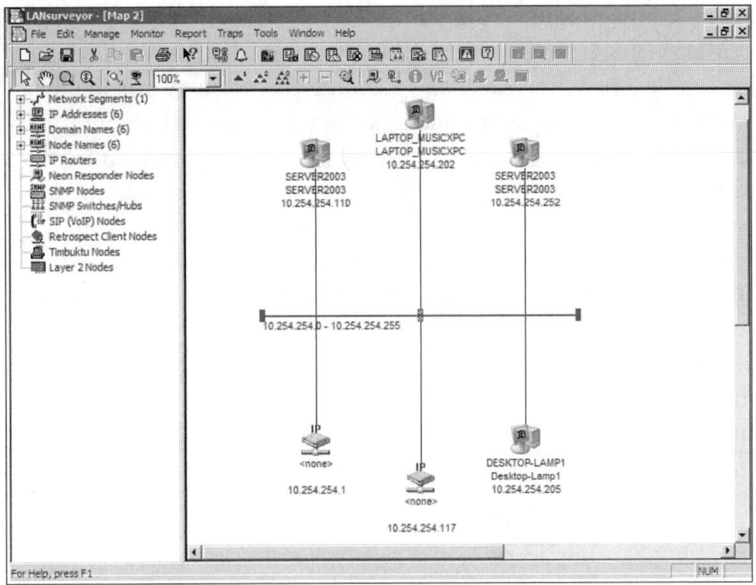

Figure 10-1 LAN Surveyor Network Map

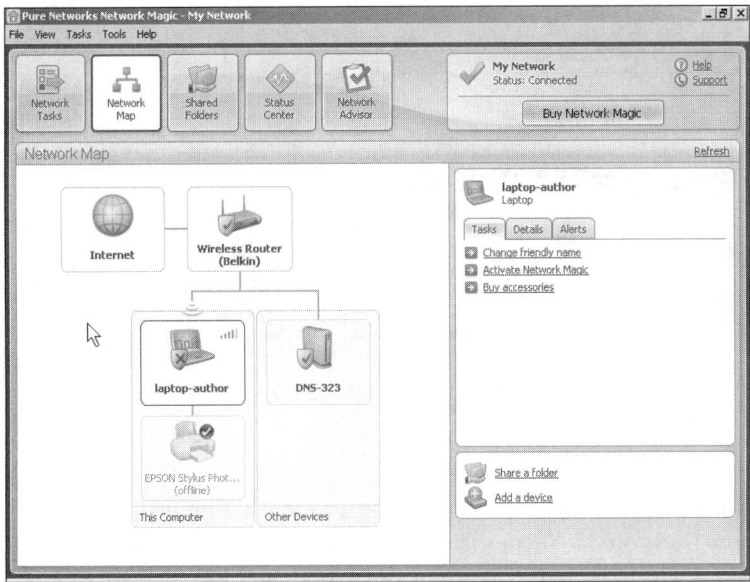

Figure 10-2 Network Magic Network Map

When you are working on your network documentation, certain areas of the network probably will need to be filled in manually. Some devices will be tough to scan, and you will have to rely on your eyes and other network administrators' knowledge to get a clear picture of the network. Network documentation can be written out or developed with a network diagramming program, such as Microsoft Visio. (A free trial is available at Microsoft's Office website.) Visio can make all kinds of diagrams and flowcharts that can be a real time-saver and planning tool for network administrators and security people. An example of a network diagram is shown in Figure 10-3. This network diagram was created by mapping a now-defunct network with LAN Surveyor, exporting those results to Visio, and then making some tweaks to the diagram manually. Names and IP addresses (among other things) were changed to protect the innocent. This documentation helped to discover a few weaknesses such as the lack of firewalling and other DMZ issues such as the lack of CIDR notation on the DMZ IP network. Just the act of documenting revealed some other issues with some of the servers on the DMZ, making it much easier to mitigate risk. When the risks were mitigated, the resulting final network documentation acted as a foundation for later security analysis and comparison to future baselines.

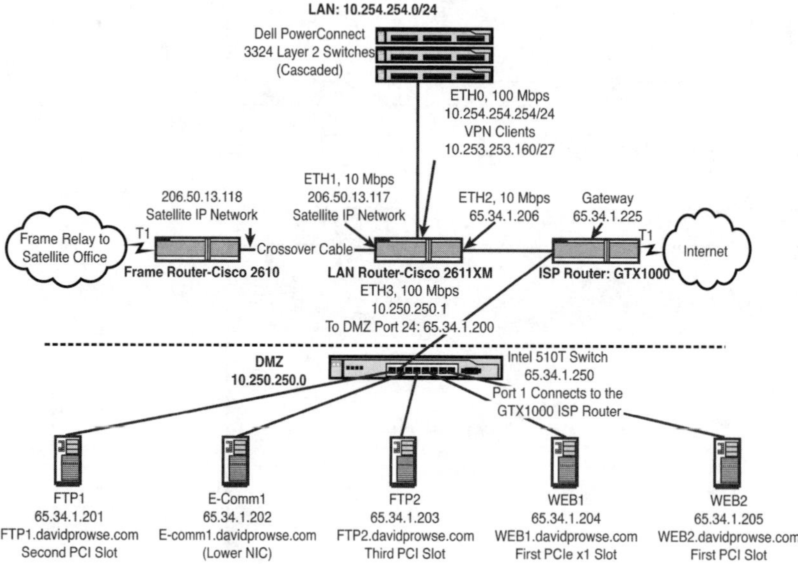

Figure 10-3 Network Diagram Created with Microsoft Visio

At times, you might be tempted to put passwords into a network diagram—don't do it! If there are too many passwords to memorize, and you need to keep passwords stored somewhere, the best way is to write them on a piece of paper and lock that paper in a fireproof, nonremovable safe, perhaps offsite. The people (admins) who know the combination to the safe should be limited. Don't keep passwords on any computers!

You might also want to keep a list of IP addresses, computer names, and so on. This can be done on paper, within Excel or Access, or can be developed within your network mapping program and exported as you want. I find that Excel works great because you can sort different categories by the column header.

To summarize, network mapping can help in several of the vulnerability assessment phases. Be sure to use network mapping programs and document your network thoroughly. It can aid you when baselining and analyzing your networks and systems.

Vulnerability Scanning

When you are ready to assess the level of vulnerability on the network, it is wise to use a general vulnerability scanner and a port scanner (or two). By scanning all the systems on the network, you can gain much insight as to the risks that you need to mitigate, and malicious activity that might already be going on underneath your nose.

One such vulnerability scanner is called Nessus. Originally developed for UNIX, you can now obtain versions for Linux and Windows as well. As of the writing of this book, Nessus 4 is the current version. It is available for home study use for free, but if you use it in the business world, there is a subscription fee. Vulnerability scanners like this one are usually active and can discover vulnerabilities within your network and beyond. Because it is a powerful, active-scanning, high-speed software tool, it should be used cautiously and most likely when there is a lull in network usage or perhaps off-hours.

The tool has a server and a client side. The server side is used to manage users and settings. The client side runs within a browser and is where you do your actual scans. To scan a host or network, you must first create a policy defining what you want to scan for. Then scan according to the policy you created. Again, these types of active scans are resource-intensive, so they take some time to complete. An example of a vulnerability scan with Nessus is shown in Figure 10-4. It shows some open ports on the IP 10.254.254.1 and their corresponding services that may or may not be vulnerabilities. The tool can also check for backdoors, denial-of-service attacks, and lots of other families of threats. If you suspect that a particular computer is the victim of a malicious attack, this is an excellent tool to use to make that determination. Even if you are not sure, scanning important hosts on the network can help to put your mind at ease or...uncover risks that you must mitigate.

Other formidable vulnerability scanners include GFI LANguard, ISS Internet Scanner, X-scan, and Sara. Sometimes, these tools are referred to as network scanners if they are used to find open ports within multiple computers on the network or the entire network.

Sometimes, a full-blown vulnerability scanner isn't necessary. There will be times when you simply want to scan ports or run other basic tests. An example of a good *port scanner* is Nmap. Although this tool has other functionality in addition to port scanning, it is probably best known for its port scanning capability. Figure 10-5 shows an example of a port scan with Nmap. This shows a scan (using the –sS parameter) to a computer that runs Kerberos (port 88), DNS (port 53), and web services (port 80) among other things. By using a port scanner like this one, you are taking a fingerprint of the operating system. The port scanner tells you what inbound ports are open on the remote computer and what services are running. From this, you can discern much more information, for example what operating system the computer is running, what applications, and so on. In the example in Figure 10-5, you can gather that the scanned computer is a Microsoft domain controller running additional services. So this is an example of OS fingerprinting.

Key Topic

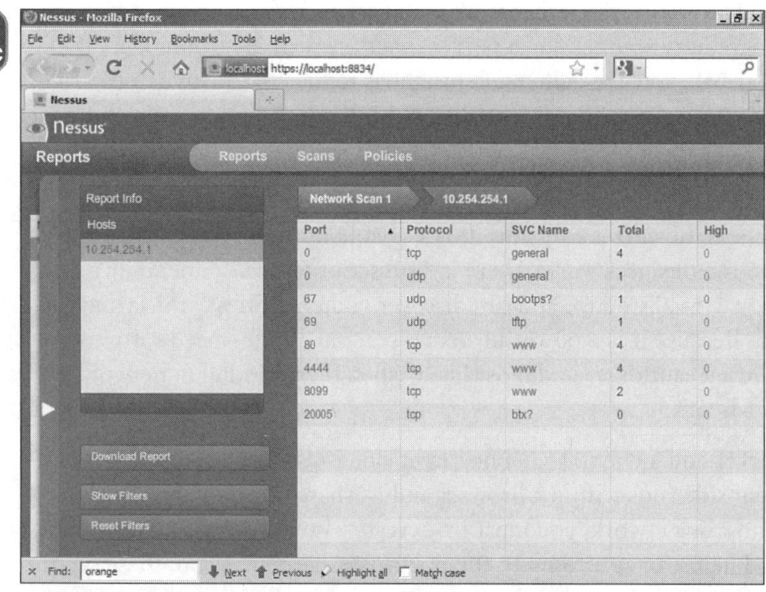

Figure 10-4 Network Vulnerability Scan with Nessus

Key Topic

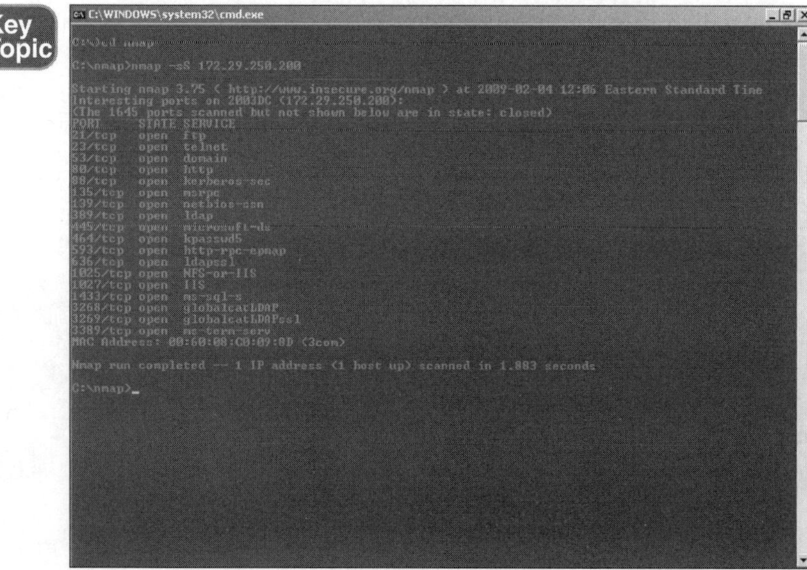

Figure 10-5 Port Scan with Nmap

Open ports should be examined. You should be fully aware of the services or processes that use those ports. If services are unnecessary, they should be stopped and disabled. For example, if this computer was indeed a domain controller but wasn't supposed to be a DNS server, the DNS service (port 53) should be stopped. Otherwise, the DNS port could act as a vulnerability of the server. Afterward, the computer should be rescanned to ensure that the risk has been mitigated.

Nonessential services are often not configured, monitored, or secured by the network administrator. It is imperative that network administrators scan for nonessential services and close any corresponding ports. Even though services may be nonessential, that doesn't necessarily mean that they are not in use, maliciously or otherwise.

Another tool that can be used to scan the ports in use is the **netstat** command. For example, the **netstat**, **netstat –a**, **netstat –n** and **netstat –an** commands. However, this is only for the local computer. More port scanners include Superscan and Angry IP Scanner among others. Some of these tools can be used as ping scanners, sending out ICMP echoes to find the IP addresses within a particular network segment.

Network Sniffing

For all intents and purposes, the terms protocol analyzer, packet sniffer, and network sniffer all mean the same thing. Sniffing the network is when you use a tool to find and investigate other computers on the network; the term is often used when capturing packets for later analysis. *Protocol analyzers* can tell you much more about the traffic that is coming and going to and from a host than a vulnerability scanner or port scanner might. In reality, the program captures Ethernet frames of information directly from the network adapter and displays the packets inside of those frames within a capture window. Each packet is *encapsulated* inside a frame.

One common example of a protocol analyzer is Wireshark, previously known as Ethereal, which is a free download that can run on a variety of platforms. By default, it captures packets on the local computer that it was installed on. Figure 10-6 shows an example of a packet capture. This capture is centered on frame number 10, which encapsulates an ICMP packet. This particular packet is a ping request sent from the local computer (10.254.254.205) to the remote host (10.254.254.1). Although my local computer can definitely send out pings, it is unknown whether 10.254.254.1 should be replying to those pings. Perhaps there is a desired policy that states that this device (which is actually a router) should not reply to pings. As we learned in Chapter 5, "Network Design Elements and Network Threats," an ICMP reply can be a vulnerability. Now, if we look at Frame 11 we see it shows an echo reply from 10.254.254.1—not what we want. So, to mitigate this risk and remove the vulnerability, we would turn off ICMP echo replies on the router.

This is just one example of many that we could show with this program. I've used this program to find unauthorized FTP, gaming, and P2P traffic among other things! You'd be surprised how often network admins and even regular old users set up these types of servers. It uses up valuable bandwidth and resources, so you can imagine that an organization would want these removed. Not only that, but they can be vulnerabilities as well. By running these services, a person opens up the computer system to a whole new set of threats. By removing these unauthorized servers, we are reducing risk. I know—I'm such a buzzkill. But really now, work is work, and play is play; that's how companies are going to look at it.

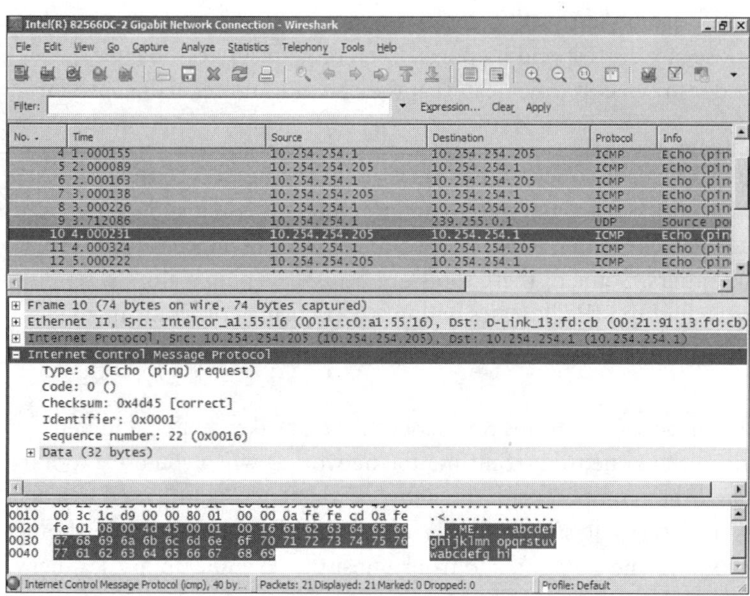

Figure 10-6 Packet Capture with Wireshark

On the other side of things, malicious users will utilize a protocol analyzer to capture passwords and other confidential information. We discuss software-based protocol analyzers more in Chapter 11, "Monitoring and Auditing."

Also, hardware-based devices can analyze your networks and hosts; for example, Fluke Networks devices such as the NetTool Inline Network Tester. Handheld computers often have a text-based menu system that can be used to monitor ports, troubleshoot authentication issues, identify network resources and IP addresses, and lots more. The name *Fluke* is used by some techs even if they use a handheld device by a different vendor; the brand is that well-known.

Password Analysis

Well, we've mapped the network, documented it, scanned for vulnerabilities, scanned ports, and analyzed packets. But wait, let's not forget about passwords. We've mentioned more than once in this book that weak passwords are the bane of today's networks. This could be because no policy for passwords was defined, and people naturally gravitate toward weaker, easier-to-remember passwords. Or it could be that a policy was defined but is not complex enough, or is out of date. Whatever the reason, it would be wise to scan computers and other devices for weak passwords with a *password cracker*, which uses comparative analysis to break passwords and systematically guesses until it cracks the password. And of course, a variety of password cracking programs can help with this. For Windows computers, there is the well-documented Cain & Abel password recovery tool. This program has a bit of a learning curve but is quite powerful. It can be used to crack all kinds of different passwords on the local system or on remote devices and computers. It sniffs out other hosts on the network the way a protocol analyzer would. This is an excellent tool to find out whether weak passwords are on the network, or to help if users forgot their passwords. Figure 10-7 shows an example of Cain & Abel. You can see hashed passwords (encrypted) that the program has discovered for various accounts on a test computer. From these hashes, the program can attempt to crack the password and deliver the original plaintext version of the password.

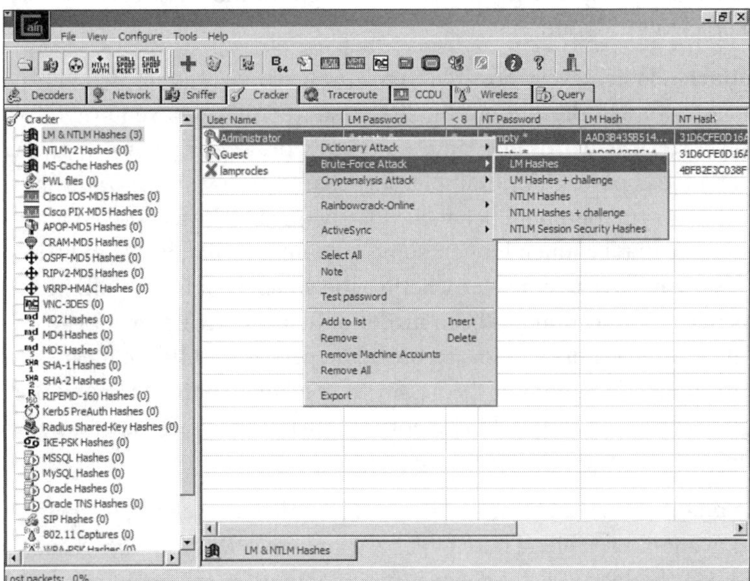

Figure 10-7 Password Cracking with Cain & Abel

We talk more about hashes and hashing algorithms in Chapter 12, "Encryption and Hashing Concepts."

Cain & Abel is a free download, and many other tools are available for various platforms; some free, some not, including John the Ripper, L0phtcrack, THC Hydra, Aircrack (and the older AirSnort), SolarWinds, and RainbowCrack. Some of these tools have additional functionality but are known best as password cracking tools, otherwise referred to as password recovery programs.

The following list shows the various password cracking methods. Password recovery (or cracking) can be done in several different ways:

- **Guessing—**Weak passwords can be guessed by a smart person, especially if the person has knowledge of the user he is trying to exploit. Blank passwords are all too common. And then there are common passwords such as password, admin, secret, love, and many more. If a guessing attacker knew the person and some of the person's details, he might attempt the person's username as the password, or someone the person knows, date of birth, and so on. Reversing letters or adding a 1 on to the end of a password are other common methods. Although guessing is not as much of a technical method as the following three options, it reveals many passwords every day all over the world.
- **Dictionary attack—**Uses a pre-arranged list of likely words, trying each of them one at a time. It can be used for cracking passwords, passphrases, and keys. It works best with weak passwords and when targeting multiple systems. The power of the dictionary attack depends on the strength of the dictionary used by the password cracking program.
- **Brute force attack—**When every possible password instance is attempted. This is often a last resort due to the amount of CPU resources it might require. It works best on shorter passwords but can theoretically break any password given enough time and CPU power. For example, a 4 -character, lowercase password with no numbers or symbols could be cracked fairly quickly. But a 10-character, complex password will take much longer; some computers will fail to complete the process. Also, you have to consider whether the attack is online or offline. Online means that a connection has been made to the host, giving the password cracking program only a short window to break the password. Offline means that there is no connection and that the password cracking computer knows the target host's password hash and hashing algorithm giving the cracking computer more (or unlimited) time to make the attempt.
- **Cryptanalysis attack—**Uses a considerable set of precalculated encrypted passwords located in a lookup table. These tables are known as *Rainbow Tables*, and the type of password attack is also known as precomputation, where all words in the dictionary (or a specific set of possible passwords) are hashed and stored. This is done in an attempt to recover passwords quicker. It is often used with the RainbowCrack application. This attack can be defeating by implementing *salting*, which is the randomization of the hashing process.

Passwords can also be obtained through viruses and Trojans, wiretapping, keystroke logging, phishing, shoulder surfing, social engineering, and dumpster diving. Yikes! It should go without mentioning that protecting passwords is just as important as creating complex passwords and complex password policies that are periodically monitored and updated. Remember that password policies created on a Windows server will not have jurisdiction where other vendor's devices are concerned, such as

Cisco routers and firewalls or Check Point security devices. These need to be checked individually or by scanning particular network segments.

We could talk about password cracking for days because there are so many types of hashes, hashing algorithms, and password cracking tools and ways to crack the passwords. But for the Security+ exam, a basic understanding of password cracking is enough.

Table 10-3 Summary of Chapter 10 Security Tools

Security Tool	Description
LAN Surveyor	Network mapping tool
Network Magic	Network mapping tool
Microsoft Visio	Network diagramming tool
Nessus	Vulnerability scanner
Nmap	Port scanner
Wireshark	Protocol analyzer
Fluke	Handheld protocol analyzer/network sniffer
Cain and Abel	Password cracking tool
John the Ripper	Password cracking tool

Exam Preparation Tasks

Review Key Topics

Review the most important topics in the chapter, noted with the Key Topics icon in the outer margin of the page. Table 10-4 lists a reference of these key topics and the page numbers on which each is found.

Table 10-4 Key Topics for Chapter 10

Key Topic Element	Description	Page Number
Table 10-1	Example of Quantitative Risk Assessment	287
Table 10-2	Summary of Risk Assessment Types	287
Numbered list	Five Steps of Vulnerability Management	289
Figure 10-1	LAN Surveyor Network Map	293
Figure 10-4	Network Vulnerability Scan with Nessus	296
Figure 10-5	Port Scan with Nmap	296
Figure 10-6	Packet Capture with Wireshark	298
Figure 10-7	Password Cracking with Cain & Abel	299
Bulleted list	Password Cracking Methods	300
Table 10-3	Summary of Chapter 10 Security Tools	301

Complete Tables and Lists from Memory

Print a copy of Appendix A, "Memory Tables," (found on the DVD), or at least the section for this chapter, and complete the tables and lists from memory. Appendix B, "Memory Tables Answer Key," also on the DVD, includes completed tables and lists to check your work.

Define Key Terms

Define the following key terms from this chapter, and check your answers in the glossary:

vulnerability, risk, risk management, residual risk, risk assessment, qualitative risk assessment, quantitative risk assessment, risk mitigation, vulnerability management, vulnerability assessment, penetration testing, Open Vulnerability and Assessment

Language (OVAL), network mapping, vulnerability scanning, port scanner, protocol analyzer, password cracker, dictionary attack, brute force attack, cryptanalysis attack, Rainbow Tables, salting

Hands-On Labs

Complete the following written step-by-step scenarios. After you finish (or if you do not have adequate equipment to complete the scenario), watch the corresponding video solutions on the DVD.

If you have additional questions, feel free to post them at my website: www.davidlprowse.com in the Ask Dave forum. (Free registration is required to post on the website.)

Equipment Needed

A Windows client computer to run tests with the following security software:

- LAN Surveyor: Trial download: www.solarwinds.com/products/lansurveyor/
- Nessus: Free download: www.nessus.org/nessus/
- Cain and Abel: Free download: www.oxid.it/cain.html
- A Windows Server (2003 or 2008 preferred) that runs at least one network service such as DNS, DHCP, and so on.
- Several other computer and network devices on the same network segment. Exactly what these are isn't important. These will be used for default mapping and scanning purposes.

Lab 10-1: Mapping and Scanning the Network

In this lab, you map your network with LAN Surveyor and then scan devices on the network with Nessus. The steps are as follows:

Step 1. Download, install, and run LAN Surveyor.

Step 2. Click **File** and select **New**. That should automatically see your network segment.

Step 3. Click **OK** to scan for hosts on the network. This takes a few minutes to locate and map all the computers and other devices on the network.

Step 4. Examine the hosts on your network. Define which host you want to analyze with Nessus. In the video, we use a 4-port SOHO router as the device to scan.

Step 5. Download, install, and run Nessus. You need to run the server side first and add users by clicking the **Manage Users** button. Then run the client (which runs in a browser) and log in.

Step 6. Click **Policies** and create a new scanning policy. Make sure that **TCP Scan** and **Ping Host** are selected. Click **Next** and complete creating the scan.

Step 7. Create a new scan:

A. Click **Scans**.

B. Click **Add**.

C. Name the scan.

D. Add the IP address of the host you want to scan into the **Scan Targets** field.

E. Click **Launch**.

Let the scan complete; it takes a few minutes.

Step 8. Double-click the scan name, and then double-click the IP address of the host scanned. Examine the open ports and associated vulnerabilities.

Step 9. In the video, we shut down DHCP on the SOHO 4-port router. If there are other threats that you find, disable or shut them down now.

Step 10. Rescan the original host and verify that the vulnerabilities have been mitigated.

Watch the solution video in the "Hands-On Scenarios" section of the DVD.

Lab 10-2: Password Cracking and Defense

In this lab, you crack a basic password on a Windows computer and then run through a couple of the precautions that can be taken to reduce the risk of passwords being cracked on your computers and network. For this lab, we use Windows Vista as the example target computer.

Be sure to run this lab on a test computer!

The steps are as follows:

Pre-lab procedure:

Step 1. Change the password policy so that you can have a noncomplex, 4-character password. See Lab 9-1 in Chapter 9 for details on how to configure the password policy.

Step 2. Change the Administrator password to a blank password.

Step 3. Select another account and change the password to **test**.

Continue with the lab:

Step 1. Download, install, and run Cain and Abel.

Step 2. Click the **Cracker** tab.

Step 3. Select **LM & NTLM Hashes**.

Step 4. Click the **+** sign on the toolbar.

Step 5. In the **Add NT Hashes from** dialog box, leave the default values, and click **Next**.

This should display the accounts on the system. Note that the Administrator account displays ***empty*** in both the LM Password and NT Password columns. This is because you changed it to blank previously.

Step 6. Examine the account that you set up with the **test** password. We will attempt to crack this password.

Step 7. Right-click the account, and select **Brute-Force Attack > NTLM Hashes**.

Step 8. Modify the Max password length to **4**.

Step 9. Click **Start**. This should deduce the password **test** in a few seconds or less.

Step 10. To mitigate this, do the following:

A. Assign a tougher policy in Windows. Make sure that complexity requirements are turned on and that the minimum password length is set to 8 characters or more.

B. Assign a complex password to the account using the **test** password.

C. Assign a complex password to the Administrator account.

D. Consider giving the Guest account a complex password also.

Watch the solution video in the "Hands-On Scenarios" section of the DVD.

View Recommended Resources

- ISO 31000: "Risk Management—Principles and Guidelines": www.iso.org/iso/catalogue_detail.htm?csnumber=43170
- OSSTMM download: www.isecom.org/osstmm/
- NIST Special Publication 800-115: "Technical Guide to Information Security Testing and Assessment": http://csrc.nist.gov/publications/nistpubs/800-115/SP800-115.pdf
- Link to all NIST Special Publication 800 Series documents (SP800): http://csrc.nist.gov/publications/PubsSPs.html

- Open Vulnerability and Assessment Language repository website: http://oval.mitre.org/
- OVAL download: http://oval.mitre.org/language/version5.7/
- LAN Surveyor trial download: www.solarwinds.com/products/lansurveyor/
- Cisco—Network Magic trial: www.purenetworks.com/download/
- Microsoft Visio trial: http://office.microsoft.com/en-us/visio/
- Nessus Network Vulnerability Scanner: www.nessus.org/nessus/
- Nmap: http://nmap.org/download.html
- Superscan: www.foundstone.com/us/resources/proddesc/superscan.htm
- Angry IP Scanner: www.angryip.org/w/Home
- Wireshark Protocol Analyzer: www.wireshark.org/download.html
- NetTool Inline Network Tester: www.flukenetworks.com/fnet/en-us/products/NetTool/Overview.htm
- Cain & Abel password recovery tool: www.oxid.it/cain.html
- John the Ripper password recovery tool: www.openwall.com/john/

Answer Review Questions

Answer the following review questions. You can find the answers at the end of this chapter.

1. Which type of vulnerability assessments software can check for weak passwords on the network?

A. Wireshark

B. Antivirus software

C. Performance Monitor

D. A password cracker

2. You are contracted to conduct a forensics analysis of the computer. What should you do first?

A. Back up the system.

B. Analyze the files.

C. Scan for viruses.

D. Make changes to the operating system.

3. Which of the following has schemas written in XML?

   A. OVAL

   B. 3DES

   C. WPA

   D. PAP

4. Russ is using only documentation to test the security of a system. What type of testing methodology is this known as?

   A. Active security analysis

   B. Passive security analysis

   C. Hybrid security analysis

   D. Hands-on security analysis

5. Of the following which is the best way for a person to find out what security holes exist on the network?

   A. Run a port scan.

   B. Use a network sniffer.

   C. Perform a vulnerability assessment.

   D. Use an IDS solution.

6. After using NMAP to do a port scan of your server, you find that several ports are open. Which of the following should you do next?

   A. Leave the ports open and monitor them for malicious attacks.

   B. Run the port scan again.

   C. Close all ports.

   D. Examine the services and/or processes that use those ports.

7. Which of the following is a vulnerability assessment tool?

   A. John the Ripper

   B. AirSnort

   C. Nessus

   D. Cain & Abel

8. You are a consultant for an IT company. Your boss asks you to determine the topology of the network. What is the best device to use in this circumstance?

   A. Network mapper

   B. Protocol analyzer

   C. Port scanner

   D. A vulnerability scanner

9. Which of the following can enable you to find all the open ports on an entire network?

A. Protocol analyzer

B. Network scanner

C. Firewall

D. Performance monitor

10. What can hackers accomplish using malicious port scanning?

A. "Fingerprint" of the operating system

B. Topology of the network

C. All the computer names on the network

D. All the usernames and passwords

11. Many companies send passwords via clear text. Which of the following can view these passwords?

A. Rainbow table

B. Port scanner

C. John the Ripper

D. Protocol analyzer

12. Which of the following persons is ultimately in charge of deciding how much residual risk there will be?

A. Chief security officer

B. Security administrator

C. Senior management

D. Disaster Recovery Plan coordinator

13. To show risk from a monetary standpoint, which of the following should risk assessments be based upon?

A. Survey of loss, potential threats, and asset value

B. Quantitative measurement of risk, impact, and asset value

C. Complete measurement of all threats

D. Qualitative measurement of risk and impact

14. The main objective of risk management in an organization is to reduce risk to a level ___________. (Fill in the blank.)

A. The organization will mitigate

B. Where the ARO equals the SLE

C. The organization will accept

D. Where the ALE is lower than the SLE

15. Why would a security administrator use a vulnerability scanner? (Select the best answer.)

A. To identify remote access policies

B. To analyze protocols

C. To map the network

D. To find open ports on a server

16. An example of a program that does comparative analysis is what?

A. Protocol analyzer

B. Password cracker

C. Port scanner

D. Event Viewer

17. Why do hacker's often target nonessential services? (Select the two best answers.)

A. Quite often, they are not configured correctly.

B. They are not monitored as often.

C. They are not used.

D. They are not monitored by an IDS.

18. Which of the following tools uses ICMP as its main underlying protocol?

A. Ping scanner

B. Port scanner

C. Image scanner

D. Barcode scanner

19. Which command would display the following output?

```
Active Connections
   Proto  Local Address          Foreign Address        State
   TCP    laptop-musicxpc:1395   8.15.228.165:http      ESTABLISHED
```

A. **Ping**

B. **Ipconfig**

C. **Nbtstat**

D. **Netstat**

Answers and Explanations

1. **D.** A password cracker can check for weak passwords on the network. Antivirus software can scan for viruses on a computer. Performance Monitor enables you to create baselines to check the performance of a computer. Wire shark is a protocol analyzer.
2. **A.** Back up the system before you do anything else. This way, you have a backup copy in the case that anything goes wrong when you analyze or make changes to the system.
3. **A.** OVAL (Open Vulnerability and Assessment Language) uses XML as a framework for the language. It is a community standard dealing with the standardization of information transfer. 3DES is an encryption algorithm. WPA is a wireless encryption standard, and the deprecated PAP is the Password Authentication Protocol, used for identifying users to a server.
4. **B.** Passive security analysis or passive security testing would be one that possibly does not include a hands-on test. It is less tangible and often includes the use of documentation only. To better protect a system or network, a person should also use active security analysis.
5. **C.** The best way to find all the security holes that exist on a network is to perform a vulnerability assessment. This may include utilizing a port scanner and using a network sniffer and perhaps using some sort of IDS.
6. **D.** If you find ports open that you don't expect, be sure to examine the services and or processes that use those ports. You may have to close some or all those ports. When you finish with your examination, and after you have taken action, run the port scan again to verify that those ports are closed.
7. **C.** Nessus is a vulnerability assessment tool. AirSnort is used to crack wireless encryption codes. John the Ripper and Cain & Abel are password cracking programs.
8. **A.** A network mapper is the best tool to use to determine the topology of the network and to find out what devices and computers reside on that network. An example of this would be LAN Surveyor.
9. **B.** A network scanner is a port scanner used to find open ports on multiple computers on the network. A protocol analyzer is used to delve into packets. A firewall protects a network, and a performance monitor is used to create baselines for and monitor a computer.
10. **A.** Port scanning can be used in a malicious way to find out all the openings to a computer's operating system; this is known as the "fingerprint" of the operating system. Port scanning cannot find out the topology of the network, computer names, usernames, or passwords.
11. **D.** A protocol analyzer can delve into the packets sent across the network that contain the clear text passwords. Rainbow tables and John the Ripper deal with crack-

ing passwords that were previously encrypted; they aren't necessary if the password were sent via clear text. Port scanners scan computers for any open ports.

12. **C.** Residual risk is the risk left over after a security and disaster recovery plan have been implemented. There is always risk, because a company cannot possibly foresee every future event, nor can it secure against every single threat. Senior management as a collective whole is ultimately responsible for deciding how much residual risk there will be in a company's network. No one person should be in charge of this, but it should be decided on as a group. If the group decides that residual risk is too high, the group might decide to get insurance in addition to its security plan. The security administrator is in charge of finding and removing risks to the network and systems and should mitigate risks if possible. The disaster recovery plan (DRP) coordinator usually assesses risks and documents them, along with creating strategies to defend against any disastrous problems that might occur from that risk, but that person does not decide on the amount of acceptable *residual* risk to a company.

13. **B.** When dealing with dollars, risk assessments should be based upon a quantitative measurement of risk, impact, and asset value.

14. **C.** The main objective of risk management is to reduce risk to a level that the organization or company will accept. Mitigation is the act of reducing threats in general.

15. **D.** The best answer for why a security administrator would use a vulnerability scanner is to find open ports on a particular computer. Although a vulnerability scanner can do more than scan for open ports, it is the best answer listed.

16. **B.** A password cracker is considered to be a program that does comparative analysis. It systematically guesses the password and compares all previous guesses before making new ones until it cracks the password.

17. **A and B.** Nonessential services are often not configured and secured by the network administrator; this goes hand-in-hand with the fact that they are not monitored as often as essential services. It is imperative that network administrators scan for nonessential services and close any corresponding ports. Even though services may be nonessential, that doesn't necessarily mean that they are not used. An IDS, if installed properly, should monitor everything on a given system.

18. **A.** A ping scanner uses the Internet Control Message Protocol (ICMP) to conduct its scans. Ping uses ICMP as its underlying protocol and IP and ARP. Image scanners are found in printers and as standalone items that scan images, photos, and text into a computer. Barcode scanners are used to scan barcodes, for example at the supermarket.

19. **D. Netstat** shows sessions including the local computer and remote computer. It shows these connections by computer name (or IP) and port name (or number).

This chapter covers the following subjects:

- **Monitoring Methodologies**—Monitoring the network is extremely important, yet often overlooked by network security administrators. In this section, you learn about the various monitoring methodologies that applications and IDS/IPS solutions use.
- **Using Tools to Monitor Systems and Networks**—Here, we delve into the hands-on again. Included in this section are performance analysis tools such as Performance Monitor and protocol analysis tools, such as Wireshark and Network Monitor.
- **Conducting Audits**—Full-blown audits might be performed by third-party companies, but you as the security administrator should be constantly auditing and logging the network and its hosts. This section gives some good tips when executing an audit and covers some of the tools you would use in a Windows server to perform audits and log them properly.

This chapter covers the CompTIA Security+ SY0-201 objectives 4.4, 4.5, 4.6, and 4.7.

CHAPTER 11

Monitoring and Auditing

In this chapter, we discuss monitoring and auditing. Key point: Monitoring alone does not constitute an audit, but audits usually include monitoring. So we cover some monitoring methodologies, and monitoring tools before we get into computer security audits. This chapter assumes that you have read through Chapter 10, "Vulnerability and Risk Assessment," and that you will employ the concepts and tools you learned about in that chapter when performing an audit. Chapter 10 and this chapter are strongly intertwined; I broke them into two chapters because there was a bit too much information for just one, and I want to differentiate somewhat between risk and audits. But regardless, these two chapters are all about putting on your sleuthing hat. You might be surprised, but many networking and operating system security issues can be solved by using that old Sherlockian adage: "When you have eliminated the impossible, whatever remains, however improbable, must be the truth." This process of elimination is one of the cornerstones of a good IT troubleshooter and works well in the actual CompTIA Security+ exam.

Foundation Topics

Monitoring Methodologies

To operate a clean, secure network, you must keep an eye on your systems, applications, servers, network devices, and the entire network in general. One way to do this is to monitor the network. This surveillance of the network will in of itself increase the security of your entire infrastructure. By periodically watching everything that occurs on the network, you become more familiar with day-to-day happenings and over time get quicker at analyzing whether an event is legitimate. It helps to think of yourself as Hercule Poirot, the Belgian detective—*seeing* everything that happens on your network, and ultimately *knowing* everything that happens. It might be a bit egotistical sounding, but whoever said that IT people don't have an ego?

This surveillance can all be done in one of two ways: manual monitoring and automated monitoring. When manually monitoring the network, you are systematically viewing log files, policies, permissions, and so on. But this can also be automated. For example, several mining programs available can mine logs and other files for the exact information you want to know. In addition, applications such as antivirus, intrusion detection systems and intrusion prevention systems can automatically scan for errors, malicious attacks, and anomalies. The three main types of automated monitoring are signature-based, anomaly-based, and behavior-based. The following acts as a review of the first two types of monitoring and adds the third type—behavior-based monitoring.

Signature-Based Monitoring

In a signature-based monitoring scenario, frames and packets of network traffic are analyzed for predetermined attack patterns. These attack patterns are known as signatures. The signatures are stored in a database that must be updated regularly to have any effect on the security of your network. Many attacks today have their own distinct signatures. However, only the specific attack that matches the signature will be detected. Malicious activity with a slightly different signature might be missed. This makes signature-based monitoring vulnerable to false negatives—when an IDS, IPS, or antivirus system fails to detect actual attack or error. To protect against this, the signature-based system should be updated to bring the system up to date with the latest signatures. When it comes to intrusion detection systems, the most basic form is the signature-based IDS. However, some signature-based monitoring systems are a bit more advanced and use heuristic signatures. These signatures incorporate an algorithm that determines if an alarm should be sounded when a specific threshold is met. This type of signature is CPU-intensive and requires fine-tuning. For example, some signature-based IDS solutions use these signatures to conform to particular networking environments.

Anomaly-Based Monitoring

An anomaly-based monitoring system (also known as statistical anomaly-based) establishes a performance baseline based on a set of normal network traffic evaluations. These evaluations should be taken when the network and servers are under an average load during regular working hours. This monitoring method then compares current network traffic activity with the previously created baseline to detect whether it is within baseline parameters. If the sampled traffic is outside baseline parameters, an alarm will be triggered and sent to the administrator (as long as the system was configured properly). This type of monitoring is dependent on the accuracy of the baseline. An inaccurate baseline increases the likelihood of obtaining false positives. Normally, false positives are when the system reads a legitimate event as an attack or other error.

Behavior-Based Monitoring

A behavior-based monitoring system looks at the previous behavior of applications, executables, and/or the operating system and compares that to current activity on the system. If an application later behaves improperly, the monitoring system will attempt to stop the behavior. This has advantages compared to signature-based and anomaly-based monitoring in that it can to a certain extent help with future events, without having to be updated. However, because there are so many types of applications, and so many types of relationships between applications, this type of monitoring could set off a high amount of false positives. Behavior monitoring should be configured carefully to avoid the system triggering alarms due to legitimate activity.

Table 11-1 Summary of Monitoring Methodologies

Monitoring Methodology	Description
Signature-based monitoring	Network traffic is analyzed for predetermined attack patterns. These attack patterns are known as signatures.
Anomaly-based monitoring	Establishes a performance baseline based on a set of normal network traffic evaluations. Requires a baseline.
Behavior-based monitoring	Looks at the previous behavior of applications, executables, and/or the operating system and compares that to current activity on the system. If an application later behaves improperly, the monitoring system will attempt to stop the behavior. Requires a baseline.

Using Tools to Monitor Systems and Networks

All the methodologies in the world won't help you unless you know how to use some monitoring tools and how to create baselines. By using performance monitoring gizmos and software, and by incorporating protocol analyzers, you can really "watch" the network and quickly mitigate threats as they present themselves.

In this section, we use the Performance tool in Windows and the Wireshark and Network Monitor protocol analyzers. These are just a couple examples of performance and network monitoring tools out there, but they are commonly used in the field and should give you a decent idea of how to work with any tools in those categories.

Performance Baselining

We mentioned in Chapter 3, "OS Hardening and Virtualization," that *baselining* is the process of measuring changes in networking, hardware, software, and so on. Let's get into baselining a little more and show one of the software tools you can use to create a baseline.

Creating a baseline consists of selecting something to measure and measuring it consistently for a period of time. For example, I might want to know what the average hourly data transfer is to and from a server's network interface. There are a lot of ways to measure this, but I could possibly use a performance monitoring tool or a protocol analyzer to find out how many packets cross through the server's network adapter. This could be run for 1 hour (during business hours of course) every day for 2 weeks. Selecting different hours for each day would add more randomness to the final results. By averaging the results together, we get a baseline. Then we can compare future measurements of the server to the baseline. This will help us define what the standard load of our server is, and the requirements our server needs on a consistent basis. It will also help when installing other like computers on the network. The term baselining is most often used to refer to monitoring network performance, but it actually can be used to describe just about any type of performance monitoring. The term *standard load* is often used when referring to servers. A configuration baseline defines what the standard load of the server is for the relevant object or objects. When it comes to performance monitoring applications objects are all of the components in the server, for example CPU, RAM, hard disk, and so on. They are measured using counters. A typical counter would be the % Processor Time of the CPU. This is used by the Task Manager.

An example of one of these tools is the Performance Monitor tool in Windows. It can help to create baselines measuring network activity, CPU usage, memory, hard drive resources used, and so on. It should also be used when monitoring changes to the baseline. Figure 11-1 shows an example of the Performance Monitor in Windows Vista. The program works basically the same in all version of Windows, be it client or server. In Windows Vista it can be found within the Reliability and Performance Monitor program in Administrative Tools.

The CPU is probably the most important component of the computer. In the figure the CPU counter has hit 100% several times. If the CPU maxes out often, as it is in the figure, a percentage of clients will cannot obtain access to resources on the computer. If the computer is a server it'll mean trouble. This CPU spiking that we see could be due to normal usage, or it could be due to malicious activity or perhaps bad design. Further analysis would be necessary to determine the exact cause. If the system is a virtual machine, there is a higher probability of CPU spikes. Proper design of VMs is critical, and they must have a strong platform to run on if they are to serve clients properly. Known as a counter, the CPU % Processor Time is just one of many. A smart security auditor will measure the activity of other objects such as the hard drive, paging file, memory (RAM), network adapter, and whatever else is specific to the organization's needs. Each object has several counters to select from. For example, if you are analyzing a web server, you would probably want to include the HTTP Service Request Queries object, and specifically the ArrivalRate and CurrentQueueSize counters, in your examination.

Now, the figure shows the Performance Monitor screen, but this only gives us a brief look at our system. The window of time is only a minute or so before the information refreshes. However, we can record this information over *x* periods of time and create reports from the recorded information. By comparing the Performance reports and logs, we ultimately create the baseline. The key is to measure the same way at the same time each day or each week. This provides accurate comparisons. However, keep in mind that performance recording can be a strain on resources. Verify that the computer in question can handle the tests first before initiating them.

Key Topic

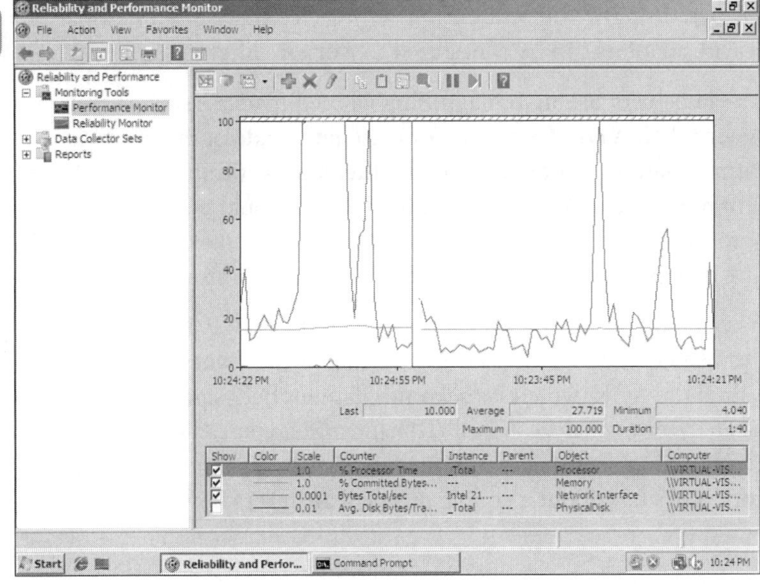

Figure 11-1 Performance Monitor in Windows Vista

Making reports is all fine and good (and necessary), but it is wise to also set up alerts. Alerts can be generated automatically by the system and sent to administrators and other important IT people. These alerts can be set off in a myriad of ways, all of your choosing, for example, if the CPU were to trip a certain threshold or run at 90% for more than a minute (although this is normal in some environments). Or maybe the physical disk was peaking at 100 MB/s for more than 5 minutes. If these types of things happen often, the system should be checked for malicious activity, illegitimate usage, or the need for an upgrade.

A tool similar to Performance Monitor used in Linux systems (for example, SuSE) is called System Monitor. The different versions of Linux also have many third-party tools that can be used for performance monitoring.

Protocol Analyzers

We've mentioned protocol analyzers a couple of times already in this book but haven't really delved into them too much. There are many protocol analyzers available, some free, some not, and some that are part of an operating system. In this section, we focus on two: Wireshark and Network Monitor. Note that network adapters can work in one of two different modes:

- **Promiscuous mode**—When the network adapter captures all packets that it has access to regardless of the destination of those packets.
- **Nonpromiscuous mode**—When a network adapter captures only the packets that are addressed to it specifically.

Packet capturing programs have different default settings for these modes. Some programs and network adapters can be configured to work in different modes.

Protocol analyzers can be very useful in diagnosing where broadcast storms are coming from on your LAN. A *broadcast storm* (or extreme broadcast radiation) is when there is an accumulation of broadcast and multicast packet traffic on the LAN coming from one or more network interfaces. These storms could be intentional or could happen due to a network application or operating system error. The protocol analyzer can specify exactly which network adapter is causing the storm.

Protocol analyzers can look inside of a packet that makes up a TCP/IP handshake. Information that can be viewed includes the SYN, which is the "synchronized sequence numbers," and the ACK, which is "acknowledgment field significant." By using the protocol analyzer to analyze a TCP/IP handshake, you can uncover attacks such as TCP Hijacking. But that is just one way to use a protocol analyzer to secure your network. Let's talk about a couple protocol analyzers now.

Wireshark

Wireshark (previously known as Ethereal) is a free download that works on several platforms including Windows and Windows portables, UNIX, and Mac. It is meant to capture packets on the local computer that it is installed on. But quite often, this is enough to find out vulnerabilities and monitor the local system and remote systems such as servers. Because Wireshark works in promiscuous mode, it can delve into packets even if they weren't addressed to the computer it runs on. To discern more information about the remote systems, simply start sessions from the client computer to those remote systems and monitor the packet stream. If that is not enough, the program can be installed on servers as well. However, you should check company policy (and get permission) before ever installing any software on a server.

Imagine that you were contracted to find out whether an organization's web server was transacting secure data utilizing TLS version 1.0. But the organization doesn't want anyone logging into the server—all too common! No problem, you could use Wireshark on a client computer, initiate a packet capture, make a connection to the web server's secure site, and verify that TLS 1.0 is being used by analyzing the packets, as shown in Figure 11-2. If you saw other protocols such as SSL 2.0, that should raise a red flag, and you would want to investigate further, most likely culminating in a protocol upgrade or change.

Key Topic

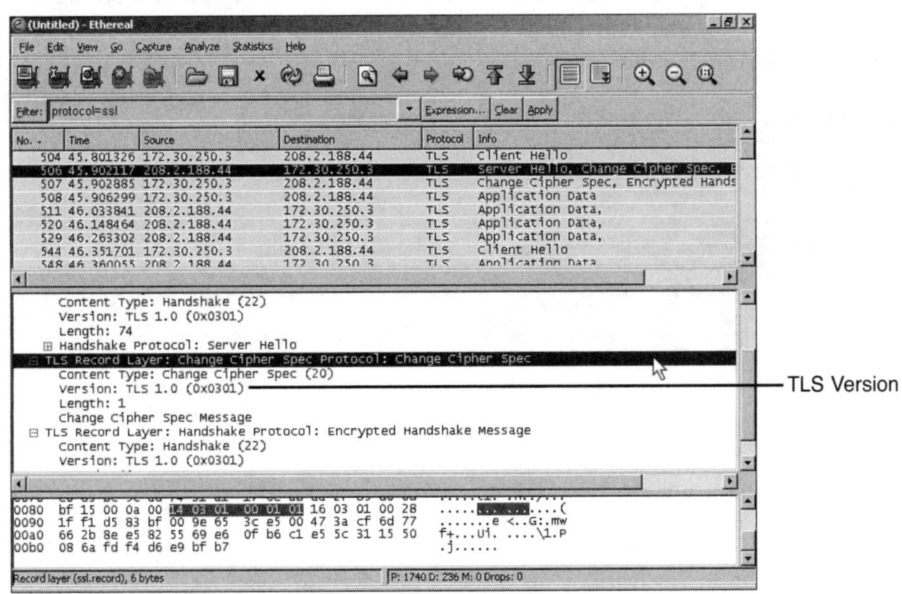

Figure 11-2 Wireshark Showing a Captured TLS Version 1.0 Packet

Always take screen captures and save your analysis as proof of the work that you did, and as proof of your conclusions and ensuing recommendations.

Remember that Wireshark can be used with a network adapter configured for promiscuous mode. It is set up by default to collect packets locally and from other sources.

Network Monitor

Network Monitor is a built-in network sniffer used in Windows Server products. Called netmon for short, it behaves in basically the same fashion as Wireshark. However, built-in versions of Network Monitor up until Windows Server 2003 work in nonpromiscuous mode by default. The full version of the program (available with SMS Server or SCCM 2007) can also monitor network adapters on remote computers. For now, we'll stick to the default Network Monitor version that comes stock with Windows Server 2003.

How about another real-world example? Let's just say you were contracted to monitor an FTP server. The organization is not sure whether FTP passwords are truly being encrypted before being sent across the network. BTW, some FTP programs with a default configuration do not encrypt the password. You could use the Network Monitor program to initiate a capture of packets on the monitoring server. Then, start up an FTP session on the monitoring server and log in to the FTP server. Afterward, stop the capture and view the FTP packets. Figure 11-3 shows an example of an FTP packet with a clear-text password. Notice that frame 1328 shows the password "locrian" in the details.

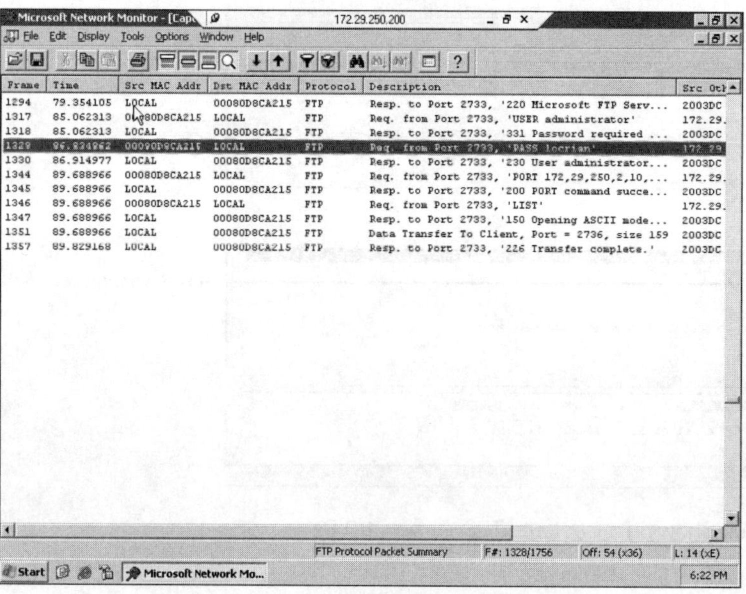

Figure 11-3 Network Monitor Showing a Captured FTP Packet with Clear-Text Password

This particular connection was made with the default FTP client within the Microsoft Command Prompt of a Windows Server 2003 to a built-in FTP server on a separate Windows Server set up with a default configuration. However, you could discern the same information by using Wireshark on a client computer and logging into the FTP server from that client computer.

Clear-text passwords being passed across the network is a definite risk. The vulnerabilities could be mitigated by increasing the level of security on the FTP server and by using more secure programs. For example, if the FTP server were part of Windows IIS, domain-based or other authentication could be implemented. Or perhaps a different type of FTP server could be used, for example Pure-FTPd. And secure FTP client programs could be used as well. Instead of using the Command Prompt or a browser to make FTP connections, the FileZilla or WS_FTP programs could be used.

For step-by-steps on using Wireshark and Network Monitor, see Lab 11-1 in the "Hands-On Labs" section.

SNMP

The *Simple Network Management Protocol (SNMP)* is a TCP/IP protocol that aids in monitoring network-attached devices and computers. It's usually incorporated as part of a network management system, such as Windows SMS, or free software, such as Net-SNMP. A typical scenario that uses SNMP can be broken down into three components:

- **Managed device—**Computers or other network-attached devices monitored through the use of agents by a network management system.
- **Agent—**An *SNMP agent* is software deployed by the network management system that is loaded on managed devices. The software redirects the information that the NMS needs to monitor the remote managed devices.
- **Network management system (NMS)—**The software run on one or more servers that control the monitoring of network attached devices and computers.

So, if the IT director asked you to install agents on several computers and network printers, and monitor them from a server, this would be an example of SNMP and the use of a network management system.

SNMP uses ports 161 and 162. SNMP agents receive requests on port 161; these requests come from the network management system or simply "manager." The manager receives notifications on port 162.

Because applications that use SNMP versions 1 and 2 are less secure, they should be replaced by software that supports SNMP version 3. SNMPv3 provides confidentiality through the use of encrypted packets that prevents snooping and provides additional message integrity and authentication.

Conducting Audits

Computer security audits are technical assessments made of applications, systems, or networks. They can be done manually or with computer programs. Manual assessments usually include the following:

- Review of security logs
- Review of access control lists
- Review of group policies
- Performance of vulnerability scans
- Review of written organization policies
- Interviewing organization personnel

Programs used to audit a computer or network could be as simple as a program such as Belarc Advisor to more complex programs such as Nsauditor to open source projects such as OpenXDAS.

When I have conducted IT security audits in the past, the following basic steps have helped me organize the entire process:

Step 1. Define exactly what is to be audited.

Step 2. Create backups.

Step 3. Scan for, analyze, and create a list of vulnerabilities, threats, and issues that have already occurred.

Step 4. Calculate risk.

Step 5. Develop a plan to mitigate risk and present it to the appropriate personnel.

Although an independent security auditor might do all these things, a network security administrator will be most concerned with the auditing of files, logs, and systems security settings.

Auditing Files

When dealing with auditing, we are interested in the who, what, and when. Basically, a network security administrator wants to know *who* did *what* to a particular resource and *when* that person did it.

Auditing files can usually be broken down into a three-step process:

Step 1. Turn on an auditing policy.

Step 2. Enable auditing for particular objects such as files, folders, and printers.

Step 3. Review the security logs to determine who did what to a resource and when.

As an example let's use Windows Vista. First, we would need to turn on a specific auditing policy such as "audit object access." This can be done within the Local Computer Policy, as shown in Figure 11-4. You can select from several different auditing policies such as logon access and privilege use, but object access is probably the most common, so we'll use that as the example.

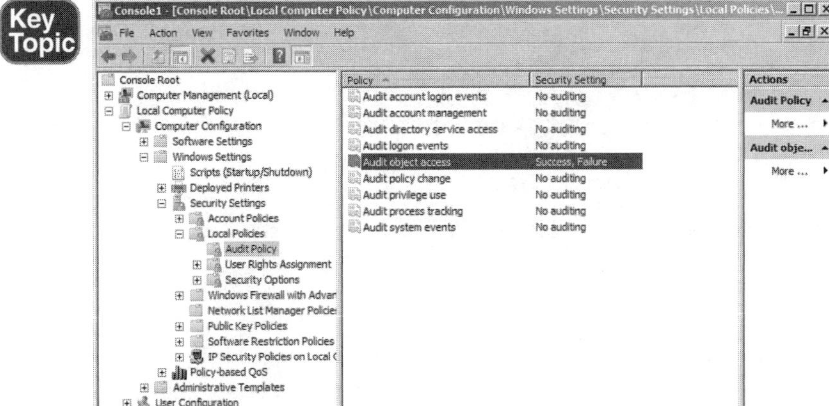

Figure 11-4 Audit Policy Within the Local Computer Policy of a Windows Vista Computer

Next, we would need to enable auditing for particular objects. Let's say that we are auditing a folder of data. We would want to go to the Properties dialog box for that folder, then navigate to the **Security** tab, then click the **Advanced** button, and finally access the **Auditing** tab, as shown in Figure 11-5.

From there, we can add users that we want to audit, and we can specify one or more of many different attributes to be audited.

Finally, we need to review the security logs to see exactly what is happening on our system and who is accessing what and when. The security logs will also tell us whether users have succeeded or failed in their attempts to access, modify, or delete objects. And if users deny that they attempted to do something, these logs act as proof that their user account was indeed involved. This is one of several ways of putting *nonrepudiation* into force. Nonrepudiation is the idea of ensuring that a person or group cannot refute the validity of your proof against them.

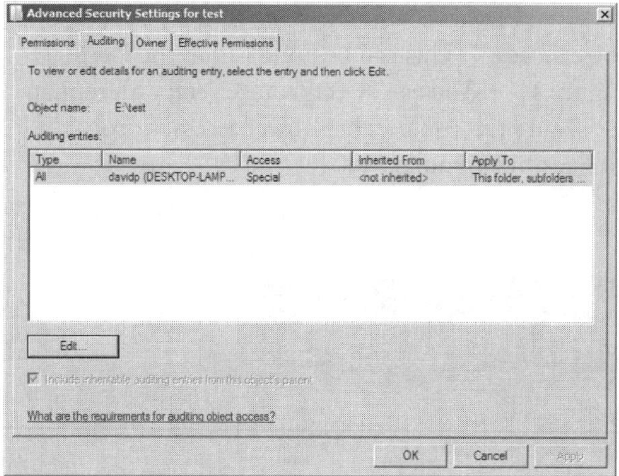

Figure 11-5 Auditing Advanced Security Settings for a Folder in Windows Vista

A common problem with security logs is that they fail to become populated, especially on older systems. If users complains to you that they cannot see any security events in the Event Viewer, you should ask yourself the following:

- Has auditing been turned on in a policy? And was it turned on in the correct policy?
- Was auditing enabled for the individual object?
- Does the person attempting to view the log have administrative capabilities?

In addition, you have to watch out for overriding policies. By default, a policy gets its settings from a parent policy; you might need to turn the override option off. On another note, perhaps the audit recording failed for some reason. Many auditing systems also have the capability to send an alert to the administrator in the case that a recording fails. Hopefully, the system attempts to recover from the failure and continue recording auditing information while the administrator fixes the issue. By answering all these questions and examining everything pertinent to the auditing scenario, you should be able to populate that security log! Now, security logs are just one component of logging that we cover in the next section.

Logging

Monitoring logs often is an important part of being a security person. Possibly the most important log file in Windows is the Security Log, as shown in Figure 11-6. The figure shows the Security log for Windows Vista, but it works in the same fashion, and can be accessed in virtually the same manner, in all versions of Windows.

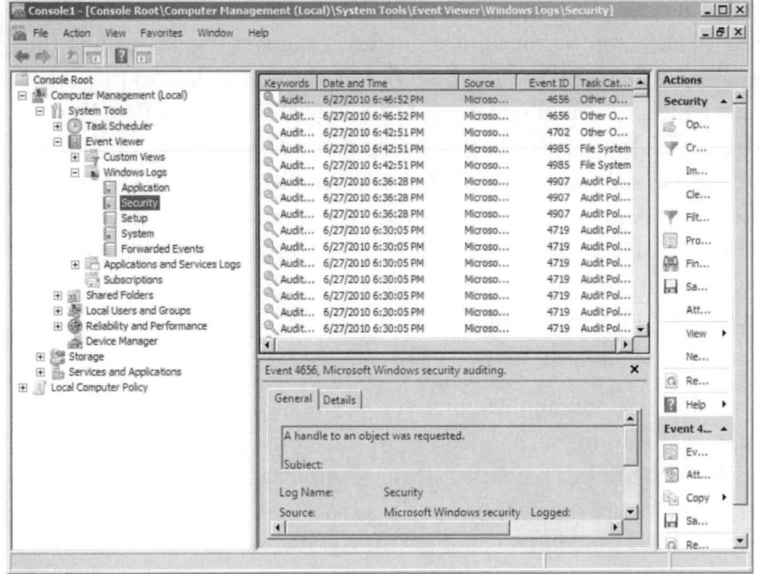

Figure 11-6 Security Log in Windows Vista

The Security log can show whether a user was successful at doing a variety of things including logging on to the local computer or domain; accessing, modifying, or deleting files; modifying policies, and so on. Of course, many of these things need to be configured first before they can be logged. Newer versions of Windows will automatically log such events as logon, or policy modification. All these security log events can be referred to as *audit trails*. Audit trails are records or logs that show the tracked actions of users, whether the user was successful in the attempt.

A network security administrator should monitor this log file often to keep on top of any breaches, or attempted breaches, of security. By periodically reviewing the logs of applications, operating systems, and network devices, we can find issues, errors, and threats quickly and increase our general awareness of the state of the network.

Several other types of Windows log files should be monitored periodically, including the following:

- **System—**Logs events such as system shut down, or driver failure.
- **Application—**Logs events for operating system applications and third-party programs.

The System and Application logs exist on client and server versions of Windows. A few log files that exist only on servers include the following:

- File Replication Service
- DNS Server
- Directory Service

The File Replication Service log exists on all Windows Servers, the Directory Service log will appear if the server has been promoted to a domain controller, and the DNS Server log will only appear if the DNS service has been installed to the server. We've mentioned the importance of reviewing DNS logs previously in Part II, "Network Infrastructure," but it is worth reminding you that examining the DNS log can uncover unauthorized zone transfers and other malicious or inadvertent activity on the DNS server. And let's not forget about web servers—by analyzing and monitoring a web server, you can determine whether the server has been compromised. A drop in CPU and hard disk speed are common indications of a web server that has been attacked. Of course, it could just be a whole lot of web traffic! It's up to you to use the log files to find out exactly what is going on.

Other types of operating systems, applications, and devices will have their own set of log files, for example applications such as Microsoft Exchange and SQL database servers, and firewalls. The firewall log especially is of importance, as shown in Figure 11-7. Note in the figure the dropped packets from addresses on the 169.254.0.0 network, which we know to be the APIPA network number. This is something that should be investigated further because most organizations will have a policy against the use of APIPA addresses.

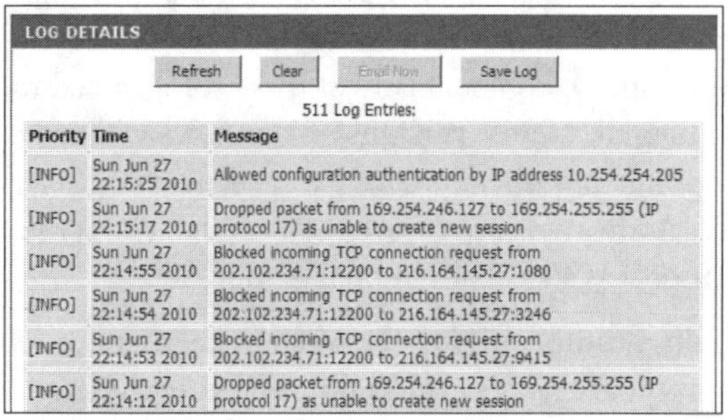

LOG DETAILS

Refresh | Clear | Email Now | Save Log

511 Log Entries:

Priority	Time	Message
[INFO]	Sun Jun 27 22:15:25 2010	Allowed configuration authentication by IP address 10.254.254.205
[INFO]	Sun Jun 27 22:15:17 2010	Dropped packet from 169.254.246.127 to 169.254.255.255 (IP protocol 17) as unable to create new session
[INFO]	Sun Jun 27 22:14:55 2010	Blocked incoming TCP connection request from 202.102.234.71:12200 to 216.164.145.27:1080
[INFO]	Sun Jun 27 22:14:54 2010	Blocked incoming TCP connection request from 202:102.234.71:12200 to 216.164.145.27:3246
[INFO]	Sun Jun 27 22:14:53 2010	Blocked incoming TCP connection request from 202.102.234.71:12200 to 216.164.145.27:9415
[INFO]	Sun Jun 27 22:14:12 2010	Dropped packet from 169.254.246.127 to 169.254.255.255 (IP protocol 17) as unable to create new session

Figure 11-7 A Basic Firewall's Log

The firewall log can show all kinds of other things such as malicious port scans and other vulnerability scans. For example, when digging into a firewall log event, and you see the following syntax, you would know that a port scan attack has occurred:

S=207.50.135.54:53 – D=10.1.1.80:0

S=207.50.135.54:53 – D=10.1.1.80:1

S=207.50.135.54:53 – D=10.1.1.80:2

S=207.50.135.54:53 – D=10.1.1.80:3

S=207.50.135.54:53 – D=10.1.1.80:4

S=207.50.135.54:53 – D=10.1.1.80:5

Note the source IP address (which is public and therefore most likely external to your network) uses port 53 outbound to run a port scan of 10.1.1.80, starting with port 0 and moving on from there. The firewall is usually the first line of defense, but even if you have an IDS or IPS in front of it, you should review those firewall logs often.

Log File Maintenance and Security

The planning, maintenance, and security of the log files should be thoroughly considered. A few things to take into account include the configuration and saving of the log files, backing up of the files, and securing and encrypting of the files.

Before setting up any type of logging system, you should consider the amount of disk space (or other form of memory) that the log requires. You should also contemplate all the different information necessary to reconstruct logged events later. Are the logs stored in multiple locations? Were they encrypted? Were they hashed for integrity? Also up for consideration is the level of detail you will allow in the log. Verbose logging is something that admins apply to get as much information as possible. Also, is the organization interested in exactly when an event occurred? If so, time stamping should be incorporated. Although many systems do this by default, some organizations will opt to not use time stamping to reduce CPU usage.

Log files can be saved to a different partition of the logging system, or saved to a different system altogether; although, the latter requires a fast secondary system and a fast network. The size and overwriting configuration of the file should play into your considerations. Figure 11-8 shows an example of the properties of a Windows Server 2003 Security log file. Currently, the file is 640 KB but can grow to a maximum size of 131072 KB (128 MB). Although 128 MB might sound like a lot, larger organizations can eat that up quickly because they will probably audit and log a lot of user actions. When the file gets this big, log mining becomes important. There can be thousands and thousands of entries making it difficult for an admin to sort through them all, but several third-party programs can make the mining of specific types of log entries much simpler. You can also note in the figure that the log is set to overwrite events if the log reaches its maximum size. Security is a growing concern with organizations in general, so the chances are that they will not want events overwritten. Instead, you would select **Do Not Overwrite Events (Clear Log Manually)**. As an admin, you would save and back up the log monthly or weekly, and clear the log at the beginning of the new time period to start a new log. If the log becomes full for any reason, you should have an alert set up to notify you or another admin.

Key Topic

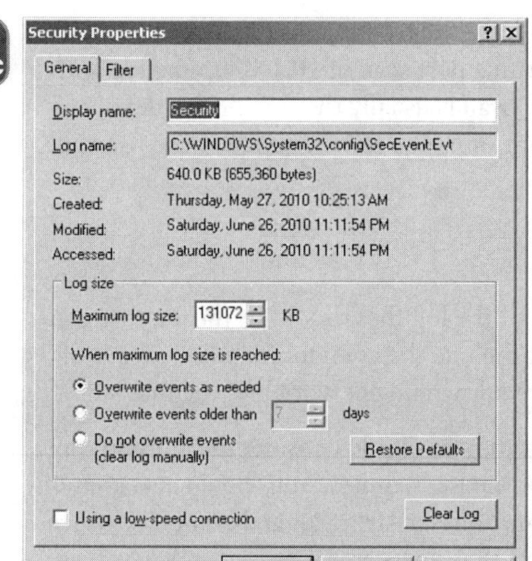

Figure 11-8 Windows Server 2003 Security Log Properties Dialog Box

As with any security configurations or files, the log files should be backed up. The best practice is to copy the files to a remote log server. The files could be backed up to a separate physical offsite location. Or WORM media types (write-once read-many) could be utilized. WORM options such as CD-R and DVD-R are good ways to back up log files, but not *re*-write optical discs mind you. USB Flash drives and USB removable hard drives should not be allowed in any area where a computer stores log files. One way or another, a retention policy should be in place for your log files—meaning they should be retained for future reference.

Securing the log files can be done in several ways: First, by employing the aforementioned backup methods. Secondly, by setting permissions to the actual log file. Figure 11-8 shows the filename for the Security log: **SecEvent.Evt** located in C:\Windows\system32\config. That is the file you would access to configure NTFS permissions. Just remember that by default, this file will inherit its permissions from the parent folder. File integrity is also important when securing log files. Encrypting the log files through the concept known as hashing is a good way to verify the integrity of the log files if they are moved and or copied. And finally, you could flat out encrypt the entire contents of the file so that other users cannot view it. We talk more about hashing and encryption in Chapter 12, "Encryption and Hashing Concepts," and Chapter 13, "PKI and Encryption Protocols."

Auditing System Security Settings

So far, we have conducted audits on object access and log files, but we still need to audit system security settings. For example, we should review user permissions and group policies.

For user access, we are most concerned with shared folders on the network and their permissions. Your file server (or distributed file system server) can easily show you all the shares it contains. This knowledge can be obtained on a Windows Server by navigating to **Computer Management > System Tools > Shared Folders > Shares**, as shown in Figure 11-9.

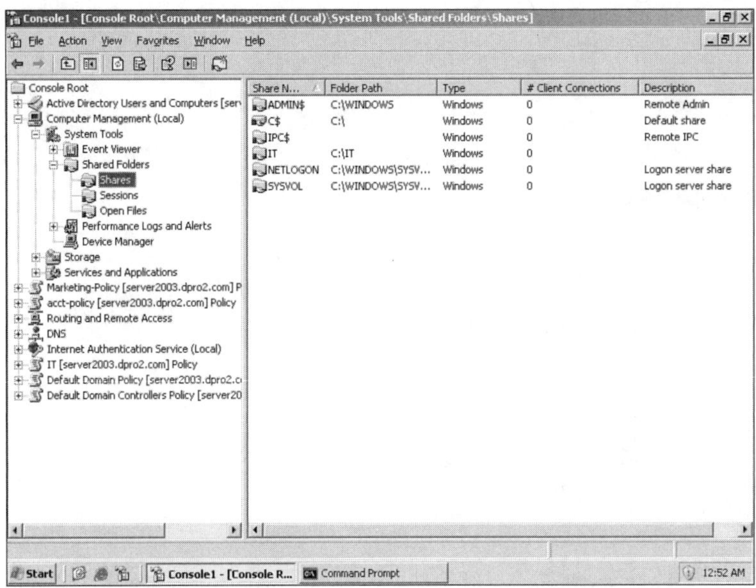

Figure 11-9 Network Shares on a Windows Server 2003

Notice the IT share. There are a couple of things that pique my interest from the get go. For starters, the shared folder is located in the C: drive of this server. Shared folders should actually be on a different partition, drive, or even a different computer. Secondly, it is in the root. That isn't a good practice, either (blame the author). Of course, this is just a test folder that we created previously, but we should definitely consider the location of our shared folders.

NOTE: Some companies opt to secure administrative shares, such as IPC$ and Admin$. Although this isn't actually an option on servers, it is a smart idea for client computers. The following link talks about hidden and administrative shares in depth: http://support.microsoft.com/kb/314984.

Either way, we now know where the IT share is located and can go to that folder in Windows Explorer and review the permissions for it, as shown in Figure 11-10.

In the figure, you can see that the IT1 group has Read & Execute, List Folder Contents, and Read permissions. It is wise to make sure that individual users and groups of users do not have more permissions than necessary, or allowed. It is also important to verify proper ownership of the folder; in this example it can be done by clicking the **Advanced** button and selecting the **Owner** tab. Figure 11-11 shows that the Administrator is the owner of this resource. We want to make sure that no one else has inadvertently or maliciously taken control.

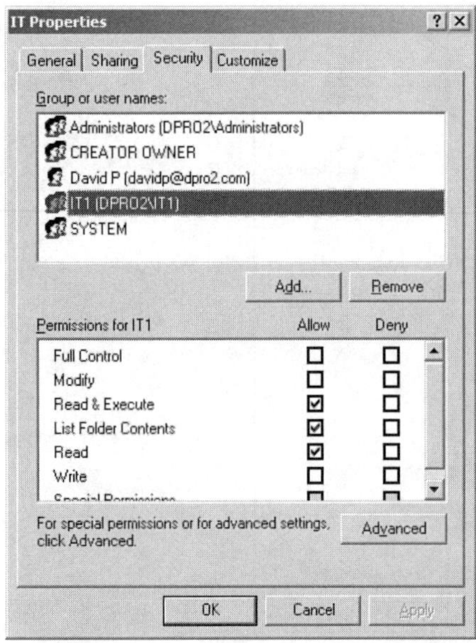

Figure 11-10 The IT Folder's Permissions

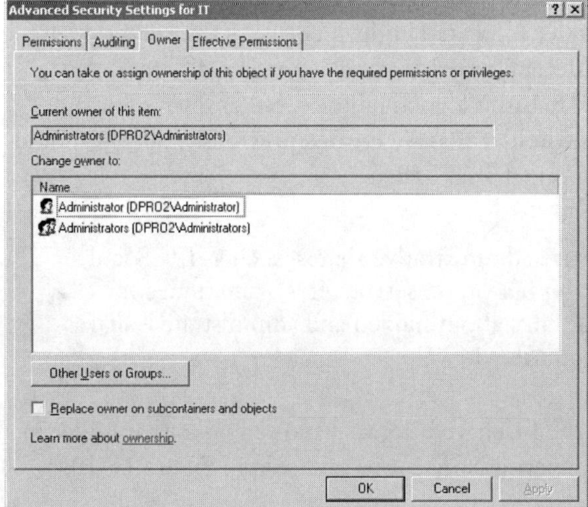

Figure 11-11 The IT Folder's Owner Tab in Advanced Security Settings

While you are in the Advanced Security Settings dialog box, you can check what auditing settings have been implemented and if they correspond to an organization's written policies.

Speaking of policies, computer policies should be reviewed as well. Remember that there might be different policies for each department in an organization. This would match up with the various organizational units on a Windows Server. Figure 11-12 shows the Security Settings section of the IT Policy we created earlier in the book. I haven't counted them, but there are probably thousands of settings. Due to this, an organization might opt to use a security template; if this is the case, verify that the proper one is being used, and that the settings included in that template take into account what the organization has defined as part of its security plan. Templates are accessed by right-clicking **Security Settings** and selecting **Import Policy**. If a template is not being used, you will need to go through as many policy objects as possible, especially things such as password policy, security options, and the audit policy itself.

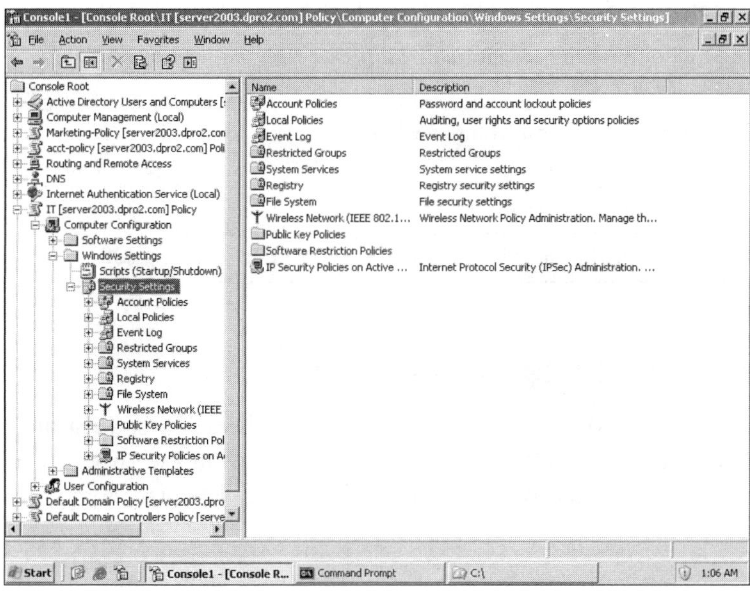

Figure 11-12 Security Settings Within the IT Policy on a Windows Server 2003

Individual computers will probably use User Account Control and adhere to the policies created on the server. A spot check should be made of individual computers to verify that they are playing by the rules. In some cases, an organization will require that all client computers are checked. Auditing can be a lot of work, so plan your time accordingly, and be ready for a few hiccups along the way.

Exam Preparation Tasks

Review Key Topics

Review the most important topics in the chapter, noted with the Key Topics icon in the outer margin of the page. Table 11-2 lists a reference of these key topics and the page numbers on which each is found.

Table 11-2 Key Topics for Chapter 11

Key Topic Element	Description	Page Number
Table 11-1	Summary of Monitoring Methodologies	315
Figure 11-1	Performance Monitor in Windows Vista	317
Figure 11-2	Wireshark Showing a Captured TLS Version 1.0 Packet	319
Figure 11-3	Network Monitor Showing a Captured FTP packet with Clear-Text Password	320
Figure 11-4	Audit Policy Within the Local Computer Policy of a Windows Vista Computer	323
Figure 11-6	Security Log in Windows Vista	325
Figure 11-8	Windows Server 2003 Security Log Properties Dialog Box	328

Complete Tables and Lists from Memory

Print a copy of Appendix A, "Memory Tables," (found on the DVD), or at least the section for this chapter, and complete the tables and lists from memory. Appendix B, "Memory Tables Answer Key," also on the DVD, includes completed tables and lists to check your work.

Define Key Terms

Define the following key terms from this chapter, and check your answers in the glossary:

Simple Network Management Protocol (SNMP), baselining, computer security audits, security log files, non-repudiation, signature-based monitoring, anomaly-based monitoring, behavior-based monitoring, audit trail, promiscuous mode, nonpromiscuous mode, broadcast storm, SNMP agent, Network Management System (NMS), audit trails

Hands-On Labs

Complete the following written step-by-step scenarios. After you finish (or if you do not have adequate equipment to complete the scenario), watch the corresponding video solutions on the DVD.

If you have additional questions, feel free to post them at my website: www.davidlprowse.com in the Ask Dave forum. (Free registration is required to post on the website.)

Equipment Needed

- Windows client (XP or higher).
- Wireshark protocol analyzer.
- Free download: www.wireshark.org/download.html.
- Windows Server (2003 or 2008 preferred) with Network Monitor installed.
- Windows Server (preferably separate and promoted to a domain controller). Used for auditing. You can use a standard member Windows server instead of a domain controller; however, you will be auditing local user accounts instead of domain user accounts. If necessary, you can use a local Windows client, but again, will be relegated to local accounts.

Lab 11-1: Using Protocol Analyzers

In this lab, you capture and analyze various types of packets with the Wireshark and Network Monitor protocol analyzers. You need to have Network Monitor installed to the server and the FTP service (part of IIS). For more information on setting up an FTP server in Windows Server 2003, see the following link: http://support.microsoft.com/kb/323384.

In the video, I use Wireshark version 1.2.8 and Windows Server 2003 Standard.

We start with the Wireshark protocol analyzer.

The steps are as follows:

Step 1. Download, install and run Wireshark. Be sure to install WinPCap if you don't already have it.

Step 2. Start a capture on the primary network adapter.

Step 3. Verify that the program is capturing packets.

Step 4. Open a browser and access a secure website, such as https://www.paypal.com.

Step 5. Return to Wireshark and stop the capture.

Step 6. Create a filter for SSL/TLS packets by typing **SSL** in the Filter field and pressing **Enter**.

Step 7. Locate a "Client Hello" TLS packet and open it.

Step 8. Drill down in the Secure Socket Layer to find out the version number of TLS. Verify that it is Version 1.0 or higher.

Now we'll move on to using Network monitor:

Step 9. Access a Windows Server 2003 or 2008 and open the Network Monitor program. If it is not installed, install it now. For more information on installing Network Monitor, see the following link: http://technet.microsoft.com/en-us/library/cc780828%28WS.10%29.aspx. When installed, to open Network Monitor, click **Start**, then **Administrative Tools**, and finally **Network Monitor**.

Step 10. Click **OK** for the pop-up window.

Step 11. Select the network adapter within Local Computer that you want to capture from; it should be the primary network adapter. Then click **OK**.

Step 12. Click **Capture** on the menu bar and click **Start**. This should start the capture.

Step 13. Go to a client computer and ping the server within the command prompt using the following syntax:

```
Ping -t -l 1500 [ServerIPaddress]
```

Step 14. Open a second command prompt and connect to the FTP server by using the following syntax:

```
ftp [ServerIPaddress]
```

As an example, type **ftp 172.29.250.200.**

Step 15. Log in as the administrator account of the server. Be sure to use the correct server. Verify that you are logged in; the FTP server should tell you whether it was successful.

Step 16. Run the **dir** command to view the contents of the FTP server.

Step 17. Return to the server. Stop the capture, and view it by clicking **Capture** on the menu bar and **Stop and View**. This should display the results of the capture.

Step 18. Filter the capture for ICMP packets:

A. Click **Display** on the menu bar and select **Filter**.

B. Then click the **Protocol == Any** subset, and click the **Edit Expression** button.

C. In the Expression window, click the **Disable All** button.

D. Scroll down to **ICMP**, select it, and click the **Enable** button.

E. Click **OK**, and click **OK** again.

Now, only ICMP information should display. Review the ICMP log and make sure that your client computer is the only one pinging the server. If other computers are pinging the server, it should be investigated.

Step 19. Filter for FTP packets only. Do this in the same manner that you filtered for ICMP.

Step 20. View the FTP packets and search for the packet containing the password. By default this should be shown in clear text.

Step 21. Drill down into the FTP password packet by double-clicking it. Examine the layers and the ASCII code underneath.

Watch the solution video in the "Hands-On Scenarios" section of the DVD.

Lab 11-2: Auditing Files on a Windows Server

In this lab, you turn on the auditing feature on a Windows Server, permit auditing for specific objects, and analyze the resulting logs and events for those audited objects. In this lab, we use Windows Server 2003, but the procedure is basically the same with other versions of Windows Server. You also need some sort of Windows client to connect to the server. The steps are as follows:

Step 1. Access the Windows Server 2003. You should have an OU and corresponding policy already created. If not, create them now. For more information on how to do this, see Lab 9-1 in Chapter 9, "Configuring Password Policies and User Account Restrictions."

Step 2. Open the MMC and snap-in the policy associated with the OU into the MMC.

Step 3. Access the policy associated with the OU.

Step 4. Navigate through the following path: **Computer Configuration > Windows Settings > Security Settings > Local Policies > Audit Policy**.

Step 5. Double-click the **Audit object access** policy. This displays a properties dialog box.

Step 6. Enable the policy by checking **Define these policy settings** and selecting the **Success** and **Failure** checkboxes. Then click **OK**.

Step 7. The policy should now show your configuration in the **Policy Setting** column.

Step 8. Access a shared folder on the server:

A. Verify that you have two basic, populated text files in the folder. If not, create them now.

B. Make sure that one or more users within the correct OU have at least the Read permission to the folder but not Full Control or Modify permissions. Right-click the folder and select **Properties**.

C. Then, select the **Security** tab. Verify the user permissions. If you have to change them, be sure to click the **Apply** button.

Step 9. Click the **Advanced** button, and click the **Auditing** tab.

Step 10. Deselect the **Allow Inheritable Auditing Entries**, button and click **Apply**.

Step 11. Click the **Add** button to add users or groups to audit. From here, you would add a person in the same manner as you would when creating permissions. Select one account from your OU. Make sure the account has only the permissions mentioned in Step 8.

Step 12. In the **Auditing Entry for [folder]** dialog box, check mark **Delete Subfolders and Files** and **Delete** in the **Successful** and **Failed** columns. Then click **OK**.

Step 13. Click **OK** for the **Advanced Security Settings Auditing** tab.

Step 14. Click **OK** for the Properties dialog box.

Step 15. Connect from a client computer to the share. In the video, we VPN in, but you could log in to the domain as you normally would, or if you are using a local computer, simply make sure that you are logged in to the local computer as the person that is to be audited.

Step 16. Map a drive to the server's share that is being audited. For example, the path might be **\\10.254.254.252\it**. It all depends on the IP of your server and the name of the share.

Step 17. Attempt to delete the text files. You should not be able to due to permissions.

Step 18. Return to the server and view the Security log. This can be accessed by navigating to **Computer Management > System Tools > Event Viewer > Security**.

Step 19. Press **F5** to refresh the Security log. This should now display Failure Audits for the audited person.

Step 20. Double-click one of the Failure Audit entries and examine the contents. It should show who did what and when.

Note: Sometimes, the parent policy (such as the Default Domain Policy) overrides any child policies such as the one we created. If necessary, turn off the override policy option by

A. Accessing the Properties page of the OU.

B. Go to the **Group Policy** tab.

C. Highlight the policy and click the **Options** button.

D. Select the **No Override** checkbox and click **OK**.

E. Click **OK** for the Properties dialog box.

Watch the solution video in the "Hands-On Scenarios" section of the DVD.

View Recommended Resources

Check out these links for more information on the topics covered in this chapter.

- Windows Vista Performance and Reliability Monitoring Step-by-Step Guide: http://technet.microsoft.com/en-us/library/cc722173%28WS.10%29.aspx
- Windows Server 2008: Windows Reliability and Performance Monitor: http://technet.microsoft.com/en-us/library/cc755081%28WS.10%29.aspx
- Wireshark download: www.wireshark.org/download.html
- Wireshark tutorial: www.wireshark.org/news/20060714.html
- How to capture network traffic with Network Monitor: http://support.microsoft.com/kb/148942
- Systems Management Server (SMS) 2003: http://technet.microsoft.com/en-us/library/cc181833.aspx
- System Center Configuration Manager (SCCM) 2007: www.microsoft.com/systemcenter/en/us/configuration-manager.aspx
- Net-SNMP: www.net-snmp.org/
- Windows Server event Logging and Viewing: http://technet.microsoft.com/en-us/library/bb726966.aspx
- How to create and delete hidden or administrative shares on client computers: http://support.microsoft.com/kb/314984

Answer Review Questions

Answer the following review questions. You can find the answers at the end of this chapter.

1. Which of the following is a record of the tracked actions of users?

A. Performance Monitor

B. Audit trails

C. Permissions

D. System and event logs

2. What tool enables you to be alerted if a server's processor trips a certain threshold?

A. TDR

B. Password cracker

C. Event Viewer

D. Performance Monitor

3. The IT director has asked you to install agents on several client computers and monitor them from a program at a server. What is this known as?

A. SNMP

B. SMTP

C. SMP

D. Performance Monitor

4. One of your coworkers complains to you that they cannot see any security events in the Event Viewer. What are three possible reasons for this? (Select the three best answers.)

A. Auditing has not been turned on.

B. The log file is only 512 KB.

C. The coworker is not an administrator.

D. Auditing for an individual object has not been turned on.

5. Which tool can be instrumental in capturing FTP GET requests?

A. Vulnerability scanner

B. Port scanner

C. Performance Monitor

D. Protocol analyzer

6. Your manager wants you to implement a type of intrusion detection system (IDS) that can be matched to certain types of traffic patterns. What kind of IDS is this?

   A. Anomaly-based IDS

   B. Signature-based IDS

   C. Behavior-based IDS

   D. Heuristic-based IDS

7. You are setting up auditing on a Windows XP Professional computer. If set up properly, which log should have entries?

   A. Application log

   B. System log

   C. Security log

   D. Maintenance log

8. You have established a baseline for your server. Which of the following is the best tool to use to monitor any changes to that baseline?

   A. Performance Monitor

   B. Antispyware

   C. Antivirus software

   D. Vulnerability assessments software

9. In what way can you gather information from a remote printer?

   A. HTTP

   B. SNMP

   C. CA

   D. SMTP

10. Which of the following can determine which flags are set in a TCP/IP handshake?

   A. Protocol analyzer

   B. Port scanner

   C. SYN/ACK

   D. Performance monitor

11. Which of following is the most basic form of IDS?

A. Anomaly based

B. Behavioral-based

C. Signature-based

D. Statistical-based

12. Which of the following deals with the standard load for a server?

A. Patch management

B. Group policy

C. Port scanning

D. Configuration baseline

13. Your boss wants you to properly log what happens on a database server. What are the most important concepts to think about while you do so? (Select the two best answers.)

A. The amount of virtual memory that you will allocate for this task

B. The amount of disk space you will require

C. The information that will be needed to reconstruct events later

D. Group policy information

14. Which of the following is the best practice to implement when securing logs files?

A. Log all failed and successful login attempts.

B. Deny administrators access to log files.

C. Copy the logs to a remote log server.

D. Increase security settings for administrators.

15. What is the main reason to frequently view the logs of a DNS server?

A. To create aliases

B. To watch for unauthorized zone transfers

C. To defend against denial of service attacks

D. To prevent domain name kiting

16. As you review your firewall log, you see the following information. What type of attack is this?

```
S=207.50.135.54:53 - D=10.1.1.80:0
S=207.50.135.54:53 - D=10.1.1.80:1
S=207.50.135.54:53 - D=10.1.1.80:2
S=207.50.135.54:53 - D=10.1.1.80:3
S=207.50.135.54:53 - D=10.1.1.80:4
S=207.50.135.54:53 - D=10.1.1.80:5
```

A. Denial of service

B. Port scanning

C. Ping scanning

D. DNS spoofing

17. Of the following, which two security measures should be implemented when logging a server? (Select the two best answers.)

A. Cyclic redundancy checks

B. The application of retention policies on log files

C. Hashing of log files

D. Storing of temporary files

18. You suspect a broadcast storm on the LAN. Which tool should you use to diagnose which network adapter is causing the storm?

A. Protocol analyzer

B. Firewall

C. Port scanner

D. Network intrusion detection system

19. Which of the following should be done if an audit recording fails?

A. Stopped generating audit records.

B. Overwrite the oldest audit records.

C. Send an alert to the administrator.

D. Shut down the server.

20. Which of the following log files should show attempts at unauthorized access?

A. DNS

B. System

C. Application

D. Security

21. To find out when a computer was shutdown, which log file would an administrator use?

A. Security log

B. System log

C. Application log

D. DNS log

22. Which of the following requires a baseline? (Select the two best answers.)

A. Behavior-based monitoring

B. Performance Monitor

C. Anomaly based monitoring

D. Signature-based monitoring

23. Jason is a security administrator for a company of 4,000 users. He wants to store 6 months of logs to a logging server for analysis. The reports are required by upper management due to legal obligations but are not time-critical. When planning for the requirements of the logging server, which of the following should not be implemented?

A. Performance baseline and audit trails

B. Time stamping and integrity of the logs

C. Log details and level of verbose logging

D. Log storage and backup requirements

24. Your manager wants you to implement a type of intrusion detection system (IDS) that can be matched to certain types of traffic patterns. What kind of IDS is this?

A. Anomaly based IDS

B. Signature-based IDS

C. Behavior-based IDS

D. Heuristic-based IDS

25. Michael has just completed monitoring and analyzing a web server. Which of the following indicates that the server might have been compromised?

A. The Web server is sending hundreds of UDP packets.

B. The Web server has a dozen connections to inbound port 80.

C. The Web server has a dozen connections to inbound port 443.

D. The Web server is showing a drop in CPU speed and hard disk speed.

Answers and Explanations

1. **B.** Audit trails are records showing the tracked actions of users. The Performance Monitor is a tool in Windows that enables you to track the performance of objects such as CPU, RAM, network adapter, physical disk, and so on. Permissions grant or deny access to resources. To see whether permissions were granted, auditing must be enabled. The system and other logs record events that happened in other areas of the system; for example, events concerning the operating system, drivers, applications, and so on.

2. **D.** The Performance Monitor can be configured in such a way where alerts can be set for any of the objects (processor, RAM, paging file) in a computer. For example, if the processor were to go beyond 90% usage for more than 1 minute, an alert would be created and could be sent automatically to an administrator. A TDR is a time-domain reflectometer, an electronic instrument used to test cables for faults. A password cracker is a software program used to recover or crack passwords; an example would be Cain & Abel. The Event Viewer is a built-in application in Windows that enables a user to view events on the computer such as warnings, errors, and other information events. It does not measure the objects in a server in the way that Performance Monitor does.

3. **A.** The Simple Network Management Protocol (SNMP) is used when a person installs agents on client computers to monitor those systems from a single remote location. SMTP is used by e-mail clients and servers. SMP is Symmetric Multi-Processing, which is not covered in the Security+ exam objectives. Performance Monitor enables a person to monitor a computer and create performance baselines.

4. **A, C, and D.** To audit events on a computer, an administrator would need to enable auditing within the computer's policy, then turn on auditing for an individual object (folder, file, and so on), and then view the events within the Security log of the Event Viewer. 512 KB is big enough for many events to be written to it.

5. **D.** A protocol analyzer captures data including things such as GET requests that were initiated from an FTP client. Vulnerability scanners and port scanners look for open ports and other vulnerabilities of a host. Performance Monitor is a Windows program that reports on the performance of the computer system and any of its parts.
6. **B.** When using an IDS, particular types of traffic patterns refer to signature-based IDS. Heuristic signatures are a subset of signature-based monitoring systems, so signature-based IDS is the best answer. Anomaly-based and behavior-based systems use different methodologies.
7. **C.** After Auditing is turned on and specific resources are configured for auditing, you need to check the Event Viewer's Security log for the entries. These could be successful logons or misfired attempts at deleting files; there are literally hundreds of options. The Application log contains errors, warnings, and informational entries about applications. The System log deals with drivers and system files and so on. A System Maintenance log can be used to record routine maintenance procedures.
8. **A.** Performance monitoring software can be used to create a baseline and monitor for any changes to that baseline. An example of this would be the Performance console window within Windows Server 2003. (It is commonly referred to as the Performance Monitor.) Antivirus and antispyware applications usually go hand-in-hand and are not used to monitor server baselines. Vulnerability assessing software such as Nessus or Nmap are used to see if open ports and other vulnerabilities are on a server.
9. **B.** SNMP (Simple Network Management Protocol) enables you to gather information from a remote printer. HTTP is the hypertext transfer protocol that deals with the transfer of web pages. A CA is a certificate authority, and SMTP is the Simple Mail Transfer Protocol.
10. **A.** A protocol analyzer can look inside of the packets that make up a TCP/IP handshake. Information that can be viewed includes SYN, which is synchronize sequence numbers, and ACK, which is acknowledgment field-significant. Port scanners and performance monitor do not have the capability to view flags set in a TCP/IP handshake, nor can they look inside of packets in general.
11. **C.** Signature-based IDS is the most basic form of intrusion detection systems, or IDS. This monitors packets on the network and compares them against a database of signatures. Anomaly-based, behavioral-based, and statistical-based are all more complex forms of IDS. Anomaly and statistical are often considered to be the same type of monitoring methodology.
12. **D.** A configuration baseline deals with the standard load of a server. By measuring the traffic that passes through the server's network adapter, you can create a configuration baseline over time.

13. **B and C.** It is important to calculate how much disk space you will require for the logs of your database server and verify that you have that much disk space available on the hard drive. It is also important to plan what information will be needed in the case that you need to reconstruct events later. Group policy information and virtual memory is not important for this particular task.
14. **C.** It is important to copy the logs to a secondary server in case something happens to the primary log server; this way you have another copy of any possible security breaches. Blocking all failed and successful login attempts might not be wise, because it will create many entries. The rest of the answers are not necessarily good ideas when working with log files.
15. **B.** Network security administrators should frequently view the logs of a DNS server to monitor any unauthorized zone transfers. Aliases are DNS names that redirects to a hostname or FQDN. Simply viewing the logs of a DNS server will not defend against denial-of-service attacks. Domain name kiting is the process of floating a domain name for up to five names without paying for the domain name.
16. **B.** Information listed is an example of a port scan. The source IP address perpetuating the port scan should be banned or blocked on the firewall. The fact that the source computer is using port 53 is of no consequence during the port scan and does not imply DNS spoofing. It is not a denial-of-service attack; note that the destination IP address ends in 80, but the number 80 is part of the IP and is not the port.
17. **B and C.** The log files should be retained in some manner either on this computer or on another computer. By hashing the log files, the integrity of the files can be checked even after they are moved. Cyclic redundancy checks or CRCs have to deal with the transmission of Ethernet frames over the network. Temporary files are normally not necessary when dealing with log files.
18. **A.** A protocol analyzer should be used to diagnose which network adapter on the LAN is causing the broadcast storm. A firewall cannot diagnose attacks perpetuated on a network. Port scanner is used to find open ports on one or more computers. A network intrusion detection system is implemented to locate and possibly quarantine some types of attacks but will not be effective when it comes to broadcast storms.
19. **C.** If an audit recording fails, there should be sufficient safeguards employed that can automatically send an alert to the administrator, among other things. Audit records should not be overwritten and in general should not be stopped.
20. **D.** The security log file should show attempts at unauthorized access to a Windows computer. The application log file must deal with events concerning

applications within the operating system and some third-party applications. The system log file deals with drivers, system files, and so on. A DNS log will log information concerning the domain name system.

21. **B.** The system log will show when a computer was shut down (and turned on for that matter or restarted). The security log shows any audited information on a computer system. The application log deals with OS apps and third-party apps. The DNS log shows events that have transpired on a DNS server.

22. **A and C.** Behavior-based monitoring and anomaly-based monitoring require creating a baseline. Many host-based IDS systems will monitor parts of the dynamic behavior and the state of the computer system. An anomaly-based IDS will classify activities as either normal or anomalous; this will be based on rules instead of signatures. Both behavior-based and anomaly-based monitoring require a baseline to make a comparative analysis. Signature-based monitoring systems do not require this baseline because they are looking for specific patterns or signatures and are comparing them to a database of signatures. The performance monitor program can be used to create a baseline on Windows computers but it does not necessarily require a baseline.

23. **A.** A performance baseline and audit trails are not necessarily needed. Because the reports are not time-critical, a performance baseline should not be implemented. Auditing this much information could be unfeasible for one person. However, it is important to implement time stamping of the logs and store log details. Before implementing the logging server, Jason should check if he has enough storage and backup space to meet his requirements.

24. **B.** When using an IDS, particular types of traffic patterns refers to signature-based IDS.

25. **D.** If the Web server is showing a drop in processor and hard disk speed, it might have been compromised. Further analysis and comparison to a pre-existing baseline would be necessary. All the other answers are common for a web server.

This chapter covers the following subjects:

- **Cryptography Concepts**—This section covers the basic terminology of cryptography including encryption, ciphers, and keys. It also discusses private versus public keys, symmetric versus asymmetric encryption, and public key encryption.
- **Encryption Algorithms**—This section delves into the various symmetric algorithms, such as DES and AES, and some of the popular asymmetric algorithms such as RSA and elliptic curve.
- **Hashing Basics**—Here, we investigate the most common way to verify the integrity of files: hashing. We cover basic hashing concepts and cryptographic hash functions, such as MD5, SHA, and NTLM.

This chapter covers the CompTIA Security+ SY0-201 objectives 5.1, 5.2, and 5.3.

CHAPTER 12

Encryption and Hashing Concepts

Chances are that the majority of you will have limited experience with encryption. Because of this, I have written this chapter, and the following one, in a very to-the-point manner with simple analogous examples. I cover only what you need to know about encryption concepts, methods, and types. Encryption by itself is an entire IT field, but the CompTIA Security+ exam requires that you know only the very basics—the exam objectives only scrape the surface of encryption concepts. Keep all this in mind as you go through this chapter and the next. At the end of this chapter, I have left some links to more advanced encryption books and websites; although, they are not necessary for the exam.

Foundation Topics

Cryptography Concepts

Cryptography is the practice of hiding information. Let's give a basic example of cryptography. When I was younger, some of the girls I knew would keep a black book with names, phone numbers, and so on. I'm still pretty sure to this day that I wasn't in any of them! Anyway, a couple of those people did something that fascinated me—they would modify phone numbers according to a code they had developed. This was done to hide the true phone number of a special friend from their parents, or from teachers, and so on. It was a basic form of encryption, although at the time I didn't realize it. I just referred to it as a "code."

Essentially, it would work like this:

The person with the black book would take a real phone number such as 555-0386. They would then modify the number by stepping each number backward or forward X amount of steps. Let's say the person decided to step each number between 0 and 9 backward by three steps, the resulting coded phone number would be 222-7053. I'm sure you see how that was done, but let's break it down so that we can make an analogy to today's data encryption. Table 12-1 shows the entire code used.

Table 12-1 Black Book Phone Number Encryption

Original Number	Modifier	Modified Number
0	Minus 3	7
1		8
2		9
3		0
4		1
5		2
6		3
7		4
8		5
9		6

In this example, each number between 0 and 9 corresponds to a number three digits behind it. BTW, the numbers cycle through: For example, the number 0 goes three steps back, starting at 0, to 9, 8, and then 7 in an "around-the-bend" fashion.

Let's analogize. Each of the components in the table can be likened to today's computer-based encryption concepts:

- The original number is like to original file data.
- The modifier is like to an encryption key.
- The modified number is like to encrypted file data.

I call this the "Black Book Example," but I would guess that others have used similar analogies. Of course, this is a basic example; however, it should serve to help you to associate actual computer-based encryption techniques with this more tangible idea.

Now, for other people to figure out the original phone numbers in the black book, they would have to do the following:

Step 1. Gain access to the black book. This is just like gaining access to data. Depending on how well the black book is secured, this by itself could be difficult.

Step 2. Break the code. This would be known as *decrypting* the data. Of course, if the owner of the black book was silly enough to put the phone number encryption table in the book, well, then game over; it would be easy to decode. But if the owner were smart enough to memorize the code (and tell it to no one), making it a secret code, it would be much more difficult for another person to crack. Plus, the person could make the code more advanced, for example look at Table 12-2.

Table 12-2 Advanced Black Book Phone Number Encryption

Original Number	Modifier	Modified Number
0	Minus 9	1
1	Minus 8	3
2	Minus 7	5
3	Minus 6	7
4	Minus 5	9
5	Minus 4	1b
6	Minus 3	3b
7	Minus 2	5b
8	Minus 1	7b
9	Minus 0	9b

In this example, there is a different modifier (or key) for each original number. Because the modified numbers have duplicates, we place a letter next to each of the various duplicates to differentiate. This is tougher to decrypt due to the increased level of variations; but on the flipside, it is that much harder to memorize. Likewise, computers have a harder time processing more advanced encryption codes, and hackers (or crackers) have a difficult time processing their decryption.

At this point, only one person has legitimate access to the encryption codes. However, what if the person wanted to share phone numbers with another person, but still keep the numbers secret from everyone else? This would be known as a secret key.

We'll be referring to this basic concept as we go through this chapter and the next.

Now that we have given a basic example, let's define some terminology in a more technical way. We'll start with cryptography, encryption, ciphers, and keys. You might want to read through this list twice because each definition builds on the last.

- **Cryptography—**By definition, *cryptography* is the practice and study of hiding information. It is used in e-commerce and with passwords. Most commonly, encryption is used to hide information and make it secret.

- **Encryption—***Encryption* is the process of changing information using an algorithm (or cipher) into another form that is unreadable by others—unless, they possess the key to that data. Encryption is used to secure communications, and to protect data as it is transferred from one place to another. The reverse, decryption, can be accomplished in two ways: First by using the proper key to unlock the data, and second, by cracking the original encryption key. Encryption enforces confidentiality of data.

- **Cipher—**A *cipher* is an algorithm that can perform encryption or decryption. A basic example would be to take the plaintext word "code" and encrypt it as a ciphertext using a specific algorithm. The end result could be anything depending on the algorithm used, but for example, let's say the end result was the ciphertext "zlab." I don't know about you, but "zlab" looks like gibberish to me. (Although if you Google it, I'm sure you'll find all kinds of endless fun.) You've probably already guessed at my cipher—each letter of the plaintext word "code" was stepped back three letters in the alphabet. Other historical ciphers would use substitution and transposition as well. However, actual algorithms used are much more complex. *Algorithms* are well-defined instructions that describe computations from their initial state to their final state. IF-THEN statements are examples of computer algorithms. The entire set of instructions is the cipher. We'll cover the various types of ciphers (again, also known as algorithms) in the section "Encryption Algorithms" later in this chapter.

- **Key—**The *key* is the essential piece of information that determines the output of a cipher. It is indispensable; without it there would be no result to the cipher computation. In the previous bullet, the key was the act of stepping back three letters. In the first black book example, the key was stepping back three numbers (a modifier of minus 3). Just like a person can't unlock a lock without the proper key, a computer can't decrypt information without the proper key (using normal methods). The only way to provide security is if the key is kept secret—or in the case that there are multiple keys, if one of them is kept secret. The terms key and cipher are sometimes used interchangeably, but you should remember that the key is the vital portion of the cipher that determines its output. The length of the key determines its strength. Shorter, weaker keys are desirable to hackers attempting to access encrypted data.

Keys can be private or public. A *private key* is only known to a specific user or users who keep the key a secret. A *public key* is known to all parties involved in encrypted transactions within a given group. An example of a private key would be the usage of an encrypted smart card for authentication. Smart cards and PCMCIA cards (PC Cards) are examples of devices that can store keys. An example of a public key would be when two people want to communicate securely with each other over the Internet; they would require a public key that each of them knows.

Encryption types, such as AES or RSA, are known as ciphers, key algorithms, or simply as algorithms; we refer to them as algorithms during the rest of this chapter and the next. There are basically two classifications of key algorithms: symmetric and asymmetric.

Symmetric Versus Asymmetric Key Algorithms

Some cryptographic systems use symmetric keys only, others use asymmetric, and some use both symmetric and asymmetric. It is important to know the differences between the two, and how they can be used together.

Symmetric Key Algorithms

The *symmetric key algorithm* is a class of cipher that uses identical or closely related keys for encryption and decryption. The term "symmetric key" is also referred to as the following: secret-key, private-key, single-key and shared-key (and sometimes as "session-key"). Examples of symmetric key algorithms include DES, 3DES, RC, and AES, all of which we discuss later in this chapter. Another example of a technology that uses symmetric keys is Kerberos. By default, Kerberos makes use of a third party known as a key distribution center for the secure transmission of symmetric keys, also referred to as tickets.

NOTE: Kerberos can optionally use public key cryptography (covered later in this chapter) by making use of asymmetric keys. This is done during specific authentication stages. Kerberos is covered in more depth in Chapter 8, "Physical Security and Authentication Models."

Following are two types of symmetric key algorithms:

- A *stream cipher* is a type of algorithm that encrypts each byte in a message one at a time.
- A *block cipher* is a type of algorithm that encrypts a group of bits collectively as individual units known as blocks. For example, the Advanced Encryption Standard (AES) algorithm uses 128-bit block ciphers.

Symmetric key algorithms require a secure initial exchange of one or more secret keys to both the sender and the receiver. In our black book example, we mentioned that people might possibly want to share their cipher with someone else. To do so, they would need to make sure that they were alone and that no one was eavesdropping. It is also so with computers. The secure initial exchange of secret keys can be difficult depending on the circumstances. It is also possible to encrypt the initial exchange of the secret keys!

Symmetric ciphers can also be used for nonrepudiation purposes by adding a message authentication code, which is a small algorithm that will check the integrity of the cipher and notify the receiver if there were any modifications to the encrypted data. This way, the data cannot be denied (repudiated) when received.

Symmetric encryption is the preferred option when encrypting and sending large amounts of data.

Asymmetric Key Algorithms

Asymmetric key algorithms use a pair of different keys to encrypt and decrypt data. The keys might be related, but they are not identical or even close to it in the way symmetric keys are. The two asymmetric keys are related mathematically. Imagine that you were the night shift security guard for a warehouse that stored CPUs. When your shift is over you are required to lock up. But the warehouse uses a special lock. Your key can only lock the warehouse door, it cannot unlock it. Conversely, the morning watchman has a key that can only unlock the door, but not lock it. There are physical and electronic locks of this manner. This is analogous to asymmetric keys used in encryption. One key is used to encrypt data; the other dissimilar key is used to decrypt the data. Examples of asymmetric key algorithms include RSA, the Diffie-Hellman system, and the elliptic curve cryptography. SSL and TLS protocols use asymmetric key algorithms but generally do so in a public key cryptographic environment.

Public Key Cryptography

Public key cryptography uses asymmetric keys alone or in addition to symmetric keys. It doesn't need the secure exchange of secret keys that was mentioned in the symmetric-key section. Instead, the asymmetric key algorithm creates a secret private key and a published public key. The public key is well known, and anyone can use it to encrypt messages. However, only the owner(s) of the paired or corresponding private key can decrypt the message. The security of the system is based on the secrecy of the private key. If the private key is compromised, the entire system will lose its effectiveness. This is illustrated in Figure 12-1.

Key Topic

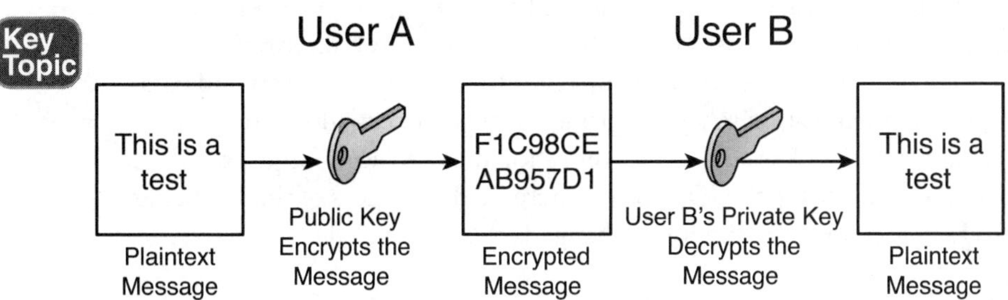

Figure 12-1 Illustration of Public Key Cryptography

Public key cryptography can become more intense. In some schemes, the private key is used to sign a message, and anyone can check the signature with the public key. This signing is done with a digital signature. A *digital signature* authenticates a document through math, letting the recipient know that the document was created and sent by the actual sender, and not someone else. It protects against forgery and tampering. The basic order of functions for the usage of asymmetric keys in this case would be encrypt, sign, decrypt, and verify. In the Diffie-Hellman scheme, each user generates a public/private key pair and distributes their public key to everyone else. After two or more users obtain a copy of the others' public keys, they can be used to create a shared secret used as the key for a symmetric cipher. Due to the varying methods of public key cryptography, the whole subject can become somewhat confusing. Remember that there will always be a private and public key involved, and that public key cryptography can use asymmetric keys alone, or in addition to symmetric keys.

Internet standards, such as SSL/TLS and PGP, use public-key cryptography. Don't confuse the term public key cryptography with Public Key Infrastructure (PKI). Although they are related, they are not the same. PKI is an entire system of hardware, software, policies, and so on, that binds public keys with user identities by way of certificates and a certificate authority (server or other such device). A *certificate* is an electronic document that uses a digital signature to bind the key with the identity. We cover PKI more in Chapter 13, "PKI and Encryption Protocols."

Key Management

Key management deals with the relationship between users and keys; it's important to manage the generation, exchange, storage, and usage of those keys. It is crucial technically, and organizationally, because issues can present themselves due to poorly designed key systems and poor management. Keys must be chosen and stored securely. The generation of strong keys is probably the most important concept. Some algorithms have weak keys that make cryptanalysis easy. For example, DES uses a considerably weaker key than AES; the stronger the key, the stronger the key management. We detail several methods for the exchange of keys later in this chapter including encapsulating one key within another, using key indicators, and exchanging symmetric session keys with an asymmetric key algorithm—in effect, ciphering our cipher. Secure storage of keys often depends on users and passwords, or other authentication schemes. Proper storage of keys allows for availability, part of the CIA triad. Finally, keys should be replaced frequently. If a particular user uses a key for too long, it will increase the chances of the key being cracked. Keys, like passwords, should be changed and/or recycled often.

Steganography

Although I have placed steganography within the cryptography section, it actually isn't cryptography, although it might be used with cryptography. *Steganography* is the science (and art) of writing hidden messages; it is a form of security through obscurity. The goal is that no one aside from the sender and receiver should even suspect that the hidden message exists. The advantage of steganography is that the clearly visible messages look to be just that, regular old messages, that wouldn't usually attract attention to themselves. Most people know when they come into contact with an encrypted message, but far fewer people identify when a steganographic message has crossed their path.

Steganography can hide messages within encrypted documents by inserting extra encrypted information. The hidden messages can also be found in sound files, image files, slowed down video files, and in regular Word documents or Excel spreadsheets. Messages can also be concealed within VOIP conversations (known as Lost Audio Packets Steganography, or LACK), and within any streaming service as well. They can also be obscured on a compromised wireless network with the HICCUPS system (Hidden Communication System for Corrupted Networks).

A common example of steganography is when using graphic files to send hidden messages. In this scenario, the least significant bit of each byte is replaced. For example, we could shade the color of a pixel (or triad) just slightly. This slight change would change the binary number associated with the color, enabling us to insert information. The color blue is represented as three bytes of data numbered 0, 0, and 255. We could change the color blue slightly to 1, 0, 255. This would not make the graphic look any different to the naked eye, but the change would be there nonetheless. This would be done in several or more pixels of the graphic to form the message. For this to work, the recipient would first need to have possession of the original file. Then the sender would transmit the modified steganographic file to be compared with the original by the recipient.

Encryption Algorithms

We mentioned previously that ciphers (or algorithms) can encrypt or decrypt data with the help of a key. We also pointed out that algorithms are well-defined instructions that describe computations from their initial state to their final state. In addition, we mentioned that there are symmetric and asymmetric algorithms. Now, let's talk about some of the actual algorithmic standards within both of those classifications. We'll start with symmetric types including DES, 3DES, AES, and RC and afterward move on to asymmetric types including RSA, Diffie-Hellman, and the elliptic curve.

DES and 3DES

The *Data Encryption Standard (DES)* is an older type of block cipher selected by the U. S. federal government back in the 1970s as its encryption standard. But due to its weak key, it is now considered deprecated and has been replaced by other standards. Being a block cipher, it groups 64 bits together into encryption units. Today, a 64-bit cipher is not considered powerful enough; also, and more important, the key size is 56-bit, which can be cracked fairly easily with a brute force or linear cryptanalysis attack. In addition to this, there are some theoretical weaknesses to the cipher itself. DES was replaced by triple DES (3DES) in 1999. The actual algorithm is sometimes referred to as the Data Encryption Algorithm (DEA). The algorithm is based on the Feistel cipher (or Feistel network) that has very similar, if not identical, encryption and decryption processes, reducing the amount of code required.

Triple DES, also known as 3DES or the Triple Data Encryption Algorithm (TDEA), is similar to DES but applies the cipher algorithm three times to each cipher block. The cipher block size is still 64-bit, but the key size can now be as much as 168-bit (three times the size of DES). This was a smart approach to defeating brute force attacks without having to completely redesign the DES protocol. However, both DES and 3DES have been overshadowed by AES, which became the preferred standard in late 2001.

AES

In the late '90s, the National Institute of Standards and Technology (NIST) started a competition to develop a more advanced type of encryption. There were 15 submissions including Serpent, Twofish, RC6, and others but the selected winner was Rijndael. This submission was then further developed into the *Advanced Encryption Standard (AES)* and became the U. S. federal government standard in 2002. AES is the successor to DES/3DES and is another symmetric key encryption standard composed of three different versions of block ciphers: AES-128, AES-192, and AES-256. Actually, each of these has the same 128-bit cipher block size, but the key sizes for each are 128-bit, 192-bit, and 256-bit, respectively.

AES is based on the substitution-permutation network, which takes plaintext and the key and applies X amount of rounds to create the ciphertext. These rounds consist of substitution boxes and permutation boxes (usually in groups of 4X4 bytes) that convert the plaintext input bits to ciphertext output bits. AES specifies 10, 12, or 14 rounds for each of the respective versions.

AES is fast, uses minimal resources, and can be used on a variety of platforms. For example, it is the encryption algorithm of choice if you have a wireless network running the WPA2 protocol; the IEEE 802.11i standard specifies the usage of AES with WPA2 and in the process deprecates WEP. In addition, AES is a good choice for transferring encrypted data quickly to a USB flash drive. It is also used in whole disk encryption techniques such as BitLocker. This software can encrypt the entire disk which, after complete, is transparent to the user. However, there are some requirements for this including the following:

- A Trusted Platform Module (TPM)—A chip residing on the motherboard that actually generates and stores the encrypted keys, and defines their use
  or
- An external USB key to store the encrypted keys
  and
- A hard drive with two volumes

AES is purportedly susceptible to the related-key attack, if the attacker has some information of the mathematical relationship between several different keys. But generally, AES is considered the strongest type of symmetric encryption for many scenarios. Possible future successors to AES include the currently named Anubis and Grand Cru. As of now, AES is used worldwide and has not been outright compromised, nor do some industry experts ever think it will be.

RC

RC stands for different things depending on who you talk to. Officially, it is known as Rivest Cipher but is playfully known as Ron's Code as well. There are multiple RC versions, most of which are not related aside from the fact that they are all encryption algorithms.

RC4 is a somewhat widely used stream cipher in such protocols such as SSL and WEP. It is known for its speed and simplicity. However, it is avoided when designing newer applications and technologies due to several vulnerabilities; when used with WEP on wireless networks, it can be cracked in under 1 minute with the use of aircrack-ptw. One way to avoid this to a certain extent is to use the Temporal Key Integrity Protocol (TKIP) with WEP. However, it still is recommended that AES and WPA2 be used in wireless networks.

RC5 is a block cipher noted for its simplicity and for its variable size (32, 64, or 128-bit). It was the predecessor to today's RC6, which is a block cipher entered into the AES competition and was one of the five finalists. Though it was not selected, it is a patented algorithm offered by RSA Security as an alternative to AES. It is similar to AES in block size and key size options but uses different mathematical methods than Rijndael.

Summary of Symmetric Algorithms

Table 12-3 gives some comparisons of the algorithms up to this point and their key strength.

Table 12-3 Summary of Symmetric Algorithms

Algorithm Acronym	Full Name	Maximum/Typical Key Size
DES	Data Encryption Standard	56-bit
3DES	Triple DES	168-bit
AES	Advanced Encryption Standard	256-bit
RC4	Rivest Cipher version 4	128-bit typical
RC5	Rivest Cipher version 5	64-bit typical
RC6	Rivest Cipher version 6	256-bit typical

RSA

Let's talk about some asymmetric key algorithms. The original and very common *RSA* (which stands for Rivest, Shamir, and Adleman, the creators) is a public key cryptography algorithm. As long as the proper size keys are used, it is considered to be a secure protocol and is used in many e-commerce scenarios. It is slower than symmetric key algorithms but has advantages being suitable for signing and for encryption. It works well with credit card security and SSL. Key lengths for RSA are much longer than in symmetric cryptosystems. For example, 512-bit RSA keys have proven to be breakable over a decade ago; however, 1,024-bit keys are currently considered unbreakable by most known technologies, but RSA still recommends using the longer 2,048-bit key, which should deter even the most powerful super hackers. It is important to note that asymmetric algorithm keys need to be much larger than their symmetric key counterparts to be as effective. For example, a 128-bit symmetric key is equal to a 2,304-bit asymmetric key in strength. The RSA algorithm uses what is known as integer factorization cryptography. It works by first multiplying two distinct prime numbers that cannot be factored, then moving on to some more advanced math, and finally it creates a private and public key pair.

RSA key distribution is vulnerable to man-in-the-middle attacks. However, these attacks are defensible through the usage of digital certificates and other parts of a

PKI system that we detail in the next chapter. It is also susceptible to timing attacks that can be defended against through the use of cryptographic blinding: This blind computation provides encryption without knowing actual input or output information. Due to other types of attacks, it is recommended that a secure padding scheme is used. Padding schemes work differently depending on the type of cryptography. In public key cryptography, padding is the adding of random material to a message to be sufficient, and incorporating a proof, making it more difficult to crack. A padding scheme is always involved, and algorithm makers such as RSA are always releasing improved versions.

In 2000, RSA Security released the RSA algorithm to the public. Therefore, no licensing fees are required if an organization decided to use or modify the algorithm.

Diffie-Hellman

The *Diffie-Hellman key exchange*, invented in the 1970s, was the first practical method for establishing a shared secret key over an unprotected communications channel. This asymmetric algorithm was developed shortly before the original RSA algorithm. It is also known as the Diffie-Hellman-Merkle key exchange due to Merkle's conceptual involvement.

Diffie-Hellman relies on secure key exchange before data can be transferred. This key exchange establishes a shared secret key that can be used for secret communications, but over a public network. Originally, names were chosen for the "users": Alice and Bob. Basically, Alice and Bob agree to initial prime and base numbers. Then, each of them selects secret integers and sends an equation based off of those to each other. Each of them computes the other's equation to complete the shared secret, which then allows for encrypted data to be transmitted. The secret integers are discarded at the end of the session, achieving perfect forward secrecy.

It is considered secure against eavesdroppers due to the difficulty of mathematically solving the Diffie-Hellman problem. However, it is vulnerable to man-in-the-middle attacks. To prevent this, some method of authentication is used such as password authentication. This algorithm is used by the Transport Layer Security (TLS) protocol during encrypted web sessions. This algorithm can also be used within a public key infrastructure, though the RSA algorithm is far more common.

Elliptic Curve

Elliptic curve cryptography (ECC) is a type of public key cryptography based on the structure of an elliptic curve. It is also based on the difficulty of certain mathematical problems. Keys are created by graphing specific points on the curve, which were generated mathematically. All parties involved must agree on the elements that define the curve. This asymmetric algorithm has a compact design and creates keys that are difficult to crack. Other algorithms have been adapted to work with elliptic curves including Diffie-Hellman and the Digital Signature Algorithm

(DSA). DSA is a Federal standard public key encryption algorithm used in digital signatures. ECC cryptography is used with smart cards, wireless security, and other communications such as VOIP and IPSec (with DSA).

ECC is susceptible to side channel attacks (SCA), which are attacks based on leaked information gained from the physical implementation (amount and type of curves) of the cryptosystem, and fault attacks (a type of side channel attack). These can be defeated by using an Elliptic Curve scalar multiplication algorithm or fixed pattern windows.

More Encryption Types

We have a couple more encryption types to speak of. They don't quite fit into the other sections, so I figured I would place them here. The first is the one-time pad and the second is the Pretty Good Privacy (PGP) application and encryption method.

One-Time Pad

A *one-time pad* is a cipher that encrypts plaintext with a secret random key that is the same length as the plaintext. Unlike other encryption types, it can be computed by hand with a pencil and paper (thus the word "pad" in the name), although today computers will be used to create a one-time pad algorithm for use with technology. It has been proven as impossible to crack if used correctly and is known as being "information-theoretically secure"; it is the only cryptosystem with theoretically perfect secrecy. This means that it provides no information about the original message to a person trying to decrypt it illegitimately. However, issues with this type of encryption have stopped it from being widely used.

One of the issues with a one-time pad is that it requires perfect randomness. The problem with computer numerical random generators is that they are usually not truly random, instead they are pseudorandom generators; high-quality random numbers are quite difficult to generate. Another issue is that the exchange of the one-time pad data must be equal to the length of the message. It also requires proper disposal, which is difficult due to data remanence.

Regardless of these issues, the one-time pad can be useful in scenarios in which two users in a secure environment are required to also communicate with each other from two other separate secure environments. The one-time pad is also used in superencryption (or multiple encryption), which is encrypting an already encrypted message. In addition it is commonly used in quantum cryptography, which uses quantum mechanics to guarantee secure communications. These last two concepts are far beyond the Security+ exam, but they show the actual purpose for this encryption type.

PGP

Pretty Good Privacy (PGP) is an encryption program used primarily for signing, encrypting and decrypting e-mails in an attempt to increase the security of e-mail communications. You might remember that we previously discussed weaknesses of e-mail client programs when sending via POP3 and SMTP servers. PGP uses (actually wrote) the encryption specifications as shown in the OpenPGP standard; other similar programs use this as well. Today, PGP has an entire suite of tools that can encrypt e-mail, accomplish whole disk encryption, and encrypt zip files and instant messages. PGP uses a symmetric session key (also referred to as a preshared key or PSK), and as such, you might hear PGP referred to as a program that uses symmetric encryption, but it also uses the asymmetric RSA for digital signatures and for sending the session key.

When encrypting data, PGP uses key sizes of at least 128-bits. Newer versions allow for RSA or DSA key sizes ranging from 512 bits to 2048 bits. The larger the key, the more secure the encryption is, but the longer it will take to generate the keys; although, this is done only once when establishing a connection with another user. The program uses a combination of hashing, data compression, symmetric key cryptography, and public key cryptography. New versions of the program are not fully compatible with older versions because the older versions cannot decrypt the data that was generated by a newer version. This is one of the issues when using PGP; users must be sure to work with the same version. Newer versions of PGP support OpenPGP and S/MIME, which allows for secure communications with just about everyone.

Because it works with RSA, the security of PGP is based on the key size. It is considered secure and uncrackable as long as a sufficient key size is used. As an example, it has been suggested that a 2,048-bit key should be safe against the strongest of well-funded adversaries with knowledgeable people and the latest in super computers until at least the year 2020; 1024-bit keys are considered strong enough for all but the most sensitive data environments.

Hashing Basics

A *hash* is a summary of a file or message. Hashes, are used in digital signatures and file and message authentication. A hash is generated through the use of a *hash function* to verify the integrity of the file or message, most commonly after transit over a network. A hash function is a mathematical procedure that converts a variable-sized amount of data into a smaller block of data. The hash function is designed to take an arbitrary data block from the file or message, use that as an input, and from that block, produce a fixed-length hash value. Basically, the hash is created at the source and is recalculated and compared with the original hash at the destination. Figure 12-2 illustrates this process. Note the hash that was created starting with ce114e and so on. This is the summary, or message digest of the file to be sent. It is an actual representation of an MD5 hash of a plaintext file with the words "This is a test," as shown in the message portion of Figure 12-2.

Key Topic

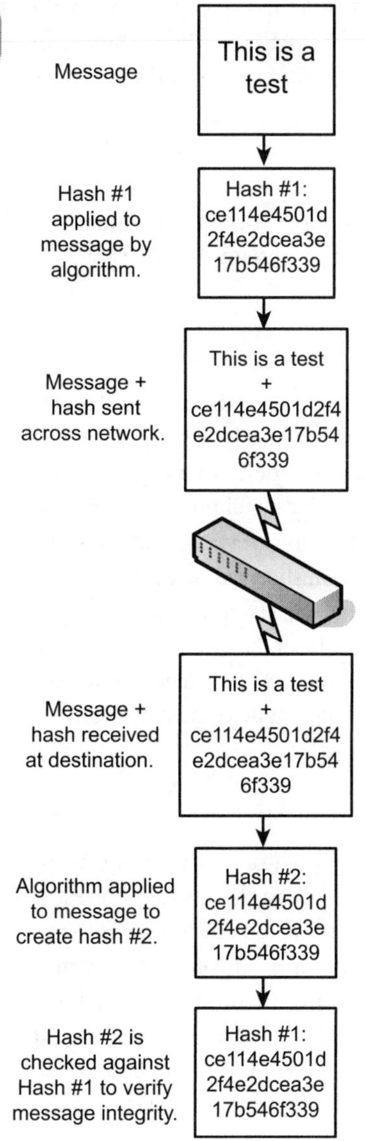

Figure 12-2 Illustration of the Hashing Process

Because the hash is a condensed version of the file/message, or a portion of it, it is also known as a message digest. It provides integrity to data so that a user knows that the message is intact, hasn't been modified during transit, and comes from the source the user expects. A hash can fall into the category of a *one-way function*. This means it is easy to compute when generated but difficult (or impossible) to compute in reverse. In the case of a hash, a condensed version of the message, initial computation is relatively easy (compared to other algorithms), but the original message should not be re-created from the hash. Contrast this concept to encryption methods that indeed can be reversed. A hash can be created without the use of an algorithm, but generally, the ones used in the field require some kind of cryptographic algorithm.

Cryptographic Hash Functions

Cryptographic hash functions are hash functions based on block ciphers. The methods used resemble that of cipher modes used in encryption. Examples of cryptographic hash functions include MD5 and SHA.

MD5

The *Message-Digest algorithm 5 (MD5)* is the latest in a series of algorithms designed by Ron Rivest. It uses a 128-bit key. This is a widely used hashing algorithm; at some point you have probably seen MD5 hashes when downloading files. This is an example of the attempt at providing integrity. By checking the hash produced by the downloaded file against the original hash, you can verify the file's integrity with a certain level of certainty. However, MD5 hashes are susceptible to collisions. A collision occurs when two different files end up using the same hash. Due to this low collision resistance, MD5 is considered to be harmful today. MD5 is also vulnerable to threats such as rainbow tables and pre-image attacks. The best solution to protect against these attacks is to use a stronger type of hashing function such as SHA-2 or higher.

SHA

The *Secure Hash Algorithm (SHA)* is one of a number of hash functions designed by the NSA and published by the NIST. They are used widely in the United States government. SHA-1 is the most commonly used version, which employs a 160-bit hash, which is reasonably secure, but uses a lot of resources on the computer generating the hash. SHA-2 is more secure; it has 256-bit and 512-bit block sizes but uses even more resources and is less widely accepted. SHA-3 is under development but is slated to be the replacement for SHA-1. An NIST hash function competition for SHA-3 (similar to the AES competition) is scheduled for completion in 2012.

It is important that a hashing algorithm be collision-resistant. If it has the capability to avoid the same output from two guessed inputs (by a hacker attempting a collision attack), it is collision-resistant. When it comes to cryptography "perfect hashing" is not possible because usually unknowns are involved, such as the data to be used to create the hash, and what hash values have been created in the past. Though perfect is not possible, it is possible to increase collision resistance by using a more powerful hashing algorithm.

Because MD5 and SHA-1 have vulnerabilities, many government agencies will start using SHA-2 in 2011 (and most likely SHA-3 after 2012).

Happy Birthday!

Not when a birthday attack is involved. A *birthday attack* is an attack on a hashing system that attempts to send two different messages with the same hash function, causing a collision. It is based on the birthday problem in probability theory (also known as the birthday paradox). This can be summed up simply as the following: A randomly chosen group of people will have a pair of persons with the same calendar date birthday. The probability of this with 365 (or 366) people is 100%, which makes sense. The paradox (thoughtfully and mathematically) comes into play when less people are involved. With only 57 people, there is a 99% probability of a match (a much higher percentage than one would think), and with only 23 people, there is a 50% probability. Imagine that and blow out your candles! And by this, I mean use hashing functions with strong collision resistance. Because if attackers can find any two messages that digest the same way (use the same hash value), they can deceive a user into receiving the wrong message. To protect against a birthday attack, use a secure transmission medium, such as SSH, or encrypt the entire message that has been hashed.

LANMAN, NTLM, and NTLM2

Passwords can also be hashed using algorithms. Some password hashes are more secure than others, whereas older ones have been cracked and are therefore compromised. This section details the LANMAN, NTLM, and NTLM2 hashes starting from the oldest. These three types of authentication are what attempts to make your logon to the computer secure, unless you log in to a domain where Kerberos is used by default.

LANMAN

The *LANMAN hash*, also known as the LAN Manager hash or simply LM hash, was the original hash used to store Windows passwords. It was used in Windows operating systems before Windows NT but is supported by some versions of Windows as a legacy backward in the attempt to be backward compatible. This backward compatibility can be a security risk because the LM hash has several weaknesses and can be cracked easily.

Its function is based off of the deprecated DES algorithm. Weaknesses also include the fact that the ASCII password is converted to uppercase, essentially removing a large portion of the character set. Brute force attacks can crack alphanumeric LM hashes in a matter of hours.

Due to all these weaknesses, it is highly recommended that it be disabled on operating systems that run it by default. It should also be checked on OSs such as Windows Vista that are supposed to have it disabled by default.

The following step-by-step procedure shows how to disable the storage of LM hashes in Windows Server 2003. It works the same in Windows XP:

Step 1. Access the Local Group Policy.

Step 2. Navigate to **Computer Configuration > Windows Settings > Security Settings > Local Policies > Security Options**.

Step 3. In the right pane, double-click the policy named **Network security: Do not store LAN Manager hash value on next password change**.

Step 4. Click **Enabled** and click **OK**. An example of this is shown in Figure 12-3.

Key Topic

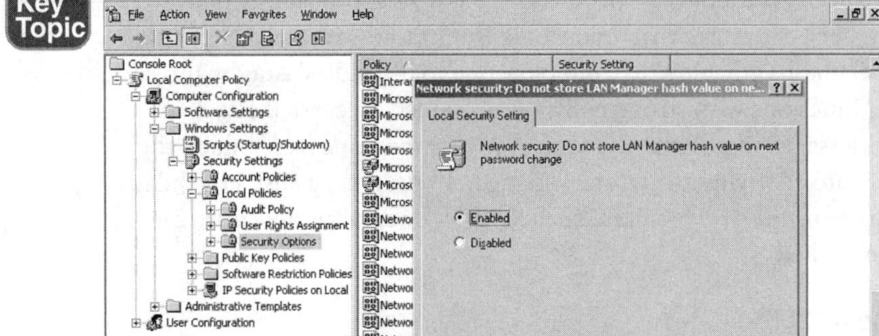

Figure 12-3 LM Hash in the Local Group Policy of a Windows Server 2003

NOTE: For Windows Server 2003 domain controllers, you need to access the Group Policy Editor, not Local Group Policy. Generally, this would be done at the default domain policy, but it could also be accomplished at a single OU's policy, if necessary.

You can also disable the storage of LM hash passwords by modifying the Registry. This process is necessary for Windows 2000 Server and Professional computers. For more information, see the link to Microsoft's website at the end of this chapter.

If, for whatever reason, the storing of LM hashes for passwords cannot be turned off, Microsoft recommends using a 15-character-minimum password. When this is done, an LM hash and a NTLM hash value are stored. In this situation, the LM hash cannot be used solely to authenticate the user; therefore, it cannot be solely cracked; the NTLM hash would have to be cracked as well. Because 15 characters might be beyond some organization's policies, it is highly recommended that the LM hash policy be disabled.

NTLM and NTLM2

Well, we talked a lot about why the LM hash is insufficient. Let's get into the replacements. The first is *NTLM hash*, also known as the NT LAN Manager hash. The NTLM algorithm was first supplied with Windows NT 3.1; it provides Unicode support, and more important to this conversation, the RC4 cipher. Although the RC4 cipher enables a more powerful hash known as NTLM for storing passwords, the systems it ran on were still configured to be backward compatible with the LM hash. So, as long as the LM hash was not disabled, those systems were still at the same risk as older systems that ran the LM hash only. Windows Vista and Windows 2008 operating systems (and higher) disable the older LM hash by default.

The issue with NTLM is that it is based off of the RC4 cipher, which has been compromised. Therefore, the NTLM hash is compromised. You probably remember the NTLM hash we cracked during the Chapter 10 labs. (It was a basic password, but it got the point across.) This was done using Cain & Abel on a Windows Vista computer with SP2, which has the LM hash disabled by default. Due to the weakness of NTLM, we need a stronger hashing algorithm: NTLM 2.

NTLM 2 uses the MD5 hash, making it difficult to crack; it is a 128-bit system. NTLM 2 (also known as NTLMv2) has been available since Windows NT 4.0 SP4 and is used by default on newer Windows operating systems. Older versions of Windows, such as Windows 98, can be upgraded to allow NTLM 2 compatibility by installing Active Directory Client Extensions. Even though NTLM 2 responds to the security issues of the LM hash and NTLM, most Microsoft domains will use Kerberos as the logon authentication scheme because of its level of security when dealing with one computer logging into another, or into an entire network.

Exam Preparation Tasks

Review Key Topics

Review the most important topics in the chapter, noted with the Key Topics icon in the outer margin of the page. Table 12-4 lists a reference of these key topics and the page numbers on which each is found.

Table 12-4 Key Topics for Chapter 12

Key Topic Element	Description	Page Number
Table 12-1	Black Book Phone Number Encryption	350
Figure 12-1	Illustration of Public Key Cryptography	355
Table 12-3	Summary of Symmetric Algorithms	359
Figure 12-2	Illustration of the Hashing Process	363
Figure 12-3	LM Hash Disabled in the Local Group Policy of a Windows Server 2003	366

Complete Tables and Lists from Memory

Print a copy of Appendix A, "Memory Tables," (found on the DVD), or at least the section for this chapter, and complete the tables and lists from memory. Appendix B, "Memory Tables Answer Key," also on the DVD, includes completed tables and lists to check your work.

Define Key Terms

Define the following key terms from this chapter, and check your answers in the glossary:

cryptography, encryption, cipher, algorithms, key, symmetric key algorithm, stream cipher, block cipher, asymmetric key algorithm, public key cryptography, private key, public key, digital signature, certificate, steganography, Data Encryption Standard (DES), Triple DES (3DES), Advanced Encryption Standard (AES), RSA, Diffie-Hellman key exchange, elliptic curve cryptography (ECC), one-time pad, Pretty Good Privacy (PGP), hash, hash function, cryptographic hash functions, Message-Digest Algorithm 5 (MD5), Secure Hash Algorithm (SHA), birthday attack, LANMAN hash, NTLM hash, NTLM2 hash

Hands-On Lab

Complete the following written step-by-step scenario. After you finish (or if you do not have adequate equipment to complete the scenario), watch the corresponding video solution on the DVD.

If you have additional questions, feel free to post them at my website: www.davidlprowse.com in the Ask Dave forum. (Free registration is required to post on the website.)

Equipment Needed

- Windows Server 2003

Lab 12-1: Disabling the LM Hash in Windows Server 2003

In this lab, you disable the LANMAN hashing algorithm within the Local Security Policy and within the Registry. The steps are as follows:

Disable the LM hash from a group policy:

Step 1. Access the Windows Server 2003.

Step 2. Access the Local Group Policy.

Step 3. Navigate to **Computer Configuration > Windows Settings > Security Settings > Local Policies > Security Options**.

Step 4. In the right pane, double-click the policy named **Network security: Do Not Store LAN Manager Hash Value on Next Password Change**.

Step 5. Click **Enabled** and click **OK**.

Disable the LM hash from the Registry:

Step 6. Start the Registry Editor by clicking **Start > Run** and typing regedit.exe.

Step 7. Navigate to the following key: HKEY_LOCAL_MACHINE\SYSTEM\CurrentControlSet\Control\Lsa

Step 8. Locate the entry named noLMHash. Double-click it and set it to **1** to enable that entry.

If the entry does not exist, create it by right-clicking the white work area in the right window pane, selecting **New > Dword**. Name the Dword **noLMHash**, and then set it to **1**.

Watch the solution video in the "Hands-On Scenarios" section of the DVD.

View Recommended Resources

Recommended reading:

- *Introduction to Modern Cryptography: Principles and Protocols*. Katz, Lindell. Chapman and Hall, 2007.
- *Cryptography Demystified*. Hershey. McGraw-Hill Professional, 2002.
- *Practical Cryptography*. Ferguson. Wiley, 2003.
- *Hiding in Plain Sight*: Cole. Wiley, 2003.
- *Malicious Cryptography: Exposing Cryptovirology*. Young, Yung. Wiley, 2004.
- *Privacy on the Line: The Politics of Wiretapping and Encryption*. Diffie, Landau. The MIT Press, 2010.
- *Schneier on Security*. Schneier. 2008 Wiley.

Recommended Internet resources:

- NIST: Data Encryption Standard (DES): http://csrc.nist.gov/publications/fips/fips46-3/fips46-3.pdf
- NIST: Recommendation for the Triple Data Encryption Algorithm (TDEA) Block Cipher: http://csrc.nist.gov/publications/nistpubs/800-67/SP800-67.pdf
- NIST: Advanced Encryption Standard (AES): http://csrc.nist.gov/publications/fips/fips197/fips-197.pdf
- RSA Laboratories: RC6 Block Cipher: www.rsa.com/rsalabs/node.asp?id=2512
- Disabling the storage of LM hashes in Windows: http://support.microsoft.com/kb/299656
- Bruce Schneier Blog: www.schneier.com/

Answer Review Questions

Answer the following review questions. You can find the answers at the end of this chapter.

1. Which of the following is the proper order of functions for asymmetric keys?

A. Decrypt, validate, and code and verify

B. Sign, encrypt, decrypt, and verify

C. Encrypt, sign, decrypt, and verify

D. Decrypt, decipher, and code and encrypt

2. Which type of encryption technology is used with the BitLocker application?
   A. Symmetric
   B. Asymmetric
   C. Hashing
   D. WPA2

3. Which of the following will provide an integrity check?
   A. Public key
   B. Private key
   C. WEP
   D. Hash

4. Why would a hacker use steganography?
   A. To hide information
   B. For data integrity
   C. To encrypt information
   D. For wireless access

5. You need to encrypt and send a large amount of data, which of the following would be the best option?
   A. Symmetric encryption
   B. Hashing algorithm
   C. Asymmetric encryption
   D. PKI

6. Imagine that you are a hacker. Which would be most desirable when attempting to compromise encrypted data?
   A. A weak key
   B. The algorithm used by the encryption protocol
   C. Captured traffic
   D. A block cipher

7. An SHA algorithm will have how many bits?
   A. 64
   B. 128
   C. 512
   D. 1,024

8. What is another term for secret key encryption?

A. PKI

B. Asymmetrical

C. Symmetrical

D. Public key

9. Your boss wants you to set up an authentication scheme in which employees will use smart cards to log into the company network. What kind of key should be used to accomplish this?

A. Private key

B. Public key

C. Cipher key

D. Shared key

10. The IT director wants you to use a cryptographic algorithm that cannot be decoded by being reversed. Which of the following would be the best option?

A. Asymmetric

B. Symmetric

C. PKI

D. One way function

11. Which of the following concepts does that Diffie-Hellman algorithm rely on?

A. Usernames and passwords

B. VPN tunneling

C. Biometrics

D. Key exchange

12. What does steganography replace in graphic files?

A. The least significant bit of each byte

B. The most significant bit of each byte

C. The least significant byte of each bit

D. The most significant byte of each bit

13. What does it mean if a hashing algorithm creates the same hash for two different downloads?

A. A hash is not encrypted.

B. A hashing chain has occurred.

C. A one-way hash has occurred.

D. A collision has occurred.

14. Which of the following methods will best verify that a download from the Internet has not been modified since the manufacturer released it?

A. Compare the final LANMAN hash with the original.

B. Download the patch file over an AES encrypted VPN connection.

C. Download the patch file through a SSL connection.

D. Compare the final MD5 hash with the original.

15. Which of the following encryption methods deals with two distinct, large prime numbers and the inability to factor those prime numbers?

A. SHA-1

B. RSA

C. WPA

D. Symmetric

16. Which of the following is not a symmetric key algorithm?

A. RC4

B. ECC

C. 3DES

D. Rijndael

17. You are attempting to move data to a USB flash drive. Which of the following enables a rapid and secure connection?

A. SHA-1

B. 3DES

C. AES256

D. MD5

18. Which of the following is used by PGP to encrypt data.

A. Asymmetric key distribution system

B. Asymmetric scheme

C. Symmetric key distribution system

D. Symmetric scheme

19. Which of the following encryption algorithms is used to encrypt and decrypt data?

A. SHA-1

B. RC5

C. MD5

D. NTLM

20. Of the following, which statement correctly describes the difference between a secure cipher and a secure hash?

A. A hash produces a variable output for any input size; a cipher does not.

B. A cipher produces the same size output for any input size; a hash does not.

C. A hash can be reversed; a cipher cannot.

D. A cipher can be reversed; a hash cannot.

21. When encrypting credit card data, which would be the most secure algorithm with the least CPU utilization?

A. AES

B. 3DES

C. SHA-1

D. MD5

22. A hash algorithm has the capability to avoid the same output from two guessed inputs. What is this known as?

A. Collision resistance

B. Collision strength

C. Collision cipher

D. Collision metric

23. Which of the following is the weakest encryption type?

A. DES

B. RSA

C. AES

D. SHA

24. Give two examples of hardware devices that can store keys. (Select the two best answers.)

A. Smartcard

B. Network adapter

C. PCI Express card

D. PCMCIA card

25. What type of attack sends two different messages using the same hash function, which end up causing a collision?

A. Birthday attack

B. Blue snarfing

C. Man-in-the-middle attack

D. Logic bomb

26. Why would a hacker use steganography?

A. To hide information

B. For data integrity

C. To encrypt information

D. For wireless access

Answers and Explanations

1. **C.** The proper order of functions for asymmetric keys is as follows: encrypt, sign, decrypt, and verify. This is the case when a digital signature is used to authenticate an asymmetrically encrypted document.
2. **A.** BitLocker uses symmetric encryption technology based off of AES. Hashing is the process of summarizing a file for integrity purposes. WPA2 is a wireless encryption protocol.
3. **D.** A hash provides integrity checks, for example, MD5 hash algorithms. Public and private keys are the element of a cipher that allows for output of encrypted information. WEP (Wired Equivalent Privacy) is a deprecated wireless encryption protocol.
4. **A.** Steganography is the act of writing hidden messages so that only the intended recipients will know of the existence of the message. This is a form of security through obscurity. Steganographers are not as concerned with data integrity or encryption because the average person shouldn't even know that a message exists. Although steganography can be accomplished by using compromised wireless networks, it is not used to gain wireless access.
5. **A.** Symmetric encryption is the best option for sending large amounts of data. It is superior to asymmetric encryption. PKI is considered an asymmetric encryption type, and hashing algorithms don't play into sending large amounts of data.
6. **A.** The easiest way for a hacker to get at encrypted data is if that encrypted data has a weak encryption key. The algorithm isn't of much use to a hacker unless it has been broken, which is a far more difficult process than trying to

crack an individual key. Captured traffic, if encrypted, still needs to be decrypted, and a weak key will aid in this process. The block cipher is a type of algorithm.

7. **C.** SHA-2 algorithm blocks will have 512 bits. SHA-1 is 160-bit. MD5 is 128-bit; 1,024-bit keys are common in asymmetric encryption.
8. **C.** Symmetric key encryption uses a secret key. The term symmetric key is also referred to as the following: private key, single key, and shared key (and sometimes as session key). PKI and public keys at their core are asymmetrical.
9. **A.** A private key should be used by users when logging in to the network with their smart card. The key should certainly not be public. A key actually determines the function of a cipher. Shared key is another term for symmetric-key encryption but does not imply privacy.
10. **D.** In cryptography, the one-way function is one option of an algorithm that cannot be reversed, or is difficult to reverse, in an attempt to decode data. An example of this would be a hash such as SHA-2, which creates only a small hashing number from a portion of the file or message. There are ways to crack asymmetric and symmetric encryptions, which enable complete decryption (decoding) of the file.
11. **D.** The Diffie-Hellman algorithm relies on key exchange before data can be sent. Usernames and passwords are considered a type of authentication. VPN tunneling is done to connect a remote client to a network. Biometrics is the science of identifying people by one of their physical attributes.
12. **A.** Steganography replaces the least significant bit of each byte. It would be impossible to replace a byte of each bit, because a byte is larger than a bit; a byte is eight bits.
13. **D.** If a hashing algorithm generates the same hash for two different messages within two different downloads, a collision has occurred and the implementation of the hashing algorithm should be investigated.
14. **D.** The purpose of the MD5 hash is to verify the integrity of a download. SHA is another example of a hash that will verify the integrity of downloads. LANMAN hashes are older deprecated hashes used by Microsoft LAN Manager for passwords. Encrypted AES and SSL connections are great for encrypting the data transfer but do not verify integrity.
15. **B.** The RSA encryption algorithm uses two prime numbers. If used properly they will be large prime numbers that will be difficult or impossible to factor. SHA-1 is an example of a Secure Hash Algorithm. WPA is the Wi-Fi Protected Access protocol, and RSA is an example of an asymmetric method of encryption.
16. **B.** ECC or elliptic curve cryptography is an example of public key cryptography that uses an asymmetric key algorithm. All the other answers are symmetric key algorithms.

17. **C.** AES256 enables a quick and secure encrypted connection for use with a USB flash drive. It might even be used with a whole disk encryption technology, such as BitLocker. SHA-1 and MD5 are examples of hashes. 3DES is an example of an encryption algorithm but would not be effective for sending encrypted information in a highly secure manner and quickly to USB flash drive.

18. **D.** Pretty Good Privacy (PGP) encryption uses a symmetric-key cryptography scheme and a combination of hashing and data compression. Key distribution systems are part of an entire encryption scheme, such as technologies such as Kerberos (key distribution center) or quantum cryptography.

19. **B.** RC5 (Rivest Cipher version 5) can encrypt and decrypt data. SHA-1 and MD5 are used as hashing algorithms, and NTLM (NT LAN Manager) is used by Microsoft as an authentication protocol and a password hash.

20. **D.** Ciphers can be reverse engineered but hashes cannot when attempting to re-create a data file. Hashing is not the same as encryption; hashing is the digital fingerprint, so to speak, of a group of data. Hashes are not reversible.

21. **A.** AES (the Advanced Encryption Standard) is fast and secure; more so than 3DES. SHA-1 and MD5 are hashing algorithms. Not listed is RSA, which is commonly implemented to secure credit card transactions.

22. **A.** A hash is collision-resistant if it is difficult to guess two inputs that hash to the same output.

23. **A.** DES or the Data Encryption Standard was developed in the 1970s; its 56-bit key has been superseded by 3DES (max 168-bit key) and AES (max 256-bit key). DES is now considered to be insecure for many applications. RSA is definitely stronger than DES even when you compare its asymmetric strength to a relative symmetric strength. SHA is a hashing algorithm.

24. **A and D.** Smart cards and PCMCIA cards can be used as devices that carry a token and store keys; this means that they can be used for authentication to systems, quite often in a multifactor authentication scenario. Network adapters and PCI Express cards are internal to a PC and would not make for good key storage devices.

25. **A.** A birthday attack exploits the mathematics behind the birthday problem in probability theory. It deals with two different messages using the same hash function, generating the same message digest. Blue snarfing deals with Bluetooth devices. The man-in-the-middle attack is when a person or computer intercepts information between a sender and the receiver. A logic bomb is a malicious attack set to go off at a particular time; quite often it is stored on a zombie computer.

26. **A.** Steganography is the act of writing hidden messages so that only the intended recipients will know of the existence of the message. This is a form of security through obscurity. Data integrity is accomplished through the use of hashing. Steganography is not the same as cryptography in that it doesn't care if a person sees the original message.

This chapter covers the following subjects:

- **Public Key Infrastructure—**In this section, we discuss PKI and its components including private and public keys, certificates, certificate authorities, and the web of trust model.
- **Security Protocols—**Here, we define more security protocols such as S/MIME, SSL, TLS, SSH, and VPN-related protocols such as PPTP, L2TP and IPsec. And three cheers if you want—these are the last of the TCP/IP security protocols in the book!

This chapter covers the CompTIA Security+ SY0-201 objectives 5.4, 5.5, and 5.6.

CHAPTER 13

PKI and Encryption Protocols

This short chapter wraps up the rest of the encryption concepts you need to know for the Security+ exam. You need to understand public key infrastructures and have the ability to explain what is entailed when a secure connection is made, for example to a secure e-commerce web server. There is an entire system involved with public key infrastructures, from the users to servers, encryption methods, and much more. It's a big topic that can be confusing due to how many and what variety of keys are used. Take it slow, and reread the section if necessary. Several protocols use public key infrastructures as well, many of which you have probably heard of, such as S/MIME, SSL, SSH, and so on. Keep in mind that the security protocols discussed in this section are intertwined with the concepts of a public key infrastructure.

Foundation Topics

Public Key Infrastructure

A *public key infrastructure (PKI)* is an entire system of hardware and software, policies and procedures, and people. It is used to create, distribute, manage, store, and revoke digital certificates. If you have connected to a secure website in the past, you have been a part of a PKI! But a PKI can be used for other things as well, such as secure e-mail transmissions and secure connections to remote computers and remote networks. The PKI is all encompassing: It includes users, client computers, servers, services, and most of all, encryption. Don't confuse PKI with public key encryption. Though they are related, PKI is a way of accomplishing public key encryption, but not all public key encryption schemes are PKI. PKI creates asymmetric key pairs, a public key and a private key: The private key is kept secret whereas the public key *can* be distributed. If the key pair is generated at a server, it is considered to be centralized, and the public key is distributed as needed. If the key pair is generated at a local computer, it is considered to be decentralized, and the keys are not distributed, instead they are used by that local system. An example of public key usage would be a certificate obtained by a web browser during an encrypted session with an e-commerce website. An example of private key usage would be when a user needs to encrypt the digital signature of a private e-mail. The difference is the level of confidentiality. The public key certificate obtained by the web browser is public and might be obtained by thousands of individuals. The private key used to encrypt the e-mail is not to be shared with anyone.

In a nutshell, public key infrastructures are set up in such a way so as to bind public keys with user identities. This is usually done through the use of certificates that are distributed by a certificate authority. Less commonly it is done by means of a web of trust.

Let's go ahead and describe these concepts in a little more detail.

Certificates

Certificates are digitally signed electronic documents that bind a public key with a user identity. The identity information might include a person's name and organization, or other details relevant to the user the certificate is to be issued to. Most certificates are based off of the *X.509 standard*, which is a common PKI standard developed by the ITU-T that often incorporates the single sign-on authentication method. This way, a recipient of a single X.509 certificate will have access to multiple resources, possibly in multiple locations. Although difficult, X.509 certificates that use MD5 and SHA-1 hashes can be compromised. For organizations worried about extremely resourceful hackers, a more powerful hashing algorithm such as SHA-2 should be implemented with the certificate. X.509 is the core of the PKIX, which is the IETF's Public Key Infrastructure (X.509) working group. Components of an X.509 certificate include the following:

- Owners (users) information including their public key
- Certificate authority information including their name, digital signature, serial number, issue and expiration date, and version.

Certificate Authorities

A *certificate authority (CA)* is the entity (usually a server) that issues certificates to users. In a PKI system that uses a CA, the CA is known as a trusted third party. Most PKI systems use a CA. The CA is also responsible for verifying the identity of the recipient of the certificate. An example of a technology that uses certificates would be secure websites. If you opened your browser and connected to a secure site, the browser would first check the certificate that comes from Verisign or another similar company, it would *validate* the certificate. You (the user) and the website are the two parties attempting to communicate. The CA is a third party that negotiates the security of the connection between you and the website. For a user to obtain a certificate from a CA, the user must present two items of information: The first is proof of the user's identity; the second is a public key. This public key is then matched to the CA's private key and if successful, the certificate is granted to the user.

A basic example of this would be if you connect to www.paypal.com. When connecting to this website it automatically redirects you to https://www.paypal.com, which is secured by way of a Verisign-issued certificate. You know you have been redirected to a secure site because the browser will have various indicators. For instance, Internet Explorer 7 shows a padlock in the locked position and the address field will has a green background. Similarly, Firefox shows a green background behind the website owner name. These examples are shown in Figures 13-1 and 13-2. The certificate information is shown in the address field, so only the top areas of the browser windows are shown.

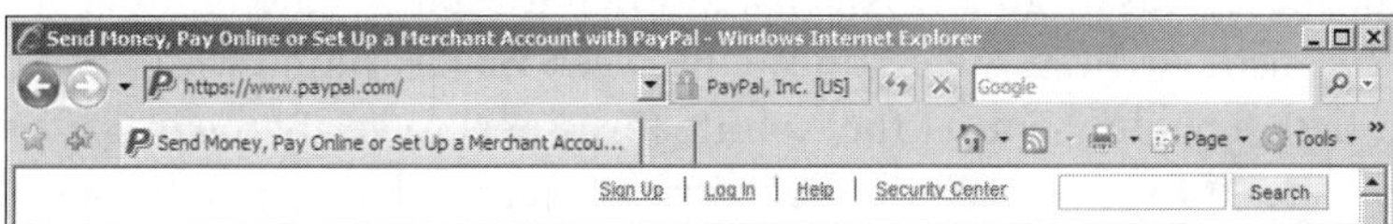

Figure 13-1 Example of a Secure Connection, Shown in Internet Explorer

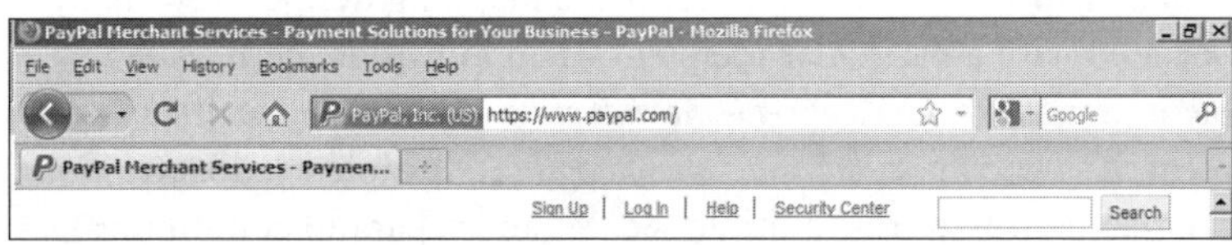

Figure 13-2 Example of a Secure Connection, Shown in Firefox

These are examples of SSL certificates. If you were to click on the green area of the address field in Firefox, it would display a drop-down information window that shows the name of the website and the issuer of the certificate. From there, you could click the **More Information** button, which tells you additional privacy and historical information, plus technical details. Finally, if you were to click the **View Certificate** button, the default General tab and the Details tab would show more details of the certificate, as shown in Figure 13-3.

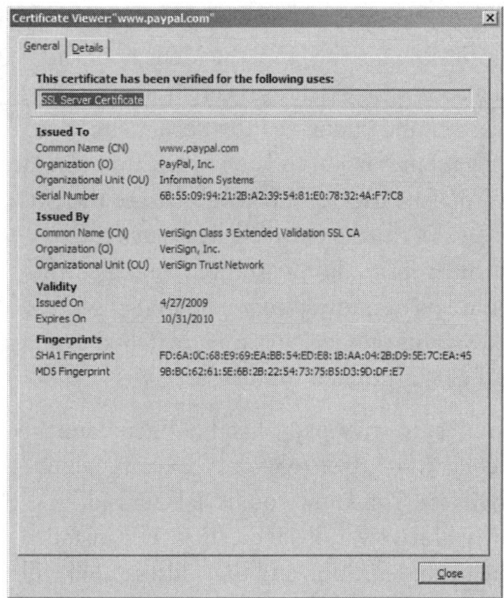

Figure 13-3 Details of a Typical Verisign Certificate

You can see that the certificate gets a super-long hexadecimal serial number and shows when the certificate was originally issued and when it expires, among other information. You can also note that the certificate has been fingerprinted with a SHA1 and a MD5 hash, enabling you or the website (or issuer) to verify the integrity of the certificate. If for some reason the certificate cannot be verified by any of the parties, and the issuer confirms this, then the issuer would need to revoke it and place it in the certificate revocation list (CRL).

Recipients can use one or more certificates. Certificate mapping defines how many certificates are associated with a particular recipient. If an individual certificate is mapped to a recipient, it is known as a *one-to-one mapping*. If multiple certificates are mapped to a recipient, it is known as *many-to-one mapping*. Multiple certificates might be used if the recipient requires multiple secure (and separate) communications channels.

In some cases, a registration authority (RA) is used to verify requests for certificates. If the request is deemed valid, the RA informs the CA to issue the certificate. An RA might also be used if the organization deals with several CAs. In this case, the RA is at the top of a hierarchical structure and verifies the identity of the user. An RA isn't necessary in a PKI, but if you are centrally storing certificates, a CA is necessary.

Certificate authorities aren't just for the rich and famous (for example, Paypal using Verisign as the issuer). You can have a CA, too! Lab 13-2 in the "Hands-On Labs" section shows how to do this on a Windows Server 2003 when implementing an L2TP VPN; more on L2TP later in this chapter. Of course, a server's built-in certificates are not necessarily secure. If you were to implement this technology in a secure environment in your organization, you would probably want to obtain proper certificates from a trusted source to use with the Windows server.

Certificate authorities can be subverted through the use of social engineering. If a person were to pose as a legitimate company and managed to obtain certificates from a trusted source, those certificates would appear to be valid certificates and could cause widespread damage due to connections made by unsuspecting users. That is, until the certificates are revoked. This happens sometimes, but the CA issuer will usually find out quickly and take steps to mitigate the problem, including revoking the certificate(s) and notifying any involved parties of the incident.

The *certificate revocation list (CRL)* is a list of certificates no longer valid or have been revoked by the issuer. There are two possible states of revocation: revoked, which is when a certificate has been irreversibly revoked and cannot be used again, and hold, which is used to temporarily invalidate a certificate. Reasons for revoking a certificate include the compromising or theft of a certificate or entire CA, unspecified certificates, superseded certificates, held certificates, and key or encryption compromise. The CRL is published periodically, usually every 24 hours. This enables users of an issuer's certificates to find out if a certificate is valid or not. CRLs, like the certificates themselves, carry digital signatures to prevent DoS and spoofing attacks; the CRL is digitally signed by the CA.

Certificate keys can also be held in escrow. *Key escrow* is when certificate keys are held in the case that third parties such as government or other organizations need access to encrypted communications.

When installing a certificate authority to a Windows Server, you can set up a recovery agent for lost or corrupted keys. To do this, you would need Windows Server 2003 Enterprise and need to set up an Enterprise level CA. In this configuration, the certificates (or private keys) are archived at the CA. If a Key Recovery Agent has been configured, lost, or corrupted, keys can be restored. It's important to use some type of software that can archive and restore keys in the case of an incident or disaster.

Another way to avoid single points of failure, such as a single CA, is to organize certificate authorities in a hierarchical manner. At the top of the tree is a root CA; underneath are subordinate CAs that offer redundancy. Though certificate authority exclusivity is common, it is not the only type of architecture used to bind public keys to users. In some cases, a centralized model for certificates is not required or desired.

Single-Sided and Dual-Sided Certificates

Most communication sessions, such as secure web sessions, use single-sided certificates. This is when the server validates itself to recipients of the certificate, for example users who are accessing the website. In these types of scenarios, users does not need to validate their own identity. This would be resource-intensive, especially for a secure web server that might have thousands of concurrent connections.

Sometimes, an organization might choose to have the server *and* the user validate their identities. This would be using a dual-sided certificate; it works well when a limited amount of computers and sessions are involved. When more computers are added to the mix, the amount of resources necessary might be a strain on the issuing CA.

Web of Trust

A *web of trust* is a decentralized trust model that addresses issues associated with the public authentication of public keys common to CA-based PKIs. It is considered peer-to-peer in that there is no root CA; instead, self-signed certificates are used that have been attested to by third parties. Users can decide what certificates they want to trust and can share those trusted certificates with others, making the web of trust grow larger. This model can also interoperate with standard CA architectures inherent to PKI. The more people that show trust of a certificate, the higher the chance that it is legitimate. This model is used by PGP, which enables users to start their own web of trust, self-publishing their own public key information.

Security Protocols

You can use a variety of security protocols to allow for more secure connections to other systems and networks. But the question is: What should be secured when connecting to other computers? I like to break it down into four categories:

- **E-mail and other communications—**This can be accomplished with the use of S/MIME or PGP.
- **E-commerce and web logins—**This can be brought about with the aid of protocols such as SSL and TLS.
- **Direct connections to other computers—**This can be done with a protocol such as SSH.
- **Virtual connections to remote networks—**This can be achieved with virtual private networks and protocols such as PPTP and L2TP.

Each of these scenarios builds on the concepts we leaned in the previous PKI section. Let's define each of these scenarios and the security protocols used in more depth.

S/MIME

Originally developed by RSA Security, *Secure/Multipurpose Internet Mail Extensions (S/MIME)* is an IETF standard that provides cryptographic security for electronic messaging such as e-mail. It is used for authentication, message integrity, and nonrepudiation of origin. Most e-mail clients have S/MIME functionality built-in.

S/MIME relies on PKI and the obtaining and validating of certificates from a CA, namely X.509v3 certificates. Is also relies on digital signatures when attempting to establish nonrepudiation. S/MIME enables users to send both encrypted and digitally signed e-mail messages.

S/MIME can be implemented in Outlook by first obtaining a certificate known as a Digital ID, publishing the certificate within Outlook, and then modifying the settings for Outlook, as shown in Figure 13-4.

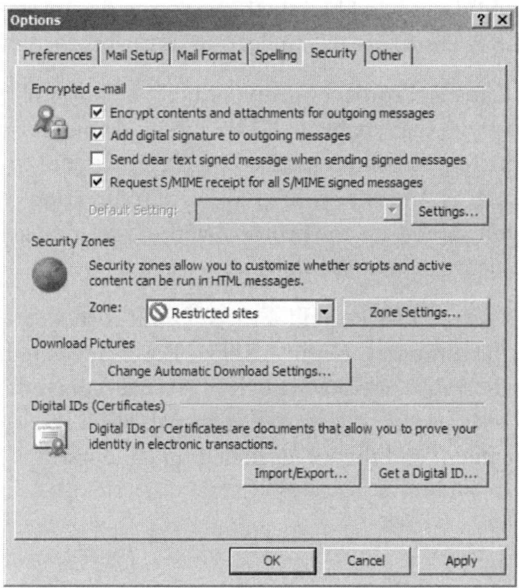

Figure 13-4 S/MIME Settings in Outlook

One of the issues with S/MIME is that it will encrypt not only messages but also any malware that found its way into the message. This could compromise systems between the sender and receiver. To defeat this, scan messages at a network gateway that has a copy of the private keys used with SMIME. Do this after decryption. If an e-mail program stores an S/MIME encrypted message and the private key used for encryption/decryption is lost, deleted, or corrupted, the message cannot be decrypted.

SSL/TLS

Secure Sockets Layer (SSL) and its successor *Transport Layer Security (TLS)* are cryptographic protocols that provide secure Internet communications such as web browsing, instant messaging, e-mail, and VoIP. These protocols rely on a PKI for the obtaining and validating of certificates.

Many people refer to the secure connections they make to websites as SSL, but in actuality some of these will be TLS. The last version of SSL, version 3, was released in 1996. TLS is a more secure solution; version 1 of TLS supersedes SSLv3. As of August 2008, the latest version of TLS is 1.2. However, they work in much the same manner. Two types of keys are required when any two computers attempt to communicate with the SSL or TLS protocols: A public key and a session key. Asymmetric encryption is used to encrypt and share session keys, and symmetric encryption is used to encrypt the session data. A recovery key will be necessary if any data is lost in an SSL/TLS session. SSL and TLS encrypt segments of network connections that start at the Transport Layer of the OSI model. The actual encryption occurs at the Session Layer. In general, SSL/TLS is known as an Application Layer protocol.

HTTPS, which stands for Hypertext Transfer Protocol Secure, is a combination of HTTP and either SSL or TLS. Web servers that enable HTTPS inbound connections must have inbound port 443 open. This is common for e-commerce. If you connect to an online shopping portal such as Amazon, your credit card transactions should be protected by HTTPS, and you should see the protocol within the address bar of your browser when you enter a secure area of the website.

HTTPS should not be confused with Secure HTTP (SHTTP). SHTTP is an alternative to HTTPS that works in much the same way. Because SHTTP was neglected by Microsoft, Netscape, and others in the 1990s, and because SHTTP encrypts only Application-Layer messages, HTTPS became the widely used standard. HTTPS can encrypt all data passed between the client and the server including data passing through Layer 3.

SSH

Secure Shell (SSH) is a protocol that can create a secure channel between two computers or network devices, enabling one computer or device to remotely control the other. Designed as a replacement for Telnet, it is commonly used on Linux and Unix systems, and nowadays also has widespread on Windows clients. It depends on public key cryptography to authenticate remote computers. One computer (the one to be controlled) will run the SSH daemon, while the other computer will run the SSH client and make secure connections to the first computer (which is known as a server), as long as a certificate can be obtained and validated.

Computers that run the SSH daemon have inbound port 22 open. If a proper SSH connection is made, files can also be transferred securely using SFTP (Secure File Transfer Protocol) or SCP (Secure Copy Protocol). Tunneling is also supported.

Vulnerabilities to SSH 1 and 1.5 such as the unauthorized insertion of content, the forwarding of client authentications to other servers (daemons), and integer overflow, precipitated the development of SSH 2.0, which is incompatible with SSH version 1. Improvements to SSH 2.0 include usage of the Diffie-Hellman key exchange and integrity checking with message authentication codes (MAC).

PPTP, L2TP, and IPsec

Virtual private networks (VPN) were developed to enable quick, secure, remote connections using the inherent capacity of the Internet. They were also developed to take advantage of faster Internet connections such as cable, DSL, and so on but still work with dial-up connections. The issue with VPNs is how to secure those connections. Basically, there are two common protocols used to do so: PPTP and L2TP (with the aid of IPsec).

PPTP

The *Point-to-Point Tunneling Protocol (PPTP)* is a protocol used in VPNs. It encapsulates PPP packets, ultimately sending encrypted traffic. PPP by itself is useful for dial-up connections but is not suitable for a VPN by itself without a protocol such as PPTP. Servers and other devices running the PPTP protocol and accepting incoming VPN connections need to have inbound port 1723 open.

Because the authentication protocol MSCHAPv1 is considered inherently insecure, and MSCHAP-v2 is vulnerable to dictionary attacks, PPTP is deemed to be vulnerable. These authentication vulnerabilities can be dismissed if PPTP is used with an authentication method such as EAP-TLS. This relies on the existence of a PKI for the client and server computers. If this infrastructure is not readily available, PEAP can be used instead, as long as the computers are running the Windows Vista operating system or newer. Otherwise, L2TP with IPsec or other tunneling protocols are recommended for environments in which session and data security are of paramount importance.

L2TP

The *Layer 2 Tunneling Protocol (L2TP)* is a tunneling protocol used to connect VPNs. In essence, it creates an unencrypted tunnel if used by itself (which would be unwise). It does not include confidentiality or encryption on its own, but when paired with a security protocol such as IPsec is considered a formidable tunneling protocol.

Its starting point is based off of the Layer 2 Forwarding Protocol (L2F) and PPTP. The latest version is L2TPv3, which has improved encapsulation and increased security features. Servers and other devices accepting incoming VPN connections need to have inbound port 1701 open.

When installed on a Windows Server, it uses a PKI. Valid certificates need to be downloaded to clients before they can make a VPN connection to the server. Security must be configured on the server and the client side. Generally, the IPsec protocol is used to accomplish the secure connection within the L2TP tunnel.

IPsec

Internet Protocol Security (IPsec) authenticates and encrypts IP packets, effectively securing communications between the computers and devices that use this protocol. IPsec operates at the Network Layer of the OSI model. It differs from SSH, SSL, and TLS in that it is the only protocol that does not operate within the upper layers of the OSI model. It can negotiate cryptographic keys and establish mutual authentication. IPsec is made up of three other protocols that perform its functions, including:

- **Security association (SA)**—This is the establishment of secure connections and shared security information, using either certificates or cryptographic keys. It is set up most often through the Internet Key Exchange (IKE) or via Kerberized Internet Negotiation of Keys. The IKE can select varying levels of security protocols for the computers in a connection, which can differ in a VPN due to the dissimilar computers (with disparate protocols) that might attempt to connect to it.
- **Authentication header (AH)**—This offers integrity and authentication. The authentication information is a keyed hash based on all of the bytes in the packet. It can be used with the Encapsulating Security Payload (ESP) protocol. It can protect against replay attacks by employing sliding window protocols, which put limits on the total amount of packets that can be transceived in a given timeframe but ultimately enables an unlimited number of packets to be communicated using fixed-size sequence numbers.
- **Encapsulating Security Payload (ESP)**—This provides integrity, confidentiality, and authenticity of packets. Protected data is encapsulated and encrypted.

IPsec uses algorithms such as SHA1 for integrity and authenticity, which hashes the packets of data; afterward the hash is encrypted. It also uses Triple DES and AES for confidentiality.

Exam Preparation Tasks

Review Key Topics

Review the most important topics in the chapter, noted with the Key Topics icon in the outer margin of the page. Table 13-1 lists a reference of these key topics and the page numbers on which each is found.

Table 13-1 Key Topics for Chapter 13

Key Topic Element	Description	Page Number
Figure 13-3	Details of a Typical Verisign Certificate	382
Bulleted list	IPsec Protocols	388

Define Key Terms

Define the following key terms from this chapter, and check your answers in the glossary:

Public Key Infrastructure, certificates, certificate authority, one-to-one mapping, many-to-one mapping, certificate revocation list (CRL), X.509, key escrow, web of trust, S/MIME, Secure Sockets Layer (SSL), Transport Layer Security (TLS), Secure Shell (SSH), Point-to-Point Tunneling Protocol (PPTP), Layer 2 Tunneling Protocol (L2TP), Internet Protocol Security (IPsec)

Hands-On Labs

Complete the following written step-by-step scenarios. After you finish (or if you do not have adequate equipment to complete the scenario), watch the corresponding video solutions on the DVD.

If you have additional questions, feel free to post them at my website: www.davidlprowse.com in the Ask Dave forum. (Free registration is required to post on the website.)

Equipment Needed

- Computer with Internet access and the Firefox web browser
- Windows Server 2003
- SuSE9 Linux installed on a computer or within a VM

- Windows client computer (preferably Windows XP) with Nmap installed and Putty downloaded (and extracted if necessary). Putty can be downloaded from: www.chiark.greenend.org.uk/~sgtatham/putty/download.html.

Lab 13-1: A Basic Example of PKI

In this lab, you view a public key infrastructure (PKI) certificate after connecting to a secure website. The steps are as follows:

Step 1. Access a Windows client computer.

Step 2. Open Firefox,

Step 3. Type the following URL into the address field: **www.paypal.com**.

Note the address automatically changes to https://www.paypal.com, with "https" indicating a secure connection with either the SSL or TLS encryption protocol. This allows for the secure, encrypted transmission of the e-mail address and password when logging in to the PayPal website.

A. Hover the mouse pointer over the green area of the address bar to find out the issuer of the certificate; in this case it is Verisign, Inc.

Step 4. Click where the domain name is listed in the address field. (This has the green background.)

Step 5. Click the **More Information** button. Examine the results.

Step 6. Click the **View Certificate** button. Examine the results. This is where the details of the certificate can be found including whom the issuer (CA) of the certificate is, its expiration date, and any hashing that was performed on the certificate to ensure integrity.

Step 7. Click the **Details** tab. Examine the results. Attempt to export the details of the certificate.

Watch the solution video in the "Hands-On Scenarios" section of the DVD.

Lab 13-2: Configuring an L2TP-Based VPN with Windows Server 2003

In this lab, you configure an L2TP-based VPN with a Windows Server 2003 and Windows client. This is an in-depth lab that will take some time to complete. Also, it's easy to make a mistake or forget a small detail. In some cases, the entire lab will need to be restarted to work properly.

The steps are as follows:

Step 1. Install a Certificate Authority on the server.

Even if your client is already set up to make L2TP connections (see step 4 for more), and you have a basic VPN server working, you would get a

781 error when attempting to connect. This is because your client requires an encryption certificate. The client must get that certificate from the server (or some other authority). Let's install and configure the Certificate Authority on the Windows Server 2003 computer now so that it can dispense certificates to clients:

A. Go to the Windows Server 2003 computer.

B. Click the **Start** button and select **Control Panel**.

C. Launch **Add/Remove Programs**.

D. Select **Add/Remove Windows Components**.

E. Click the **Certificate Services** check box to select it. A pop-up window opens; click **Yes**.

F. Click **Next**.

G. When asked what type of Certificate Authority you will be installing, choose the default option, **Enterprise root CA**. Then click **Next**.

H. In the **Common Name for This CA** field, type **test**. Leave the rest of the information as is, and click **Next**.

I. Leave the **Certificate Database Settings** window as is and click **Next**.

J. A pop-up window might ask you about IIS, which needs to be stopped during the installation of the CA. Click **OK**. The installation of the CA will begin.

K. If you are asked for the CD, you can get the necessary information from X:\i386 (where X is the letter of your disc drive). This could be from the Windows Server 2003 disc, the Service Pack disc, or the Server 2003 disc with slipstreamed service pack, it depends on your setup.

NOTE: If IIS is not yet installed, Server 2003 will warn you that Certificate Services Web Enrollment Support will not work until IIS is installed. Click **OK** for this message and be sure to install IIS before continuing with this lab. This can be done from **Add/Remove Windows Components > Application Server > Internet Information Services (IIS)**. IIS can be installed simultaneously with Certificate Services.

L. Click **Finish**. The Certificate Authority is now installed. You should see it within your Administrative Tools. A restart is not normally necessary, but might be a good idea, especially if you have a lot of other services running on the server.

Step 2. Configure the Certificate Authority (CA) on the server.

Now you need to set up the CA to hand out certificates automatically and turn on the IP Security policy:

A. First, though, set up an MMC if you have not already and add the Certificate Authority snap-in (for the local computer) and the Default Domain Policy. (Select the **Group Policy Object editor** snap-in, **Browse**, and then **Default Domain Policy**.)

B. Set up the server to hand out certificates automatically:

   i. In the MMC, click the Default Domain Policy entry, select Computer Configuration, choose Windows Settings, click Security Settings, select Public Key Policies, and choose Automatic Certificate Request Settings.

   ii. Right-click the Automatic Certificate Request Settings entry, select New, and then select Automatic Certificate Request.

   iii. A wizard is launched. Click Next.

   iv. When asked what type of auto certificate template you want to install, select Computer. Then click Next.

   v. Click Finish. You should see a certificate template called Computer on the right side window pane in the MMC.

   vi. Save the MMC.

C. Turn on the IP Security Policy.

   i. Within the MMC expand the following options in the left window pane: Default Domain Policy > Computer Configuration > Windows Settings > Security Settings. Click once on IP Security Policies on Active Directory.

   ii. This should bring up three policies on the right side. None of these are yet assigned.

   iii. Right-click the Secure Server (require Security) option and select Assign. This should assign the security policy allowing clients to connect.

   iv. Save the MMC and close it.

Step 3. Configure MS-CHAP on the client.

Let's configure your client to connect to the VPN server using a more complex level of authentication—username and password verification. This will be MS-CHAP II:

A. Go to the Windows XP computer.

B. Right-click **My Network Places** and select **Properties** to find your VPN adapter. If it is not there, create a new one, and point it toward your existing VPN server.

C. Right-click the VPN adapter and select **Properties**.

D. Click the **Security** tab and select **Advanced (Custom Settings)**.

E. Click the **Settings** button. This opens the **Advanced Security Settings** dialog box.

F. Make sure that Require encryption is selected in the Data encryption drop-down list and that the Microsoft CHAP (MS-CHAP) and Microsoft CHAP Version 2 (MS-CHAP v2) checkboxes are selected. MS-CHAPII is already accepted by the server. MS-CHAPII will now be your challenge authentication scheme; it will work automatically.

Step 4. Configure L2TP and IPsec on the client:

Connect through L2TP as opposed to PPTP. L2TP is a more secure way of connecting than PPTP when L2TP is used with IPsec:

A. Click OK to close the Advanced Security Settings dialog box.
B. In the VPN Properties window, click the Networking tab.
C. Open the Type of VPN: Drop-Down List and choose L2TP IPsec VPN.
D. Click OK to close the VPN Properties window.

Step 5. Install a certificate on the client.

In some cases, you have to connect through a custom-made MMC, but in this scenario you retain your certificate within the browser:

A. Go to the Windows XP computer.
B. Open Internet Explorer and, in the address bar, type **http://*servername*/certsrv** (where *servername* is the actual hostname of your server). A web page with information opens.

NOTE: You might need to configure the client so that it has the server's IP address as the DNS settings within IP properties. In addition, it might be necessary to connect the client to the domain that the Certificate Authority server is a member of. How your client is configured will all depend on the setup of your particular network. Also, make sure that all your computers have the latest service packs installed.

C. Click the Request a Certificate link.
D. On the next screen, click User Certificate.
E. On the User Certificate – Identifying Information screen click Submit.
F. Click Yes in the pop-up window(s) that appears.
G. The browser should talk to the server and retrieve a certificate. Choose to install it now by clicking the Install this Certificate link.
H. Click Yes in the pop-up window that appears to add the certificate to the store. You'll be informed that the certificate has been installed.

Step 6. Make the new VPN connection.

Now you can connect from your client to the server through the VPN connection using L2TP and MS-CHAP II. Connect to the VPN the way you normally would by double-clicking the VPN adapter and logging in with your username and password. There you have it!

NOTE: This is an in-depth lab, and as such, there are a lot of things that can go wrong. You might decide to run the various necessary services on separate servers, for example a Domain Controller, a VPN server, and a Certificate server. In addition, when it comes to certificates, there is a lot to talk about! Depending on the order of services you installed, you might have to install a certificate on the server as well. Be ready for many different variables when performing this lab. Remember, if you have questions, post them on my website.

Watch the solution video in the "Hands-On Scenarios" section of the DVD.

Lab 13-3: Making an SSH Connection

In this lab, you install SSH and allows the SSH daemon on a SuSE 9 Linux computer to be later remotely accessed and controlled by a Windows XP computer or other Windows client. The steps are as follows:

Step 1. Access the SuSE9 Linux computer and open the **Shell – Konsole**.

Step 2. Because this version of Linux already has SSH installed by default, verify that it is running by typing the following command:

```
/etc/init.d/sshd start
```

That should start the SSH daemon, if it weren't started already.

Step 3. Access the Windows client computer, open the **Command Prompt**, and navigate to the Nmap folder.

Step 4. Type the following command: **nmap –sS [IPAddress]** where IPAddress is the IP address of the Linux computer. Actually, any port scanner will do; in the video we use Nmap as the example.

This should discern the services that are running on the Linux computer. Port 22 should be open at this point indicating that SSH is running.

Step 5. Return to the Linux computer.

Step 6. Download and run OpenSSH. Even though I just demonstrated how to start SSH in Linux, I'd like to show how to download OpenSSH in the case that you don't have SSH built in to your version of Linux. It is a common type of SSH that technicians should know how to use:

A. Open the web browser.

B. Access the following link: ftp://ftp5/usa.openbsd.org/pub/OpenBSD/OpenSSH/portable/.

   If the link doesn't work, try running a search with the query **OpenSSH download**.

C. Double-click the **openssh-5.1p1.tar.gz** file and select **Save As**.

D. Save it where you want. The root is fine.

E. Decompress and extract the contents of the file:
   i. In the command-line, type Dir and locate the file.
   ii. Now type tar xvzf openssh-5.1p1.tar.gz to extract and decompress the contents.
   iii. Run a Dir again to see the new folder that was extracted.

F. Run OpenSSH:
   i. Change to the new folder by typing cd openssh-5.1p1.
   ii. Type sshd to start up the OpenSSH program.

Step 7. Access the Windows client computer.

Step 8. Download Putty if you haven't done so already.

Step 9. Locate the putty.exe download within Windows Explorer, and double-click it to run it. This should bring up the PuTTY Configuration window.

Step 10. Type the IP address of the Linux computer, and click the **Open** button to connect and have a lot of fun!

Step 11. At the PuTTY command-line window displayed, log in as the root account of the Linux computer. If you have a password, be sure to type it correctly.

Step 12. Run various commands to examine the remote Linux computer such as ifconfig, cd, dir, and so on.

Step 13. Access the Windows Command Prompt and run the **netstat –an** command. View the connection to the remote Linux computer. You should see a session with port 22 used on the remote computer.

Watch the solution video in the "Hands-On Scenarios" section of the DVD.

View Recommended Resources

- Microsoft TechNet: Configuring the Key Recovery Agent Certificate: http://technet.microsoft.com/en-us/library/cc780525%28WS.10%29.aspx

Answer Review Questions

Answer the following review questions. You can find the answers at the end of this chapter.

1. Which of the following does not apply to an x.509 certificate?
   A. Certificate version
   B. The Issuer of the certificate
   C. Public key information
   D. Owner's symmetric key

2. What two items are included in a digital certificate? (Select the two best answers.)
   A. User's private key
   B. Certificate Authority's digital signature
   C. The user's public key
   D. Certificate Authority's IP address

3. Rick has a local computer that uses software to generate and store key pairs. What type of PKI implementation is this?
   A. Distributed key
   B. Centralized
   C. Hub and spoke
   D. Decentralized

4. Which of the following is usually used with L2TP?
   A. IPsec
   B. SSH
   C. PHP
   D. SHA

5. What ensures that a CRL is authentic and has not been modified?
   A. The CRL can be accessed by anyone.
   B. The CRL is digitally signed by the CA.
   C. The CRL is always authentic.
   D. The CRL is encrypted by the CA.

6. Which of the following encryption concepts is PKI based on?

A. Asymmetric

B. Symmetric

C. Elliptical curve

D. Quantum

7. You are in charge of PKI certificates. What should you implement so that stolen certificates cannot be used?

A. CRL

B. CAD

C. CA

D. CRT

8. Which of the following are certificate-based authentication mapping schemes? (Select the two best answers.)

A. One to-many mapping

B. One-to-one mapping

C. Many-to-many mapping

D. Many-to-one mapping

9. Which of the following network protocols sends data between two computers while using a secure channel?

A. SSH

B. SMTP

C. SNMP

D. P2P

10. Which of the following protocols uses port 443?

A. SFTP

B. HTTPS

C. SSHTP

D. SSLP

11. Which of the following protocols creates an unencrypted tunnel?

A. L2TP

B. PPTP

C. IPsec

D. VPN

12. In a public key infrastructure setup, which of the following should be used to encrypt the signature of an e-mail?

A. Private key

B. Public key

C. Shared key

D. Hash

13. Two computers are attempting to communicate with the SSL protocol. Which two types of keys will be used? (Select the two best answers.)

A. Recovery key

B. Session key

C. Public key

D. Key card

14. Which layer of the OSI model does IPsec operate at?

A. Data Link

B. Network

C. Transport

D. Application

15. Which layer of the OSI model is where SSL provides encryption?

A. Network

B. Transport

C. Session

D. Application

16. Which of the following details one of the primary benefits of using S/MIME?

A. S/MIME expedites the delivery of e-mail messages.

B. S/MIME enables users to send e-mail messages with a return receipt.

C. S/MIME enables users to send both encrypted and digitally signed e-mail messages.

D. S/MIME enables users to send anonymous e-mail messages.

17. What should you do to make sure that a compromised PKI key cannot be used again?

A. Renew the key.

B. Reconfigure the key.

C. Revoke the key.

D. Create a new key.

18. Which of the following statements is correct about IPsec authentication headers?

A. The authentication information is a keyed hash based on half of the bytes in the packet.

B. The authentication information is a keyed hash based on all the bytes in the packet.

C. The authentication information hash will remain the same even if the bytes change on transfer.

D. The authentication header cannot be used in combination with the IP Encapsulating Security Payload.

19. Which of the following protocols is not used to create a VPN tunnel and not used to encrypt VPN tunnels?

A. PPTP

B. L2TP

C. PPP

D. IPsec

20. Which of the following answers are not part of IPsec? (Select the two best answers.)

A. TKIP

B. Key exchange

C. AES

D. Authentication header

Answers and Explanations

1. **D.** In x.509, the owner does not use a symmetric key. All the other answers apply to x.509.
2. **B and C.** A digital certificate will include the Certificate Authority's (CA) digital signature and the user's public key. A user's private key should be kept private and should not be within the digital certificate. The IP address of the CA should have been known to the user's computer before obtaining the certificate.
3. **D.** When creating key pairs, PKI has two methods: centralized and decentralized. Centralized is when keys are generated at a central server and are transmitted to hosts. Decentralized is when keys are generated and stored on a local computer system for use by that system.

4. **A.** IPsec is usually used with L2TP. SSH is a more secure way of connecting to remote computers. PHP is a type of language commonly used on the web. SHA is a type of hashing algorithm.
5. **B.** Certificate revocation lists or CRLs are digitally signed by the certificate authority for security purposes. If a certificate is compromised, it will be revoked and placed on the CRL. CRLs are later generated and published periodically.
6. **A.** The public key infrastructure, or PKI, is based on the asymmetric encryption concept. Symmetric, elliptical curve, and quantum cryptography are all different encryption schemes that PKI is not associated with.
7. **A.** You should implement a certificate revocation list or CRL so that stolen certificates, or otherwise revoked or held certificates, cannot be used.
8. **B and D.** When dealing with certificate authentication, asymmetric systems use one-to-one mappings and many-to-one mappings.
9. **A.** SSH, or the secure Shell, enables two computers to send data via a secure channel. SMTP is the Simple Mail Transfer Protocol that deals with e-mail. SNMP is the Simple Network Management Protocol that enables the monitoring of remote systems. P2P is the abbreviated version of peer-to-peer network.
10. **B.** Port 443 is used by HTTPS, which implements TLS/SSL for security. SFTP is the Secure File Transfer Program. There are no protocols named SSHTP and SSLP.
11. **A.** In Virtual Private Networks (VPN), Layer Two Tunneling Protocol (L2TP) creates an unencrypted tunnel between two IP addresses. It is usually used with IPsec to encrypt the data transfer. PPTP is the Point-to-Point Tunneling Protocol that includes encryption.
12. **A.** A private key should be used to encrypt the signature of an e-mail in an asymmetric system such as PKI. Public keys and shared keys should never be used to encrypt this type of information. A hash is not used to encrypt in this fashion; it is used to verify the integrity of the message.
13. **B and C.** In an SSL session, a session key and a public key are used. A recovery key is not necessary unless data has been lost. A key card would be used as a physical device to gain access to a building or server room.
14. **B.** IPsec is a dual mode, end-to-end security scheme that operates at Layer 3, the Network Layer of the OSI model, also known as the Internet Layer within the Internet Protocol Suite. It is often used with L2TP for VPN tunneling among other protocols.
15. **C.** SSL, or the Secure Sockets Layer, and its successor Transport Layer Security (TLS) encrypt segments of network connections that start at the

Transport Layer. The actual encryption is done at the Session Layer, and the protocol is known as an Application Layer protocol.

16. **C.** S/MIME enables users to send both encrypted and digitally signed e-mail messages enabling a higher level of e-mail security. It does not make the delivery of e-mail any faster nor does it have anything to do with return receipts. Return receipts are usually controlled by the SMTP server. Anonymous e-mail messages would be considered spam, completely insecure, and something that a security administrator wants to reduce, and certainly does not want their users to implement.

17. **C.** Key revocation is the proper way to approach the problem of a compromised PKI key. The revoked key will then be listed in the CRL (Certificate Revocation List).

18. **B.** The only statement that is true is that the authentication information is a keyed hash that is based on all the bytes in the packet. A hash will not remain the same if the bytes change on transfer; a new hash will be created for the authentication header (AH). The authentication header can be used in combination with the Encapsulating Security Payload (ESP).

19. **C.** PPP, or point-to-point protocol, does not provide security and is not used to create VPN connections. You will see PPP used in dial-up connections, and it is an underlying protocol used by L2TP, PPTP, and IPsec, which are all used in VPN connections.

20. **A and C.** IPsec contains (or uses) a key exchange (either Internet Key Exchange or Kerberized Internet Negotiation of Keys) and an authentication header (in addition to many other components). TKIP and AES are other encryption protocols.

This chapter covers the following subjects:

Redundancy Planning—This section is all about ensuring your network and servers are fault tolerant. By setting up redundant power, data, servers, and even ISPs, you can avoid many disasters that could threaten the security of your organization.

Disaster Recovery Planning and Procedures—A disaster is when something happens to your network that your fault-tolerant methods cannot prevent. To help recovery after a disaster, data should be backed up, and a proper disaster recovery plan should be designed, practiced, and implemented if necessary.

This chapter covers the CompTIA Security+ SY0-201 objectives 6.1 and 6.2.

CHAPTER 14

Redundancy and Disaster Recovery

The typical definition of "redundant" means superfluous or uncalled for. However, it is not so in the IT field. Being redundant is a way of life. It is a way of enhancing your servers, network devices, and other equipment. It is a way of developing fault tolerance—the capability to continue functioning even if there is an error.

This chapter discusses how to prevent problems that might occur which could threaten the security of your servers, network equipment, and server room in general. A good network security administrator should have plenty of redundancy and fault-tolerant methods in place that can help combat threats and help avoid disaster.

However, no matter how much redundancy you implement, there is always a chance that a tragedy could arise—a disaster if you will. A disaster could be the loss of data on a server, a fire in a server room, or the catastrophic loss of access to an organization's building. To prepare for these events, a disaster recovery plan should be designed, but with the thought in mind that redundancy and fault tolerance can defend against most "disasters." The best admin is the one that avoids disaster and in the rare case that it does happen, has a plan in place to recovery quickly from it. This chapter also covers how to plan for disasters and discusses a plan of action for recovering swiftly.

Foundation Topics

Redundancy Planning

Most networks could do with a little more redundancy. I know...a lot of you are probably wondering why I keep repeating myself! It's because so many customers of mine in the past, and network admins that have worked for, and with me, insist on avoiding the issue. Redundancy works—use it!

This section discusses redundant power in the form of power supplies, UPS, and backup generators. It also talks about redundant data, servers, ISPs, and sites. All these things, when planned properly, will create an environment that can withstand most failures barring total disaster.

The whole concept revolves around single points of failure. A *single point of failure* is an element, object, or part of a system that, if it fails, will cause the whole system to fail. By implementing redundancy, you can bypass just about any single point of failure.

There are two methods to combating single points of failure. The first is to use redundancy. If employed properly, redundancy will keep a system running with no downtime. However, this can be pricey, and we all know there is only so much IT budget to go around. So, the alternative is to make sure you have plenty of spare parts lying around. This is a good method if your network and systems are not time-critical. Installing spare parts often requires you to down the server or portion of a network. If this risk is not acceptable to an organization, you'll have to find the cheapest redundant solutions available. Research is key, and don't be fooled by the hype—sometimes the simplest sounding solutions are the best.

Here's the scenario (and we will apply this to the rest of this "Redundancy Planning" section). Your server room has the following powered equipment:

- 9 servers
- 2 Microsoft domain controllers
- 1 DNS server
- 2 file servers
- 1 database server
- 2 Web servers (which second as FTP servers)
- 1 Mail server
- 5 48-port switches
- 1 master switch

- 3 routers
- 2 CSU/DSUs
- 1 PBX
- 2 client workstations (for remote server access without having to work directly at the server), these are within the server room as well.

It appears that there is already some redundancy in place in your server room. For example, there are two domain controllers. One of them has a copy of the Active Directory and acts as a secondary DC in the case that the first one fails. There are also two web servers, one ready to take over for the other if the primary one fails. This type of redundancy is known as fail-over redundancy. The secondary system is inactive until the first one fails. Also, there are two client workstations that are used to remotely control the servers; if one fails, another one is available.

Otherwise, the rest of the servers and other pieces of equipment are one-offs; single instances in need of something to prevent failure. There are a lot of them, so we truly need to redundacize! Hey, it's a word if IT people use it! Try to envision the various upcoming redundancy methods used with each of the items listed previously in our fictitious server room.

Redundant Power

Let's begin with power because that is what all our devices and computers gain "sustenance" from. Power is so important—when planning for redundancy it should be at the top of your list. When considering power implications, think like an engineer; you might even need to enlist the help of a coworker who has engineering background or a third party to help plan your electrical requirements and make them a reality.

We are most interested in the server room. Smart companies will store most of their important data, settings, apps, and so on in that room. So power is critical here whereas it is not as important for client computers and other client resources. If power fails in a server room or in any one component within the server room, it could cause the network to go down, or loss of access to resources. It could also cause damage to a server or other device.

When considering power, think about it from the inside out. For example, start with individual computers, servers, and networking components. How much power does each of these things require? Make a list and tally your results. Later, this will play into the total power needed by the server room. Remember that networking devices such as IP phones, cameras, and some wireless access points are powered over Ethernet cabling, which can require additional power requirements at the Ethernet switch(s) in the server room. Think about installing redundant power supplies in some of your servers and switches. Next, ponder using UPS devices as a way of defeating short-term power loss failures. Then, move on to how many circuits you will need, total power, electrical panel requirements, and also the cleanliness of power coming in from your municipality. Finally, consider backup generators for longer term power failures.

Using proper power devices is part of a good preventative maintenance/security plan and helps to protect a computer. You need to protect against several things:

- **Surges—**A *surge* in electrical power means that there is an unexpected increase in the amount of voltage provided. This can be a small increase or a larger increase known as a spike.
- **Spikes—**A *spike* is a short transient in voltage that can be due to a short circuit, tripped circuit breaker, power outage, or lightning strike.
- **Sags—**An unexpected decrease in the amount of voltage provided. Typically, sags are limited in time and in the decrease in voltage. However, when voltage reduces further, a brownout could ensue.
- **Brownouts—**The voltage drops to such an extent that it typically causes the lights to dim and causes computers to shut off.
- **Blackouts—**A total loss of power for a prolonged period occurs. Another problem associated with blackouts is the spike that can occur when power is restored. In the New York area, it is common to have an increased amount of tech support calls during July; this is attributed to lightning storms! Quite often, this is due to improper protection.
- **Power supply failure—**Power supplies are like hard drives in two ways: One, they will fail; it's not a matter of if, it's a matter of when. Two, they can cause intermittent issues when they begin to fail, issues that are hard to troubleshoot. If you suspect a power supply failure then you should replace the supply. Also consider using a redundant power supply.

Some devices have specific purposes, and others can protect against more than one of these electrical issues. Let's talk about three of them now: redundant power supplies, uninterruptible power supplies, and backup generators.

Redundant Power Supplies

A proper *redundant power supply* is an enclosure that contains two (or more) complete power supplies. You make one main power connection from the AC outlet to the power supply, and there is one set of wires that connect to the motherboard and devices. However, if one of the power supplies in the enclosure fails, the other takes over immediately without computer failure. These are common on servers, especially RAID boxes. They are not practical for client computers, but you might see them installed in some powerful workstations. In our scenario, we should install redundant power supplies to as many servers as possible, starting with the file servers and domain controllers. If possible, we should implement redundant power supplies for any of our switches or routers that will accept them, or consider new routers and switches that are scalable for redundant power supplies.

In some cases (pun intended), it is possible to install two completely separate power supplies so that each has a connection to an AC outlet. This will depend on your server configuration but is less common due to the amount of redundancy it requires of the devices inside the server. Either look at the specifications for your server's case, or open it up during off hours to see if redundant power supplies are an option.

Vendors such as HP, and manufacturers such as Thermaltake, and Enlight offer redundant power supply systems for servers, and vendors such as Cisco offer redundant AC power systems for its networking devices.

This technology is great in the case that a power supply failure occurs but does not protect from scenarios when power *to* the computer is disrupted.

Uninterruptible Power Supplies

It should go without saying, but surge protectors are not good enough to protect power issues that might occur in your server room. A UPS is the proper device to use. An *uninterruptible power supply (UPS)* takes the functionality of a surge suppressor and combines that with a battery backup. So now, our server is protected not only from surges and spikes, but also from sags, brownouts, and blackouts. Most UPS devices also act as line conditioners that serve to clean up dirty power. Noise and increases/decreases in power make up dirty power. Dirty power can also be caused by too many devices using the same circuit, or because power coming from the electrical panel or from the municipal grid fluctuates, maybe because the panel or the entire grid is under/overloaded. If a line conditioning device such as a UPS doesn't fix the problem, a quick call to your company's electrician should result in an answer and possibly a long-term fix.

If you happen to be using a separate line conditioning device *in addition to* a UPS, it should be tested regularly. Line conditioning devices are always supplying power to your devices. A UPS backup battery will kick in only if a power loss occurs.

Battery backup is great, but the battery can't last indefinitely! It is considered emergency power and typically keeps your computer system running for 5 to 30 minutes depending on the model you purchase. UPS devices today, have a USB connection so that your computer can communicate with the UPS. When there is a power outage, the UPS sends a signal to the computer telling it to shut down, suspend, or stand-by before the battery discharges completely. Most UPSs come with software that you can install that enables you to configure the computer with these options.

The more devices that connect to the UPS, the less time the battery can last if a power outage occurs; if too many devices are connected, there may be inconsistencies when the battery needs to take over. Thus many UPS manufacturers limit the amount of battery backup-protected receptacles. Connecting a laser printer to the UPS is *not* recommended due to the high current draw of the laser printer; and *never* connect a surge protector or power strip to one of the receptacles in the UPS, to protect the UPS from being overloaded.

The UPS normally has a lead-acid battery that, when discharged, requires 10 hours to 20 hours to recharge. This battery is usually shipped in a disconnected state. Before charging the device for use, you must first make sure that the leads connect. If the battery ever needs to be replaced, a red light will usually appear accompanied by a beeping sound. Beeping can also occur if power is no longer supplied to the UPS by the AC outlet.

There are varying levels of UPS devices, which incorporate different technologies. For example, the cheaper standby UPS (known as an SPS) might have a slight delay when switching from AC to battery power, possibly causing errors in the computer operating system. If a UPS is rack mounted, it will usually be a full-blown UPS (perhaps not the best choice of words!); this would be known as an "online" or "continuous" UPS—these cost in the hundreds or even thousands. If it is a smaller device that plugs into the AC outlet and lays freely about, it is probably an SPS—these cost between $25 and $100. You should realize that some care should be taken when planning the type of UPS to be used. When data is crucial, you had better plan for a quality UPS!

Just about everything in the server room should be connected to a UPS (you will most likely need several) to protect from power outages. This includes servers, monitors, switches, routers, CSU/DSUs, PBX equipment, security cameras, workstations, and monitors—really, everything in the server room!

Backup Generators

What if power to the building does fail completely? Most would consider this a disaster, and over the long term it could possibly be. However, most power outages are 5 minutes or less on the average, and most of the time a UPS can pick up the slack for these short outages, but not for the less common, longer outages that might last a few hours or days. And, a UPS powers only the devices you plug into it. If your organization is to keep functioning, it will need a backup generator to power lights, computers, phones, and security systems over short-term outages, or longer ones.

A *backup generator* is a part of an emergency power system used when there is an outage of regular electric grid power. Some emergency power systems might include special lighting and fuel cells, whereas larger more commercial backup generators can power portions of, or an entire building, as long as fuel is available. For our scenario we should make sure that the backup generator powers the server room at the very least.

Backup generator fuel types include gasoline, diesel, natural gas, propane, and solar. Smaller backup generators will often use gasoline, but these are not adequate for most companies. Instead, many organizations will use larger natural gas generators. Some of these generators need to be started manually, but the majority of them are known as *standby generators*. These are systems that will turn on automatically within seconds of a power outage. Transfer switches sense any power loss and instruct the generator to start. Standby generators may be required by code for certain types of buildings with standby lighting, or building with elevators, fire-suppression systems, and life-support equipment. You should always check company policy and your municipal guidelines before planning and implementing a backup generator system.

Backup generators can be broken into three types:

- **Portable gas-engine generator**—The least expensive and run on gasoline or could be solar powered. They are noisy, high maintenance, must be started manually, and usually require extension cords. They are a carbon monoxide risk and are only adequate for small operations and in mobile scenarios.
- **Permanently installed generator**—Much more expensive with a complex installation. These almost always run on either natural gas or propane. They are quieter and can be connected directly to the organization's electrical panel. Usually, these are standby generators and as such require little user interaction.
- **Battery-inverter generator**—These are based off of lead-acid batteries, are quiet, and require little user interaction aside from an uncommon restart and change of batteries. They are well matched to environments that require a low amount of wattage or are the victims of short power outages only. Battery-inverter systems can be stored indoors, but because the batteries can release fumes, the area they are stored in should be well ventilated, such as an air conditioned server room with external exhaust. Uninterruptible power supplies fall into the battery inverter generator category.

Some of the considerations you should take into account when selecting a backup generator include the following:

- **Price**—As with any organizational purchase, this will have to be budgeted.
- **How unit is started**—Does it start automatically? Most organizations will require this.
- **Uptime**—How many hours will the generator stay on before needing to be refueled? This goes hand-in-hand with the next bullet.
- **Power output**—How many watts does the system offer? Before purchasing a backup generator, you should measure the total maximum load your organization might use by running all computers, servers, lights, and other devices simultaneously, and measure this at the main electrical panel. Alternatively, you

could measure the total on paper by adding the estimated power requirements of all devices together.

- **Fuel source**—Does it run on natural gas, gasoline, and so on? If it is an automatically starting system, the options will probably be limited to natural gas and propane.

Some vendors that offer backup generators include Generac, Gillette, and Kohler. These devices should be monitored periodically; most companies will attempt to obtain a service contract from you, which might be wise depending on the size of your organization. We discuss service contracts and service level agreements in Chapter 15, "Policies, Procedures, and People."

Remember that your mission-critical devices, such as servers, should constantly be drawing power from a line conditioning device. Then, if there is a power outage to the server, a UPS should kick in. (In some cases, the UPS will also act as the line conditioning device.) Finally, if necessary a backup generator will come online and feed all your critical devices with power.

Redundant Data

Now that we have power taken care of, we can move on to the heart of the matter—data. Data can fail due to file corruption and malicious intent among other things. Power failures, hard drive failures, and user error can all lead to data failure. As always, it's the data that we are most interested in securing, so it stands to reason that the data should be redundant as well. But which data? There is so much of it! Well, generally file servers should have redundant data sets of some sorts. If an organization has the budgeting, next on the list would be databases and then web and file servers. However, in some instances these additional servers might be better off with failover systems as opposed to redundant data arrays. And certainly, the majority of client computers' data does not constitute a reason for RAID. So we'll concentrate on the file servers in our original scenario in the beginning of the chapter.

The best way to protect file servers' data is to use some type of redundant array of disks. This is referred to as RAID (an acronym for redundant array of independent disks, or inexpensive disks). RAID technologies are designed to either increase the speed of reading and writing data or to create one of several types of fault tolerant volumes, or do both. From a security viewpoint, we are most interested in the fault tolerance (the capability to withstand failure) of our disks. A RAID array can be internal or external to a computer. Historically, RAID arrays were configured as SCSI chains, but nowadays you will also find SATA, eSATA, and Fibre Channel. Either way, the idea is that data is being stored on multiple disks that work with each other. The amount of disks and the way they work together will be dependent on the level of RAID. For the exam, you need to know several levels of RAID including RAID 0, RAID 1, RAID 5, RAID 6, and RAID 10. Table 14-1 describes each of these. Note that RAID 0 is the only one listed that is *not* fault-tolerant, so from a security perspective it is not a viable option. Nevertheless, you should know it for the exam.

Table 14-1 RAID Descriptions

RAID Level	Description	Fault Tolerant?	Minimum Number of Disks
RAID 0	Striping Data is striped across multiple disks to increase performance.	No	Two
RAID 1	Mirroring Data is copied to two identical disks. If one disk fails, the other continues to operate. See Figure 14-1 for an illustration. This RAID version allows for the least amount of downtime because there is a complete copy of the data ready to at a moment's notice. When each disk is connected to a separate controller, this is known as disk duplexing.	Yes	Two (and two only)
RAID 5	Striping with Parity Data is striped across multiple disks; fault-tolerant parity data is also written to each disk. If one disk fails, the array can reconstruct the data from the parity information. See Figure 14-2 for an illustration.	Yes	Three
RAID 6	Striping with Double Parity Data is striped across multiple disks as it is in RAID 5, but there are two stripes of parity information. This usually requires another disk in the array. This system can operate even with two failed drives and is more adequate for time-critical systems.	Yes	Four

continues

Table 14-1 RAID Descriptions (continued)

RAID Level	Description	Fault Tolerant?	Minimum Number of Disks
RAID 0+1	Combines the advantages of RAID 0 and RAID 1. Requires a minimum of four disks. This system contains two RAID 0 striped sets. Those two sets are mirrored.	Yes	Four
RAID 1+0	Combines the advantages of RAID 1 and RAID 0. Requires a minimum of two disks but will usually have four or more. This system contains at least two mirrored disks that are then striped.	Yes	Two (usually four)

Figure 14-1 shows an illustration of RAID 1; you can see that data is written to both disks and that both disks collectively are known as the M: drive or M: *volume*. Figure 14-2 displays an illustration of RAID 5. In a RAID 5 array, blocks of data are distributed to the disks (A1 and A2 are a block, B1 and B2 are a block, and so on), and parity information is written for each block of data. This is written to each disk in an alternating fashion (A^P, B^P, and such) so that the parity is also distributed. If one disk fails, the parity information from the other disks will reconstruct the data. It is important to make the distinction between fault tolerance and backup. Fault tolerance means that the hard drives can continue to function (with little or no downtime) even if there is a problem with one of the drives. Backup means that we are taking the data and copying it (and possibly compressing it) to another location for archival in the event of a disaster. An example of a disaster would be if *two* drives in a RAID 5 array were to fail. If an organization is worried that that could happen, they should consider RAID 6, RAID 0+1, or the less common RAID 1+0.

Key Topic

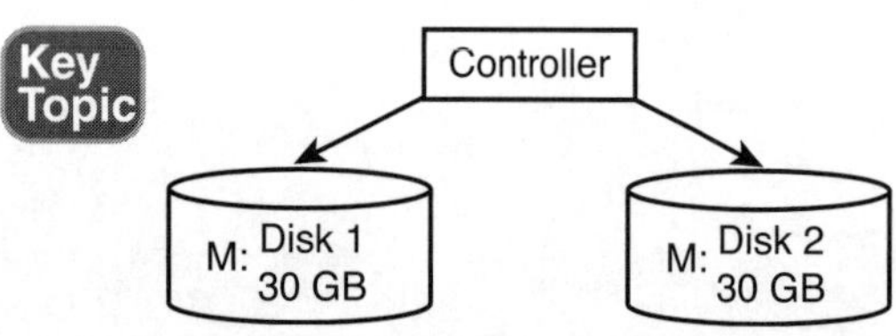

Figure 14-1 RAID 1 Illustration

Windows servers support RAID 0, 1, and 5 (and possibly 6 depending on the version) within the operating system. But most client operating systems cannot support RAID 1, 5, and 6. However, they *can* support hardware controllers that can create these arrays. Some motherboards have built in RAID functionality as well.

Key Topic

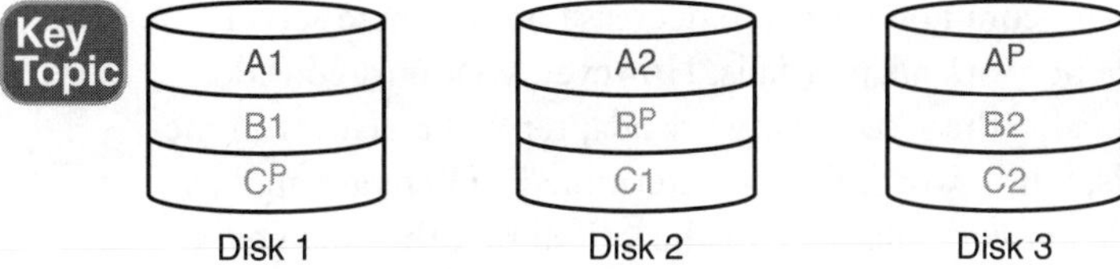

Figure 14-2 RAID 5 Illustration

Hardware is always the better way to go when it comes to RAID. Having a separate interface that controls the RAID configuration and handling is far superior than trying to control it with software within an operating system. The hardware could be an adapter card installed inside the computer, or an external box that connects to the computer or even to the network. When it comes to RAID in a network storage scenario, you are now dealing with network attached storage (NAS). These NAS points can be combined to form a storage area network (SAN), but any type of network attached storage will cost more money to an organization.

You can classify RAID in three different ways; these classifications can help when you plan which type of RAID system to implement.

- **Failure-resistant disk systems—**Protect against data loss due to disk failure. An example of this would be RAID 1 Mirroring.
- **Failure-tolerant disk systems—**Protect against data loss due to any single component failure. An example of this would be RAID 1 mirroring with duplexing.
- **Disaster-tolerant disk systems—**Protect data by the creation of two independent zones, each of which provides access to stored data. An example of this would be RAID 0+1.

Of course, no matter how well you protect the data from failure, users still need to access the data, and to do so might require some redundant networking.

Redundant Networking

Network connections can fail as well. And we all know how users need to have the network up and running—or there will be heck to pay. The security of an organization can be compromised if networking connections fail. Some of the types of connections you should consider include the following:

- Server network adapter connections
- Main connections to switches and routers
- The Internet connection

So basically, when I speak of redundant networking, I'm referring to any network connection of great importance that could fail. Generally, these connections will be located in the server room.

Redundant network adapters are commonly used to decrease or eliminate server downtime in the case that one network adapter fails. However, you must consider how they will be set up. Optimally, the second network adapter will take over immediately when the first one fails, but how will this be determined? There are applications that can control multiple network adapters, or the switch that they connect to can control where data is directed in the case of a failure. Also, multiple network adapters can be part of an individual collective interface. What you decide will be dictated by company policy, budgeting, and previously installed equipment. As a rule of thumb, you should use like network adapters when implementing redundancy; check the model and the version of the particular model to be exact. When installing multiple network adapters to a server, that computer than becomes known as a multihomed machine. It is important to consider how multiple adapters (and their operating systems) will behave normally and during a failure. Microsoft has some notes about this; I left a link at the end of the chapter. In some cases, you will install multiple physical network adapters, and in others you might opt for a single card that has multiple ports such as the Intel PRO/1000 MT Dual Port Server Adapter. This is often a cheaper solution than installing multiple cards but provides a single point of failure in the form of one adapter card and one adapter card slot. In our original scenario we had domain controllers, database servers, web servers, and file servers; these would all do well with the addition of redundant network adapters.

Companies should always have at least one backup switch sitting on the shelf. If the company has only one switch, it is a desperate single point of failure. If a company has multiple switches stacked in a star-bus fashion, the whole stack can be a single point of failure unless special backup ports are used (only available on certain switches). These special ports are often fiber optic-based and are designed either for high-speed connections between switches or for redundancy. This concept should be employed at the master switch in a hierarchical star as well to avoid a complete network collapse. However, the hierarchical star is more secure than a star-bus configuration when it comes to network failure. In a hierarchical star, certain areas of the network will still function even if one switch fails. This is a form of redundant topology.

Finally, your ISP is susceptible to failure as well—as I'm sure you are well aware. Most organizations rely on just one Internet connection for their entire network. This is another example of a single point of failure. Consider secondary connections to your ISP; known as a *redundant ISP*. If you have a T-1 line, perhaps a BRI connection will do. Or if you have a T-3, perhaps a PRI connection would be best. At the very least, a set of dial-up connections can be used for redundancy. Some companies will install completely fault-tolerant, dual Internet connections, the second of which comes online immediately following a failure. If you use a web host for your website and/or e-mail, consider a mirror site or more than one. Basically, in a nutshell, it's all about not being caught with your pants down. If an organization is without its Internet connection for more than a day (or hours in some cases), you know it will be the network admin and security admin that will be the first on the chopping block, most likely followed by the ISP.

Redundant Servers

Let's take it to the next level and discuss redundant servers. When redundant network adapters and disks are not enough, you might decide to cluster multiple servers together that act as a single entity. This will be more costly and require more administration but can provide a company with low downtime and a secure feeling. Two or more servers that work with each other are a *cluster*.

The clustering of servers can be broken down into two types:

- **Failover clusters—**Otherwise known as high-availability clusters are designed so that a secondary server can take over in the case that the primary one fails, with limited or no downtime. An example of a failover cluster would be the usage of two Microsoft domain controllers. When the first domain controller fails, the secondary domain controller should be ready to go at a moment's notice. There can be tertiary and quaternary servers and beyond as well. It all depends on how many servers you think might fail concurrently.
- **Load-balancing clusters—**Load balancing clusters are when multiple computers are connected together in an attempt to share resources such as CPU, RAM, and hard disks. In this way, the cluster can share CPU power, along with other resources, and balance of the CPU load among all the servers. Microsoft's Cluster Server is an example of this (although it can also act in failover mode), enabling for parallel, high performance computing. Several third-party vendors offer clustering software for operating systems and virtual OSs as well.

Data can also be replicated back and forth between servers as it often is with database servers and web servers. This is actually a mixture of redundant data (data replication) and server clustering.

However, it doesn't matter how many servers you install in a cluster. If they are all local, they could all be affected by certain attacks or worse yet, disasters. Enter the redundant site concept.

Redundant Sites

Well, we have implemented redundant arrays of disks, redundant network adapters, redundant power, and even redundant servers. What is left? Devising a mirror of the entire network! That's right, a redundant site, if you will. In the case of a disaster, a redundant site can act as a safe haven for your data and users. Redundant sites are sort of a gray area between redundancy and a disaster recovery method. If you have one and need to use it, a "disaster" has probably occurred. But, the better the redundant site, the less time the organization loses, and the less it seems like a disaster and more like a failure that you have prepared for. Of course, this all depends on the type of redundant site your organization decides on.

When it comes to the types of redundant sites, I like to refer to the story of Goldilocks and the three bears' three bowls of porridge. One was too hot, one too cold—and one just right. Most organizations will opt for the warm redundant site as opposed to the hot or cold. Let's discuss these three now.

- **Hot site—**A near duplicate of the original site of the organization that can be up and running within minutes (maybe longer). Computers and phones are installed and ready to go, a simulated version of the server room stands ready, and vast majority of the data is replicated to the site on a regular basis in the event that the original site is not accessible to users for whatever reason. Hot sites are used by companies that would face financial ruin in the case that a disaster makes their main site inaccessible for a few days of even a few hours. This is the only type of redundant site that can facilitate a *full* recovery.
- **Warm site—**Will have computers, phones, and servers, but they might require some configuration before users can start working on them. The warm site will have backups of data that might need to be restored; they will probably be several days old. This is chosen the most often by organizations because it has a good amount of configuration, yet remains less inexpensive than a hot site.
- **Cold site—**Has tables, chairs, bathrooms, and possibly some technical setup; for example basic phone, data, and electric lines. Otherwise, a lot of configuration of computers and data restoration is necessary before the site can be properly utilized. This type of site is used only if a company can handle the stress of being nonproductive for a week or more.

Although they are redundant, these types of sites are generally known as backup sites because if they are required, a disaster has probably occurred. A good network security administrator will try to plan for, and rely on, redundancy and fault tolerance as much as possible before having to resort to disaster recovery methods.

Disaster Recovery Planning and Procedures

Regardless of how much you planned out redundancy and fault tolerance, when disaster strikes, it can be devastating. There are three things that you should be concerned with as a network security administrator when it comes to disasters—your data, your server room, and the site in general. You need to have a powerful backup plan for your data and a comprehensive disaster recovery plan as well.

Data Backup

Disaster recovery (or DR for short) is pretty simple in the case of data. If disaster strikes you better have a good data backup plan; one that fits your organization's needs and budget. Your company might have a written policy as to what should be backed up, or you might need to decide what is best. Data can be backed up to a lot of different types of media (or to other computers), but generally the best method is tape backup.

There are three tape backup types you should be aware of for the exam. Keep in mind that this list is not the end all of backup types, but it gives a basic idea of the main types of backups used in the field. When performing any of these types of backups, the person must select what to backup. It could be a folder or an entire volume. For the sake of simplicity we will call these folders.

- **Full backup—**When all the contents of a folder are backed up. It can be stored on one or more tapes. If more than one is used, the restore process would require starting with the oldest tape and moving through the tapes chronologically one by one. Full backups can use a lot of space, causing a backup operator to make use of a lot of backup tapes which can be expensive. Full backups can also be time-consuming if there is a lot of data. So, quite often, incremental and differential backups are used with full backups as part of a backup plan.
- **Incremental backup—**Backs up only the contents of a folder that has changed since the last full backup or the last incremental backup. An incremental backup must be preceded by a full backup. Restoring the contents of a folder or volume would require a person to start with the full backup tape and then move on to each of the incremental tapes chronologically, ending with the latest incremental backup tape. Incremental backups started in the time of floppy disks when storage space and backup speed were quite limited. Some operating systems and backup systems will associate an archive bit (or archive flag) to any file that has been modified; this indicates to the backup program that it should be backed up during the next backup phase. If this is the case, the incremental backup will reset the bit after backup is complete.
- **Differential backup—**Backs up only the contents of a folder that has changed since the last full backup. A differential backup must be preceded by a full backup. To restore data, a person would start with the full backup tape and then move on to the differential tape. Differential backups do not reset the archive bit when backing up. This means that incremental backups will not see or know that a differential backup has occurred.

Table 14-2 shows an example of a basic one-week backup schedule using these three backup types.

Table 14-2 Example Backup Schedule

Day	Backup Type	Time
Monday	Full backup	6 p.m.
Tuesday	Incremental backup	6 p.m.
Wednesday	Incremental backup	6 p.m.

continues

Table 14-2 Example Backup Schedule (continued)

Day	Backup Type	Time
Thursday	Incremental backup	6 p.m.
Friday	Differential backup	6 p.m.

In this schedule, five backup tapes are required, one for each day. Let's say that the backups are done at 6 p.m. daily. Often an organization might employ a sixth tape, which is a dummy tape. This tape is put in the tape drive every morning by the backup operator and is replaced with the proper daily tape at 5:30 p.m. when everyone has left the building. This prevents data theft during the day. The real tapes are kept locked up until needed. Tapes might be reused when the cycle is complete, or an organization might opt to archive certain tapes each week, for example the full and differential tapes, and use new tapes every Monday and Friday. Another option is to run a complete full backup (which might be time-consuming) over the weekend and archive that tape every Monday. As long as no data loss is reported, this is a feasible option.

Let's say that this backup procedure was used to backup a server. Now, let's say that the server crashed on Wednesday at 9 p.m., and the hard drive data was lost. A backup operator arriving on the scene Thursday morning would need to review any logs available to find out when the server crashed. Then, after an admin fixes the server, the backup operator would need to restore the data. This would require starting with the Monday full backup tape and continuing on to the Tuesday and Wednesday incremental backup tapes. So three tapes in total would be needed to complete the restore.

Another example would be if the backup operator needed to restore data on Monday morning due to a failure over the weekend. The backup operator would need only two backup tapes, the Monday full backup and the Friday differential backup, because the differential backup would have backed up everything since the last full backup.

Windows Server operating systems have the capability to do full backups, incrementals, and differentials, as shown in Figure 14-3. Windows refers to a full backup as "normal." You will note that Windows also enables copy backups and daily backups.

Now, the schedule we just showed in Table 14-2 is a basic backup method, also known as a backup rotation scheme. Organizations might also do something similar in a 2-week period. However, you should also be aware of a couple of other backup schemes used in the field. These might use one or more of the backup types mentioned previously.

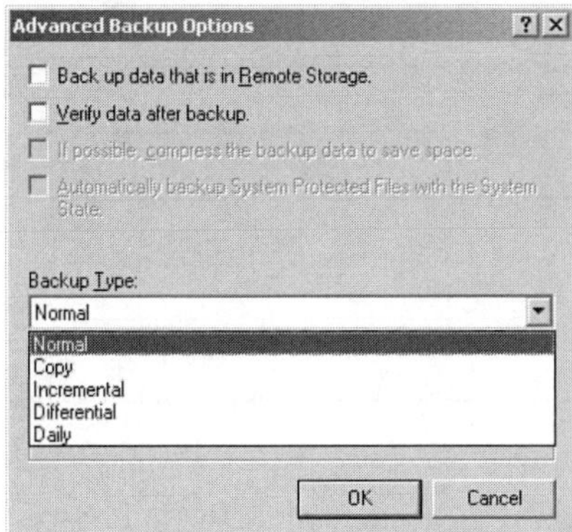

Figure 14-3 Windows Server 2003 Backup Types

- **10 tape rotation—**This method is simple and provides easy access to data that has been backed up. It can be accomplished during a 2-week backup period, each tape is used once per day for 2 weeks. Then the entire set is recycled. Generally, this will be similar to the one-week schedule shown previously, however, the second Monday might be a differential backup instead of a full backup. And the second Friday might be a full backup, which is archived. There are several options; you would need to run some backups and see which is best for you given the amount of tapes required and time spent running the backups.
- **Grandfather-father-son—**This backup rotation scheme is probably the most common backup method used. When attempting to use this scheme, three sets of backup tapes must be defined—usually they are daily, weekly, and monthly, which correspond to son, father, and grandfather. Backups are rotated on a daily basis; normally the last one of the week will be graduated to father status. Weekly (father) backups are rotated on a weekly basis with the last one of the month being graduated to grandfather status. Quite often, monthly (grandfather) backups, or a copy of them, are archived offsite.
- **Towers of Hanoi—**This backup rotation scheme is based on the mathematics of the Towers of Hanoi puzzle. This also uses three backup sets, but they are rotated differently. Without getting into the mathematics behind it, the basic idea is that the first tape is used every 2nd day, the second tape is used every 4th day, and the third tape is used every 8th day. Table 14-3 shows an example of this. Keep in mind that this can go further; a fourth tape can be used every 16th day, and a fifth tape every 32nd day, and so on, although it gets much more complex to remember what tapes to use to backup and which order to go by when restoring. The table shows an example with three tape sets represented as set A, B, and C.

Table 14-3 Example of Towers of Hanoi 3 Tape Schedule

	Day of the Cycle							
	1	**2**	**3**	**4**	**5**	**6**	**7**	**8**
Tape	A		A		A		A	
		B				B		
				C				C

To avoid the rewriting of data, start on the 4th day of the cycle with tape C. This rotation scheme should be written out and perhaps calculated during the planning stage before it is implemented. Also, due to the complexity of the scheme, a restore sequence should be tested as well.

Tapes should be stored in a cool, dry area, away from sunlight, power lines, and other power sources. Most tape backup vendors will have specific guidelines as to the temperature and humidity ranges for storage, along with other storage guidelines.

Tape backup methods and tape integrity should always be tested by restoring all or part of a backup.

It's also possible to archive data to a third-party. This could be for backup purposes or for complete file replication. Several companies offer this type of service, and you can usually select to archive data over the Internet or by courier.

Whatever your data backup method, make sure that there is some kind of archival offsite in the case of a true disaster. Optimally, this will be in a sister site in another city but regardless should be geographically distant from the main site.

DR Planning

Before we can plan for disasters, we need to define exactly what disasters are possible and list them in order starting with the most probable. Sounds a bit morbid, but it's necessary to ensure the long-term welfare of your organization.

What could go wrong? Let's focus in on the server room in the beginning of the chapter as our scenario. As you remember, we had nine servers, networking equipment, a PBX, and a few workstations—a pretty typical server room for a mid-sized company. Keep in mind that larger organizations will have more equipment, bigger server rooms, and more to consider when it comes to DR planning.

Disasters can be divided into two categories: natural and man-made. Some of the disasters that could render your server room inoperable include the following:

- **Fire**—Fire is probably the number one planned for disaster. This is partially because most municipalities will require some sort of fire suppression system, as well as the fact that most organizations' policies will define the usage of a proper fire suppression system. You probably recall the three main types of fire extinguishers: A (for ash fires), B (for gas and other flammable liquid fires), and C (for electrical fires). Unfortunately, these and the standard sprinkler system in the rest of the building are not adequate for a server room. If there were a fire, the material from the fire extinguisher or the water from the sprinkler system would damage the equipment, making the disaster even worse! Instead, a server room should be equipped with a proper system of its own such as DuPont FM-200. This uses a large tank that stores a clean agent fire extinguishant that is sprayed from one or more nozzles in the ceiling of the server room. It can put out fires of all types in seconds. A product such as this can be used safely when people are present; however, most systems will also employ a *very* loud alarm that tells all personnel to leave the server room. It is wise to run through several fire suppression alarm tests and fire drills, ensuring that the alarm will sound when necessary and that personnel know what do to when the alarm sounds. We'll talk more about fire in Chapter 15.

- **Flood—**The best way to avoid server room damage in the case of a flood is to locate the server room on the first floor or higher, not in a basement. There's not much you can do about the location of a building, but if it is in a flood zone, it makes the use of a warm or hot site that much more imperative. And a server room could also be flooded by other things such as boilers. The room should not be adjacent to, or on the same floor as, a boiler room. It should also be located away from other water sources such as bathrooms and any sprinkler systems. The server room should be thought of three-dimensionally; the floors, walls, and ceiling should be analyzed and protected. Some server rooms are designed to be a room within a room and might have drainage installed as well.
- **Long-term power loss—**Short-term power loss should be countered by the UPS, but long-term power loss requires a backup generator and possibly a redundant site.
- **Theft and malicious attack—**Theft and malicious attack can also cause a disaster, if the right data is stolen. Physical security such as door locks/access systems and video cameras should be implemented to avoid this. Servers should be cable-locked to their server racks, and removable hard drives (if any are used) should have key access. Physical security is covered in more depth in Chapter 8, "Physical Security and Authentication Models." Malicious network attacks also need to be warded off; these are covered in depth in Chapter 5, "Network Design Elements and Network Threats."
- **Loss of building—**Temporary loss of the building due to gas leak, malicious attack, inaccessibility due to crime scene, or natural event will require personnel to access a redundant site. Your server room should have as much data archived as possible, and the redundant site should be warm enough to keep business

running. A plan should be in place as to how data will be restored at the redundant site and how the network will be made functional.

Disaster recovery plans should include information regarding redundancy such as sites and backup but will not include information that deals with the day-to-day operations of an organization such as updating computers, patch management, monitoring and audits, and so on. It is important to include only what is necessary in a disaster recovery plan. Too much information can make it difficult to use when a disaster does strike.

Although not an exhaustive set, the following written disaster recovery policies, procedures, and information should be part of your disaster recovery plan:

- **Contact information**—Who you should contact if a disaster occurs and how employees will contact the organization.
- **Impact determination**—A procedure to determine a disaster's full impact on the organization. This will include an evaluation of assets lost and the cost to replace those assets.
- **Recovery plan**—This will be based on the determination of disaster impact. This will have many permutations depending on the type of disaster. Although it is impossible to foresee every possible event, the previous list gives a good starting point. The recovery plan will include an estimated time to complete recovery and a set of steps defining the order of what will be recovered and when.
- **Business continuity plan**—A BCP defines how the business will continue to operate if a disaster occurs; this plan is often carried out by a team of individuals.
- **Copies of agreements**—Copies of any agreements with vendors of redundant sites, ISPs, building management, and so on should be stored with the DR plan.
- **Disaster recovery drills and exercises**—Employees should be drilled on what to do if a disaster occurs. These exercises should be written out step-by-step and should conform to safety standards.

This information should be accessible at the company site and should have a copy stored offsite as well. It might be that your organization conforms to special compliance rules; these should be consulted when designing a DR plan. Depending on the type of organization, there might be other items that go into your DR plan. We will cover these in more depth in Chapter 15.

Exam Preparation Tasks

Review Key Topics

Review the most important topics in the chapter, noted with the Key Topics icon in the outer margin of the page. Table 14-4 lists a reference of these key topics and the page numbers on which each is found.

Table 14-4 Key Topics for Chapter 14

Key Topic Element	Description	Page Number
Bulleted list	Power Failures	406
Table 14-1	RAID Descriptions	411–412
Figure 14-1	RAID 1 Illustration	412
Figure 14-2	RAID 5 Illustration	413
Bulleted list	Server Cluster Types	415
Bulleted list	Types of Redundant Sites	416
Bulleted list	Backup Types	417
Table 14-2	Example Backup Schedule	417
Bulleted list	Backup Rotation Schemes	419

Complete Tables and Lists from Memory

Print a copy of Appendix A, "Memory Tables," (found on the DVD), or at least the section for this chapter, and complete the tables and lists from memory. Appendix B, "Memory Tables Answer Key," also on the DVD, includes completed tables and lists to check your work.

Define Key Terms

Define the following key terms from this chapter, and check your answers in the glossary:

single point of failure, surge, spike, sag, brownout, blackout, redundant power supply, uninterruptible power supply (UPS), backup generator, standby generator, RAID 1, disk duplexing, RAID 5, redundant ISP, cluster, failover clusters, load-balancing clusters, hot site, warm site, cold site, full backup, differential backup, incremental backup, 10 tape rotation, grandfather-father-son, Towers of Hanoi, disaster recovery plan

Hands-On Labs

Complete the following written step-by-step scenarios. After you finish (or if you do not have adequate equipment to complete the scenario), watch the corresponding video solutions on the DVD.

If you have additional questions, feel free to post them at my website: www.davidlprowse.com in the Ask Dave forum. (Free registration is required to post on the website.)

Equipment Needed

- Windows Server 2003 with a minimum of three drives for data. These drives should be separate from the drive(s) used to store the operating system.

Lab 14-1: Backing Up Data on a Windows Server

In this lab, you will back up information on a Windows Server 2003 through the use of the built-in NTbackup program. The steps are as follows:

Step 1. Create a folder called **admin**. Stock it with a few files.

Step 2. Open the NTbackup program by clicking **Start > Run** and typing **ntbackup**. Deselect Wizard mode and restart the program to run it in regular mode.

Step 3. Click the **Backup** tab.

Step 4. Expand the + sign for the C: drive.

Step 5. Click the **admin** folder to view the contents.

Step 6. Checkmark the **admin** folder to back up all the contents within the admin folder.

Step 7. Click the **Browse** button to select where you will back up the data. This could be to tape, removable media, or elsewhere on the drive. For this procedure, back up to another folder on the C: drive.

Step 8. Name the backup. Consider adding the date into the filename of the backup. Then click **Save**.

Step 9. Click the **Start Backup** button. This displays the Backup Job Information window. Leave the default settings.

Step 10. Click the **Advanced** button.

Step 11. Select the **Verify data after backup** checkbox.

Step 12. Click **OK**.

Step 13. Click the **Start Backup** button.

Step 14. When the backup is complete, jot down the amount of bytes that were backed up. Next, view the report by clicking the **Report** button. Make sure that the data was verified within the Verified Status portion of the report.

Step 15. To represent the loss of data because of an unexpected event, go to Windows Explorer and delete the admin folder. Delete it from the Recycle Bin as well.

Step 16. Restore the deleted data from the backup file.

Step 17. Return to the NTbackup program.

Step 18. Click the **Restore** and **Manage Media** tab.

Step 19. Click the + sign next to File.

Step 20. Click the + sign for the backup that you just completed. View the contents inside the backup.

Step 21. Checkmark the backup and click the **Start Restore** button. Compare the amount of bytes that were restored to the amount of bytes that was originally backed up.

Step 22. Return to Windows Explorer and view your **admin** folder. Verify that all the contents of the folder were restored properly.

Watch the solution video in the "Hands-On Scenarios" section of the DVD.

Lab 14-2: Configuring RAID 1 and 5

In this lab, you configure RAID 1 (mirroring) and RAID 5 (striping with parity) on a Windows Server 2003. You will use the built-in software functionality to do this. The server needs to have three extra hard drives separate from the operating system drive. RAID 1 requires two individual drives; RAID 5 requires a minimum of 3, although you could use more.

The steps are as follows:

Configure a RAID 1 Mirror

Step 1. Access Disk Management within Computer Management or your MMC. The extra disks in your computer should be listed.

Step 2. Right-click the unallocated section of one of the blank disks to be used in your mirror and select **New Volume**.

Step 3. Click **Next** for the wizard.

Step 4. Click the **Mirrored** radio button and click **Next**.

Step 5. Add the disks you want to use to the Selected area by highlighting the disk(s) and clicking **Add**. Then click **Next**.

Step 6. Assign the drive letter **M:** for the mirror and click **Next**.

Step 7. In the Format Volume screen:

A. Change the name of the Volume Label to **Mirror for Data**.

B. Select the **Perform a quick format** checkbox.

C. Click **Next**.

If the system runs slowly, consider doing the format afterward.

Step 8. Verify the data and click **Finish**. That should create the mirror between the two disks (shown in a reddish color) and will begin formatting. This may take a few minutes. It should display the status **Healthy** when complete. Try saving data to the new mirror!

Configure a RAID 5 Mirror

Step 9. Delete the previously created mirror volume by right-clicking either of the disks in the mirror and selecting **Delete**.

Step 10. Confirm that you have three disks (each showing as Unallocated) available for the RAID 5 stripe set. It is recommended that you use disks of the same size; optimally they would be the same model.

Step 11. Right-click the unallocated section of one of the blank disks to be used in your mirror and select **New Volume**.

Step 12. Click **Next** for the wizard.

Step 13. Click the **RAID-5** radio button and click **Next**.

Step 14. Add the disks you want to use to the Selected area by highlighting the disk(s) and clicking **Add**. (You will have to select three in total.) Then click **Next**.

Step 15. Assign the drive letter P: for the RAID 5 array, and click **Next**.

Step 16. In the Format Volume screen:

A. Change the name of the Volume Label to **RAID 5 Stripe**.

B. Select the **Perform a quick format** checkbox.

C. Click **Next**.

If the system runs slowly, consider doing the format afterward.

Step 17. Verify the data and click **Finish**. That should create the RAID 5 stripe set from the three disks (shown in a light blue color) and will begin formatting. This may take a few minutes. It should display the status **Healthy** when complete for each of the disks in the stripe. Try saving some data to the new array!

Watch the solution video in the "Hands-On Scenarios" section of the DVD.

View Recommended Resources

- Thermaltake redundant power supply: www.tt-server.com/Product.aspx?S=82&ID=28
- Enlight redundant power supply: http://us.enlightcorp.com/Product/Product_list_server_power.aspx
- APC enterprise-level UPS devices: www.apc.com/products/family/index.cfm?id=163
- Gillette Generators: www.gillettegenerators.com/
- Generac generators: www.generac.com/Commercial/
- Intel PRO/1000 MT Dual Port Server Adapter" www.intel.com/products/server/adapters/pro1000mt-dualport/pro1000mt-dualport-overview.htm
- Expected Behavior of Multiple Adapters on the same Network" http://support.microsoft.com/kb/175767
- Data Backup and Recovery article: http://technet.microsoft.com/en-us/library/bb727010.aspx
- DuPont FM-200 web page: www2.dupont.com/FE/en_US/products/FM200.html

Answer Review Questions

Answer the following review questions. You can find the answers at the end of this chapter.

1. Which of the following RAID versions enable the least amount of downtime?
   A. RAID 0
   B. RAID 1
   C. RAID 4
   D. RAID 5

2. Which of the following can facilitate a full recovery within minutes?
   A. Warm site
   B. Cold site
   C. Reestablishing a mirror
   D. Hot site

3. What device should be used to ensure that a server does not shut down when there is a power outage?
   A. RAID 1 box
   B. UPS
   C. Redundant NIC
   D. Hot site

4. Which of the following tape backup methods enable daily backups, weekly full backups, and monthly full backups?
   A. Towers of Hanoi
   B. Incremental
   C. Grandfather-father-son
   D. Differential

5. To prevent electrical damage to a computer and its peripherals, the computer should be connected to what?
   A. Power strip
   B. Power inverter
   C. AC to DC converter
   D. UPS

6. Which of the following would not be considered part of a disaster recovery plan?
   A. Hot site
   B. Patch management software
   C. Backing up computers
   D. Tape backup

7. Which of the following factors should you consider when evaluating assets to a company? (Select the two best answers.)
   A. Its value to the company
   B. Its replacement cost
   C. Where they were purchased from
   D. Their salvage value

8. You are using the following backup scheme. A full backup is made every Friday night at 6 p.m. Differential backups are made every other night at 6 p.m. Your database server fails on Thursday afternoon at 4 p.m. How many tapes will you need to restore the database server?

A. One

B. Two

C. Three

D. Four

9. Of the following, what is the worst place to store a backup tape?

A. Near a bundle of fiber-optic cables

B. Near a power line

C. Near a server

D. Near an LCD screen

10. Critical equipment should always be able to get power. What is the correct order of devices that your critical equipment should draw power from?

A. Generator, line conditioner, UPS battery

B. Line conditioner, UPS battery, generator

C. Generator, UPS battery, line conditioner

D. Line conditioner, generator, UPS battery

11. What is the best way to test the integrity of a company's backed up data?

A. Conduct another backup

B. Use software to recover deleted files

C. Review written procedures

D. Restore part of the backup

12. Your company has six web servers. You are implementing load balancing. What is this an example of?

A. UPS

B. Redundant servers

C. RAID

D. Warm site

13. Your company has a T-1 connection to the Internet. Which of the following can enable your network to remain operational even if the T-1 fails?

A. Redundant network adapters

B. RAID 5

C. Redundant ISP

D. UPS

14. Which action should be taken to protect against a complete disaster in the case that a primary company's site is permanently lost?

A. Back up all data to tape, and store those tapes at a sister site in another city.

B. Back up all data to tape, and store those tapes at a sister site across the street.

C. Back up all data to disk, and store the disk in a safe deposit box at the administrator's home.

D. Back up all data to disk, and store the disk in a safe in the building's basement.

15. Of the following backup types, which describes the back up of files that have changed since the last full or incremental backup?

A. Incremental

B. Differential

C. Full

D. Copy

16. Michael's company has a single web server that is connected to three other distribution servers. What is the greatest risk involved in this scenario?

A. Fraggle attack

B. Single point of failure

C. Denial of service

D. Man-in-the-middle attack

Answers and Explanations

1. B. RAID 1 is known as mirroring. If one drive fails, the other will still function and there will be no downtime. All the rest of the answers are striping-based and therefore have downtime associated with them.

2. D. A hot site can facilitate a full recovery of communications software and equipment within minutes. Warm and cold sites cannot facilitate a *full* recovery but may have some of the options necessary to continue business. Reestablishing a mirror will not necessarily implement a full recovery of data communications or equipment.

3. **B.** An Uninterruptible Power Supply (UPS) ensures that a computer will keep running even if a power outage occurs. The amount of minutes the computer can continue in this fashion depends on the type of UPS and battery it contains. A backup generator can also be used, but it does not guarantee 100% uptime, because there might be a delay between when the power outage occurs and when the generator comes online. RAID 1 has to do with the fault tolerance of data. Redundant NICs (network adapters) are used on servers in the case that one of them fails. Hot sites are completely different places that a company can inhabit. Although the hot site can be ready in minutes, and although it may have a mirror of the server in question, they do not ensure that the original server will not shut down during a power outage.
4. **C.** The grandfather-father-son (GFS) backup scheme generally uses daily backups (the son), weekly backups (the father), and monthly backups (the grandfather). The Towers of Hanoi is a more complex strategy based on a puzzle. Incremental backups are simply one-time backups that back up all data that has changed since the last incremental backup. These might be used as the son in a GFS scheme. Differential backups back up everything since the last differential or full backup.
5. **D.** A UPS (uninterruptible power supply) protects computer equipment against surges, spikes, sags, brownouts, and blackouts. Power strips, unlike surge protectors, do not protect against surges.
6. **B.** Patching a system is part of the normal maintenance of a computer. In the case of a disaster to a particular computer, the computer's OS and latest service pack would have to be reinstalled. The same would be true in the case of a disaster to a larger area, like the building. Hot sites, backing up computers, and tape backup are all components of a disaster recovery plan.
7. **A and B.** When evaluating assets to a company, it is important to know the replacement cost of those assets and the value of the assets to the company. If the assets were lost or stolen, the salvage value is not important, and although you may want to know where the assets were purchased from, it is not one of the best answers.
8. **B.** You need two tapes to restore the database server—the full backup tape made on Friday and the differential backup tape made on the following Wednesday. Only the last differential tape is needed. When restoring the database server, the technician must remember to start with the full backup tape.
9. **B.** Backup tapes should be kept away from power sources including power lines, CRT monitors, speakers, and so on. And the admin should keep backup

tapes away from sources that might emit EMI. LCD screens, servers, and fiber optic cables have low EMI emissions.

10. **B.** The line conditioner is constantly serving critical equipment with clean power. It should be first and should always be on. The UPS battery should kick in only if there is a power outage. Finally, the generator should kick in only when the UPS battery is about to run out of power. Quite often, the line conditioner and UPS battery will be the same device. However, the line conditioner function will always be used, but the battery comes into play only when there is a power outage, or brownout.
11. **D.** The best way to test the integrity of backed up data is to restore part of that backup. Conducting another backup will tell you if the backup procedure is working properly, and if necessary after testing the integrity of the backup and after the restore a person might need to use software to recover deleted files. It's always important to review written procedures and amend them if need be.
12. **B.** Load balancing is a method used when you have redundant servers. In this case, the six web servers will serve data equally to users. The UPS is an uninterruptible power supply, and RAID is the redundant array of inexpensive disks. A warm site is a secondary site that a company can use if a disaster occurs that can be up and running within a few hours or a day.
13. **C.** A secondary ISP enables the network to remain operational and still gain Internet access even if the T-1 connection fails. This generally means that there will be a second ISP and a secondary physical connection to the Internet. Redundant network adapters are used on servers so that the server can have a higher percentage of uptime. RAID 5 is used for redundancy of data and spreads the data over three or more disks. A UPS is used in the case of a power outage.
14. **A.** In the case that a building's primary site is lost, data should be backed up to tape stored at a sister site in another city. Storing information across the street might not be good enough especially if the area has to be evacuated. Company information should never be stored at an employee's home. And of course if the data were stored in the primary building's basement and there were a complete disaster at the primary site, that data would also be lost.
15. **A.** An incremental backup backs up only the files that have changed since the last incremental or full backup. Generally it is used as a daily backup. Differential backups back up files that have changed since the last differential backup or the last full backup. A full backup backs up all files in a particular folder or drive, depending on what has been selected; this is regardless of any previous differential or incremental backups. Copies of data can be made, but they will not affect backup rotations that include incremental, differential, and full backups.

16. B. The greatest risk involved in this scenario is that the single web server is a single point of failure regardless that it is connected to three other distribution servers. If the web server goes down or is compromised, no one can access the company's website. A Fraggle is a type of denial-of-service attack. Although denial-of-service attacks are a risk to web servers, they are not the greatest risk in this particular scenario. A company should implement as much redundancy as possible.

This chapter covers the following subjects:

- **Environmental Controls—**When dealing with the environment, it is important for a security person to consider fire suppression methods, heating, cooling, and ventilation, and shielding, and how to protect server room. This section covers fire suppression methods such as fire extinguishers, sprinkler systems, and special hazard protection, and HVAC, shielding, and the Faraday cage concept.
- **Social Engineering—**This section delves into the methods and techniques that social engineers can employ to gain access to buildings and systems and obtain company data and personal information. It also covers the various ways that these social engineers can be defeated.
- **Legislative and Organizational Policies—**In this section, you learn about ways to classify data, laws that protect individual privacy, personnel security policies and how to implement them, service level agreements, the safe disposal of computers, and incident response procedures.

This chapter covers the CompTIA Security+ SY0-201 objectives 6.3, 6.4, 6.5 and 6.6.

CHAPTER 15

Policies, Procedures, and People

The idea behind this chapter is to examine the people who work for an organization, and how to protect their privacy, while still protecting your infrastructure, from *them*! Environmental controls, policies, and procedures can help to protect legitimate individuals and help protect the infrastructure from malicious individuals and social engineers.

This is the last chapter of actual objective content for the Security+ exam, but you will no doubt see several questions on the exam about these topics. The concepts covered in this chapter are a bit of a hodge-podge, covering concepts less about computers, and more on the periphery of technology security, but I have tried to line them up in a way that will make for easy reading and recall. We start with fire suppression, and social engineering, which are first and second sections. That's not to say that policies and procedures are not important, and we do indeed move on to those in the third section.

When going through this chapter, try to keep an open-mind as to the different roles a security person might be placed in. Imagine branching out beyond computers, servers, and networks, and developing security for the entire organization and its personnel.

Foundation Topics

Environmental Controls

Although it is usually the duty of the IT director and building management to take care of the installation, maintenance, and repair of environmental controls, you also should have a basic knowledge of how these systems function. Significant concepts include fire suppression, HVAC, and shielding of equipment. By far, the concept a person would spend the most time dealing with when planning a server room is fire suppression.

Fire Suppression

We talked about fire suppression somewhat in Chapter 14, "Redundancy and Disaster Recovery," but we need to dig a bit deeper into the types you can employ, and some of the policies and procedures involved with fire suppression. *Fire suppression* is the process of controlling and/or extinguishing fires to protect an organization's employees and its data and equipment. There are basically three types of fire suppression you need to know for the CompTIA Security+ exam: handheld fire extinguisher solutions, sprinkler systems, and special hazard protection systems such as those used in server rooms.

Fire Extinguishers

Be careful when selecting a handheld fire extinguisher. There are several types to choose from; they vary depending on what type of environment you work in. Keep in mind that any one of these will probably cause damage to computers, phones, and other electronics. With only a couple exceptions, these solutions should not be used in a server room or other critical areas of your organization. Here are some of the classifications of fires and their indicators on corresponding fire extinguishers:

- **Fire Class A—**Denoted by a green triangle, this class defines use for ordinary fires consuming solid combustibles such as wood. Think A for "ash" to help remember this type. Water-based extinguishers are suitable for Class A fires only and should not be used in a server room.
- **Fire Class B—**Represented by a red square, this type defines use for flammable liquid and gas fires. I like to remember this by associating B with "butane" because butane is a highly flammable gas.
- **Fire Class C—**Indicated with a blue circle, this type defines use for electrical fires, for example when an outlet is overloaded. Think C for "copper" as in copper electrical wiring to aid in memorizing this type. If a fire occurs in a server room, and you don't have a special hazard system (not wise), the multipurpose

BC extinguisher (CO_2) is the best handheld extinguisher to use. Electrical fires are the most likely type of fire in a server room.

- **Fire Class D**—Designated with a yellow decagon, this type defines use for combustible metal fires such as magnesium, titanium, and lithium. A class D extinguisher is effective in case a laptop's batteries spontaneously ignite. Chemical laboratories and PC repair labs should definitely have one of these available. Metal fires can easily and quickly spread to become ordinary fires. These fire extinguishers are usually yellow; it is one of only a couple that deviates from the standard red color. Also, this is the only other exception when it comes to the use of extinguishers in a critical area of your organization. Because of those two reasons, I like to remember it by associating D with "deviate."
- **Fire Class K**—Symbolized as a black hexagon, this type is for cooking oil fires. This is one type of extinguisher that should be in any kitchen. This is important if your organization has a cafeteria with cooking equipment. Think K for "kitchen" when remembering this type.

The previous bulleted list is not an official standard but is used by most manufacturers of fire extinguishers in the United States. Other countries might have a slightly different system.

In general, the most common type of fire extinguisher used in a building is the multipurpose dry-chemical ABC extinguisher. However, this is extremely messy—it gets into everything! Plus, it can cause corrosion to computer components over time. For server rooms, BC extinguishers are sometimes employed; the most common is the carbon dioxide (CO_2) extinguisher. The CO_2 extinguisher displaces oxygen, which is needed for a fire to burn, in addition to heat and fuel, which collectively make up the fire triangle. CO_2 extinguishers are relatively safe for computer components, especially compared to ABC extinguishers. However, the CO_2 extinguisher can possibly cause damage to computer components from electro-static discharge (ESD), although this is rare. Also, if carbon dioxide is released in an enclosed space where people are present, there is a risk of suffocation. If the organization has the money, it is far more preferable to use an ABC-rated Halotron extinguisher in the server room—or better yet, a special hazard protection system.

Older extinguishants, such as Halon, are not used anymore because they are harmful to the environment. Less-developed countries might still use them, but most governments have banned the use of Halon. If you see one of these, it should be replaced with a newer extinguisher that uses environment-safe halocarbon agents such as Halotron or FE-36. These are known as gaseous clean agents that are not only safe on humans and safe for IT equipment, but are better for the environment as well. Gaseous fire suppression systems are the best for server rooms.

Sprinkler Systems

The most common type of fire sprinkler system consists of a pressurized water supply system that can deliver a high quantity of water to an entire building via a piping distribution system. This is known as a *wet pipe system*. Typical to these systems are sprinkler heads with glass bulbs (often red) or two-part metal links. When a certain amount of predetermined heat reaches the bulb or link, it causes it to shatter or break, applying pressure to the sprinkler cap and initiating the flow of water from that sprinkler and perhaps others in the same zone. The entire system is usually controlled by a valve assembly, often located in the building's basement. Some organizations might have a need for a dry pipe system, which is necessary in spaces where the temperature of that area of the building can be cold enough to freeze the water in a wet pipe system. In this type of system, the pipes are pressurized with air, and water is sent through the system only if necessary; for example, during a fire.

Regardless of the system, an organization should conduct periodic fire drills to simulate a real fire and sprinkler system activation. Afterward, the network security administrator should simulate disaster recovery procedures, as detailed in Chapter 14.

Most local municipalities require that organizations possess a sprinkler system that covers all the building's floor space. However, the standard wet pipe or dry pipe systems are not acceptable in server rooms because if set off, they will most likely damage the equipment within. If a person were working in the server room and somehow damaged a pipe, it could discharge; possibly sending a few servers to the scrap heap. Instead, another option for a server room would be a pre-action sprinkler system (and possibly a special hazard protection system in addition to that). A pre-action system is similar to a dry pipe system, but there are requirements for it to be set off such as heat or smoke. So, even if a person were to damage one of the pipes in the sprinkler system, the pre-action system would not be set off.

Special Hazard Protection Systems

I've mentioned several times that your server room contains the livelihood of your organization—its data. If you don't protect the data, you'll be out of a job. One way to protect the server room is by installing a clean agent fire suppression system. Special clean agent fire extinguishers, such as Halotron and FE-36, are recommended for server rooms because they leave no residue after the fire is extinguished, reducing the likelihood of damage to computer systems and networking equipment. Also, they are rated as ABC, so not only can they put out electrical fires, but they can also put out the ash fire that will most likely ensue. All the other systems mentioned up to this point can easily cause computer failure if they are discharged.

The ultimate solution would be to equip the server room with a special hazard protection, clean agent system, such as a FM-200 system. This gaseous system would be installed in addition to the pre-action system (or other dry pipe system) if the organization can afford it. This system uses a large tank that stores a clean agent fire extinguishant in the form of liquid. It is sprayed from one or more nozzles in the ceiling of the server room in gas form. A system such as this can put out most classes of fires in seconds. This type of product does not do damage to equipment and can be used safely when people are present. However, most of these systems also employ a *very* loud alarm that tells all personnel to leave the server room; it's usually so loud and abrasive that you are compelled to leave! It is wise to run through fire suppression alarm tests and fire drills, ensuring that the alarm will sound when necessary and that IT personnel know what do to when the alarm sounds, namely leave. In some cases, these systems will shut the door automatically after a certain timeout. In these cases, procedures should be written out specifying what to do if a fire occurs. Drilling is of utmost importance in these environments to make certain that everyone knows to leave the server room quickly if a fire occurs. Again, after drills have been completed, the appropriate IT personnel should simulate disaster recovery procedures, if necessary. If the system were installed properly and does its job, this simulation should be minimal.

HVAC

HVAC, or heating, ventilating, and air conditioning, is important for server rooms and other technology-oriented areas of your building. Servers run hot—their CPUs can make the temperature inside the case skyrocket. This heat needs to be dissipated and exhausted outside the case. All the heat from servers and other networking equipment is enough to make your server room fry!

To alleviate the situation, organizations will install a heavy duty air conditioning system used solely for the server room. Often times, the system will also include a humidity control. As we know, static electricity is our enemy. By increasing humidity, we decrease the buildup of static electricity and the chance of ESD. Also, this can enable us to keep our equipment from getting too humid, which can also cause failure. It is important to have this system on its own dedicated circuit that is rated properly. Another way to improve the heat situation is to install an exhaust system. The biggest server rooms have enormous exhaust ducts that lead up and over the building. Because most AC systems use refrigerant, it is important to locate the device and any pipes away from where servers and other equipment will be situated, or use a pipeless system. The controls for this system should be within the server room, perhaps protected by a key code. This way, only authorized IT personnel (who have access to the server room) can change the temperature or humidity. This control can also be hooked up to the door access system or other monitoring systems to log who made changes and when.

Heat is rarely needed in server room, unless the organization's building is in the coldest of environments. This is due to the amount of heat that all the servers give off.

If there is a power failure that cannot be alleviated by use of a UPS and/or backup generator, you might opt to shut down all but the most necessary of systems temporarily. Some organizations will enforce this by way of a written policy.

These types of systems are usually beyond the knowledge of the IT people, and any maintenance or repair of such systems should be directed to qualified professionals. Sometimes, the building management is responsible for such systems, but more than likely it is the organization who is responsible for the installation, repair, and maintenance.

Shielding

We have already established that EMI and RFI can corrupt legitimate signals and can possible create unwelcome emanations. Shielding can help to prevent these problems. Let's give a few examples:

- **Shielded twisted-pair (STP) cable—**By using STP cable, you employ a shield around the wires inside the cable reducing the levels of interference on the cable segment.
- **HVAC shielding—**By installing a shield around air conditioners and other similar equipment, you end up shielding them, and thereby keep EMI generated by that equipment inside the shield.
- **Faraday cage—**There are several types of Faraday cages. Screened cables such as coaxial cables for TV are basic examples. Booster bags lined with aluminum foil would be another example. But the term *Faraday cage* is usually applied to an entire room. If an entire room is shielded, electromagnetic energy cannot pass through the walls in either direction. So, if a person attempts to use a cell phone inside the cage, it will not function properly, because the signal cannot go beyond the cage walls; the cell phone cannot acquire a signal from a cell phone tower. More important, devices such as cell phones, motors, and wireless access points that create electromagnetic fields and are outside the cage cannot disrupt electromagnetic-sensitive devices that reside inside the cage.

By using shielding effectively, you can limit just about any type of interference. Some server rooms are shielded entirely to stop any type of wireless transmissions from entering or exiting the room. This can be an expensive proposition and is more common in data centers and advanced technology computer rooms. The pinnacle of shielding technology and research is TEMPEST, which according to some organizations stands for Transient ElectroMagnetic Pulse Emanations Standard, though the U.S. government has denied that the word is an acronym at all. The TEMPEST standards (as defined by the U.S. government) deal with the studies into compromising emissions, which are broken down into different levels according to particular environments and strictness of shielding necessary to those environments. Because computers and monitors give off electromagnetic radiation, there is a chance, if a hacker uses the proper antenna, that information could be recorded.

TEMPEST is a set of standards that govern the limiting of EM radiation, reducing the chance of the leakage of data. A TEMPEST-certified building can prevent wireless devices from being hacked by war-driving attacks and other similar wireless attacks.

If it were only so easy to shield people from the con: from what we call social engineering.

Social Engineering

Let's discuss a low note in our society. Because that is what social engineering is—a low form of behavior, but an effective one. It is estimated that 1 out of 10 people is conned every year through social engineering, and as many as half of them don't even know it has occurred.

We mentioned in Chapter 1, "Introduction to Security," that *social engineering* is the act of manipulating users into revealing confidential information or performing other actions detrimental to the user. Examples of social engineering are common in everyday life. A basic example would be a person asking for your username and password over the phone; often they will use flattery to gain the information they seek. Malicious people will use various forms of social engineering in an attempt steal whatever you have of value: your money, information, identity, confidential company data, or IT equipment. Social engineering experts use techniques such as bold impersonation, company jargon, embedding of questions, grooming trust, persistence and patience, and even emergency to gain their ends. The main reason that social engineering succeeds is due to lack of user awareness. But social engineering can also be effective in environments in which the IT personnel have little training and in public areas, for example public buildings with shared office space. Let's discuss some of the more common types of social engineering.

Pretexting

Pretexting is when a person invents a scenario, or pretext, in the hope of persuading a victim to divulge information. Preparation and some prior information are often needed before attempting a pretext; impersonation is often a key element. By impersonating the appropriate personnel or third-party entities, a person performing a pretext hopes to obtain records about an organization, its data, and its personnel. IT people and employees should always be on the lookout for impersonators and always ask for identification. If there is any doubt, the issue should be escalated to your supervisor and/or a call should be made to the authorities.

Diversion Theft

Diversion theft is when a thief attempts to take responsibility for a shipment by diverting the delivery to a nearby location. This happens more often than you would think, and millions of dollars of IT equipment are stolen in this manner everyday. It is important that couriers and other shippers know exactly where they are supposed to be delivering items, and that they are given an organization contact name, number, and possibly security code in the case that there is any confusion.

Phishing

Phishing is the attempt at fraudulently obtaining private information. A phisher usually masquerades as someone else, perhaps another entity. There are two main differences between phishing and pretexting. First, phishing is usually done by electronic communication/phone, not in person. Second, little information about the target is necessary. A phisher may target thousands of individuals without much concern as to their background. An example of phishing would be an e-mail that requests verification of private information. The e-mail will probably lead to a malicious website designed to lure people into a false sense of security to fraudulently obtain information. The website will often look like a legitimate website. While writing this chapter a common phishing technique is to pose as a vendor (such an online retailer or domain registrar) and send the target e-mail confirmations of orders that they supposedly placed.

This is a triple-whammy. First, the orders are obviously fake; a person might say "Hey wait! I didn't place these orders!" and perhaps click the link(s) in the e-mail leading them to the false web page. Second, if a person thinks it's a legitimate order (perhaps they do lots of orders, and the fraudulent one will look like another legitimate one) the person might click a link to track the order, again leading to the bogus web page. Third, once at the web page, they will be attempted to enter their credentials for their account (which then leads to credit card fraud and ID theft), and in addition to that the page might have Trojans and other malicious scripts. Sheesh. This same concept is also done by phone. Phone phishing (or vishing) works in the same manner but by phone; the phone call will sound like a prerecorded message from a legitimate institution (bank, online retailer, donation collector, and so on).

A lot of different types of social engineering are often lumped into what is referred to as phishing, but actual phishing for private information is normally limited to e-mail, websites, and phone. To defend against this, a phishing filter or add-on should be installed and enabled on the web browser. Also, a person should be trained to realize that institutions will *not* call or e-mail requesting private information. If people is not sure, they should hang up the phone or simply delete the e-mail. A quick way to find out if an e-mail is phishing for information is to hover over a link. You will see a URL domain name that is far different from the institution that the phisher is claiming to be, probably a URL located in a distant country.

Hoaxes

A *hoax* is the attempt at deceiving people into believing something that is false. The differences between hoaxes and phishing can be quite gray. However, hoaxes can come in person, or through other means of communication, whereas phishing is generally relegated to e-communication and phone. Although phishing can occur at any time, and with the specific goal of obtaining private information, a hoax can often be perpetuated on holidays or other special days and could be carried out simply for fun. Regardless, they can use up valuable organization resources: e-mail replies, Internet bandwidth used, time spent, and so on. An example of a "harmless" hoax was Google's supposed name change to "Topeka" on April Fools' Day, 2010. An example of a financially harmful hoax was the supposed assassination of Bill Gates on April Fools' Day, 2003. This hoax led to stock market fluctuations and loss of profit in Asia. Some companies place a time limit on jokes and hoaxes indicating that the affected person has become nonproductive; for example 3% of the workday.

Pretexting, diversion theft, phishing, and hoaxes are all known as *confidence tricks*, thus the term *con*, and are committed by "bunko" artists. However, there are even lower ways to get access to people's information; these will often be used with the previous methods. These include shoulder surfing, eavesdropping, dumpster diving, baiting, and piggybacking.

Shoulder Surfing

Shoulder surfing is when a person uses direct observation to find out a target's password, PIN, or other such authentication information. The simple resolution for this is for the user to shield the screen, keypad, or other authentication requesting devices. A more aggressive approach is to courteously ask the assumed shoulder surfer to move along. Also, private information should never be left on a desk or out in the open. Computer's should be locked or logged off when the user is not in the immediate area. Shoulder surfing and the following two sections are examples of no tech hacking.

Eavesdropping

Eavesdropping is when a person uses direct observation to "listen" in to a conversation. This could be a person hiding around the corner or a person tapping into a phone conversation. Sound proof rooms are often employed to stop eavesdropping, and encrypted phone sessions can also be implemented. For other phone eavesdropping mitigations, see Chapter 7, "Securing Network Media and Devices."

Dumpster Diving

Dumpster diving is when a person literally scavenges for private information in garbage and recyclable containers. Any sensitive documents should be stored in a safe place as long as possible. When they are no longer necessary, they should be shredded. (Some organizations will incinerate their documents.) Information might not only be found on paper, but also on hard drives or removable media. Proper recycling and/or destruction of hard drives is covered later in this chapter.

Baiting

Baiting is when a malicious individual leaves malware-infected removable media such as a USB drive or optical disc lying around in plain view. It might have an interesting logo or distinctive look about it. When a person takes it and connects it to their computer, the malware infects the computer and attempts to take control of it and/or the network the computer is a member of.

Piggybacking

Piggybacking is when an unauthorized person tags along with an authorized person to gain entry to a restricted area. This can be defeated through the use of turnstiles, double entry doors and by employing security guards.

Summary of Social Engineering Types

Table 15-1 summarizes the various types of social engineering we have discussed in this section.

Table 15-1 Summary of Social Engineering Types

Type	Description
Pretexting	When a person invents a scenario, or pretext, in the hope of persuading a victim to divulge information.
Diversion theft	When a thief attempts to take responsibility for a shipment by diverting the delivery to a nearby location.
Phishing	The attempt at fraudulently obtaining private information, usually done electronically.
Hoax	The attempt at deceiving people into believing something that is false.
Shoulder surfing	When a person uses direct observation to find out a target's password, PIN, or other such authentication information.
Eavesdropping	When a person uses direct observation to "listen" in to a conversation. This could be a person hiding around the corner or a person tapping into a phone conversation.
Dumpster diving	When a person literally scavenges for private information in garbage and recyclable containers.
Baiting	When a malicious individual leaves malware-infected removable media such as a USB drive or optical disc lying around in plain view in the hopes that unknowing people will bring it back to their computer and access it.
Piggybacking	When an unauthorized person tags along with an authorized person to gain entry to a restricted area.

In some cases, social engineering is an easier method than other more technical ways of hacking information. For example, if a malicious individual wanted a person's password, it might be a lot easier to trick people into giving their password than to try to crack it.

User Education and Awareness

User education and awareness training are the keys to helping reduce social engineering success. The following is a basic list of rules you can use when training employees:

- Never, under any circumstances, give out any authentication details such as passwords, PINs, company ID, and so on.
- Always shield keypads and screens when entering authentication information.
- Always screen your e-mail and phone calls carefully and keep a log of events.
- Use encryption when possible to protect e-mails and phone calls.
- If there is any doubt as to the legitimacy of a person, e-mail, or phone call, document the situation and escalate it to your supervisor, security, or the authorities.
- Never pick up, and make use of, any removable media.
- Always shred any sensitive information destined for the garbage or recycling.
- Always track and expedite shipments.

When training employees, try to make keep them interested; infuse some fun and examples. Use examples of social engineering so that your trainees can make the connection between actual social engineering methods and their defenses. Make them understand that social engineers don't care how powerful an organization's firewall is or how many armed guards they have. They get past technology and other types of security by exploiting the weaknesses inherent in human nature.

This previous lists of social engineering methods and defenses are in no way finite. There are so many ways to con a person and so many ways to defend against the con. However, some of the best weapons against social engineering, aside from user education and awareness, are policies and procedures, and their constant analysis. The next two sections detail some policies and procedures designed to protect sensitive information.

Legislative and Organizational Policies

There is a myriad of legislative laws and policies. For the Security+ exam, we are concerned only with a few that affect, and protect, the privacy of individuals. In this section, we cover those and some associated security standards.

More important for the Security + exam are organizational policies. Organizations usually define policies that concern how data is classified, expected employee behavior, and how to dispose of IT equipment that is no longer needed. These policies will begin with a statement or goal that is usually short and to the point and open-ended. They are normally written in clear language that can be understood by most everyone. They are followed by procedures (or guidelines) that detail how the policy will be implemented.

Table 15-2 shows an example of a basic policy and corresponding procedure.

Table 15-2 Example of a Company Policy

Policy	Procedure
Employees will identify themselves in a minimum of two ways when entering the complex.	**1.** When employees enter the complex, they will first enter a guard room. This will begin the authentication process. **2.** In the guard room, they must prove their identification in two ways: ■ By showing their ID badge to the on-duty guard. ■ By being visible to the guard so that the guard can compare their likeness to the ID badge's photo. The head of the employee should not be obstructed by hats, sunglasses, and so on. In essence, the employee should look similar to the ID photo. If the employee's appearance changes for any reason, that person should contact human resources for a new ID badge. * If guards cannot identify the "employee," they will contact the employee's supervisor, human resources, or security in an attempt to confirm the person's identity. If employees is not confirmed, they will be escorted out of the building by security. **3.** After the guard has acknowledged the identification, employees will swipe their ID badge against the door scanner to complete the authentication process and gain access to the complex.

Keep in mind that this is just a basic example; technical documentation specialists will tailor the wording to fit the feel of the organization. Plus, the procedure will be different depending on the size and resources of the organization and the type of authentication scheme used, which could be more or less complex. However, the *policy* (which is fairly common) is written in such a way as to be open-ended, allowing for the *procedure* to change over time. We'll talk about many different policies as they relate to the Security+ exam in this section.

Data Sensitivity and Classification of Information

Sensitive data is information that can result in a loss of security, or loss of advantage to a company, if accessed by unauthorized persons. Quite often, information is broken down into two groups: classified (which requires some level of security clearance) and nonclassified.

ISO/IEC 27002:2005 (which revises the older ISO/IEC 17799:2005) is a security standard that among other things can aid companies in classifying their data. Although you don't need to know the contents of that document for the Security+ exam, you should have a basic idea of how to classify information. For example, classification of data can be broken down, as shown in Table 15-3.

Table 15-3 Example of Data Sensitivity Classifications

Class	Description
Public information	Information available to anyone.
Internal information	Used internally by a company, but if it becomes public, no critical consequences results.
Confidential information	Information that can cause financial and operational loss to the company.
Secret information	Data that should never become public and is critical to the company.
Top secret information	The highest sensitivity of data, few should have access, security clearance may be necessary. Information is broken into sections on a *need-to-know* basis.

In this example, loss of public and internal information probably won't affect the company very much. However, unauthorized access, misuse, modification, or loss of confidential, secret, or top secret data can affect users' privacy, trade secrets, financials, and the general security of the company. By classifying data and enforcing policies that govern who has access to what information, a company can limit its exposure to security threats.

Many companies need to be in compliance with specific laws when it comes to the disclosure of information. In the United States there are a few acts you should know about, as shown in Table 15-4. In addition, there are several bills in process that will probably be passed in the near future regarding data breach notification.

Table 15-4 Acts Passed Concerning the Disclosure of Data and PII

Act	Acronym	Description
Privacy act of 1974	n/a	Establishes a code of fair information practice. Governs the collection, use, and dissemination of personally identifiable information about persons' records maintained by federal agencies.
Sarbanes-Oxley	SOX	Governs the disclosure of financial and accounting information. Enacted in 2002.
Health Insurance Portability and Accountability Act	HIPAA	Governs the disclosure and protection of health information. Enacted in 1996.
Gramm-Leach-Bliley Act	GLB	Enables commercial banks, investment banks, securities firms, and insurance companies to consolidate. Protects against pretexting. Individuals need proper authority to gain access to nonpublic information such as Social Security numbers.

Many computer technicians have to deal with SOX and HIPAA at some point in their careers, and although these types of acts create a lot of paperwork and protocol, the expected result is that, in the long run, they will help companies protect their data and keep sensitive information private.

Personnel Security Policies

Most organizations have policies governing employees. The breadth and scope of these policies will vary from organization to organization. For example, a small company might have a few pages defining how employees should behave (a code of ethics) and what to do in an emergency. Other larger organizations might go so far as to certify to a particular standard such as ISO 9001:2000 or ISO 9001:2008. This means that the organization will comply with a set of standards that is all-encompassing, covering all facets of the business. An organization would have to be examined and finally accredited by an accrediting certification body to state that it is ISO 9001:2000-certified. This is a rigorous process and is not for the average organization. For many companies, this would create too much documentation and would bog the company down in details and minutia.

We as IT people are more interested in policies that deal with the security of the infrastructure and its employees. As a network security administrator, you might deal with procedural documentation specialists, technical documentation specialists, and even outside consultants. You should become familiar with policies and as many procedures as possible, focusing on policies that take security into account, but remember that actual work must take precedence!

Let's define a few types of policies that are common to organizations. We'll focus on the security aspect of these policies.

Acceptable Use

Acceptable usage policies define the rules that restrict how a computer, network, or other system may be used. They state what users are, and are not, allowed to do when it comes to the technology infrastructure of an organization. Quite often, an AUP must be signed by the employees before they begin working on any systems. This protects the organization, but it also defines to employees exactly what they should, and should not, be working on. If a director asks a particular employee to repair a particular system that was outside of the AUP parameters, the employee would know to refuse. If employees are found working on a system that is outside the scope of their work, and they signed an AUP, it is grounds for termination. As part of an AUP, employees should understand that they are not to take any information or equipment home without express permission from the various parties listed in the policy.

Change Management

Change Management is a structured way of changing the state of a computer system, network, or IT procedure. The idea behind this is that change is necessary, but that an organization should adapt with change, and be knowledgeable of it. Any change that a person wants to make must be introduced to each of the heads of various departments that it might affect. They must approve the change before it goes into effect. Before this happens, department managers will most likely make recommendations and/or give stipulations. When the necessary people have signed off on the change, it should be tested and then implemented. During implementation, it should be monitored and documented carefully.

Because there are so many interrelated parts and people in an IT infrastructure, it is sometimes difficult for the left hand to know what the right hand is doing, or has done in the past. For example, after a network analysis, a network engineer might think that an unused interface on a firewall doesn't necessarily need to exist anymore. But does he know this for sure? Who installed and configured the interface? When was it enabled? Was it ever used? Perhaps it is used only rarely by special customers making a connection to a DMZ; perhaps it is used with a honeynet; or maybe it is for future use or for testing purposes. It would be negligent for the network engineer to simply modify the firewall without at least asking around to find out if the interface is necessary. More likely, there will be forms involved that require the network engineer to state the reason for change and have signed by several other people before making the change. In general this will slow down progress, but in the long run it will help to cover the network engineer. People were warned, and as long as the correct people involved have signed off on the procedure or technical change, the network engineer shouldn't have to worry. In a larger organization that complies with various certifications such as ISO 9001:2000, it can be a complex task. IT people should have charts of personnel and department heads. There should also be current procedures in place that show who needs to be contacted in the case of a proposed change.

Separation of Duties/Job Rotation

Separation of duties is when more than one person is required to complete a particular task or operation. This distributes control over a system, infrastructure, or particular task. Job rotation is one of the checks and balances that might be employed to enforce the proper separation of duties. It is used to increase user insight and skill level. Both of these policies are enforced to increase the security of an organization by limiting the amount of control a person has over a situation and by increasing employees' knowledge of what other employees are doing. For more information on these and similar concepts, see Chapter 9, "Access Control Methods and Models."

Mandatory Vacations

Some organizations require employees to take X amount of consecutive days vacation over the course of a year as part of their annual leave. For example, a company might require an IT director to take 5 consecutive days vacation at least once per year to force another person into their role for that time period. Although a company might state that this helps the person to rest and focus on their job, and incorporate job rotation, the underlying security concept is that it can help to stop any possible malicious activity that might occur such as sabotage, embezzlement, and so on. Because IT people are smart, and often access the network remotely in a somewhat unobserved fashion, auditing becomes very important.

Due Diligence

When it comes to information security, *due diligence* is ensuring that IT infrastructure risks are known and managed. An organization needs to spend time assessing risk and vulnerabilities and might state in a policy how it will give due diligence to certain areas of its infrastructure.

Due Care

Due care is the mitigation action that an organization takes to defend against the risks that have been uncovered during due diligence.

Due Process

Due process is the principle that an organization must respect and safeguard personnel's rights. This is to protect the employee from the state and from frivolous lawsuits.

User Education and Awareness Training

With so many possible organizational policies, employees need to be trained to at least get a basic understanding of them. Certain departments of an organization require more training than others. For example, Human Resources personnel need to understand many facets of the business and their corresponding policies, especially policies that affect personnel. HR people should be thoroughly trained in guidelines and enforcement. Sometimes the HR people train management and other employees on the various policies that those trainees are expected to enforce. In other cases, the trainer would be an executive assistant or outside consultant.

In addition, all employees should be trained on personally identifiable information (PII). This is information used to uniquely identify, contact, or locate a person. This type of information could be a name, Social Security number, biometric information, and so on. They should know what identifies them to the organization and how to keep that information secret and safe from outsiders. Another key element of user education is the dissemination of the password policy. They should understand that passwords should be complex, and know the complexity requirements. They should also understand never to give out their password or ask for another person's password to any resource.

IT personnel should be trained on what to do in the case of account changes. For example, temporarily disabling the account of employees when they take a leave of absence or disabling the account (or deleting it, less common) of an employee that has been terminated. All IT personnel should be fluent in the organization's password policy, lockout policy, and other user-related policies so that they can explain them to any other employees.

Summary of Personnel Security Policies

Table 15-5 breaks down and summarizes the various policy types mentioned in this section.

Table 15-5 Summary of Policy Types

Type	Description
Acceptable use	Policy that defines the rules that restrict how a computer, network, or other system may be used.
Change management	A structured way of changing the state of a computer system, network, or IT procedure.
Separation of duties	When more than one person is required to complete a task.
Job rotation	When a particular task is rotated among a group of employees.
Mandatory vacations	When an organization requires employees to take X amount of consecutive days vacation over the course of a year as part of their annual leave.

continues

Table 15-5 Summary of Policy Types (continued)

Type	Description
Due diligence	Ensuring that IT infrastructure risks are known and managed.
Due care	The mitigation action that an organization takes to defend against the risks that have been uncovered during due diligence.
Due process	The principle that an organization must respect and safeguard personnel's rights.

How to Deal with Vendors

Before we begin, I should mention that the following information is *not* intended as legal advice. Before signing any contracts, an organization should strongly consider consulting with an attorney.

An organization will often have in-depth policies concerning vendors. I can't tell you how many times I've seen issues occur because the level of agreement between the organization and the vendor was not clearly defined. A proper *service level agreement (SLA)* that is analyzed by the organization carefully before signing can be helpful. A basic service contract is usually not enough; a service contract with an SLA will have a section within it that formally and clearly defines exactly what a vendor is responsible for and what the organization is responsible for—a demarcation point so to speak. It might also define performance expectations and what the vendor will do if a failure of service occurs, timeframes for repair, backup plans, and so on. To benefit the organization, these will usually be legally binding and not informal. Due to this, it would benefit the organization to scrutinize the SLA before signing, and an organization's attorney should be involved in that process.

For instance, a company might use an ISP for its T3 connection. The customer will want to know what kind of fault-tolerant methods are on hand at the ISP and what kind of uptime they should expect, which should be monitored by a network admin. The SLA might have some sort of guarantee of measurable service that can be clearly defined. Perhaps a minimum level of service and a target level of service. Before signing an SLA such as this, it is recommended that an attorney, the IT director, and other organizational management review the document carefully and make sure that it covers all the points required by the organization.

How to Dispose of Computers and Other IT Equipment Securely

Organizations might opt to recycle computers and other equipment or donate them. Rarely do organizations throw away equipment. It might be illegal to do so depending on your location and depending on what IT equipment is to be thrown away. The first thing an IT person should do is consult the organization's policy regarding computer disposal, and if necessary, consult local municipal guidelines.

A basic example of a policy and procedure that an organization enforces might look like the following:

Policy: Recycle or donate IT equipment that has been determined to be outdated and nonproductive to the company.

Step 1. Define what equipment is to be disposed of.

Step 2. Obtain a temporary storage place for the equipment.

Step 3. Have appropriate personnel analyze the equipment.

- Verify whether the equipment is indeed outdated and if it can be used somewhere else in the organization.
- If a device can be used in another area of the organization, it should be formatted, flashed, or otherwise reset back to the original default, and then transported to its new location. See the procedure named "Resetting a device or computer to factory defaults" within document S-536 for more information.
- If a device cannot be reused in the organization, move to Step 4.

Step 4. Sanitize the devices or computers.

- Check for any removable media inside, or connected to, the computer. These should be analyzed and recycled within the organization if possible.
- Remove any RAM, label it with the computer name, and store it.
- Remove the hard drive, sanitize it, and store it.
- Reset any BIOS or other passwords to the default setting.

Step 5. Recycle or donate the item as required. See the procedure named "Recycling and donating IT equipment" within document S-536 for more information on whether to select recycling or donating.

Again, this is just an example of a basic recycle policy and procedure, but it gives you an idea of the type of method an organization might employ to best make use of their IT equipment and to organize the entire recycling/donating process.

In Step 4, we mentioned to "sanitize the hard drive." Sanitizing the hard drive is a common way of removing data but not the only one. The way data is removed might vary depending on its proposed final destination. Data removal is the most important element of computer recycling. Proper data removal goes far beyond file deletion or the formatting of digital media. The problem with file deletion/formatting is data remanence, or the residue, that is left behind, from which re-creation of files can be accomplished with the use of software such as SpinRite or Ontrack Data

Recovery. Companies typically employ one of three options when met with the prospect of data removal:

- **Clearing**—This is the removal of data with a certain amount of assurance that it cannot be reconstructed. The data is actually recoverable with special techniques. In this case, the media is recycled and used within the company again. The data wiping technique (also known as shredding) is used to clear data from media by overwriting new data to that media. In some cases, patterns of ones and zeros are written to the entire drive. Several software programs are available to accomplish this.
- **Purging**—Also known as sanitizing, this is once again the removal of data, but this time, it's done in such a way so that it cannot be reconstructed by any known technique; in this case the media is released outside the company. Special software (or other means) is employed to completely destroy all data on the media. It is also possible to degauss the disk, which will render the data unreadable but might also cause physical damage to the drive.
- **Destruction**—This is when the storage media is physically destroyed through pulverizing, incineration, and so on. At this point, the media can be disposed of in accordance with municipal guidelines.

The type of data removal used will be dictated by the data stored on the drive. If there is no personally identifiable information, or other sensitive information, it might simply be cleared and released outside the company. But in many cases, organizations will specify purging of data if the drive is to leave the building. In cases where a drive previously contained confidential or top secret data, the drive will usually be destroyed.

Incident Response Procedures

Incident response is a set of procedures that an investigator will go by when examining a computer security incident. Incident response procedures are a part of computer security incident management, which can be defined as the monitoring and detection of security events on a computer network and the execution of proper responses to those security events.

However, quite often, IT employees of the organization will discover the incident. Sometimes they will act as the investigators also. It depends on the resources and budget of the organization. So it is important for the IT personnel to be well briefed on policies regarding the reporting and disclosure of incidents.

Don't confuse an incident with an event. An example of a single event might be a single stop error on a Windows computer. In many cases, the BSOD won't occur again, and regardless, it has been logged in the case that it does. The event should be monitored but that is about all. An example of an incident would be when several DDOS attacks are launched at an organization's web servers over the course of a work day. This will require an incident response team that might include the network security administrator, IT or senior management, and possibly a liaison to the public and local municipality.

The seven main steps of the incident response process can be summed up simply as the following:

Step 1. **Identification**—The recognition of whether an event that occurs should be classified as an incident.

Step 2. **Containment**—Isolating the problem. For example, if it is a network attack, the attacker should be extradited to a padded cell. Or if only one server has been affected so far by a worm or virus, it should be physically disconnected from the network.

Step 3. **Evidence gathering**—Evidence of the incident is gathered by security professionals in a way that will preserve the evidence's integrity.

Step 4. **Investigation**—Investigators within the organization and perhaps consultants will ascertain exactly what happened and why.

Step 5. **Eradication**—Removal of the attack, threat, and so on.

Step 6. **Recovery**—Retrieve data, repair systems, re-enable servers, networks, and so on.

Step 7. **Documentation & Monitoring**—Document the process and make any changes to procedures and processes that are necessary for the future. Damage and loss should be calculated and that information should be shared with the accounting department of the organization. The affected systems should be monitored for any repercussions.

However, an organization might have more or less steps, and their procedures might vary. An organization's typical incident response policy and procedures will generally detail the following:

- **Initial incident management process—**This includes who first found the problem, tickets, and various levels of change controls. It also defines *first responders* (also known as first-level responders) who perform preliminary analysis of the incident data and determine whether the incident is actually an incident or just an event, and the criticality of the incident.
- **Emergency response detail—**If the incident is deemed to be an emergency, this details how the event is escalated to an emergency incident. It also specifies a coordinator of the incident, in which the incident team will meet, lock-down procedures, containment of the incident, repair and test of systems, and further investigation procedures to find the culprit (if there is one).
- **Computer forensics—**The incident response policy might define how computer forensics (or digital forensics) should be carried out. It might detail how

information is to be deciphered from a hard disk or other device. It might also specify a list of rules to go by when investigating what an attacker did. For example, forensics investigators will verify the integrity of data to ensure that it has not been tampered with. It is important that computer forensics investigations are carried out properly in the case that legal action is taken. Policies detailing the proper collection and preservation of evidence can be of assistance when this is the case.

- **Collection and preservation of evidence—**Sherlock Holmes based his investigations on traditional clues such as footprints, fingerprints, and cigar ash. Analogous to this, a security investigator needs to collect log files, alerts, captured packets, and so on and preserve the integrity of this information. Modification of any information during the investigative process will most likely void its validity in a court of law. One way to preserve evidence properly is to establish a *chain of custody*—the chronological documentation or paper trail of evidence. This is something that should be set up immediately at the start of an investigation; it documents who had custody of evidence all the way up to litigation or a court trial (if necessary) and verifies that the evidence has not been modified. An incident response policy will list proper procedures when it comes to the procurement of evidence.
- **Damage and loss control—**The incident response policy will also cover how to stop the spread of damage to other IT systems and how to minimize or completely curtail loss of data.

Of course, this type of policy will be much more in depth, specify exact procedures, and vary in content from organization to organization. To find out more about common practices and standards for incident response, see the ISO/IEC 27002:2005 standard. Due to the length and breadth of the information, there is far too much to cover in this book. (I left a link at the end of the chapter to this. You can also search the Internet for one of several documents that whittles down the content to a more manageable size—but still pretty hefty reading material!) The Security+ exam expects you to know t only he basics of incident response.

Now, I know what you are thinking. With all these policies and procedures in place, how does anything ever get done?! And how do incidents get analyzed quickly enough so as not to become a disaster? Well, training is important. Personnel need to be trained quickly and efficiently without getting too much into the minutia of things. They also need to be trained to *take action* quickly. By narrowing down an organization's policies to just what an employee needs to know, you can create a short but sweet list of key points for the employee to remember. Need-to-know is in itself an important security concept in companies. It is designed as much to hide information from people as it is to prevent information overload. For example, if a person were choking, the information you want to know is how to perform the Heimlich Maneuver; you don't care why a person chokes, what they ate for breakfast, or how specifically the maneuver works. This concept helps when there is an event or incident; the employees don't need to sift through wads of policies to find the right action to take, because they are on a need-to-know basis and will quickly execute what they have been trained to do. Need-to-know also comes into play when confidential or top secret information is involved. In classified environments, top secret information will be divided into pieces, only some of which particular people will have access to.

So that wraps up this chapter about policies, procedures, and people. It was a bit helter-skelter as far as the listing of content, but in a way, all the concepts are intertwined. When you are involved in any type of policing, investigative work, or other security-based IT work, consider the safety of personnel and data and the integrity of organizational information.

Exam Preparation Tasks

Review Key Topics

Review the most important topics in the chapter, noted with the Key Topics icon in the outer margin of the page. Table 15-6 lists a reference of these key topics and the page numbers on which each is found.

Table 15-6 Key Topics for Chapter 15

Key Topic Element	Description	Page Number
Bulleted list	Fire Extinguisher Types	436
Table 15-1	Summary of Social Engineering Types	444
Table 15-4	Acts Passed Concerning the Disclosure of Data and PII	448
Table 15-5	Summary of Policy Types	451
Numbered list	Seven Steps of Incident Response Process	455

Complete Tables and Lists from Memory

Print a copy of Appendix A, "Memory Tables," (found on the DVD), or at least the section for this chapter, and complete the tables and lists from memory. Appendix B, "Memory Tables Answer Key," also on the DVD, includes completed tables and lists to check your work.

Define Key Terms

Define the following key terms from this chapter, and check your answers in the glossary:

fire suppression, wet pipe sprinkler system, pre-action sprinkler system, special hazard protection system, pretexting, diversion theft, phishing, hoax, shoulder surfing, eavesdropping, dumpster diving, baiting, piggybacking, acceptable use, mandatory vacations, due diligence, due care, due process, change management, personally identifiable information (PII), service level agreement (SLA), first responders, chain of custody

View Recommended Resources

- ISO/IEC 27002:2005: Information technology—Security techniques—Code of practice for information security management: www.iso.org/iso/catalogue_detail?csnumber=50297

- Privacy Act of 1974: http://epic.org/privacy/laws/privacy_act.html and www.justice.gov/opcl/privstat.htm
- SpinRite data recovery software: www.grc.com/sr/spinrite.htm
- Ontrack Data Recovery: www.ontrackdatarecovery.com/file-recovery-software/
- *Journal of Digital Forensics, Security and Law*: www.jdfsl.org/
- *The International Journal of Forensic Computer Science*: www.ijofcs.org/
- *CISSP Video Mentor*: Shon Harris: www.pearsonitcertification.com/store/product.aspx?isbn=0789740303

Answer Review Questions

Answer the following review questions. You can find the answers at the end of this chapter.

1. Which method would you use if you were disposing hard drives as part of a company computer sale?

A. Destruction

B. Purging

C. Clearing

D. Formatting

2. Which of these governs the disclosure of financial data?

A. SOX

B. HIPAA

C. GLB

D. Top secret

3. Jeff wants to employ a Faraday cage. What will this accomplish?

A. It will increase the level of wireless encryption.

B. It will reduce data emanations.

C. It will increase EMI.

D. It will decrease the level of wireless emanations.

4. If a fire occurs in the server room, which device is the best method to put it out?

A. Class A extinguisher

B. Class B extinguisher

C. Class C extinguisher

D. Class D extinguisher

5. What device will not work in a Faraday cage? (Select the best two answers.)

A. Cell phones

B. Computers

C. Pagers

D. TDR

6. You go out the back door of your building and noticed someone looking through your company's trash. If this person were trying to acquire sensitive information, what would this attack be known as?

A. Browsing

B. Dumpster diving

C. Phishing

D. Hacking

7. You are told by your manager to keep evidence for later use at a court proceeding. Which of the following should you document?

A. Disaster recovery plan

B. Chain of custody

C. Key distribution center

D. Auditing

8. Which law protects your Social Security number and other pertinent information?

A. HIPAA

B. SOX

C. The National Security Agency

D. The Gramm-Leach-Bliley Act

9. User education can help to defend against which of the following? (Select the three best answers.)

A. Social engineering

B. Phishing

C. Rainbow tables

D. Dumpster diving

10. Which of these is an example of social engineering?

A. Asking for a username and password over the phone

B. Using someone else's unsecured wireless network

C. Hacking into a router

D. Virus

11. What is the most common reason that social engineering succeeds?

A. Lack of vulnerability testing

B. People share passwords

C. Lack of auditing

D. Lack of user awareness

12. Which of the following is *not* one of the steps of the incident response process?

A. Eradication

B. Recovery

C. Containment

D. Non-Repudiation

13. In which two environments would social engineering attacks be most effective? (Select the two best answers.)

A. Public building with shared office space

B. Company with a dedicated IT staff

C. Locked building

D. Military facility

E. An organization whose IT personnel have little training

14. Of the following definitions, which would be an example of eavesdropping?

A. Overhearing parts of a conversation

B. Monitoring network traffic

C. Another person looking through your files

D. A computer capturing information from a sender

15. Your company expects its employees to behave in a certain way. How could a description of this behavior be documented?

A. Chain of custody

B. Separation of duties

C. Code of ethics

D. Acceptable use policy

16. You are a forensics investigator. What is the most important reason for you to verify the integrity of acquired data?

A. To ensure that the data has not been tampered with

B. To ensure that a virus cannot be copied to the target media

C. To ensure that the acquired data is up-to-date

D. To ensure that the source data will fit on the target media

17. Of the following, which type of fire suppression can prevent damage to computers and servers?

A. Class A

B. Water

C. CO_2

D. ABC extinguishers

18. You are the security administrator for your organization. You have just identified a malware incident. Of the following, what should be your first response?

A. Containment

B. Removal

C. Recovery

D. Monitoring

19. A man pretending to be a data communications repair technician enters your building and states that there is networking trouble and he needs access to the server room. What is this an example of?

A. Man-in-the-middle attack

B. Virus

C. Social engineering

D. Chain of custody

20. Employees are asked to sign a document that describes the methods of accessing a company's servers. Which of the following best describes this document?

A. Acceptable use policy

B. Chain of custody

C. Incident response

D. Privacy Act of 1974

21. One of the developers for your company asks you what he should do before making a change to the code of a program's authentication. Which of the following processes should you instruct him to follow?

A. Chain of custody

B. Incident response

C. Disclosure reporting

D. Change management

22. As a network administrator, one of your jobs is to deal with Internet service providers. You want to ensure that the provider guarantees end-to-end traffic performance. What is this known as?

A. SLA

B. VPN

C. DRP

D. WPA

23. Turnstiles, double entry doors, and security guards are all preventative measures for what kind of social engineering?

A. Dumpster diving

B. Impersonation

C. Piggybacking

D. Eavesdropping

24. When it comes to security policies, what should HR personnel be trained in?

A. Maintenance

B. Monitoring

C. Guidelines and enforcement

D. Vulnerability assessment

25. In a classified environment, clearance to top secret information that enables access to only certain pieces of information is known as what?

A. Separation of duties

B. Chain of custody

C. Non-repudiation

D. Need to know

26. In addition to bribery and forgery, which of the following are the most common techniques that attackers used to socially engineer people? (Select the two best answers.)

A. Flattery

B. Assuming a position of authority

C. Dumpster diving

D. Whois search

27. What is documentation that describes minimum expected behavior known as?

A. Need to know

B. Acceptable usage

C. Separation of duties

D. Code of ethics

28. You are the security administrator for your company. You have been informed by human resources that one of the employees in accounting has been terminated. What should you do?

A. Delete the user account.

B. Speak to the employee's supervisor about the person's data.

C. Disable the user account.

D. Change the user's password.

Answers and Explanations

1. **B.** Purging (or sanitizing) removes all the data from a hard drive so that it cannot be reconstructed by any known technique. If a hard drive were destroyed, it wouldn't be of much value at a company computer sale. Clearing is the removal of data with a certain amount of assurance that it cannot be reconstructed; this method is usually used when recycling the drive within the organization. Formatting is not nearly enough to actually remove data because it leaves data residue which can be used to reconstruct data.
2. **A.** SOX, or Sarbanes-Oxley, governs the disclosure of financial and accounting data. HIPAA governs the disclosure and protection of health information. GLB, or the Gramm-Leach-Bliley Act of 1999, enables commercial banks, investment banks, securities firms, and insurance companies to consolidate. Top secret is a classification given to confidential data.
3. **B.** The Faraday cage will reduce data emanations. The cage is essentially an enclosure (of which there are various types) of conducting material that can block external electric fields and stop internal electric fields from leaving the cage, thus reducing or eliminating data emanations from such devices as cell phones.

4. **C.** When you think Class C, think Copper. Extinguishers rated as Class C can suppress electrical fires, which are the most likely kind in a server room.
5. **A and C.** Signals cannot emanate outside a Faraday cage. Therefore, cell phones and pagers will not work inside the Faraday cage.
6. **B.** Dumpster diving is when a person goes through a company's trash to find sensitive information about an individual or a company. Browsing is not an attack but something you do when connecting to the Internet. Phishing is known as acquiring sensitive information through the use of electronic communication. Nowadays, hacking is a general term used with many different types of attacks.
7. **B.** A chain of custody is the chronological documentation or paper trail of evidence. A disaster recovery plan details how a company will recover from a disaster with such methods as backup data and sites. A key distribution center is used with the Kerberos protocol. Auditing is the verification of logs and other information to find out who did what action and when and where.
8. **D.** The Gramm-Leach-Bliley Act protects private information such as Social Security numbers. HIPAA deals with health information privacy. SOX, or the Sarbanes Oxley Act of 2002, applies to publicly held companies and accounting firms and protects shareholders in the case of fraudulent practices.
9. **A, B, and D.** Rainbow tables are lookup tables used when recovering passwords. User education and awareness can help defend against social engineering attacks, phishing, and dumpster diving.
10. **A.** Social engineering is the practice of obtaining confidential information by manipulating people. Using someone else's network is just theft. Hacking into a router is just that, hacking. And a virus is a self-spreading program that may or may not cause damage to files and applications.
11. **D.** User awareness is extremely important when attempting to defend against social engineering attacks. Vulnerability testing and auditing are definitely important as part of a complete security plan but will not necessarily help defend against social engineering and definitely not as much as user awareness training. People should *not* share passwords.
12. **D.** Nonrepudiation, although an important of security, is not part of the incident response process. Eradication, containment, and recovery are all parts of the incident response process.
13. **A and E.** Public buildings, shared office space, and companies with employees that have little training are all environments in which social engineering attacks are common and would be most successful. Social engineering will be less successful in secret buildings, buildings with a decent level of security such as military facilities, and organizations with dedicated and well-trained IT staff.

14. **A.** Eavesdropping is when people listen to a conversation that they are not part of. A security administrator should keep in mind that someone could always be listening and to try to protect against this.

15. **C.** The code of ethics describes how a company wants its employees to behave. A chain of custody is a legal and chronological paper trail. Separation of duties means that more than one person is required to complete a job. Acceptable use policy is a set of rules that restrict how a network or a computer system may be used.

16. **A.** Before analyzing any acquired data, you need to make sure that the data has not been tampered with, so you should verify the integrity of the acquired data before analysis.

17. **C.** CO_2 is the best answer that will prevent damage to computers because it is air-based, not water-based. CO_2 displaces oxygen; fire needs oxygen, without it the fire will go out. All the others have substance that can damage computers. However, because CO_2 can possibly cause ESD damage, the best solution in a server room would be Halotron or FE-36.

18. **A.** Most organizations incident response procedures will specify that containment of the malware incident should be first. Next would be the removal, then recovery of any damaged systems, and finally monitoring that should actually be going on at all times.

19. **C.** Any person pretending to be a data communications repair person would be attempting a social engineering attack.

20. **A.** Acceptable use (or usage) policies set forth the principles for using IT equipment such as computers, servers, and network devices. Employees are commonly asked to sign such a document that is a binding agreement that they will try their best to adhere to the policy.

21. **D.** He should follow the change management process as dictated by your company's policies and procedures. This might include filing forms in paper format and electronically, and notifying certain departments of the proposed changes before they are made.

22. **A.** An SLA, or service-level agreement, is the agreement between the Internet service provider and you, finding how much traffic you are allowed, and what type of performance you can expect. A VPN is a virtual private network. A DRP is a disaster recovery plan. And WPA is Wi-Fi protected access.

23. **C.** Turnstiles, double entry doors, and security guards are all examples of preventative measures that attempts to defeat piggybacking. Dumpster diving is when a person looks through a coworkers trash or a buildings trash to retrieve information. Impersonation is when a person attempts to represent another person possibly with their identification. Eavesdropping is when a person overhears another person's conversation.

24. C. Human resource personnel should be trained in guidelines and enforcement. A company's standard operating procedures will usually have more information about this. However, a security administrator might need to train these employees in some of the areas of guidelines and enforcement.

25. D. In classified environments, especially when accessing top secret information, a person can get access to only what they need to know.

26. A and C. The most common techniques that attackers use to socially engineer people include flattery, dumpster diving, bribery, and forgery. Although assuming a position of authority is an example of social engineering, it is not one of the most common. A WHOIS search is not necessarily malicious, it can be accomplished by anyone and can be done for legitimate reasons. This type of search can tell a person who runs a particular website or who owns a domain name.

27. D. A code of ethics is documentation that describes the minimum expected behavior of employees of a company or organization. Need to know deals with the categorizing of data and how much an individual can access. Acceptable usage defines how a user or group of users may use a server or other IT equipment. Separation of duties refers to a task that requires multiple people to complete.

28. C. When an employee has been terminated, their account should be disabled, and the employees data should be stored for a certain amount of time, which should be dictated by the companies policies and procedures. There is no need to speak to the employee's supervisor. It is important not to delete the user account because the company may need information relating to that account later on. Changing the user's password is not enough; the account should be disabled.

This chapter covers the following subjects:

- **Getting Ready and the Exam Preparation Checklist**—This section give you a step-by-step list on how to go about taking the exam. It also shows one of my favorite study methods—the cheat sheet.
- **Tips for Taking the Real Exam**—In this section, you learn all my certification test taking techniques that I have developed over the past 15 years.
- **Beyond the CompTIA Security+ Certification**—This section briefly discusses your future and the possibilities that are out there.

CHAPTER 16

Taking the Real Exam

Now you've done it! You've accessed the final chapter. We are at the final countdown! This chapter shows you how to go about taking the exam. Then it goes over some tips and tricks I have used over the years that have helped me to pass the exam. Finally, we discuss some of the possible future avenues that can lead you to a career in IT security.

Foundation Topics

Getting Ready and the Exam Preparation Checklist

The CompTIA Security+ certification exams can be taken by anyone. There are no prerequisites; although, CompTIA recommends prior networking experience and the Network+ certification. For more information on CompTIA and the Security+ exam, go to www.comptia.org/certifications/listed/security.aspx.

To acquire your Security+ certification, you need to pass the SY0-201 exam, which is approximately 100 questions. As of the publishing of this book, the passing score is 750 on a scale of 100–900. You get 90 minutes to complete the exam. The exam is administered by two testing agencies: Sylvan Prometric (www.2test.com) and Pearson Vue (www.vue.com). You need to register with one of those test agencies to take the exam. The exam can be taken in English or Spanish.

NOTE: There is also a bridge exam available to *only* persons who have passed the 2002 version of the Security+ exam. It is exam code BR0-001, 50 questions, 60 minutes long, and requires a passing score of 560 on a scale of 100–900.

Because of the somewhat unorthodox grading scale, it is difficult to estimate exactly what percentage of questions you need to get correct to pass the exam. The best bet is to attempt to know as much as possible and shoot for 85% correct when *first* taking a practice exam.

It is important to be fully prepared for the exam, so I created a checklist that you can use to make sure you have covered all the bases. The checklist is shown in Table 16-1. Place a check in the status column as each item is completed. Historically, my readers and students have benefited greatly from this type of checklist.

Table 16-1 Exam Preparation Checklist

Step	Item	Details	SY0-201 Status
1.	Complete the Practice Exams in the book.	Directly after this chapter are two 100-question practice exams. Your goal should be to get at least 85% correct on each exam. Do not continue to another exam until you can get at least 85% correct on the first one. When using the practice exams, be sure to understand why the correct answer is correct and also why incorrect answers are incorrect. The explanations should help you in this regard. However, if any names, acronyms, or concepts seem new to you, go back to the chapter and section where the concept is covered and review them.	
2.	Complete the Practice Exam on the DVD.	The DVD contains one more 100-question practice exam. Keep taking it until you have reached 85% accuracy or better.	
3.	*(Optional)* Purchase and take the two additional exams.	Two additional 100-question practice exams are available for purchase online (written by yours truly). I get frequent requests from my readers and students asking for additional practice exams to get more preparation before taking the real exam. These can be purchased at www.pearsonitcertification.com/0132303381.	
4.	Visit my website.	Make use of my website (www.davidlprowse.com) to ask questions about any of the practice exam questions and explanations (or other questions about this book). That's why I am here! On the site you can find book errata, videos, and other materials, plus plenty of other questions that other readers and students have asked in the past. Your question might have been answered previously, but if not then I welcome you to start a new thread in the Ask Dave section.	
5.	Create a cheat sheet.	A cheat sheet can be very helpful for late-stage studying. See Table 16-2 for an example. The act of writing down important details helps to commit them to memory. This sheet should have facts that are tough to memorize. Due to this, each person's cheat sheet will vary. Keep in mind that you will not be allowed to take this into the actual testing room. (It's not actually for "cheating"!)	

Table 16-1 Exam Preparation Checklist

Step	Item	Details	SY0-201 Status
6.	Register for the exam.	Do not register until you have completed the previous steps; you shouldn't register until you are fully prepared. When you are ready, schedule the exam to commence within a day or two so that you won't forget what you learned! Registration can be done over the phone or online; although, online is much easier for many people. Register at one of the two websites: ■ Sylvan Prometric: www.2test.com ■ Pearson Vue: www.vue.com You need to input your personal information into a secure website. Afterward, you will be assigned an ID#, which you can refer to for all your exams. They accept payment by major credit card for the exam fee. To save some money, consider purchasing discounted exam vouchers from places such as www.getcertify4less.com/. If you choose to do this, you pay the company that provides you with the voucher (which is sent to you by email). Then, when you register for the exam with Sylvan or Vue, you input the voucher number, instead of paying by credit card.	
7.	Study the cheat sheet.	Study from the cheat sheet during the day or two between when you registered and the day of the exam. If your exam gets delayed for any reason, reschedule, then go back to steps 1 and 2 (and optionally 3), and retake the practice exams until the test day is a day or two away.	
8.	Take the exam!	Good luck! Check mark the column to the right when you pass! Feel free to shout out on my website when you have passed the exam.	

Table 16-2 gives a partial example of a cheat sheet that you can create to aid in your studies. For example, the first row shows common ports. Add information that you think is important or difficult to memorize. Keep the descriptions short and to the point. A few examples are listed in the table.

Table 16-2 Example Cheat Sheet

Concept	Fill in the Appropriate Information Here
Common Port numbers	Echo—Port 7 CHARGEN—Port 19 FTP—Port 21 (Complete for all ports.)
Access Control Models	MAC—Mandatory Access Control—Uses labels, has predefined privileges. DAC—Discretionary Access Control—Uses ACLs, or Access Control Lists. Owner of list establishes access permissions. RBAC—Role-Based Access Control—Permissions are assigned to roles instead of individual users. Users are assigned roles.
NIDS and NIPS	(Spell out the acronym and give a brief description)
The CIA of computer security	(Spell out the acronym and give a brief description)
Etc.*	

**Continue Table 16-2 in this fashion on paper. The key is to write down various technologies, processes, step-by-steps, and so on to commit them to memory.*

Tips for Taking the Real Exam

Some of you will be new to exams. This section is for you. For others who have taken exams before, feel free to skip this section or use it as a review.

The exam is conducted on a computer and is generally multiple choice. You have the option to skip questions. If you do so, be sure to "mark" them before moving on. There will be a small checkbox that you can select to mark them. Feel free to mark any other questions that you have answered but are not completely sure about. When you get to the end of the exam, there will be an item review section, which shows you any questions that you did not answer and any that you marked. Though you shouldn't mark a lot of items and don't want to skip around too much, sometimes it is unavoidable and can save time in the long run if a question is overly difficult. A good rule of thumb is to keep the marked questions between 10% and 20%.

The following list includes tips and tricks that I have learned over the years when it comes to taking exams. By utilizing these points, you can easily increase your score.

First, let's talk about some good general practices for taking exams:

- **Pick a good time for the exam—**It would appear that the least amount of people are at test centers on Monday and Friday mornings. Consider scheduling during these times. Otherwise, schedule a time that works well for you, when you don't have to worry about anything else. Keep in mind that Saturdays can be busy.
- **Don't over-study the day before the exam—**Some people like to study hard the day before; some don't. My recommendations are to study off the cheat sheet you created, but in general, don't overdo it. It's not a good idea to go into overload the day before the exam.
- **Get a good night's rest—**A good night's sleep (7 hours to 9 hours) before the day of the exam is probably the best way to get your mind ready for an exam.
- **Eat a decent breakfast—**Eating is good! Breakfast is number two when it comes to getting your mind ready for an exam, especially if it is a morning exam. Just watch out for the coffee and tea. Too much caffeine for a person who is not used to it can be detrimental to the thinking process.
- **Show up early—**Both testing agencies recommend that you show up 30 minutes prior to your scheduled exam time. This is important; give yourself plenty of time, and make sure you know where you are going. You don't want to have to worry about getting lost or being late. Stress and fear are the mind killers. Work on reducing any types of stress the day of and the day before the exam. By the way, you really do need extra time because when you get to the testing center, you need to show ID, sign forms, get your personal belongings situated, and be escorted to the your seat. Have two forms of ID (signed) ready for the administrator of the test center. Turn your cell phone or PDA off when you get to the test center; they'll check that, too.
- **Bring ear plugs—**You never know when you will get a loud testing center—or worse yet, a loud test taker next to you. Ear plugs help to block out any unwanted noise that might show up. Just be ready to show your ear plugs to the test administrator.

- **Brainstorm before starting the exam—**Write down as much as you can remember from the cheat sheet before starting the exam. The testing center is obligated to give you *something* to write on; make use of it! By getting all the memorization out of your head and on "paper" first, it clears the brain somewhat so that it can tackle the questions. I put paper in quotation marks because it might not be paper; it could be a mini dry erase board or something similar.
- **Take small breaks while taking the exam—**Exams can be brutal. You have to answer one hundred questions while staring at a screen for an hour. Sometimes these screens are old and have seen better days; these older flickering monitors can cause a strain on your eyes. I recommend small breaks and breathing techniques. For example, after going through every 25 questions or so, close your eyes, and slowly take a few deep breaths, holding each one for 5 seconds or so, and releasing each one slowly. Think about nothing while doing so. Remove the test from your mind during these breaks. It takes only half a minute but can really help to get your brain refocused.
- **Be confident—**You have studied hard, gone through the practice exams, created your cheat sheet—done everything you can to prep. These things alone should build confidence. But really, you just have to *be* confident. You are great...I am great...there is no disputing this!

Now let's talk about some methods to use when faced with difficult questions. Use the following methods in the face of all difficult questions.

- **Use the process of elimination—**If you are not sure about an answer, first eliminate any answers that are definitely *incorrect*. You might be surprised how often this works. This is one of the reasons why it is recommended that you not only know the correct answers to the practice exams' questions, but also know *why* the wrong answers are wrong. The testing center should give you something to write on; use it by writing down the letters of the answers that are incorrect to keep track.

NOTE: Check out this chapter's Hands-On Lab. It shows me going through five questions as if I were taking an exam and shows some of my tips and tricks to taking the exam.

- **Be logical in the face of adversity—**The most difficult questions are when two answers appear to be correct, even though the test question requires you to select only one answer. Real exams do not rely on "trick" questions. Sometimes you need to slow down, think logically, and really *compare* the two possible correct answers.

- **Use your gut instinct**—Sometimes a person taking a test just doesn't know the answer; it happens to everyone. If you have read through the question and all the answers and used the process of elimination, sometimes the gut instinct is all you have left. In some scenarios you might read a question and instinctively know the answer, even if you can't explain why. Tap into this ability. Some test takers write down their gut instinct answer before delving into the question and then compare their thoughtful answer with their gut instinct answer.
- **Don't let one question beat you!**—Don't let yourself get stuck on one question. Mark it, move on to the next question, and return to it later. When you spend too much time on one question, the brain gets sluggish. The thing is, with these exams you either know it or you don't. And don't worry too much about it; chances are you are not going to get a perfect score. Remember that the goal is only to pass the exams; how many answers you get right after that is irrelevant. If you have gone through this book thoroughly, you should be well prepared, and you should have plenty of time to go through all the exam questions with time to spare to return to the ones you skipped and marked.
- **If all else fails, guess**—Remember that the exams might not be perfect. A question might seem confusing or appear not to make sense. Leave questions like this until the end, and when you have gone through all the other techniques mentioned, make an educated, logical guess. Try to imagine what the test is after, and why they would be bringing up this topic, vague or strange as it might appear.

And when you finish:

- **Review all your answers**—Use the time allotted to you to review the answers. Chances are you will have time left over at the end, so use it wisely! Make sure that everything you have marked has a proper answer that makes sense to you. But try not to over think! Give it your best shot and be confident in your answers.

Beyond the CompTIA Security+ Certification

After you pass the exams, consider thinking about your technical future. Technical growth is important. Keeping up with new technology and keeping your technical skills sharp are what can keep you in demand. This technical growth equals job security.

Information Technology (IT) people need to keep learning to foster good growth in the field. Consider taking other certification exams after you complete the Security+. The CompTIA Security+ certification acts as a springboard to other certifications. For example, you might choose to go for other more difficult nonvendor certifications such as the CISSP. And of course, there are vendor-specific certifications from Microsoft, Cisco, Check Point, and many others. Now that you know exactly how to go about passing a security-based certification exam, consider more certifications to bolster your resume.

The best advice I can give is to do what you love. From an IT perspective, I usually break it down by technology, as opposed to by the vendor. For example, you might want to learn more about firewalls. If that is the case, you should delve into Check Point appliances, Cisco PIX and ASA devices, Microsoft ISA Server/Forefront, and as many of the SOHO router/firewalls that you can get your hands on. And that is just a small sample of what is out there where firewalls are concerned. Plus, that is just one portion of the security field. Whatever segment (or segments) of security you decide to pursue, learn as much as you can about that field(s) and all its vendors to stay ahead. Read up on the latest technologies, visit security websites, read security periodicals, and keep in touch with other fellow security people. Consider security conferences and seminars and ongoing training. Taking it to the next level, you might decide that there is a security threat that you would like to address. Who knows, in the future you might be interested in developing a security application or secure hardware device. My advice is this: Good engineering can usually defy malicious individuals; the better you plan your security product, the less chance of it being hacked.

Whatever you decide, I wish you the best of luck in your IT career endeavors. And remember that I am available to answer any of your questions about this book via my website: www.davidlprowse.com.

Hands-On Lab

Lab 16-1, "How to Approach Exam Questions," has only a video solution. There is no step-by-step lab to go through first, so just proceed to watching the video.

There are no other Exam Preparation Tasks for this chapter as there are for the other chapters. After you have watched the video, move on to the two practice exams after this chapter.

The 100 multiple-choice questions provided here help you to determine how prepared you are for the actual exam, and which topics you need to review further. Write down your answers on a separate sheet of paper so that you can take this exam again if necessary. Compare your answers against the answer key that follows this exam.

Practice Exam 1: CompTIA Security+ SY0-201

1. What are the three main goals of information security? (Select the three best answers.)

   A. Auditing

   B. Integrity

   C. Nonrepudiation

   D. Confidentiality

   E. Risk Assessment

   F. Availability

2. Which method would you use if you were disposing of hard drives as part of a company computer sale?

   A. Destruction

   B. Purging

   C. Clearing

   D. Formatting

3. Which of these governs the disclosure of financial data?

   A. SOX

   B. HIPAA

   C. GLB

   D. Top secret

4. Virtualization technology is often implemented as operating systems and/or applications that run in software. Quite often, it is implemented as a virtual machine. Of the following, which can be a security benefit when using virtualization?

A. Patching a computer will patch all virtual machines running on the computer.

B. If one virtual machine is compromised, none of the other virtual machines can be compromised.

C. If a virtual machine is compromised, the adverse effects can be compartmentalized.

D. Virtual machines cannot be affected by hacking techniques.

5. Jeff wants to employ a Faraday cage. What will this accomplish?

A. It will increase the level of wireless encryption.

B. It will reduce data emanations.

C. It will increase EMI.

D. It will decrease the level of wireless emanations.

6. Which of the following is the verification of a person's identity?

A. Authorization

B. Accountability

C. Authentication

D. Password

7. If a fire occurs in the server room, which device is the best method to put it out?

A. Class A extinguisher

B. Class B extinguisher

C. Class C extinguisher

D. Class D extinguisher

8. Which of the following would you set up utilizing a router?

A. DMZ

B. DOS

C. OSI

D. ARP

9. Which of the following is a group of compromised computers that have software installed by a worm?

   A. Botnet
   B. Virus
   C. Honeypot
   D. Zombie

10. Which of the following is the strongest password?

    A. |ocrian#
    B. Marqu1sD3S0d
    C. This1sV#ryS3cure
    D. Thisisverysecure

11. Which of the following is an example of a nonessential protocol?

    A. DNS
    B. ARP
    C. HTTPS
    D. TFTP

12. Which of the following would fall into the category of "something a person is"?

    A. Passwords
    B. Passphrases
    C. Fingerprints
    D. Smart cards

13. What are some of the drawbacks to using HIDS instead of NIDS on a server? (Select the two best answers.)

    A. HIDS may use a lot of resources that can slow server performance.
    B. HIDS cannot detect operating system attacks.
    C. HIDS have a low level of detection of operating system attacks.
    D. HIDS cannot detect network attacks.

14. Which of these is a security component of Windows Vista?

A. UAC

B. UPS

C. Gadgets

D. Control Panel

15. What Windows key combination helps to secure the logon process?

A. Windows+R

B. Ctrl+Shift+Esc

C. Ctrl+Alt+Del

D. Alt+F4

16. Which of the following computer security threats can be updated automatically and remotely? (Select the best answer).

A. A Virus

B. A Worm

C. A Zombie

D. Malware

17. Which of the following is the best utility or process to use when scanning for viruses?

A. Safe Mode

B. Last Known Good Configuration

C. Command Prompt only

D. Boot into Windows normally

18. Which of the following is a common symptom of spyware?

A. Infected files

B. Computer shuts down

C. Applications freeze

D. Pop-up windows

19. Eric wants to install an isolated operating system. What is the best tool to use?

A. UAC

B. Virtualization

C. HIDS

D. NIDS

20. Which of the following is one way of preventing spyware?

A. Use firewall exceptions.

B. Adjust web browser security settings.

C. Adjust the web browser home page.

D. Remove the spyware from Add/Remove Programs.

21. What Windows key combination should be used to close a pop-up window?

A. Windows+R

B. Ctrl+Shift+Esc

C. Ctrl+Alt+Del

D. Alt+F4

22. Where would you turn off file sharing in Windows Vista?

A. Control Panel

B. Local area connection

C. Network and Sharing Center

D. Firewall properties

23. Which type of encryption technology is used with the BitLocker application?

A. Symmetric

B. Asymmetric

C. Hashing

D. WPA2

24. Which tool would you use if you want to view the contents of a packet?

A. TDR

B. Port scanner

C. Protocol analyzer

D. Loopback adapter

25. Which option enables you to hide ntldr?

A. Enable Hide protected operating system files

B. Disable Show hidden files and folders

C. Disable Hide protected operating system files

D. Remove the –R attribute

26. A person attempts to access a server during a zone transfer to get access to a zone file. What type of server is he trying to manipulate?

A. Proxy server

B. DNS server

C. File server

D. Web serverA

27. Which of the following is a private IP address?

A. 11.16.0.1

B. 127.0.0.1

C. 172.16.0.1

D. 208.0.0.1

28. Which of these hides an entire network of IP addresses?

A. SPI

B. NAT

C. SSH

D. FTP

29. Which command would display the following output?

```
Active Connections
   Proto  Local Address          Foreign Address        State
   TCP    laptop-musicxpc:1395   8.15.228.165:http      ESTABLISHED
```

A. Ping

B. Ipconfig

C. Nbtstat

D. Netstat

30. Which of the following is the most secure protocol to use when accessing a wireless network?

A. WEP

B. WPA

C. WPA2

D. WEP2

31. Which of the following are good practices for tracking user identities? (Select the two best answers.)

A. Video cameras

B. Key card door access systems

C. Sign-in sheets

D. Security guards

32. What are two examples of common single sign-on authentication configurations?

A. Biometrics-based

B. Multifactor authentication

C. Kerberos-based

D. Smart card-based

33. Which of the following answers are not part of IPSec? (Select the two best answers.)

A. TKIP

B. Key exchange

C. AES

D. Authentication header

34. Which protocol can be used to secure the e-mail login from an Outlook client using POP3 and SMTP?

A. SMTP

B. SPA

C. SAP

D. Exchange

35. What are two ways to secure the computer within the BIOS? (Select the two best answers.)

A. Configure a supervisor password.

B. Turn on BIOS shadowing.

C. Flash the BIOS.

D. Set the hard drive first in the boot order.

36. What type of cabling is the most secure for networks?

A. STP

B. UTP

C. Fiber optic

D. Coaxial

37. Dan is a network administrator. One day he notices that his DHCP server is flooded with information. He analyzes it and finds that the information is coming from more than 50 computers on the network. Which of the following is the most likely reason?

A. Virus

B. Worm

C. Zombie

D. PHP script

38. Which one of the following can monitor and protect a DNS server?

A. Ping the DNS server.

B. Block port 53 on the firewall.

C. Purge PTR records daily.

D. Check DNS records regularly.

39. The honeypot concept is enticing to administrators because

A. It enables them to observe attacks.

B. It traps an attacker in a network.

C. It bounces attacks back at the attacker.

D. It traps a person physically between two locked doors.

40. Which of the following is not an example of malicious software?

A. Rootkits

B. Spyware

C. Viruses

D. Browser

41. Which of the following can provide an integrity check?

A. Public key

B. Private key

C. WEP

D. Hash

42. Which two devices do not work in a Faraday cage? (Select the two best answers.)

A. Cell phones

B. Computers

C. Pagers

D. TDR

43. Which of the following is a record of the tracked actions of users?

A. Performance Monitor

B. Audit trails

C. Permissions

D. System and event logs

44. Which of the following is the most common authentication model?

A. Username and password

B. Biometrics

C. Key cards

D. Tokens

45. Which of the following access control methods uses rules to govern whether object access will be allowed?

A. Discretionary access control

B. Role-based access control

C. Rule-based access control

D. Mandatory access control

46. Which TCP port does LDAP use?

A. 389

B. 80

C. 443

D. 143

47. When using the mandatory access control model, what component is needed?

A. Labels

B. Certificates

C. Tokens

D. RBAC

48. Which type of vulnerability assessments software checks for weak passwords on the network?

A. Antivirus software

B. Password cracker

C. Performance Monitor

D. Wireshark

49. Which of the following RAID versions provides for the least amount of downtime in the event of a disk failure?

A. RAID 0

B. RAID 1

C. RAID 4

D. RAID 5

50. Which of the following authentication methods uses a KDC?

A. Kerberos

B. SSL

C. CHAP

D. Biometrics

51. Of the following, which authentication model enables a user to access to multiple resources without giving multiple credentials?

A. Mandatory access control

B. Three-factor authentication

C. Single sign-on

D. DAC

52. Which ports are used for e-mail? (Select the two best answers.)

A. 110

B. 3389

C. 143

D. 389

53. Kerberos uses which of the following? (Select the two best answers.)

A. Ticket distribution service

B. The Faraday cage

C. Port 389

D. Authentication service

54. You go out the back door of your building and notice someone looking through your company's trash. If this person were trying to acquire sensitive information, what is the type of attack?

A. Browsing

B. Dumpster diving

C. Phishing

D. Hacking

55. Why would a hacker use steganography?

A. To hide information

B. For data integrity

C. To encrypt information

D. For wireless access

56. You are told by your manager to keep evidence for later use at a court proceeding. Which of the following should you document?

A. Disaster recovery plan

B. Chain of custody

C. Key distribution center

D. Auditing

57. Which law protects your Social Security number and other pertinent information?

A. HIPAA

B. SOX

C. National Security Agency

D. Gramm-Leach-Bliley Act

58. What should you configure to improve wireless security?

A. Enable the SSID

B. IP spoofing

C. Remove repeaters

D. MAC filtering

59. Which type of attack uses more than one computer?

A. Virus

B. DoS

C. Worm

D. DDoS

60. To protect against malicious attacks, what should you think like?

A. Hacker

B. Network admin

C. Spoofer

D. CEO

61. Tom sends out many e-mails containing secure information to competing companies. What concept should be implemented to prove that Tom did indeed send the e-mails?

A. Authenticity

B. Nonrepudiation

C. Confidentiality

D. Integrity

62. Which of the following does not apply to an x.509 certificate?

A. Certificate version

B. Issuer of the certificate

C. Public key information

D. Owner's symmetric key

63. User education can help to defend against which of the following? (Select the three best answers.)

A. Social engineering

B. Phishing

C. Rainbow tables

D. Dumpster diving

64. What are the two ways that you can stop employees from using USB flash drives? (Select the two best answers.)

A. Use RBAC.

B. Disable USB devices in the BIOS.

C. Disable the USB root hub.

D. Employee MAC filtering.

65. Which of the following does not need updating?

A. HIDS

B. Antivirus software

C. Pop-up blockers

D. Antispyware

66. The Domain Name System uses which port number?

A. 53

B. 80

C. 110

D. 88

67. Which of the following are Bluetooth threats? (Select the two best answers.)

A. Blue snarfing

B. Blue bearding

C. Bluejacking

D. Distributed denial of service

68. A malicious attack that executes at the same time every week would be known as what?

A. Virus

B. Worm

C. Bluejacking

D. Logic bomb

69. Which of the following should be implemented to harden a Windows operating system? (Select the two best answers.)

A. Install the latest service pack.

B. Install Windows Defender.

C. Install a virtual operating system.

D. Execute PHP scripts.

70. Which of these is true for active inception?

A. When a computer is put between a sender and receiver

B. When a person overhears a conversation

C. What a person looks through files

D. When a person hardens an operating system

71. James has detected an intrusion in his company. What should he check first?

A. DNS logs

B. Firewall logs

C. The Event Viewer

D. Performance logs

72. Which of the following statements best describes a static NAT?

A. Static NAT uses a one-to-one mapping.

B. Static NAT uses a many-to-many mapping.

C. Static NAT uses a one-to-many mapping.

D. Static NAT uses a many-to-one mapping.

73. You need to encrypt and send a large amount of data. Which of the following would be the best option?

A. Symmetric encryption

B. Hashing algorithm

C. Asymmetric encryption

D. PKI

74. Which of the following can facilitate a full recovery within minutes?

A. Warm site

B. A Cold site

C. Reestablishing a mirror

D. Hot site

75. What does a virtual private network use to connect one host to another? Select the best answer.

A. Modem

B. Network adapter

C. Internet

D. Cell phone

76. Which of the following statements regarding the mandatory access control model is true?

A. Mandatory access control is a dynamic model.

B. Mandatory access control enables an owner to establish access privileges to a resource.

C. Mandatory access control is not restrictive.

D. Mandatory access control users cannot share resources dynamically.

77. Tim believes that his computer has a worm. What is the best tool to use to remove that worm?

A. Antivirus software

B. Antispyware software

C. HIDS

D. NIDS

78. Imagine that you are a hacker. Which would be most desirable when attempting to compromise encrypted data?

A. Weak key

B. Algorithm used by the encryption protocol

C. Captured traffic

D. Block cipher

79. What is the best practice to use to code applications in a secure manner?

A. Cross site scripting

B. Flash version 3

C. Input validation

D. HTML version 5

80. An SHA algorithm block size will have how many bits?

A. 64

B. 128

C. 512

D. 1024

81. Which of the following protocols is the least suitable for a VPN?

A. PPTP

B. L2TP

C. PPP

D. IPSec

82. In Windows XP and Windows Vista, what is the best file system to use?

A. FAT

B. NTFS

C. DFS

D. FAT32

83. In a wireless network, why is an SSID used?

A. To secure the wireless access point

B. To identify the network

C. To encrypt data

D. To enforce MAC filtering

84. In the DAC model, how are permissions identified?

A. Role membership.

B. Access control lists.

C. They are predefined.

D. It is automatic.

85. You are contracted to conduct a forensics analysis of the computer. What should you do first?

A. Back up the system.

B. Analyze the files.

C. Scan for viruses.

D. Make changes to the operating system.

86. This tool enables you to be alerted if a server's processor trips a certain threshold.

A. TDR

B. Password cracker

C. Event Viewer

D. Performance Monitor

87. The IT director has asked you to install agents on several client computers and monitor them from a program at a server. What is this known as?

A. SNMP

B. SMTP

C. SMP

D. Performance Monitor

88. One of your coworkers complains to you that she cannot see any security events in the Event Viewer. What are three possible reasons for this? (Select the three best answers.)

A. Auditing has not been turned on.

B. The log file is only 512 KB.

C. The coworker is not an administrator.

D. Auditing for an individual object has not been turned on.

89. What is another term for secret key encryption?

A. PKI

B. Asymmetrical

C. Symmetrical

D. Public key

90. What two items are included in a digital certificate? (Select the two best answers.)

A. User's private key

B. Certificate Authority's digital signature

C. User's public key

D. Certificate Authority's IP address

91. What device should be used to ensure that a server does not shut down when a power outage occurs?

A. RAID 1 box

B. UPS

C. Redundant NIC

D. Hot site

92. Which of the following tape backup methods enables for daily backups, weekly full backups, and monthly full backups?

A. Towers of Hanoi

B. Incremental

C. Grandfather-father-son

D. Differential

93. Which tool can be instrumental in capturing FTP GET requests?

A. Vulnerability scanner

B. Port scanner

C. Performance Monitor

D. Protocol analyzer

94. What are two ways to secure Internet Explorer? (Select the two best answers.)

A. Set the Internet zone's security level to **High**.

B. Disable the pop-up blocker.

C. Disable ActiveX controls.

D. Add malicious sites to the Trusted Sites zone.

95. Which of the following devices should you employ to protect your network? (Select the best answer)

A. Protocol analyzer

B. Firewall

C. DMZ

D. Proxy server

96. Which of the following is an example of two-factor authentication?

A. L2TP and IPSec

B. Username and password

C. Thumb print and key card

D. Client and server

97. Which of the following has schemas written in XML?

A. OVAL

B. 3DES

C. WPA

D. PAP

98. Your boss wants you to set up an authentication scheme in which employees will use smart cards to log into the company network. What kind of key should be used to accomplish this?

A. Private key

B. Public key

C. Cipher key

D. Shared key

99. When it comes to information security, what is the I in CIA?

A. Integrated

B. Interface

C. Integrity

D. Infrared

100. When is a system completely secure?

A. When it is updated

B. When it is assessed for vulnerabilities

C. When all anomalies have been removed

D. Never

Answers to Practice Exam 1

Answers at a Glance

1. B, D, and F	**26.** B	**51.** C	**76.** D
2. B	**27.** C	**52.** A and C	**77.** A
3. A	**28.** B	**53.** A and D	**78.** A
4. C	**29.** D	**54.** B	**79.** C
5. B	**30.** C	**55.** A	**80.** C
6. C	**31.** A and B	**56.** B	**81.** C
7. C	**32.** C and D	**57.** D	**82.** B
8. A	**33.** A and C	**58.** D	**83.** B
9. A	**34.** B	**59.** D	**84.** B
10. C	**35.** A and D	**60.** A	**85.** A
11. D	**36.** C	**61.** B	**86.** D
12. C	**37.** B	**62.** D	**87.** A
13. A and D	**38.** D	**63.** A, B, and D	**88.** A, C, and D
14. A	**39.** A	**64.** B and C	**89.** C
15. C	**40.** D	**65.** C	**90.** B and C
16. C	**41.** D	**66.** A	**91.** B
17. A	**42.** A and C	**67.** A and C	**92.** C
18. D	**43.** B	**68.** D	**93.** D
19. B	**44.** A	**69.** A and B	**94.** A and C
20. B	**45.** C	**70.** A	**95.** B
21. D	**46.** A	**71.** B	**96.** C
22. C	**47.** A	**72.** A	**97.** A
23. A	**48.** B	**73.** A	**98.** A
24. C	**49.** B	**74.** D	**99.** C
25. A	**50.** A	**75.** C	**100.** D

Answers with Explanations

1. Answers: B, D, and F. Confidentiality, Integrity, and Availability (known as CIA or the CIA triad) are the three *main* goals of information security. Another goal within information security is Accountability. See the section titled "Security 101" in Chapter 1, "Introduction to Security," for more information.

2. Answer: B. Purging (or sanitizing) removes all the data from a hard drive so that it cannot be reconstructed by any known technique. See the section titled "Legislative and Organizational Policies" in Chapter 15, "Policies, Procedures, and People," for more information.

3. Answer: A. SOX, or Sarbanes-Oxley, governs the disclosure of financial and accounting data. See the section titled "Legislative and Organizational Policies" in Chapter 15, "Policies, Procedures, and People," for more information.

4. Answer: C. By using a virtual machine (which is one example of a virtual instance) any ill effects can be compartmentalized to that particular virtual machine, usually without any ill effects to the main operating system on the computer. This is because the virtual machine is isolated from the main OS. Patching a computer does not automatically patch virtual machines existing on the computer. Other virtual machines can be compromised, especially if nothing is done about the problem. If a particular piece of spyware finds its way to one virtual machine from the Internet, chances are the same spyware can do the same to other virtual machines. Finally, virtual machines can definitely be affected by hacking techniques. Be sure to secure them! See the section titled "Virtualization Technology" in Chapter 3, "OS Hardening and Virtualization," for more information.

5. Answer: B. The Faraday cage will reduce data emanations. The cage is essentially an enclosure (of which there are various types) of conducting material that can block external electric fields and stop internal electric fields from leaving the cage, thus reducing or eliminating data emanations devices such as cell phones. See the section titled "Environmental Controls" in Chapter 15, "Policies, Procedures, and People," for more information.

6. Answer: C. Authentication is the verification of a person's identity. Authorization to specific resources cannot be accomplished without previous authentication of the user. See the section titled "Authentication Models and Components" in Chapter 8, "Physical Security and Authentication Models," for more information.

7. Answer: C. When you think Class C, think "Copper." Class C extinguishers can suppress electrical fires, which are the most likely kind in a server room. See the section titled "Environmental Controls" in Chapter 15, "Policies, Procedures, and People," for more information.

8. Answer: A. A DMZ, or demilitarized zone, can be set up utilizing a router to create a sort of safe haven for servers. It is neither the LAN nor the Internet, but instead, a location in between, or parallel, to the two. See the section titled “Network Design” in Chapter 5, “Network Design Elements and Network Threats,” for more information.

9. Answer: A. A botnet is a group of compromised computers, usually working together, with malware installed by a worm or a Trojan horse. See the section titled “Computer Systems Security Threats” in Chapter 2, “Computer Systems Security,” for more information.

10. Answer: C. This1sV#ryS3cure incorporates case-sensitive letters, numbers, and special characters and has 16 characters. See the section titled “ Rights, Permissions, and Policies” in Chapter 9, “Access Control Methods and Models,” for more information.

11. Answer: D. The Trivial File Transfer Protocol (TFTP) is a simpler version of FTP that uses a small amount of memory and is generally considered to be a nonessential protocol. The Domain Name System service (or DNS service) is required for Internet access and on Microsoft domains. The Address Resolution Protocol (ARP) is necessary in Ethernets that use TCP/IP. HTTPS (Hypertext Transfer Protocol Secure) uses the SSL or TLS protocols to protect the HTTP session. See the section titled “Ports, Protocols, and Malicious Attacks” in Chapter 5, “Network Design Elements and Network Threats,” for more information.

12. Answer: C. Fingerprints are an example of something a person is. The process of measuring that characteristic is known as biometrics. See the section titled “Authentication Models and Components” in Chapter 8, “Physical Security and Authentication Models,” for more information.

13. Answers: A and D. Host-based intrusion detection systems (HIDS) run within the operating system of a computer. Due to this, they can slow a computer’s performance. Most HIDS do not detect network attacks well (if at all). However, a HIDS can detect operating system attacks and will usually have a high level of detection when it comes to those attacks. See the section titled “Implementing Security Applications” in Chapter 2, “Computer Systems Security,” for more information.

14. Answer: A. User Account Control (UAC) adds a layer of security to Windows Vista to protect against malware and user error, and conserve resources. See the section titled “Access Control Models Defined” in Chapter 9, “Access Control Methods and Models,” for more information.

15. Answer: C. Ctrl+Alt+Del is the key combination that is used to help secure the logon process. It can be added by configuring the Local Security policy. See the

section titled "Rights, Permissions, and Policies" in Chapter 9, "Access Control Methods and Models," for more information.

16. Answer: C. Zombies (also known as zombie computers) are systems that have been compromised without the knowledge of the owner. A prerequisite is the computer must be connected to the Internet so that the hacker or malicious attack can make its way to the computer and be controlled remotely. Multiple zombies working in concert often form a botnet. See the section titled "Computer Systems Security Threats" in Chapter 2, "Computer Systems Security," for more information.

17. Answer: A. Safe Mode should be used (if your AV software supports it) when scanning for viruses. See the section titled "Implementing Security Applications" in Chapter 2, "Computer Systems Security," for more information.

18. Answer: D. Pop-up windows are common in spyware. The rest of the answers are more common symptoms of viruses. See the section titled "Computer Systems Security Threats " in Chapter 2, "Computer Systems Security," for more information.

19. Answer: B. Virtualization enables a person to install operating systems (or applications) in an isolated area of the computer's hard drive, separate from the computer's main operating system. See the section titled "Virtualization Technology" in Chapter 3, "OS Hardening and Virtualization," for more information.

20. Answer: B. Adjust the web browser security settings so that security is at a higher level, and in Internet Explorer add trusted and restricted websites. See the section titled "Securing the Browser" in Chapter 4, "Application Security," for more information.

21. Answer: D. Alt+F4 is the key combination that closes an active window. Sometimes it is okay to click the X, but because malware creators are getting smarter all the time, the X could be a ruse. See the section titled "Securing other Applications" in Chapter 4, "Application Security," for more information.

22. Answer: C. The Network and Sharing Center is where you would disable file sharing in Windows Vista. See the section titled "Hardening Operating Systems" in Chapter 3, "OS Hardening and Virtualization," for more information.

23. Answer: A. BitLocker uses symmetric encryption technology based off of AES. See the section titled "Encryption Algorithms" in Chapter 12, "Encryption and Hashing Concepts," for more information.

24. Answer: C. A protocol analyzer has the capability to "drill" down through a packet and show the contents of that packet as they correspond to the OSI model. See the section titled "Protocol Analyzers" in Chapter 6, "Network Perimeter Security," for more information.

25. Answer: A. To hide ntldr you need to enable the **Hide protected operating system files** check box. Keep in mind that you should have already enabled the **Show hidden files and folders** radio button. See the section titled "Hardening Operating Systems" in Chapter 3, "OS Hardening and Virtualization," for more information.

26. Answer: B. DNS servers are the only types of servers listed that do zone transfers. The purpose of accessing the zone file is to find out what hosts are on the network. See the section titled "Ports, Protocols, and Malicious Attacks" in Chapter 5, "Network Design Elements and Network Threats," for more information.

27. Answer: C. 172.16.0.1 is the only private address. The private assigned ranges can be seen in Table 1 listed after this explanation. 11.16.0.1 is a public IP address, as is 208.0.0.1; 127.0.0.1 is the loopback address. See the section titled "Network Design" in Chapter 5, "Network Design Elements and Network Threats," for more information.

28. Answer: B. Network Address Translation hides an entire network of IP Addresses. SPI, or Stateful Packet Inspection, is the other type of firewall that today's SOHO routers incorporate. See the section titled "Network Design" in Chapter 5, "Network Design Elements and Network Threats," for more information.

29. Answer: D. **Netstat** shows sessions like the preceding output, including the local computer and remote computer. It shows these connections by computer name (or IP) and port name (or number). See the section titled "Assessing Vulnerability with Security Tools" in Chapter 10, "Vulnerability and Risk Assessment," for more information.

30. Answer: C. Wi-Fi Protected Access 2 (WPA2) is the most secure protocol listed for connecting to wireless networks. It is more secure than WPA and WEP. Wired Equivalent Privacy (WEP) is actually a deprecated protocol that should be avoided, as is WEP2. The WEP and WEP2 algorithms are considered deficient when it comes to encrypted wireless networks. See the section titled "Securing Wireless Networks" in Chapter 7, "Securing Network Media and Devices," for more information.

31. Answers: A and B. Video cameras enable a person to view and visually identify users as they enter and traverse through a building. Key card access systems can be configured to identify a person as well, as long as the right person is carrying the key card! See the section titled "Physical Security" in Chapter 8, "Physical Security and Authentication Models," for more information.

32. Answers: C and D. Kerberos and smart card setups are common single sign-on configurations. See the section titled "Authentication Models and Components" in Chapter 8, "Physical Security and Authentication Models," for more information.

33. Answers: A and C. IPSec contains a key exchange and an authentication header (in addition to many other components). TKIP and AES are other encryption protocols. See the section titled "Authentication Models and Components" in Chapter 8, "Physical Security and Authentication Models," for more information.

34. Answer: B. SPA (Secure Password Authentication) is a Microsoft protocol used to authenticate e-mail clients. S/MIME and PGP can be used to secure the actual e-mail transmissions. See the section titled "Securing other Applications" in Chapter 4, "Application Security," for more information.

35. Answers: A and D. Configuring a supervisor password in the BIOS disallows any other user from entering the BIOS and make changes. Setting the hard drive first in the BIOS boot order disables any other devices from being booted off of floppy drives, optical drives, and USB flash drives. BIOS shadowing doesn't have anything to do with computer security, and although flashing the BIOS may include some security updates, it's not the best answer. See the section titled "Securing Computer Hardware and Peripherals" in Chapter 2, "Computer Systems Security," for more information.

36. Answer: C. Fiber optic is the most secure because it cannot be tapped like the other three copper-based cables; it does not emit EMI. Although shielded twisted pair (STP) offers a level of security due to it's shielding, it is not as secure as fiber optic and is not the best answer. See the section titled "Securing Wired Networks and Devices" in Chapter 7, "Securing Network Media and Devices," for more information.

37. Answer: B. A worm is most likely the reason that the server is bombarded with information by the clients; perhaps it is perpetuated by a botnet. Because worms self-replicate, the damage can quickly become critical. See the section titled "Computer Systems Security Threats" in Chapter 2, "Computer Systems Security," for more information.

38. Answer: D. By checking a DNS server's records regularly, a security admin can monitor *and* protect it. Blocking port 53 on a firewall might protect it (it also might make it inaccessible depending on the network configuration) but won't allow you to monitor it. Pinging the server will simply tell you if the server is alive. Purging pointer records (PTR) will not help to secure or monitor the server. See the section titled "Ports, Protocols, and Malicious Attacks" in Chapter 5, "Network Design Elements and Network Threats," for more information.

39. Answer: A. By creating a honeypot, the administrator can lure potential attackers away and monitor attacks without sustaining damage to a server or other computer. Don't confuse this with a honeynet (answer B), which is meant to attract and trap malicious attackers in an entire false network. Answer C is not something that an administrator would normally do, and answer D is defining a man trap. See the section titled "Firewalls and Network Security" in Chapter 6, "Network Perimeter Security," for more information.

40. Answer: D. A web browser (for example, Internet Explorer) is the only one listed that is not an example of malicious software. Although a browser can be compromised in a variety of ways by malicious software, the application itself is not the malware. See the section titled "Computer Systems Security Threats" in Chapter 2, "Computer Systems Security," and the section titled "Securing the Browser" in Chapter 4, "Application Security," for more information.

41. Answer: D. A hash provides integrity checks, for example, MD5 hash algorithms. See the section titled "Hashing Basics" in Chapter 12, "Encryption and Hashing Concepts," for more information.

42. Answers: A and C. Signals cannot emanate outside a Faraday cage. Therefore, cell phones and pagers do not work inside the Faraday cage. See the section titled "Environmental Controls" in Chapter 15, "Policies, Procedures, and People," for more information.

43. Answer: B. Audit trails are records showing the tracked actions of users. See the section titled "Conducting Audits" in Chapter 11, "Monitoring and Auditing," for more information.

44. Answer: A. By far, the username and password combination is the most common authentication model. Although biometrics, key cards, and tokens are also used, the password is still the most common. See the section titled "Rights, Permissions, and Policies" in Chapter 9, "Access Control Methods and Models," for more information.

45. Answer: C. Rule-based access control (RBAC) uses rules to govern if an object can be accessed. See the section titled " Access Control Models Defined" in Chapter 9, "Access Control Methods and Models," for more information.

46. Answer: A. The Lightweight Directory Access Protocol (LDAP) uses port TCP 389. Port 80 is used by HTTP. Port 443 is used by HTTPS. Port 143 is used by IMAP. See the section titled "Ports, Protocols, and Malicious Attacks" in Chapter 5, "Network Design Elements and Network Threats," for more information.

47. Answer: A. Labels are required in the mandatory access control model (MAC). See the section titled "Access Control Models Defined" in Chapter 9, "Access Control Methods and Models," for more information.

48. Answer: B. A password cracker checks for weak passwords on the network. Antivirus software can scan for viruses on a computer. Performance Monitor enables you to create baselines to check the performance of a computer. Wire shark is a protocol analyzer. See the section titled "Assessing Vulnerability with Security Tools" in Chapter 10, "Vulnerability and Risk Assessment," for more information.

49. Answer: B. RAID 1 is known as mirroring. If one drive fails the other will still function and there will be no downtime. All the rest of the answers have downtime associated with them. See the section titled "Redundancy Planning" in Chapter 14, "Redundancy and Disaster Recovery," for more information.

50. Answer: A. The KDC or key distribution center is used by Kerberos. None of the other answers use KDC. See the section titled "Security Protocols" in Chapter 13, "PKI and Encryption Protocols," for more information.

51. Answer: C. Single sign-on is used so that a user does not have to give multiple credentials. The single sign-on could be a signature, voice print, key code, or username and password, and so on. If a user uses three of these credentials, it would be known as three-factor authentication. See the section titled "Authentication Models and Components" in Chapter 8, "Physical Security and Authentication Models," for more information.

52. Answers: A. and C. POP3 uses port 110; IMAP uses port 143; 3389 is used by the remote desktop protocol; and 389 is used by LDAP. See the section titled "Ports, Protocols, and Malicious Attacks" in Chapter 5, "Network Design Elements and Network Threats," for more information.

53. Answers: A. and D. Kerberos uses a ticket distribution service and an authentication service. This is provided by the Key Distribution Center. A Faraday cage is used to block data emanations. Port 389 is used by LDAP. One of the more common ports that Kerberos uses is port 88. See the section titled "Security Protocols" in Chapter 13, "PKI and Encryption Protocols," for more information.

54. Answer: B. Dumpster diving is when a person goes through a company's trash to find sensitive information about an individual or a company. Browsing is not an attack but something you do when connecting to the Internet. Phishing is

known as acquiring sensitive information through the use of electronic communication. Nowadays, hacking is a general term used with many different types of attacks. See the section titled "Social Engineering" in Chapter 15, "Policies, Procedures, and People," for more information.

55. Answer: A. Steganography is the act of writing hidden messages so that only the intended recipients know of the existence of the message. This is a form of security through obscurity. See the section titled "Cryptography Concepts" in Chapter 12, "Encryption and Hashing Concepts," for more information.

56. Answer: B. A chain of custody is the chronological documentation or paper trail of evidence. See the section titled "Legislative and Organizational Policies" in Chapter 15, "Policies, Procedures, and People," for more information.

57. Answer: D. The Gramm-Leach-Bliley Act protects private information such as Social Security numbers. HIPAA deals with health information privacy. SOX, or the Sarbanes-Oxley Act of 2002, applies to publicly held companies and accounting firms and protects shareholders in the case of fraudulent practices. See the section titled "Legislative and Organizational Policies" in Chapter 15, "Policies, Procedures, and People," for more information.

58. Answer: D. MAC filtering disallows connections from any wireless clients unless the wireless client's MAC address is on the MAC filtering list. See the section titled "Securing Wireless Networks" in Chapter 7, "Securing Network Media and Devices," for more information.

59. Answer: D. DDoS, or distributed denial of service attack, uses multiple computers to make its attack, usually perpetuated on a server. None of the other answers use multiple computers. See the section titled "Computer Systems Security Threats" in Chapter 2, "Computer Systems Security," for more information.

60. Answer: A. To protect against malicious attacks, think like a hacker; then protect and secure like a network security administrator. See the section titled "Think Like a Hacker" in Chapter 1, "Introduction to Security," for more information.

61. Answer: B. You should use nonrepudiation to prevent Tom from denying that he sent the e-mails. See the section titled "Security 101" in Chapter 1, "Introduction to Security," for more information.

62. Answer: D. In x.509, the owner does not use a symmetric key. All the other answers apply to x.509. See the section titled "Public Key Infrastructure" in Chapter 13, "PKI and Encryption Protocols," for more information.

63. Answers: A, B, and D. Rainbow tables are lookup tables used when recovering passwords. User education and awareness can help defend against social engineering attacks, phishing, and dumpster diving. See the section titled "Social Engineering" in Chapter 15, "Policies, Procedures, and People," for more information.

64. Answers: B. and C. By disabling all USB devices in the BIOS, users cannot utilize their flash drive. Also, users cannot use the device if you disable the USB root hub within the operating system. See the section titled "Securing Computer Hardware and Peripherals" in Chapter 2, "Computer Systems Security," for more information.

65. Answer: C. Pop-up blockers do not require updating to be accurate. However, host-based intrusion detection systems, antivirus software, and antispyware all need to be updated to be accurate. See the section titled "Implementing Security Applications" in Chapter 2, "Computer Systems Security," for more information.

66. Answer: A. The Domain Name System, or DNS, uses port 53. Port 80 is used by HTTP, port 110 is used by POP3, and port 88 is used by Kerberos. See the section titled "Ports, Protocols, and Malicious Attacks" in Chapter 5, "Network Design Elements and Network Threats," for more information.

67. Answers: A and C. Blue snarfing and bluejacking are the names of a couple of Bluetooth threats. Another attack could be aimed at a Bluetooth device's discovery mode. To date, there is no such thing as blue bearding, and a distributed denial of service attack is one that uses multiple computers attacking one host. See the section titled "Computer Systems Security Threats" in Chapter 2, "Computer Systems Security," for more information.

68. Answer: D. A logic bomb is a malicious attack that executes at a specific time. Viruses normally execute when a user inadvertently runs them. Worms can self-replicate at will. And bluejacking deals with Bluetooth devices. See the section titled "Computer Systems Security Threats" in Chapter 2, "Computer Systems Security," for more information.

69. Answers: A and B. Two ways to harden an operating system include installing the latest service pack and installing Windows Defender. However, virtualization is a separate concept altogether, and PHP scripts are generally not used to harden an operating system. See the section titled "Hardening Operating Systems" in Chapter 3, "OS Hardening and Virtualization," for more information.

70. Answer: A. Active inception (aka active interception) normally includes a computer placed between the sender and the receiver to capture information. See the section titled “Computer Systems Security Threats” in Chapter 2, “Computer Systems Security,” for more information.

71. Answer: B. If you find that there was an intrusion, the first thing you should check are the firewall logs. DNS logs in the Event Viewer and the performance logs will most likely not show intrusions to the company. The best place to look first is the firewall logs. See the section titled “Firewalls and Network Security” in Chapter 6, “Network Perimeter Security,” for more information.

72. Answer: A. Static network address translation normally uses a one-to-one mapping when dealing with IP addresses. See the section titled “Network Design” in Chapter 5, “Network Design Elements and Network Threats,” for more information.

73. Answer: A. Symmetric encryption is the best option for sending large amounts of data. It is superior to asymmetric encryption. PKI is considered an asymmetric encryption type, and hashing algorithms don’t play into sending large amounts of data. See the section titled “Cryptography Concepts” in Chapter 12, “Encryption and Hashing Concepts,” for more information.

74. Answer: D. A hot site can facilitate a full recovery of communications software and equipment within minutes. Warm and cold sites cannot facilitate a full recovery but might have some of the options necessary to continue business. Reestablishing a mirror will not necessarily implement a full recovery of data communications or equipment. See the section titled “Redundancy Planning” in Chapter 14, “Redundancy and Disaster Recovery,” for more information.

75. Answer: C. The Internet connects hosts to each other in virtual private networks. A particular computer will probably also use a VPN adapter and/or a network adapter. Modems are generally used in dial-up connections and are less commonly used in VPNs. See the section titled “Network Design” in Chapter 5, “Network Design Elements and Network Threats,” for more information.

76. Answer: D. In MAC (mandatory access control), users cannot share resources dynamically. MAC is not a dynamic model, it is a static model. Owners cannot establish access privileges to a resource; this would be done by the administrator. MAC is indeed very restrictive, as restrictive as the administrator wants it to be. See the section titled “Access Control Models Defined” in Chapter 9, “Access Control Methods and Models,” for more information.

77. Answer: A. Antivirus software is the best option when removing a worm. It may be necessary to boot into safe mode to remove this worm when using antivirus software. See the section titled “Implementing Security Applications” in Chapter 2, “Computer Systems Security,” for more information.

78. Answer: A. The easiest way for a hacker to get at encrypted data is if that encrypted data has a weak encryption key. See the section titled "Cryptography Concepts" in Chapter 12, "Encryption and Hashing Concepts," for more information.

79. Answer: C. Input validation is the best practice to use when coding applications. This is important when creating web applications or web pages that require information to be inputted by the user. See the section titled "Implementing Security Applications" in Chapter 2, "Computer Systems Security," for more information.

80. Answer: C. SHA algorithm blocks will have 512 bits. All other answers are incorrect. See the section titled "Hashing Basics" in Chapter 12, "Encryption and Hashing Concepts," for more information.

81. Answer: C. PPP, or point-to-point protocol, does not provide security and is not used in VPN connections. You will see PPP used in dial-up connections. L2TP, PPTP, and IPSec are all used in VPN connections. See the section titled "Network Design" in Chapter 5, "Network Design Elements and Network Threats," for more information.

82. Answer: B. NTFS is the most secure file system for use with Windows XP and Windows Vista. FAT and FAT32 are older file systems, and DFS is the distributed file system used in more advanced networking. See the section titled "Hardening Operating Systems" in Chapter 3, "OS Hardening and Virtualization," for more information.

83. Answer: B. The SSID is used to identify the wireless network. It does not secure the wireless access point; one of the ways to secure a wireless access point is by masking the SSID or disabling the SSID broadcast. The SSID does not encrypt data or enforce MAC filtering. See the section titled "Securing Wireless Networks" in Chapter 7, "Securing Network Media and Devices," for more information.

84. Answer: B. In the discretionary access control model, permissions to files are identified by access control lists, or ACLs. Role membership is used in RBAC. The mandatory access control model predefines permissions. Either way, it is not identified automatically. See the section titled "Access Control Models Defined" in Chapter 9, "Access Control Methods and Models," or more information.

85. Answer: A. Back up the system before you do anything else. This way, you have a backup copy in the case that anything goes wrong when you analyze or make changes to the system. See the section titled "Assessing Vulnerability with Security Tools" in Chapter 10, "Vulnerability and Risk Assessment," or more information.

86. Answer: D. The Performance Monitor can be configured in such a way where alerts can be set for any of the objects (processor, RAM, paging file) in a computer. For example, if the processor was to go beyond 90% usage for more than a minute, an alert would be created and could be sent automatically to an administrator. See the section titled "Using Tools to Monitor Systems and Networks" in Chapter 11, "Monitoring and Auditing," for more information.

87. Answer: A. The Simple Network Management Protocol (SNMP) is used when a person installs agents on client computers to monitor those systems from a single remote location. SMTP is used by e-mail clients and servers. SMP is Symmetric Multi-Processing, which is not covered in the Security+ exam objectives. Performance Monitor enables a person to monitor a computer and create performance baselines. See the section titled "Using Tools to Monitor Systems and Networks" in Chapter 11, "Monitoring and Auditing," for more information.

88. Answers: A, C, and D. To audit events on a computer, an administrator would need to enable auditing within the computer's policy, turn on auditing for an individual object (folder, file, and so on), and then view the events within the Security log of the Event Viewer. 512 KB is big enough for many events to be written to it. See the section titled "Conducting Audits" in Chapter 11, "Monitoring and Auditing," for more information.

89. Answer: C. Symmetric key encryption uses a secret key. PKI and public keys at their core are asymmetrical. See the section titled "Cryptography Concepts" in Chapter 12, "Encryption and Hashing Concepts," for more information.

90. Answers: B and C. A digital certificate will include the Certificate Authority's (CA) digital signature and the user's public key. A user's private key should be kept private and should not be within the digital certificate. The IP address of the CA should have been known to the user's computer before obtaining the certificate. See the section titled "Public Key Infrastructure" in Chapter 13, "PKI and Encryption Protocols," for more information.

91. Answer: B. An Uninterruptible Power Supply (UPS) ensures that a computer keeps running even if a power outage occurs. The amount of minutes the computer can continue in this fashion depends on the type of UPS and battery it contains. A backup generator can also be used but do not guarantee 100% uptime, because there might be a delay between when the power outage occurs and when the generator comes online. RAID 1 has to do with the fault tolerance of data. Redundant NICs (network adapters) are used on servers in the case that one of them fails. Hot sites are completely different places that a company can inhabit. Although the hot site can be ready in minutes, and although it may have a mirror of the server in question, they do not ensure that the original server will not shut down during a power outage. See the section titled

"Redundancy Planning" in Chapter 14, "Redundancy and Disaster Recovery," for more information.

92. Answer: C. The grandfather-father-son (GFS) backup scheme generally uses daily backups (the son), weekly backups (the father), and monthly backups (the grandfather). The Towers of Hanoi is a more complex strategy based on a puzzle. Incremental backups are simply one-time backups that back up all data that has changed since the last incremental backup. These might be used as the son in a GFS scheme. Differential backups back up everything since the last differential or full backup. See the section titled "Disaster Recovery Planning and Procedures" in Chapter 14, "Redundancy and Disaster Recovery," for more information.

93. Answer: D. A protocol analyzer captures data including things such as GET requests initiated from an FTP client. See the section titled "Using Tools to Monitor Systems and Networks" in Chapter 11, "Monitoring and Auditing," for more information.

94. Answers: A and C. By increasing the Internet zone security level to high, you employ the maximum safeguards for that zone. ActiveX controls can be used for malicious purposes; disabling them makes it so that they do not show up in the browser. Disabling a pop-up blocker and adding malicious sites to the Trusted Sites zone would make Internet Explorer less secure. See the section titled "Securing the Browser" in Chapter 4, "Application Security," for more information.

95. Answer: B. Install a firewall to protect the network. Protocol analyzers will not help to protect a network but are valuable as vulnerability assessment and monitoring tools. Although a DMZ and a proxy server could possibly help to protect a portion of the network to a certain extent, the best answer is a firewall. See the section titled "Firewalls and Network Security" in Chapter 6, "Network Perimeter Security," for more information.

96. Answer: C. Two-factor authentication (or dual-factor) means that two pieces of identity are needed prior to authentication. A thumb print and key card would fall into this category. L2TP and IPSec are protocols used to connect through a VPN, which by default require only a username and password. Username and password is considered one-factor authentication. There is no client and server authentication model. See the section titled "Authentication Models and Components" in Chapter 8, "Physical Security and Authentication Models," for more information.

97. Answer: A. OVAL (Open Vulnerability and Assessment Language) uses XML as a framework for the language. It is a community standard dealing with the standardization of information transfer. 3DES is an encryption algorithm.

WPA is a wireless encryption standard, and the deprecated PAP is the Password Authentication Protocol used for identifying users to a server. See the section titled "Assessing Vulnerability with Security Tools" in Chapter 10, "Vulnerability and Risk Assessment," for more information.

98. Answer: A. A private key should be used by users when logging in to the network with their smart card. The key should certainly not be public. A key actually determines the function of a cipher. Shared key is another term for symmetric-key encryption. See the section titled "Cryptography Concepts" in Chapter 12, "Encryption and Hashing Concepts," for more information.

99. Answer: C. The "I" in CIA stands for Integrity. Together CIA stands for Confidentiality, Integrity, and Availability. Accountability is also a core principle of information security. See the section titled "Security 101" in Chapter 1, "Introduction to Security," for more information.

100. Answer: D. A system can never truly be completely secure. The scales are always tipping back and forth; a hacker develops a way to break into a system, an administrator finds a way to block that attack, the hacker looks for an alternative method, and so on. See the section titled "Think Like a Hacker" in Chapter 1, "Introduction to Security," for more information.

The 100 multiple-choice questions provided here help you to determine how prepared you are for the actual exam, and which topics you need to review further. Write down your answers on a separate sheet of paper so that you can take this exam again if necessary. Compare your answers against the answer key that follows this exam.

Practice Exam 2: CompTIA Security+ SY0-201

1. A customer's computer is using FAT16 as its file system. What file system can you upgrade it to when using the **convert** command?

   A. NTFS

   B. HPFS

   C. FAT32

   D. NFS

2. Which of the following is a benign list of entries?

   A. Access control list

   B. Blacklist

   C. Whitelist

   D. Spam list

3. Which of these is an example of social engineering?

   A. Asking for a username and password over the phone

   B. Using someone else's unsecured wireless network

   C. Hacking into a router

   D. Virus

4. Robert needs to access a resource. In the DAC model, what is used to identify him or other users?

   A. Roles

   B. ACLs

   C. MAC

   D. Rules

5. To prevent damage to a computer and its peripherals, the computer should be connected to what?

A. Power strip
B. Power inverter
C. AC to DC converter
D. UPS

6. Which device's log file can show access control lists and who was allowed access and who wasn't?

A. Firewall
B. PDA
C. Performance Monitor
D. IP proxy

7. Russ is using only documentation to test the security of a system. What type of testing methodology is this known as?

A. Active security analysis
B. Passive security analysis
C. Hybrid security analysis
D. Hands-on security analysis

8. Which of the following is not an advantage of NTFS over FAT32?

A. NTFS supports file encryption.
B. NTFS supports larger file sizes.
C. NTFS supports larger volumes.
D. NTFS supports more file formats.

9. John needs to install a web server that can offer SSL-based encryption. Which of the following ports is required for SSL transactions?

A. Port 80 inbound
B. Port 80 outbound
C. Port 443 inbound
D. Port 443 outbound

10. What is the most common reason that social engineering succeeds?

A. Lack of vulnerability testing

B. People share passwords

C. Lack of auditing

D. Lack of user awareness

11. Where are software firewalls usually located?

A. On routers

B. On servers

C. On clients

D. On every computer

12. Which of the following would not be considered part of a disaster recovery plan?

A. Hot site

B. Patch management software

C. Backing up computers

D. Tape backup

13. Where is the optimal place to have a proxy server?

A. In between two private networks

B. In between a private and a public network

C. In between two public networks

D. On all the servers

14. If a person takes control of a session between a server and a client, it is known as what type of attack?

A. DDoS

B. Smurf

C. Session hijacking

D. Malicious software

15. Rick has a local computer that uses software to generate and store key pairs. What type of PKI implementation is this?

A. Distributed key

B. Centralized

C. Hub and Spoke

D. Decentralized

16. You administer a bulletin board system for a rock and roll band. While reviewing logs for the board, you see one particular IP address posting spam multiple times per day. What is the best way to prevent this type of problem?

A. Block the IP address of the user.

B. Ban the user.

C. Disable ActiveX.

D. Implement CAPTCHA.

17. Making data appear as if it is coming from somewhere other than its original source is known as what?

A. Hacking

B. Phishing

C. Cracking

D. Spoofing

18. Which of the following tools uses ICMP?

A. Ping scanner

B. Port scanner

C. Image scanner

D. Barcode scanner

19. Which of the following types of scanners can locate a rootkit on a computer?

A. Image scanner

B. Barcode scanner

C. Malware scanner

D. Adware scanner

20. Your manager wants you to implement a type of intrusion detection system (IDS) that can be matched to certain types of traffic patterns. What kind of IDS is this?

A. Anomaly-based IDS

B. Signature-based IDS

C. Behavior-based IDS

D. Heuristic-based IDS

21. You are setting up auditing on a Windows XP Professional computer. If set up properly, which log should have entries?

A. Application log
B. System log
C. Security log
D. Maintenance log

22. Which type of malware does *not* require a user to execute a program to distribute the software?

A. Worm
B. Virus
C. Trojan horse
D. Stealth

23. A company has a high staff attrition rate. What should you as the network administrator do first? (Select the best answer.)

A. Review user permissions and access control lists.
B. Review group policies.
C. Review Performance logs.
D. Review the Application log.

24. Which of the following is *not* one of the steps of the incident response process?

A. Eradication
B. Recovery
C. Containment
D. Nonrepudiation

25. In which two environments would social engineering attacks be most effective? (Select the two best answers.)

A. Public building with shared office space
B. Company with a dedicated IT staff
C. Locked building
D. Military facility
E. Organization that has IT personnel with little training

26. Two items are needed before a user can be given access to the network. What are these two items? (Select the two best answers.)

A. Authentication and authorization

B. Authorization and identification

C. Identification and authentication

D. Password and authentication

27. Of the following, which is the best way for a person to find out what security holes exist on the network?

A. Run a port scan.

B. Use a network sniffer.

C. Perform a vulnerability assessment.

D. Use an IDS solution.

28. The IT director wants you to use a cryptographic algorithm that cannot be decoded by being reversed. Which of the following would be the best option?

A. Asymmetric

B. Symmetric

C. PKI

D. One-way function

29. Of the following definitions, which would be an example of eavesdropping?

A. Overhearing parts of a conversation

B. Monitoring network traffic

C. Another person looking through your files

D. A computer capturing information from a sender

30. Which of the following concepts does that Diffie-Hellman algorithm rely on?

A. Usernames and passwords

B. VPN tunneling

C. Biometrics

D. Key exchange

31. Which of the following is usually used with L2TP?

A. IPSec

B. SSH

C. PHP

D. SHA

32. Of the following, which best describes the difference between RADIUS and TACACS?

A. RADIUS is a remote access authentication service.

B. RADIUS separates authentication, authorization, and auditing capabilities.

C. TACACS is a remote access authentication service.

D. TACACS separates authentication, authorization. and auditing capabilities.

33. What is the most commonly seen security risk of using coaxial cable?

A. Data that emanates from the core of the cable

B. Crosstalk between the different wires

C. Chromatic dispersion

D. Time domain reflection

34. Heaps and stacks can be affected by which of the following attacks?

A. Buffer overflows

B. Root kits

C. SQL injection

D. Cross-site scripting

35. As part of your user awareness training, you recommend that users remove which of the following when they are done accessing the Internet?

A. Instant messaging

B. Cookies

C. Group policies

D. Temporary files

36. Which of these is not considered to be an in-line device?

A. Firewall

B. Router

C. CSU/DSU

D. HIDS

37. Your company expects its employees to behave in a certain way. How could a description of this behavior be documented?

A. Code of ethics
B. Chain of custody
C. Separation of duties
D. Acceptable use policy

38. What is the main purpose of a physical access log?

A. To enable authorized employee access
B. To show who exited the facility
C. To show who entered the facility
D. To prevent unauthorized employee access

39. After using NMAP to do a port scan of your server, you find that several ports are open. Which of the following should you do next?

A. Leave the ports open and monitor them for malicious attacks.
B. Run the port scan again.
C. Close all ports.
D. Examine the services and or processes that use those ports.

40. You have established a baseline for your server. Which of the following is the best tool to use to monitor any changes to that baseline?

A. Performance monitor
B. Antispyware
C. Antivirus software
D. Vulnerability assessments software

41. Which of the following factors should you consider when evaluating an asset of a company? (Select the two best answers.)

A. Its value to the company
B. Its replacement cost
C. Where it was purchased
D. Its salvage value

42. What ensures that a CRL is authentic and has not been modified?

A. The CRL can be accessed by anyone.

B. The CRL is digitally signed by the CA.

C. The CRL is always authentic.

D. The CRL is encrypted by the CA.

43. Your company has 1,000 users. Which of the following password management systems will work best for your company?

A. Multiple access methods

B. Synchronize passwords

C. Historical passwords

D. Self-service password resetting

44. You are using the following backup scheme. A full backup is made every Friday night at 6 P.M. Differential backups are made every other night at 6 P.M. Your database server fails on Thursday afternoon at 4 P.M. How many tapes will you need to restore the database server?

A. One

B. Two

C. Three

D. Four

45. What is the most common problem with UTP cable?

A. Crosstalk

B. Data emanation

C. Chromatic dispersion

D. Vampire tapping

46. What two security precautions can best help to protect against wireless network attacks?

A. Authentication and the WEP

B. Access control lists and WEP

C. Identification and WPA2

D. Authentication and WPA

47. In what way can you gather information from a remote printer?

A. HTTP

B. SNMP

C. CA

D. SMTP

48. Which of the following will an Internet filtering appliance analyze? (Select the three best answers.)

A. Content

B. Certificates

C. Certificate revocation lists

D. URLs

49. You are a forensics investigator. What is the most important reason for you to verify the integrity of acquired data?

A. To ensure that the data has not been tampered with

B. To ensure that a virus cannot be copied to the target media

C. To ensure that the acquired data is up-to-date

D. To ensure that the source data will fit on the target media

50. Which of the following is the proper order of functions for asymmetric keys?

A. Decrypt, validate, and code and verify

B. Sign, encrypt, decrypt, and verify

C. Encrypt, sign, decrypt, and verify

D. Decrypt, decipher, and code and encrypt

51. Which of the following is not a common criteria when authenticating users?

A. Something you do

B. Something you are

C. Something you know

D. Something you like

52. What does steganography replace in graphic files?

A. The least significant bit of each byte

B. The most significant bit of each byte

C. The least significant byte of each bit

D. The most significant byte of each bit

53. Of the following, what is the worst place to store a backup tape?

A. Near a bundle of fiber-optic cables

B. Near a power line

C. Near a server

D. Near an LCD screen

54. Critical equipment should always be able to get power. What is the correct order of devices that your critical equipment should draw power from?

A. Generator, line conditioner, UPS battery

B. Line conditioner, UPS battery, generator

C. Generator, UPS battery, line conditioner

D. Line conditioner, generator, UPS battery

55. In a discretionary access control model, who is in charge of setting permissions to a resource?

A. Owner of the resource

B. Administrator

C. Any user of the computer

D. Administrator and the owner

56. Jason needs to add several users to a group. Which of the following can help him to get the job done faster?

A. Propagation

B. Inheritance

C. Template

D. Access control lists

57. Michael has just completed monitoring and analyzing a web server. Which of the following indicates that the server might have been compromised?

A. The web server is sending hundreds of UDP packets.

B. The web server as a dozen connections to inbound port 80.

C. The web server has a dozen connections to inbound port 443.

D. The web server is showing a drop in CPU access speed., and hard disk access speed.

58. Which of the following is a vulnerability assessment tool?

A. John the Ripper

B. AirSnort

C. Nessus

D. Cain & Abel

59. Which of the following can determine which flags are set in a TCP/IP handshake?

A. Protocol analyzer

B. Port scanner

C. SYN/ACK

D. Performance monitor

60. You are a consultant for an IT company. Your boss asks you to determine the topology of the network. What is the best device to use in this circumstance?

A. Network mapper

B. Protocol analyzer

C. Port scanner

D. Vulnerability scanner

61. Whitelisting, blacklisting, and closing open relays are all mitigation techniques addressing what kind of threat?

A. Spyware

B. Spam

C. Viruses

D. Botnets

62. Which of the following enables a hacker to float a domain registration for a maximum of 5 days?

A. Kiting

B. DNS poisoning

C. Domain hijacking

D. Spoofing

63. From the following, select the best definition for ARP.

A. Resolves IP addresses to DNS names

B. Resolves IP addresses to hostnames

C. Resolves IP addresses to MAC addresses

D. Resolves IP addresses to DNS addresses

64. How are permissions defined in the mandatory access control model?

A. Access control lists

B. User roles

C. Defined by the user

D. Predefined access privileges

65. Which of the following cables suffers from chromatic dispersion if the cable is too long?

A. Twisted-pair cable

B. Fiber optic cable

C. Coaxial cable

D. USB cables

66. Which of following is the most basic form of IDS?

A. Anomaly based

B. Behavioral-based

C. Signature-based

D. Statistical-based

67. Which of the following encryption concepts is PKI based on?

A. Asymmetric

B. Symmetric

C. Elliptical curve

D. Quantum

68. Of the following, which type of fire suppression can prevent damage to computers and servers?

A. Class A

B. Water

C. CO2

D. Halon

69. You are in charge of PKI certificates. What should you implement so that stolen certificates cannot be used?

A. CRL

B. CAD

C. CA

D. CRT

70. You are the security administrator for your organization. You have just identified a malware incident. What should be your first response?

A. Containment

B. Removal

C. Recovery

D. Monitoring

71. Which of the following deals with the standard load for a server?

A. Patch management

B. Group policy

C. Port scanning

D. Configuration baseline

72. Which of the following cable media is the least susceptible to a tap?

A. Coaxial cable

B. Twisted-pair cable

C. Fiber-optic cable

D. CATV cable

73. Which of the following would lower the level of password security?

A. After a set number of failed attempts, the server will lock the user out, forcing them to call the administrator to reenable their account.

B. Passwords must be greater than eight characters and contain at least one special character.

C. All passwords are set to expire after 30 days.

D. Complex passwords that users cannot change are randomly generated by the administrator.

74. Which of the following are certificate-based authentication mapping schemes? (Select the two best answers.)

A. One-to-many mapping

B. One-to-one mapping

C. Many-to-many mapping

D. Many-to-one mapping

75. Of the following access control models, which use object labels?

A. Discretionary access control

B. Role-based access control

C. Rule-based access control

D. Mandatory access control

76. What is the best way to test the integrity of a company's backed up data?

A. Conduct another backup.

B. Use software to recover deleted files.

C. Review written procedures.

D. Restore part of the backup.

77. Which of the following should be placed between the LAN and the Internet?

A. DMZ

B. HIDS

C. Domain controller

D. Extranet

78. Which of the following, when removed, will increase the security of a wireless access point?

A. MAC filtering

B. SSID

C. WPA

D. Firewall

79. Of the following, what two authentication mechanisms require something you physically possess? (Select the two best answers.)

A. Smart card

B. Certificate

C. USB flash drive

D. Username and password

80. Which of the following network protocols sends data between two computers while utilizing a secure channel?

A. SSH

B. SMTP

C. SNMP

D. P2P

81. What is the greatest risk of a virtual computer?

A. If a virtual computer fails, all other virtual computers immediately go offline.

B. If a virtual computer fails, the physical server goes offline.

C. If the physical server fails; all other physical servers immediately go offline.

D. If the physical server fails, all the virtual computers immediately go offline.

82. Of the following, which is a collection of servers that was set up to attract hackers?

A. DMZ

B. Honeypot

C. Honeynet

D. VLAN

83. Which of the following is the final step a user needs to take before that user can access domain resources?

A. Verification

B. Validation

C. Authorization

D. Authentication

84. Your company has six web servers. You are implementing load-balancing. What is this an example of?

A. UPS

B. Redundant servers

C. RAID

D. A warm site

85. The term Java Applet is best described by which of the following?

A. It increases the usability of web-enabled systems.

B. It is a programming language.

C. A web browser must have the capability to run Java applets.

D. It uses digital signatures for authentication.

86. You have three e-mail servers. What is it called when one server forwards e-mail to another?

A. SMTP relay

B. Buffer overflows

C. POP3

D. Cookies

87. How do most network-based viruses spread?

A. By CD and DVD

B. Through e-mail

C. By USB flash drive

D. By floppy disk

88. To gain access to your network, users must provide a thumbprint, username, and password. What type of authentication model is this?

A. Biometrics

B. Domain logon

C. Multifactor

D. Single sign-on

89. The IT director has asked you to set up an authentication model where users can enter their credentials one time, yet still access multiple server resources. What type of authentication model should you implement?

A. Smart card and biometrics

B. Three-factor authentication

C. SSO

D. VPN

90. A man pretending to be a data communications repair technician enters your building and states that there is networking trouble and he needs access to the server room. What is this an example of?

A. A man-in-the-middle attack

B. A virus

C. Social engineering

D. Chain of custody

91. Which of the following about authentication is false?

A. RADIUS is a client/server system that provides authentication, authorization, and accounting services.

B. PAP is insecure because usernames and passwords are sent as clear text.

C. MS-CHAPv1 is capable of mutual authentication of the client and server.

D. CHAP is more secure than PAP because it encrypts usernames and passwords.

92. Which of the following methods could identify when an unauthorized access has occurred?

A. Two factor authentication

B. Session termination

C. Previous logon notification

D. Session lock

93. Your boss wants you to properly log what happens on a database server. What are the most important concepts to think about while you do so? (Select the two best answers.)

A. The amount of virtual memory that you will allocate for this task

B. The amount of disk space you will require

C. The information that will be needed to reconstruct events later

D. Group policy information

94. Which of the following can enable you to find all the open ports on an entire network?

A. Protocol analyzer

B. Network scanner

C. Firewall

D. Performance monitor

95. Which of the following is the best practice to implement when securing log files?

A. Log all failed and successful login attempts.

B. Deny administrators access to log files.

C. Copy the logs to a remote log server.

D. Increase security settings for administrators.

96. What do hackers use malicious port scanning to accomplish?

A. The "fingerprint" of the operating system

B. The topology of the network

C. All the computer names on the network

D. All the usernames and passwords

97. Many companies send passwords via clear text. Which of the following can be used to view these passwords?

A. Rainbow table

B. port scanner

C. John the Ripper

D. Protocol analyzer

98. What does it mean if a hashing algorithm creates the same hash for two different downloads?

A. A hash is not encrypted.

B. A hashing chain has occurred.

C. A one-way hash has occurred.

D. A collision has occurred.

99. What would you use to control the traffic allowed in or out of a network? (Select the best answer.)

A. Access control lists

B. Firewall

C. Address resolution protocol

D. Discretionary access control

100. Which one of the following, originally used for ease of administration, can be the victim of malicious attack.

A. Zombies

B. Backdoors

C. Buffer overflow

D. Group policy

Answers to Practice Exam 2

Answers at a Glance

1. A
2. C
3. A
4. B
5. D
6. A
7. B
8. D
9. C
10. D
11. C
12. B
13. B
14. C
15. D
16. D
17. D
18. A
19. C
20. B
21. C
22. A
23. A
24. D
25. A and E
26. C
27. C
28. D
29. A
30. D
31. A
32. D
33. A
34. A
35. B
36. D
37. A
38. C
39. D
40. A
41. A and B
42. B
43. D
44. B
45. A
46. D
47. B
48. A, B, and D
49. A
50. C
51. D
52. A
53. B
54. B
55. A
56. C
57. D
58. C
59. A
60. A
61. B
62. A
63. C
64. D
65. B
66. C
67. A
68. C
69. A
70. A
71. D
72. C
73. D
74. B and D
75. D
76. D
77. A
78. B
79. A and C
80. A
81. D
82. C
83. C
84. B
85. C
86. A
87. B
88. C
89. C
90. C
91. C
92. C
93. B and C
94. B
95. C
96. A
97. D
98. D
99. A
100. B.

Answers with Explanations

1. Answer: A. The **convert** command is used to upgrade FAT and FAT32 volumes to the more secure NTFS without loss of data. HPFS is the High Performance File System developed by IBM, and not used by Windows. NFS is the Network File System, something you would see in a storage area network. See the section titled "Hardening Operating Systems" in Chapter 3, "OS Hardening and Virtualization," for more information.

2. Answer: C. A whitelist is a trusted list, usually concerning e-mail addresses. A blacklist is a list of entries that are denied access. An access control list (ACL) defines what levels of access particular users and groups have. A spam list could be considered a blacklist as well. See the section titled "Rights, Permissions and Policies" in Chapter 9, "Access Control Methods and Models," for more information.

3. Answer: A. Social engineering is the practice of obtaining confidential information by manipulating people. Using someone else's network is just theft. Hacking into a router is just that, hacking. And a virus is a self-spreading program that may or may not cause damage to files and applications. See the section titled "Social Engineering" within Chapter 15 "Policies, Procedures, and People," for more information.

4. Answer: B. Access control lists (ACL) are used in the Discretionary Access Control model. This is different from role-based, rule-based, and MAC (Mandatory Access Control) models. See the section titled "Access Control Models Defined " in Chapter 9, "Access Control Methods and Models," for more information.

5. Answer: D. A UPS (uninterruptible power supply) protects computer equipment against surges, spikes, sags, brownouts, and blackouts. Power strips, unlike surge protectors do not protect against surges. See the section titled "Redundancy Planning" in Chapter 14, "Redundancy and Disaster Recovery," for more information.

6. Answer: A. A firewall contains one or more access control lists (ACL) defining who is allowed access to the network. The firewall also shows attempts at access and whether they succeeded or failed. A personal digital assistant (PDA) might list who called or e-mailed, but as of the writing of this book does not use ACLs. Performance Monitor analyzes the performance of a computer, and an IP proxy deals with network address translation, hiding many private IP addresses behind one public address. Although the function of an IP proxy is often built into a firewall, the best answer would be firewall. See the section titled "Firewalls and Network Security" in Chapter 6, "Network Perimeter Security," for more information.

7. Answer: B. Passive security analysis or passive security testing would be one that possibly does not include a hands-on test. It is less tangible and often includes the use of documentation only. To better protect a system or network, you should also use active security analysis. See the section titled "Conducting Risk Assessments" in Chapter 10, "Vulnerability and Risk Assessment," for more information.

8. Answer: D. NTFS and FAT32 support the same number of file formats. See the section titled "Hardening Operating Systems" within Chapter 3, "OS Hardening and Virtualization," for more information.

9. Answer: C. For clients to connect to the server via SSL, the server must have inbound port 443 open. The outbound ports on the server are of little consequence for this concept, and inbound port 80 is used by HTTP. See the section titled "Ports, Protocols, and Malicious Attacks" in Chapter 5, "Network Design Elements and Network Threats," for more information.

10. Answer: D. User awareness is extremely important when attempting to defend against social engineering attacks. Vulnerability testing and auditing are definitely important as part of a complete security plan, but will not necessarily help defend against social engineering, and definitely not as much as user awareness training. People should *not* share passwords. See the section titled "Social Engineering" in Chapter 15, "Policies, Procedures, and People," for more information.

11. Answer: C. Software-based firewalls, such as the Windows Firewall, are normally running on the client computers. Though a software-based firewall could also be run on a server, it is not as common. Also, a SOHO router might have a built-in firewall, but not all routers will have firewalls. See the section titled "Firewalls and Network Security" within Chapter 6 "Network Perimeter Security," for more information.

12. Answer: B. Patching a system is part of the normal maintenance of a computer. In the case of a disaster to a particular computer, the computer's OS and latest service pack would have to be reinstalled. The same would be true in the case of a disaster to a larger area, such as the building. Hot sites, backing up computers, and tape backup are all components of a disaster recovery plan. See the section titled "Disaster Recovery Planning and Procedures" in Chapter 14, "Redundancy and Disaster Recovery," for more information.

13. Answer: B. Proxy servers should normally be between the private and the public network. This way, they can act as a go between for all the computers located on the private network. This applies especially to IP proxy servers but might also include HTTP proxy servers. See the section titled "Firewalls and Network Security" in Chapter 6, "Network Perimeter Security," for more information.

14. Answer: C. Session hijacking (or TCP/IP hijacking) is when an unwanted mediator takes control of the session between a client and a server (for example, an FTP or HTTP session). See the section titled "Ports, Protocols, and Malicious Attacks" in Chapter 5, "Network Design Elements and Network Threats," for more information.

15. Answer: D. When creating key pairs, PKI has two methods: centralized and decentralized. Centralized is when keys are generated at a central server and are transmitted to hosts. Decentralized is when keys are generated and stored on a local computer system for use by that system. See the section titled "Public Key Infrastructure" in Chapter 13, "PKI and Encryption Protocols," for more information.

16. Answer: D. By implementing CAPTCHA, another level of security is added that users have to complete before they can register to and/or post to a bulletin board. Although banning a user or the user's IP address can help to eliminate that particular person from spamming the site, the best way is to add another level of security such as CAPTCHA. This applies to all persons who attempt to attack the bulletin board. See the section titled "Rights, Permissions, and Policies " in Chapter 9, "Access Control Methods and Models," for more information.

17. Answer: D. Spoofing is when a malicious user makes data or e-mail appear to be coming from somewhere else. See the section titled "Ports, Protocols, and Malicious Attacks" in Chapter 5, "Network Design Elements and Network Threats," for more information.

18. Answer: A. A ping scanner uses the Internet Control Message Protocol (ICMP) to conduct its scans. Ping uses ICMP as its underlying protocol and IP and ARP. Image scanners are found in printers and as standalone items that scan images, photos, and text into a computer. Barcode scanners scan barcodes, for example at the supermarket. See the section titled "Firewalls and Network Security" in Chapter 6, "Network Perimeter Security," for more information.

19. Answer: C. Malware scanners can locate rootkits and other types of malware. These types of scanners are often found in antimalware software from manufacturers such as McAfee, Norton, Viper, and so on. Adware scanners (quite often free) only scan for adware. Always have some kind of antimalware software running on live client computers! See the section titled "Computer Systems Security Threats" in Chapter 2, "Computer Systems Security," for more information.

20. Answer: B. When using an IDS, particular types of traffic patterns refers to signature-based IDS. See the section titled "NIDS Versus NIPS" in Chapter 6, "Network Perimeter Security," and "Monitoring Methodologies" in Chapter 11, "Monitoring and Auditing," for more information.

21. Answer: C. After Auditing is turned on and specific resources are configured for auditing, you need to check the Event Viewer's Security log for the entries. These could be successful logons or misfired attempts at deleting files; there are literally hundreds of options. The Application log contains errors, warnings, and informational entries about applications. The System log deals with drivers, system files, and so on. A maintenance log can be used to record routine maintenance procedures. See the section titled "Conducting Audits" in Chapter 11, "Monitoring and Auditing," for more information.

22. Answer: A. Worms self-replicate and do not require a user to execute a program to distribute the software across networks. All the other answers do require user intervention. Stealth refers to a type of virus. See the section titled "Computer Systems Security Threats" in Chapter 2, "Computer Systems Security," for more information.

23. Answer: A. The first thing an administrator should do when he notices that the company has a high attrition rate is to conduct a thorough review of user permissions, rights, and access control lists. A review of group policies might also be necessary but is not as imperative. Performance logs and the Application log will probably not pertain to that the company has a lot of employees being hired and leaving the company. See the section titled "Rights, Permissions, and Policies" in Chapter 9, "Access Control Methods and Models," for more information.

24. Answer: D. Nonrepudiation, although an important part of security, is not part of the incident response process. Eradication, containment, and recovery are all parts of the incident response process. See the section titled "Legislative and Organizational Policies" in Chapter 15, "Policies, Procedures, and People," for more information.

25. Answer: A and E. Public buildings, shared office space, and companies with employees that have little training are all environments where social engineering attacks are common and would be most successful. See the section titled "Social Engineering" in Chapter 15, "Policies, Procedures, and People," for more information.

26. Answer: C. Before a user can be given access to the network, the network needs to identify them and authenticate them. Later users may be authorized to use particular resources on the network. Part of the authentication scheme may include a username and password. This would be known as an access control method. See the section titled "Access Control Models Defined" in Chapter 9, "Access Control Methods and Models," for more information.

27. Answer: C. The best way to find all the security holes that exist on a network is to perform a vulnerability assessment. This may include using a port scanner

and a network sniffer and perhaps using some sort of IDS. See the section titled “Assessing Vulnerability with Security Tools” in Chapter 10, “Vulnerability and Risk Assessment,” for more information.

28. Answer: D. In cryptography, the one-way function is one option of an algorithm that cannot be reversed in an attempt to decode data. See the section titled “Cryptography Concepts” in Chapter 12, “Encryption and Hashing Concepts,” for more information.

29. Answer: A. Eavesdropping is when someone is listening to a conversation that she is not part of. A security administrator should keep in mind that someone could always be listening and try to protect against this. See the section titled “Social Engineering” in Chapter 15, “Policies, Procedures, and People,” or more information.

30. Answer: D. The Diffie-Hellman algorithm relies on key exchange before data can be sent. Usernames and passwords are considered a type of authentication. VPN tunneling is done to connect a remote client to a network. Biometrics is the science of identifying a person by one of his physical attributes. See the section titled “Encryption Algorithms” in Chapter 12, “Encryption and Hashing Concepts,” for more information.

31. Answer: A. IPSec is usually used with L2TP. SSH is a more secure way of connecting to remote computers. PHP is a type of language commonly used on the web. SHA is a type of hashing algorithm. See the section titled “Security Protocols” in Chapter 13, “PKI and Encryption Protocols,” for more information.

32. Answer: D. Unlike RADIUS, TACACS separates authentication, authorization. and auditing capabilities. The other three answers are incorrect and are not differences between RADIUS and TACACS. See the section titled “Security Protocols” in Chapter 13, “PKI and Encryption Protocols.” for more information.

33. Answer: A. Coaxial cable suffers from the emanation of data from the core of the cable, which can be accessed. Crosstalk occurs on twisted-pair cable. Chromatic dispersion occurs on fiber optic cable. Time domain reflection is a concept used by a TDR. See the section titled “Securing Wired Networks and Devices” in Chapter 7, “Securing Network Media and Devices,” for more information.

34. Answer: A. Stacks and heaps are data structures that can be affected by buffer overflows. Value types are stored in a stack, whereas reference types are stored in a heap. A good coder will try to keep these running efficiently. See the section titled “Securing Other Applications” in Chapter 4, “Application Security,” for more information.

35. Answer: B. The best answer is cookies. Cookies can be used for authentication and session tracking and can be read as plain text. They can be used by spyware and can track people without their permission. It is also wise to delete temporary Internet files as opposed to temporary files. See the section titled "Securing the Browser" in Chapter 4, "Application Security," for more information.

36. Answer: D. HIDS, or host-based intrusion detection systems, are not considered to be an inline device. This is because they run on an individual computer. Firewalls, routers, and CSU/DSUs are inline devices. See the section titled "Implementing Security Applications" in Chapter 2, "Computer Systems Security," for more information.

37. Answer: A. The code of ethics describes how a company wants its employees to behave. A chain of custody is a legal and chronological paper trail. Separation of duties means that more than one person is required to complete a job. Acceptable use policy is a set of rules that restrict how a network or a computer system may be used. See the section titled "Legislative and Organizational Policies" in Chapter 15, "Policies, Procedures, and People," for more information.

38. Answer: C. A physical access log's main purpose is to show who entered the facility and when. Different access control and authentication models will be used to enable or prevent employee access. See the section titled "Physical Security" in Chapter 8, "Physical Security and Authentication Models," for more information.

39. Answer: D. If you find ports open that you don't expect, be sure to examine the services and or processes that use those ports. You may have to close some or all those ports. When you finish with your examination, and after you have taken action, run the port scan again to verify that those ports are closed. See the section titled "Assessing Vulnerability with Security Tools" in Chapter 10, "Vulnerability and Risk Assessment," for more information.

40. Answer: A. Performance monitoring software can be used to create a baseline and monitor for any changes to that baseline. An example of this would be the Performance console within Windows Server 2003. See the section titled "Using Tools to Monitor Systems and Networks" in Chapter 11, "Monitoring and Auditing," for more information.

41. Answer: A. and B. When evaluating assets of a company, it is important to know the replacement cost of those assets and the value of the assets to the company. If the assets were lost or stolen, the salvage value is not important, and although you may want to know where the assets were purchased from, it is not one of the best answers. See the section titled "Disaster Recovery Planning and Procedures" in Chapter 14, "Redundancy and Disaster Recovery," for more information.

42. Answer: B. Certificate revocation lists or CRLs are digitally signed by the certificate authority for security purposes. If a certificate is compromised, it will be revoked and placed on the CRL. CRLs are later generated and published periodically. See the section titled "Public Key Infrastructure" in Chapter 13, "PKI and Encryption Protocols," or more information.

43. Answer: D. It would be difficult for administrators to deal with thousands of users passwords; therefore, the best management system for a company with 1,000 users would be self-service password resetting. See the section titled "Rights, Permissions, and Policies" in Chapter 9, "Access Control Methods and Models," for more information.

44. Answer: B. You need two tapes to restore the database server, the full backup tape made on Friday and the differential backup tape made on Wednesday. Only the last differential tape is needed. When restoring the database server, the technician must remember to start with the full backup tape. See the section titled "Disaster Recovery Planning and Procedures" in Chapter 14, "Redundancy and Disaster Recovery," or more information.

45. Answer: A. Of the listed answers, crosstalk is the most common problem with UTP cable. Although data emanation can be a problem with UTP cable, it is more common with coaxial cable, as is vampire tapping. Chromatic dispersion is a problem with fiber optic cable. See the section titled "Securing Wired Networks and Devices" in Chapter 7, "Securing Network Media and Devices," for more information.

46. Answer: D. The best two security precautions are authentication and WPA. Although WPA2 is more secure than WPA, the term identification is not correct. WEP is a deprecated wireless encryption protocol and should be avoided. See the section titled "Securing Wireless Networks" in Chapter 7, "Securing Network Media and Devices," for more information.

47. Answer: B. SNMP (Simple Network Management Protocol) enables you to gather information from a remote printer. HTTP is the hypertext transfer protocol that deals with the transfer of web pages. A CA is a certificate authority, and SMTP is the Simple Mail Transfer Protocol. See the section titled "Using Tools to Monitor Systems and Networks" in Chapter 11, "Monitoring and Auditing," for more information.

48. Answer: A, B, and D. Internet filtering appliances will analyze just about all the data that comes through. However, certificate revocation lists will most likely not be analyzed. Remember that CRLs are published only periodically. See the section titled "Public Key Infrastructure" in Chapter 13, "PKI and Encryption Protocols," for more information.

49. Answer: A. Before analyzing any acquired data, you want to make sure that the data has not been tampered with, so you should verify the integrity of the acquired data before analysis. See the section titled “Legislative and Organizational Policies” in Chapter 15, “Policies, Procedures, and People,” for more information.

50. Answer: C. The proper order of functions for asymmetric keys is as follows: encrypt, sign, decrypt, and verify. See the section titled “Cryptography Concepts” in Chapter 12, “Encryption and Hashing Concepts,” for more information.

51. Answer: D. Common criteria when authenticating users includes something you do, something you are, something you know, and something you have. A person’s likes and dislikes are not common criteria; although, they may be asked as secondary questions when logging into a system. See the section titled “Authentication Models and Components” in Chapter 8, “Physical Security and Authentication Models,” for more information.

52. Answer: A. Steganography replaces the least significant bit of each byte. It would be impossible to replace a byte of each bit, because a byte is larger than a bit; a byte is eight bits. See the section titled “Cryptography Concepts” in Chapter 12, “Encryption and Hashing Concepts,” or more information.

53. Answer: B. Backup tapes should be kept away from power sources including power lines, CRT monitors, speakers, and so on. And admin should keep backup tapes away from sources that might emit EMI. LCD screens, servers, and fiber optic cables have low EMI emissions. See the section titled “Disaster Recovery Planning and Procedures” in Chapter 14, “Redundancy and Disaster Recovery,” for more information.

54. Answer: B. The line conditioner is constantly serving critical equipment with clean power. It should be first and should always be on. The UPS battery should kick in only if there is a power outage. Finally, the generator should kick in only when the UPS battery is about to run out of power. Quite often, the line conditioner and UPS battery will be the same device. However, the line conditioner function will always be used, but the battery comes into play only when there is a power outage, or brownout. See the section titled “Redundancy Planning” in Chapter 14, “Redundancy and Disaster Recovery,” for more information.

55. Answer: A. In the discretionary access control model (DAC), the owner of the resource is in charge of setting permissions. In a mandatory access control (MAC) model, the administrator is in charge. See the section titled “Access Control Models Defined” in Chapter 9, “Access Control Methods and Models,” for more information.

56. Answer: C. By using a template, you can add many users to a group at one time simply by applying the template to the users. Propagation and inheritance deal with how permissions are exchanged between parent folders and subfolders. Access control lists show who was allowed access to a particular resource. See the section titled "Rights, Permissions, and Policies" in Chapter 9, "Access Control Methods and Models," for more information.

57. Answer: D. If the web server is showing a drop in processor and hard disk access speed, it might have been compromised. Further analysis and comparison to a pre-existing baseline would be necessary. All the other answers are common for a web server. See the section titled "Using Tools to Monitor Systems and Networks" in Chapter 11, "Monitoring and Auditing," for more information.

58. Answer: C. Nessus is a vulnerability assessment tool. AirSnort is used to crack wireless encryption codes. John the Ripper and Cain & Abel are password cracking programs. See the section titled "Assessing Vulnerability with Security Tools" in Chapter 10, "Vulnerability and Risk Assessment," for more information.

59. Answer: A. A protocol analyzer can look inside of the packets that make up a TCP/IP handshake. Information that can be viewed includes SYN, which is synchronize sequence numbers, and ACK, which is acknowledgment field significant. Port scanners and performance monitor do not have the capability to view flags set in a TCP/IP handshake, nor can they look inside of packets in general. See the section titled "Using Tools to Monitor Systems and Networks" in Chapter 11, "Monitoring and Auditing," for more information.

60. Answer: A. A network mapper is the best tool to use to determine the topology of the network and to find out what devices and computers reside on that network. An example of this would be LAN Surveyor. See the section titled "Assessing Vulnerability with Security Tools" in Chapter 10, "Vulnerability and Risk Assessment," for more information.

61. Answer: B. Closing open relays, white listing, and blacklisting are all mitigation techniques that address spam. Spam e-mail is a serious problem for all companies and must be filtered as much is possible. See the section titled "Computer Systems Security Threats" in Chapter 2, "Computer Systems Security," or more information.

62. Answer: A. Kiting is the practice of monopolizing domain names without paying for them. Newly registered domain names can be canceled with a full refund during an initial 5-day window, which is known as an AGP, or add grace period. See the section titled "Ports, Protocols, and Malicious Attacks" in Chapter 5, "Network Design Elements and Network Threats," for more information.

63. Answer: C. The address resolution protocol, or ARP, resolves IP addresses to MAC addresses. DNS resolves from IP addresses to hostnames' word domain names, and vice versa. RARP resolves MAC addresses to IP addresses. See the section titled "Ports, Protocols, and Malicious Attacks" in Chapter 5, "Network Design Elements and Network Threats," for more information.

64. Answer: D. The mandatory access control model uses predefined access privileges to define which users have permission to resources. See the section titled "Access Control Models Defined" in Chapter 9, "Access Control Methods and Models," for more information.

65. Answer: B. Fiber optic cable is the only one listed that might suffer from chromatic dispersion because it is the only cable based on light. All the other answers are based on electricity. See the section titled "Securing Wired Networks and Devices" in Chapter 7, "Securing Network Media and Devices," for more information.

66. Answer: C. Signature-based IDS is the most basic form of intrusion detection system (IDS). This monitors packets on the network and compares them against a database of signatures. Anomaly based, behavioral-based, and statistical-based are all more complex forms of IDS. See the section titled "Monitoring Methodologies" in Chapter 11, "Monitoring and Auditing," for more information.

67. Answer: A. The public key infrastructure, or PKI, is based on the asymmetric encryption concept. Symmetric, elliptical curve, and quantum are all different encryption schemes that PKI does not use. See the section titled "Public Key Infrastructure" in Chapter 13, "PKI and Encryption Protocols," for more information.

68. Answer: C. CO2 is the best answer because it displaces oxygen; fire needs oxygen; without it the fire will go out. CO2 is the only answer that will not damage computers because it is a gas. All the others have substances that can damage computers. See the section titled "Environmental Controls" in Chapter 15, "Policies, Procedures, and People," for more information.

69. Answer: A. You should implement a certificate revocation list or CRL so that stolen certificates cannot be used. See the section titled "Public Key Infrastructure" in Chapter 13, "PKI and Encryption Protocols," for more information.

70. Answer: A. Most organizations' incident response procedures specify that containment of the malware incident should be first. Next would be the removal, then recovery of any damaged systems, and finally monitoring, which should be going on at all times. See the section titled "Legislative and Organizational Policies" in Chapter 15, "Policies, Procedures, and People," or more information.

71. Answer: D. A configuration baseline deals with the standard load of a server. By measuring the traffic that passes through the server's network adapter, you can create a configuration baseline over time. See the section titled "Using Tools to Monitor Systems and Networks" in Chapter 11, "Monitoring and Auditing," for more information.

72. Answer: C. Fiber-optic cable is the least susceptible to a tap because it operates on the principle of light as opposed to electricity. All the other answers suffer from data emanation because they are all copper-based. See the section titled "Securing Wired Networks and Devices" in Chapter 7, "Securing Network Media and Devices," for more information.

73. Answer: D. To have a secure password scheme, passwords should be changed by the user. They should not be generated by the administrator. All the other answers would increase the level of password security. See the section titled "Rights, Permissions, and Policies" in Chapter 9, "Access Control Methods and Models," for more information.

74. Answer: B and D. When dealing with certificate authentication, asymmetric systems use one-to-one mappings and many-to-one mappings. See the section titled "Public Key Infrastructure" in Chapter 13, "PKI and Encryption Protocols," for more information.

75. Answer: D. The mandatory access control (MAC) model uses object and subject labels; DAC and RBAC do not. See the section titled "Access Control Models Defined" in Chapter 9, "Access Control Methods and Models," for more information.

76. Answer: D. The best way to test the integrity of backed up data is to restore part of that backup. Conducting another backup will tell you whether the backup procedure is working properly; if necessary after testing the integrity of the backup and after the restore, a person might need to use software to recover deleted files. It's always important to review written procedures and amend them if needed. See the section titled "Disaster Recovery Planning and Procedures" in Chapter 14, "Redundancy and Disaster Recovery," for more information.

77. Answer: A. A demilitarized zone, or DMZ, should be placed between the LAN and the Internet. In many cases it will be part of a three-leg firewall scheme. Host-based intrusion detection systems are placed on an individual computer, usually within the LAN. Domain controllers should be protected and are normally on the LAN as well. An extranet can include parts of the Internet and parts of one or more LANs; normally it connects two companies utilizing the power of the Internet. See the section titled "Network Design" in Chapter 5, "Network Design Elements and Network Threats," for more information.

78. Answer: B. By removing the security set identifier, or SSID, the wireless access point will be more secure and will be tougher for wardrivers to access that network. Of course, no new clients can connect to the wireless access point. MAC filtering, WPA, and firewalls are all components that increase the security of a wireless access point. See the section titled "Securing Wireless Networks" in Chapter 7, "Securing Network Media and Devices," for more information.

79. Answer: A and C. Two of the authentication mechanisms that require something you physically possess include smart cards and USB flash drives. Key fobs and card keys would also be part of this category. Certificates are granted from a server and are stored on a computer as software. The username/password mechanism is a common authentication scheme, but they are something that you type and not something that you physically possess. See the section titled "Physical Security" in Chapter 8, "Physical Security and Authentication Models," for more information.

80. Answer: A. SSH, or Secure Shell, enables two computers to send data via a secure channel. SMTP is the Simple Mail Transfer Protocol, which deals with e-mail. SNMP is the Simple Network Management Protocol, which enables the monitoring of remote systems. P2P is the abbreviated version of peer-to-peer network. See the section titled "Security Protocols" in Chapter 13, "PKI and Encryption Protocols," for more information.

81. Answer: D. The biggest risk of running a virtual computer is that it will go offline immediately if the server that it is housed on fails. All other virtual computers on that particular server will also go offline immediately. See the section titled "Virtualization Technology" in Chapter 3, "OS Hardening and Virtualization," for more information.

82. Answer: C. A honeynet is a collection of servers that is set up to attract hackers. A honeypot is usually one computer or one server that has the same purpose. A DMZ is the demilitarized zone, which is in between the LAN and the Internet. A VLAN is a virtual LAN. See the section titled "Network Design" in Chapter 5, "Network Design Elements and Network Threats," for more information.

83. Answer: C. Before a user can gain access to domain resources, the final step is to be authorized to those resources. Previously the user should have provided identification to be authenticated. See the section titled "Authentication Models and Components" in Chapter 8, "Physical Security and Authentication Models," for more information.

84. Answer: B. Load balancing is a method used when you have redundant servers. In this case, the six web servers will serve data equally to users. The UPS is an uninterruptible power supply, and RAID is a redundant array of inexpensive disks. A warm site is a secondary site that a company can use in the case of a disaster that can be up and running within a few hours or a day. See the section titled "Redundancy Planning" in Chapter 14, "Redundancy and Disaster Recovery," for more information.

85. Answer: C. To run Java applets, a web browser must have that option enabled. Java itself is what increases the usability of web-enabled systems, and Java is a programming language. It does not use digital signatures for authentication. See the section titled "Securing the Browser" in Chapter 4, "Application Security," for more information.

86. Answer: A. The SMTP relay is when one server forwards e-mail to other e-mail servers. Buffer overflows are attacks that can be perpetuated on web pages. POP3 is another type of e-mail protocol, and cookies are small text files stored on the client computer that remember information about which computers session with a website. See the section titled "Network Design" in Chapter 5, "Network Design Elements and Network Threats," for more information.

87. Answer: B. E-mail is the number one reason why network-based viruses spread. All a person needs to do is double-click the attachment within the e-mail and the virus will do its thing, which is most likely to spread through the user's address book. Removable media such as CDs, DVDs, USB flash drives, and floppy disks can spread viruses, but they are not nearly as common as e-mail. See the sections titled "Computer Systems Security Threats" and "Securing Computer Hardware and Peripherals," in Chapter 2, "Computer Systems Security" for more information.

88. Answer: C. Multifactor authentication means that the user must provide two different types of identification. The thumbprint is an example of biometrics. Username and password are example of a domain logon. Single sign-on would be only one type of authentication that enables the user access to multiple resources. See the sections titled "Authentication Models and Components" and "Physical Security" in Chapter 8, "Physical Security and Authentication Models," for more information.

89. Answer: C. Single sign-on or SSO enables users to access multiple servers and multiple resources while entering their credentials only one time. The type of authentication can vary but will generally be a user name and password. Smart cards and biometrics are examples of two-factor authentication. VPN is short for virtual private network. See the section titled "Authentication Models and Components" in Chapter 8, "Physical Security and Authentication Models," for more information.

90. Answer: C. Any person pretending to be a data communications repair person would be attempting a social engineering attack. See the section titled "Social Engineering" in Chapter 15, "Policies, Procedures, and People," for more information.

91. Answer: C. MS-CHAPv1 is not capable of mutual authentication of the client and server. All the other statements are true. See the section titled "Authentication Models and Components" in Chapter 8, "Physical Security and Authentication Models," for more information.

92. Answer: C. Previous logon notification can identify if unauthorized access has occurred. Two-factor authentication means that person will supply two forms of identity before being authenticated to a network or system. Session termination is a mechanism that can be implemented to end an unauthorized access. Session lock mechanisms can be employed to lock a particular user or IP address out of the system. See the section titled "Access Control Models Defined" in Chapter 9, "Access Control Methods and Models," for more information.

93. Answer: B and C. It is important to calculate how much disk space you will require for the logs of your database server and verify that you have that much disk space available on the hard drive. It is also important to plan what information will be needed in the case that you need to reconstruct events later. Group policy information and virtual memory is not important for this particular task. See the section titled "Monitoring Methodologies" in Chapter 11, "Monitoring and Auditing," for more information.

94. Answer: B. A network scanner is a port scanner used to find open ports on multiple computers on the network. A protocol analyzer is used to delve into packets. A firewall protects a network, and a performance monitor is used to create baselines for and monitor a computer. See the section titled "Assessing Vulnerability with Security Tools" in Chapter 10, "Vulnerability and Risk Assessment," for more information.

95. Answer: C. It is important to copy the logs to a secondary server in case something happens to the primary log server; this way you have another copy of any possible security breaches. Blocking all failed and successful login attempts might not be wise, because it will create many entries. The rest of the answers are not necessarily good ideas when working with log files. See the section titled "Using Tools to Monitor Systems and Networks" in Chapter 11, "Monitoring and Auditing," or more information.

96. Answer: A. Port scanning can be used in a malicious way to find out all the openings to a computer's operating system; this is known as the "fingerprint" of the operating system. Port scanning cannot find out the topology of the network, computer names, usernames, or passwords. See the section titled "Assessing Vulnerability with Security Tools" in Chapter 10, "Vulnerability and Risk Assessment," for more information.

97. Answer: D. A protocol analyzer can delve into the packets that were sent across the network that contain the clear text passwords. Rainbow tables and John the Ripper deal with cracking passwords that were previously encrypted; they aren't necessary if the password were sent via clear text. Port scanners scan computers for any open ports. See the section titled "Assessing Vulnerability with Security Tools" in Chapter 10, "Vulnerability and Risk Assessment," for more information.

98. Answer: D. If a hashing algorithm generates the same hash for two different messages within two different downloads, a collision has occurred, and the implementation of the hashing algorithm should be investigated. See the section titled "Hashing Basics" in Chapter 12, "Encryption and Hashing Concepts," for more information.

99. Answer: A. Access control lists can be used to control the traffic allowed in or out of a network. They are usually included as part of a firewall and are the better answer because they specifically will control the traffic. Address resolution protocol, or ARP, resolves IP addresses to MAC addresses. In the discretionary access control model, the owner controls permissions of resources. See the section titled "Access Control Models Defined" in Chapter 9, "Access Control Methods and Models," for more information.

100. Answer: B. Backdoors were originally created to ease administration. However, hackers quickly found that they could use these backdoors for a malicious attack. See the section titled "Securing Other Applications" in Chapter 4, "Application Security," for more information.

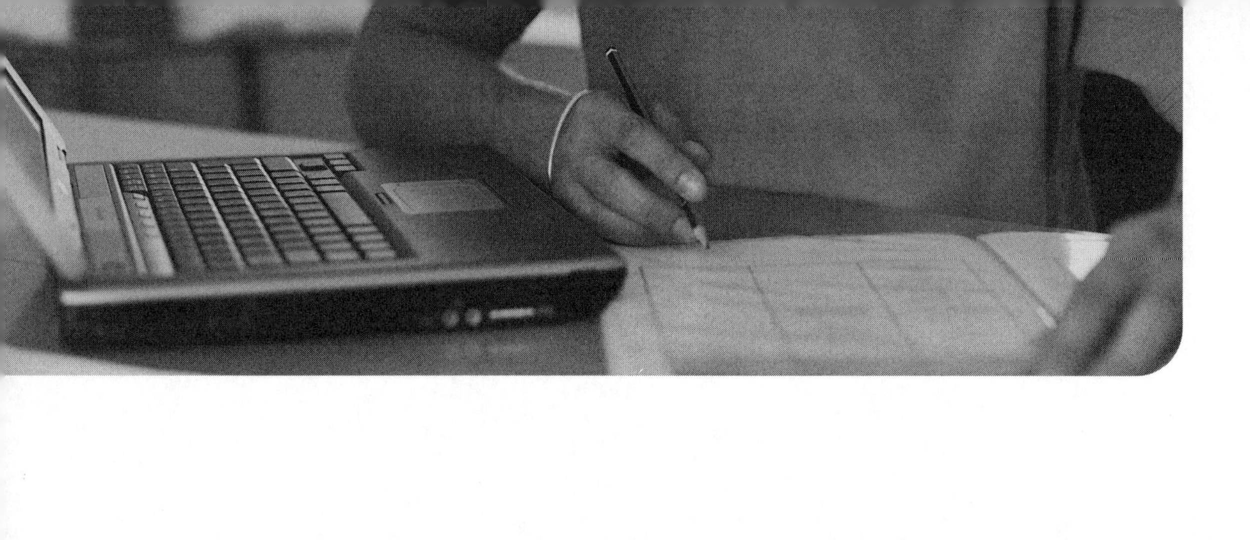

Glossary

This glossary contains the key terms from the book. All the terms from each chapter's "Define Key Terms" tasks are defined here.

10 tape rotation
A backup rotation scheme in which 10 backup tapes are used over the course of 2 weeks.

802.1X
An authentication technology used to connect devices to a LAN or WLAN. It is an example of port-based NAC.

acceptable use
Acceptable usage policies define the rules that restrict how a computer, network, or other system may be used.

access control list (ACL)
A list of permissions attached to an object. They specify what level of access a user, users, or groups have to an object. When dealing with firewalls, an ACL is a set of rules that apply to a list of network names, IP addresses. and port numbers.

access control model
Methodologies in which admission to physical areas, and more important computer systems, is managed and organized.

account expiration
The date when users' accounts they use to log on to the network expires.

accounting
The tracking of data, computer usage, and network resources. Often it means logging, auditing, and monitoring of the data and resources.

active interception
Also known as active inception in the CompTIA 2008 Security+ objectives; normally includes a computer placed between the sender and the receiver in an effort to capture and possibly modify information.

ad filtering
Ways of blocking and filtering out unwanted advertisement; pop-up blockers and content filters are considered to be ad filtering methods.

Advanced Encryption Standard (AES)
An encryption standard used with WPA and WPA2. The successor to DES/3DES and is another symmetric key encryption standard composed of three different block ciphers: AES-128, AES-192, and AES-256.

adware
Type of spyware that pops up advertisements based on what it has learned about the user.

algorithms
Well-defined instructions that describe computations from their initial state to their final state.

anomaly based monitoring
Also known as statistical anomaly–based; establishes a performance baseline based on a set of normal network traffic evaluations.

application-level gateway (ALG)
Applies security mechanisms to specific applications, such as FTP and/or BitTorrent. It supports address and port translation and checks if the type of application traffic is allowed.

ARP poisoning
An attack that exploits Ethernet networks, and it may enable an attacker to sniff frames of information, modify that information, or stop it from getting to its intended destination.

asymmetric key algorithm
This type of cipher uses a pair of different keys to encrypt and decrypt data.

audit trails
Records or logs that show the tracked actions of users, whether the user was successful in the attempt.

authentication
When a person's identity is confirmed. Authentication is the verification of a person's identity.

authorization
When a user is granted access to specific resources when authentication is complete.

availability
Data is obtainable regardless of how information is stored, accessed, or protected.

backdoors
Used in computer programs to bypass normal authentication and other security mechanisms in place.

back-to-back perimeter
A type of DMZ where the DMZ is located between the LAN and the Internet.

backup generator
Part of an emergency power system used when there is an outage of regular electric grid power.

baiting
When a malicious individual leaves malware-infected removable media, such as a USB drive or optical disc, lying around in plain view.

baselining
The process of measuring changes in networking, hardware, software, and so on.

behavior-based monitoring
A monitoring system that looks at the previous behavior of applications, executables, and/or the operating system and compares that to current activity on the system.

biometrics
The science of recognizing humans based on one or more physical characteristics.

birthday attack
An attack on a hashing system that attempts to send two different messages with the same hash function, causing a collision.

blackout
When a total loss of power for a prolonged period occurs.

block cipher
A type of algorithm that encrypts a number of bits as individual units known as blocks.

bluejacking
The sending of unsolicited messages to Bluetooth-enabled devices such as mobile phones and PDAs.

bluesnarfing
The unauthorized access of information from a wireless device through a Bluetooth connection.

botnet
A group of compromised computers used to distribute malware across the Internet; the members are usually zombies.

broadcast storm
When there is an accumulation of broadcast and multicast packet traffic on the LAN coming from one or more network interfaces.

brownout
When the voltage drops to such an extent that it typically causes the lights to dim and causes computers to shut off.

brute force attack
A password attack where every possible password is attempted.

buffer overflow
When a process stores data outside of the memory that the developer intended. This could cause erratic behavior in the application, especially if the memory already had other data in it.

butt set (or lineman's handset)
A device that looks similar to a phone but has alligator clips that can connect to the various terminals used by phone equipment, enabling a person to listen in to a conversation.

CAM table
The Content Addressable Memory table, a table that is in a switch's memory that contains ports and their corresponding MAC addresses.

certificate authority
The entity (usually a server) that issues digital certificates to users.

certificate revocation list (CRL)
A list of certificates no longer valid or have been revoked by the issuer.

certificates
Digitally signed electronic documents that bind a public key with a user identity.

chain of custody
Documents who had custody of evidence all the way up to litigation or a court trial (if necessary) and verifies that the evidence has not been modified.

Challenge-Handshake Authentication Protocol (CHAP)
An authentication scheme used by the Point-to-Point Protocol (PPP) that is the standard for dial-up connections.

change management
A structured way of changing the state of a computer system, network, or IT procedure.

chromatic dispersion
The refraction of light as in a rainbow. If light is refracted in such a manner on fiber optic cables, the signal cannot be read by the receiver.

cipher
An algorithm that can perform encryption or decryption.

circuit-level gateway
Works at the Session layer of the OSI model and applies security mechanisms when a TCP or UDP connection is established; they act as a go-between for the Transport and Application Layers in TCP/IP.

cluster
Two or more servers that work with each other.

cold site
This has tables, chairs, bathrooms, and possibly some technical setup; for example basic phone, data, and electric lines, but will require days if not weeks to set up properly.

computer security audits
Technical assessments made of applications, systems, or networks.

confidentiality
Preventing the disclosure of information to unauthorized persons.

content filters
Individual computer programs that block external files that use JavaScript or images from loading into the browser.

cookies
Text files placed on the client computer that store information about it, which could include your computer's browsing habits and credentials. Tracking cookies are used by spyware to collect information about a web user's activities. Session cookies are used by attackers in an attempt to hijack a session.

cross-site scripting
A type of vulnerability found in web applications used with session hijacking.

crosstalk
When a signal transmitted on one copper wire creates an undesired effect on another wire; the signal "bleeds" over, so to speak.

cryptanalysis attack
A password attack uses a considerable set of precalculated encrypted passwords located in a lookup table.

cryptographic hash functions
Hash functions based on block ciphers.

cryptography
The practice and study of hiding information.

data emanation (or signal emanation)
The electromagnetic field generated by a network cable or network device, which can be manipulated to eavesdrop on conversations or to steal data.

Data Encryption Standard (DES)
An older type of block cipher selected by the United States federal government back in the 1970s as its encryption standard; due to its weak key, it is now considered deprecated.

default account
An account installed by default on a device or within an operating system with a default set of user credentials that are usually insecure.

demilitarized zone (DMZ)
A special area of the network (sometimes referred to as a subnetwork) that houses servers that host information accessed by clients or other networks on the Internet.

Denial of Service (DoS)
A broad term given to many different types of network attacks that attempts to make computer resources unavailable.

dictionary attack
A password attack that uses a prearranged list of likely words, trying each of them one at a time.

differential backup
Type of backup that backs up only the contents of a folder that have changed since the last full backup.

Diffie-Hellman key exchange
Invented in the 1970s, it was the first practical method for establishing a shared secret key over an unprotected communications channel.

digital signature
A signature that authenticates a document through math, letting the recipient know that the document was created and sent by the actual sender and not someone else.

disaster recovery plan
A plan that details the policies and procedures concerning the recovery and/or continuation of an organization's technology infrastructure.

discretionary access control (DAC)
An access control policy generally determined by the owner.

disk duplexing
When each disk is connected to a separate controller.

Distributed Denial of Service (DDoS)
An attack in which a group of compromised systems attack a single target, causing a DoS to occur at that host, usually using a botnet.

diversion theft
When a thief attempts to take responsibility for a shipment by diverting the delivery to a nearby location.

DNS poisoning
The modification of name resolution information that should be in a DNS server's cache.

domain name kiting
The process of deleting a domain name during the 5-day grace period (known as the add grace period or AGP) and immediately reregistering it for another 5-day period to keep a domain name indefinitely and for free.

due care
The mitigation action that an organization takes to defend against the risks that have been uncovered during due diligence.

due diligence
Ensuring that IT infrastructure risks are known and managed.

due process
The principle that an organization must respect and safeguard personnel's rights.

dumpster diving
When a person literally scavenges for private information in garbage and recyclable containers.

Easter egg
A platonic extra added to an OS or application as a sort of joke; the harmless cousin of the logic bomb.

eavesdropping
When a person uses direct observation to "listen" in to a conversation.

electromagnetic interference (EMI)
A disturbance that can affect electrical circuits, devices, and cables due to electromagnetic conduction or radiation.

elliptic curve cryptography (ECC)
A type of public key cryptography based on the structure of an elliptic curve.

encryption
The process of changing information using an algorithm (or cipher) into another form that is unreadable by others—unless they possess the key to that data.

Extensible Authentication Protocol (EAP)
Not an authentication mechanism in itself but instead defines message formats. 802.1X would be the authentication mechanism and defines how EAP is encapsulated within messages.

failopen mode
When a switch broadcasts data on all ports the way a hub does.

failover clusters
Also known as high-availability clusters, these are designed so that a secondary server can take over in the case that the primary one fails, with limited or no downtime.

false negative
When a system denies a user who actually should be allowed access to the system. For example, when an IDS/IPS fails to block an attack, thinking it is legitimate traffic.

false positive
When a system authenticates a user who should not be allowed access to the system. For example, when an IDS/IPS blocks legitimate traffic from passing on to the network.

Faraday cage
An enclosure formed by conducting material or by a mesh of such material; it blocks out external static electric fields and can stop emanations from cell phones and other devices within the cage to leak out.

fire suppression
The process of controlling and/or extinguishing fires to protect people and an organization's data and equipment.

firewall
A part of a computer system or network designed to block unauthorized access while permitting authorized communications. It is a device or set of devices configured to permit or deny computer applications based on a set of rules and other criteria.

first responders
People who perform preliminary analysis of the incident data and determine whether the incident is an incident or just an event, and the criticality of the incident.

fork bomb
An attack that works by creating a large number of processes quickly to saturate the available processing space in the computer's operating system. It is a type of wabbit.

fraggle
A type of DoS similar to the Smurf attack, but the traffic sent is UDP echo traffic as opposed to ICMP echo traffic.

full backup
Type of backup where all the contents of a folder are backed up.

grandfather-father-son
A backup rotation scheme in which three sets of backup tapes must be defined—usually they are daily, weekly, and monthly, which correspond to son, father, and grandfather.

grayware
A general term used to describe applications that are behaving improperly but without serious consequences; often describes types of spyware.

group policy
Used in Microsoft environments to govern user and computer accounts through a set of rules.

hardening
Hardening of the operating system is the act of configuring an OS securely, updating it, creating rules and policies to help govern the system in a secure manner, and removing unnecessary applications and services.

hash function
A mathematical procedure that converts a variable-sized amount of data into a smaller block of data.

hash
A summary of a file or message. It is generated to verify the integrity of the file or message.

hoax
The attempt at deceiving people into believing something that is false.

honeynet
One or more computers, servers, or an area of a network, used to attract and trap potential attackers to counteract any attempts at unauthorized access of the network.

honeypot
Generally is a single computer but could also be a file, group of files, or an area of unused IP address space used to attract and trap potential attackers to counteract any attempts at unauthorized access of the network.

host-based intrusion detection system (HIDS)
A type of system loaded on an individual computer; it analyzes and monitors what happens inside that computer, for example if any changes have been made to file integrity.

hot site
A near duplicate of the original site of the organization, complete with phones, computers, networking devices, and full backups.

hotfix
Originally, a hotfix was defined as a single problem fixing patch to an individual OS or application that was installed live while the system was up and running, and without a reboot necessary. However, this term has changed over time and varies from vendor to vendor.

HTTP proxy (web proxy)
The HTTP proxy, also known as a web proxy, which caches web pages from servers on the Internet for a set amount of time.

identification
When a person is in a state of being identified. It can also be described as something that identifies a person such as an ID card.

identity proofing
An initial validation of an identity.

implicit deny
Denies all traffic to a resource unless the users generating that traffic are specifically granted access to the resource. For example, when a device denies all traffic unless a rule is made to open the port associated with the type of traffic desired to be let through.

incremental backup
Type of backup that backs up only the contents of a folder that have changed since the last full backup or the last incremental backup.

input validation
Input validation or data validation is a process that ensures the correct usage of data.

integrity
This means that authorization is necessary before data can be modified.

Internet content filter
An Internet content filter, or simply a content filter, is usually applied as software at the Application Layer and can filter out various types of Internet activities such as websites accessed, e-mail, instant messaging, and more. It is used most often to disallow access to inappropriate web material.

Internet Protocol Security (IPsec)
A TCP/IP protocol that authenticates and encrypts IP packets, effectively securing communications between computers and devices using the protocol.

IP proxy
Secures a network by keeping machines behind it anonymous; it does this through the use of NAT.

job rotation
When users are cycled through various assignments.

Kerberos
An authentication protocol that enables computers to prove their identity to each other in a secure manner.

key escrow
When certificate keys are held in case third parties, such as government or other organizations, need access to encrypted communications.

key
The essential piece of information that determines the output of a cipher.

LANMAN hash
The original hash used to store Windows passwords, known as LM hash, based off the DES algorithm.

Layer 2 Tunneling Protocol (L2TP)
A tunneling protocol used to connect virtual private networks. It does not include confidentiality or encryption on its own. It uses port 1701 and can be more secure than PPTP is used in conjunction with IPsec.

least privilege
When a user is given only the amount of privileges needed to do their job.

Lightweight Directory Access Protocol (LDAP)
An Application Layer protocol used for accessing and modifying directory services data.

load-balancing clusters
When multiple computers are connected in an attempt to share resources such as CPU, RAM, and hard disks.

logic bomb
Code that has, in some way, been inserted into software; it is meant to initiate some type of malicious function when specific criteria are met.

MAC filtering
A method used to filter out which computers can access the wireless network; the WAP does this by consulting a list of MAC addresses that have been previously entered.

MAC flooding
An attack that sends numerous packets to a switch, each of which has a different source MAC address, in an attempt to use up the memory on the switch. If this is successful, the switch will change state to failopen mode.

malware
Software designed to infiltrate a computer system and possibly damage it without the user's knowledge or consent.

mandatory access control (MAC)
An access control policy determined by a computer system, not by a user or owner, as it is in DAC.

mandatory vacations
When an organization requires that an employee take a certain amount of days vacation consecutively.

man-in-the-middle (MITM) attack
A form of eavesdropping that intercepts all data between a client and a server, relaying that information back and forth.

mantrap
An area between two doorways, meant to hold people until they are identified and authenticated.

many-to-one mapping
When multiple certificates are mapped to a single recipient.

Message-Digest Algorithm 5 (MD5)
A 128-bit key hash used to provide integrity of files and messages.

multifactor authentication
When two or more types of authentication are used when dealing with user access control.

mutual authentication
When two computers, for example a client and a server, both verify each other's identity.

Network Access Control (NAC)
Sets the rules by which connections to a network are governed.

network address translation (NAT)
The process of changing an IP address while it is in transit across a router. This is usually so one larger address space (private) can be remapped to another address space, or single IP address (public).

network intrusion detection system (NIDS)
A type of IDS that attempts to detect malicious network activities—for example, port scans and DoS attacks—by constantly monitoring network traffic.

network intrusion prevention system (NIPS)
Designed to inspect traffic and based on their configuration or security policy, they can remove, detain, or redirect malicious traffic.

Network Management System (NMS)
The software run on one or more servers that controls the monitoring of network attached devices and computers.

network mapping
The study of physical and logical connectivity of networks.

network perimeter
The border of a computer network, commonly secured by devices such as firewalls and NIDS/NIPS solutions.

nonce
A random number issued by an authentication protocol that can only be used once.

nonpromiscuous mode
When a network adapter captures only the packets that are addressed to it.

nonrepudiation
The idea of ensuring that a person or group cannot refute the validity of your proof against them.

NTLM hash
Successor to the LM hash. A more advanced hash used to store Windows passwords, based off the RC4 algorithm.

NTLM2 hash
Successor to the NTLM hash. Based off the MD5 hashing algorithm.

null session
When used by an attacker, a malicious connection to the Windows interprocess communications share (IPC$).

one-time pad
A cipher that encrypts plaintext with a secret random key that is the same length as the plaintext.

one-to-one mapping
When an individual certificate is mapped to a single recipient.

open mail relay
Also known as a SMTP open relay; it enables anyone on the Internet to send e-mail through an SMTP server.

Open Vulnerability and Assessment Language (OVAL)
A standard and a programming language designed to standardize the transfer of secure public information across networks and the Internet utilizing any security tools and services available.

packet filtering
Packet filtering as it applies to firewalls inspects each packet passing through the firewall and accepts or rejects it based on rules. Two types of packet filtering include stateless packet filters and stateful packet inspection (SPI).

password cracker
Software tool used to recover passwords from hosts or to discover weak passwords.

patch
Updates to a system. They generally carry the connotation of a small fix in the mind of the user or system administrator, so larger patches will often be referred to as software updates, service packs. or something similar.

patch management
The planning, testing, implementing, and auditing of patches.

penetration testing
A method of evaluating the security of a system by simulating one or more attacks on that system.

permanent DoS (PDoS) attack
Generally consists of an attacker exploiting security flaws in routers and other networking hardware by flashing the firmware of the device and replacing it with a modified image.

permissions
File system permissions control what resources a person can access on the network.

personal firewall
Applications that protect an individual computer from unwanted Internet traffic; they do so by way of a set of rules and policies.

personally identifiable information (PII)
Information used to uniquely identify, contact, or locate a person.

phishing
The criminally fraudulent process of attempting to acquire sensitive information such as usernames, passwords, and credit card details by masquerading as a trustworthy entity in an electronic communication.

piggybacking
When an unauthorized person tags along with an authorized person to gain entry to a restricted area.

ping flood
A ping flood, also known as an ICMP flood attack, is when an attacker attempts to send many ICMP echo request packets (pings) to a host in an attempt to use up all available bandwidth.

Ping of Death (POD)
A type of DoS that sends an oversized and/or malformed packet to another computer.

Point-to-Point Tunneling Protocol (PPTP)
A tunneling protocol used to support VPNs. Generally includes security mechanisms and no additional software or protocols need to be loaded. A VPN device or server must have inbound port 1723 open to enable incoming PPTP connections.

policy
Rules or guidelines used to guide decisions and achieve outcomes. They can be written or configured on a computer.

pop-up blocker
An application or add-on to a web browser that blocks pop-up windows that usually contain advertisements.

port address translation (PAT)
Like NAT but it translates both IP addresses and port numbers.

port scanner
Software used to decipher which ports are open on a host.

pre-action sprinkler system
Similar to a dry pipe system, but there are requirements for it to be set off such as heat or smoke.

pretexting
When a person invents a scenario, or pretext, in the hope of persuading a victim to divulge information.

Pretty Good Privacy (PGP)
An encryption program used primarily for signing, encrypting, and decrypting e-mails in an attempt to increase the security of e-mail communications.

private key
A type of key that is known only to a specific user or users who keep the key a secret.

privilege escalation
The act of exploiting a bug or design flaw in a software or firmware application to gain access to resources that normally would've been protected from an application or user.

promiscuous mode
In a network adapter, this passes all traffic to the CPU, not just the frames addressed to it. When the network adapter captures all packets that it has access to regardless of the destination for those packets.

protocol analyzer
Software tool used to capture and analyze packets.

proxy server
Acts as an intermediary for clients usually located on a LAN and the servers that they want to access that are usually located on the Internet.

public key cryptography
Uses asymmetric keys alone or in addition to symmetric keys. The asymmetric key algorithm creates a secret private key and a published public key.

Public Key Infrastructure
An entire system of hardware and software, policies and procedures, and people, used to create, distribute, manage, store, and revoke digital certificates.

public key
A type of key that is known to all parties involved in encrypted transactions within a given group.

qualitative risk assessment
An assessment that assigns numeric values to the probability of a risk and the impact it can have on the system or network.

quantitative risk assessment
An assessment that measures risk by using exact monetary values.

radio frequency interference (RFI)
Interference that can come from AM/FM transmissions and cell towers.

RAID 1
Mirroring. Data is copied to two identical disks. If one disk fails, the other continues to operate.

RAID 5
Striping with Parity. Data is striped across multiple disks; fault tolerant parity data is also written to each disk.

Rainbow Tables
In password cracking, a set of precalculated encrypted passwords located in a lookup table.

redundant ISP
Secondary connections to another ISP; for example, a backup T-1 line.

redundant power supply
An enclosure that contains two complete power supplies, the second of which will turn on when the first fails.

Remote Access Service (RAS)
A networking service that allows incoming connections from remote dial-in clients. It is also used with VPNs.

Remote Authentication Dial-In User Service (RADIUS)
Used to provide centralized administration of dial-up, VPN, and wireless authentication.

replay attack
An attack in which valid data transmission is maliciously or fraudulently repeated or delayed.

residual risk
The risk that is left over after a security and disaster recovery plan have been implemented.

risk
The possibility of a malicious attack or other threat causing damage or downtime to a computer system.

risk assessment
The attempt to determine the amount of threats or hazards that could possibly occur in a given amount of time to your computers and networks.

risk management
The identification, assessment, and prioritization of risks, and the mitigating and monitoring of those risks.

risk mitigation
When a risk is reduced or eliminated altogether.

role-based access control (RBAC)
An access model that works with sets of permissions, instead of individual permissions that are label-based. So roles are created for various job functions in an organization.

rootkit
A type of software designed to gain administrator-level control over a computer system without being detected.

RSA
A public key cryptography algorithm created by Rivest, Shamir, Adleman. It is commonly used in e-commerce.

S/MIME
An IETF standard that provides cryptographic security for electronic messaging such as e-mail.

sag
An unexpected decrease in the amount of voltage provided.

salting
The randomization of the hashing process to defend against cryptanalysis password attacks and Rainbow Tables.

sandbox
When a Web script runs in its own environment for the express purpose of not interfering with other processes, possibly for testing.

Secure Hash Algorithm (SHA)
A group of hash functions designed by the NSA and published by the NIST, widely used in government. The most common currently is SHA-1.

Secure Shell (SSH)
A protocol that can create a secure channel between two computers or network devices.

Secure Sockets Layer (SSL)
A cryptographic protocol that provides secure Internet communications such as web browsing, instant messaging, e-mail, and VoIP.

security log files
Files that log activity of users. They show who did what and when, plus whether they succeeded or failed in their attempt.

security template
Groups of policies that can be loaded in one procedure.

security tokens
Physical devices given to authorized users to help with authentication. These devices might be attached to a keychain or are part of a card system.

Separation of Duties (SoD)
This is when more than one person is required to complete a particular task or operation.

service level agreement (SLA)
Part of a service contract where the level of service is formally defined.

service pack (SP)
A group of updates, bug fixes, updated drivers, and security fixes that are installed from one downloadable package or from one disc.

service set identifier (SSID)
The name of a wireless access point (or network) to which network clients will connect; it is broadcast through the air.

shoulder surfing
When a person uses direct observation to find out a target's password, PIN, or other such authentication information.

signature-based monitoring
Frames and packets of network traffic are analyzed for predetermined attack patterns. These attack patterns are known as signatures.

Simple Network Management Protocol (SNMP)
A TCP/IP protocol that monitors network-attached devices and computers. It's usually incorporated as part of a network management system.

single point of failure
An element, object, or part of a system that, if it fails, will cause the whole system to fail.

single sign-on (SSO)
When a user can log in once but gain access to multiple systems without being asked to log in again.

Smurf attack
A type of DoS that sends large amounts of ICMP echoes, broadcasting the ICMP echo requests to every computer on its network or subnetwork. The header of the ICMP echo requests will have a spoofed IP address. That IP address is the target of the Smurf attack. Every computer that replies to the ICMP echo requests will do so to the spoofed IP.

SNMP agent
Software deployed by the network management system that is loaded on managed devices. The software redirects the information that the NMS needs to monitor the remote managed devices.

spam
The abuse of electronic messaging systems such as e-mail, broadcast media, and instant messaging.

special hazard protection system
A clean agent sprinkler system such as FM-200 used in server rooms.

spike
A short transient in voltage that can be due to a short circuit, tripped circuit breaker, power outage, or lightning strike.

spoofing
When an attacker masquerades as another person by falsifying information.

spyware
A type of malicious software either downloaded unwittingly from a website or installed along with some other third-party software.

standby generator
Systems that turn on automatically within seconds of a power outage.

stateful packet inspection
Type of packet inspection that keeps track of network connections by examining the header in each packet, also known as SPI.

static NAT
When a single private IP address translates to a single public IP address. This is also called one-to-one mapping.

steganography
The science (and art) of writing hidden messages; it is a form of security through obscurity.

stream cipher
A type of algorithm that encrypts each byte in a message on at a time.

surge
Means that there is an unexpected increase in the amount of voltage provided.

symmetric key algorithm
A class of cipher that uses identical or closely related keys for encryption and decryption.

SYN flood
A type of DoS where an attacker sends a large amount of SYN request packets to a server in an attempt to deny service.

TCP reset attack
Sets the reset flag in a TCP header to 1, telling the respective computer to kill the TCP session immediately

TCP/IP hijacking
When a hacker takes over a TCP session between two computers without the need of a cookie or any other type of host access.

teardrop attack
A type of DoS that sends mangled IP fragments with overlapping and oversized payloads to the target machine.

TEMPEST
Refers to the investigations of conducted emissions from electrical and mechanical devices, which could be compromising to an organization.

Temporal Key Integrity Protocol (TKIP)
An algorithm used to secure wireless computer networks; meant as a replacement for WEP.

Terminal Access Controller Access-Control System (TACACS)
A remote authentication protocol similar to RADIUS used more often in UNIX networks.

3-leg perimeter
A type of DMZ where a firewall has three legs that connect to the LAN, Internet, and the DMZ.

Tickets
Part of the authentication process used by Kerberos.

time bomb
Trojans set off on a certain date.

time of day restriction
When a user's logon hours are configured to restrict access to the network during certain types of the day and week.

Towers of Hanoi
A backup rotation scheme based on the mathematics of the Towers of Hanoi puzzle. Uses three backup sets. For example, the first tape is used every second day, the second tape is used every fourth day, and the third tape is used every eighth day.

Transport Layer Security (TLS)
The successor to SSL. Provides secure Internet communications. This is shown in a browser as HTTPS.

Triple DES (3DES)
Similar to DES but applies the cipher algorithm three times to each cipher block.

Trojan horse
Applications that appear to perform desired functions but are actually performing malicious functions behind the scenes.

Trusted Computer System Evaluation Criteria (TCSEC)
A DoD standard that sets basic requirements for assessing the effectiveness of computer security access policies. Also known as The Orange Book.

UDP flood attack
A similar attack to the Fraggle. It uses the connectionless User Datagram Protocol. It is enticing to attackers because it does not require a synchronization process.

uninterruptible power supply (UPS)
Takes the functionality of a surge suppressor and combines that with a battery backup, protecting our computer not only from surges and spikes, but also from sags, brownouts, and blackouts.

User Account Control (UAC)
A security component of Windows Vista that keeps every user (besides the actual Administrator account) in standard user mode instead of as an administrator with full administrative rights—even if they are a member of the administrators group.

vampire tap
A device used to add computers to a 10BASE5 network. It pierces the copper conductor of a coaxial cable and can also be used for malicious purposes.

virtual machine (VM)
Created by virtual software; they are images of operating systems or individual applications.

virtual private network (VPN)
A connection between two or more computers or devices that are not on the same private network.

virtualization
The creation of a virtual entity, as opposed to a true or actual entity.

virus
Code that runs on a computer without the user's knowledge; it infects the computer when the code is accessed and executed.

VLAN hopping
The act of gaining access to traffic on other VLANs that would not normally be accessible by jumping from one VLAN to another

vulnerability
Weaknesses in your computer network design and individual host configuration.

vulnerability assessment
Baselining of the network to assess the current security state of computers, servers, network devices, and the entire network in general.

vulnerability management
The practice of finding and mitigating software vulnerabilities in computers and networks.

vulnerability scanning
The act of scanning for weaknesses and susceptibilities in the network and on individual systems.

wardialing
The act of scanning telephone numbers by dialing them one at a time and adding them to a list, in an attempt to gain access to computer networks.

wardriving
The act of searching for wireless networks by a person in a vehicle through the use of a device with a wireless antenna, often a particularly strong antenna.

warm site
This will have computers, phones, and servers, but they might require some configuration before users can start working on them.

web of trust
A decentralized model used for sharing certificates without the need for a centralized CA.

wet pipe sprinkler system
Consists of a pressurized water supply system that can deliver a high quantity of water to an entire building via a piping distribution system.

Wi-Fi Protected Access (WPA)
A security protocol created by the Wi-Fi Alliance to secure wireless computer networks, more secure than WEP.

Wired Equivalent Privacy (WEP)
A deprecated wireless network security standard, less secure than WPA.

wiretapping
Tapping into a network cable in an attempt to eavesdrop on a conversation or steal data.

worm
Code that runs on a computer without the user's knowledge; they self-replicate whereas a virus does not.

X.509
A common PKI standard developed by the ITU-T that incorporates the single sign-on authentication method.

zombie
The individual compromised computers in a botnet.

Index

B

C

D

E

F

G

H

I

J

K

L

N

O

P

Q

R

S

T

U

V

W